DISTORTIONS TO AGRICULTURAL INCENTIVES IN ASIA

DISTORTIONS TO AGRICULTURAL INCENTIVES IN ASIA

Kym Anderson
and Will Martin, Editors

THE WORLD BANK
Washington, D.C.

© 2009 The International Bank for Reconstruction and Development / The World Bank
1818 H Street NW
Washington DC 20433
Telephone: 202-473-1000
Internet: www.worldbank.org
E-mail: feedback@worldbank.org

1 2 3 4 12 11 10 09

This volume is a product of the staff of the International Bank for Reconstruction and Development / The World Bank. The findings, interpretations, and conclusions expressed in this volume do not necessarily reflect the views of the Executive Directors of The World Bank or the governments they represent.

The World Bank does not guarantee the accuracy of the data included in this work. The boundaries, colors, denominations, and other information shown on any map in this work do not imply any judgement on the part of The World Bank concerning the legal status of any territory or the endorsement or acceptance of such boundaries.

Cover design: Tomoko Hirata/World Bank.
Cover photo: © Tran Thi Hoa/World Bank Photo Library.

ISBN: 978-0-8213-7662-1
eISBN: 978-0-8213-7663-8
DOI: 10.1596/978-0-8213-7662-1

Library of Congress Cataloging-in-Publication Data
Distortions to agricultural incentives in Asia / edited by Kym Anderson and Will Martin.
    p. cm.
  Includes bibliographical references and index.
  ISBN 978-0-8213-7662-1 — ISBN 978-0-8213-7663-8 (electronic)
  1. Agriculture—Economic aspects—Asia. 2. Agriculture and state—Asia. 3. Agriculture—Taxation—Asia. 4. Agricultural subsidies—Asia. I. Anderson, Kym. II. Martin, Will, 1953-
    HD2056.Z8D57 2008
    338.1'85—dc22

                                                                            2008029534

DEDICATION

To the authors of the country case studies and their assistants,
especially for generating the time series of distortion estimates
that underpin the chapters, and, in particular,
to Yujiro Hayami for his insights and advice during this project
and his related and influential work on Asia over several decades.

CONTENTS

Figures

Tables

FOREWORD

Three-quarters of the world's poorest households depend on farming for their livelihoods, and the majority live in Asia where 81 percent of the poor (more than 900 million people earn less than US$1.25/day) are engaged directly or indirectly in agriculture. During the 1960s and 1970s, many developing countries had in place pro-urban and anti-agricultural policies, while many high-income countries restricted agricultural imports and subsidized their farmers. Although progress has been made over the past two decades to reduce those policy biases, particularly the anti-agricultural bias in Asia, the extent of reform has not been systematically quantified. Nor has it been clear how many trade- and welfare-reducing price distortions remain in Asian agriculture, both within and between countries, and whether later developing countries have followed Japan and the Republic of Korea in replacing past anti-agricultural policies with not a neutral regime but a pro-agricultural set of policies—which could be just as wasteful of national resources.

To help fill this lacuna, the World Bank launched a major research project in 2006 aimed at quantifying the changing extent of distortions to agricultural incentives over recent decades. This volume is one of a series of four regional books that summarizes the findings. By including all the large Asian economies as case studies, no less than 95 percent of Asian GDP and agricultural output is covered.

These estimates are used to help address questions such as the following: Where is there still a policy bias against agricultural production? To what extent has there been overshooting in the sense that some developing-country farmers are now being protected from import competition? What are the political and economic forces behind the more successful reformers, and how do these forces compare with those in less successful countries where major distortions in agricultural incentives remain? How important have domestic political forces been in bringing about reform, compared with international forces? What explains the cross-commodity pattern of distortions within the agricultural sector of each country? What policy lessons and trade implications can be drawn from these differing experiences with a view to ensuring better growth-enhancing and poverty-reducing outcomes in other still-distorted developing countries during their reforms in the future?

In Asia more than anywhere else, the reforms have been truly transformational. The world's most populous nations, China and India, have been among the most ambitious in raising incentives for farmers, albeit from a very low base in each case. Vietnam also has undertaken major and rapid reforms, while in other Southeast Asian economies the reforms have been more gradual (or nonexistent in the cases of Myanmar and the Democratic People's Republic of Korea, but they were not able to be included as case studies because of lack of access to data). Meanwhile, the Republic of Korea has moved from taxing agriculture relative to other tradable sectors in the 1950s to increasingly protecting it beginning in the 1970s. This development has raised concerns that other emerging economies may follow suit and pursue the same agricultural protection growth path of more-advanced economies.

The new empirical indicators summarized in these case studies provide a strong evidence-based foundation for assessing the successes and failures of policies of the past and for evaluating policy options for the years ahead. The analytical narratives reveal that the reforms to agricultural price and trade policies were sometimes undertaken unilaterally. In other cases, they were also partly in response to international pressures such as the Uruguay Round (for example, the Republic of Korea), commitments required for accession to the World Trade Organization (WTO) (for example, China), and structural adjustment loan conditionality by international financial institutions (for example, the Philippines in the 1980s).

The study is timely because the WTO is in the midst of the Doha round of multilateral trade negotiations, and agricultural policy reform is one of the most contentious issues in those talks. Hopefully China and South and Southeast Asian countries will not make use of the legal wiggle room they have allowed themselves in their WTO bindings and follow Japan and the Republic of Korea into high agricultural protection. It might be argued, on one hand, that a laissez-faire strategy could increase rural-urban inequality and poverty and thereby generate social unrest. On the other hand, policies that lead to high prices for staple foods, in particular, involve potentially serious risks for the urban and rural poor who are net buyers of food in developing countries. Available evidence suggests that problems of rural-urban poverty gaps have been alleviated in parts of Asia by some of the more-mobile members of farm households finding full- or part-time work off the farm and repatriating part of their higher earnings back to those remaining in farm households. Efficient ways of assisting any left-behind groups of poor (non-farm as well as farm) households include public investment measures that have high social payoffs, such as in basic education and health and in rural infrastructure, as well as in agricultural research and development. As argued in the World Bank's *World Development Report 2008*, the latter also provide more sustainable and more equitable ways of securing domestic food supplies than artificially propping up prices.

Justin Yifu Lin
Senior Vice President and Chief Economist
The World Bank

ACKNOWLEDGMENTS

This book provides an overview of the evolution of the distortions to agricultural incentives caused by price and trade policies in the World Bank–defined regions of East Asia and South Asia. The volume includes an introduction and summary chapter and commissioned studies of three Northeast Asian, five Southeast Asian, and four South Asian economies. The chapters are followed by two appendixes. The first appendix describes the methodology we have used to measure the nominal and relative rates of assistance for farmers and the taxes and subsidies on food consumption. The second appendix provides summaries of our annual estimates of these rates of assistance across the focus economies. Together, the 12 economies we study account for no less than 95 percent of the region's agricultural value added, farm households, total population, and total gross domestic product.

To the authors of the case studies, who are listed on the following pages, we are extremely grateful for the dedicated way in which they have delivered far more than we could have reasonably expected. We are particularly grateful to Yujiro Hayami for his insights and advice during this project and his influential, related work over several decades. Staff at the World Bank's East Asia and Pacific Department and South Asia Department have provided generous and insightful advice and assistance throughout the project. This has included participation in two Bank-wide seminars that provided helpful suggestions on the draft studies. We offer thanks likewise to the World Bank directors in the focus economies, who examined and cleared the working paper versions of each chapter. We have similarly benefited from the feedback provided by many participants at workshops and conferences in which drafts have been presented over the past year or so. Johanna Croser, Francesca de Nicola, Esteban Jara, Marianne Kurzweil, Signe Nelgen, Damiano Sandri, and Ernesto Valenzuela have generously assisted in compiling material for the opening overview chapter, and Johanna Croser and Marie Damania assisted in copyediting the case study chapters.

We wish to extend our thanks to the Organisation for Economic Co-operation and Development and the International Food Policy Research Institute for sharing methodological insights, and also to the members of the project's Senior Advisory Board, who have provided sage advice and much encouragement throughout the planning and implementation stages. The board is comprised of Yujiro Hayami, Bernard Hoekman, Anne Krueger, John Nash, Johan Swinnen, Stefan Tangermann, Alberto Valdés, Alan Winters, and, until his untimely death in 2008, Bruce Gardner.

Our thanks go also to the Development Research Group and to the Trust Funds of the governments of Ireland, Japan, the Netherlands, and the United Kingdom for financial assistance. This support has made it possible for this set of economies to be included as part of a wider study that also encompasses more than 30 other developing countries, 18 economies in transition from central planning, and 20 high-income countries. Three companion volumes examine case studies of other emerging economies in a similar way and for a similar time period (back to the mid-1950s or early 1960s, except for the transition economies). Also published by the World Bank in 2008 or 2009, they cover Africa (coedited by Kym Anderson and Will Masters), Latin America (coedited by Kym Anderson and Alberto Valdés), and Europe's transition economies (coedited by Kym Anderson and Johan Swinnen). A global overview volume edited by Kym Anderson will be published in 2009.

Kym Anderson and Will Martin
November 2008

CONTRIBUTORS

Nazneen Ahmed is a research fellow at the Bangladesh Institute of Development Studies, Ministry of Planning in Dhaka, Bangladesh.

Kym Anderson is George Gollin Professor of Economics at the University of Adelaide and a fellow of the Center for Economic Policy Research, London. During 2004–07, he was on an extended sabbatical as lead economist (trade policy) in the Development Research Group of the World Bank in Washington, DC.

Prema-Chandra Athukorala is professor of economics in the Research School of Pacific and Asian Studies at the Australian National University in Canberra.

Arsenio M. Balisacan is professor of agricultural economics and director of the Southeast Asian Regional Center for Graduate Study and Research in Agriculture in Los Baños, Laguna, the Philippines.

Zaid Bakht is research director at the Bangladesh Institute of Development Studies, Ministry of Planning in Dhaka, Bangladesh.

Jayatilleke Bandara is associate professor of economics at Griffith University in Brisbane, Australia.

Johanna Croser has been a consultant with this project and is a PhD student in the Department of Economics of the University of British Columbia in Vancouver, Canada.

Cristina David is a senior research fellow at the Philippine Institute for Development Studies in Makati City, the Philippines.

Paul A. Dorosh is a senior rural development economist at the Agriculture and Rural Development Department (South Asia Agriculture and Rural Development Group) at the World Bank in Washington, DC.

George Fane is an adjunct professor of economics in the Research School of Pacific and Asian Studies, Australian National University in Canberra.

Ashok Gulati is the Asian Director for the International Food Policy Research Institute in New Delhi. Previously, he headed the institute's Markets, Trade, and Institutions Division.

Kanupriya Gupta is a senior research analyst with the International Food Policy Research Institute in New Delhi.

Yujiro Hayami is chairman of the graduate faculty of the Foundation for Advanced Studies on International Development. He is also visiting professor in the National Graduate Institute of Policy Studies, Tokyo.

Masayoshi Honma is professor of agricultural and resource economics at the University of Tokyo. He is also a member of the Board of Trustees of the International Food Policy Research Institute in Washington, DC.

Jikun Huang is director and professor, Center for Chinese Agricultural Policy, Chinese Academy of Sciences in Beijing.

Pham Lan Huong is a researcher with the Central Institute of Economic Management in Hanoi, Vietnam.

Ponciano Intal is professor and director, Angelo King Institute for Economic and Business Studies, De La Salle University in Manila.

Sisira Jayasuriya was director, Asian Economics Center and associate professor in the Department of Economics, University of Melbourne at the time of the study and is now professor of economics at La Trobe University (Bundoora) in Victoria, Australia.

Archanun Kohpaiboon is lecturer in the economics department of Thammasat University in Bangkok.

Marianne Kurzweil is a young professional at the African Development Bank in Tunis. During 2006–07, she was consultant with this project at the Development Research Group at the World Bank in Washington, DC.

Yu Liu is researcher at the Center for Chinese Agricultural Policy, Chinese Academy of Sciences in Beijing.

Wai-Heng Loke is lecturer at the Department of Economics, Faculty of Economics and Administration at the University of Malaya in Kuala Lumpur, Malaysia.

Will Martin is lead economist in the Development Research Group at the World Bank in Washington, DC. He specializes in trade and agricultural policy issues globally, especially in Asia.

Signe Nelgen has been a consultant with this project and is a PhD student in the School of Economics of the University of Adelaide in Australia.

Garry Pursell is visiting fellow at the Australia South Asia Research Center, Australian National University in Canberra. Previously, he was with the South Asia Department of the World Bank.

Scott Rozelle holds the Helen Farnsworth Endowed Professorship and is senior fellow and professor at the Freeman Spogli Institute for International Studies at Stanford University in Stanford, California.

Abdul Salam is professor of economics at the Federal Urdu University and is former chairman of the Agricultural Prices Commission in Islamabad, Pakistan.

Damiano Sandri is a PhD candidate in economics at Johns Hopkins University in Baltimore, Maryland. During 2006–07, he was a consultant with this project at the Development Research Group at the World Bank in Washington, DC.

Quazi Shahabuddin is director general of the Bangladesh Institute of Development Studies, Ministry of Planning in Dhaka, Bangladesh.

Vo Tri Thanh is a researcher with the Central Institute of Economic Management in Hanoi, Vietnam.

Ernesto Valenzuela is lecturer in economics and research fellow at the University of Adelaide in Australia. During 2005–07, he was consultant at the Development Research Group of the World Bank in Washington, DC.

Peter Warr is the John Crawford Professor of Agricultural Economics and founding Director of the Poverty Research Centre in the Division of Economics, Research School of Pacific and Asian Studies at the Australian National University in Canberra.

ABBREVIATIONS

CTE   consumer tax equivalent
GDP   gross domestic product
GVA   gross value added
IMF   International Monetary Fund
NRA   nominal rate of assistance
NRP   nominal rate of protection
NTB   nontariff barrier
OECD   Organisation for Economic Co-operation and Development
RRA   relative rate of assistance
TBI   trade bias index
WTO   World Trade Organization

Note: All dollar amounts are U.S. dollars (US$) unless otherwise indicated.

The Focus Economies of Asia

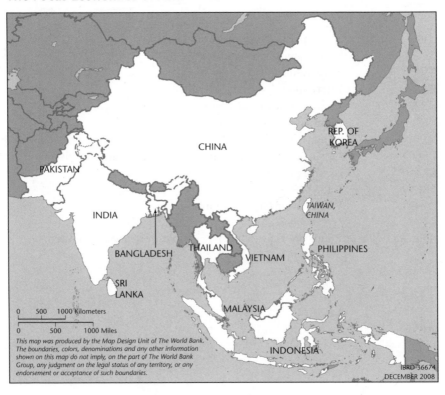

CHINA

REP. OF KOREA

PAKISTAN

TAIWAN, CHINA

INDIA

BANGLADESH

THAILAND

VIETNAM

PHILIPPINES

SRI LANKA

MALAYSIA

0   500   1000 Kilometers

0   500   1000 Miles

INDONESIA

This map was produced by the Map Design Unit of The World Bank.
The boundaries, colors, denominations and any other information
shown on this map do not imply, on the part of The World Bank
Group, any judgment on the legal status of any territory, or any
endorsement or acceptance of such boundaries.

IBRD 36674
DECEMBER 2008

PART I

INTRODUCTION

1

INTRODUCTION
AND SUMMARY

Kym Anderson and Will Martin

Farm earnings in developing countries have often been depressed by a pro-urban, antiagricultural bias in government policies. Progress has been made since the 1980s in reducing the policy bias in many countries, however. In some cases, the changes have been modest and intermittent, but, in China and, to a lesser extent, India, they have been transformational. Many trade-reducing price distortions nonetheless remain within the agricultural sector in low- and middle-income economies, including in Asia. This is important for the majority of households in the world because 45 percent of the global workforce is employed in agriculture, and 75 percent of the world's poorest households depend directly or indirectly on farming for livelihoods. It is even more important in Asia's developing economies, where 60 percent of the workforce and 81 percent of the poor (625 million people each earning less than US$1 a day) are engaged in agriculture (World Bank 2007; Chen and Ravallion 2007).

This study is part of a global research project seeking to understand the changing scope and impact of the policy bias against agriculture and the reasons behind agricultural policy reforms in Africa, Europe's transition economies, Latin America and the Caribbean, and Asia.[1] One purpose of the project is to obtain quantitative indicators of the effects of recent policy interventions. A second objective is to gain a deeper understanding of the political economy of trends in the distortions in agricultural incentives in various national settings. The third goal is to use this deeper understanding to explore the prospects for reducing the distortions in agricultural incentives and discover the likely implications for agricultural competitiveness, equality, and poverty reduction in many countries, large and small.

The compilation of new annual time series estimates of the protection and taxation of farmers over the past half century is a core component of the first stage of our research project. These estimates are used to help address questions such as the following: Where is the policy bias against agricultural production? To what extent has there been overshooting in that some food producers are now being protected from import competition in developing countries in much the same way they were protected in Europe and Japan during earlier periods of industrialization? What are the political economy forces behind successful reforms in some countries? How do they compare with the forces in other countries where reforms are less successful and major distortions in agricultural incentives remain? Over the past two decades, how important have domestic political forces been in generating reform relative to forces operating in earlier decades or international forces, such as loan conditionality, rounds of multilateral trade negotiations in the World Trade Organization (WTO), regional integration agreements, accession to the WTO, and the globalization of supermarkets and other firms along the value chain? What has caused the patterns of distortion within the agricultural sectors of individual countries? What policy lessons and trade implications may be drawn from these differing experiences so that we may seek to ensure growth-enhancing and poverty-reducing outcomes, including less overshooting and fewer protectionist regimes, during future reforms in still-distorted developing economies in Asia and elsewhere?

Our study is timely for at least four reasons. First, the WTO is in the midst of the Doha Round of multilateral trade negotiations, and agricultural policy reform is one of the most contentious issues in these talks. Second, countries are also seeking to position themselves favorably in preferential trade negotiations in the wake of other forces in globalization, including revolutions in information, communications, agricultural biotechnology, and supermarketing. Third, poorer countries and their development partners are striving to achieve the United Nations Millennium Development Goals by 2015, including the prime goals of alleviating hunger and reducing poverty. Fourth, the outputs of our study are timely also because world food prices spiked at high levels in 2008, and governments in some developing countries, in their panic to deal with the inevitable protests from consumers, have reacted in ways that are not optimal. Spikes have occurred in the past, most notably in 1973–74, and lessons on appropriate policy responses may be drawn from the experiences then. The empirical estimates reported in our study reveal that governments in Asia have differed in their responses to such shocks, although this is less the case of rice, the region's main staple.

This study on Asia is based on a sample of 12 developing economies. We exclude Japan, which has been a high-income country throughout our review period and, so, is analyzed separately as part of the high-income group in the project's global overview volume. In Northeast Asia, we include China, the Republic of Korea (hereafter referred to as Korea), and Taiwan, China. In Southeast Asia, we include the five large economies of Indonesia, Malaysia, the Philippines, Thailand, and Vietnam, and, in South Asia, we include the four largest economies: Bangladesh, India, Pakistan, and Sri Lanka. In 2000–04, these economies (all of them now WTO members) accounted for more than 95 percent of Asia's agricultural value added, total farm households, total population, and total gross domestic product (GDP).[2] The distortion estimates are provided for as many years as data permit over the past five decades (an average of 42 years), and they are presented for an average of eight crop and livestock products per economy, which, in aggregate, amounts to about 70 percent of the gross value of agricultural production in each of these economies. The time series and country coverage in our study greatly exceed the data and country coverage of earlier studies, including Anderson and Hayami (1986); Krueger, Schiff, and Valdés (1991); Orden et al. (2007); and the Organisation for Economic Co-operation and Development (OECD 2007). The product coverage is broader in each of our case studies than in all earlier case studies other than the study by the OECD (2007).[3]

The key characteristics of these economies—accounting in 2000–04 for only 10 percent of worldwide GDP, but 37 percent of global agricultural value added, 51 percent of the world's population, and 73 percent of the world's farmers—are shown in table 1.1. The table reveals the considerable diversity within the region in development, relative resource endowments, comparative advantage, trade specialization, and the incidence of poverty and income inequality. These economies thus provide a rich sample for comparative study.

Per capita incomes in Bangladesh, India, and Vietnam are barely 8 percent of the world average. In Indonesia, the Philippines, and Sri Lanka, they are around 16 percent. In China, they are over 25 percent. In Thailand, they are more than 30 percent. In Malaysia, they are about 75 percent of the world average. Korea and Taiwan, China appear exceptional in that average per capita incomes are currently twice the global average; however, in the 1950s, at the start of the period of our study, these two economies were among the poorest in the world.

Korea and Taiwan, China are also exceptional in the per capita endowment of agricultural land; they have only around 5 percent of the world average endowment ratio. Bangladesh has a little more, followed by Sri Lanka and the Philippines. Even India, Indonesia, and Pakistan have only about 25 percent of the global average endowment, while Malaysia and Thailand have about 40 percent, and China, over 50 percent.[4] Thus, these Asian economies are not relatively well endowed with cropland or pastureland; on a per capita basis, the region has only

Table 1.1. Key Economic and Trade Indicators, Asian Focus Economies, 2000–04

Economy or subregion	Share of world, %				Index, world = 100			Agricultural trade specialization index[b]	Poverty incidence[c]	Gini index, per capita income[d]	
	Population	Total GDP	Agricultural GDP	Agricultural workers	GDP per capita	Agricultural land per capita	RCA[a]			1984	2004
East Asia	29.09	8.38	24.76	47.1	29	45	75	−0.12	9	24	37
China	20.60	4.33	16.62	38.4	21	54	58	−0.05	10	20	36
Indonesia	3.41	0.59	2.62	3.8	17	27	173	0.08	4	30	35
Korea, Rep. of	0.77	1.62	1.69	0.2	212	5	26	−0.78	0	—	—
Malaysia	0.39	0.28	0.73	0.1	74	41	107	−0.18	0	49	49
Philippines	1.27	0.22	0.91	1.0	18	19	67	−0.10	13	41	44
Taiwan, China	0.36	0.84	0.45	0.1	232	5	28	−0.72	0	—	—
Thailand	1.01	0.38	1.05	1.5	38	39	204	0.38	1	45	42
Vietnam	1.29	0.11	0.69	2.1	8	14	301	0.61	1	36	37
South Asia	21.67	1.99	11.90	25.3	9	20	145	0.07	31	31	35
Bangladesh	2.16	0.14	0.90	2.9	7	8	93	−0.69	35	26	33
India	16.87	1.57	9.32	20.2	9	22	143	0.24	36	31	33
Pakistan	2.33	0.23	1.43	1.9	10	23	137	—	17	33	31
Sri Lanka	0.31	0.05	0.24	0.3	16	15	254	0.45	6	32	40
Total	50.76	10.37	36.65	72.5	20	34	80	−0.15	19	27	36

Sources: Sandri, Valenzuela, and Anderson 2007; World Development Indicators Database 2008; PovcalNet 2008.

Note: — = no data are available.

a. The index of revealed comparative advantage (RCA) for agriculture and processed foods is the share of agriculture and processed food in national exports as a ratio of such products in worldwide exports.

b. The index of primary agricultural trade specialization is defined as net exports, divided by the sum of the exports and imports of agricultural and processed food products (the world average = 0.0).

c. The percentage of the population living on less than US$1 a day.

d. Poverty incidence and the 2004 Gini index are for the most recent year available between 2000 and 2004. The 1984 Gini index is for the available year nearest 1984 (PovcalNet). The weighted averages for the focus economies use population as the basis for weights.

34 percent of the global average. This might suggest that the comparative advantage of the Asian economies in agricultural goods is low, were it not for the variations in these economies in the level of industrial development, the quality of land and water, and the related institutional arrangements and entitlements. As a result, the strengths of these economies in agricultural competitiveness are diverse. The differences are reflected in the index of revealed comparative advantage and the agricultural trade specialization index (table 1.1). A majority of our focus economies have an index of revealed comparative advantage well above 100, indicating the extent to which the share of agricultural and food products in an economy's merchandise trade exceeds the global average share of these products. For Korea and Taiwan, China, the index is below 30, and, for China and the Philippines, it is around 60. The index of agricultural trade specialization measures net exports as a ratio of exports, plus imports of farm products, and, so, it is bounded between -1 and $+1$. It is positive for half of our focus economies, but is -0.7 for Bangladesh, Korea, and Taiwan, China.

Income inequality has risen slightly over the past two decades, but is still low throughout much of the region relative to the rest of the world. In 2004, the Gini coefficient was between 0.40 and 0.49 in Malaysia, the Philippines, Sri Lanka, and Thailand and averaged between 0.31 and 0.37 in the rest of the region. The regional average of 0.36 contrasts with, for example, the average of 0.52 in Latin America. Likewise, the Gini coefficient for land distribution is relatively low in Asia, at only 0.41 for China and Pakistan and below 0.50 also in Bangladesh; Indonesia; Korea; Taiwan, China; and Thailand. Even in India, the coefficient for land distribution is only 0.58, and it is 0.50 in Vietnam. However, these coefficients imply that the distribution of land is more equal in Asia than it is in Latin America, where the Gini coefficient for land distribution is above 0.70 for major countries such as Argentina and Brazil and possibly for the region as a whole (World Bank 2007). A significant proportion of the rural population is landless in South Asia, however; so 31 percent of the population of South Asia was still living on less than US$1 a day in 2004 compared with only 9 percent in East Asia (table 1.1).

The extent of the decline in poverty in Asia has been unprecedented. The number of people living on less than US$1 a day has been reduced by half since 1981 (in 1993 purchasing power parity dollars). Most of the decline has occurred in East Asia, especially China. In East Asia, the poverty rate declined from 58 percent to less than 10 percent of the population; but, even in South Asia, the proportion has fallen from 50 to around 30 percent (table 1.2). During the 10 years to 2002, no less than 75 percent of the decline in the share of the poor among the population in Asia occurred in rural areas, and another 15 percent of the decline was generated by a movement out of poverty among rural people who had migrated because of better opportunities in urban areas (Chen and Ravallion 2007).

Table 1.2. Poverty Levels[a] in Asia, 1981–2004

Economy, indicator	1981	1987	1993	1999	2004
Poor people, millions					
Asia	1,251	900	857	740	615
China	634	310	334	223	128
Other East Asia	162	119	86	53	41
India	364	369	376	376	371
Other South Asia	91	102	61	87	75
Population share, %					
East Asia	58	28	25	15	9
South Asia	50	45	37	35	31

Source: Chen and Ravallion 2007.

a. People living on less than US$1 a day at 1993 international purchasing power parity.

Policy developments have made nontrivial contributions to the growth, structural change, and poverty reduction observed in Asia over the past five decades. The transformational shift from central planning and state-owned enterprises to greater dependence on markets and private entrepreneurship has had a particularly dramatic effect in China and Vietnam since the 1980s, but India has also benefited from similar reforms beginning in the early 1990s. Also important has been the abandonment in market economies of import-substituting industrialization in favor of export-oriented development strategies, beginning in Taiwan, China around 1960 and followed by Korea, then by several Southeast Asian economies, and now also by economies in South Asia. Agricultural policies have not been the only or even the main target of these reforms, but they have been an integral part of the process.

We begin with a brief summary of economic growth and the structural changes in the region since the 1950s. We also examine the agricultural and other economic policies that have affected agriculture before and after the various reforms and, in several cases, after fundamental regime changes during the past half century.[5] We then introduce the methodology used by the authors of the individual country studies to estimate the nominal rates of assistance (NRAs) and relative rates of assistance (RRAs) for farmers delivered by national farm and nonfarm policies over the past several decades (depending on data availability), as well as the impact of these policies on the consumer prices of farm products. Farmer assistance and consumer taxation will be negative during periods of antiagricultural, pro-urban bias in a policy regime. We subsequently provide a synopsis of the empirical results detailed in the country studies in this volume, though we do not attempt to survey the myriad policy changes discussed in detail in the following chapters. The final sections of this chapter summarize what we have learned and draw out the implications of the findings for poverty, inequality, and the possible future direction of policies affecting agricultural incentives in Asia.

Growth and Structural Change

The most striking economic characteristic of the developing economies in Asia, particularly East Asia, is the rates of economic growth and industrial development in Korea; Taiwan, China; and elsewhere over the past three decades or more (Anderson 2008). The recent report of the Commission on Growth and Development (2008) has noted that 13 of the world's economies have had sustained growth in real per capita income of more than 7 percent for at least 25 consecutive years since World War II, and nine of these economies are in East Asia.[6] Between 1980 and 2004, per capita GDP grew 6.3 percent per year in East Asia and 3.4 percent per year in South Asia, while the global average was only 1.4 percent. Asia's industrial growth during this period was 8.6 percent per year. This compares with the world average of 2.5 percent. Even the agricultural growth rate was more than half again as high in Asia relative to the world average (3.1 percent and 2.0 percent per year, respectively; see table 1.3). As a consequence of this growth performance, per capita incomes in some Asian economies have been converging rapidly, albeit from a low base, toward incomes in rich countries, while other developing and transition economies have, on average, been slipping away from the performance of rich countries such as the United States (figure 1.1).

A key driver of the rapid growth and industrialization in Asia has been the decision by many governments in the region to open up economies and abandon an import-substituting development strategy in favor of an export-oriented approach. This shift occurred at different times in our focus economies, beginning with Korea and Taiwan, China in the 1960s. China joined the group in the late 1970s, Vietnam in the mid-1980s, and India haltingly in the early 1980s and more concertedly in 1991. As a result, export volumes grew at double-digit rates (last column of table 1.3). The share of exports in GDP rose steadily in the region, more than doubling in the 30 years to 2004 (table 1.4). East Asia's share in worldwide exports of nonfood manufactures has quadrupled since 1990, thanks especially to industrialization in China. China accounted for 11 percent of the world's manufacturing exports in 2006, compared with less than 1 percent in 1990: a 20-fold increase in current U.S. dollar terms. Our other focus economies experienced an average fivefold increase, and all the economies have contributed to the region's growing share in global manufacturing exports since 1990 (table 1.5).[7]

Along with the export-led growth has come a dramatic restructuring of Asia's economies that has involved a shift from agriculture toward manufacturing and service activities. In East Asia, the share of the agricultural sector in GDP is now

Table 1.3. Real Growth in GDP and Exports, Asian Focus Economies, 1980–2004
(at constant 2000 prices, trend-based, % per year)

Economy	GDP (1980–2004)					Export volume, 1985–95
	Agriculture	Industry	Services	Total	Per capita	
East Asia	3.1	9.0	7.9	7.6	6.3	13.7
China	4.4	12.1	11.3	9.9	8.6	15.1
Indonesia	2.9	6.6	5.3	5.4	3.7	10.4
Korea, Rep. of	1.3	8.2	7.2	7.1	6.1	10.6
Malaysia	1.7	7.8	6.9	6.6	3.9	10.3
Philippines	1.7	2.0	3.5	2.7	0.4	12.8
Taiwan, China	0.5	5.3	8.3	6.7	5.6	17.0
Thailand	2.4	8.5	5.8	6.3	4.9	17.3
Vietnam	3.9	9.7	7.5	7.0	5.1	—
South Asia	3.0	6.2	6.4	5.4	3.4	—
Bangladesh	2.7	6.6	4.4	4.4	2.1	13.4
India	3.0	6.3	7.0	5.7	3.7	—
Pakistan	4.0	5.5	4.8	4.7	2.1	9.8
Sri Lanka	1.8	5.6	5.1	4.5	3.3	6.3
Total	3.1	8.6	7.5	7.1	5.5	—
World	2.0	2.5	3.2	3.0	1.4	—

Sources: Sandri, Valenzuela, and Anderson 2007; World Development Indicators Database 2008.

Note: — = no data are available.

Figure 1.1. Index of Real Per Capita GDP, Asia Relative to the United States, 1950–2006

a. Asian focus economies

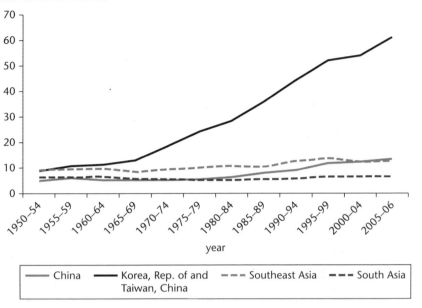

b. Asia and other developing and transition regions

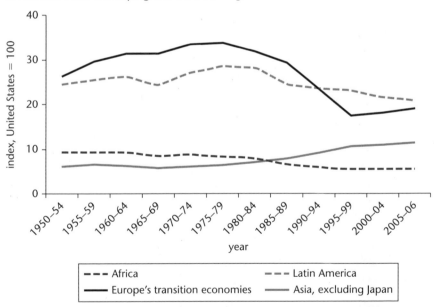

Sources: Author calculations; Maddison 2003; World Development Indicators Database 2008.

Note: The charts are based on 1990 Geary-Khamis international dollars up to 2001, taken from Maddison (2003), and updated using real GDP per capita growth data from the World Development Indicators Database. The economies and regions are indicated relative to the United States, which is set as the numeraire at 100. Southeast Asia is Indonesia, Malaysia, the Philippines, Thailand, and Vietnam. South Asia is Bangladesh, India, Pakistan, and Sri Lanka.

Table 1.4. Exports of Goods and Services as a Share of GDP, Asian Focus Economies, 1965–2004
(percent)

Economy	1965–69[a]	1975–79	1980–84	1985–89	1990–94	1995–99	2000–04
East Asia[b]	8	19	22	25	28	34	39
China	3	6	11	14	22	21	28
Indonesia	10	23	25	23	26	32	35
Korea, Rep. of	13	32	34	35	27	33	39
Malaysia	37	49	53	63	82	103	117
Philippines	11	20	21	25	28	47	53
Taiwan, China	22	49	53	54	45	48	59
Thailand	18	21	23	30	38	49	68
Vietnam	—	—	—	—	—	44	55
South Asia	—	7	7	7	11	12	14
Bangladesh	—	5	5	6	8	13	15
India	3	6	6	6	9	11	13
Pakistan	—	12	12	14	17	16	16
Sri Lanka	19	24	29	26	32	36	37
Total[a]	—	16	19	22	25	30	34

Sources: Sandri, Valenzuela, and Anderson 2007; World Development Indicators Database 2008.

Note: — = no data are available.

a. Only merchandise exports in 1965–69, except for Taiwan, China. In 1960–64, the shares of Korea and Taiwan, China were 6 and 15 percent, respectively. In 1955–59, the share of Taiwan, China was 10 percent.

b. Ignores Vietnam in 1980–94, when the weight of Vietnam in Asian GDP was less than 1 percent.

**Table 1.5. Share of Nonfood Manufactures in World Exports,
Asian Focus Economies, 1990–2006**

(percent)

Economy	1990–94	1995–99	2000–04	2006	2006 value as % of 1990
East Asia	5.1	10.3	15.6	20.4	790
China	1.0	2.4	6.1	10.8	2,020
Indonesia	0.1	0.5	0.6	0.5	490
Korea, Rep. of	1.7	2.6	3.1	3.5	480
Malaysia	0.2	1.0	1.5	1.4	750
Philippines	0.1	0.2	0.6	0.5	730
Taiwan, China	1.8	2.7	2.5	2.3	310
Thailand	0.2	0.8	1.0	1.2	670
Vietnam	0.0	0.1	0.2	0.2	—
South Asia	0.6	0.9	1.1	1.4	470
Bangladesh	0.0	0.1	0.1	0.1	800
India	0.4	0.5	0.7	1.0	550
Pakistan	0.1	0.2	0.2	0.2	310
Sri Lanka	0.0	0.1	0.1	0.1	480
Total	5.7	11.2	16.7	21.8	760

Sources: Sandri, Valenzuela, and Anderson 2007; WTO 2007; World Development Indicators Database 2008.

Note: — = no data are available.

less than 30 percent of the sector's share in the late 1960s. In slower-growing South Asia, the share has fallen by less than 50 percent over the period. The biggest changes have occurred in China and Indonesia, where agriculture's share in GDP dropped from more than 40 and 50 percent, respectively, in the 1960s to 13 percent in 2005. Bangladesh has also been transformed remarkably: agriculture's share was 54 percent in 1965–69, and all other nonservice industries accounted for only 9 percent; now, industry's share is higher than the share of agriculture (27 versus 20 percent in 2005). Pakistan, the Philippines, and Sri Lanka are the focus economies that have been growing the most slowly, and they have also been the slowest in moving away from agriculture since the 1960s. At the other extreme are Korea and Taiwan, China; only 2 or 3 percent of the GDP of these economies is now derived from farming. For Asia as a whole, agriculture now accounts for only around 12 percent of GDP, down from about 36 percent in the late 1960s. Meanwhile, the share of industry has risen from 27 to 38 percent, and the share of services from 35 to 49 percent (table 1.6).

The share of overall employment accounted for by farming activities has fallen somewhat more slowly than agriculture's GDP share, according to statistics in the

Table 1.6. Sectoral Shares of GDP, Asian Focus Economies, 1965–2004
(percent)

Economy	Agriculture				Industry				Services			
	1965–69	1975–79	1985–89	2000–04	1965–69	1975–79	1985–89	2000–04	1965–69	1975–79	1985–89	2000–04
East Asia[a]	34	26	19	10	29	40	40	42	34	32	41	48
China	39	31	27	14	35	47	44	46	26	22	30	41
Indonesia	49	29	23	16	16	35	36	45	35	36	41	40
Korea, Rep. of	30	21	10	4	22	30	37	35	48	49	53	61
Malaysia	29	26	20	9	27	37	39	49	44	37	42	42
Philippines	27	29	24	14	27	36	35	32	46	35	42	53
Taiwan, China	20	10	5	2	34	44	45	31	47	46	50	67
Thailand	30	25	16	10	24	29	34	43	46	46	50	48
Vietnam	—	—	41	23	—	—	27	39	—	—	32	38
South Asia	43	36	29	21	18	21	23	24	39	42	48	55
Bangladesh	54	55	31	22	9	14	21	25	36	31	48	52
India	44	36	29	21	19	22	24	24	38	43	47	55
Pakistan	35	29	24	22	19	21	21	22	46	50	55	56
Sri Lanka	29	28	24	17	21	26	24	24	51	46	51	59
Total[a]	36	28	22	12	27	36	35	38	35	34	43	49

Sources: Sandri, Valenzuela, and Anderson 2007; World Development Indicators Database 2008.

Note: — = no data are available.

a. Ignores Vietnam in 1965–69 and 1975–79, when the weight of Vietnam in Asian GDP was less than 1 percent.

Table 1.7. Agriculture's Share in Employment, Asian Focus Economies, 1965–2004

(percent)

Economy	1965–69	1975–79	1985–89	2000–04
East Asia	77	72	68	60
China	79	75	73	66
Indonesia	69	60	56	47
Korea, Rep. of	53	41	24	9
Malaysia	57	45	31	18
Philippines	60	54	48	39
Taiwan, China	45	25	15	7
Thailand	81	74	66	55
Vietnam	79	74	72	67
South Asia	74	70	65	57
Bangladesh	85	76	67	54
India	73	70	66	59
Pakistan	65	64	55	46
Sri Lanka	55	53	49	45
Total	76	71	67	59

Sources: Sandri, Valenzuela, and Anderson 2007; FAOSTAT Database 2008.

FAOSTAT Database of the Food and Agriculture Organization of the United Nations (which, because of definitional differences, is not always consistent with official national databases). The employment share remains at much higher levels than the GDP share, implying relatively low labor productivity on farms. The most rapid declines have occurred in Korea and Taiwan, China, where the employment share in agriculture has fallen from around 50 percent to less than 10 percent over the past 40 years. Malaysia, too, has experienced a major decline, from 57 to 18 percent of the workforce. Elsewhere in Asia, however, the share of employment remains large in farming (table 1.7). The share would be somewhat less in full-time equivalent terms if more careful account were taken of part-time off-farm activities (for example, see Otsuka and Yamano 2006), but the share nonetheless underscores the importance of the incentives faced by farmers in the well-being of the majority of Asia's households.

The average share of agriculture in Asia's merchandise exports has declined even more dramatically than the GDP share over the past four decades, from 45 percent to only 7 percent. During this period, the share of nonprimary goods in exports has doubled, to 85 percent. Among our 12 focus economies, only the exports of such goods from natural resource-rich Indonesia represent less than 75 percent of the total exports of the economy (table 1.8). The declining relative

Table 1.8. Sectoral Shares of Merchandise Exports, Asian Focus Economies, 1965–2004
(percent)

Economy	Agriculture and processed food				Other primary goods				Other goods			
	1965–69	1975–79	1985–89	2000–04	1965–69	1975–79	1985–89	2000–04	1965–69	1975–79	1985–89	2000–04
East Asia[a]	46	30	18	7	10	16	12	7	43	53	62	85
China	51	35	19	5	5	17	14	4	44	48	53	90
Indonesia	49	26	21	15	48	72	55	29	2	2	24	55
Korea, Rep. of	21	11	5	2	9	2	2	6	70	87	92	92
Malaysia	61	55	36	10	32	27	24	11	5	17	40	78
Philippines	78	55	27	6	16	17	11	3	7	18	32	83
Taiwan, China	39	13	6	3	2	2	2	3	59	85	92	94
Thailand	79	67	46	18	14	10	3	4	4	20	50	75
Vietnam	—	—	—	27	—	—	—	23	—	—	—	48
South Asia	42	40	26	13	9	8	7	8	49	52	66	78
Bangladesh	—	37	28	8	—	1	1	0	—	61	71	91
India	38	35	22	13	11	9	9	11	50	55	67	75
Pakistan	53	38	30	12	2	5	1	2	45	57	68	85
Sri Lanka	96	79	47	23	2	8	5	2	1	9	46	75
Total[a]	45	32	18	7	10	14	12	7	44	53	62	85

Sources: Sandri, Valenzuela, and Anderson 2007; World Development Indicators Database 2008.

Note: — = no data are available.

a. Ignores Vietnam in 1985–89, when the weight of Vietnam in Asian merchandise trade was less than 1 percent.

importance of farm exports has been much more rapid in Asia than in the rest of the world: the index of the revealed agricultural comparative advantage for Asia—defined as the share of agriculture and processed food in national exports as a ratio of the share of such products in worldwide merchandise exports—has fallen since the 1980s by about two-thirds in East Asia and one-third in South Asia. The index of agricultural trade specialization (defined as net exports, divided by the sum of imports and exports of agricultural and processed food products) has also fallen. The latter index, by definition, ranges from -1 to $+1$. It has become increasingly less positive, or it has become negative in virtually all our Asian focus economies in recent decades (table 1.9).

This apparent decline in agricultural comparative advantage is evident in the self-sufficiency data on primary farm products. Until 30 years ago, the region was almost exactly 100 percent self-sufficient in farm products; but, since then, the indicator has declined to less than 85 percent. The share of farm production that is exported has not changed much, averaging in the 4–6 percent range. However, there have been substantial changes in individual economies, including declines in Malaysia, the Philippines, Sri Lanka, and Taiwan, China and increases in China, Thailand, and Vietnam. In contrast, since the late 1970s, the share of imports in the domestic consumption of farm products has quadrupled, to around 20 percent (table 1.10).

The growing dependence on imports of farm products in Asia has occurred despite reductions in the taxation of agricultural exports and increases in the incentives provided to farmers through government policy reforms (discussed below). These reforms have probably contributed to poverty reduction in Asia. Using a price indicator that is simpler than the one developed by us below, Ravallion and Chen (2007) show that the reduction in the antiagricultural bias in farm price policies has contributed significantly to poverty reduction in China. Rural growth is also a key contributor to the reduction in poverty in India (Ravallion and Datt 1996). One may revisit these and other, similar studies using the more comprehensive measures of the extent of changes in distortions to agricultural incentives summarized below. To generate these measures, a common methodology has been adopted by the authors of the country case studies in this volume. A summary of the methodology follows, and additional details may be found in Anderson et al. (2008) and in appendix A.

Methodology for Measuring Rates of Assistance or Taxation

The NRA is defined as the percentage by which government policies have raised (or lowered if the NRA is less than 0) the gross returns to producers above (or below) the gross returns they would have received without government intervention. If a

(*Text continues on page 22.*)

Table 1.9. Indexes of Comparative Advantage in Agriculture and Processed Food, Asian Focus Economies, 1965–2004

a. Revealed comparative advantage index (world = 1.0)[a]

Economy	1965–69	1975–79	1985–89	2000–04
East Asia	2.2	2.2	1.1	0.7
China	2.1	2.1	1.3	0.6
Indonesia	2.0	1.3	1.4	1.7
Korea, Rep. of	0.8	0.6	0.3	0.3
Malaysia	2.4	2.9	2.4	1.1
Philippines	3.1	2.8	1.9	0.7
Taiwan, China	1.5	0.6	0.4	0.3
Thailand	3.1	3.5	3.1	2.0
Vietnam	—	—	—	3.0
South Asia	1.9	2.0	1.8	1.4
Bangladesh	—	1.9	1.9	0.9
India	1.5	1.8	1.5	1.4
Pakistan	2.1	1.9	2.1	1.4
Sri Lanka	3.8	4.1	3.2	2.5
Total	2.2	2.2	1.2	0.8

b. Trade specialization index (world = 0.0)[b]

Economy	1965–69	1975–79	1985–89	2000–04
East Asia	—	—	—	−0.03
China	—	—	0.07	−0.16
Indonesia	0.48	0.42	0.43	0.16
Korea, Rep. of	−0.63	−0.41	−0.45	−0.53
Malaysia	0.44	0.60	0.56	0.29
Philippines	0.47	0.51	0.25	−0.18
Taiwan, China	0.08		−0.27	−0.35
Thailand	0.68	0.69	0.57	0.44
Vietnam	—	—	—	0.44
South Asia	—	0.05	0.03	−0.06
Bangladesh	—	−0.37	−0.46	−0.62
India	−0.18	0.13	0.16	0.10
Pakistan	0.20	−0.13	−0.05	−0.24
Sri Lanka	0.34	0.30	0.21	0.08
Total	—	—	—	−0.03

Sources: Sandri, Valenzuela, and Anderson 2007; World Development Indicators Database 2008.

Note: — = no data are available.

a. The share of agriculture and processed food in national exports as a ratio of such products in worldwide merchandise exports. The world average is 1.0.

b. The ratio of net exports to the sum of the exports and imports of agricultural and processed food products. The world average is 0.0.

Table 1.10. Export Orientation, Import Dependence, and Self-Sufficiency in Primary Agricultural Production, Asian Focus Economies, 1961–2004

(%, at undistorted prices)

a. Exports, as a share of production

Economy	1961-64	1965-69	1970-74	1975-79	1980-84	1985-89	1990-94	1995-99	2000-04
Korea, Rep. of	0	0	0	0	0	0	0	2	1
Taiwan, China	5	9	13	14	10	10	6	5	6
China	2	2	2	3	5	5	7	7	7
Indonesia	—	—	6	5	5	6	4	5	4
Malaysia	70	64	54	41	35	34	19	12	9
Philippines	13	11	14	8	7	2	1	1	1
Thailand	—	—	13	20	24	26	25	25	30
Vietnam	—	—	—	—	—	3	4	9	11
Bangladesh	—	—	3	3	3	3	2	1	1
India	1	1	1	1	1	1	1	1	2
Pakistan	7	5	5	2	5	8	4	2	1
Sri Lanka	68	62	44	52	36	34	24	31	39
Total	3	4	4	4	4	6	6	5	5

(Table continues on the following page.)

· **Table 1.10. Export Orientation, Import Dependence, and Self-Sufficiency in Primary Agricultural Production, Asian Focus Economies, 1961–2004 (continued)**

b. Imports, as a share of apparent consumption

Economy	1961–64	1965–69	1970–74	1975–79	1980–84	1985–89	1990–94	1995–99	2000–04
Korea, Rep. of	4	5	12	8	11	9	11	11	13
Taiwan, China	24	33	56	66	76	81	86	90	93
China	2	2	2	3	5	5	7	7	7
Indonesia	—	—	0	1	1	1	1	2	2
Malaysia	13	6	3	1	1	1	2	3	6
Philippines	0	0	1	0	1	0	0	2	1
Thailand	—	—	0	0	0	0	0	2	5
Vietnam	—	—	—	—	—	0	0	0	0
Bangladesh	—	—	—	3	4	5	3	3	5
India	3	4	2	2	1	1	1	1	2
Pakistan	6	5	3	5	2	5	5	6	4
Sri Lanka	7	5	1	0	1	4	1	3	5
Total	3	4	4	5	7	12	17	17	19

c. Self-sufficiency ratio

Economy	1961–64	1965–69	1970–74	1975–79	1980–84	1985–89	1990–94	1995–99	2000–04
Korea, Rep. of	96	95	88	92	89	91	90	91	87
Taiwan, China	80	73	51	40	27	21	15	11	7
China	99	101	100	99	98	101	101	99	98
Indonesia	—	—	106	105	104	106	104	103	102
Malaysia	293	265	215	167	152	150	122	110	104
Philippines	115	112	116	108	106	101	101	99	99
Thailand	—	—	115	125	131	135	133	130	137
Vietnam	—	—	—	—	—	103	104	110	112
Bangladesh	—	—	98	99	99	98	99	98	96
India	98	97	99	99	99	99	100	100	100
Pakistan	101	100	102	97	103	104	99	96	97
Sri Lanka	297	298	194	221	155	144	131	142	157
Total	100	100	100	99	97	94	88	87	85

Sources: Author compilation; FAO Agricultural Trade Database 2008.

Note: Compiled using estimates of the total agricultural production of covered and noncovered products, valued at undistorted prices, plus total agricultural trade value data. Self-sufficiency is defined for each product as the ratio of production to production, plus imports, minus exports. — = no data are available.

trade measure is the sole government intervention, then the measured NRA will also be the consumer tax equivalent (CTE) rate at that same point in the value chain. Where there are also domestic producer or consumer taxes or subsidies, the NRA and CTE will no longer be equal, and at least one of them will be different from the price distortion at the border caused by trade measures.[8]

NRAs and CTEs may be used for several purposes, and the purpose affects the appropriate choice of methodology. In our project, we rely on NRAs and CTEs to achieve three purposes. One purpose is to generate a comparable set of numbers across a wide range of countries and over a long time period. This means the methodology must be both simple and somewhat flexible. Another purpose is to provide a single number, the NRA, to indicate the total extent of transfers to or from farmers because of government agricultural policies and another number, the CTE, to indicate the extent of the transfers to or from consumers. The NRA and the CTE are both expressed as a percentage of the undistorted price or in dollar terms. This is also the purpose of the OECD's producer and consumer support estimates, which may be negative if the transfers from the relevant group exceed the transfers to the relevant group. Our research project's agricultural NRAs and CTEs are similar in spirit to the OECD estimates, but there are also important differences, which are outlined below. Our third purpose is to enable economic modelers to use the NRAs as producer price wedges for individual primary and lightly processed agricultural products and to use the CTEs as consumer price wedges in single-sector, multisector, and economy-wide policy simulation models by allocating these wedges to particular policy instruments such as trade taxes or domestic producer or consumer subsidies or taxes.

The NRAs are based on our estimates of assistance to individual industries. Great care has gone into generating the NRAs for each covered agricultural industry, particularly in countries where trade costs are high, the pass-through along the value chain is affected by imperfect competition, and the markets for foreign currency have been highly distorted to varying degrees at various times.

Most distortions in industries producing tradables arise from trade measures such as quantitative trade restrictions or tariffs imposed on the import cost, insurance, and freight price or export subsidies or taxes imposed on the free on board price at the country's border. An ad valorem tariff or export subsidy is the equivalent of a production subsidy and a consumption tax at the same rate expressed as a percentage of the border price. For this reason, such tariffs and subsidies are captured in the NRAs and CTEs at the point in the value chain at which a product is first traded. To obtain the NRAs for farmers, the authors of the country studies have estimated or guessed the extent of pass-through back to the farmgate and added any domestic farm output subsidies. To obtain the CTEs, they have also added any product-specific domestic consumer taxes to the distortions caused by border measures. Note that the NRAs and CTEs differ from the OECD's producer and consumer support estimates in that the latter pair is expressed as a percentage of the distorted price and, hence, will be lower (for positive protection rates) than the former pair, which is expressed as a percentage of the undistorted price.

We have decided not to seek estimates of the more complex effective rate of assistance even though it is, in principle, a better single partial equilibrium measure of the distortions in producer incentives. To establish these alternative estimates, we must know, for each product, the value added and various intermediate input shares in output. These data are not available in most developing countries even for a few years, let alone for every year in the long time series that is the focus of our study. Moreover, in most countries, the distortions in farm input prices are small compared with the distortions in farm output prices. Nonetheless, if the product-specific distortions to input costs are significant, they may be captured by estimating their equivalent values in terms of a higher output price and then including this estimate in the NRA for individual agricultural industries wherever data allow. We also add any non-product-specific distortions, including distortions in farm input prices, into the estimate for the overall sectoral NRA for agriculture.

The targeted minimum product coverage of our NRA estimates is 70 percent based on the gross value of farm production at undistorted prices. This target coverage is similar to the coverage of the OECD producer support estimates. Unlike the OECD, however, we do not routinely assume that the nominal assistance for covered products applies equally to the farm products we do not cover. This is because, in developing countries, agricultural policies affecting our noncovered products are often different from those affecting our covered products. For example, nontradables among noncovered farm goods—often highly perishable products or products of low value relative to the transport cost—are frequently not subject to direct distortionary policies. We have asked the authors of the country case studies to provide three sets of NRA guesstimates for noncovered farm products, one each for the import-competing, exportable, and nontradable subsectors. Weighted averages for all agricultural products have then been generated using the gross values of production at unassisted prices as weights. For countries that also provide non-product-specific agricultural subsidies or taxes—assumed to be shared on a pro rata basis between tradables and nontradables—or assistance decoupled from production, the net assistance from these measures is then added to the product-specific assistance to obtain NRAs for total agriculture. We apply the same procedure to obtain NRAs also for tradable agriculture for use in generating RRAs (which are defined below).

How best to present regional aggregate NRA and RRA estimates depends on the purpose for which the averages are required. We generate weighted average NRAs for covered products for each country because only then are we able to add the NRAs for noncovered products and the non-product-specific assistance to obtain the NRAs for all agriculture. In averaging across countries, we consider each polity as an observation of interest. So, a simple average is meaningful for the purpose of political economy analysis. However, if one wishes to acquire a sense of the distortion in the agriculture of an entire region, one needs a weighted average. The weighted average NRAs for covered primary agriculture may be generated by multiplying the share of each primary industry in the gross value of production (valued at farmgate equivalent undistorted prices) by the corresponding NRAs and adding across industries.[9] The overall sectoral rate, which we denote as *NRAag,* may be obtained by also adding the actual or assumed information for noncovered farm commodities and, where it exists, the aggregate value of non-product-specific and decoupled assistance in agriculture.

A weighted average can be similarly generated for the tradables part of agriculture, including those industries producing products such as milk and sugar that require only light processing before they are traded. This is accomplished by assuming that the product's share of non-product-specific assistance equals the product's weight in the total. Call this $NRAag^t$.

In addition to the mean, it is important also to provide a measure of the dispersion or variability of the NRA estimates across the covered products. The cost of government policy distortions in incentives in terms of resource misallocation tends to be greater, the greater the degree of substitution in production (Lloyd 1974). In the case of an agricultural sector that involves a use of farmland that is sector specific, but transferable among farm activities, the greater the variation of NRAs across industries within the sector, then the higher will be the welfare cost of the market interventions. A simple indicator of dispersion is the standard deviation in the NRAs of the covered industries.

Each industry is classified as import-competing, or as a producer of exportables, or as a producer of nontradables. This status sometimes changes over time. It is possible to generate for each year the weighted average NRAs for the two groups of tradables (import-competing products and exportables). These NRAs are used to generate a trade bias index (TBI), which is defined as follows:

$$TBI = [(1 + NRAag_x/100)/(1 + NRAag_m/100) - 1], \qquad (1.1)$$

where $NRAag_m$ and $NRAag_x$ are the average percentage NRAs for the import-competing and exportable parts of the agricultural sector. The TBI indicates, in a single number, the extent to which the (typically) antitrade bias (negative TBI) in agricultural policies changes over time.

Farmers are affected not only by the prices for their own outputs, but also, albeit indirectly, through changes in factor market prices and the exchange rate because of the incentives nonagricultural producers face. Thus, it is the *relative* prices and, hence, the *relative* rates of government assistance that affect producer incentives. More than 70 years ago, Lerner (1936) provided the symmetry theorem, which proved that, in a two-sector economy, an import tax has the same effect as an export tax. This carries over to a model that also includes a third sector producing only nontradables and to a model with imperfect competition, regardless of the economy's size (Vousden 1990). If one assumes that there are no distortions in the markets for nontradables and that the value shares of agricultural and nonagricultural nontradable products remain constant, then the economy-wide effect of distortions in agricultural incentives may be captured by measuring the extent to which the tradable parts of agricultural production are assisted or taxed relative to the producers of other tradables. Because we are able to generate estimates of the average NRAs for nonagricultural tradables, we are then able to calculate an RRA, which is defined in percentage terms as follows:

$$RRA = 100[(1 + NRAag^t/100)/(1 + NRAnonag^t/100) - 1], \qquad (1.2)$$

where $NRAag^t$ and $NRAnonag^t$ are the weighted average percentage NRAs for the tradable parts of the agricultural and nonagricultural sectors, respectively. Since the NRA cannot be less than -100 percent if producers are to earn anything, neither can the RRA (assuming $NRAnonag^t$ is positive). If both of those sectors are equally assisted, the RRA is zero. This measure is useful in that, if it is below (above) zero, it provides an internationally comparable indication of the extent to which a country's policy regime has an anti- or proagricultural bias.

In calculating the NRAs for producers of agricultural and nonagricultural tradables, we use the methodology outlined in appendix A to seek to include distortions generated by dual or multiple exchange rates. Direct interventions in the markets for foreign currency were common in some Asian countries, including China in the 1970s and 1980s. However, authors of some of the focus country studies have experienced difficulty in determining an appropriate estimate of the extent of this distortion. So, the impact of such interventions on the NRAs has not been included in all the studies. The exclusion of this impact in some countries (for example, India) means that the estimated (typically) positive NRAs for importables and (typically) negative NRAs for exportables are smaller than they should be in these studies. In cases where the NRAs for importables dominate the NRAs for exportables, this omission would lead to an underestimate of the average (positive) NRAs for such tradables. The converse would also be true. In either case, this leads also to an underestimate of the (anti-)TBI.

To obtain U.S. dollar values for farmer assistance and consumer taxation, Valenzuela, Kurzweil, Croser, Nelgen, and Anderson (see appendix B) have multiplied the country author NRA estimates by the gross value of production at undistorted prices to obtain an estimate, in current U.S. dollars, of the direct gross subsidy equivalents of assistance to farmers. These estimates are then added across the products of a country and across countries for all products to obtain regional aggregate transfer estimates for the economies under study. These values are calculated in constant dollars and are also expressed as estimates per farmworker.

To obtain comparable U.S. dollar value estimates of consumer transfers, the CTE estimate at the point at which a product is first traded is multiplied by consumption (obtained from the FAO SUA-FBS Database), which is valued at undistorted prices, to obtain an estimate in constant U.S. dollars of the tax equivalent to consumers of primary farm products. This is then added across the products of a country and across countries for any or all products to obtain regional aggregate transfer estimates on the economies under study. These values are also expressed on a per capita basis.

Estimates of Asian Policy Indicators

We begin with the NRAs in agriculture and compare them with the NRAs for nonagricultural tradables. We also present constant U.S. dollar equivalents of the assistance and taxation among farmers, as well as the CTEs of policies as they affect the buyers of farm products.

NRAs in agriculture

Agricultural price and trade policies reduced average farmer earnings in developing Asia throughout the period up to the 1980s by more than 20 percent.[10] This implicit taxation declined beginning in the early 1980s, and, in the mid-1990s, the NRAs switched sign and became increasingly positive. The averages hide considerable diversity within the region, however. The nominal assistance for farmers in Korea and Taiwan, China was positive starting in the early 1960s (although small initially). The NRAs were slightly above zero in Indonesia during some years in the 1970s and 1980s, as they were in Pakistan prior to the independence of Bangladesh (East Pakistan) in 1971. The average NRAs in India and the Philippines became positive in the 1980s (table 1.11). A visual impression of the differences across countries and the rise in average NRAs is supplied in figure 1.2, in which the situation in 2000–04 is compared with the situation in 1980–84. This trend is evident among the vast majority of the commodity NRAs for the region, too. Meat and milk were the only products for which the assistance rates were cut over 1980–2004 (figure 1.3).

Table 1.11. NRAs for Agricultural Products, Asian Focus Economies, 1955–2004
(percent)

Economy, indicator	1955–59	1960–64	1965–69	1970–74	1975–79	1980–84	1985–89	1990–94	1995–99	2000–04
Northeast Asia	-42.8	-42.6	-41.7	-41.2	-39.5	-38.2	-25.7	-1.7	14.4	11.9
Korea, Rep. of	-3.2	4.0	13.4	35.7	56.3	89.4	126.1	152.8	129.8	137.3
Taiwan, China[a]	-12.0	3.6	3.0	9.3	7.1	14.9	27.1	38.1	46.4	61.3
China[b]	-45.2	-45.2	-45.2	-45.2	-45.2	-45.2	-35.5	-14.3	6.6	5.9
Southeast Asia	—	-6.8	5.9	-8.8	0.0	4.6	-0.4	-4.2	0.0	11.1
Indonesia	—	—	—	-2.6	9.3	9.2	-1.7	-6.6	-8.6	12.0
Malaysia	—	-7.2	-7.5	-9.0	-13.0	-4.6	1.3	2.3	-0.2	1.2
Philippines	—	-5.3	14.4	-5.1	-7.1	-1.0	18.7	18.5	32.9	22.0
Thailand	—	—	—	-20.3	-14.0	-2.0	-6.2	-5.7	1.7	-0.2
Vietnam[a]	—	—	—	—	—	—	-13.9	-25.4	0.6	21.2
South Asia	0.0	-0.5	0.6	0.4	-5.5	0.6	20.9	0.7	0.2	13.6
Bangladesh	—	—	—	-16.0	1.4	-3.3	11.7	-1.5	-5.2	2.7
India[b]	0.1	0.1	0.1	0.2	-5.6	1.9	24.9	1.8	0.7	15.8
Pakistan[a]	—	-0.7	15.3	6.8	-8.5	-6.4	-4.0	-6.9	-1.6	1.2
Sri Lanka	-2.3	-22.8	-24.5	-16.3	-25.5	-13.5	-9.9	-1.2	12.2	9.5
Unweighted average[c]	-12.3	-10.2	-3.9	-4.7	-4.1	3.2	11.5	12.1	16.8	21.7
Weighted average	-27.3	-26.7	-25.1	-25.3	-23.8	-20.6	-9.0	-2.0	7.5	12.0
Dispersion, country NRAs[d]	25.3	25.2	31.2	29.9	32.5	39.9	43.8	47.5	36.6	38.0
Product coverage[e]	52	65	63	64	68	74	78	75	73	66

Sources: Author compilation; Anderson and Valenzuela, 2008; estimates reported in chapters 2–12 of this volume.

Note: For each economy, the figure shows weighted averages, including product-specific input distortions, non-product-specific assistance, and guesstimates by the authors of chapters 2–12 of the averages for noncovered farm products. The weights are based on the gross value of total agricultural production at undistorted prices. — = no data are available.

a. Pakistan: 1960–64 is 1961–64. Taiwan, China: 2000–04 is 2000–03. Vietnam: 1985–89 is 1986–89.

b. The estimates for China before 1981 and India before 1965 are based on the assumption that the NRAs were the same as the average NRAs for those economies in 1981–84 and 1965–69, respectively, and that the gross value of production of those economies in the missing years is the same as the average share of the value of the production of the economies in total world production in 1981–84 and 1965–69, respectively. This assumption is conservative in that, in both countries, the average NRAs were probably even lower in earlier years.

c. The unweighted average is the simple average across the 12 economies of the national weighted NRA averages.

d. Dispersion is a simple five-year average of the annual standard deviation around the weighted mean of the national NRAs.

e. Weighted averages for the covered products.

Figure 1.2. NRAs in Agriculture, Asian Focus Economies, 1980–84 and 2000–04

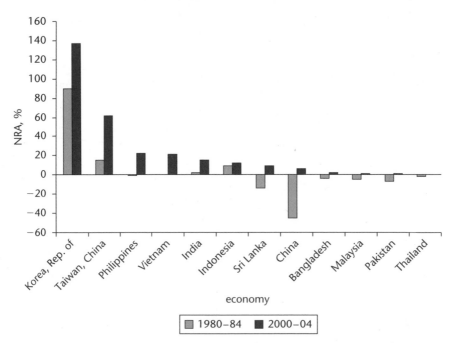

Sources: Author compilation; Anderson and Valenzuela, forthcoming; estimates reported in chapters 2–12 of this volume.

Note: There are no data for Vietnam in 1980–84. The estimates for China before 1981 are based on the assumption that the NRAs were the same as the average NRAs in 1981–84 and that the gross value of production in the missing years is the same as the average share of the value of production of the economy in total world production in 1981–84.

Figure 1.3 also illustrates the diversity of the region's average NRAs across farm commodities. In Asia, as in other regions, the product NRAs for rice pudding— rice, milk, and sugar—are among the highest, but, even among these three products, there is great diversity across economies in the NRAs. The five-year averages range from almost zero to as much as 400 percent for rice and 140 percent for milk in Korea and to 230 percent for sugar in Bangladesh (figure 1.4). This suggests that the production of these products in Asia is not optimally allocated for efficient resource use.

There is a great deal of diversity across economies in the average NRAs and across commodities within the farm sector of each economy. Measured through the standard deviation, the extent of both types of diversity has grown rather than diminished over the past five decades. The cross-economy diversity of average

Figure 1.3. NRAs, by Product, Asian Focus Economies, 1980–84 and 2000–04

a. Unweighted average

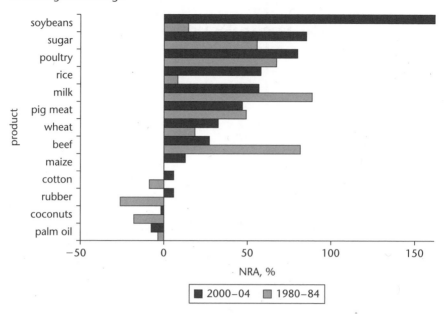

b. Weighted average[a]

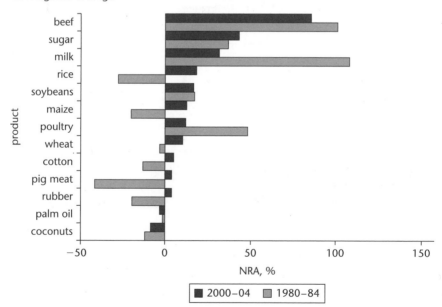

Sources: Author compilation; Anderson and Valenzuela, forthcoming; estimates reported in chapters 2–12 of this volume.

a. Weights are based on the gross value of total agricultural production at undistorted prices. Each NRA by economy and by product has been weighted by the value of the production in the economy of that commodity in a given year. Products representing less than 1 percent of the gross value of regional production are excluded. These include cocoa, onions, chilies, barley, jute, sunflower seeds, garlic, peppers, cabbages, cassava, potatoes, eggs, tea, coffee, sorghum, rapeseeds, chickpeas, groundnuts, and beef.

Figure 1.4. NRAs for Rice, Milk, and Sugar, Asian Focus Economies, 1980–84 and 2000–04

a. Rice

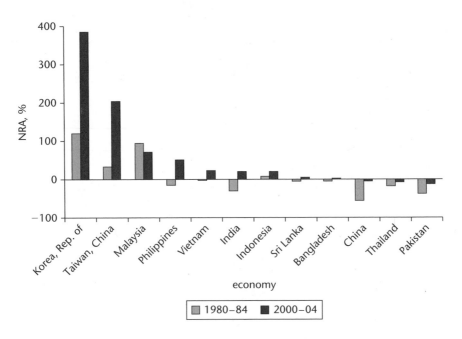

b. Milk

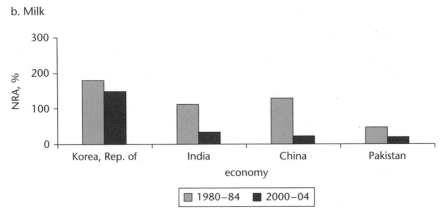

Figure 1.4. (*continued*)

c. Sugar

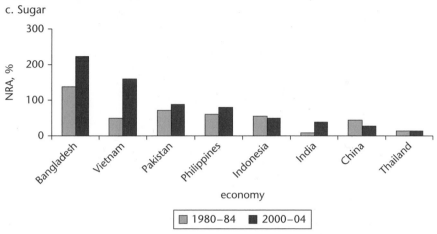

Sources: Author compilation; Anderson and Valenzuela, 2008; estimates reported in chapters 2–12 of this volume.

Note: Vietnam: 1980–84 is 1986–89 for rice and 1990–95 for sugar.

NRAs is evident at the bottom of table 1.11: the dispersion indicator rises from around 25 percent in the early years we are studying to around 40 percent in recent years. The cross-commodity diversity within each economy is clear in table 1.12 (unweighted averages), where the standard deviation among NRAs is reported for covered products (which account for up to 75 percent of the value of agricultural production at undistorted prices). This means that much could be gained through improved resource reallocation among economies and within the agricultural sector of each economy if the differences in rates of assistance were reduced.

A striking feature of the distortion pattern within the farm sector is the strong antitrade bias. This is evident in figure 1.5, which depicts the average NRAs in the region for agriculture's import-competing and export subsectors. The average NRAs for import-competing products are always positive, and the trend is upward-sloping, whereas the average NRAs for exportables are negative before gradually approaching zero after the 1980s. While the gap between the NRAs for these two subsectors has diminished little in the region since the 1960s, there are nonetheless several countries—Malaysia, Pakistan, Sri Lanka, Thailand—in which the gap has narrowed and, hence, the TBIs have approached zero (table 1.13).

The rise in the average NRAs since the 1980s is too large to be explained only by loses in the comparative advantage of farm products as economies industrialize. The export shares indicated in table 1.13 show that the share of the export

(*Text continues on page 37.*)

Table 1.12. NRA Dispersion across Covered Agricultural Products, Asian Focus Economies, 1955–2004

(percent)

Economy	1955–59	1960–64	1965–69	1970–74	1975–79	1980–84	1985–89	1990–94	1995–99	2000–04
Northeast Asia[a]	38.5	38.5	66.8	61.7	68.6	64.0	67.1	80.5	102.3	116.6
Korea, Rep. of	34.1	40.5	85.0	82.5	89.0	80.1	114.8	164.2	200.1	225.4
Taiwan, China[b]	42.8	36.4	48.7	40.9	48.2	37.5	34.3	56.5	88.4	109.0
China	—	—	—	—	—	74.3	52.3	20.7	18.4	15.3
Southeast Asia[a]	—	21.1	30.4	23.9	32.7	46.2	47.9	42.5	39.7	40.4
Indonesia	—	—	—	29.1	49.4	53.6	35.0	40.5	49.0	33.3
Malaysia	—	19.8	10.6	11.0	34.8	58.6	90.5	71.9	33.7	40.1
Philippines	—	22.5	50.2	28.3	24.2	42.7	50.9	30.1	40.6	37.6
Thailand	—	—	—	27.5	22.4	30.1	29.3	25.1	22.9	16.7
Vietnam[b]	—	—	—	—	—	—	33.6	44.7	52.4	74.3
South Asia[a]	44.2	46.3	64.9	51.8	55.2	51.5	86.2	55.4	45.0	58.7
Bangladesh	—	—	—	—	71.4	67.6	190.7	77.5	67.9	101.2
India	—	35.5	68.0	45.8	49.8	39.2	46.9	28.5	19.4	21.5
Pakistan[b]	—	74.6	105.8	77.6	45.0	52.2	69.4	34.4	29.4	43.1
Sri Lanka	44.2	28.7	20.9	31.9	54.6	46.9	37.9	81.3	63.3	69.1
Unweighted average[a]	39.0	36.8	55.5	41.5	48.0	51.1	66.9	55.9	55.6	64.4

Sources: Author compilation; Anderson and Valenzuela, 2008; estimates reported in chapters 2–12 of this volume.

Note: Dispersion for each country is a simple five-year average of the annual standard deviation around the weighted mean of the NRAs across covered products. — = no data are available.

a. The unweighted average is the simple average across the relevant economies of the simple five-year dispersion measure averages.

b. Pakistan: 1960–64 is 1961–64. Taiwan, China: 2000–04 is 2000–03. Vietnam: 1985–89 is 1986–89.

Figure 1.5. NRAs for Exportable, Import-Competing, and All Agricultural Products, Asian Focus Economies, 1955–2004

a. Unweighted averages

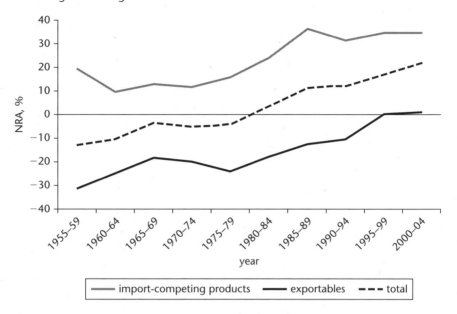

b. Weighted averages

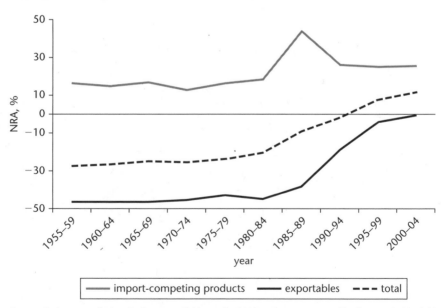

Sources: Author compilation; Anderson and Valenzuela, 2008; estimates reported in chapters 2–12 of this volume.

Note: Total NRAs may be above or below the exportable and importable averages because assistance to nontradables and non-product-specific assistance are also included. The values used in the NRA estimates are based on the assumption that the NRAs in agriculture in China before 1981 and in India before 1965 are the same as the average NRAs in those economies in 1981–84 and 1965–69, respectively, and that the gross value of production of those economies in the missing years is the same as the average share of the value of the production of the economies in total world production in 1981–84 and 1965–69, respectively.

Table 1.13. NRAs for Agricultural Exportable and Import-Competing Products and the TBI, Asian Focus Economies, 1955–2004

(percent)

Economy, indicator	1955–59	1960–64	1965–69	1970–74	1975–79	1980–84	1985–89	1990–94	1995–99	2000–04
Korea, Rep. of										
NRA, exportable	-3.3	—	—	—	—	—	—	—	—	—
NRA, import-competing	—	4.9	16.3	46.1	71.8	118.6	159.8	197.6	164.8	171.9
TBI[a]	0.03	-0.05	-0.14	-0.32	-0.42	-0.54	-0.62	-0.66	-0.62	-0.63
Export share[b]	0	0	0	0	0	0	0	0	0	0
Taiwan, China[c]										
NRA, exportable	-18.1	5.7	4.3	15.4	10.3	25.1	48.9	57.1	57.0	70.3
NRA, import-competing	-3.6	0.5	2.3	3.3	5.2	9.2	18.1	42.0	54.3	71.3
TBI[a]	-0.15	0.05	0.02	0.12	0.05	0.15	0.27	0.11	0.02	0.00
Export share[b]	85	80	78	74	70	61	47	28	25	24
China										
NRA, exportable	—	—	—	—	—	-56.9	-46.0	-21.8	-0.8	-0.1
NRA, import-competing	—	—	—	—	—	-11.0	20.4	2.2	17.0	7.3
TBI[a]	—	—	—	—	—	-0.50	-0.55	-0.23	-0.15	-0.07
Export share[b]	—	—	—	—	—	79	88	80	75	72
Northeast Asia										
NRA, exportable	-18.1	5.7	4.3	15.4	10.3	-40.0	-44.2	-20.5	-0.2	0.2
NRA, import-competing	-3.4	3.9	14.4	38.3	59.7	21.2	51.8	42.8	40.5	26.4
TBI[a]	-0.15	0.02	-0.09	-0.17	-0.31	-0.50	-0.63	-0.44	-0.29	-0.21
Export share[b]	35	31	32	29	29	76	83	74	70	69
Indonesia										
NRA, exportable	—	—	—	-3.3	-0.3	-7.0	-16.5	-24.6	-17.2	-3.3
NRA, import-competing	—	—	—	-1.3	16.5	19.5	5.1	-0.7	-5.8	24.7
TBI[a]	—	—	—	0.01	-0.14	-0.21	-0.20	-0.24	-0.12	-0.22
Export share[b]	—	—	—	57	37	34	32	29	34	37
Malaysia										
NRA, exportable	—	-11.4	-9.0	-12.7	-18.7	-11.8	-5.0	-4.1	-3.0	-1.3
NRA, import-competing	—	13.0	-1.8	2.5	21.6	36.7	44.1	33.2	10.8	12.3

TBI[a]	—	—	-0.22	-0.06	-0.14	-0.31	-0.35	-0.33	-0.28	-0.12	-0.12
Export share[b]	—	—	84	79	78	86	86	86	82	80	81
Philippines											
NRA, exportable	—	—	-6.2	35.4	-10.2	-9.9	-3.8	6.2	4.8	-0.7	-3.7
NRA, import-competing	—	—	-5.3	10.1	-2.7	-6.1	0.6	30.0	27.6	47.9	30.8
TBI[a]	—	—	0.00	0.23	-0.04	-0.04	-0.04	-0.18	-0.17	-0.32	-0.25
Export share[b]	—	—	21	22	30	41	41	39	33	25	22
Thailand											
NRA, exportable	—	—	—	—	-26.7	-19.4	-11.1	-11.7	-9.2	-3.8	-0.6
NRA, import-competing	—	—	—	—	-4.8	1.9	45.3	22.0	6.4	34.4	4.7
TBI[a]	—	—	—	—	-0.18	-0.20	-0.37	-0.24	-0.14	-0.27	-0.03
Export share[b]	—	—	—	—	83	83	84	84	81	85	86
Vietnam[c]											
NRA, exportable	—	—	—	—	—	—	—	-17.5	-27.1	-2.0	17.7
NRA, import-competing	—	—	—	—	—	—	—	37.1	25.8	65.4	67.3
TBI[a]	—	—	—	—	—	—	—	-0.37	-0.42	-0.40	-0.29
Export share[b]	—	—	—	—	—	—	—	98	96	96	94
Southeast Asia											
NRA, exportable	—	—	-10.8	4.4	-13.9	-10.8	-8.7	-11.0	-14.9	-7.6	1.0
NRA, import-competing	—	—	4.5	8.2	-2.7	11.1	18.4	10.6	5.8	8.0	24.9
TBI[a]	—	—	-0.15	-0.03	-0.12	-0.20	-0.23	-0.19	-0.20	-0.14	-0.19
Export share[b]	—	—	57	44	61	51	48	51	48	51	53
Bangladesh											
NRA, exportable	—	—	—	—	—	-34.6	-26.2	-32.4	-33.0	-9.9	-33.2
NRA, import—competing	—	—	—	—	—	6.5	-1.9	24.4	-0.1	-7.9	6.0
TBI[a]	—	—	—	—	—	-0.30	-0.23	-0.45	-0.33	0.00	-0.37
Export share[b]	—	—	—	—	—	13	9	7	11	7	5
India											
NRA, exportable	—	—	—	-37.4	-22.3	-35.9	-27.8	-6.0	-15.3	-12.4	-6.4
NRA, import-competing	—	—	—	41.7	52.7	74.5	58.8	81.4	38.3	22.5	34.2
TBI[a]	—	—	—	-0.55	-0.50	-0.63	-0.54	-0.47	-0.38	-0.28	-0.30
Export share[b]	—	—	—	58	74	73	63	43	70	71	51

(*Table continues on the following page.*)

Table 1.13. NRAs for Agricultural Exportable and Import-Competing Products and the TBI, Asian Focus Economies, 1955–2004 *(continued)*

Economy, indicator	1955–59	1960–64	1965–69	1970–74	1975–79	1980–84	1985–89	1990–94	1995–99	2000–04
Pakistan[c]										
NRA, exportable	—	−33.3	−35.3	−20.1	−33.5	−29.1	−32.1	−16.7	−4.4	−5.6
NRA, import-competing	—	1.8	45.0	19.2	−4.3	−1.9	5.4	−7.9	−1.9	3.7
TBI[a]	—	−0.38	−0.55	−0.27	−0.31	−0.28	−0.35	−0.10	−0.02	−0.08
Export share[b]	—	31	29	24	25	27	30	24	21	22
Sri Lanka										
NRA, exportable	−22.8	−40.0	−38.6	−41.1	−45.2	−31.1	−21.4	−24.2	−2.0	5.9
NRA, import-competing	62.5	11.9	−5.9	9.0	−3.7	−0.6	−2.1	22.4	31.8	12.8
TBI[a]	−0.52	−0.45	−0.35	−0.45	−0.43	−0.31	−0.18	−0.38	−0.25	−0.05
Export share[b]	76	72	68	50	62	58	52	51	58	58
South Asia										
NRA, exportable	−22.8	−37.5	−37.2	−30.0	−36.1	−27.9	−20.6	−15.8	−12.0	−6.2
NRA, import-competing	62.5	39.2	41.2	39.4	45.1	37.9	63.3	25.1	14.5	26.5
TBI[a]	−0.52	−0.55	−0.56	−0.50	−0.56	−0.48	−0.51	−0.33	−0.23	−0.26
Export share[b]	76	27	53	61	63	56	32	63	64	46
Asia, unweighted average[d]										
NRA, exportable	−20.4	−16.3	−12.5	−15.5	−20.8	−17.3	−12.5	−10.4	0.1	0.9
NRA, import-competing	18.9	6.8	15.2	13.2	17.7	24.6	36.4	31.4	34.5	34.5
TBI	−0.33	−0.22	−0.24	−0.25	−0.33	−0.34	−0.36	−0.32	−0.26	−0.25
Asia, weighted average[d]										
NRA, exportable	−20.2	−12.6	−27.2	−20.7	−25.4	−41.7	−38.1	−19.1	−4.3	−0.6
NRA, import-competing	5.9	4.7	33.9	26.6	31.3	20.8	43.8	25.8	24.8	25.4
TBI	−0.25	−0.17	−0.46	−0.37	−0.43	−0.52	−0.57	−0.36	−0.23	−0.21
Export share[b]	47	37	50	58	55	65	69	66	65	63

Sources: Author compilation; Anderson and Valenzuela, 2008; estimates reported in chapters 2–12 of this volume.

Note: — = no data are available.

a. The TBI is defined as $(1 + NRAag_x/100)/(1 + NRAag_m/100) - 1$, where $NRAag_m$ and $NRAag_x$ are the average percentage NRAs for the import-competing and exportable parts of the agricultural sector, respectively.

b. The export share is the share of exportables in the gross value of the production of all agricultural tradables at undistorted prices.

c. Pakistan: 1960–64 is 1961–64. Taiwan, China: 2000–04 is 2000–03. Vietnam: 1985–89 is 1986–89.

d. These NRAs differ from those in figure 1.5 because these do not include backcast estimates for China and India. The regional TBI averages are calculated from the regional NRA averages for the exportable and import-competing parts of the agricultural sector.

subsector in total tradable farm production has not declined much in most Asian economies. This suggests that the main motive for intervention cannot have been to raise revenue by taxing trade; nor can it have only been to reduce distortions. Otherwise, there would have been no overshooting in the transition from taxing to assisting farmers, on average, nor would there have been the increase in assistance to import-competing farmers.

The contributions to overall agricultural NRAs by input subsidies, domestic output taxes or subsidies, and trade measures at the border are summarized in table 1.14. (Non-product-specific assistance, which is not shown in the table, added only around 2 percentage points during the period of our study.) The distortions in product-specific input prices contributed little, on average, to the overall regional NRAs in agriculture. They reduced the negative value slightly in the 1960s and have added slightly to the positive value during the past decade or so. The contribution of input subsidies is largest in India, especially in recent years when it has added almost 10 percentage points to the sector's NRAs and has been a nontrivial item in overall government budgets. Earlier, the contribution of input subsidies was high in Indonesia, too, peaking at 7 percentage points in the 1980s, before reforms sent them back to only 2 percentage points more recently. There are fewer domestic output subsidies, on average, in the region now, although such subsidies were implemented in India and Sri Lanka during earlier decades (table 1.14). In China, output taxes in kind were prevalent until recently.

The U.S. dollar value equivalents of the positive or negative assistance to farmers because of agricultural price and trade policies have been nontrivial. The antiagricultural bias peaked in the region in the late 1970s at more than US$130 billion per year at constant 2000 U.S. dollars (2000 U.S. dollars; see the bottom row of table 1.15, panel a). This is equivalent to a gross tax of around US$170 for each person engaged in agriculture. Most of the US$130 billion was generated by China's antiagricultural policies. India was the second most important contributor in the 1960s and 1970s. Thanks to the reforms of the past two decades, this taxation has gradually disappeared in all our focus economies. This reform does not mean there is no intervention now. Rather, the negative influence has been replaced by positive assistance to farmers in most countries, totaling around US$60 billion per year in recent years. China, India, and Korea each contributed about one-quarter of the total. In recent years, the total has averaged around US$60 per farmworker in Asia (table 1.15, panel b). This is not insignificant relative to per capita income in the region, but the amount is unevenly distributed. It ranges from around US$6,900 and US$5,300 in Korea and Taiwan, China (more than one-third of per capita income in those economies) to around $150 in the Philippines, $90 in Indonesia, $60 in India, Malaysia, and Vietnam, and virtually zero in Bangladesh, Pakistan, and Thailand.

(*Text continues on page 44.*)

Table 1.14. NRAs for Covered Agricultural Products, by Policy Instrument, Asian Focus Economies, 1955–2004
(percent)

Economy, indicator	1955–59	1960–64	1965–69	1970–74	1975–79	1980–84	1985–89	1990–94	1995–99	2000–04
Korea, Rep. of										
NRA, inputs	0.0	0.0	0.0	0.0	0.0	0.0	0.0	0.0	0.0	0.0
NRA, domestic MS[a]	−0.2	−0.4	0.9	4.2	7.1	5.3	5.5	5.9	6.1	5.2
NRA, border MS[a]	−3.7	4.7	15.7	43.4	66.7	117.5	161.2	196.0	176.9	208.5
NRA, total agriculture	−3.9	4.4	16.6	47.6	73.8	122.8	166.7	201.9	182.9	213.6
Taiwan, China[b]										
NRA, inputs	0.0	0.0	0.0	0.0	0.0	0.0	0.0	0.0	0.0	0.0
NRA, domestic MS[a]	0.0	0.0	0.0	0.0	0.0	0.0	0.0	0.0	0.0	0.0
NRA, border MS[a]	−23.6	7.3	6.3	20.4	14.4	36.9	82.4	117.4	142.2	178.4
NRA, total agriculture	−23.6	7.3	6.3	20.4	14.4	36.9	82.4	117.4	142.2	178.4
China										
NRA, inputs	—	—	—	—	—	0.3	0.3	0.2	0.7	0.5
NRA, domestic MS[a]	—	—	—	—	—	−12.6	−6.3	−6.2	−1.1	−1.4
NRA, border MS[a]	—	—	—	—	—	−38.5	−34.6	−12.9	2.7	1.8
NRA, total agriculture	—	—	—	—	—	−50.8	−40.6	−18.9	2.3	0.9
Northeast Asia[c]										
NRA, inputs	0.0	0.0	0.0	0.0	0.0	0.2	0.3	0.2	0.7	0.5
NRA, domestic MS[a]	−0.1	−0.2	0.6	2.6	4.6	−8.4	−5.8	−5.5	−0.8	−1.2
NRA, border MS[a]	−12.1	5.7	12.3	34.9	48.3	−11.4	−26.6	−1.5	10.9	9.0
NRA, total agriculture	−12.3	−5.5	12.9	37.5	53.0	−19.6	−32.2	−6.8	10.7	8.3
Indonesia										
NRA, inputs	—	—	—	6.0	6.8	7.3	6.0	3.2	2.6	2.3
NRA, domestic MS[a]	—	—	—	0.0	0.0	0.0	0.0	0.0	0.0	0.0
NRA, border MS[a]	—	—	—	−8.7	4.3	4.8	−6.3	−8.8	−11.7	13.3
NRA, total agriculture	—	—	—	−2.7	11.1	12.2	−0.3	−5.5	−9.1	15.6
Malaysia										
NRA, inputs	—	0.0	0.0	0.0	0.0	0.0	0.0	0.0	0.0	0.0
NRA, domestic MS[a]	—	−9.0	−8.1	−10.2	−17.0	−6.9	0.4	2.5	−0.1	1.5

NRA, border MS[a]	—	-0.6	-0.3	1.8	1.3	1.3	1.0	-0.3	0.6
NRA, total agriculture	—	-8.7	-10.5	-15.3	-5.7	1.8	3.4	-0.3	2.1
Philippines									
NRA, inputs	0.0	0.0	0.0	0.0	0.0	0.0	0.0	0.0	0.0
NRA, domestic MS[a]	0.0	0.0	0.0	0.0	0.0	0.0	0.0	0.0	0.0
NRA, border MS[a]	-6.7	16.7	-6.0	-8.7	-1.6	21.9	21.4	37.8	24.9
NRA, total agriculture	-6.7	16.7	-6.0	-8.7	-1.6	21.9	21.4	37.8	24.9
Thailand									
NRA, inputs	—	—	-1.3	-1.2	-1.1	-2.7	-1.8	-1.4	-0.8
NRA, domestic MS[a]	—	—	0.0	0.0	0.0	0.0	0.0	0.0	0.0
NRA, border MS[a]	—	—	-24.5	-17.2	-7.3	-7.0	-5.9	0.3	0.2
NRA, total agriculture	—	—	-25.8	-18.4	-8.4	-9.7	-7.7	-1.1	-0.6
Vietnam[b]									
NRA, inputs	—	—	—	—	—	0.0	0.0	0.0	0.0
NRA, domestic MS[a]	—	—	—	—	—	-0.9	-0.7	0.0	1.7
NRA, border MS[a]	—	—	—	—	—	-24.6	-12.6	0.6	19.0
NRA, total agriculture	—	—	—	—	—	-25.4	-13.3	0.7	20.6
Southeast Asia[c]									
NRA, inputs	0.0	0.0	2.1	3.5	4.0	2.7	1.3	1.0	0.9
NRA, domestic MS[a]	-6.3	-3.3	-1.4	-2.1	-0.9	0.0	0.1	0.0	0.4
NRA, border MS[a]	-1.8	9.6	-11.2	-2.1	1.5	-2.2	-4.5	-0.1	11.9
NRA, total agriculture	-8.1	6.4	-10.5	-0.6	4.7	0.5	-3.0	0.9	13.1
Bangladesh									
NRA, inputs	—	—	—	1.1	1.2	1.2	1.5	2.2	2.6
NRA, domestic MS[a]	—	—	—	0.0	0.0	0.0	0.0	0.0	0.0
NRA, border MS[a]	—	—	—	1.7	-4.9	15.5	-3.7	-9.8	1.3
NRA, total agriculture	—	—	—	2.8	-3.8	16.8	-2.2	-7.6	3.9
India									
NRA, inputs	—	0.0	0.0	0.0	0.7	4.4	5.7	7.2	9.5
NRA, domestic MS[a]	—	18.1	17.8	3.7	2.1	4.3	3.4	-0.1	0.2
NRA, border MS[a]	—	-17.9	-17.7	-9.3	-0.8	16.2	-7.3	-6.4	6.1
NRA, total agriculture	—	0.3	0.2	-5.6	1.9	24.9	1.8	0.7	15.8

(Table continues on the following page.)

Table 1.14. NRAs for Covered Agricultural Products, by Policy Instrument, Asian Focus Economies, 1955–2004 (continued)

Economy, indicator	1955–59	1960–64	1965–69	1970–74	1975–79	1980–84	1985–89	1990–94	1995–99	2000–04
Pakistan[b]										
NRA, inputs	—	−4.5	−2.1	−1.6	4.6	3.5	2.9	2.3	1.9	1.4
NRA, domestic MS[a]	—	0.0	0.0	0.0	0.0	0.0	0.0	0.0	0.0	0.0
NRA, border MS[a]	—	−1.3	23.9	10.9	−16.4	−12.8	−8.8	−12.5	−4.5	0.1
NRA, total agriculture	—	−5.8	21.7	9.3	−11.8	−9.3	−5.9	−10.2	−2.6	1.5
Sri Lanka										
NRA, inputs	0.0	0.0	0.0	0.0	0.0	0.0	0.0	0.0	0.0	0.0
NRA, domestic MS[a]	4.2	8.1	6.9	5.0	5.1	5.0	3.6	1.5	0.7	0.9
NRA, border MS[a]	−14.5	−38.0	−36.9	−25.4	−37.0	−24.2	−16.3	−3.1	10.8	7.8
NRA, total agriculture	−10.3	−29.9	−30.0	−20.3	−31.9	−19.2	−12.6	−1.7	11.5	8.6
South Asia[c]										
NRA, inputs	0.0	−1.5	−0.2	−0.1	0.4	0.9	4.0	5.0	6.3	8.3
NRA, domestic MS[a]	4.2	8.3	16.3	16.1	3.1	1.8	3.6	2.8	−0.1	0.2
NRA, border MS[a]	−14.5	−14.7	−14.9	−15.4	−9.2	−2.5	13.5	−7.5	−6.2	5.2
NRA, total agriculture	−10.3	−7.8	1.2	0.6	−5.7	0.2	21.0	0.3	0.0	13.6
Asia, unweighted average										
NRA, inputs	0.0	−0.6	−0.3	0.3	1.1	1.1	1.0	0.9	1.1	1.3
NRA, domestic MS[a]	1.4	0.6	2.4	1.4	−0.8	−0.9	0.1	0.0	−0.1	0.2
NRA, border MS[a]	−13.4	−6.1	1.1	−0.9	0.3	6.5	17.7	20.8	26.2	30.9
NRA, total agriculture	−12.0	−6.2	3.2	0.9	0.6	6.6	18.8	21.7	27.3	32.4
Asia, weighted average[d]										
NRA, inputs	0.0	−0.5	−0.1	0.4	1.4	1.1	1.5	1.7	2.3	2.6
NRA, domestic MS[a]	1.4	2.0	13.0	10.6	1.0	−5.3	−2.9	−2.5	−0.6	−0.7
NRA, border MS[a]	−12.4	−4.2	−10.2	−10.8	−2.8	−17.4	−13.7	−4.0	4.3	8.2
NRA, total agriculture	−11.1	−2.7	2.6	0.3	−0.4	−21.6	−15.2	−4.8	6.0	10.2

Sources: Author compilation; Anderson and Valenzuela, 2008; estimates reported in chapters 2–12 of this volume.

Note: — = no data are available.

a. MS = market support, which is provided through domestic subsidies (or taxes) or through a border measure such as an import tariff (or subsidy) or an export subsidy (or tax).

b. Pakistan: 1960–64 is 1961–64. Taiwan, China: 2000–04 is 2000–03. Vietnam: 1985–89 is 1986–1989.

c. The weights for the subregional averages are based on the gross value of agricultural production at undistorted prices.

d. The weight is the gross value of the production of covered products at undistorted prices.

Table 1.15. Gross Subsidy Equivalents of Agricultural Assistance, Total and Per Farm Worker, Asian Focus Economies, 1955–2004

a. Total (at constant 2000 US$, millions, using the U.S. GDP deflator)

Economy	1955–59	1960–64	1965–69	1970–74	1975–79	1980–84	1985–89	1990–94	1995–99	2000–04
Korea, Rep. of	−154	107	854	1,672	6,943	9,335	13,306	18,594	17,536	15,289
Taiwan, China[a]	−394	133	132	439	605	1,342	2,500	3,849	4,170	3,725
China[b]	−52,857	−69,648	−70,671	−98,931	−124,086	−118,224	−75,780	−28,381	15,667	15,644
Indonesia	—	—	—	−848	3,783	4,131	−785	−2,729	−4,101	4,286
Malaysia	—	−250	−246	−547	−1,097	−456	75	156	3	100
Philippines	—	−225	735	−1,082	−903	−299	1,399	1,850	3,832	1,951
Thailand	—	—	—	−2,434	−2,148	−324	−645	−719	260	−14
Vietnam[a]	—	—	—	—	—	—	−726	−1,815	−18	1,602
Bangladesh	—	—	—	—	583	−672	882	−103	−448	189
India[b]	46	61	−993	−7,803	−8,653	−49	21,607	1,600	281	15,433
Pakistan[a]	—	−91	1,089	−34	−815	−787	−380	−755	−260	95
Sri Lanka	−68	−461	−455	−396	−571	−344	−194	−27	245	154
Total	−53,426	−70,373	−69,554	−109,965	−126,359	−106,348	−38,740	−8,481	37,169	58,455
All Asian economies[c]	−56,836	−74,865	−73,994	−116,984	−134,424	−113,136	−41,213	−9,023	39,541	62,186

(Table continues on the following page.)

Table 1.15. Gross Subsidy Equivalents of Agricultural Assistance, Total and Per Farm Worker, Asian Economies, 1955–2004 *(continued)*

b. Per person engaged in agriculture (at constant 2000 US$ using the U.S. GDP deflator)

Economy	1960–64	1965–69	1970–74	1975–79	1980–84	1985–89	1990–94	1995–99	2000–04
Korea, Rep. of	20	155	293	1,196	1,716	3,041	5,618	6,445	6,899
Taiwan, China[a]	76	76	261	390	1,045	2,077	3,699	4,795	5,329
China[b]	−235	−222	−281	−319	−280	−163	−57	31	31
Indonesia	—	—	−27	113	113	−19	−60	−86	86
Malaysia	−135	−126	−267	−515	−213	36	79	2	56
Philippines	−33	99	−132	−99	−30	132	163	318	155
Thailand	—	—	−163	−130	−18	−34	−36	13	−1
Vietnam[a]	—	—	—	—	—	−33	−73	−1	57
Bangladesh	—	—	—	20	−22	26	−3	−12	5
India[b]	0	−6	−43	−43	0	97	7	1	57
Pakistan[a]	−7	78	−2	−47	−41	−19	−35	−11	4
Sri Lanka	−217	−195	−155	−207	−116	−60	−8	66	40
Total	−125	−115	−166	−174	−136	−46	−9	40	61
All Asian economies[c]	−125	−115	−166	−174	−136	−46	−9	40	61

c. By subsector (at undistorted farmgate prices, constant US$, billions)

Year	Focus economies			Guesstimate, other Asian economies[c]	All Asian economies, from direct assistance to farmers[e]		
	Covered products[d]	Noncovered farm products[d]	Non-product-specific assistance		Total	Exportables	Import-competing products
1955–59	–0.7	0.1	0.4	–56.6	–56.8	–58.6	10.1
1960–64	0.8	–0.1	–1.0	–74.4	–74.7	–74.4	12.0
1965–69	1.4	–0.3	–0.8	–74.4	–74.0	–78.6	14.8
1970–74	–7.7	–3.7	0.3	–106.3	–117.4	–113.9	11.1
1975–79	–0.9	–1.4	–0.7	–131.4	–134.4	–142.9	26.5
1980–84	–76.4	–6.2	14.0	–44.6	–113.1	–140.3	26.6
1985–89	–50.0	6.2	15.4	–12.8	–41.1	–97.1	48.4
1990–94	–14.9	1.1	4.4	0.3	–9.1	–49.5	33.7
1995–99	21.7	8.1	–0.1	9.8	39.5	–13.4	41.1
2000–04	32.0	14.3	–1.5	15.8	60.6	–2.0	42.0

Sources: Author compilation; Anderson and Valenzuela, 2008; estimates reported in chapters 2–12 of this volume.

Note: — = no data are available.

a. Pakistan: 1960–64 is 1961–64. Taiwan, China: 2000–04 is 2000–03. Vietnam: 1985–89 is 1986–89.

b. See table 1.11, note b.

c. Assumes that the rates of assistance in the Asian economies not under study are the same as the average for the focus economies and that the share of the former economies in the value of Asian agricultural production at undistorted prices is the same as the average share of the former economies in the region's agricultural GDP at distorted prices, which was 6 percent. (It was actually only 4 percent in 2004, but was somewhat larger in earlier decades.)

d. Including assistance for nontradables and non-product-specific assistance.

e. Including product-specific input subsidies and non-product-specific assistance.

Which products contribute to the positive or negative assistance to farmers because of agricultural price and trade policies? Panel c in table 1.15 shows that the negative contribution arises mainly from policies directly affecting the exportable parts of agriculture, while most of the positive contribution arises from the protection for import-competing producers. The product NRAs, shown in table 1.16, panel a, offer insights into the products that are responsible. This information is combined with information on each product's share of the gross value of production to obtain the U.S. dollar contributions by product that are shown in table 1.16, panel b (also see appendix B). Rice, milk, and sugar are clearly still the most well assisted industries. Note that, in the early 1980s, when China was still heavily taxing farmers, the net contribution of rice was negative and large. At that time, policies affecting pig meat, fruits, and vegetables were equally important contributors to the effective taxation of Asian farmers, and this was almost entirely because of the influence of China.

Assistance to nonfarm sectors and RRAs

The antiagricultural policy bias of past decades was not generated only by agricultural policies. Likewise, the significant reductions in the border protection for the manufacturing sector, which have represented the dominant intervention in the tradables part of the nonagricultural sector, have also been important in the changes in the incentives affecting intersectorally mobile resources. Reductions in the assistance for producers of nonfarm tradables have been even more responsible for the improvement in farmer incentives than the reductions in the direct taxation on agricultural industries.

It has not been possible to quantify the distortions in nonfarm tradables as carefully as we have done in agriculture. Authors have typically been obliged to rely on the applied trade taxes for exports and imports rather than price comparisons, and they therefore usually do not capture the quantitative restrictions on trade that were once important, but have been decreasingly so through recent times.[11] Nor do they capture distortions in services, and services are also now generating tradables (or would be generating them in the absence of interventions preventing the emergence of service tradables). As a result, the NRA estimates for nonfarm importables are smaller and decline less rapidly than the actual NRAs. The same is true of the estimated NRAs for nonfarm exportables, except that the NRAs would have sometimes been negative. Of these two elements of underestimation, the former bias certainly dominates. Thus, the author estimates of the overall NRAs for nonagricultural tradables should be considered lower-bound estimates, especially in the past, and the declines are therefore less rapid than they should be.[12]

Table 1.16. NRA and Gross Subsidy Equivalents of Farmer Assistance, by Product, Asian Focus Economies, 1955–2004

a. NRA (at primary product level, %)

Product	1955–59	1960–64	1965–69	1970–74	1975–79	1980–84	1985–89	1990–94	1995–99	2000–04
Barley	41	84	72	120	101	166	357	524	543	563
Beef	38	25	34	44	95	101	94	145	106	85
Cassava	—	—	—	−23	−1	−9	−17	−11	−14	−10
Chickpeas	—	50	24	1	0	8	12	9	15	19
Cocoa	—	—	−2	−3	−2	−2	−1	−2	−2	0
Coconuts	−29	−29	−24	−8	−3	−11	−19	−34	−22	−8
Coffee	—	—	—	−7	−4	−9	−5	−5	−1	−2
Cotton	—	−19	12	63	7	−12	−2	−3	0	5
Eggs	−25	−21	19	0	−6	10	22	27	23	51
Fruits and vegetables[a]	—	0	0	0	0	−8	−3	−11	−6	−4
Jute	—	—	—	−30	−37	−29	−35	−38	−6	−39
Maize	—	−10	50	19	8	−20	−6	−15	8	13
Milk	—	—	71	122	139	108	124	40	23	32
Oilseeds[b]	—	24	31	11	−5	22	35	21	22	22
Palm oil	—	−11	−11	−15	−14	−1	−2	2	−9	−3
Pig meat	−10	16	59	51	47	−41	−39	−3	7	4
Poultry	−25	0	69	18	58	48	−2	20	17	12
Rice	−10	−6	−25	−17	−13	−27	−6	−9	2	18
Rubber	−16	−16	−14	−8	−19	−19	−14	−16	5	4
Sorghum	—	82	42	55	12	7	36	7	21	16
Sugar	—	96	163	13	2	37	39	13	20	43
Tea	−22	−39	−39	−28	−22	−18	−19	−10	−8	−7
Wheat	−33	−12	24	15	−3	−3	12	4	18	11
Total[c]	−11.1	−2.7	2.6	0.3	−0.4	−21.6	−15.2	−4.8	6.0	10.2

(Table continues on the following page.)

Table 1.16. NRA and Gross Subsidy Equivalents of Farmer Assistance, by Product, Asian Focus Economies, 1955–2004 (continued)

b. Gross subsidy equivalent (at undistorted farmgate prices, constant US$, millions)

Product	1955–59	1960–64	1965–69	1970–74	1975–79	1980–84	1985–89	1990–94	1995–99	2000–04
Barley	96	307	439	588	546	436	444	331	198	140
Beef	21	49	107	162	670	893	822	1,410	1,236	831
Cassava	—	—	—	-86	-7	-87	-136	-84	-80	-41
Chickpea	—	1201	499	40	0	193	268	149	224	255
Cocoa	—	0	0	0	-1	-1	-4	-2	-1	0
Coconut	-135	-104	-110	-543	-256	-841	-841	-1,103	-1,017	-273
Coffee	—	—	—	-18	-42	-56	-34	-28	-14	-11
Cotton	—	-72	338	1,820	302	-1,008	-147	-227	-20	197
Egg	-28	-29	33	-13	-41	70	150	213	199	282
Fruits and vegetables[a]	—	0	0	-5	19	-23,014	-45,349	-14,769	-1,304	-1,239
Jute	—	—	—	-338	-275	-147	-193	-118	-12	-66
Maize	—	-36	991	620	230	-4,041	-977	-2,530	1,336	1,926
Milk	—	—	605	756	9,163	9,044	10,865	5,162	4,405	6,459
Oilseeds[b]	—	1,212	1,150	455	-260	1,582	2,609	2,015	2,176	1,743
Palm oil	—	-13	-20	-210	-380	-70	-101	63	-680	-210
Pig meat	-62	136	668	897	1,464	-35,274	-16,203	-1,232	3,443	2,019
Poultry	-26	10	217	78	831	1,603	-354	1,700	2,806	2,023
Rice	-353	-299	-8,741	-13,809	-10,843	-32,220	-5,945	-7,328	2,150	11,789
Rubber	-51	-438	-322	-356	-1,389	-1,230	-734	-813	-121	48
Sorghum	—	2,036	1,017	1,240	359	186	568	30	231	125
Sugar	-160	476	2,875	-36	-395	3,665	3,186	1,605	1,969	3,738
Tea	-160	-210	-158	-125	-140	-112	-100	-53	-42	-40
Wheat	-19	243	1,732	928	-443	-513	2,457	719	4,593	2,322
Total[d]	-704	771	1,377	-7,690	-902	-76,336	-50,000	-14,889	21,676	32,010

Sources: Author compilation; Anderson and Valenzuela, 2008; estimates reported in chapters 2–12 of this volume.

Note: — = no data are available.

a. Fruits and vegetables include fruit and vegetable aggregates for China and India and bananas, cabbages, chilies, garlic, onions, peppers, and potatoes for other economies.

b. Oilseeds include groundnuts, rapeseeds, soybeans, and sunflower seeds.

c. For covered products only. The weights are the value of production at undistorted prices.

d. For covered products only, hence, less than the totals in table 1.15, panel a.

Despite these methodological limitations, the estimated NRAs for nonfarm tradables were sizable prior to the 1990s. For Asia as a whole, the average NRA value has steadily declined throughout the past four or five decades as policy reforms have spread. This has therefore contributed to a decline in the estimated negative RRAs for farmers. The weighted average RRAs were below −50 percent up to the early 1970s, but improved to an average of −32 percent in the 1980s, −9 percent in the 1990s, and, now positive, were averaging 7 percent in 2000–04 (or 15 percent if the average is unweighted). The five-decade trends in the RRAs and the two component sets of NRAs for each economy are summarized in table 1.17. It is clear from figure 1.6 that the contribution of the falling positive NRAs among nonfarm producers to the rise in RRAs is greater than the corresponding contribution of the gradual disappearance of the negative NRAs among farmers.

Has the location of the production of farm products within Asia become more efficient or less efficient as a result of policy changes over the past five decades? A set of global computable general equilibrium models relying on a time series of databases is required to answer this question properly. In the absence of such models, one crude method of addressing the question involves examining the standard deviation in RRAs across the economies of the region over time. This suggests that distortions have become more dispersed over time. The dispersion averaged 35 percent in 1960–74, 50 percent in 1975–89, and 55 percent in 1990–2004 (table 1.17, bottom row).

Among the striking changes in the RRAs in individual economies in the past two decades is the shift from negative to positive RRAs in China and India (figure 1.7). This is significant for the region and, indeed, for the world. The extent of the decline in nonagricultural NRAs since the early 1980s is similar in these two key countries. However, the agricultural NRAs in the two economies have differed. In China, the five-year averages have risen steadily from −45 to 6 percent. In India, they have been close to zero except for a rise in the present decade and an upward spike when international food prices collapsed in the mid-1980s (figure 1.8).

This dramatic rise in the RRAs in the world's two most populous economies is significant for those examining the causes of the recent increases in international food prices. One of the contributors to the increases is said to be the growing appetite for food imports in these two economies as they industrialize and per capita incomes grow. Yet, as table 1.10 shows, both economies have remained close to self-sufficient in agricultural products over the past four decades. Undoubtedly, the steady rise in the RRAs of these two economies has supported this outcome. The rise in the RRAs may have also helped ensure that the trend in the ratio of urban to rural mean incomes, adjusted for differences in the cost of living, has been flat in China since 1980 (Ravallion and Chen 2007). Meanwhile, the rise in the RRAs in India helped ensure that the Gini coefficient hardly changed between

(*Text continues on page 52.*)

Table 1.17. RRAs in Agriculture, Asian Focus Economies, 1955–2004
(percent)

Economy, indicator	1955–59	1960–64	1965–69	1970–74	1975–79	1980–84	1985–89	1990–94	1995–99	2000–04
Korea, Rep. of										
NRA, agriculture	−3.3	4.9	16.3	46.1	71.8	118.6	159.8	197.6	164.8	171.9
NRA, nonagriculture	45.6	37.1	22.3	11.4	11.7	6.8	5.7	3.3	2.3	1.7
RRA[a]	−32.6	−21.4	−4.8	30.5	53.9	104.8	145.9	188.2	158.8	167.3
Taiwan, China[b]										
NRA, agriculture	−15.8	4.7	3.9	12.0	8.9	18.7	33.8	46.3	54.9	70.9
NRA, nonagriculture	8.8	9.3	8.8	7.5	7.0	5.2	4.5	2.6	1.8	1.0
RRA[a]	−22.5	−4.2	−4.5	4.2	1.7	12.9	28.0	42.5	52.2	69.0
China[c]										
NRA, agriculture	−45.2	−45.2	−45.2	−45.2	−45.2	−45.2	−35.5	−14.3	6.6	5.9
NRA, nonagriculture	41.6	41.6	41.6	41.6	41.6	41.6	28.3	24.9	9.9	5.0
RRA[a]	−60.5	−60.5	−60.5	−60.5	−60.5	−60.5	−49.9	−31.1	−3.0	0.9
Northeast Asia										
NRA, agriculture	−43.1	−42.5	−42.2	−41.3	−40.0	−18.4	−26.2	−1.7	14.7	12.0
NRA, nonagriculture	40.9	40.8	40.0	39.7	39.4	71.1	18.8	15.0	6.8	3.3
RRA[a]	−58.2	−57.7	−56.6	−55.7	−53.7	−51.9	−38.0	−14.2	7.4	8.5
Indonesia										
NRA, agriculture	—	—	—	−3.8	10.4	10.5	−1.9	−7.5	−9.7	13.9
NRA, nonagriculture	—	—	—	27.7	27.7	27.7	26.5	17.6	10.6	8.1
RRA[a]	—	—	—	−24.7	−13.6	−13.5	−22.5	−21.3	−18.3	5.4
Malaysia										
NRA, agriculture	—	−7.6	−7.9	−9.4	−13.7	−4.9	1.4	2.6	−0.2	1.5
NRA, nonagriculture	—	7.4	7.0	7.1	6.5	5.2	3.9	2.8	2.0	0.9
RRA[a]	—	−14.0	−13.9	−15.5	−18.9	−9.6	−2.4	−0.3	−2.2	0.6
Philippines										
NRA, agriculture	—	−1.7	14.3	−6.0	−7.2	−4.0	15.8	16.7	35.7	23.5
NRA, nonagriculture	—	19.0	20.3	16.3	16.3	12.9	11.0	9.9	8.6	6.4
RRA[a]	—	−17.4	−5.0	−19.8	−20.3	−14.9	4.3	6.1	24.9	15.9

Thailand										
NRA, agriculture	—	—	—	-23.1	-15.9	-2.3	-6.9	-6.4	1.8	-0.2
NRA, nonagriculture	—	—	—	16.1	16.0	14.2	11.1	10.0	8.9	7.8
RRA[a]	—	—	—	-33.7	-27.5	-14.4	-16.3	-14.9	-6.5	-7.4
Vietnam[b]										
NRA, agriculture	—	—	—	—	—	—	-15.9	-26.4	0.0	20.7
NRA, nonagriculture	—	—	—	—	—	—	4.3	-11.2	1.5	20.8
RRA[a]	—	—	—	—	—	—	-19.2	-17.4	-1.3	0.0
Southeast Asia										
NRA, agriculture	—	-5.8	5.6	-10.2	0.1	4.9	-0.9	-4.7	0.0	12.1
NRA, nonagriculture	—	11.5	15.4	20.2	22.0	21.1	18.0	11.5	8.2	8.1
RRA[a]	—	-15.5	-8.5	-25.3	-18.0	-13.4	-16.1	-14.5	-7.7	3.7
Bangladesh										
NRA, agriculture					3.1	-3.9	17.5	-2.4	-8.0	4.0
NRA, nonagriculture					28.4	22.4	28.5	33.3	29.0	23.4
RRA[a]					-19.7	-21.5	-8.6	-26.7	-28.6	-15.8
India[c]										
NRA, agriculture	5.2	5.2	5.2	12.6	-7.4	4.1	67.5	2.0	-2.3	15.4
NRA, nonagriculture	113.0	113.0	113.0	83.1	64.8	59.3	48.6	15.9	12.6	5.2
RRA[a]	-56.3	-56.3	-56.3	-38.3	-43.8	-33.5	11.7	-12.1	-12.9	12.5
Pakistan[b]										
NRA, agriculture	—	-1.0	21.7	9.3	-11.8	-9.3	-5.9	-10.2	-2.6	1.5
NRA, nonagriculture	—	169.7	224.5	146.7	44.0	48.3	45.1	39.3	27.0	14.6
RRA[a]	—	-63.8	-62.4	-55.9	-38.6	-38.6	-35.1	-35.2	-23.0	-11.5
Sri Lanka										
NRA, agriculture	-2.7	-25.7	-27.6	-18.5	-29.0	-15.4	-11.2	-1.3	14.0	10.8
NRA, nonagriculture	104.9	124.6	138.4	70.7	52.9	57.1	59.0	47.1	36.4	22.9
RRA[a]	-52.5	-66.6	-68.0	-51.6	-53.5	-46.2	-44.3	-32.9	-16.3	-9.8

(Table continues on the following page.)

Table 1.17. RRAs in Agriculture, Asian Focus Economies, 1955–2004 (*continued*)

Economy, indicator	1955–59	1960–64	1965–69	1970–74	1975–79	1980–84	1985–89	1990–94	1995–99	2000–04
South Asia										
NRA, agriculture	4.7	4.1	4.4	9.7	−7.7	1.8	47.1	0.2	−2.4	12.7
NRA, nonagriculture	112.7	114.4	135.9	81.7	57.8	54.6	39.9	18.6	15.0	10.1
RRA[a]	−50.7	−51.5	−56.0	−39.8	−41.6	−33.3	5.1	−15.5	−14.9	3.4
Asia, unweighted average[d]										
NRA, agriculture	−12.1	−8.3	−2.5	−3.1	−3.6	5.9	18.0	15.5	19.6	25.2
NRA, nonagriculture	62.8	65.2	72.0	42.8	28.8	22.1	19.3	12.3	10.0	8.4
RRA[a]	−44.7	−38.0	−34.4	−27.0	−22.2	−13.2	−1.2	2.9	8.7	15.5
Asia, weighted average[e]										
NRA, agriculture	−29.0	−27.7	−26.9	−24.3	−31.3	−18.8	−11.2	−2.6	7.5	11.7
NRA, nonagriculture	66.8	67.1	70.9	50.3	50.3	38.3	15.4	14.9	9.6	4.3
RRA[a]	−57.5	−56.4	−55.3	−47.9	−44.7	−40.8	−22.8	−15.2	−1.9	7.1
Dispersion, national RRAs[f]	21.9	30.7	36.2	37.6	41.5	51.9	56.0	65.1	50.5	50.8

Sources: Author compilation; Anderson and Valenzuela, 2008; estimates reported in chapters 2–12 of this volume.

Note: — = no data are available.

a. The RRA is defined as 100*[(100 + $NRAag^t$)/(100 + $NRAnonag^t$) − 1], where $NRAag^t$ and $NRAnonag^t$ are the percentage NRAs for the tradables parts of the agricultural and nonagricultural sectors, respectively.

b. Pakistan: 1960–64 is 1961–64. Taiwan, China: 2000–04 is 2000–03. Vietnam: 1985–89 is 1986–1989.

c. See table 1.11, note b.

d. Simple averages of the weighted national average RRAs.

e. Weighted averages of the national average RRAs. The weights are based on the gross value of national agricultural production at undistorted prices.

f. Dispersion is a simple five-year average of the annual standard deviation around the weighted mean of the national NRAs.

Figure 1.6. NRAs for Agricultural and Nonagricultural Tradables and the RRA, Asian Focus Economies, 1955–2004

a. Unweighted averages

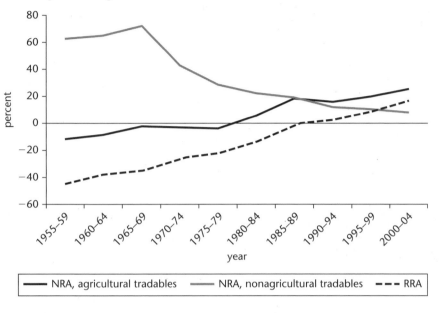

b. Weighted averages

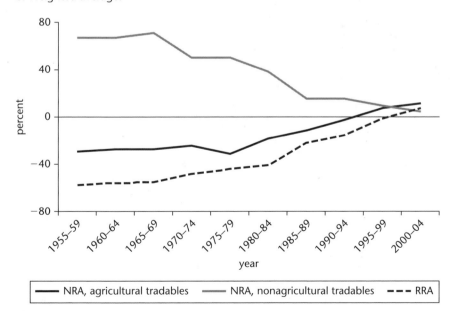

Sources: Author compilation; Anderson and Valenzuela, 2008; estimates reported in chapters 2–12 of this volume.

Note: For the definition of the RRA, see table 1.17, note a.

Figure 1.7. RRAs in Agriculture, Asian Focus Economies, 1980–84 and 2000–04

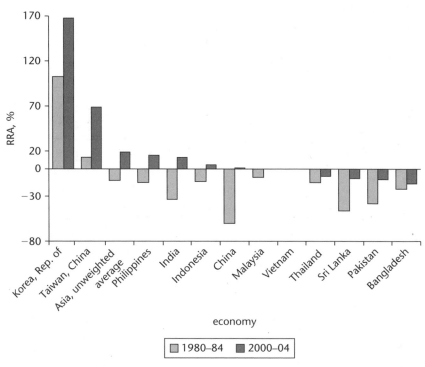

Sources: Author compilation; Anderson and Valenzuela, 2008; estimates reported in chapters 2–12 of this volume.

Note: For the definition of the RRA, see table 1.17, note a. There are no estimates for Vietnam in 1980–84.

1984 and 2004 (table 1.1). A major issue is: Will their RRAs remain at the current neutral level of close to zero (in which case, the self-sufficiency of these economies in farm products may begin to fall)? Or will their RRAs continue to rise in the same way as they have risen in Korea and Taiwan, China and, before them, Japan and Western Europe? (We return to this issue at the end of the chapter.)

Comparisons with other regions

The recent regional upward shift in agricultural NRAs and RRAs toward zero and even to positive numbers is not unique to Asia. Figure 1.9 shows that similar trends, albeit less steep, have resulted from policy reforms in other developing-country regions over the past four decades. This suggests that similar political

Figure 1.8. NRAs and RRAs, China and India, 1965–2004

a. India

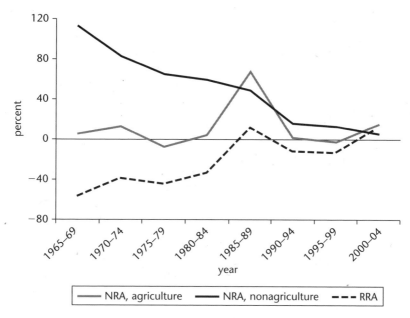

b. China

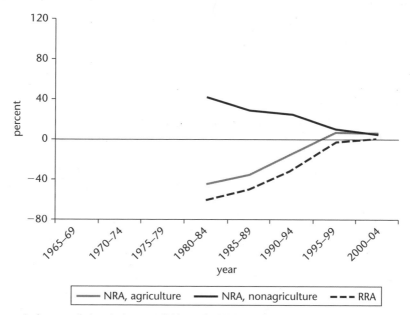

Sources: Author compilation; Anderson and Valenzuela, 2008; estimates reported in chapters 2–12 of this volume.

Figure 1.9. NRAs and RRAs, Africa, Asia, and Latin America, 1965–2004

a. NRAs

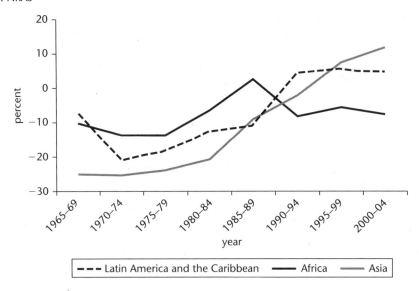

b. RRAs

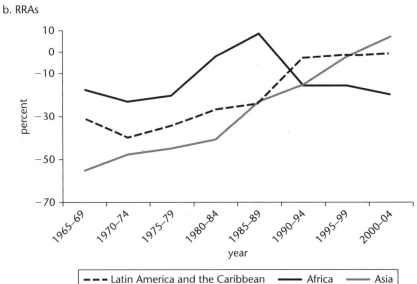

Sources: Author compilation; Anderson and Valenzuela, 2008; estimates reported in chapters 2–12 of this volume.

Note: The five-year averages are weighted. The weights are based on the gross value of total agricultural production at undistorted prices. The estimates for China before 1981 and India before 1965 are based on the assumption that the NRAs were the same as the average NRAs for those economies in 1981–84 and 1965–69, respectively, and that the gross value of production of those economies in the missing years is the same as the average share of the value of the production of the economies in total regional production in 1981–84 and 1965–69, respectively.

economy trends may be at work as economies develop, although farm-nonfarm household income inequality is different in Asia relative to the rest of the world (figure 1.10). In the past, it has been found that agricultural NRAs and RRAs are positively correlated with per capita incomes and agricultural comparative disadvantage (Anderson 1995). A glance at table 1.18 suggests that Asian economies have been contributors to the trend. This is confirmed statistically in the simple regressions with country fixed effects shown in figures 1.11 and 1.12 and the multiple regressions with country and time fixed effects shown in table 1.19.

The CTEs of agricultural policies

The extent to which farm policies have impacts on retail consumer prices for food and on prices for livestock feedstuffs depends on a wide range of elements, including the degree of processing undertaken and the extent of competition along the value chain. Like the OECD (2007), we therefore attempt only to ask about the impacts of policies on the prices buyers pay at the point on the value chain where the farm product is first traded internationally and, hence, where comparisons are made between domestic and international prices (for example, as milled rice, or

Figure 1.10. Income Distribution, Asian Subregions and the World, 2000

a. East Asia

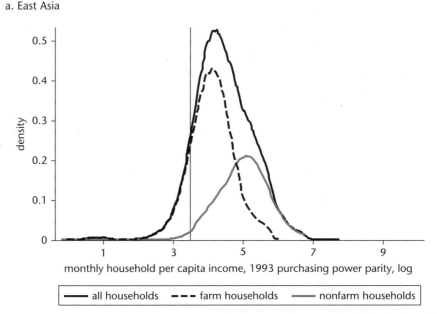

monthly household per capita income, 1993 purchasing power parity, log

——— all households   – – – farm households   ——— nonfarm households

(Figure continues on the following page.)

Figure 1.10. (*continued*)

b. South Asia

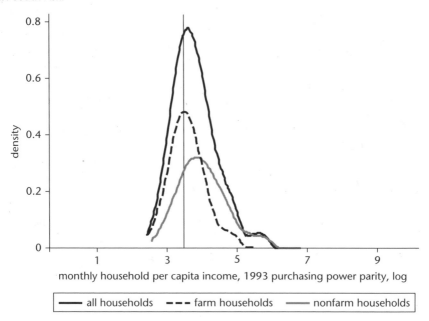

c. World

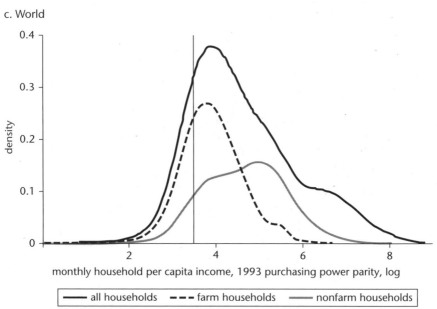

Source: Bussolo, de Hoyes, and Medledev, forthcoming.

Note: The vertical line is the US$1-a-day poverty line in 1993 purchasing power parity terms.

Table 1.18. Relative Per Capita Income, Agricultural Comparative Advantage, and NRAs and RRAs for Agricultural Tradables, Asian Focus Economies, 2000–04

Economy	Relative per capita income[a]	Agricultural comparative advantage[b]	NRA, %	RRA, %
Korea, Rep. of	212	26	137.3	167.3
Taiwan, China	232	28	61.3	69.0
China	21	58	5.9	0.9
Indonesia	17	173	12.0	5.4
Malaysia	74	107	1.2	0.6
Philippines	18	67	22.0	15.9
Thailand	38	204	−0.2	−7.4
Vietnam	8	301	21.2	0.0
Bangladesh	7	93	2.7	−15.8
India	9	143	15.8	12.5
Pakistan	10	137	1.2	−11.5
Sri Lanka	16	254	9.5	−9.8
Total[c]	20	80	12.0	7.1

Sources: Author compilation based on Sandri, Valenzuela, and Anderson 2007; Anderson and Valenzuela, 2008; estimates reported in chapters 2–12 of this volume.
a. Income per capita relative to the world average, 2000–04. World = 100.
b. The ratio of the share of agriculture and food in national exports to the share of agriculture and food in worldwide exports, 2000–04.
c. The unweighted averages for relative per capita income and agricultural comparative advantage. The weighted averages for the NRAs and RRAs.

raw sugar, or beef). If they are not supplied by national sources, we have obtained consumption data directly from the food balance sheets of the Food and Agriculture Organization or, in the case of minor products, indirectly by using data of the Food and Agriculture Organization on the value of trade (see FAOSTAT Database 2008) and assuming that the undistorted value of consumption is production valued at undistorted prices, plus imports, minus exports. We used this information to construct weights so that we could sum across commodities and countries.

If there were no farm input distortions and no domestic output price distortions so that NRAs were entirely the result of border measures such as import or export taxes or other restrictions and if there were no domestic consumption taxes or subsidies, then the CTEs would equal the NRAs for each covered product. However, such domestic distortions exist in several Asian economies. In Korea, for example, producer prices have been well above consumer prices for several important crop products. In China, the opposite was true at least until the early 1990s. In

Figure 1.11. Regressions of Real GDP per Capita and Agricultural NRAs and RRAs, Asian Focus Economies, 1955–2005

a. Regression of ln real GDP per capita on NRAs, with country fixed effects

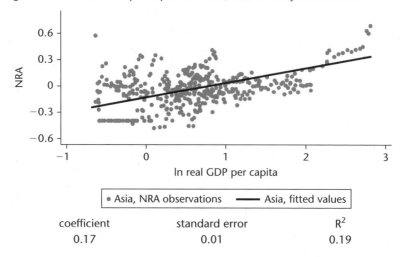

coefficient	standard error	R^2
0.17	0.01	0.19

b. Regression of ln real GDP per capita on RRAs, with country fixed effects

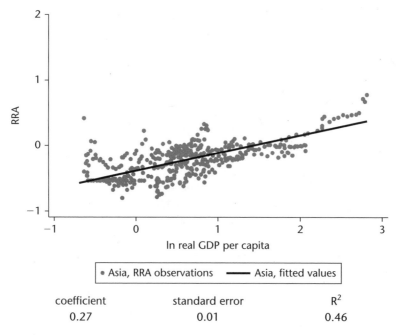

coefficient	standard error	R^2
0.27	0.01	0.46

Sources: Author compilation based on Sandri, Valenzuela, and Anderson 2007; Anderson and Valenzuela, 2008; estimates reported in chapters 2–12 of this volume.

Note: The dependent variable for the regressions is the NRAs or RRAs by country and year expressed as a fraction. The results are ordinary least squares estimates. The explanatory variable is the natural log of real GDP per capita expressed in US$10,000s.

China, the producers of food staples were taxed more than the consumers were subsidized even if we take into account the in-kind partial wage payment received by many urban workers (the iron rice bowl).[13] Also, because of international trade, the weights one uses to aggregate product distortion rates on the consumption side of the market differ from the weights one uses on the production side. Hence, aggregate CTEs differ somewhat from aggregate NRAs in each economy. This may be seen by comparing the CTEs in panel a, table 1.20 with the NRAs in table 1.11. The weighted average CTEs in the region were negative until the early 1990s, but were above zero thereafter and have increased in recent years. The variance in CTEs across products is even greater now than it was before the reforms of the past two decades (see table 1.20, panel b, including the bottom row).

In proportional and in per capita terms, the current transfers from consumers are clearly largest in Korea and Taiwan, China (panel a, table 1.20 and panel b,

Figure 1.12. Regressions of Real Comparative Advantage and Agricultural NRAs and RRAs, Asian Focus Economies, 1960–2004

a. Regression of revealed comparative advantage on NRAs, with country fixed effects

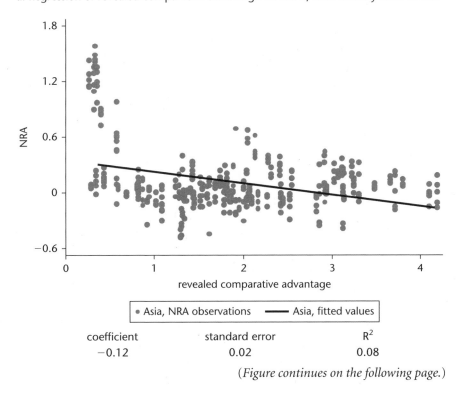

coefficient	standard error	R^2
−0.12	0.02	0.08

(Figure continues on the following page.)

Figure 1.12. (*continued*)

b. Regression of revealed comparative advantage on RRAs, with country fixed effects

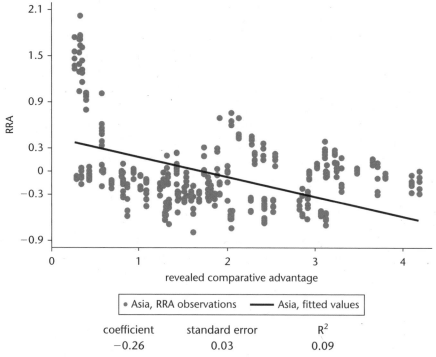

coefficient	standard error	R²
−0.26	0.03	0.09

Sources: Author compilation based on Sandri, Valenzuela, and Anderson 2007; Anderson and Valenzuela, forthcoming; estimates reported in chapters 2–12 of this volume.

Note: The dependent variable for the regressions is the NRAs or RRAs by country and year expressed as a fraction. The results are ordinary least squares estimates. The explanatory variable is the revealed comparative advantage, which is the ratio of the share of agriculture and processed food in national exports to the share of agriculture and processed food in worldwide merchandise exports. The revealed comparative advantage is expressed in five-year averages.

table 1.21), but, in constant (2000) U.S. dollar terms, they are also large in China, India, and Indonesia (table 1.21, panel a). In the present decade, the average transfers from consumers to producers in the region have amounted to around US$35 billion per year. In the early 1980s, in contrast, the transfers were from producers to consumers, and they amounted to about US$50 billion per year at the producer level for the products covered in our project. Among the covered products, the biggest transfers are related to milk, rice, and sugar (table 1.21, panel c).

The role of agricultural policies in stabilizing domestic prices

An often-stated objective of food policies in Asia and elsewhere is to reduce fluctuations in domestic food prices and in the quantities available for consumption.

(*Text continues on page 69.*)

Table 1.19. Regressions of NRAs and Selected Determinants, Asian Focus Economies, 1960–2004

Explanatory variable	(1)	(2)	(3)	(4)	(5)	(6)	(7)	(8)	(9)	(10)	(11)	(12)
Ln GDP per capita	-0.28* (-0.03)	-0.21* (-0.03)	-0.23* (-0.03)	-0.22* (-0.03)	-0.11 (-0.05)	-0.06 (-0.05)	-0.14 (-0.06)	-0.16* (-0.06)	-0.38* (-0.10)	-0.28* (-0.9)	-0.44* (-0.10)	-0.38* (-0.11)
Ln GDP per capita squared	0.23* (-0.02)	0.20* (-0.01)	0.21* (-0.01)	0.21* (-0.01)	0.19* (-0.02)	0.15* (-0.02)	0.21* (-0.03)	0.18* (-0.02)	0.23* (-0.03)	0.19* (-0.02)	0.22* (-0.03)	0.21* (-0.03)
Import-competing products		0.33* (-0.04)	0.34* (-0.04)	0.32* (-0.04)		0.40* (-0.04)	0.41* (-0.04)	0.40* (-0.04)		0.39* (-0.04)	0.39* (-0.04)	0.39* (-0.04)
Exportables		-0.13 (-0.04)	-0.12 (-0.04)	-0.14 (-0.04)		-0.03 (-0.04)	-0.03 (-0.04)	-0.03 (-0.04)		-0.04 (-0.04)	-0.04 (-0.04)	-0.04 (-0.04)
Revealed comparative advantage[a]				0.03* (-0.01)				-0.07* (-0.02)				-0.04 (-0.03)
Trade specialization index[b]			0.11* (-0.03)				-0.13 (-0.09)				-0.03 (-0.10)	
Constant	0.14* (-0.01)	0.03 (-0.03)	0.00 (-0.03)	-0.02 (-0.04)	0.07* (-0.02)	-0.11 (-0.04)	-0.05 (-0.05)	0.07 (-0.07)	-0.49* (-0.12)	0.23* (-0.11)	-0.19 (-0.09)	-0.08 (-0.10)
R^2	0.10	0.27	0.27	0.27	0.07	0.23	0.22	0.22	0.14	0.28	0.29	0.29
Number of observations	2,766	2,766	2,594	2,594	2,766	2,766	2,594	2,594	2,766	2,766	2,594	2,594
Country fixed effect	No	No	No	No	Yes	Yes	Yes	Yes	Yes	Yes	Yes	Yes
Time fixed effect	No	No	No	No	No	No	No	No	Yes	Yes	Yes	Yes

Sources: Author compilation based on Sandri, Valenzuela, and Anderson 2007; Anderson and Valenzuela, 2008; estimates reported in chapters 2–12 of this volume.

Note: The dependent variable for the regressions is the NRAs by commodity and year. The results are ordinary least squares estimates. Standard errors are indicated in parentheses. The main explanatory variable is ln GDP per capita in $10,000s.

a. The ratio of the share of agriculture and processed food in national exports to the share of agriculture and processed food in worldwide exports. World = 1.

b. Net exports as a ratio of the sum of exports and the sum of imports of agricultural and processed food products. World = 1.

*Significance levels at 99 percent.

Table 1.20. CTEs for Policies Assisting the Producers of Covered Agricultural Products, Asian Focus Economies, 1960–2004

(at the primary product level, %)

a. Aggregate CTEs, by country

Economy, indicator	1960–64	1965–69	1970–74	1975–79	1980–84	1985–89	1990–94	1995–99	2000–04
Korea, Rep. of	5.4	14.5	39.7	63.9	114.3	148.5	176.4	144.9	154.1
Taiwan, China[a]	7.7	6.9	19.0	15.2	38.4	82.7	116.5	136.8	166.5
China	—	—	—	—	-40.3	-37.1	-14.3	3.3	2.4
Indonesia	—	—	-9.0	6.4	8.4	-4.3	-6.7	-11.2	17.3
Malaysia	12.0	1.4	3.6	18.1	18.1	28.8	15.7	2.8	5.6
Philippines	-5.5	12.0	-4.5	-7.4	-3.1	23.7	22.3	40.2	26.0
Thailand	—	—	-27.3	-19.6	-5.7	-6.1	-6.8	3.1	2.0
Vietnam[a]	—	—	—	—	—	-11.5	-24.3	1.0	20.8
Bangladesh	—	—	—	3.1	-4.6	17.0	-2.9	-9.3	1.9
India	—	-19.1	-21.8	-10.8	-0.6	14.1	-8.7	-7.4	5.3
Pakistan[a]	0.2	28.3	9.0	-17.6	-11.8	-6.2	-13.3	-5.6	1.6
Sri Lanka	-5.7	-14.7	-2.6	-19.8	-11.5	-6.1	3.5	20.4	14.5
Unweighted average	2.3	4.2	0.7	3.1	9.2	20.3	21.5	26.6	34.8
Weighted average[b]	-0.1	-12.3	-14.9	-2.2	-15.5	-13.9	-3.1	5.4	10.2
Dispersion, national CTEs[c]	7.7	24.4	26.3	26.1	47.6	61.4	66.3	59.5	64.6

b. Regional CTEs, by product

Product	1965–69	1970–74	1975–79	1980–84	1985–89	1990–94	1995–99	2000–04
Barley	65	97	57	120	326	411	341	327
Beef	33	43	98	106	95	156	106	105
Cassava	—	-22	1	-8	-13	-8	-12	-9
Chickpeas	5	0	0	3	5	0	3	6
Cocoa	-3	-4	-1	-2	-2	-3	-3	0
Coconuts	-24	-9	-3	-12	-22	-36	-25	-10
Coffee	—	-17	-11	-18	-13	-8	-3	-1
Cotton	-5	14	-4	-16	-11	-15	-6	-4
Eggs	19	0	-6	10	22	27	23	51
Fruit and vegetables[d]	0	0	0	-26	-45	-17	-2	-1
Jute	—	-30	-37	-30	-36	-39	-7	-42
Maize	23	-1	6	-4	17	-7	8	14
Milk	71	122	139	108	123	39	23	31
Oilseeds[e]	5	-5	-9	18	32	19	22	23
Palm oil	-1	-9	-3	10	1	12	-15	-5
Pig meat	58	49	47	-37	-38	-4	7	4
Poultry	69	18	58	49	-2	21	17	12
Rice	-41	-37	-17	-18	-8	-9	0	16
Rubber	-52	-6	-19	-23	-19	-11	2	1
Sorghum	9	30	7	0	23	-5	10	1

(Table continues on the following page.)

Table 1.20. CTEs for Policies Assisting the Producers of Covered Agricultural Products, Asian Focus Economies, 1960–2004 (continued)

b. Regional CTEs, by product

Product	1965–69	1970–74	1975–79	1980–84	1985–89	1990–94	1995–99	2000–04
Sugar	121	0	–3	32	31	8	16	27
Tea	–58	–29	–19	–14	–17	–10	–15	–17
Wheat	8	–1	–7	5	21	14	8	2
Weighted average[b]	–12	–15	–2	–15	–14	–3	5	10
Dispersion, regional product CTEs[f]	53	45	44	52	85	96	76	73

Sources: Author compilation; Anderson and Valenzuela, 2008; estimates reported in chapters 2–12 of this volume.

Note: The figure is based on the assumption that the CTE is the same as the NRA derived from trade measures (that is, not including any input taxes or subsidies or any domestic producer price subsidies or taxes), except for rice, barley, wheat, and sorghum in Korea and wheat in Taiwan, China. — = no data are available.

a. Pakistan: 1960–64 is 1961–64. Taiwan, China: 2000–04 is 2000–03. Vietnam: 1985–89 is 1986–89.

b. The weights are consumption valued at undistorted prices, where consumption (from the FAOSTAT Database) is production, plus imports, net of exports, plus changes in the stocks of the covered products.

c. A simple five-year average of the annual standard deviation around the weighted mean of the average national CTEs.

d. Fruits and vegetables include fruit and vegetable aggregates for China and India and bananas, cabbages, chilies, garlic, onions, peppers, and potatoes for other economies.

e. Oilseeds include groundnuts, rapeseeds, soybeans, and sunflower seeds.

f. A simple five-year average of the annual standard deviation around the weighted mean of the average regional CTEs for the covered products indicated.

Table 1.21. Value of CTEs for Policies Assisting the Producers of Covered Agricultural Products, Asian Focus Economies, 1965–2004

(at the primary product level, using the U.S. GDP deflator, constant 2000 US$, millions)

a. Aggregate CTEs

Economy	1965–69	1970–74	1975–79	1980–84	1985–89	1990–94	1995–99	2000–04
Korea, Rep. of	677	1,690	6,070	9,710	12,300	17,900	15,500	14,500
Taiwan, China[a]	149	417	638	1,390	2,400	3,660	4,290	2,380
China	—	—	—	−57,500	−68,600	−22,800	6,240	4,090
Indonesia	—	−1,330	1,760	2,360	−1160	−1720	−3,280	3,490
Malaysia	5	2	163	196	207	170	43	65
Philippines	467	−890	−607	−318	1,230	1,630	3,760	1,910
Thailand	—	−1,550	−1,250	−347	−229	−349	168	71
Vietnam[a]	—	—	—	—	−300	−1040	−5	668
Bangladesh	—	−334	527	−744	948	−167	−632	92
India	−13,300	−22,000	−9,540	−1,850	8,800	−6,440	−7,280	3,790
Pakistan[a]	1,390	−1,100	−1,380	−960	−410	−989	−546	83
Sri Lanka	−111	50	−208	−131	−65	35	190	108
Total	−10,723	−25,144	−3,737	−48,194	−44,870	−10,110	18,358	31,267
All Asian economies[b]	−11,407	−26,749	−3,976	−51,270	−47,734	−10,755	19,530	33,263

(Table continues on the following page.)

Table 1.21. Value of CTEs for Policies Assisting the Producers of Covered Agricultural Products, Asian Focus Economies, 1965–2004 (continued)

b. CTEs per capita

Economy	1965–69	1970–74	1975–79	1980–84	1985–89	1990–94	1995–99	2000–04
Korea, Rep. of	22.4	51.9	164.6	247.7	294.9	408.5	339.5	305.5
Taiwan, China[a]	11.1	27.3	37.9	75.4	121.9	176.9	202.4	105.1
China	—	—	—	−69.3	−61.5	−19.4	5.0	3.1
Indonesia	—	−10.3	13.0	14.8	−6.3	−9.2	−16.3	16.1
Malaysia	0.7	0.4	12.6	13.3	12.7	9.0	2.1	2.7
Philippines	14.0	−21.6	−13.9	−6.7	21.6	25.2	51.7	24.6
Thailand	—	−39.7	−29.1	−7.4	−4.4	−6.2	2.9	1.1
Vietnam[a]	—	—	—	—	−6.0	−15.3	−0.1	8.5
Bangladesh	—	−22.8	8.0	−8.8	9.5	−1.4	−4.9	0.7
India	−25.6	−37.3	−14.7	−2.9	11.3	−7.3	−7.8	3.6
Pakistan[a]	24.0	−14.9	−19.0	−11.6	3.9	−8.7	−4.3	0.6
Sri Lanka	−5.9	−3.7	−14.8	−8.9	−3.9	2.0	10.5	5.8
Total	−6.4	−13.1	−1.7	−20.8	−17.6	−3.6	6.1	9.8
All Asian economies[b]	−6.8	−13.9	−1.8	−22.1	−18.7	−3.9	6.5	10.4

c. Regional CTEs, by product

Product	1965–69	1970–74	1975–79	1980–84	1985–89	1990–94	1995–99	2000–04
Barley	430	577	442	376	440	405	276	225
Beef	112	164	982	1,430	1,110	2,980	2,260	2,120
Cassava	0	−8	0	−5	−7	−5	−6	−3
Chickpeas	150	0	0	91	121	0	58	100
Cocoa	0	0	0	0	0	0	0	0
Coconuts	−76	−564	−239	−878	−879	−1,120	−1,087	−322
Coffee	0	−23	−22	−23	−15	−10	−12	−3
Cotton	−211	564	−165	−1,289	−643	−1,045	−477	−232
Eggs	34	−13	−41	70	150	215	200	284
Fruits and vegetables[c]	0	−8	1	−18,700	−45,800	−15,100	−1,252	−1,230
Jute	0	−47	−189	−92	−146	−86	−9	−48
Maize	578	−118	186	−1,140	1,500	−837	1,690	2,037
Milk	608	759	9,183	9,099	10,904	5,550	4,422	6,470
Oilseeds[d]	211	−446	−674	1,748	3,003	2,380	2,945	3,150
Palm oil	0	−8	−9	50	−17	98	−255	−70
Pig meat	636	839	1,418	−28,008	−14,856	−1,510	3,270	2,140
Poultry	217	79	830	1,630	−313	1,810	2,840	2,100
Rice	−16,500	−26,199	−13,700	−17,600	−7,020	−7,680	−628	9,670
Rubber	−3	−3	−49	−72	−77	−87	−21	10

(Table continues on the following page.)

67

Table 1.21. Value of CTEs for Policies Assisting the Producers of Covered Agricultural Products, Asian Focus Economies, 1965–2004 (*continued*)

c. Regional CTEs, by product

Product	1965–69	1970–74	1975–79	1980–84	1985–89	1990–94	1995–99	2000–04
Sorghum	343	854	230	−8	379	−118	99	13
Sugar	2,173	−835	−913	3,294	2,470	1,029	1,565	4,240
Tea	−17	−24	−27	−16	−16	−10	−22	−22
Wheat	590	−905	−957	1,710	4,870	3,310	2,530	614
Total	−10,729	−25,168	−3,712	−48,216	−44,892	−10,137	18,354	31,263

Sources: Author compilation; Anderson and Valenzuela, 2008; estimates reported in chapters 2–12 of this volume.

Note: — = no data are available.

a. Pakistan: 1960–64 is 1961–64. Taiwan, China: 2000–04 is 2000–03. Vietnam: 1985–89 is 1986–1989.
b. Assumes that the rates of assistance for covered products in the Asian economies not under study are the same as the average for the focus economies and that the share of the former economies in the value of Asian agricultural production at undistorted prices is the same as the average share of the former economies in the region's agricultural GDP at distorted prices during 1990–2004, which was 6 percent. These dollar amounts do not include noncovered farm products, which account for almost one-third of agricultural output (see the bottom row of Table 1.11), nor any markup that might be applied along the value chain.
c. Fruits and vegetables include fruit and vegetable aggregates for China and India and bananas, cabbages, chilies, garlic, onions, peppers, and potatoes for other economies.
d. Oilseeds include groundnuts, rapeseeds, soybeans, and sunflower seeds.

68

Nowhere is this more obvious than in rice. Rather than using trade as a source of less expensive imports or an opportunity for export earnings, governments frequently use fluctuations in trade barriers in rice as a buffer against domestic or international shocks. Because Asia produces and consumes four-fifths of the world's rice (compared with about one-third of the world's wheat and maize), this market-insulating behavior of Asian policy makers means that, even by 2000–04, only 6.9 percent of global rice production was being traded internationally, compared with 14 and 24 percent for maize and wheat, respectively.[14] International prices are thus much more volatile for rice than for these other grains. This means that the nominal rates of protection for rice would be above trend in years of low international prices for rice and below trend in years of high international prices for rice.

Figure 1.13 reveals that this has been the case. Even if we average over all our focus economies in Southeast or South Asia, the negative correlation between the rice NRAs and the international prices for rice is high, at −0.59 for Southeast Asia and −0.75 for South Asia. This behavior is evident whether the NRA trend is upward or downward. A clear illustration is provided in the case of Malaysia,

Figure 1.13. NRAs and International Prices, Rice, Asian Focus Economies, 1970–2005

a. South Asian focus economies (correlation coefficient = −0.75)

(Figure continues on the following page.)

Figure 1.13. (*Continued*)

b. Southeast Asian focus economies (correlation coefficient = −0.59)

Sources: Author compilation; Anderson and Valenzuela, 2008; estimates reported in chapters 2–12 of this volume.

where policies were reformed during a financial crisis in 1985–87; the growth in rice protection was reversed at that time (figure 1.14).

This beggar-thy-neighbor dimension of each government's food policies reduces hugely the international role that trade among nations might play in bringing stability to the world's food markets. The more countries insulate their domestic markets, the more they export the volatility in these markets to the international marketplace. This creates a perceived need among other countries to do likewise. In most cases, volatility is exported through changes in import tariffs, but export taxes and export controls are also used by exporting countries. As domestic NRAs are adjusted by these means to changes in international prices, world prices change again in reaction so that even larger adjustments in domestic NRAs become desirable. This is a classic collective action problem.

A multilateral agreement to desist is thus needed. This was sought through the Uruguay Round Agreement on Agriculture, which established tariff bindings and disciplines on administered domestic prices. Tariff bindings help reduce the extent of the problem by imposing limits on the range of tariff increases implemented in response to low prices. However, the bindings are so far beyond the applied import tariffs that the discipline facing food-importing members in years of low international prices is weak. Moreover, there is no corresponding WTO

Figure 1.14. NRAs for Rice, Malaysia, 1960–2004

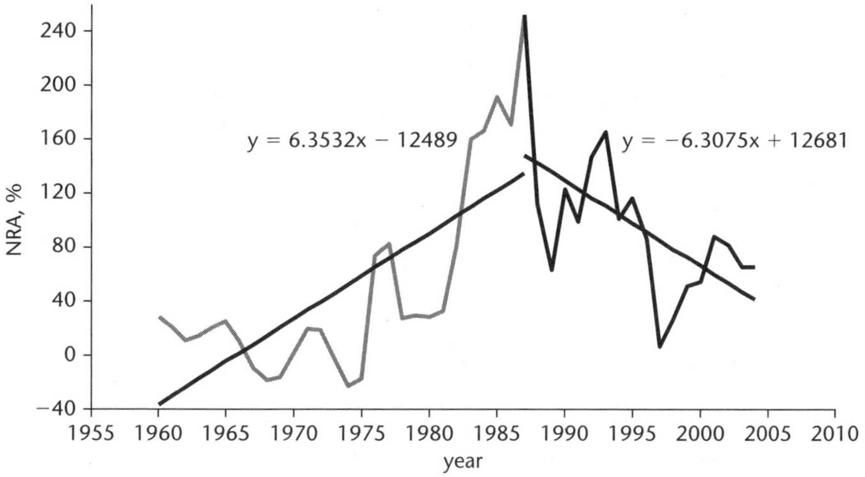

$y = 6.3532x - 12489$

$y = -6.3075x + 12681$

Sources: Author compilation; Anderson and Valenzuela, 2008; estimates reported in chapters 2–12 of this volume.

discipline on food export restrictions, which, as 2008 has starkly revealed, can be a serious problem in years of high international prices.

Summary: what have we learned?

A salient feature of price and trade policies in Asia since the 1960s is the spate of major economic reforms, including significant trade liberalization. Overall levels of nonagricultural protection have declined considerably, and this has improved the competitiveness of the agricultural sector in many economies, especially China and India. Other salient features include the gradual policy shift away from taxing agricultural exportables and, at the same time (in contrast to the situation in nonagricultural sectors), the rise in agricultural import protection.

These features are captured in figure 1.15, which shows agricultural TBIs on the horizontal axis and the RRAs on the vertical axis. An economy with no antiagricultural bias (RRA = 0) and no antitrade bias within the farm sector (TBI = 0) would be located at the intersection of lines extending from the 0 point on each of the axes in figure 1.15 (indicated by a large +). China and the focus economies of South and Southeast Asia were to the southwest of this neutral point in 1980–84, but, by 2000–04, most had moved toward the northeast, closer to the neutral point. This indicates they had reduced the antitrade bias in agriculture. Most had also shifted up, closer to RRA = 0, but some are now above rather than below zero. This indicates they are assisting farmers relative to producers of other tradable products, which, similar to the antiagricultural policy bias, can lead to wasted resources.

Figure 1.15. RRAs and TBIs in Agriculture, Asian Focus Economies, 1980–84 and 2000–04

a. 1980–84

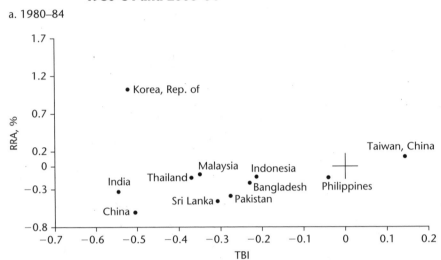

b. 2000–04

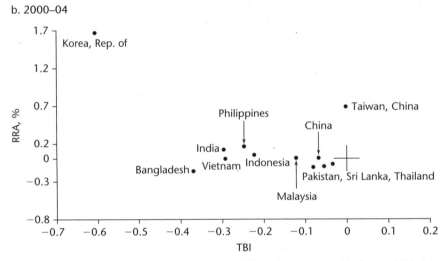

Sources: Author compilation; Anderson and Valenzuela, 2008; estimates reported in chapters 2–12 of this volume.

Note: Vietnam, 1980–84: no data are available.

The following features of the Asian experience over the past five decades are worth highlighting by way of a summary of the key findings of our regional study.

Since the 1950s, the region has shown a gradual shift away from the taxation of farmers relative to nonagricultural producers and the emergence, during the most recent decade, of positive assistance, on average, among farmers. The decline in the estimated (negative) RRAs in the region—from less than −50 percent until the early 1970s to small positive rates in the past decade—has not been dissimilar to the trends in Africa and Latin America, though it has been more dramatic. Asian farmers were effectively taxed more than US$130 billion per year in the late 1970s and early 1980s (US$170 per person working in agriculture). Asian farmers now enjoy support worth more than US$60 billion per year (nearly US$60 per person employed on farms).

Despite reforms, the dispersion in the NRAs and RRAs among farmers across Asian economies has increased rather than diminished. This means there is still scope for reducing the distortions in the use of resources in agriculture though more intensive international relocation in production, especially rice production. This finding also suggests there are political economy forces at work among economies that do not change greatly over time. In particular, the econometric results reported above suggest that the NRAs and RRAs in agriculture tend to rise as per capita incomes rise and to be higher in economies with less agricultural comparative advantage.

The dispersion in NRAs among farmers has also increased rather than diminished within each Asian economy under study. This means there is still scope for reducing distortions in resource use within agriculture even in economies with average NRAs and RRAs in agriculture close to zero. As in other regions, the products in Asia showing the highest rates of distortion and gross subsidy equivalent values are rice, sugar, and milk.

The antitrade bias in assistance rates within the farm sector remains strong. The NRAs for import-competing farm industries have increased over the decades we study, while the NRAs for agricultural exportables have become less negative. The fact that the average NRAs for import-competing and exportable agricultural industries have risen almost in parallel means that the TBIs have not fallen much from the peaks in the 1980s. This may be understandable from a political economy viewpoint, but it means that resources are not being allocated efficiently within the farm sector. Because openness tends to promote economic growth (Commission on Growth and Development 2008), it also means that total factor productivity growth in agriculture is slower than it would have been if the remaining policy interventions were ended.

Measures that restrict trade are still the most important instruments of farm assistance and taxation. Non-product-specific assistance and domestic taxes and subsidies on farm inputs and outputs made only minor contributions to the NRA estimates for the region as a whole. Input subsidies have played a significant role in India and, occasionally, in other parts of the region; but, as in Latin America, there has been comparatively little assistance provided through public investments in rural infrastructure and agricultural research and development, even though the social rates of return from such investments are high (Fan and Hazell 2001; Lopez and Gallinato 2006; Fan 2008).[15] This suggests these other instruments could play a bigger role in boosting farm output and productivity in Asia.

Movements in the CTEs closely follow changes in farm taxation and support because agricultural taxation and assistance are mostly generated through trade measures. This means that, before the reforms, food prices were kept artificially low in Asia, but, in recent years, they have been above international levels, on average. This also means there is considerable variation in the CTEs across products and countries in the region. The current level of taxation of food consumers is rising in the region. In 2000–04, it amounted to US$11 per capita per year. This contrasts with the subsidy of US$22 per capita per year in 1980–84.

The reductions in negative RRAs have been caused by cuts in the protection for nonagricultural sectors as much as by reforms in agricultural policies. Thus, the reductions in the distortions to agricultural incentives in the region have been caused not merely by reforms in farm policies, but are part of economy-wide reform programs.

Governments continue to seek to reduce fluctuations in domestic food prices and in the quantities of food available for consumption by adding to or reducing barriers to trade. This beggar-thy-neighbor dimension of each economy's food policies reduces the role that trade among nations can play in encouraging stability in the world's food markets. This is especially the case in rice. Rice is the main staple in Asia; and Asia accounts for more than 80 percent of the global market for rice.

Where To from Here?

The expectation is that, provided they remain open, continue to free up domestic markets, and practice good macroeconomic governance, Asia's developing economies will grow rapidly in the foreseeable future. The growth will be more rapid in manufacturing and service activities than in agriculture. In the more densely populated economies of the region, growth will be accompanied by increases in incomes among low-skilled workers wherever labor-intensive exports boom. Agricultural comparative advantage is thus likely to decline in these economies. Whether these economies become more dependent on imports of farm products depends, however, on the RRAs. The first wave of Asian industrializers (Japan, then Korea, and Taiwan, China) chose to slow the growth of food import dependence by raising the NRAs in agriculture even as they reduced the NRAs for nonfarm tradables so that the RRAs rose above the neutral zero level. A key question is: will later industrializers follow suit, given the close associations among RRAs, rising per capita incomes, and declining agricultural comparative advantage?

Figure 1.16. RRAs and Real Per Capita GDP, India, Japan, and Northeast Asian Focus Economies, 1955–2005

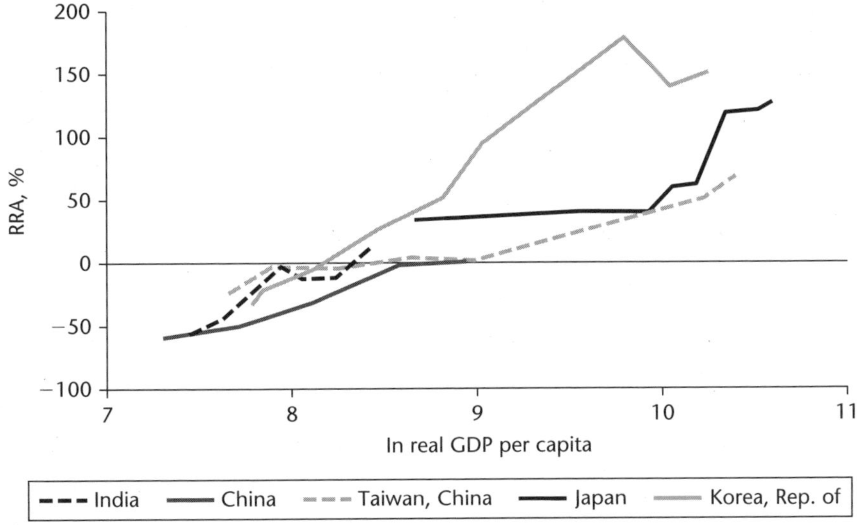

Sources: Author compilation; Anderson and Valenzuela, 2008; estimates reported in chapters 2–12 of this volume.

We have mapped the RRAs for Japan, Korea, and Taiwan, China against real per capita GDP and then superimposed on the same map the RRAs for lower-income economies to understand the extent to which the latter economies are tracking the former economies. Figure 1.16 shows the results for China and India. It indicates that the RRA trends of the past three decades in these two economies are on the same trajectory as the earlier trends in the richer economies of Northeast Asia. This represents a reason to expect the governments of later industrializing economies to follow suit, all else being equal.

One reason we might expect different government behavior now is because the earlier industrializers were not bound under the General Agreement on Tariffs and Trade to keep agricultural protection down. Had there been strict discipline on farm trade measures at the time Japan and Korea joined the General Agreement on Tariffs and Trade in 1955 and 1967, respectively, their NRAs might have plateaued at less than 20 percent (figure 1.17). At the time of China's accession to the WTO in December 2001, the average national NRAs were below 5 percent, according to our study, or 7.3 percent for import-competing agriculture alone. The average bound import tariff commitment of China was about twice this level (16 percent in 2005), but more important were China's out-of-quota bindings on the items the imports of which were restricted through tariff rate quotas. In 2005,

Figure 1.17. NRAs for China, Japan, and the Republic of Korea and GATT/WTO Accession, 1955–2005

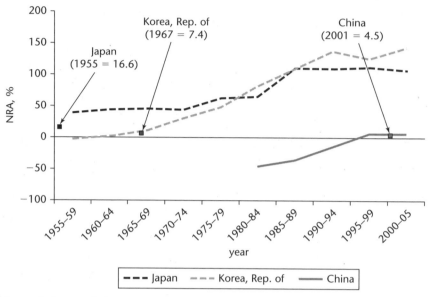

Sources: Author compilation.

Note: WTO accession also refers to accession to the WTO predecessor organization, the General Agreement on Tariffs and Trade.

the latter tariff bindings were 65 percent for grains, 50 percent for sugar, and 40 percent for cotton (WTO, ITC, and UNCTAD 2007). The Chinese government also had bindings on product-specific domestic supports in agriculture of 8.5 percent and was able to provide another 8.5 percent as non-product-specific assistance if it so wished. This sums to an NRA of 17 percent through domestic support measures alone, which is in addition to the assistance available through out-of-quota tariff protection.

Clearly, the legal commitments the Chinese government made on acceding to the WTO are distant from the current levels of domestic and border support it provides to its farmers. The commitments are therefore unlikely to constrain the government much in the next decade or so, and the legal commitments made by the Asian developing economies that joined the WTO earlier (except Korea) are even less constraining (Anderson, Martin, and Valenzuela 2008). In Bangladesh, India, and Pakistan, for example, the estimated NRAs for agricultural importables in 2000–04 are 6, 34, and 4 percent, respectively, whereas the average bound tariffs on the agricultural imports in these economies were 189, 114, and 96 percent, respectively (WTO, ITC, and UNCTAD 2007). Also, like other developing-economy governments, the governments of these economies have significant bindings, 10 percent, on product-specific domestic supports and another 10 percent for non-product-specific assistance, a total of 20 extra percentage points of NRA that legally could be applied through domestic support measures. This compares with the 10 percent in India and the less than 3 percent in the rest of South Asia (tables 1.13 and 1.14).

One can only hope that China and South and Southeast Asia will not make use of the legal wiggle room they have allowed themselves in their WTO bindings and thereby follow Japan, Korea, and Taiwan, China into substantial agricultural protection.[16] A much more efficient and equitable strategy would involve treating agriculture in the same way they have been treating nonfarm tradables. This would involve opening the sector to international competition and relying on more-efficient domestic taxes (for example, taxes on income and consumption or value added taxes) rather than trade taxes to raise government revenue.

It might be argued that such a laissez faire strategy might increase rural-urban inequality and poverty and thereby generate social unrest. Nonetheless, policies that lead to high prices for staple foods, in particular, involve potentially serious risks for the urban and rural poor who are net buyers of food in developing countries, as has been demonstrated during the recent increases in the prices for these goods (Ivanic and Martin 2008). The available evidence suggests that rural-urban poverty gaps have been reduced in parts of Asia when more mobile members of farm households are able to find full- or part-time work off the farm and repatriate a portion of their higher earnings among other farm household members (Otsuka and Yamano 2006; World Bank 2007). Concerted government intervention through social policy measures are hugely important in reducing the gaps between rural and urban incomes and in raising national incomes overall (Winters, McCulloch, and McKay 2004; Hayami 2007). Efficient ways of assisting any poor (nonfarm or farm) households left behind include public investment measures that have high social payoffs, such as in basic education and health care, and investments in rural infrastructure and agricultural research and development.[17]

What do the above lessons and implications suggest developing-country policy makers should do when confronted, as in recent years, by a sharp upward movement in international food prices? In the past, as illustrated for rice in figures 1.13 and 1.14, many governments have simply increased export restrictions or lowered import restrictions on food staples for the duration of the spike. What if the recent rise in international prices is more prolonged than the short-lived spikes of the past? Outlook projections issued by international agencies suggest that prices might remain high for the foreseeable future and that growth in net food imports by the rapidly industrializing economies of Asia is a significant contributor to this phenomenon.[18] Yet, as we see in figure 1.8, China and India over the past two or three decades have steadily raised the RRAs, though these had been adequate to keep both countries close to self-sufficiency in primary agricultural products over the previous four decades. However, in 2000–04, China became a net importer in all trade in agriculture and processed food for the first time, while, in South Asia, the net exports of India were less than the net imports of Bangladesh and Pakistan for the first time since the late 1960s (Sandri, Valenzuela, and Anderson 2007).[19] Should these governments choose to maintain RRAs at current levels (close to zero), the import dependence of these economies in agriculture might rise. If this occurs, other developing economies might reconsider their current position in the WTO's Doha Round of trade negotiations. By agreeing to lower substantially their bound tariffs and their subsidies on agricultural products, they could extract greater concessions from high-income countries without having to reduce their actual applied rates in the foreseeable future.

We have dealt little in this chapter with the effects of the trends and fluctuations in the NRAs and RRAs, especially on economic welfare, price stability, income equality, or poverty, and we have dealt little with the underlying causes of these effects. The analytical narratives in the chapters that follow touch on these issues, but more in-depth empirical analysis may now be undertaken with the help of our assistance estimates. Some analysis will appear in our project's publications. Specifically, Anderson, Valenzuela, and van der Mensbrugghe (forthcoming) provide results from a global economy-wide model of the impacts on agricultural markets, national economic welfare, and net farm incomes of distortions to the world's goods markets as of 2004. They use the new agricultural distortion estimates in this volume and its companion volumes. How these distortions, both within an economy and in the rest of the world, affect poverty and inequality are explored in a series of country case studies brought together in Anderson, Cockburn, and Martin (forthcoming), who use national economy-wide models that have been enhanced with detailed earning and spending information on numerous types of urban and rural households. In Anderson (*Political Economy*, forthcoming), a broad range of theoretical and econometric analyses are assembled to shed light on the political economy forces that have generated the evolving pattern of inter- and intrasectoral distortions in farmer and food consumer incentives over the past half century. Our hope is that these and others results of this study and its companion volumes will spawn much more analysis in the years to come.

Notes

1. The other three regional studies are Anderson and Masters (forthcoming), Anderson and Swinnen (2008), and Anderson and Valdés (2008). Together with comparable studies of high-income countries, including Japan, they have formed the basis for a global overview volume (Anderson, *A Global Perspective*, forthcoming).

2. Apart from the urban islands of Hong Kong, China and Singapore, the region's economies that have populations above 1 million each and that we have omitted are Afghanistan, Cambodia, the Democratic People's Republic of Korea, the Lao People's Democratic Republic, Mongolia, Myanmar, Nepal, and Papua New Guinea, which, in 2004, contributed less than 5 percent of the population, 4 percent of the agricultural GDP, and 2 percent of the total GDP of all the developing economies in the region.

3. Anderson and Hayami (1986) only examine Japan, the Republic of Korea, and Taiwan, China and only from 1955 to 1982 (apart from the rice distortion estimates, which are provided for an additional five decades). Krueger, Schiff, and Valdés (1991) analyze Korea, Malaysia, Pakistan, the Philippines, Sri Lanka, and Thailand, but for only four or five crops and only from 1960 to 1984. Orden et al. (2007) supply producer support estimates only for China, India, Indonesia, and Vietnam and only since 1985. The OECD (2007) has been covering its two Asian members, Japan and Korea, since 1986, but has also begun examining China (see OECD 2005). All these earlier studies find that the average nominal rates of assistance (NRAs) for farmers are higher in higher-income settings and in settings in which agricultural comparative advantage is weaker. They find that the NRAs in each economy are also much higher in the import-competing subsector than among exporters of farm products.

4. In overall land endowment per capita rather than only cropland and pastureland, China has around 30 percent of the global average.

5. The regime changes that have occurred during this period have included the shift from socialism to the market in China and Vietnam and the opening of India and several other economies. The region saw the end of colonization between the late 1940s and late 1950s. The Korean Peninsula and Taiwan, China obtained independence from Japan in 1945, India and Pakistan from Britain in 1947, Indonesia from the Netherlands in 1949, Indochina from France in 1954, and Malaya from Britain in 1957.

6. The nine are China; Hong Kong, China; Indonesia; Japan; Korea; Malaysia; Singapore; Taiwan, China; and Thailand. Brazil is the only other large economy in the set of 12; the other three economies are Botswana, Malta, and Oman.

7. By contrast, the share of our focus economies in the global exports of agricultural and food products grew only a little, from 11.0 to 13.5 percent between 1990 and 2006.

8. Our definition of a policy-induced price distortion follows Bhagwati (1971) and Corden (1997). It includes any policy measure at the border (such as a trade tax or subsidy, a quantitative restriction on trade, or a dual or multiple foreign exchange rate system, assuming the country is small enough to have no monopoly power in international markets) or any domestic producer or consumer tax, subsidy, or restraint on output, intermediate inputs, or primary factors of production (except where these are needed to overcome directly an externality, or where it is set optimally across all products or factors, for example as a value added tax to raise government revenue).

9. Corden (1971) proposed that the volume of free trade might be used as weights, but because this is not observable (and an economy-wide model is needed to estimate the weights), the usual practice is to compromise by using actual distorted volumes, but undistorted unit values or, equivalently, distorted values, divided by (1 + NRA). If estimates of own and cross-price elasticities of demand and supply are available, a partial equilibrium estimate of the quantity at undistorted prices might be generated, but, if the estimated elasticities are unreliable, this may introduce more error to the error one seeks to correct.

10. Recall that, unless otherwise noted, Asia is shorthand throughout this volume for our focus developing economies and thus excludes Japan.

11. Also ignored are distortions in the prices for the inputs into the production of nonfarm goods, which is in contrast to the treatment of these prices in agricultural NRA estimates.

12. This bias is accentuated in cases in which distortions in exchange rates are not included, as noted also in the section on methodology. Exchange rate distortions have been included in the studies that form the basis of the chapters on China, Malaysia, Pakistan, Sri Lanka, and Vietnam. Their impact was greatest in China, where they caused the RRAs to be more negative by about 2 percentage points in the 1970s, 6 percentage points in the 1980s, and 3 percentage points in the 1990s (see chapter 3, table 3.5 in this volume).

13. It is also true that consumers in South Asia received staple foods at prices that were effectively subsidized through the fair price shops. However, these government handouts were sufficiently

rationed to be mostly inframarginal and, so, are considered here as implicit income transfers rather than additional distortive consumer subsidies.

14. The number for the share of rice production represented an increase over the pre-1990s half-decade global shares, which were all less than 4.5 percent (for example, 4.1 percent in 1985–89) and is greater than the Asian share of only 5.7 percent in 2000–04 according to our estimates.

15. Data in Pardey et al. (2006) suggest that public research and development expenditure in Asia since the late 1970s has averaged less than 0.5 percent of the gross value of production at undistorted prices. This is trivial compared with the NRAs for the region that are generated through price-distorting measures. These NRAs are 25 to 40 times this share of the gross value of production (below −20 percent until the mid-1980s and 12 percent in 2000–04).

16. The indications in the ongoing Doha Round of multilateral trade negotiations at the WTO are not encouraging. The Group of 33 developing countries, led by Indonesia, but strongly supported by India and the Philippines, among others, is arguing for additional special and differential treatment for developing countries in the form of exemptions from agricultural tariff cuts for special products and for a special safeguard mechanism that would allow these countries to impose tariffs that are even higher than the bound tariffs in years of likely import surges.

17. As implied by the estimates reported in note 15 above, even if only 5 percent of the current NRAs provided to Asian farmers through farm price support policies were replaced by agricultural research and development expenditure, this would more than double current public spending on this research and development. The latter would increase regional economic welfare, whereas price-distortionary policies reduce welfare. Such a boost in research and development might generate another Green Revolution, especially if it took full advantage of the new developments in biotechnology. (For rice, for example, see Anderson, Jackson, and Nielsen 2005.)

18. The World Bank's commodity forecasts indicate that, by 2020, grain prices will still be 10 percent above 2006 levels in real terms (Prospects for the Global Economy Database 2008). The 2006 levels were 20 percent above the average for 2001–05. The International Food Policy Research Institute, the OECD, and the Food and Agriculture Organization similarly expect food prices to remain high well into the next decade and beyond (von Braun 2007; OECD and FAO 2008).

19. The change in China was largely caused by increases in the cotton imports needed to supply the economy's rising production in textiles and clothing for export.

References

Anderson, K. 1995. "Lobbying Incentives and the Pattern of Protection in Rich and Poor Countries." *Economic Development and Cultural Change* 43 (2): 401–23.

———. 2008. "Distorted Agricultural Incentives and Economic Development: Asia's Experience." 2008 World Economy Lecture, Leverhulme Center for Research on Globalization and Economic Policy, University of Nottingham, Semenyih, Malaysia, January 16. Forthcoming in *The World Economy* 32 (2009).

———, ed. forthcoming. *Distortions to Agricultural Incentives: A Global Perspective, 1955 to 2007.*

———, ed. forthcoming. *Political Economy of Distortions to Agricultural Incentives.*

Anderson, K., J. Cockburn, and W. Martin, eds. forthcoming. *Agricultural Price Distortions, Inequality, and Poverty.*

Anderson, K., and Y. Hayami, eds. 1986. *The Political Economy of Agricultural Protection: East Asia in International Perspective.* London: Allen and Unwin.

Anderson, K., L. A. Jackson, and C. P. Nielsen. 2005. "GM Rice Adoption: Implications for Welfare and Poverty Alleviation." *Journal of Economic Integration* 20 (4): 771–88.

Anderson, K., M. Kurzweil, W. Martin, D. Sandri, and E. Valenzuela. 2008. "Measuring Distortions to Agricultural Incentives, Revisited." *World Trade Review* 7 (4): 675–704.

Anderson, K., W. Martin, and E. Valenzuela. 2008. "Long Run Implications of WTO Accession for Agriculture in China." In *China's Agricultural Trade: Issues and Prospects*, ed. C. Carter and I. Sheldon. London: CABI.

Anderson, K., and W. Masters, eds. forthcoming. *Distortions to Agricultural Incentives in Africa.* Washington, DC: World Bank.

Anderson, K., and J. Swinnen, eds. 2008. *Distortions to Agricultural Incentives in Europe's Transition.* Washington, DC: World Bank.

Anderson, K., and A. Valdés, eds. 2008. *Distortions to Agricultural Incentives in Latin America.* Washington, DC: World Bank.

Anderson, K., and E. Valenzuela. 2008. "Estimates of Global Distortions to Agricultural Incentives, 1955 to 2007." World Bank. http://go.worldbank.org/5XY7A7LH40.

Anderson, K., E. Valenzuela, and D. van der Mensbrugghe. forthcoming. "Effects of Distortions on Global Welfare, Farm Incomes, and Agricultural Markets." In *Distortions to Agricultural Incentives: A Global Perspective, 1955 to 2007*, ed. K. Anderson, chap. 12. London: Palgrave Macmillan; Washington, DC: World Bank.

Bhagwati, J. N. 1971. "The Generalized Theory of Distortions and Welfare." In *Trade, Balance of Payments and Growth: Papers In International Economics in Honor of Charles P. Kindleberger*, ed. J. N. Bhagwati, R. W. Jones, R. A. Mundell, and J. Vanek, 265–86. Amsterdam: North-Holland.

Bussolo, M., R. de Hoyes, and D. Medledev. forthcoming. "Policy Impacts on Global Income Distribution, Inequality, and Poverty Using Microsimulation with the Linkage Model." In *Agricultural Price Distortions, Inequality, and Poverty*, ed. K. Anderson, J. Cockburn, and W. Martin, chap. 4.

Chen, S., and M. Ravallion. 2007. "Absolute Poverty Measures for the Developing World, 1981–2004." Policy Research Working Paper 4211, World Bank, Washington, DC.

Commission on Growth and Development. 2008. *The Growth Report: Strategies For Sustained Growth and Inclusive Development.* Washington, DC: Commission on Growth and Development, World Bank.

Corden, W. M. 1971. *The Theory of Protection.* Oxford: Clarendon Press.

———. 1997. *Trade Policy and Economic Welfare.* 2nd ed. Oxford: Clarendon Press.

Fan, S., ed. 2008. *Public Expenditures, Growth, and Poverty: Lessons from Developing Countries.* Baltimore: Johns Hopkins University Press; Washington, DC: International Food Policy Research Institute.

Fan, S., and P. Hazell. 2001. "Returns to Public Investments in the Less-Favored Areas of India and China." *American Journal of Agricultural Economics* 83 (5): 1217–22.

FAO Agricultural Trade Database (FAOSTAT). Food and Agriculture Organization of the United Nations. http://faostat.fao.org/site/342/default.aspx (accessed May 2008).

FAOSTAT Database. Food and Agriculture Organization of the United Nations. http://faostat.fao.org/default.aspx (accessed May 2008).

FAO SUA-FBS Database (Supply Utilization Accounts and Food Balance Sheets Database, FAOSTAT). Food and Agriculture Organization of the United Nations. http://faostat.fao.org/site/354/default.aspx (accessed May 2008).

Hayami, Y. 2007. "An Emerging Agricultural Problem in High-Performing Asian Economies." Policy Research Working Paper 4312, World Bank, Washington, DC.

Ivanic, M., and W. Martin. 2008. "Implications of Higher Global Food Prices for Poverty in Low-Income Countries." Policy Research Working Paper 4594, World Bank, Washington, DC.

Krueger, A. O., M. Schiff, and A. Valdés. 1988. "Agricultural Incentives in Developing Countries: Measuring the Effect of Sectoral and Economywide Policies." *World Bank Economic Review* 2 (3): 255–72.

———. 1991. *Asia.* Vol. 2 of *The Political Economy of Agricultural Pricing Policy.* World Bank Comparative Study. Baltimore: Johns Hopkins University Press; Washington, DC: World Bank.

Lerner, A. P. 1936. "The Symmetry between Import and Export Taxes." *Economica* 3 (11): 306–13.

Lloyd, P. J. 1974. "A More General Theory of Price Distortions in an Open Economy." *Journal of International Economics* 4 (4): 365–86.

Lopez, R., and G. I. Gallinato. 2006. "Should Governments Stop Subsidies to Public Goods? Evidence from Latin America." *Journal of Public Economics* 91 (5–6): 1071–94.

Maddison, A. 2003. *The World Economy: Historical Statistics.* Paris: Development Centre, Organisation for Economic Co-operation and Development.

OECD (Organisation for Economic Co-operation and Development). 2005. *Review of Agricultural Policies: China.* Paris: OECD.

———. 2007. *Agricultural Policies in OECD Countries: Monitoring and Evaluation 2007.* Paris: OECD.

OECD (Organisation for Economic Co-operation and Development) and FAO (Food and Agriculture Organization of the United Nations). 2008. *OECD-FAO Agricultural Outlook 2008–2017.* Paris: OECD.

OECD PSE-CSE Database (Producer and Consumer Support Estimates, OECD Database 1986–2005). Organisation for Economic Co-operation and Development. http://www.oecd.org/document/55/0,3343,en_2649_33727_36956855_1_1_1_1,00.html (accessed December 2007).

Orden, D., F. Cheng, H. Nguyen, U. Grote, M. Thomas, K. Mullen, and D. Sun. 2007. *Agricultural Producer Support Estimates for Developing Countries: Measurement Issues and Evidence from India, Indonesia, China, and Vietnam.* Research Report 152. Washington, DC: International Food Policy Research Institute.

Otsuka, K., and T. Yamano. 2006. "Introduction to the Special Issue on the Role of Nonfarm Income in Poverty Reduction: Evidence from Asia and East Africa." *Agricultural Economics* 35 (3) (supplement): 373–97.

Pardey, P. G., N. Beintima, S. Dehmer, and S. Wood. 2006. "Agricultural Research: A Growing Global Divide?" Food Policy Report 17, International Food Policy Research Institute, Washington, DC.

PovcalNet. World Bank. http://go.worldbank.org/7X6J3S7K90 (accessed May 2008).

Prospects for the Global Economy Database. World Bank. http://go.worldbank.org/PF6VWYXS10 (accessed May 2008).

Ravallion, M., and S. Chen. 2007. "China's (Uneven) Progress against Poverty." *Journal of Development Economics* 82 (1): 1–42.

Ravallion, M., and G. Datt. 1996. "How Important to India's Poor is the Sectoral Composition of Economic Growth?" *World Bank Economic Review* 10 (1): 1–26.

Sandri, D., E. Valenzuela, and K. Anderson. 2007. "Economic and Trade Indicators for Asia, 1960 to 2004." Agricultural Distortions Working Paper 20, World Bank, Washington, DC.

von Braun, J. 2007. "The World Food Situation: New Driving Forces and Required Actions." Food Policy Report 18, International Food Policy Research Institute, Washington, DC.

Vousden, N. 1990. *The Economics of Trade Protection.* Cambridge, UK: Cambridge University Press.

Winters, L. A., N. McCulloch, and A. McKay. 2004. "Trade Liberalization and Poverty: The Empirical Evidence." *Journal of Economic Literature* 62 (1): 72–115.

World Bank. 2007. *World Development Report 2008: Agriculture for Development.* Washington, DC: World Bank.

World Development Indicators Database. World Bank. http://go.worldbank.org/B53SONGPA0 (accessed May 2008).

WTO (World Trade Organization). *International Trade Statistics 2007.* Geneva: WTO.

WTO (World Trade Organization), ITC (International Trade Center), and UNCTAD (United Nations Conference on Trade and Development). 2007. *World Tariff Profiles 2006.* Geneva: WTO.

PART II

NORTHEAST ASIA

REPUBLIC OF KOREA
AND TAIWAN, CHINA

Masayoshi Honma and Yujiro Hayami

The story of agricultural policies over the past 50 years in the Republic of Korea (the southern part of the Korean Peninsula, hereafter referred to as Korea) and Taiwan, China includes the dramatic changes in the distortions to agricultural incentives that producers and consumers have face in the course of the development of these economies. In this study, we estimate the degree of distortions for key agricultural products, as well as for the agricultural sector as a whole, over a period when these economies transitioned from low- to high-income economies (from 1955 to 2004).

Schultz (1978) established that, as economies advance from low-income to high-income status, price and trade policies tend to switch from taxing to subsidizing agriculture relative to other tradable sectors. During the 50 years of our analysis, Korea and Taiwan, China jumped from the status of low-income to middle-income economies and toward the status of high-income economies. Policy switching—shifting from negative to positive assistance for agricultural producers in the course of economic development—is clearly observable in the time series on these two economies.

We compare the switching processes in the two economies—which grew at about the same speed—to obtain insights into the effects of policies and the underlying causes of the changes in the distortions in agricultural incentives. Our findings shed light on the process of change in agricultural distortions that occurs during the stages in economic development.

In the following sections, we first briefly describe the structure of agriculture in the course of the development of these two economies. Next, the evolution of agricultural policies in these economies is reviewed. Distortions to agricultural

85

incentives are measured in terms of the nominal and relative rates of assistance to agriculture (NRAs and RRAs to agriculture, respectively). We then discuss the policy implications of the estimates for the two economies and draw lessons for less-developed economies that are currently experiencing structural transformation in the course of growth.

Economic Development and Structural Change

The available choices among agricultural policies, particularly price-distorting policies, are closely linked to the process of economic development. As identified by Schultz (1978), there are two agricultural problems. The food problem underlies the policies commonly adopted in low-income countries that exploit or tax agriculture. Such policies are in contrast to policies in many high-income countries that protect or subsidize agriculture to solve the farm problem. The hypothesis of Schultz became an established paradigm among agricultural economists and found support in several empirical studies (Anderson and Hayami 1986; Hayami 1988; Krueger, Schiff, and Valdés 1991). More recently, Hayami and Godo (2004) and Hayami (2005) have added the disparity problem, which is specific to middle-income economies. They suggest that one should examine the ways distortions in agricultural incentives change in all three types of economies over the stages of development.

The most distinguishing characteristic of Korea and Taiwan, China during the period of analysis is the unusually rapid rates of economic growth generated by success in industrial development. Indeed, during the East Asian miracle (World Bank 1993), while Japan was first, Korea and Taiwan, China—together with Hong Kong, China and Singapore—comprised the runner-up group; and China and members of the Association of Southeast Asian Nations are now following these economies. Since economic growth is a fundamental determinant of the nature of distortions to agricultural incentives, it is useful, in this section, to offer an overview of development processes in Korea and Taiwan, China.

An historical perspective

Because of regular monsoon rains and the mountainous, undulated topography in which water may be controlled relatively easily through cooperation at the family and community levels, this region is well suited to rice production on small family farms organized into village communities. The agrarian structure therefore became characterized by a uni-modal distribution of smallholders who farmed an average plot of about 1 hectare. Relative to Southeast Asia, large agribusiness plantations based on hired labor were almost completely absent not only in Korea, which is located in the temperate zone, but also in Taiwan, China, where tropical cash crops such as sugar and bananas occupy a significant agricultural subsector. The rural community was traditionally stratified across landlords, landowning cultivators, and landless tenants. Agricultural laborers subsisting on hired labor wages were not a significant component of the rural population in this region. Land reforms after World War II significantly changed the distribution of landownership, but the distribution of operational landholdings was essentially intact.

There is a high degree of similarity in the agrarian structures of the two economies partly because Japan brought its own institutions to its colonies: Taiwan, China was ceded by China to Japan in 1895, and the Korean Peninsula was annexed by Japan in 1910. The biggest reform during Japanese colonization was the transfer of fee simple titles to landowners through cadastral surveys in return for the commitment of the new landowners to pay the land tax. Japanese efforts to develop the colonies concentrated on agriculture, especially rice, when shortages within Japan became evident after the Rice Riots of 1918. The promotion of rice production through agricultural research and extension systems, as well as improvements in irrigation and drainage infrastructure, plus protection from rice imports from the rest of the world (see Anderson and Tyers 1992), was a major success from the viewpoint of the colonists in that Japan's rice imports from the two colonies rose from 5 to 20 percent of the country's consumption between 1915 and 1935.

Rising exports of rice and other primary commodities and the corresponding inflows of manufactured commodities meant that dependency on agriculture remained significant in the two economies. This was especially so in the southern half of the Korean Peninsula because Japanese efforts in industrial development in Korea were concentrated in the north to exploit the hydroelectric power of the Yalu River and feed a network of chemical industries that was larger than the one in Japan. The heavy dependency on agriculture in the south was intensified by the urban destruction during the Korean War (1950–53). In Taiwan, China, commerce and industry were more active because the relatively larger cash crop subsector required larger amounts of processing and marketing relative to Korean agriculture, which was dominated by subsistence crops such as rice and barley. Today, the wide dispersion of small and medium industries in rural areas in Taiwan, China contrasts with the concentration of Korean industry in large-scale establishments in urban areas and seems to be, at least in part, rooted in the cash crop tradition.

We discuss elsewhere why Japan, Korea, and Taiwan, China were able to achieve remarkable success in economic development as forerunners to the East Asian miracle (see Hayami and Aoki 1998; Hayami and Godo 2005). Here, it suffices to say that their success was the result of borrowing technology from advanced economies. Gerschenkron (1962) suggested that the later the start of industrialization, the larger the scope for achieving economic growth by borrowing technology. Why then were Korea and Taiwan, China, in particular, so successful in this borrowing in the midst of many other late starters? One reason is that the two economies were endowed with cheap, but relatively well-educated labor because of the diffusion of compulsory elementary education systems during the colonial period. This made the initial borrowing of labor-intensive industrial technologies more rewarding in these resource-poor economies. The accumulation of human capital through education investments by the newly independent governments smoothed the way for the switch to capital- and knowledge-intensive technologies that occurred later. Another reason was the constant danger of Communist aggression, which compelled leaders to adopt policies to achieve economic success for the sake of maintaining legitimacy and viability. The success of development based on industrial technology borrowing by their neighbor Japan was an added motive for adopting this strategy.

There are many similarities, but also significant differences in the industrialization strategies followed by Korea and Taiwan, China. In the latter, although the Nationalist Party exerted strong control over formal sectors, the government did not attempt to intervene in the activities of small and medium entrepreneurs in informal sectors. Informal sectors were able to grow by developing various marketing and financial links among themselves and with foreign firms. These enterprises were dispersed widely over urban and rural areas and were able to achieve substantial international competitive strength (Ho 1979, 1982). In contrast, government control in Korea was stronger and more complete, especially under the military administration of Pak Chong-hui (1961–79). All formal credits were channeled from nationalized banks to large industries, while foreign direct investment was tightly controlled. The strategy was the reason for the high concentration of industrial production in Korea in a small number of large enterprises located predominantly in urban areas (Cole and Park 1983; Amsden 1989).

Economic growth and structural transformation

We now provide a quantitative summary of economic development in Korea and Taiwan, China during the past five decades. Table 2.1 shows selected indicators of economic development. The first rows provide data on real gross domestic product (GDP) per capita in 2000 constant prices in purchasing power parity dollars in Korea and Taiwan, China. Until 1960, the two economies showed a low level of per capita GDP, at less than US$1,500. Thereafter, income levels rose rapidly,

Table 2.1. Economic Growth and Structural Transformation, Republic of Korea and Taiwan, China, 1955–2004

Indicator	Economy	1955	1960	1970	1980	1990	2000	2004
Real GDP per capita, 2000 constant prices, US$	Korea, Rep. of	1,429	1,458	2,552	4,497	9,593	15,702	18,424
	Taiwan, China	1,241	1,444	2,846	5,963	11,248	19,184	20,868
Agriculture in GDP,[a] %	Korea, Rep. of	46.9	39.1	29.2	16.2	8.9	4.9	3.8
	Taiwan, China	28.9	28.2	15.3	7.5	4.0	2.0	1.7
Agriculture among the economically active population,[a] %	Korea, Rep. of	79.7	60.2	49.1	37.1	18.1	10.0	7.7
	Taiwan, China	53.6	50.2	36.7	19.5	12.8	8.9	7.5
Farm household population in total population, %	Korea, Rep. of	61.9	58.2	44.7	28.4	15.5	8.6	7.1
	Taiwan, China	50.7	49.8	40.9	30.3	21.1	16.5	14.3
Agricultural GDP per worker in total GDP per worker, %	Korea, Rep. of	58.8	65.0	59.5	43.7	49.2	49.0	49.4
	Taiwan, China	53.9	56.2	41.7	38.5	31.3	22.5	22.7

Sources: Heston, Summers, and Aten 2006; MAF, various; Department of Agriculture and Forestry, various.

a. The shares of agriculture in GDP and in the labor force include forestry and fisheries.

exceeding US$2,500 in the 1970s, US$5,000 in the 1980s, and US$10,000 in the 1990s.[1] The economic growth paths were largely parallel, but, after 1960, Taiwan, China went slightly ahead, with a lead of about five years.

It is convenient to review the development of the two economies in four stages, as follows:

- Low-income stage (US$1,500 or less), before 1960
- Lower-middle-income stage (US$1,500–US$5,000), 1960–80
- Upper-middle-income stage (US$5,000–US$10,000), 1980–90
- High-income stage (US$10,000 or more), after 1990

The criteria are not applicable to all economies; they are tentatively adopted here for the sake of a comparison in a limited context: the development processes in these two economies.[2]

Although Korea and Taiwan, China experienced similar changes in real per capita GDP over the four stages, significant differences may be observed in economic structures. The GDP share of agriculture in Korea in 1955 was nearly 50 percent, whereas, in Taiwan, China, it was below 30 percent. This reflects Korea's greater dependency on agriculture. In both economies, the share of agriculture in GDP declined significantly (to 3.8 percent in Korea and to 1.7 percent in Taiwan, China by 2004), although Korea's share remained at nearly double the share in Taiwan, China.

Historical differences may be observed in the shares of agriculture in the labor force. In 1955, up to 80 percent of workers were employed in agriculture in Korea versus about 50 percent in Taiwan, China. The difference in the share of the labor force employed in agriculture disappeared over time: in 2004, about 7.7 percent of workers were employed in agriculture in the former versus 7.5 percent in the latter. Relatively more rapid declines in the labor force share compared to the GDP share in Korea reflect the urban concentration of industry. In Taiwan, China, there is a wide dispersion of industries over rural areas, and farmers were able to increase their incomes through off-farm employment. While engaging in nonfarm activities much of the time, they continued to be classified as farmers. In contrast, in Korea, rural people had to quit farming and migrate to urban areas to obtain nonfarm employment. Such differences are also reflected in the much more rapid decrease in the share of farm household population in the total population in Korea versus Taiwan, China.

The last rows in table 2.1 report the ratios of agricultural GDP per worker to total GDP per worker. This may be considered an indicator of the labor productivity of agriculture relative to the labor productivity of the total economy in nominal value. It may also be regarded as an indicator of the income gap between the agricultural sector and the whole economy. This measure must be interpreted with care. It declined much more quickly in Taiwan, China than in Korea, which may appear to indicate more rapid growth in agricultural labor productivity in Korea. In fact, however, this apparently more rapid relative growth of agricultural labor productivity in Korea was caused by more rapid relative decreases in the size of the farm labor force owing to steadier out-migration of farm labor to urban occupations. The number of agricultural workers decreased more slowly in Taiwan, China because these workers continued to farm, while increasing the allocation of their labor to nonfarm activities. Thus, growth in the labor productivity of farmers engaging in agricultural activities relative to that of other workers would not have been slower and might even have been more rapid in Taiwan, China if the ratio is calculated using output per hour of labor instead of output per worker according to the official sectoral labor force classification.

Changes in the structures of agriculture

How did the structure of agriculture in Korea and Taiwan, China change through the process of economic growth outlined above? Tables 2.1 and 2.2 show that, in 1955, Korea had 2.2 million farm households, which accounted for 62 percent of the total population, while Taiwan, China had 0.73 million farm households, which accounted for 51 percent of the population. The number of farm households has been relatively stable in the latter, whereas it has decreased rapidly in the former. The number of people in farm households in Korea also declined at more rapid rates because of steadier decreases in the number of farm households and the number of persons per farm household. These observations represent additional evidence for the scarcity of nonfarm employment opportunities in rural areas in Korea because of urban-centered industrialization. Indeed, from 1970 to 2004, the share of agricultural income in the total income of farm households declined from 49 to 22 percent in Taiwan, China, whereas, in Korea, it peaked at 76 percent in 1970 and was still 39 percent in 2004.

The amount of arable land increased in Korea from about 2 million hectares in 1955 to 2.3 million hectares by 1970, but declined to 1.8 million hectares in 2004. In Taiwan, China, the amount increased from 0.87 million hectares in 1955 to 0.91 million hectares in 1980, but declined to 0.84 million hectares in 2004.

Changes in operational farm size in Korea and Taiwan, China during the past five decades have resulted almost exclusively from changes in the number of farm households. In Korea, the average farm size increased from 0.9 hectares of arable land in 1955 to 1.5 hectares in 2004. Meanwhile, the farm size in Taiwan, China remained close to constant at around 1.2 hectares. The much more rapid increase in farm size in Korea was the result of greater out-migration of the farm population to urban areas owing to more urban-centered industrialization.

Table 2.2. Changes in Agricultural Structure, Republic of Korea and Taiwan, China, 1955–2004

Indicator	Economy	1955	1960	1970	1980	1990	2000	2004
Farm households, 1,000s	Korea, Rep. of	2,218	2,350	2,483	2,155	1,768	1,383	1,240
	Taiwan, China	733	786	880	891	860	721	721
Population in farm households, 1,000s	Korea, Rep. of	13,300	14,559	14,422	10,827	6,661	4,031	3,415
	Taiwan, China	4,603	5,373	5,997	5,389	4,289	3,669	3,225
Persons per farm household	Korea, Rep. of	6.00	6.20	5.81	5.02	3.77	2.91	2.75
	Taiwan, China	6.28	6.84	6.81	6.05	4.99	5.09	4.47
Arable land, 1,000s hectares	Korea, Rep. of	1,995	2,025	2,298	2,196	2,109	1,918	1,836
	Taiwan, China	873	869	905	907	890	852	836
Arable land per farm household, hectares	Korea, Rep. of	0.90	0.86	0.93	1.02	1.19	1.39	1.48
	Taiwan, China	1.19	1.11	1.03	1.02	1.03	1.18	1.16
Agricultural income in total farm household income, %	Korea, Rep. of	—	—	75.8	65.2	56.8	47.2	39.3
	Taiwan, China	—	—	48.7	24.8	20.1	17.6	22.0
Rice in the total value of agricultural production, %	Korea, Rep. of	—	59.3	37.3	34.1	36.9.	32.9	27.6
	Taiwan, China	37.4	36.5	25.7	19.8	12.1	9.6	7.1

Sources: MAF, various; Department of Agriculture and Forestry, various.

Note: — = no data are available.

This distinguishing characteristic of industrialization in Korea is clearly reflected in the high share of agricultural income in total farm household income. The ratio fell with increases in off-farm employment among members of farm households. In Taiwan, China, the share of agricultural income was already below 50 percent in 1970, when the economy was in the low-income stage, and it fell to about 20 percent in the 1990s, when the economy approached the high-income stage. In contrast, in Korea, the share of agricultural income in total farm household income was 76 percent in 1970 and still nearly 40 percent in 2004; this was not only higher than the share in Taiwan, China, but also higher than the share in Japan at comparable development stages.

Major differences in the adjustments undertaken in agriculture in the face of economic growth based on industrial development are also observable in the changes in the commodity mix in farm production. Rice was traditionally the most important crop in both economies, and this importance tended to decline as per capita income rose. However, the changes in the relative importance of rice was different in the two economies. In Korea from 1960 to 2004, the share of rice in the total value of agricultural production declined from 59 to 28 percent. In Taiwan, China, the share was initially low, at 37 percent in 1960, but fell more rapidly, to only 7 percent in 2004. The difference reflects the greater opportunity to grow tropical cash crops there. It also reflects the economy's success in achieving greater agricultural diversification toward high-valued commodities such as vegetables, fruits, chicken, and pork in response to the shift in demand toward more income-elastic commodities.

The Evolution of Agricultural Policy

We now outline changes in agricultural policies over the different stages of development in the two economies.

Korea

Before 1960, Korea was a low-income country, with a per capita income below US$1,500.[3] The economy had been severely damaged during the Korean War. The agricultural policy adopted at this stage aimed to maintain low domestic consumer prices for staple foods, notably rice and barley, as well as for fertilizer. The Grain Management Law, enacted in 1950, gave the government the authority to regulate price on staple foods. However, government control was not effective during the 1950s, given that the market share of government-controlled rice was less than 10 percent. The government was supposed to purchase grain directly from farmers, but it was unable to purchase sufficient amounts; there were budgetary constraints, and inflation had caused grain prices to spiral upward in the mid-1950s. Schemes to collect rice in payment of the land tax and to barter fertilizer for rice were initiated. The first type of scheme was successful, but the second type failed because the implicit barter price of rice was lower than the market price. Grain imports from the United States under Public Law 480, which amounted to 8 to 12 percent of total domestic grain in 1956–65, helped the government keep grain prices low.

In the 1960s, under the development autocracy of Pak Chong-hui, Korea launched an energetic policy to promote industrialization. Rather than supporting adequate incomes among farmers, agricultural policies at the time were designed to keep prices on staple food crops low so as to maintain low wage rates and a low cost of living among industrial workers. Government purchase prices were set below market prices; this was considered necessary to raise industrial profits and foster capital formation. The government's price interventions gradually became more intense. The market share of government-controlled rice was expanded to 20–25 percent during the 1960s; this was used principally to maintain low domestic prices. These agricultural-taxing policies continued during the initial part of the lower-middle-income stage.

The Korean economy advanced quickly toward the upper-middle-income stage. Meanwhile, the direction of agricultural policy gradually moved toward the provision of support for farmers. In the early 1970s, the buffer-stock operation for noncereal products was set in motion to counteract price declines in the subsector. Chemical fertilizers, pesticides, and farm machinery were added to the list of subsidized inputs (alleviating the adverse impact on farmers of the import protection provided to the manufacturers of these inputs). The government's purchase prices for rice and barley were steadily raised with the aim of increasing food production, as well as reducing the urban-rural income gap. Although the government allowed an increase in the producer prices on staple food grains, this occurred without a comparable rise in the market prices for rice and barley, thereby preventing a rise in the cost of living and the wage rates among industrial workers. Likewise, the government assisted livestock producers in part by using import quotas rather than tariffs to protect them from import competition; the rents from the quotas were captured by the producer-managed meat import agency.[4]

The implementation of the two-price system, however, conflicted with the need to maintain financial and monetary stability. When the difference between the purchase prices and the sale prices of rice and barley widened, the deficit in the grain management fund increased. Because a large portion of the deficit was financed through long-term overdrafts at the Bank of Korea, the policy came to represent a major addition in inflationary pressure. The expansion in the government deficit caused by the two-price policy became a serious constraint on the policy.

When the economy entered the upper-middle-income stage in the 1980s, the government took a step toward reducing both tariff and nontariff protection for manufacturing industries. In contrast, agricultural policies that tended to protect farmers were strengthened. The producer prices of farm products were raised far above border prices by means of quantitative import restrictions on most agricultural commodities.

After Korea entered the high-income stage in the early 1990s, significant policy changes were mostly related to the Uruguay Round Agreement on Agriculture, which was stipulated in 1995. According to the provisions of the agreement, Korea's quantitative restrictions were converted to tariffs for all agricultural products except rice. In the Uruguay Round negotiations, Korea retained the status of a developing country, which assigned it special treatment in the implementation of the commitments to reduce border protection. The agricultural products under tariffication were subject to a protection reduction commitment of 24 percent, on average, within 10 years, and a minimum cut of 10 percent. The tariff rates on Korean agricultural products were over 60 percent, on average. The tariffs on products that were considered particularly important in Korea were cut by the minimum rate of 10 percent.

In addition, many agricultural products began to be imported under the minimum market access commitment. This commitment required that, for all agricultural products, at least 3 percent of consumption must be purchased internationally during the first year, and the import share must increase annually up to 5 percent of consumption within 10 years. Low tariff rates were applied to the in-quota volume so as to guarantee easy market access from exporting countries. Many key agricultural products such as rice, barley, oranges, red peppers, garlic, and onions were newly imported under this commitment.

Rice, the most important item in Korean agriculture, was temporarily exempted from tariffication as provided in the Uruguay Round Agreement on Agriculture, annex 5.B. As an exception, rice was subject to an import quota, beginning at 1 percent of total consumption and gradually increasing up to 4 percent in 2004, the final implementation year. If Korean rice had not been exempted from tariffication, Korea would have complied with the standard market access commitment, 3 to 5 percent. The temporary exemption from tariffication expired in 2004, but Korea opted to continue invoking a rice exemption from tariffication for another 10 years, to 2014.

Taiwan, China

After World War II, Taiwan, China suffered high inflation rates, serious shortages of food and other necessities, and a heavy defense burden.[5] The government gave the highest priority to economic stabilization, food production increases, and the repair of war damage. To alleviate the intense population pressure on the limited land, it decided to grant incentives to farmers. Together with the land reform program implemented between 1949 and 1953, war-damaged irrigation and drainage facilities were repaired, fertilizers and other farm inputs were made available, and farmer organizations were strengthened.

During the recovery stage of the economy, the Sino-American Joint Commission on Rural Reconstruction, established in Nanjing in 1948, played an important role. The commission served as a nonpermanent agency for the postwar rural reconstruction of China. From 1951 to 1965, the United States provided US$1.5 billion in aid in Taiwan, China through the commission. Approximately one-third of the aid went to agriculture, where the aid was used to build infrastructure and enhance human resources. Also, substantial imports of commodities financed by U.S. aid and increases in domestic production, especially food production, helped relieve demand pressure.

During the low-income stage of economic development (before 1960), agricultural policy in Taiwan, China was designed mainly to supply rice to the nonfarm population at low, stable prices. In those days, two important taxes were imposed on farmers: the farm land tax and the hidden rice tax. Implementation was achieved by means of compulsory rice purchases and a rice-fertilizer barter system. The compulsory purchase of paddy from landowners at official prices was another method used to exert government control over rice. All paddy lands were subject to the paddy land tax, plus the compulsory procurement of rice. The compulsory procurement was assessed on the basis of tax units determined according to land productivity. The difference between the government procurement prices and farmer market prices constituted a hidden tax on paddy landowners, who, after the land reform program, were mostly farm operators. The hidden tax was gradually reduced as per capita incomes rose, but it continued to be imposed until 1973.

The government's rice collection by all these means during 1950–70 averaged 50 to 60 percent of the total amount of rice produced, minus the home consumption of farm families. By 1973, however, the share had declined to 20 percent. In subsequent years, it rose again because of the launch of the guaranteed rice price policy.

The total value of the hidden rice tax was more than twice the value of the farm land tax before 1961 (except in 1954) and was larger than the total income tax before 1963. After 1961, when the economy moved to the lower-middle-income stage, the hidden rice tax decreased rapidly: in 1971, the ratio of the hidden rice tax to the total income tax was only 8.5 percent (Kuo 1975).

Agricultural policy geared to exploit agriculture for the sake of supporting industrial development (and military development) largely ended during the 1970s, when the shift toward the subsidization of agriculture was initiated. This was the period when labor-intensive light industries were rapidly expanding in response to increases in export demand. Because many light industries such as garments and footwear were located in rural areas, nonfarm incomes became increasingly important among farm households. Farmers were able to take advantage of employment in manufacturing without leaving home; and, moreover, many farmers also engaged in nonfarm self-employed activities during less busy farm seasons. Therefore, the need for farmers to rely on agricultural protection policies was less substantial in Taiwan, China than in Korea.

In 1978, Taiwan entered the upper-middle-income stage at a real GDP per capita above US$5,000. To help raise the incomes of farm workers to levels comparable to the incomes of workers in the rapidly expanding industrial sector, the government offered loans and subsidies to promote farm mechanization; the scheme was designed to raise farm labor productivity. At this time, the growth in rice production began to slow in response to renewed emphasis on livestock and fishery products and high-value export crops. Increases in industrial employment were also pushing up the costs of farm labor. Agriculture continued to lag behind the industrial sector in labor productivity, and the gap between farm and nonfarm per capita incomes was widening, to the disadvantage especially of farmers who relied mainly on rice production. The problems faced in Taiwan, China in agriculture were similar to those experienced by many industrial countries at comparable stages of development, especially Japan in the early 1960s and Korea in the late 1970s.

The annual per capita consumption of rice in Taiwan, China fell from 140 to 74 kilograms between 1968 and 1988. The accumulation in rice reserves became a serious problem. To reduce production, farm extension workers encouraged farmers to plant other crops in rice fields. The effort was unsuccessful because no economic incentive was provided. A six-year rice-crop substitution plan was inaugurated in 1984 that involved direct subsidies of 1 metric ton of paddy rice per hectare to farmers who shifted their rice fields to corn or sorghum, or 1.5 metric tons of paddy rice per hectare to farmers who shifted to crops other than corn and sorghum. In addition, corn and sorghum were purchased by the government at guaranteed prices. Under the program, rice production declined to 1.8 million metric tons in 1988, which was 0.9 million metric tons less than the peak, which had been reached in 1976. The in-kind subsidy was altered to a cash payment in 1988 to improve efficiency in the management of the program.

The economy entered the high-income stage in the late 1980s. Real GDP per capita exceeded US$10,000 beginning in 1988. The most important changes in agricultural policy during the high-income stage were related to the accession of Taiwan, China to the World Trade Organization, which became effective on January 1, 2002. In line with the level of development of the economy, Taiwan, China agreed to adjust its tariff rates so that they were between the rates in Japan and the rates in Korea. It also agreed to reduce tariffs from the average nominal rate of 20 percent in 2001 to 14 percent in the first year of accession and to 13 percent by 2004. The target date for tariff reductions was 2002 except for 137 items that were under tariff rate quotas. Of the 41 products that were under import quota restrictions before accession to the World Trade Organization, 18 were moved to tariffication after accession. Rice received a special exemption, and the remaining 22 items were governed by the tariff rate quota regime.

As in the case of Korea, the special treatment of rice is based on the rules of the Uruguay Round Agreement on Agriculture, annex 5. The quota of rice imports was set in 2002 at 8 percent of the average domestic consumption between 1990 and 1992 (144,720 tons of brown rice). By negotiation, this amount was divided into governmental and private import quotas. The government rice quota (65 percent of rice imports) was subject to the same treatment as rice purchased from local growers. The imported rice cannot be exported for food aid, nor can it be used for animal feed. The remainder (35 percent) was imported by private firms and was allocated on a first-come-first-served basis. For both private and government quotas, there is a ceiling on the price markup of NT (New Taiwan) $23.26 per kilogram for rice and NT$25.59 for rice products sold on the domestic market. If the sale of quota rice is slow, the price markup can be cut by NT$3 every two weeks. The markup reduction may be continued until all quantities are sold.

The Measurement of Distortions to Agricultural Incentives

The main focus of this study is the measurement of the extent of distortions to agricultural prices brought about by government-imposed policy measures. The measures examined are those that create a gap between domestic prices and prices as they would be under free markets. Since it is not possible to understand the characteristics of agricultural development from a sectoral perspective alone, the project's methodology estimates the effects of direct agricultural policy measures (including any distortions in the foreign exchange market) and, for comparative evaluation, also generates estimates of distortions in nonagricultural sectors. Specifically, our study computes NRAs for farmers that reflect an adjustment for direct interventions on inputs, such as border protection for fertilizers. Via the calculation of an RRA, it also generates NRAs for nonagricultural tradables for comparison with the NRAs for agricultural tradables (see appendix A).

The commodities for which we calculate NRAs include rice, wheat, barley, beef, soybeans, pig meat, poultry, eggs, and milk for Korea. For Taiwan, China we estimate NRAs for rice, wheat, beef, pig meat, poultry, and eggs. Domestic prices have been converted to U.S. dollars using market rates for foreign exchange rates except for 1955–64 in Korea and 1955–61 in Taiwan, China. The shadow exchange rates estimated for Korea by Frank, Kim, and Westphal (1975) and for Taiwan, China by Scott (1979) are used to take into account the distortions in foreign exchange markets during those earlier years. Aggregate NRAs for output for each county are calculated using weights based on the domestic production of commodities valued at undistorted prices.

In addition to the commodities covered in this study, three other crops—peppers, garlic, and Chinese cabbages—are included in the NRA calculations for Korea. The estimates for these products come from the producer and consumer support estimates in the OECD PSE-CSE Database (2007). The data for these crops are available only beginning in 1986. We assume that the distortions affecting these crops prior to 1986 were equivalent to about 90 percent of the distortions affecting the available products that are covered.

Valued at distorted prices, the share of agricultural output surveyed in this study is between 50 and 70 percent for Korea and somewhat less for Taiwan, China. It is difficult to judge the NRAs for the residual products that are not covered. We assume they are made up of the following share trends (at distorted prices) between 1955 and the present: import-competing at 50 to 80 percent and nontradables at 50 to 20 percent in Korea. The distortions to the residual products are assumed at zero for nontradables and, to import-competing products, at the same level applied in the four products in the Organisation for Economic Co-operation and Development study. For Taiwan, China, we assume that the distortions of all the noncovered residual products are zero because most of these products are nontradable or exportable.

To compute the RRAs, we estimate the NRAs for nonagricultural industries. For the latter, weighted tariffs were available for the two economies only for selected years. We linearly interpolated data for the years for which data are not available. For the early years, the tariff rates are estimated as the value of total tariff revenue, divided by the value of imports. Assuming the exportable industries receive no assistance, we then multiply the weighted average tariff by the share of import-competing industries in the value of all nonagricultural tradables. This procedure undoubtedly underestimates the assistance to nonagricultural industries (and thereby the implicit taxation of agriculture) in the 1950s and, to a lesser extent, the 1960s. This is so because it does not account for the nontariff import restrictions that were rife, nor for Korea's subsidized credit for target industries.

The estimation results for the NRAs on the covered farm products are summarized as five-year averages in tables 2.3 and 2.4 for Korea and Taiwan, China, respectively, while table 2.5 reports the RRAs for both economies.[6] The annual movements in the NRAs and RRAs are shown separately for the two economies in figures 2.1 to 2.6.

Table 2.3. NRAs for Covered Agricultural Products, Republic of Korea, 1955–2004
(percent)

Product, indicator	1955–59	1960–64	1965–69	1970–74	1975–79	1980–84	1985–89	1990–94	1995–99	2000–04
Exportables[a]	n.a.	n.a.	n.a.	n.a.	n.a.	n.a.	n.a.	n.a.	n.a.	n.a.
Import-competing products[a]	−3.9	4.4	16.6	47.6	73.8	122.8	166.7	201.9	182.9	213.6
Wheat	−43.0	−26.7	−11.2	0.4	26.5	92.2	144.4	216.0	122.8	135.4
Barley	41.2	83.5	72.3	120.3	101.2	165.9	357.0	524.3	543.0	562.8
Rice	−8.2	−7.0	−5.4	31.3	59.6	118.4	214.4	265.9	294.3	385.9
Beef	38.8	34.4	64.9	73.9	162.6	163.2	126.2	200.8	159.9	167.8
Pig meat	−15.2	21.7	158.7	204.1	202.9	169.1	124.7	149.3	116.2	134.4
Poultry	−11.8	6.9	131.4	103.5	161.7	94.2	86.6	155.6	171.7	179.2
Eggs	−32.3	−24.7	23.0	0.1	−7.5	14.9	19.4	28.0	26.6	54.3
Milk	—	—	173.3	108.8	189.0	179.8	185.2	203.7	140.7	149.8
Cabbages	—	—	—	—	—	—	30.0	30.0	29.1	27.6
Peppers	—	—	—	—	—	—	175.0	245.4	145.5	197.0
Soybeans	−13.0	18.8	58.8	80.0	122.2	253.0	361.8	508.2	625.6	757.4
Garlic	—	—	—	—	—	—	250.3	288.8	213.3	122.6
Total, covered products[a]	−3.9	4.4	16.6	47.6	73.8	122.8	166.7	201.9	182.9	213.6
Dispersion, covered products[b]	33.4	40.0	82.7	81.0	87.2	64.7	112.4	164.2	200.1	225.4
% coverage, at undistorted prices	45	55	64	61	61	56	60	57	52	46

Source: Honma and Hayami 2007a.

Note: — = no data are available; n.a. = not applicable.

a. Weighted averages; weights are based on the unassisted value of production.
b. Dispersion is a simple five-year average of the annual standard deviation around the weighted mean of the NRAs of the covered products.

Table 2.4. NRAs for Covered Agricultural Products, Taiwan, China, 1955–2002
(percent)

Product, indicator	1955–59	1960–64	1965–69	1970–74	1975–79	1980–84	1985–89	1990–94	1995–99	2000–02
Exportables[a]	−23.5	7.5	5.7	20.7	13.4	35.9	89.5	161.4	167.6	203.1
Rice	−29.6	−6.6	−17.9	−9.4	−7.6	32.5	103.3	161.4	167.6	203.1
Pig meat[b]	−8.1	64.0	99.7	98.3	60.6	42.6	64.8	n.a.	n.a.	n.a.
Import-competing products[a]	−33.0	5.3	21.7	26.7	32.5	49.1	55.4	93.6	126.3	160.0
Wheat	48.2	36.0	39.4	32.2	57.2	92.3	—	—	—	—
Beef	13.7	41.2	28.8	22.0	79.6	77.0	101.3	98.5	82.6	72.8
Pig meat[b]	n.a.	n.a.	n.a.	n.a.	n.a.	n.a.	n.a.	107.1	131.3	173.2
Poultry	−47.5	−3.7	21.2	27.1	30.0	63.6	84.6	143.0	228.7	279.5
Eggs[c]	n.a.	n.a.	n.a.	n.a.	n.a.	0.7	26.8	23.9	17.9	24.7
Nontradables[a]	0.0	0.0	0.0	0.0	0.0	0.0	n.a.	n.a.	n.a.	n.a.
Eggs[c]	0.0	0.0	0.0	0.0	0.0	0.0	n.a.	n.a.	n.a.	n.a.
Total, covered products[a]	−23.2	7.2	6.2	20.0	14.0	35.1	76.1	109.5	134.0	167.8
Dispersion, covered products[d]	33.4	35.3	47.5	40.5	40.5	34.5	56.9	66.1	86.9	106.4
Coverage, at undistorted prices, %	53	49	49	48	50	42	35	34	35	36

Source: Honma and Hayami 2007a.

Note: — = no data are available; n.a. = not applicable; the applicable data are shown elsewhere in the table under another trade status.

a. Weighted averages; weights are based on the unassisted value of production.

b. In 1989, the trade status of pig meat was changed from import-competing to exportable. The period average reported here corresponds to 1985–88 for the import-competing product and to 1989–94 for the exportable product.

c. Eggs were assumed to be a nontradable, with zero distortions, prior to 1983.

d. Dispersion is a simple five-year average of the annual standard deviation around the weighted mean of the NRAs of the covered products.

Table 2.5. NRAs in Agriculture Relative to Nonagricultural Industries, Republic of Korea and Taiwan, China, 1955–2004

(percent)

Indicator	1955–59	1960–64	1965–69	1970–74	1975–79	1980–84	1985–89	1990–94	1995–99	2000–04
Korea, Rep. of										
Covered products[a]	−3.9	4.4	16.6	47.6	73.8	122.8	166.7	201.9	182.9	213.6
Noncovered products	−1.7	−0.2	7.0	15.3	25.3	37.4	64.3	88.0	74.6	71.7
All agricultural products[a]	−3.2	4.0	13.4	35.7	56.3	89.4	126.1	152.8	129.8	137.3
Non-product-specific assistance	—	—	—	—	—	—	—	—	—	—
Total agricultural NRA[b]	−3.2	4.0	13.4	35.7	56.3	89.4	126.1	152.8	129.8	137.3
Trade bias index[c]	n.a.	n.a.	n.a.	n.a.	n.a.	n.a.	n.a.	n.a.	n.a.	n.a.
NRA, all agricultural tradables	−3.3	4.9	16.3	46.1	71.8	118.6	159.3	197.6	164.8	171.9
NRA, all nonagricultural tradables	45.6	37.1	22.3	11.4	11.7	6.8	5.7	3.3	2.3	1.7
RRA[d]	−32.6	−21.4	−4.8	30.5	53.9	104.8	145.5	188.2	158.8	167.3

Indicator	1955–59	1960–64	1965–69	1970–74	1975–79	1980–84	1985–89	1990–94	1995–99	2000–02
Taiwan, China										
Covered products[a]	−23.2	7.2	6.2	20.0	14.0	35.1	76.1	109.5	134.0	167.8
Noncovered products	0.0	0.0	0.0	0.0	0.0	0.0	0.0	0.0	0.0	0.0
All agricultural products[a]	−11.8	3.5	3.0	9.2	7.0	14.6	26.4	37.2	45.5	60.0
Non-product-specific assistance	—	—	—	—	—	—	—	—	—	—
Total agricultural NRA[b]	−11.8	3.5	3.0	9.2	7.0	14.6	26.4	37.2	45.5	60.0
Trade bias index[c]	−0.15	0.05	0.02	0.12	0.05	0.15	0.27	0.11	0.02	0.00
NRA, all agricultural tradables	−15.8	4.7	3.9	12.0	8.9	18.5	32.7	45.0	53.6	69.2
NRA, all nonagricultural tradables	8.8	9.3	8.8	7.5	7.0	5.2	4.5	2.6	1.8	1.1
RRA[d]	−22.5	−4.2	−4.5	4.2	1.7	12.7	27.0	41.3	51.0	67.3

Source: Honma and Hayami 2007a.

Note: — = no data are available; n.a. = not applicable.

a. Including product-specific input subsidies.

b. Including product-specific input subsidies and non-product-specific assistance. The total assistance to primary factors and intermediate inputs, divided by the total value of primary agriculture production at undistorted prices.

c. The trade bias index is defined as $(1 + NRAag_x/100)/(1 + NRAag_m/100) - 1$, where $NRAag_m$ and $NRAag_x$ are the average percentage NRAs for the import-competing and exportable parts of the agricultural sector, respectively.

d. The RRA is defined as $100*[(100 + NRAag^t)/(100 + NRAnonag^t) - 1]$, where $NRAag^t$ and $NRAnonag^t$ are the percentage NRAs for the tradables parts of the agricultural and nonagricultural sectors, respectively.

The estimated RRAs for the two economies in the 1950s and 1960s—during the low-income and lower-middle-income stages of development—were low; the RRAs involved negative rates for most years before the 1970s. If one were able to include in the calculations the nontariff barriers limiting industrial imports during the period, the resulting RRAs would have been even more negative. In any case, the RRAs suggest that, in Korea in the later 1950s, the relative prices for outputs faced by farmers were over 30 percent below the output prices they would have faced under free-market conditions, while they were over 20 percent below in Taiwan, China. Output prices were still low in the 1960s, when RRAs averaged about −15 percent in Korea and −5 percent in Taiwan, China (table 2.5 and figure 2.1). In Korea, there was a rapid increase in agricultural assistance and a decline in the protection for manufacturing beginning in the 1970s when the economy moved from the lower- to the upper-middle-income stages.[7] In Taiwan, China, the transition was similar, but less rapid. Thus, the RRA lines in figure 2.1 crossed in the late 1960s, and—apart from 1974, when world food prices spiked—the RRAs for Taiwan, China thereafter remained below and grew less rapidly than the RRAs for Korea, although Korea lagged slightly in terms of per capita income.

Figure 2.1. RRAs for Agricultural and Nonagricultural Tradables, Japan, Republic of Korea, and Taiwan, China, 1955–2004

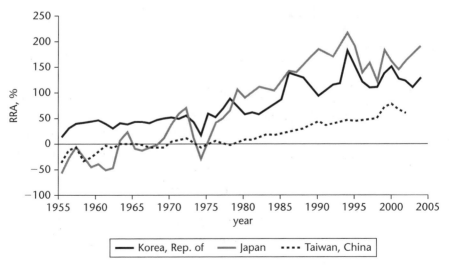

Source: Honma and Hayami 2007b.

Note: For the definition of the RRA, see table 2.5, note d.

Figure 2.2. NRAs for Agricultural Products, Republic of Korea and Taiwan, China, 1955–2004

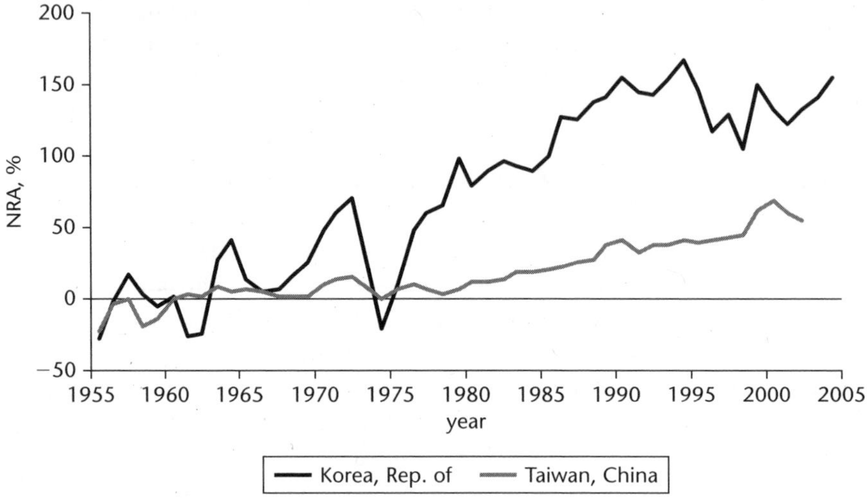

Source: Honma and Hayami 2007a.

Even after the two economies entered the high-income stage of development in the 1990s, the trend continued in the rising RRAs, reaching nearly 170 percent for Korea (above the 125 percent for Japan) and almost 70 percent for Taiwan, China in the first years after 2000 (table 2.5).

Figure 2.2 shows the movements in the weighted average NRAs for agricultural products in the two economies. They are similar to the movements in the RRAs in both economies after the 1970s because the impact of nonagricultural NRAs on the RRA calculation became trivial.

For Korea, the NRAs refer only to import-competing products because there have been no significant farm exports from Korea for decades. Two additional issues are worthy of note in the case of Taiwan, China. First, tradable products show estimated NRAs that are higher than the NRAs of the sector as a whole. This is because we assume that the products not covered explicitly in our study are exportable or nontradable and show a zero average NRA. Second, in Taiwan, China, the exportables covered (predominantly rice) show average NRAs that are higher than the average NRAs for the import-competing products covered (figure 2.3). This generates the positive trade bias index shown in table 2.5 and is possibly a unique situation; typically, governments find it much easier politically to provide assistance to import-competing industries (via import restrictions) rather than to exporting industries.

Figure 2.3. NRAs for Exportable, Import-Competing, and All Agricultural Products, Taiwan, China, 1955–2002

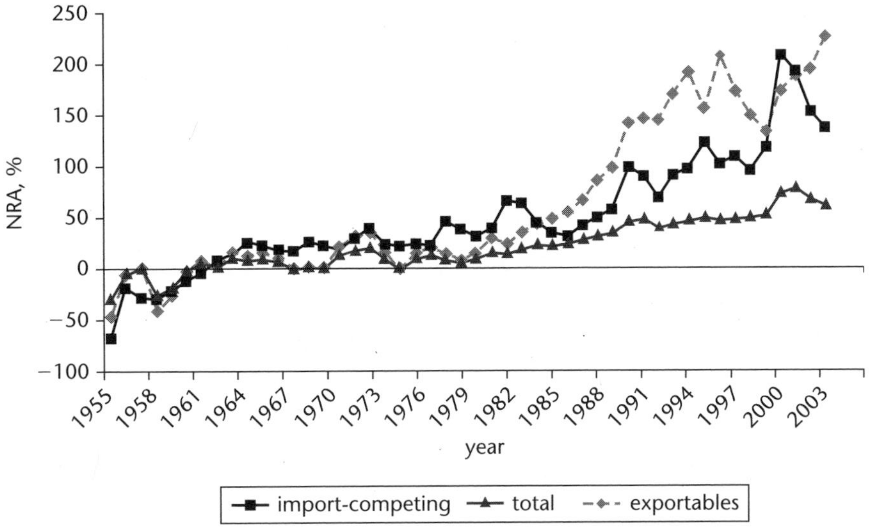

Source: Honma and Hayami 2007a.

There were wide fluctuations in the RRAs for Korea in the late 1990s because of the currency crises in Asia that began in 1997. The sharp increases in the RRAs for Taiwan, China in 1999 and 2000 were caused by shortages in livestock products after the September 1999 earthquake and the reductions in the production of pig meat resulting from the spread of foot-and-mouth disease among pigs in 1997.

Fluctuations in the RRAs and NRAs arose mainly from changes in the NRAs of individual farm commodities and changes in the weights of each commodity (figure 2.4). In both economies, the most important agricultural product was rice. The protection of rice therefore exercised a large influence on the RRAs. The movements in the NRAs for rice in the two economies, shown in figure 2.5, are clear: a strong upward trend from the mid-1970s as both economies began to move out of the lower-middle-income stage. Over the past three decades, the weight of rice in agricultural production in Korea has been twice the corresponding weight in Taiwan, China (see table 2.2). Korea was exempted from the tariffication of rice under the Uruguay Round Agreement on Agriculture; this allowed rice NRAs to grow despite Korea's commitment to the World Trade Organization to lower the protection on farm products.

Figure 2.4. NRAs for Agricultural and Nonagricultural Tradables and the RRA, Republic of Korea and Taiwan, China, 1955–2004

a. Republic of Korea

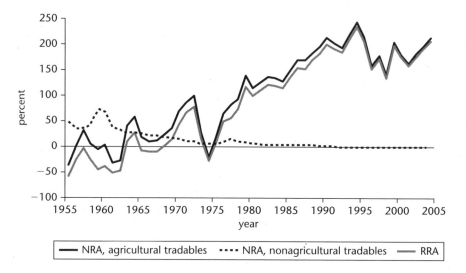

b. Taiwan, China

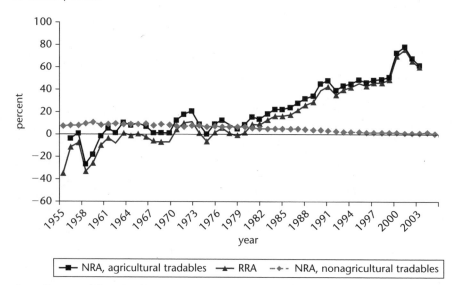

Source: Honma and Hayami 2007a.

Note: For the definition of the RRA, see table 2.5, note d.

Figure 2.5. NRAs for Rice, Republic of Korea and Taiwan, China, 1955–2004

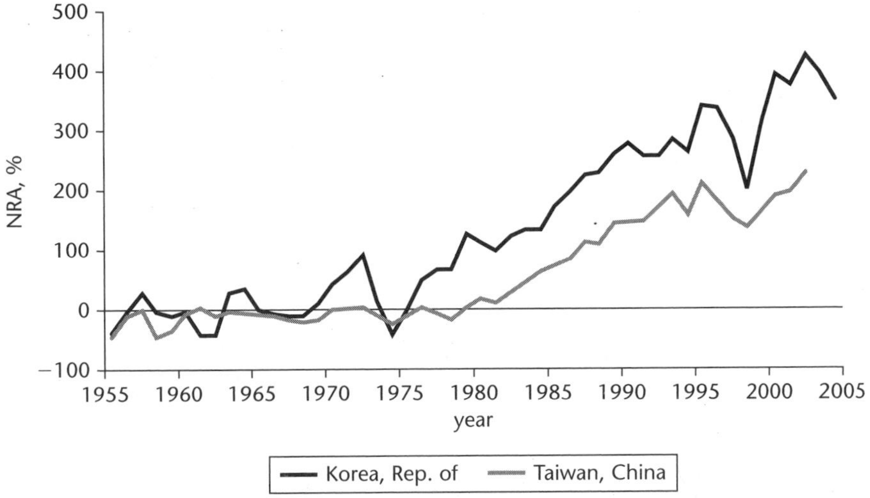

Source: Honma and Hayami 2007a.

In the two economies, support for farmers has been mostly provided through restrictions on food imports. In addition, there have been schemes whereby crop producer prices have been supported above the prices charged to grain and soybean consumers, including feedmixers that supply livestock producers with animal feedstuffs. Thus, the consumer tax equivalents for food are below the NRAs for some crop products. This, combined with the different weights of various products in consumption and production, has meant that, for Korea in 2000–04, the average NRA for the products covered is more than 30 percent above the consumer tax equivalent, while, for Taiwan, China in 2000–02, it is more than 65 percent above the consumer tax equivalent (compare tables 2.3, 2.4, and 2.6). Thus, consumers have been spared some of the implicit tax that otherwise would have been imposed on them had border measures alone been used to raise producer prices above international levels.

Sources of Growth in Agricultural Protection

The experiences of Korea and Taiwan, China offer good illustrations of the policy shift from the exploitation of agriculture to the protection of agriculture as economies grow and industrialize. In these two economies, agricultural protection

Table 2.6. CTEs for Covered Agricultural Products, Republic of Korea and Taiwan, China, 1955–2004
(percent)

a. Republic of Korea

Product	1955–59	1960–64	1965–69	1970–74	1975–79	1980–84	1985–89	1990–94	1995–99	2000–04
Wheat	−46.2	−22.5	−11.1	1.1	16.2	46.0	132.8	167.4	80.5	80.6
Barley	40.8	77.8	64.9	96.6	57.3	119.6	325.6	411.5	341.2	327.5
Rice	−7.7	−5.5	−5.0	29.1	54.5	113.4	211.5	261.7	290.8	385.3
Beef	38.8	34.4	64.9	73.9	162.6	163.2	122.1	200.7	153.9	167.7
Pig meat	−15.0	21.7	158.7	204.1	202.9	169.1	124.7	149.3	116.2	134.4
Poultry	−11.6	7.0	131.4	103.5	161.7	94.2	86.6	155.6	171.7	179.2
Eggs	−27.1	−24.7	23.0	0.1	−7.5	14.9	19.4	28.0	26.6	54.3
Milk	—	—	130.0	108.8	189.0	179.8	185.2	203.7	140.7	149.8
Soybeans	−19.8	8.2	51.6	63.2	95.2	245.4	112.2	75.5	63.6	66.8
Total, covered products[a]	—	6.6	13.6	39.2	63.3	110.6	150.8	185.9	159.6	163.9

b. Taiwan, China

Product	1955–59	1960–64	1965–69	1970–74	1975–79	1980–84	1985–89	1990–94	1995–99	2000–02
Rice	−29.6	−6.6	−17.9	−9.4	−7.6	32.5	103.3	161.4	167.6	203.1
Wheat	33.9	23.5	29.3	14.7	−1.1	40.3	183.4	—	—	—
Beef	13.7	41.2	28.8	22.0	79.6	77.0	101.3	98.5	82.6	72.8
Pig meat	−8.1	64.0	99.7	98.3	60.6	42.6	64.8	107.1	131.3	173.2
Poultry	−47.5	−3.7	21.2	27.1	30.0	63.6	84.6	143.0	228.7	279.5
Eggs	0.0	0.0	0.0	0.0	0.0	0.7	26.8	23.9	17.9	24.7
Total, covered products[a]	26.2	27.0	21.7	23.2	18.6	39.9	82.6	116.4	136.7	99.8

Source: Honma and Hayami 2007a.

Note: CTE = consumer tax equivalent. — = no data are available.
a. Weighted averages; weights are based on the undistorted value of consumption. For the Republic of Korea, this includes cabbages, peppers, and garlic.

levels were negative in the 1950s and the 1960s and began to rise sharply in the late 1970s following successes in industrial development.

Anderson, Hayami, and Honma (1986) found the growth of agricultural protection during the three decades to the early 1980s far more rapid in these economies than in the pioneers of industrialization in the West or even Japan. Moreover, the two economies were not exceptional in their bent toward growth in agricultural protection, and the growth was unusually rapid because the industrial development and the associated structural changes were also unusually rapid. The growth in protection continued at the same pace to the early 1990s, when the two economies were in the middle-income stage, but it began to decelerate thereafter, particularly in Korea when that economy reached the high-income stage.

The rapid growth in agricultural protection is largely explained by the shift in comparative advantage away from agriculture to industry as the result of successful industrialization. This shift was most pronounced during the middle-income stage. Relative to population, the two economies are characterized by meager endowments of natural resources, including land for cultivation. Industrialization was the only possible route to sufficient economic growth to catch up with advanced economies. Economic growth through the exploitation of abundant natural resources—vent-for-surplus growth (Myint 1965)—was not an option in these economies, unlike in Southeast Asian countries such as Malaysia and Thailand (Douangngeune, Hayami, and Godo 2005). The decline in agriculture's comparative advantage because of successful industrialization increased intersectoral resource adjustment costs and led to a widening rural-urban income disparity that, if left to the solutions of competitive markets, would have been shouldered by farmers. This raised demands among farmers for agricultural protection.

The association between the rise in agricultural protection and the decline in agriculture's comparative advantage was tested by Honma and Hayami (1986) using multiple regression analysis and a pooled data set on 15 countries at six points of time ending in 1980. They found a strong correlation between the aggregate nominal rate of protection and the index of agriculture's labor productivity relative to the total economy's labor productivity.[8] Based on the results, Honma and Hayami concluded that the high level of agricultural protection in East Asia was caused not so much by factors unique to East Asia, but mainly by factors common to all industrial countries.

One may argue that high rates of agricultural protection hinder adjustments aimed at raising agricultural productivity and thereby slow the growth in agriculture's comparative disadvantage. However, it is doubtful that the needed adjustments in agriculture in the face of the rapid industrial development experienced by East Asia's top performers could have been achieved sufficiently quickly under free markets to avoid major disruptions and social instability. This is particularly so because, in these economies, the agrarian structure involves a large number of small, independent family farms possessing unfavorable resource endowments.

Korea and Taiwan, China were at the low-income stage of economic development in the 1950s and entered the middle-income stage in the 1960s. During the middle-income stage, productivity growth in agriculture lagged relative to nonagriculture because of successful industrialization. Farm incomes declined relative to the incomes of nonfarm households. Nonetheless, during the lower-middle-income stage, it was not possible for the government to secure sufficient financing to close the income gap because the share of agriculture in the national income and in the labor force was still large. Thus, before Korea and Taiwan, China reached the upper-middle-income stage, agricultural protection remained low despite growing rural-urban income disparity.

The basic agricultural problem confronted by middle-income economies such as these in the 1960s and 1970s is known as the disparity problem (Hayami and Godo 2004; Hayami 2005). In this case, it revolves around the income disparity between farm and nonfarm households brought about by a lag in productivity growth in agriculture relative to nonagriculture. This lag was caused by the industrialization that successfully raised these economies to the middle-income stage. With respect to the low-income stage, food supply capacity rises during this stage because of both the productivity growth in domestic agriculture and the higher foreign exchange earnings, which enable more food imports. Meanwhile, factors causing growth in the demand for food, such as high population growth and high demand elasticities, are weakened. The terms of trade between agriculture and nonagriculture thus worsen.

Farmer incomes tend to decline relative to nonfarmer incomes. This reflects the widening intersectoral productivity gap. Observing the rapid escape of nonfarm workers from poverty, farmers begin to realize the relative extent of their poverty even if their incomes have not fallen or have risen only slightly since the previous stage. The dissatisfaction of these farmers who have remained poor often becomes a significant source of social instability.

Thus, at the middle-income stage, preventing growth in rural-urban income disparity is a prime concern of policy makers. To achieve this goal, the government might adopt agricultural protection measures to appease farmers so that their dissatisfaction is not transformed into a serious antigovernmental movement.

This protection may not be sufficient, however, to close the income gap between farmers and urban workers until the country graduates from the lower middle-income stage. Because the share of agriculture in national income and in the labor force is still large, it is difficult to raise sufficient revenue from the nonfarm sectors to close the growing farm-nonfarm income gap through direct support payments. It is also difficult to pass on the cost of agricultural protection to consumers by raising food import barriers; increases in food prices erode the real wages paid by the large number of small-scale enterprises that rely heavily on cheap labor.

Faced with the disparity problem, policy makers in middle-income countries are forced to search for ways to protect farmers within the constraints of the food problem. The food problem binds because a large number of urban workers have remained absolutely poor and food still accounts for a high share in their household expenditures.

Per capita incomes rose rapidly in the late 1970s and early 1980s as Korea and Taiwan, China approached the upper-middle-income stage. Both the government and the nonagricultural sectors became capable of shouldering the cost of agricultural protection during the upper-middle-income stage. It may be argued that high protection contributed to the loss in agricultural comparative advantage in these two economies by reducing the incentives to improve agricultural productivity. The effect of high protection on comparative advantage was much smaller than the effect of industrial productivity growth, which was unusually rapid among the high performers in East Asia. The conditions necessary for growth in agricultural protection were created by the increases in industrial productivity growth, which occurred far more quickly than agricultural productivity growth and provided the higher earnings capable of supporting agriculture.

There were also differences in the policy approaches toward agricultural protection in the two economies. During the upper-middle-income stage, agricultural protection rose more quickly and to higher levels in Korea. This seems to reflect the differences in the cost of the intersectoral adjustments required by farmers because of the shifts in comparative advantage. In Korea, the shift of labor from agriculture to nonagriculture involved the migration of workers from rural to urban areas; whereas, in Taiwan, China, much of the shift was absorbed by farm households, which increased their nonfarm activities in their home villages and towns. The pecuniary and psychological costs of the intersectoral labor reallocation would have been correspondingly higher in the farm sector in Korea.

The ratio of agricultural GDP per worker to total GDP per worker in nominal terms decreased more rapidly in Taiwan, China (see table 2.1). This does not mean that agricultural adjustment occurred more slowly there. One should make allowance for the fact that output per hour of labor in agricultural activities differs from output per farm worker as carried in official statistics. Since farmers in Taiwan, China depended more heavily on earnings from nonfarm activities (table 2.2), it is likely that household incomes per capita were not lower, but

Figure 2.6. RRAs in Agriculture and Relative GDP per Agricultural Worker, Republic of Korea and Taiwan, China, 1955–2004

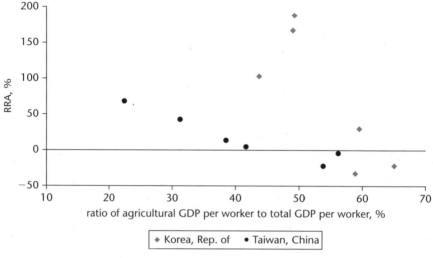

Source: Honma and Hayami 2007a.

Note: Calculated at 2000 constant prices in U.S. dollars.

higher than the corresponding incomes in Korea, although, in Taiwan, China, GDP per farm worker was lower relative to GDP per worker in the total economy.

The negative relationship between the relative GDP per worker and the RRA in the two economies in 1955–2004 is shown in figure 2.6.[9] Korea intensified agricultural protection despite the relatively high incomes among farmers. In addition to the high cost of intersectoral adjustment shouldered by Korean farmers, the constant menace of Communist aggression from the north caused citizens to feel the need to support farmers to maintain political stability.

In their analysis, Honma and Hayami (1986) found that political power is maximized in the agricultural sector when the share of agriculture declines to 4 to 5 percent of GDP or to 5 to 8 percent of the labor force. Korea recently entered this peak zone in terms of both GDP and labor force. Taiwan, China recently entered it in terms of the labor share (having entered this zone in 1990 in terms of GDP share). Political economy factors may underlie the rise in agricultural protectionism in Korea at the high-income stage since 1990, as observed through NRAs at the farmgate, despite the lack of an apparent additional increase in agricultural comparative disadvantage.[10]

Concluding Remarks

This chapter examines changes in the distortions to agricultural incentives in terms of price distortions in Korea and Taiwan, China in a manner consistent with the methodology described in Anderson et al. (2008) and appendix A. Rates of assistance to the agricultural sector are estimated for the half-century since 1955. These are based on estimates of the NRAs for selected individual commodities and RRAs in agriculture and industry. The estimates show that the growth of agricultural protection in Northeast Asia, together with the decline in industrial protection rates, caused RRAs there to rise over the five postwar decades under investigation. The data indicate that agricultural protection rates were negative in the two economies during the low-income stage of development and were low during the lower-middle-income stage, but rose sharply after the economies reached the upper-middle-income stage. The experience seems to be explained by two factors common to rapidly industrializing economies: first, the strong demand for protection among farmers, who shoulder the high cost of intersectoral adjustments in resource allocations in a context of rapidly declining comparative advantage in agriculture; and, second, the enhanced capacity of nonagriculture to support agriculture. The latter is associated with a growing tolerance among nonfarmers for policies to protect farmers. The first factor emerged at the beginning of the lower-middle-income stage; the second emerged when the economies reached the upper-middle-income stage.

Following the sharp increase in agricultural protection during the upper-middle-income stage, the two economies began to suffer from problems arising because of the high level of protection. These included the misallocation of resources and a high fiscal burden in the domestic economy, as well as serious international trade frictions, which are common among high-income economies. These problems might have been less serious if the farm-nonfarm income gap had been addressed properly during the middle-income stage.

The agricultural problem in the middle-income stage is known as the disparity problem. The challenge is to balance the conflicting need to support farm incomes and the need to supply low-cost food to a large population of urban workers in view of the weak capacity of the government to raise sufficient revenue for this purpose among nonagricultural sectors.

Contrasting patterns in agricultural and industrial growth in Korea and Taiwan, China provide a key to solving this problem. Despite their largely parallel progress in industrial and economic development, the growth in agricultural protection was significantly lower in the latter. The difference seems to be largely explained by differences in industrial and agricultural structures. Industrial structures have been characterized in Taiwan, China by the wide diffusion of small and medium industries in rural areas and, in Korea, by urban-centered industrialization. The cost of intersectoral labor reallocation that had to be shouldered by farmers was therefore considerably lower in the former. The advantage this represented for Taiwan, China was augmented by the success of agricultural diversification there toward highly income-elastic commodities such as horticultural and livestock products and away from traditional subsistence crops, especially rice. The demand for farming assistance was thus significantly less in Taiwan, China despite the pressures of rapid industrial expansion. Developing economies currently pursuing rapid development and relying on a similar strategy of borrowing industrial technology may benefit from closer analysis of the contrasting experiences in Korea and Taiwan, China.

Notes

1. Korea and Taiwan, China exceeded US$5,000 per capita GDP in 1983 and 1978, respectively, and US$10,000 per capita GDP in 1991 and 1988, respectively.

2. In terms of real GDP per capita in 2000 constant prices, for example, China exceeded US$1,500 in 1990 and US$5,000 in 2004, whereas Thailand passed the US$1,500 level in 1968 and the US$5,000 level in 1991. In the high-income stage, the United Kingdom and France exceeded US$10,000 in 1960 and 1964, respectively, whereas the United States had already exceeded US$10,000 in 1950.

3. This subsection draws heavily on Moon and Kang (1989).

4. This drove a small wedge between the NRA for producers and the consumer tax equivalent for beef (Anderson 1986). The scheme was similar to one operating in Japan in the 1970s. The reason the government chose the scheme rather than a more efficient, equally protective tariff, plus a consumer subsidy funded with the tariff revenue, is discussed in Hayami (1979) and Anderson (1983a).

5. This section draws heavily on Mao and Schive (1995).

6. Our NRAs for commodities differ from the estimates for Korea in the OECD PSE-CSE Database (2007). There are two key differences. First, our domestic prices are wholesale prices, whereas the database relies on farmgate prices. Second, border prices in our calculations are based on the study in Anderson and Hayami (1986), whereas the database relies on a different set of reference prices. The fact that producer prices were above wholesale (consumer) prices in the case of grains and soybeans in Korea is captured by setting the NRA equal to the measured consumer tax equivalent, times the ratio of the NRA to the consumer tax equivalent in Anderson (1989) for the period to 1985 and times the negative of the ratio of producer support estimates to consumer support estimates in the OECD PSE-CSE Database (2007) for the period thereafter. Most of the differences between the database and our measures arise from the differences in the border prices used. For example, our border price for rice in Japan and Korea is the world import unit value, adjusted by a quality coefficient. But the border price for rice in Korea in the database is China's export price for rice, adjusted by transportation costs and, beginning in 2001, the average of the import prices for rice from China, Thailand, and the United States. This means that our NRA series for rice is more stable than the database series in recent years; and, so, this explains the stability of our NRAs for Korean rice compared with the information in the database. For meat products, the border prices are also different. In the estimation of the NRAs for beef, pork, and chicken, the database relies on border prices derived ultimately from data on border prices for meat in Canada or the United States, while we use Japan's import price for beef and own-country unit values for pork and chicken (or, for the 1950s, the import prices in Hong Kong, China). Our approach is preferred for estimating NRAs consistently over longer periods, particularly during the period when Korean imports were absent or negligible. Also, our approach is necessary if one wishes to compare the NRAs of Korea and Taiwan, China on a similar basis.

7. Fertilizer price subsidies were also being provided to farmers in Korea, but they only partially offset the protection from import competition that was provided to the domestic fertilizer man-

ufacturing industry, which meant that farmers were effectively taxed in this respect, too, to support manufacturing (Anderson 1983b).

8. The actual data used to measure the level of agricultural protection in the regression analysis are the nominal protection coefficients $(NPC = 1 + NRP/100)$.

9. The average RRA in 1955–59 is paired with the agricultural GDP per worker relative to the total GDP per worker in 1955, and so on.

10. The shares of agriculture in GDP and the labor force in Korea were 3.8 and 7.7 percent, respectively, in 2004, while the corresponding shares in Taiwan, China in that year were 1.7 and 7.5 percent (see table 2.1, rows 2 and 3).

References

Amsden, A. 1989. *Asia's Next Giant: South Korea and Late Industrialization.* New York: Oxford University Press.

Anderson, K. 1983a. "The Peculiar Rationality of Beef Import Quotas in Japan." *American Journal of Agricultural Economics* 65 (1): 108–12.

———. 1983b. "Fertilizer Policy in Korea." *Journal of Rural Development* 6 (1): 43–57.

———. 1986. "The Peculiar Rationality of Beef Import Quotas in Japan and Korea." In *The Political Economy of Agricultural Protection: East Asia in International Perspective*, ed. K. Anderson and Y. Hayami, chap. 7. London: Allen and Unwin.

———. 1989. "Korea: A Case of Agricultural Protection." In *Food Price Policies in Asia*, ed. T. Sicular, chap. 4. Ithaca, NY: Cornell University Press.

Anderson, K., and Y. Hayami, eds. 1986. *The Political Economy of Agricultural Protection: East Asia in International Perspective.* London: Allen and Unwin.

Anderson, K., Y. Hayami, and M. Honma. 1986. "The Growth of Agricultural Protection." In *The Political Economy of Agricultural Protection: East Asia in International Perspective*, ed. K. Anderson and Y. Hayami, chap. 2. London: Allen and Unwin.

Anderson, K., M. Kurzweil, W. Martin, D. Sandri, and E. Valenzuela. 2008. "Measuring Distortions to Agricultural Incentives, Revisited." *World Trade Review* 7 (4): 675–704.

Anderson, K., and R. Tyers. 1992. "Japanese Rice Policy in the Interwar Period: Some Consequences of Imperial Self Sufficiency." *Japan and the World Economy* 4 (2): 103–27.

Cole, D. C., and Y. C. Park. 1983. *Financial Development in Korea, 1945–1978.* Cambridge, MA: Harvard University Press.

Department of Agriculture and Forestry. Various issues. *Taiwan Agricultural Yearbook.* Tapei: Department of Agriculture and Forestry.

Douangngeune, B., Y. Hayami, and Y. Godo. 2005. "Education and Natural Resources in Economic Development: Thailand Compared with Japan and Korea." *Journal of Asian Economics* 16 (2): 179–204.

Frank, C. R., K. S. Kim, and K. Westphal. 1975. *Foreign Trade Regimes and Economic Development: South Korea.* New York: Colombia University Press; Washington, DC: National Bureau of Economic Research.

Gerschenkron, A. 1962. *Economic Backwardness in Historical Perspective.* Cambridge, MA: Harvard University Press.

Hayami, Y. 1979. "Trade Benefits to All: A Design of the Beef Import Liberalization in Japan." *American Journal of Agricultural Economics* 62 (2): 342–47.

———. 1988. *Japanese Agriculture under Siege: The Political Economy of Agricultural Policies.* London: Macmillan.

———. 2005. "Emerging Agricultural Problem in High-Performing Economies in Asia." Presidential address at the Fifth Conference of the Asian Society of Agricultural Economists, "Prospects of Asian Agriculture in the New Millennium," University of Sistan and Baluchestan, Zahedan, Iran, August 29–31.

Hayami, Y., and M. Aoki, eds. 1998. *The Institutional Foundation of East Asian Economic Development.* London: Macmillan.

Hayami, Y., and Y. Godo. 2004. "The Three Agricultural Problems in the Disequilibrium of World Agriculture." *Asian Journal of Agriculture and Development* 1 (1): 3–16.

———. 2005. *Development Economics: From the Poverty to the Wealth of Nations*, 3rd ed. London: Oxford University Press.

Heston, A., R. Summers, and B. Aten. 2006. "Penn World Table Version 6.2." Center for International Comparisons of Production, Income and Prices, University of Pennsylvania. http://pwt .econ.upenn.edu/php_site/pwt_index.php (version of September).

Ho, S. P. S. 1979. "Decentralized Industrialization and Rural Development: Evidence from Taiwan." *Economic Development and Cultural Change* 28 (1): 77–96.

———. 1982. "Economic Development and Rural Industry in South Korea and Taiwan." *World Development* 10 (11): 973–90.

Honma, M., and Y. Hayami. 1986. "Determinants of Agricultural Protection Levels: An Econometric Approach." In *The Political Economy of Agricultural Protection: East Asia in International Perspective*, ed. K. Anderson and Y. Hayami, chap. 4. London: Allen and Unwin.

———. 2007a. "Distortions to Agricultural Incentives in Korea and Taiwan." Agricultural Distortions Working Paper 30, World Bank, Washington, DC.

———. 2007b. "Distortions to Agricultural Incentives in Japan, Korea, and Taiwan." Agricultural Distortions Working Paper 35, World Bank, Washington, DC.

Krueger, A. O., M. Schiff, and A. Valdés, eds. 1991. *The Political Economy of Agricultural Pricing Policies.* 3 vols. Baltimore: Johns Hopkins University Press; Washington, DC: World Bank.

Kuo, S. W. Y. 1975. "Effects of Land Reform, Agricultural Pricing Policy, and Economic Growth on Multiple Crop Diversification in Taiwan." *Philippine Economic Journal* 14 (1 and 2).

MAF (Ministry for Food, Agriculture, Forestry, and Fisheries, Republic of Korea). various issues. "Major Statistics of Agriculture, Forestry and Fisheries." MAF, Seoul.

Mao, Y.-K., and C. Schive. 1995. "Agricultural and Industrial Development in Taiwan." In *Agriculture on the Road to Industrialization*, ed. J. Mellor, 23–66. Baltimore: Johns Hopkins University Press.

Moon, P. Y., and B. S. Kang. 1989. *Trade, Exchange Rate, and Agricultural Pricing Policies in the Republic of Korea.* World Bank Comparative Study. Washington, DC: World Bank.

Myint, H. 1965. *The Economic Theory of the Developing Countries.* New York: Praeger.

OECD PSE-CSE Database (Producer and Consumer Support Estimates, OECD Database 1986–2005). Organisation for Economic Co-operation and Development. http://www.oecd.org/document/ 55/0,3343,en_2649_33727_36956855_1_1_1_1,00.html (accessed December 2007).

Schultz, T. W., ed. 1978. *Distortions of Agricultural Incentives.* Bloomington, IN: Indiana University Press.

Scott, M. 1979. "Foreign Trade." In *Economic Growth and Structural Change in Taiwan: The Postwar Experience of the Republic of China*, ed. J. Galenson, 308–83. Ithaca, NY: Cornell University Press.

Tyers, R., and K. Anderson. 1992. *Disarray in World Food Markets: A Quantitative Assessment.* New York: Cambridge University Press.

World Bank. 1993. *The East Asian Miracle: Economic Growth and Public Policy.* World Bank Policy Research Reports. New York: Oxford University Press.

3

CHINA

Jikun Huang, Scott Rozelle,
Will Martin, and Yu Liu

The purpose of this chapter is to present estimates of indicators of the effects on agriculture in China of direct and indirect government interventions. To put these indicators in context, we review China's experience with policy reforms since the 1950s and measure the extent of these reforms in the agricultural sector. Because of data constraints, we are only able to produce quantitative measures of price distortions since the early 1980s, that is, for the past 25 years, but we also summarize the country's agricultural experience over previous decades. Our review emphasizes the sectoral and macroeconomic policies and the elements of the institutional framework that have influenced the incentive framework facing the sector's product and factor markets. The changes over the past quarter century in trade, pricing, and marketing policies as these affect incentives for producing and consuming various farm products are reflected in our estimated rates of government assistance to or taxation of producers and consumers.

The main finding of our study is that the nature of policy interventions has changed dramatically in China over the past 25 years, propelling agriculture from a sector characterized by significant distortions to one that is relatively liberal. In the 1980s and early 1990s (the early reform period), there were distortions in domestic and external policies that isolated farmers and food consumers from international markets. Importantly, during this period, domestic marketing and pricing policies caused the prices that domestic producers and consumers faced also to become almost independent of the effects of trade policy. Because of this, even in the case of an exportable commodity such as rice, a commodity that appears to have been subject to little distortion at the border (meaning that the international price and the free-market price were nearly identical), domestic

117

pricing and marketing policies did not allow producers to reap the profits from international prices. Instead, they forced farmers to sell much of their surplus to the state at an artificially low price. Hence, domestic policies levied a tax on farmers although there was little distortion at the border. Similar dynamics characterized importable commodities such as wheat and soybeans, where, despite fairly high rates of protection erected by trade policies, producers were receiving much less protection than they would have received had there been a free domestic market for these importables.

In contrast, after the 1980s and early 1990s, the liberalization of domestic markets resulted in a reduction in the distortions arising from domestic policies. During this late reform period, the market gradually replaced the government procurement system as the primary mechanism for allocating resources, and market-generated prices became the basis for production and marketing decisions by farmers. At the same time, especially in the case of importable commodities, trade policy also became more liberal, and the distortions caused by border measures were substantially reduced. As a result, we find that, since the end of the late reform period (that is, after 2000), China's agriculture has become much less distorted in two ways. First, the differences between international and domestic market prices have narrowed considerably for many commodities because of trade policy liberalization. Second, the elimination of domestic policy distortions has meant that, when trade liberalization allows for increased imports or exports of agricultural commodities, prices in the domestic market change and farmer incentives are directly affected.

In addition, we also examine the effect of input-oriented policies and exchange rate policies. We find that input-related policies have generated few distortions since 1980. However, exchange rate policy, like changes in pricing, marketing, and trade policies, has played an important role. In the early reform period, exchange rates were highly distorted and served to add an implicit tax on agricultural trade. By the late reform period, however, the system of exchange rates was being reformed gradually, which reinforced the gradual shift toward a more liberal agricultural economy.

Despite the finding that considerable liberalization has occurred because of policy reforms in the domestic and external economy, there were still distortions in agriculture in the mid-2000s (25 years after the reforms were initiated). In some cases, the remaining distortions have arisen mainly through import tariffs, which, while low by international standards, are still providing a degree of protection for a number of importables (for example, sugar and dairy products). In the case of other importable commodities (for example, maize), the use of export subsidies has created a wedge between the domestic price and the international price. These subsidies are mostly disguised as domestic marketing, transport, and storage subsidies, which are allowed under World Trade Organization (WTO) rules for developing countries.

To show these results and provide the reader with a fuller discussion of recent changes in the structure of China's economy, the policy environment within which the changes have been occurring, and the analytical approach and findings of our analysis of price distortions, we have organized the rest of the chapter as follows. We begin below by examining the changes in the performance of the economy and reviewing the policy environment and reform agenda during periods of change. We examine the changes for two separate periods: the socialist era (1950–79) and the reform era (since 1980). The periods are split in this way not only because of the differences in the performance and the policy changes between the two periods, but also because, in the subsequent distortion analysis, we are only able to quantify the effect of China's liberalizing domestic and external changes after 1980. We discuss our quantitative approach and the sources of our data. The results of the distortion analysis are then presented and discussed. The final section provides concluding remarks.

Growth and Structural Change in Agriculture since 1949

The history of the Chinese economy since World War II may be clearly divided into a socialist era that lasted until December 1978 and the era since then during which China has implemented a transition toward a market economy.

The socialist era, 1949–78

Socialist policies dominated in China from the 1950s to the 1970s. They had profound and complicated effects on agriculture. In this section, we briefly review the performance of the agricultural sector during the socialist era by laying out the sector's successes and failures. We then describe the major policies—inside and outside agriculture—that we believe are responsible for producing the outcomes that were realized.

Performance during the socialist era

The record of the performance of agriculture in producing food and other raw materials for industry during the socialist era is mixed, although the record partly depends on the standard against which the sector's performance is being judged. Aggregate trends show that agriculture played an important role in increasing food availability, especially in the staple grains (Huang et al. 2007). Between 1952 and 1978, the total area sown only changed marginally, increasing 6.3 percent; the area sown in grain also changed little, declining 2.7 percent. In contrast, grain yields increased by 91 percent from 1952 to 1978, an annual growth rate of 2.8 percent. In aggregate, China's grain production rose by 86 percent, a rise of 2.5 percent a year. Indeed, the growth rate of grain production outpaced that of the population (1.9 percent), meaning that the agricultural sector increased per capita calorie availability during the socialist era.

To the country's credit, the increases in the absolute and per capita levels of availability of food and agricultural raw materials occurred during a time when many other nations were suffering from falling food production. Nonetheless, it is difficult to argue that agriculture's performance was sufficiently stellar to be considered a transformative force in the socialist era economy. Throughout the 1950s, 1960s, and 1970s, China's consumers remained on strictly rationed diets. Coarse grains—maize, millet, and sorghum—and sweet potatoes made up much of the average citizen's staple food intake. Cooking oil, sugar, meat, and vegetables were not available to the typical consumer on a daily basis. Most tellingly, despite the growth, the average level of consumption in the 1970s remained low in urban areas, at only 2,330 calories per capita, while the calorie intake of the average rural resident was only slightly more than the United Nations average minimum requirement of 2,100 calories. Moreover, food production systems were so fragile that they were subject to catastrophic failure, such as occurred during the famine in 1959–61, which reportedly killed more than 30 million people (Ashton et al. 1984).

Food availability became such an issue during the late 1960s and the 1970s that China turned to international markets to supplement domestic production. Between 1973 and 1980, China imported an average of more than 6 million tons of grain a year, mostly wheat. In peak import years, grain accounted for a large share of the value of the country's imports. At the time, planners were trying to jump-start industrialization by importing machinery and other technologies. The inability of the agricultural sector to produce sufficient food (and foreign exchange earnings from exports) obviously represented a drag on development.

The performance of the food production subsector in the rural economy was mixed, at best. Almost everything else about the record of structural change during agricultural development in China up to about the late 1970s is negative (Huang et al. 2007). For example, the production structure of cropping showed almost no change at all. In 1952, grain accounted for 88 percent of the total area sown; in 1970, grain was still being sown on 83 percent of the total area sown. Likewise, there was little change in the structure of the agricultural sector according to a broader definition. The value of the cropping subsector as a share of the value of total agricultural output was 83 percent in 1952; it was still 75 percent in 1970. Perhaps of greatest importance, the income per capita of rural farmers and other metrics of wealth also reflected the stagnation in the agricultural sector. Despite the rise in grain output, rural earnings per capita in the 1970s were almost the same as they had been in the mid-1950s (Lardy 1983). Even by 1978, nearly 30 years after the start of the socialist era, the annual rural per capita consumption of almost every food item was low, amounting to only 1.1 kilograms of edible oil and 6.4 kilograms of meat (Huang and Bouis 1996). The poverty rate was between 30 and 40 percent.

The stagnation in incomes, given the (even modest) rising output, suggests that farm productivity growth was slow. Although the data sources do not facilitate a rigorous analysis of total factor productivity, there appears to have been a complete absence of any gain in productivity and of any increase in allocative efficiency. The work of Stone and Rozelle (1995) and Wen (1993) supports such a conclusion. Using aggregate data, both studies find that total factor productivity growth between 1950 and 1978 was zero or close to zero.

Finally, there also was almost no sign of a shift in the structure of employment in the economy. Other rapidly developing countries in East Asia were diversifying the sources of the incomes of rural populations and expanding employment in the off-farm sector, but there was little of this in China's rural sector (Lardy 1983). In 1957, about 84 percent of the population was in the agricultural sector; by 1970, the share had risen to 85 percent; and, in 1980, it was still 83 percent. Of the more than 400 million people in China's rural labor force in 1980, only 4 percent had full-time off-farm employment (deBrauw et al. 2002). In fact, the share of people living and working in the agricultural sector was greater in China than in any other country at a similar level of income (World Bank 1985).

Socialist policies and institutions

Blame for the poor performance of the agricultural sector may almost certainly be placed squarely on poor policy. Even while local leaders were experimenting with privatized land through ambitious land-to-the-tiller policies in the early 1950s, other factions in the socialist leadership were already developing policies that would threaten the incentives embodied in private landownership (Lardy 1983). The levels of investment believed to be required to promote industrialization were partly obtained through transfers from the agricultural sector. During the planning era, prices for agricultural products were depressed so food could be sold to consumers at rationed prices. The scissors effect was reportedly large (that is, the extent to which the agricultural sector is taxed if the prices of agricultural goods are set below market value and the prices of industrial goods are set above market price). Realized primarily through the direct taxation imposed on the prices of agricultural goods, the estimated taxation rate was 26 percent in 1957 and 27 percent in 1978 (Yao 1994).

After the early 1950s, farmers were organized into collectives and then communes, eliminating the household farm in China. The main negative effect of the communization movement was the absence of incentives. The basic problem was that individual families were not the residual claimants of production, and decision making was left to a collective leadership (Putterman 1993). Farm workers were assigned points based on tasks that were difficult to monitor. There is a debate over the extent to which the collectives were able to motivate farmers to exert effort and attempt to increase the efficiency of production on their farms (Dong and Dow 1993; Chang and Wen 1997; Lin and Yang 2000). Most scholars believe, however, that free riding and the inability to monitor agricultural labor undermined the incentives in agriculture.

Socialist era pricing and marketing policies also did little to encourage the efficient production and allocation of goods and services. Prices were fixed by the government (Sicular 1988a). Between 1962 and 1978, the price of grain was adjusted only three times and rose by a total of less than 20 percent. Input prices played mainly an accounting function because shortages kept most producers from receiving the quantities they demanded. Marketing institutions—monopolized by government parastatals—did not encourage the development of agriculture. There was little competition, and marketing officials did not have an incentive to search out low-cost or high-quality producers. Through plans directed via the marketing system, production was carried out based on (mostly) planned acreage, target volumes, and the quality and variety of production. Even the ratio between home consumption and marketed surplus was stipulated.

The system also served to support—at least in the short run—the government's effort at forced industrialization by keeping down the price of staples, thereby allowing wages to be kept low. Except for the amount used by farm households for food, feed, and seeds at home, all production of grains, edible oils, and fiber crops was procured exclusively by the state at quota prices for a specified (compulsory) amount (Sicular 1988a). After the early 1960s, the government also procured—at a somewhat higher, above-quota price (to provide an incentive to increase production)—any surplus output beyond the quota and beyond consumption by farm families. The incentives, however, were targeted at collective leaders and not at the farmers on whose effort labor depended. To suppress the demand for agricultural products that were in short supply (because they were priced low), marketing policy also exercised tight control over food marketing in urban areas. Almost all major commodities were sold by government agencies to urban consumers and rural households in grain-deficit regions at low prices upon presentation of the appropriate ration coupons.

Fertilizers, pesticides, and other material inputs, where available, were also sold during this same period through marketing channels monopolized by the state

(Stone 1988). The Agricultural Inputs Corporation, the government retailer for fertilizer, sold fertilizer to villages on the basis of a carefully formulated plan. Collective leaders needed fertilizer coupons to buy fertilizer and other inputs that were in short supply.

In an agricultural system dominated by either tens of millions of individual farmers or hundreds of thousands of brigades and teams, there is a need for the government to play a major role in organizing wide-ranging investments because individuals have little incentive to make these investments. In several areas, the government made such investments between 1950 and 1978. National leaders arguably put their greatest effort into water conservation (Nickum 1998). In the early 1950s, China's irrigation and flood control systems were a shambles. The irrigated area was less than 20 percent of the total cultivated area (Stone 1988). By 1978, after more than 20 years of investment by local and national governments and the aid of uncountable man-years of corvée labor, more than 40 percent of the country's cropland was being irrigated. By the mid-1970s, every major river system was also protected by intricate networks of dikes, dams, and flood diversion projects.

In addition, led by a publicly funded research and development system, China's agricultural scientists led the developing world in many areas and were responsible for generating many scientific breakthroughs. Breeders developed high-yielding semidwarf varieties of rice several years before the Green Revolution began in other parts of Asia (Stone 1988). Farmers were able to use hybrid maize and disease-resistant varieties of wheat in the 1960s and 1970s, long before such technologies were available elsewhere in the developing world. In 1976, Yuan Longping created and commercialized the world's first hybrid rice variety (Lin 1991; Huang and Rozelle 1996). An extension system with nearly 500,000 agents was in charge of introducing the technology to brigade technicians (Hu and Huang 2001). By the mid-1970s, most of the country's cereals were improved varieties.

The government's approach to planning, including the placement of the rural economy in the unplanned sector, also had dramatic effects on the nature of employment and on the structural stagnation in the country (Lyons 1987). Because the agricultural sector was large and underdeveloped, leaders decided to make a sharp distinction between people who lived in rural areas and people who lived in urban areas. Agriculture became part of the collective sector. In return for shipments of fertilizer and small amounts of capital and other inputs, the agricultural sector was expected to supply food and nonfood commodities to the urban-industrial portion of the economy. The rest of the needs of the collective agricultural sector were supposed to be satisfied by the leadership of the collectives through their own resources. Farmers were not allowed to move freely from their collectives. The scope and magnitude of the gap in housing, education, health care, welfare, and other services between rural and urban areas widened throughout the socialist era. Without doubt, these *hukou* policies—policies tied to the household registration system (hukou)—and other restrictions prevented rural people from moving into manufacturing and service provision. They also artificially limited structural changes during the socialist era and depressed rural incomes and rural productivity.

Two key external policies had a negative effect on agriculture in the socialist era. First, in the prereform period, agricultural trade was subject to the planning system (Huang and Chen 1999a, 1999b; Lardy 2001). It was used to supplement the planning for the domestic economy. Given the nation's commitment to self-sufficiency in all areas of the economy, imports were to be used only for procuring those items—most of which were machinery and other productive investments—that could not be produced domestically and that facilitated realization of the goals of the plan. Almost all trade occurred through eight state-owned trading firms. In the 1970s, the state agricultural trading firms monopolized nearly all food imports and exports. Hence, it was not in the nature of the institutional structure of the trade apparatus to allow specialization in labor-intensive export crops that could be offset by imports of land-intensive staple crops. Agricultural trade was looked upon primarily as a means to generate foreign exchange.

Summary: socialist agriculture was a policy-driven disaster

After nearly 30 years of development, agriculture was not effective in fulfilling any of its roles. Although output was increasing, this was because of enormous central and local government investments, as well as mostly corvée labor financed predominantly through the sweat of farmers. Productivity and incomes were stagnant. There had been no structural shift toward more productivity and higher efficiency. A large share of the population was locked into agriculture.

The clearest finding arising from our analysis of the socialist era is that the dismal performance of agriculture was mainly the result of more than two decades of socialist policies inside and outside the agricultural sector. Production structures, the pricing system, and marketing institutions did not provide adequate incentives. Some investments were effective, but there were far too few of these to offset the negative impact of poor incentives. Perhaps most negative was the effects of a system that treated the rural population as second-class citizens and excluded them from a fair share of investments, services, and opportunities. In short, the agricultural and nonagricultural policy environment failed to allow agriculture to contribute to the establishment of a healthy modern economy.

Performance during the transition era, post-1978

We first describe the performance of the agricultural sector and the role it has played since the onset of reform in the late 1970s. We then analyze in greater depth the policy initiatives—inside and outside agriculture—that have helped launch and guide China's agricultural transition. We examine the reform strategy by looking at its various components, including implementation, objectives, and rationale.

The ups and downs that characterized the performance of agriculture during the prereform period ceased after 1978. All the best indicators achieved in agricultural production from the 1950s to the 1970s were surpassed after the launch of the reforms, and agriculture finally began to play a positive role in the development process. In the early and mid-1970s, agricultural gross domestic product (GDP) rose by 2.7 percent a year. The annual growth rate almost doubled, to 7.1 percent, during the initial reform period, from 1978 to 1984, before declining to 4.0 percent in 1985–95 and 3.4 percent in 1996–2004 (table 3.1). By world standards, these are high rates of agricultural growth over such a sustained period.

At least during the early reform period, output growth—driven by increases in yields—was experienced in all subsectors of agriculture. Between 1978 and 1984, grain production increased, in aggregate, by 4.7 percent a year (table 3.1). Production rose for each of the major grains, namely, rice, wheat, and maize. The success of agriculture in playing its role of supplying inexpensive food is illustrated by grain prices. During the reforms, with the exception of price spikes in 1988 and 1995, the real prices of rice, wheat, and maize fell by between 33 percent (maize) and 45 percent (wheat) from the late 1970s to the early 2000s.

Another change was far more fundamental than the higher yields in grains. As it achieved success in grain production, the agricultural economy was steadily remaking itself from a grain-first economy to an economy producing higher-valued cash crops, horticultural goods, and livestock and aquaculture products. Like the grain subsector, the output of cash crops in general, especially cotton, edible oils, fruits, and vegetables, also grew more rapidly in the early reform period than in the 1970s (table 3.1). Unlike grains, the growth in the nongrain subsector continued throughout the reform era (with the exception of land-intensive staples such as cotton). The rise in some subsectors was dramatic. For example, between 1990 and 2004, the increase in vegetable production was so rapid that the country was adding the equivalent of the production capacity of California (the world's most productive vegetable region) every two years. In the total cultivated area in China, the share that is planted in fruit orchards (over 5 percent) is more than double the share in the next closest major agricultural nation. Today, agriculture in China is following the dictum "make apples and onions the key link" rather than the dictum "grains first" that was applied to agriculture in the socialist era.

Livestock production rose 9.1 percent in the early reform period and has continued to grow at 4.5 to 8.8 percent annually since 1985. The fishery subsector is the most rapidly growing component of food production, growing at more than 10 percent a year between 1985 and 2000. Today, over 70 percent of the world's

Table 3.1. Real Average Annual Rates of Economic Growth, China, 1970–2004

(percent)

Indicator	Prereform 1970–78	Reform 1979–84	1985–95	1996–2000	2001–04
GDP	4.9	8.8	9.7	8.2	8.7
Agriculture	2.7	7.1	4.0	3.4	3.4
Industry	6.8	8.2	12.8	9.6	10.6
Services	—	11.6	9.7	8.3	8.3
Population	1.80	1.40	1.37	0.91	0.63
Per capita GDP	3.1	7.4	8.3	7.2	8.1
Grain production	2.8	4.7	1.7	0.03	−0.2
Rice					
Production	2.5	4.5	0.6	0.3	−0.9
Area	0.7	−0.6	−0.6	−0.5	−1.2
Yield	1.8	5.1	1.2	0.8	0.2
Wheat					
Production	7.0	8.3	1.9	−0.4	−1.9
Area	1.7	−0.0	0.1	−1.4	−5.1
Yield	5.2	8.3	1.8	1.0	3.3
Maize					
Production	7.4	3.7	4.7	−0.1	5.5
Area	3.1	−1.6	1.7	0.8	2.5
Yield	4.2	5.4	2.9	−0.9	2.8
Other production					
Cotton	−0.4	19.3	−0.3	−1.9	6.5
Soybeans	−2.3	5.2	2.8	2.6	2.4
Other oil crops	2.1	14.9	4.4	5.6	0.6
Fruit	6.6	7.2	12.7	8.6	29.5
Meat	4.4	9.1	8.8	6.5	4.6
Fishery	5.0	7.9	13.7	10.2	3.5
Planted area					
Vegetables	2.4	5.4	6.8	6.8	3.8
Fruits	8.1	4.5	10.4	1.5	2.2

Sources: Data of the National Bureau of Statistics and the Ministry of Agriculture.

Note: Growth rates are computed using the regression method. The growth rates of individual commodities and groups of commodities are based on production data. GDP in real terms in 1970–78 is the growth rate of national income in real terms. — = no data are available.

freshwater aquaculture is produced in China. The sustained and rapid rise in livestock and fishery output has steadily eroded the predominance of cropping. After remaining fairly static during the socialist era, the share of agriculture contributed by cropping fell from 76 to 51 percent between 1985 and 2005. Meanwhile, the

Table 3.2. Structure of the Agricultural Economy, China, 1970–2005

(share in agricultural output, %)

Subsector	1970	1980	1985	1990	1995	2000	2005
Crop	82	80	76	65	58	56	51
Livestock	14	18	22	26	30	30	35
Fisheries	2	2	3	5	8	11	10
Forestry	2	4	5	4	3	4	4

Source: Data of the National Bureau of Statistics of China.

combined share of livestock and fisheries rose to 45 percent, more than doubling the 1980 share of 20 percent. The expansion in the livestock and fishery subsectors is also outpacing the growth in most of the cropping subcategories (tables 3.1 and 3.2). It is projected that, beginning in 2008, cropping will account for less than 50 percent of agricultural output in China.

Moving off the farm

The reform era has also generated other fundamental transformative changes. One sees this by examining the rural economy based on a definition that is broader than agriculture. While the annual growth in agriculture averaged about 5 percent throughout the reform era, the growth rates of the economy as a whole and in the industrial and services sectors were more rapid (table 3.1). In fact, since 1985, the growth in industry and services has been two to three times more rapid than the growth in agriculture. Because of the differences in the sectoral growth rates, agriculture's share of GDP fell from 40 percent in 1970 to less than 13 percent in 2005 (data of the National Bureau of Statistics). Given the current growth of agricultural GDP and overall GDP, the share of agriculture will fall below 10 percent after 2010. The shifts in the economy may also be seen in employment. Agriculture employed 81 percent of the labor force in 1970. By 2005, however, as the industrial and services sectors grew in importance, the share of employment in agriculture fell to a reported 45 percent.

Agricultural trade liberalization

While much has been made of China's accession to the WTO as a turning point in its relationship with the world, the country's open-door policy was undertaken much earlier (Huang and Chen 1999a, 1999b). During the process, China has abandoned isolation and become one of the world's great trading nations, including in agricultural trade. From 1980 to 2000, the total value of the country's agricultural trade grew by about 6.0 percent a year. It has more than doubled since 2000, making China the fourth largest importer of agricultural commodities in

Figure 3.1. Agricultural Trade Balance, by Factor Intensity, China, 1985–2002

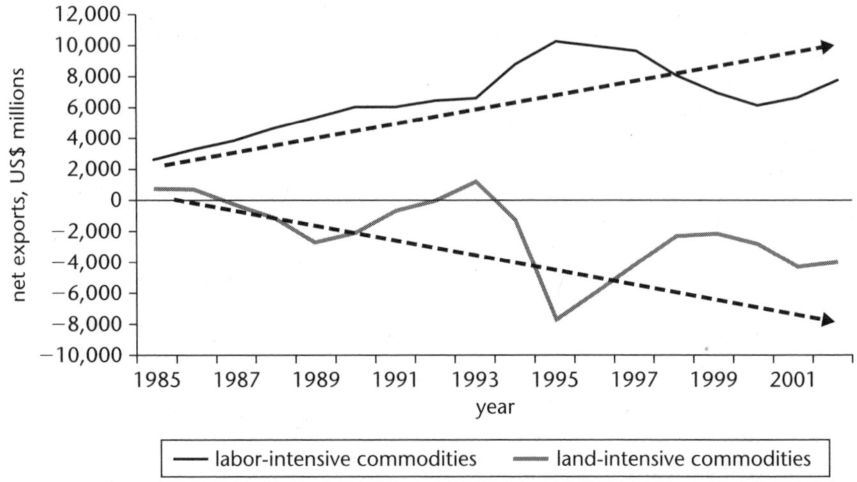

Source: Rosen, Huang, and Rozelle 2004.

Note: Labor-intensive commodities include fruits, vegetables, meat products, and aquaculture products. Land-intensive commodities include food and feed grains, soybeans, edible oils, and cotton.

the world (Gale 2006). In agriculture, the level of exports has exceeded that of imports almost every year since the reforms were launched (Huang and Chen 1999a, 1999b).

Perhaps more remarkable is the shift in the composition of trade over the past 25 years. Figure 3.1 shows that net exports of land-intensive bulk commodities, such as grains, oilseeds, and sugar, have fallen, while exports of higher-valued, more labor-intensive products, such as horticultural, livestock, and aquaculture products, have risen. The country has thus begun to export those commodities in which it has a comparative advantage and import those in which it does not have an advantage. Disaggregated, crop-specific trade trends show the same sharp shifts (Anderson, Huang, and Ianchovichina 2004).

The production and marketing environment

After more than 25 years of reform, one of the most striking changes in the nature of agriculture in China is the change in the role of local and national government regulation in production and marketing. During the socialist era, bureaucrats in government supply and marketing agencies and local commune and brigade officials were deeply involved in all aspects of pre- and postharvest decision making. By 2005, the situation had changed dramatically. Indeed, a notable feature of

China's agricultural economy today is the limited extent of government intervention (with several exceptions). Restrictions on landownership aside, agriculture in China may now be one of the least regulated domestic agricultural economies in the world. In a recent survey carried out by the Center for Chinese Agricultural Policy, all farmers who were not renting village-owned orchards planted in the early reform period indicated that they had made the planting decision and had not been compelled by local officials (Rozelle, Huang, and Sumner 2006). All farmers in a survey of households in eight provinces stated that they had purchased all their chemical fertilizers on their own and that local officials had no role in the transactions (Zhang, Li, and Rozelle 2005). Moreover, all purchases had been made through private suppliers.

On the procurement side, government parastatals used to be responsible for purchasing farm output, but, today, a large majority of the grains, oilseeds, and fiber crops and all the horticultural and livestock products are sold to small private traders (H. Wang et al. 2006). Indeed, despite the impressive rise of supermarkets and processing firms catering to the retail needs of urban populations, a recent survey found that almost all purchases of fruit, vegetables, nuts, livestock, and other agricultural products are made by individual entrepreneurs who are trading on their own account. The existence of millions of small traders who are competing in a market virtually without regulations has meant that the market has become well integrated and efficient (Park et al. 2002; Huang, Rozelle, and Chang 2004; Rozelle and Huang 2004, 2005).

Productivity trends and rural incomes

While it is possible that trends in agricultural productivity tell a story about the effects of transition on agricultural performance that is somewhat different from the story told by output (as they did during the prereform period), this is not the case. First, as shown in table 3.1, output per unit of land rose sharply (that is, all yields). In addition, trends in agricultural labor productivity—measured as output per farm worker—paralleled those in yields during the entire reform period. Moreover, several series of estimates of total factor productivity have been produced for China's agriculture (McMillan, Whalley, and Zhu 1989; Fan 1991; Lin 1992; Wen 1993; Huang and Rozelle 1996; Fan 1997; Jin et al. 2002). The studies uniformly demonstrate that, in the first years after reform (1978–84), comprehensive measures of productivity (either constructed total factor productivity indexes or their regression-based equivalents) rose 5 to 10 percent a year.

Rural incomes during the reforms steadily increased partly because of rising productivity and, perhaps even more, because of the increasing efficiency associated with specialization, the shift to more production of higher-value crops and

Table 3.3. Rural Income per Capita, China, 1980–2001
(real 2000 yuan)

Income group	1980	1985	1990	1995	2000	2001	Annual growth, 1980–2001, %
Average	711	1,248	1,305	1,702	2,253	2,347	6
Bottom decile (poorest)	312	448	442	493	579	578	3
Top decile (richest)	1,530	2,486	3,253	4,763	6,805	7,159	8

Source: Compiled based on data of the National Bureau of Statistics.

livestock commodities, and the expansion of off-farm work (table 3.3). Between 1980 and 2001, average real rural per capita income rose by a remarkable 6 percent per year, which is as high as the growth rates experienced in Japan and the Republic of Korea during the take-off years of those economies. The amount of attention given to the rural income problem by the media might seem surprising, but the attention has been generated by the more rapid rise in urban incomes relative to rural incomes. Inequality is increasing between rural and urban areas, but it is also increasing between those people within the rural economy who were relatively rich at the outset of reform and those who were relatively poor. The growth rate in rural per capita income in the richest decile, at more than 8 percent annually, is far higher than the average (3 percent annually), which means that the growth rate among other segments of the rural population is correspondingly lower than 3 percent. In relative terms, the poorest of the rural poor are falling behind.

Summary of agriculture's performance during the transition era
Whereas the socialist era witnessed few transformations, the agricultural sector in China has changed dramatically during the transition. The sector has grown, but the decline in its importance in employment and in the value of output in the overall economy has been characteristic of the growth. The structure of the sector itself is also changing; it is diversifying out of coarse grains into fine grains, out of staple grains into higher-valued crops, and out of cropping into livestock and aquaculture. Trade patterns are changing and are now more reflective of the country's comparative advantages. One of the largest shifts has occurred in production and marketing, which have become almost laissez-faire, that is, there is little government intervention. Although the most dramatic changes have taken place most rapidly among wealthier households, changes are also occurring among the poor.

Institutions and the Policy Foundation of Reform

Unlike leaders in the transitional economies in Europe, leaders in China did not seek to dismantle the planned economy in favor of liberalized markets during the initial stages of reform (Rozelle and Swinnen 2004). Policy makers in China only began to shift their focus toward market liberalization in 1985 after decollectivization was complete. Even then, liberalization was start-stop (Sicular 1995). Lin, Cai, and Li (1996) argue that the leaders were afraid of disruptive social effects. The institutions through which the leadership controlled the main goods in the food economy (such as grains, fertilizers, and meat products) could not be eliminated before the institutions were in place that would support more efficient market exchanges. Throughout the reforms, leaders were investing in the economy and changing the rules governing those domestic producers and consumers who were interacting with the external economy.

Pricing policies

Early during the reforms, although China's leaders had no concrete plan to liberalize markets, they did take steps to change the producer incentives that were embodied in the prices producers received for their marketed surplus. Perhaps one of the least appreciated initiatives of the early reformers was their bold decision to increase the administered prices received by farmers (Lardy 1983; Sicular 1988a). Between 1978 and 1983, in a number of separate actions, the government-set above-quota prices (the payments farmers received for voluntary sales beyond the mandatory deliveries) were increased by 41 percent for grain and by around 50 percent for cash crops (Sicular 1988a). According to National Bureau of Statistics data, the price of grain relative to fertilizer rose by more than 60 percent during the first three years after the reform. During the early reform period, the rise in the above-quota price represented a higher output price at the margin for farmers (Sicular 1995).

The important contribution of pricing policy was in the timing and breadth of the policy change. The first major price rise occurred in 1979, close to the moment when reformers were deciding to decollectivize. However, following the decision of the leadership to implement the household responsibility system gradually, beginning first in the poorest areas of China, the price increases immediately affected all farmers, regardless of whether they had been decollectivized. By 1981, the period of the second major price increase, less than half of all farmers had been allowed to dismantle their communes (Lin 1992). Hence, as long as there was a link, albeit weak, between the output price and production, the plan-based price rise would have led to increases in farm output. Empirical studies confirm the strong impact of these price changes on output during the first years of transition (Fan 1991; Lin 1992; Huang and Rozelle 1996; Fan and Pardey 1997).

Greater incentives

The rural economic reforms initiated in 1979 were founded on the household responsibility system. The reforms of this system led to the dismantlement of the communes. Agricultural land was contracted to households, mostly on the basis of family size and the number of people in the household labor force. Most importantly, after the reforms of the system, income and control rights over farmland belonged to individual households (though the right to sell was excluded).

There is little doubt that the changes in incentives resulting from the reforms in property rights triggered strong growth in farm output and productivity. In the most definitive study on the subject, Lin (1992) estimates that China's household responsibility system accounted for 42 to 46 percent of the total rise in output during 1978–84. Fan (1991) and Huang and Rozelle (1996) find that, even accounting for technological change, institutional change during the late 1970s and early 1980s contributed about 30 percent of output growth. Empirical researchers have also documented impacts that go beyond output. For example, McMillan, Whalley, and Zhu (1989) demonstrate that the early reforms raised total factor productivity, accounting for 90 percent of the rise (23 percent) in 1978–84. Jin et al. (2002) show that the reforms had a large effect on productivity, contributing substantially to a rise in total factor productivity that exceeded 7 percent annually.

Domestic market liberalization policies

In addition to pricing changes and decollectivization, another major task of the reformers was to create efficient institutions of exchange. Whether they are classic and competitive or only workable substitutes, efficient markets facilitate transactions among agents to allow specialization and trade and, through pricing mechanisms, provide information to producers and consumers about the relative scarcity of resources and products.

The major changes to agricultural commerce in the early 1980s almost exclusively centered on increasing crop purchase prices (Sicular 1988a; Watson 1994). The decision to raise prices should not be considered part of a strategy to liberalize markets. Planners in the Ministry of Commerce made the price changes administratively, and the changes were mostly executed by the national network of grain procurement stations under the direction of the State Grain Bureau.

An examination of policies and marketing activities in the early 1980s reveals the limited changes in the marketing environment in China's food economy before 1985. It is true that reformers allowed farmers greater discretion in producing and marketing crops in 10 planning categories, including vegetables, fruits, and coarse grains. Moreover, by 1984, the state only claimed control over 12 commodities, including rice, wheat, maize, soybeans, peanuts, rapeseeds, and several other cash crops (Sicular 1988a). While this may seem to represent a significant step toward liberalization, the crops remaining almost entirely under the planning authority of the government still accounted for more than 95 percent of the total sown area in 1984. Hence, in policy and practice, the output of almost all the sown area and the related marketing decisions were still directly influenced by government planners. The planners proceeded with equal caution in reducing the restrictions on free-market trade, and the process was start-stop-start at first.

Market liberalization began in earnest after 1985. Changes in the procurement system, additional reductions in the restrictions on commodity trading, steps to commercialize the state trading system for grains, and calls for expansion in the establishment of markets in rural and urban areas led to a surge in market-oriented activity (Sicular 1995). For example, only around 240,000 private and semi-private trading enterprises were registered with the State Markets Bureau in 1980; by 1990, there were more than 5.2 million (deBrauw, Huang, and Rozelle 2004).

Private trading gradually expanded to include all categories of agricultural output remaining after contractual obligations to the government had been fulfilled. This eventually undermined the state marketing system (Rozelle et al. 2000). The reformers eliminated the planned procurement of all agricultural products except rice, wheat, maize, and cotton. Government commercial departments were able to continue to buy and sell only if they did so through the market. Incentives were introduced for grains through reductions in the volume of compulsory quotas and increases in procurement prices. Even among grains, after the share of compulsory quota procurement reached 29 percent in 1984, it declined to 18 percent in 1985 and 13 percent in 1990. The share of negotiated procurement at market prices rose from 3 percent in 1985 to 6 percent in 1985 and 12 percent in 1990.

Agricultural technology and water infrastructure development

Plant breeding and agricultural research are almost universally organized and managed by the government. Reflecting the urban bias of food policy, most crop breeding programs emphasize fine grains (rice and wheat). The traditional focus of research has been on quantity because of concerns about food self-sufficiency, but quality improvement has recently been emphasized because of a shift in demand toward higher-quality food. There have been several joint ventures and private domestic investment initiatives in agricultural research and development, but government policy still discriminates against the practice.

The record of the reforms in agricultural technology is mixed, and the impact of the reforms in terms of new technological development and greater crop productivity is unclear. Empirical evidence indicates that the effectiveness of the country's agricultural research system is declining (Jin et al. 2002). Our previous work has shown that, while competitive grant programs probably boosted the effectiveness of the system, the reliance on revenues from commercialization to make up for falling budgetary commitments weakened the system.[1] It is possible that imperfections in the seed industry contributed to the lack of success in the reforms in research on crop breeding.

Since the late 1990s, there has been a sharp rise in spending on agricultural research and development. However, government investments in the development of water management for irrigation and flood control swamp the investments in agricultural research. From the 1950s to the 1970s, most of the government's efforts were focused on building dams and canals, often with the input by farmers of corvée labor. Since the end of the 1970s, greater attention has been focused on increasing the use of the country's massive groundwater resources (Wang, Huang, and Rozelle 2005). By 2005, China had more tube wells than any other country in the world, with the possible exception of India. Initially, the investments were made by local governments, which were assisted by county and provincial water bureaus. But, by the 1990s, the government was encouraging the huge shift in ownership that was already occurring, as pump sets, wells, and other irrigation equipment were being taken over by families on private farms (J. Wang et al. 2005). Meanwhile, private water markets—whereby farmers would sell water pumped from their own wells to other farmers in the village—were also encouraged. The main policy initiative after the mid-1990s in the surface water subsector was a management reform that sought to raise efficiency in water use.

Trade policy

There were important changes during the 1980s and 1990s in foreign exchange policy that saw the nation's currency depreciate steeply and trading rights become more accessible to traders. A number of other fundamental reforms were also undertaken in China's international trading system. The lower agricultural tariffs and the rising imports and exports of agricultural products began to affect the domestic terms of trade in the 1980s. During the initial reform years, most of the fall in protection was caused by a reduction in the commodities that were controlled by single-desk state traders (Huang and Chen 1999a, 1999b). In many products, competition among nonstate foreign trade corporations started to stimulate imports and exports (Martin 2002). Although many major agricultural commodities were not included in the effort to decentralize trade, the effort spurred the export of many agricultural goods. In addition, policy shifts in the 1980s and 1990s also altered the trading behavior of state traders. Thus, the policy leadership allowed state traders to boost imports during these decades.

Steps to relax restrictions on the right of access to import and export markets were matched by steps to reduce the taxes assessed at the border. After the elimination of limits on the imports and exports of many agricultural commodities, a new effort was undertaken in the early 1990s to lower the level of formal protection. The simple average agricultural import tariff fell from 42 percent in 1992 to 24 percent in 1998 and 21 percent in 2001 (Rosen, Huang, and Rozelle 2004).

Overall protection in the agricultural sector has declined in the past 20 years. Much of the drop has been caused by the decentralization of authority over imports and exports, a relaxation in the licensing procedures for some crops (for example, the shift away from state trading firms in importing oil and oilseeds), and changes in the foreign exchange rate. Other trade policies have reduced the scope of nontariff barriers, relaxed the real tariff rates at the border, and changed quotas (Huang and Chen 1999a, 1999b). Despite these real and, in some areas, rapid reforms, the control over commodities that policy leaders consider of national strategic importance, such as rice, wheat, and maize, remains largely with government officials (Nyberg and Rozelle 1999).

The accession to the WTO has been a major event in the country and will continue to have a substantial impact on many sectors. Nonetheless, given the trends in reform, the WTO accession agreement in the agricultural sector, in its most basic terms, represents a continuation of previous agricultural policies. Importantly, though, the commitments embodied in this agricultural part of the agreement—market access, domestic support, and export subsidies—are a binding confirmation and codification of steps the government took in the 1990s while it was negotiating the accession to the WTO.

Summary: China's transition era agricultural policies

The scope of China's policy efforts during the transition is impressive. Policy shifts were realized in pricing, production management, marketing, investments, technology, and trade. Although the rate of investment has risen during the reforms, the country is probably still underinvesting in agriculture relative to other sectors and other countries. Explicit taxes and the taxes implicit in pricing and trade policies have also fallen. The government is not assisting the agricultural economy in the substantial ways that characterize the country's neighbors in East Asia (see Honma and Hayami 2008). However, it appears to have headed in the direction noted by Timmer (1998), whereby developing nations, after they reach a certain point in development, begin to shift from making net extractions from agriculture to making net investments in the sector.

Many policies and other factors outside agriculture have affected the sector. Other rural policies, such as those that govern fiscal reform, the emergence of township and village enterprises, privatization, and rural governance, almost certainly have a large, albeit indirect effect on agriculture. Urban employment policies, residency restrictions, exchange rate management, and many other policy initiatives also affect agriculture by influencing relative prices in the economy, access to jobs off the farm, and the overall attractiveness of staying on the farm.

Taken together, these policies have had a dramatic impact on the agricultural sector. They have increased the output of food, driven prices down, and improved the supplies of nongrain food and raw materials for industry. The mix of policies—pricing, enhanced property rights, market liberalization, investment, trade—has also made producers more efficient. It has freed up their labor and resources, and these have supported the structural transformation in the agricultural economy and the rural economy more generally. There are several pieces of convincing evidence that agriculture is beginning to play a more effective role in the nation's development: the importance of grain in the cropping subsector is shrinking; the importance of the cropping subsector in the overall agricultural sector is shrinking; and the importance of agriculture in the general economy is shrinking. Productivity is up, and rural incomes are up. Many of the increases in welfare, however, are being generated by individuals—there have been more than 200 million of them—who have been able to shift from grain production to high-valued crops or from cropping to livestock and fisheries production or, perhaps most importantly, who have been able to leave agriculture and the rural economy altogether and obtain employment in cities.

Quantifying the Distortions to Agricultural Incentives since 1980

We introduce our quantification of the policy-imposed distortions in the incentives faced by farmers in China by explaining our methodology and, in particular, the way we deal with distortions in the market for foreign currency. We also outline our data sources. We then discuss our results in detail.

Methodology and data sources

The main focus of our study is government-imposed distortions that create a gap between domestic prices and prices as they would be under free markets. It is not possible to understand the characteristics of agricultural development through a sectoral view alone. For comparative evaluation, the project's methodology therefore involves estimates of the effects of direct agricultural policy measures, including distortions in the foreign exchange market, but also estimates of distortions in nonagricultural sectors. Specifically, we compute nominal rates of assistance (NRAs) to farmers that reflect an adjustment for direct interventions on tradable and nontradable inputs. We also generate NRAs for nonagricultural tradables for comparison with the NRAs for agricultural tradables via the calculation of a relative rate of assistance (RRA) (see Anderson et al. 2008 and appendix A).

This approach is not well suited to the analysis of the prereform period because prices played only an accounting function at the time, and key prices involving currency exchange rates were enormously distorted. During the reform period, however, the price comparison approach has provided valuable indicators of distortions to the incentives for production, consumption, and trade. as well as indicators of the income transfers associated with policy interventions. Such an approach is necessary because of the low inframarginal procurement prices, but also because of the complexity and lack of transparency in the trade barriers in agriculture, including tariffs, licenses, quotas, tariff rate quotas, and government trading. Exchange rate distortions present particular measurement problems and require detailed analysis if we expect measures based on price comparisons not to be misleading.

NRAs and CTEs

NRAs are constructed in three steps. The NRAs on agricultural output are based partly on a comparison of the price of a commodity in the domestic economy at the port and the international price of the commodity at that same border point (that is, including, cost, insurance, and freight in port for an import good and free on board in port for an exportable good), taking into account inherent differences in product quality, where appropriate. Conceptually, we need this part of the NRA on output to measure the extent, at the border, of the distortions caused by tariffs, exchange rate policies, and other nontariff barriers. A positive NRA measure indicates that the sector is being protected from import competition, while a negative NRA measure indicates the sector is subject to some form of (possibly implicit) taxation at the border.

Because we have independent observations on the prices obtained by farmers in local markets, the second step involves estimating NRAs on output at the farmgate by also taking into account any domestic distortions affecting the returns to farmers. This part of the NRA is calculated after allowing for quality adjustments, taxes, subsidies, and the costs of domestic transport, storage, and handling in delivering products from the farm to the wholesale market. This part of the NRA on output arises from subsidy or transfer payments that cause the prices received by farmers to differ from the prices they would receive under competitive internal market conditions. As we show below, these internal subsidies and tax measures had an enormous impact on the returns to farmers, particularly during the early reform period.

An important component of this second part of the NRA evolved during the period when domestic incentives were distorted by the requirement to deliver a fixed quota of output at a (low) planned price, although producers were allowed to sell above-quota output (surplus) at a higher market price. Clearly, the delivery requirements reduced the incomes of farm households, but the impact on the level of output is less clear. Sicular (1988b) makes the point that, in the short run, the output decision of a firm is determined by the marginal return rather than the average return. Under these circumstances, the inframarginal tax imposed by the plan delivery requirement may not have reduced the incentive to produce. However, more recent work on decoupled price incentives, by taking into account the incentives for firm entry and exit, suggests that average returns may actually have a greater impact on output in the longer term (de Gorter, Just, and Kropp 2008). Nonetheless, the inability of farm households to sell their land probably reduced the extent to which these households exited from agriculture in response to reductions in incomes.

The third step in our NRA measurement captures distortions in farm input markets. To realize this step, we provide measures that take into account direct subsidies and differences between international input prices and the input prices that farmers pay. While these forms of protection (or taxation) may be important in other countries, we find that they are generally relatively small in China and so contribute little to the overall NRA.

While most of our focus is on agricultural producers, we also consider the extent to which consumers are taxed or subsidized. To achieve this, we use a measure called the consumer tax equivalent (CTE). In principle, this measure compares the price that consumers pay for food commodities and the international price at the border. As with the NRAs, differences arise between NRAs and CTEs because of distortions in the domestic economy, as well as at the border. The domestic distortions are caused by transfer policies, taxes, and subsidies that generate gaps between the prices paid by consumers (adjusted to the wholesale level) and domestic market prices. If a CTE is negative, then consumers are paying prices that are below the international market prices and the consumers are being subsidized. (For more details on the methodology used to calculate these measures, see Anderson et al. 2008 and appendix A.)

The foreign exchange regime

Prior to 1981, China's official exchange rate was seriously overvalued. While this did not directly affect exports and imports because decisions on these were made by planners, it did create serious accounting difficulties given that exports generally incurred losses (Lardy 1992). If the official exchange rate is used, it will provide misleading indicators of the incentives created by the foreign exchange regime. Because it made all foreign goods appear inexpensive in terms of the domestic currency, it overestimated the extent of protection provided to any importable good.

In 1981, an internal settlement rate was introduced that was intended to be aligned with the average cost of foreign exchange. This supplied at least some basis for meaningful comparisons between domestic and international prices. The internal settlement rate, at 2.8 yuan per U.S. dollar for trade transactions in 1981, represented nearly a 50 percent devaluation relative to the official exchange rate. It was used only for nontrade transactions. This internal rate remained at Y 2.8 until January 1985, when it was merged with the official exchange rate.

During most of the reform period, the effects of the foreign exchange regime were relatively transparent. The regime between the late 1970s and 1994 was included among those found by Kiguel and O'Connell (1995) to involve differential rates for different types of current account transactions. The overvalued official exchange rate was a key element of this system. Prior to 1979, enterprises had to surrender all their foreign exchange earnings at the official rate. However, beginning in that year, exporting enterprises were allowed to retain some of their foreign exchange earnings (Lardy 1992). Because of the pervasive shortage of foreign exchange in the economy, the value of these retained earnings was, on average, considerably above the value as measured by the official exchange rate, although there were restrictions on trading retained foreign exchange among enterprises, which inevitably exposed the variation in the demand of enterprises for foreign exchange.

The restrictions on trade in retained foreign exchange were gradually liberalized, and a legal secondary-market exchange rate emerged that was higher (more depreciated) than the official exchange rate. There was always a shortage of foreign exchange at the official exchange rate, forcing importers to meet their needs for additional foreign exchange at the secondary-market rate. Under these circumstances, the exchange rate system created a distortion analogous to a tariff and an export tax. The exchange rate received by exporters was lower than that paid, at the margin, by importers.

To account for the effects of the exchange rate system, we construct an exporter exchange rate series by using the retention ratio to calculate a weighted average of the official and the secondary-market exchange rates. We use the secondary-market exchange rate as an indicator of the price paid for foreign exchange, at the margin, by importers. Following the methodology outlined in Anderson et al. (2008) and appendix A, we calculate an estimated equilibrium exchange rate as the simple average of the importer and the exporter exchange rates. This method arbitrarily assumes equal elasticities of demand and supply for foreign exchange, though this assumption does not affect the results for any trade impacts because taxes on imports and taxes on exports have the same effect (the Lerner symmetry theorem).

The share of export earnings eligible to be retained rose gradually, and the extent to which these eligibility rights were tradable increased. Initially, there were only limited opportunities to trade the rights, and the shadow value varied from firm to firm depending upon the firm's foreign exchange earnings and need for foreign exchange. Policy makers quickly recognized that it was important to be able to able to transfer foreign exchange among firms. Lardy (1992) notes that foreign exchange trading outlets were first established in Guangzhou (1980) and Shanghai (1981). However, the exchange rates in these markets tended to be heavily managed; the government was seeking to set the selling price at, for example, the internal settlement rate (Lardy 1992).

Formal foreign exchange adjustment centers were established on a large scale after 1985. The centers allowed firms with excess foreign exchange earnings to sell to ventures that sold their output domestically and needed foreign exchange. Over the next few years, a large network of these centers was established, and the markets became more closely integrated over time. By 1988, Lardy (1992) concludes, the price in the Shanghai market followed the strictures of supply and demand, subject to the conditions on the use of foreign exchange, including licensing requirements and duties on imported goods. The pricing policies for imported goods were also becoming more liberal, and, by 1990, the prices of close to 90 percent of all imported goods were based on the import price, plus transport costs and tariffs (Lardy 1992).

During the transition, the exchange rate regime had an extremely important influence on the returns obtainable through exported goods and on the prices paid for imported goods. Even in the absence of explicit trade policies, overvalued official exchange rates tended to lower the returns to exported goods and increase the costs of imported goods, often by large amounts. The combination of an overvalued official exchange rate and a secondary-market exchange rate at which importers could purchase foreign exchange legally allows us to assess the effects of the foreign exchange regime and then to begin to assess the impacts of other trade policies.

The analytics of a multiple exchange rate system are relatively clear and are easily understood in a partial equilibrium setting. Figure 3.2 shows the exchange rates in a market that is characterized by an upward-sloping supply of foreign exchange (perhaps determined by the marginal costs of generating additional assets) and a downward-sloping demand for foreign exchange (perhaps determined by the extent of substitutability among imports and domestic goods). If there is an official

Figure 3.2. The Domestic Market for Foreign Currency, China

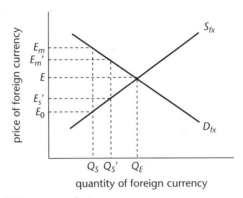

Source: Anderson et al. 2008; see appendix A.

Note: See the text for an explanation of the figure. S_{fx} = the supply of foreign exchange. D_{fx} = the demand for foreign exchange.

exchange rate, E_0, at which exporters must surrender their foreign currency to the central bank and a secondary-market exchange rate, E_m, at which importers may buy foreign exchange, then the two-tier exchange rate system functions as a uniform tax on all exports or (equivalently) a uniform tax on all imports. Figure 3.2 shows the effect of such a regime. Setting the official exchange rate at E_0 reduces the returns to exporters relative to the equilibrium rate, E. The resulting shortage of foreign exchange drives up the foreign exchange's scarcity value, and, in the presence of a secondary market, its market price in sales to importers becomes E_m. Under these circumstances, the two-tier exchange rate reduces export earnings from Q_E to Q_S.

A foreign exchange retention scheme of the type used in China during the transition raises the return to exports by allowing exporters to convert some of their foreign exchange earnings at the higher secondary-market rate. As a result, the supply of foreign exchange rises from Q_S to Q_S'. The increase in supply allows the price of foreign exchange on the secondary market to fall to E_m'. This reduces the cost of imported goods, and it also raises the demand for imports from Q_S to Q_S'.

The tax on exporters was lowered because exporters were allowed to retain a portion of their foreign exchange earnings and sell foreign exchange on the secondary market. The retention rates have been estimated roughly at 20 percent in 1981–84, 25 percent in 1985–86, 44 percent in 1987–90, and 80 percent in 1991–94 (World Bank 1994). The resulting blended average exchange rate received by exporters is indicated in the figure as E_s'. The introduction of the foreign exchange retention scheme reduced the secondary-market rate because of the increased incentive to supply foreign exchange.

We use several different series to obtain secondary-market exchange rate data: the internal settlement rate in 1981–84, an estimated secondary-market exchange rate in 1985–86, and the Foreign Exchange Adjustment Center rate in 1987–94. We use the difference between the importer exchange rate and the estimated equilibrium rate as a measure of the component of the protection for import-competing products that is represented by exchange rate distortion. Similarly, we use the difference between the exporter exchange rate and the equilibrium rate as a measure of the exchange rate distortion affecting exportable goods. Relying on these principles and data, we obtain the results described in Huang et al. (2007).[2]

The data used

In compiling price data, we first had to make choices about our study's coverage of commodities. We have included 11 commodities: rice, wheat, maize, soybeans, cotton, pig meat, milk, poultry, fruit (we use apples as a representative product), vegetables (we use tomatoes as a representative product), and sugar (sugar beets and sugarcane). Over the period we study, these commodities account for between 75 percent (in the late 1980s) and 60 percent (during the early 2000s) of the total value of agricultural output (Huang et al. 2007). Because decisions on production and consumption were only gradually being allowed to respond to domestic market prices and because we do not have access to reliable data on secondary-market exchange rates prior to 1981, we focus on data for the period beginning in 1981.

The data in our study have been gathered from diverse sources, depending on the period of analysis and the commodity (see the references). We have taken commodity balance data (production, utilization, trade, and others) from the CAPSiM database of the Center for Chinese Agricultural Policy. These data have been compiled mainly by the Ministry of Agriculture (production), the National Bureau of Statistics (consumption and others), and the Ministry of Commerce (trade). The data on domestic prices are from several ministries. Specifically, farmgate output prices have been taken from the cost of production surveys conducted by the National Development and Reform Commission. Data on the wholesale and retail prices of most products have been collected from the Center for Price Monitoring, the National Development and Reform Commission, the Ministry of Agriculture, and the Department of Rural Survey at the National Bureau of Statistics. If wholesale and retail prices for some commodities are not available for some years, we have estimated the price margins from farmgate to wholesale and to retail. Much of the data on margins, transportation costs, and other transaction costs have been taken from extensive surveys conducted by Huang and Rozelle during the 1990s and the early 2000s. The surveys have also served to identify the commodity price series that provide an appropriate foundation for price comparisons. Some of this material has been examined in Rozelle, et al. (2000) and Huang, Rozelle, and Chang (2004), who provide information on substantial quality differences between imported and domestic commodities and the resulting biases in price comparisons as a measure of protection. Survey teams from the Center for Chinese Agricultural Policy interviewed traders in 10 cities around China in 2006, and this has provided additional data on more recent years. The data for all the commodities are summarized in appendix B, table B.3.

International price data for all commodities except milk—free on board prices and cost, insurance, and freight prices—represent the unit values of exports or imports, with adjustments for quality, where needed. We have taken these data from the Ministry of Commerce and China Customs. For the border price of milk, because no import prices for milk are available, we adjust the farmgate price of milk in New Zealand according to international transportation and insurance rates to create a series for the international price of milk (cost, insurance, and freight included), which we refer to as the reference price.

Other data used in this study include tariff rates and information on taxes and subsidies. The tariff rates have been compiled from the Office of Tariff Regulation (1998, 2005). Agricultural tax data have been collected from cost of production surveys conducted by the National Development and Reform Commission. Information on subsidies (for example, recent grain subsidies) is taken from various government documents. Aggregate input subsidies are based on producer support estimates by the Organisation for Economic Co-operation and Development (OECD), which are disaggregated into individual commodities based on shares in total crop area (see OECD 2005 and the OECD PSE-CSE Database 1986–2005).

Results

An indirect indication of the success of China's reform policies may be gained by examining the domestic free-market prices for four of the country's most important crops (Huang et al. 2007). Prices were relatively stable despite the sharp rise in demand after 1980 for all commodities because of increases in the population, rapidly rising incomes, the shift of the population from rural to urban areas, and gradual marketization. The overall self-sufficiency rate for rice, wheat, maize, and soybeans during the 1980s and 1990s was nearly 100 percent (Huang and Chen 1999a, 1999b). It is clear that domestic production was keeping up with the growth in demand. Many studies have found that the rise in supply, as well as in total factor productivity, was generated by a reduction in the distortions in production incentives that was driven by reforms such as improved property rights and more open access to new technologies (Lin 1992; Fan 1991; Huang and Rozelle 1996; Jin et al. 2002).

The role of domestic price and marketing policy

It is useful to examine the relationship between the available domestic price series for farmgate procurement and the urban and rural retail prices for the major grain crops (Huang et al. 2007). The importance and role of the government's domestic price and marketing policy for rice, wheat, and maize—the three largest crops in China—may be understood through a comparison of the urban retail price, the rural farmgate procurement price, and the rural retail price. The first two are set by the government, while the third is a free-market price. Until 1992, the urban retail price for rice was usually substantially below the price on the free market in rural areas, despite the costs associated with transferring rice to urban areas. This was a consequence of a procurement price system designed to provide urban residents with relatively inexpensive (that is, subsidized) food. Only urban residents were allowed to buy rice at these low prices, and they were allowed to do so only on the basis of ration coupons that were available in limited quantities.

The marketing and procurement system may have been the source of additional distortions. In the 1980s, the relatively low selling price for grain by farmers at the farmgate shows that the food system was transferring income from rural to urban areas. The prices paid to farmers for the output they delivered based on government quotas were far below free-market prices. Nonetheless, given the inframarginal nature of many of the transfers, there is some uncertainty about the effect on the incentives for production and consumption (Sicular 1988b). This is because, after the mid-1980s, farmers were able to sell surplus output at higher market prices once they had met their quota obligations. If a farmer could sell surplus grain at an above-quota price determined by market forces, then the farmer may have faced a less severe distortion. However, the inframarginal transfers were not fully decoupled from incentives. It appears, for instance, that they represented an incentive to move out of agriculture (Wang, Rozelle, and Huang 1999). The domestic marketing and procurement system may thus have also distorted incentives relative to international prices.

Beginning in 1992, however, changes in the domestic marketing and procurement system appear to have eliminated this additional layer of regulation for producers of rice, wheat, and maize. In the early 1990s, the urban price began to rise above the farmgate price, and urban and rural retail prices also moved closer together. This reflects the phasing out of the implicit taxation of farmers through the grain procurement system. The gap between urban and rural retail prices eventually disappeared, and the gap between the rural retail price and the farmgate price declined, suggesting that there had been an improvement in marketing efficiency (Park et al. 2002). The distortions remaining after the mid-1990s, following the disappearance of the distortions caused by the marketing and procurement system, reflect only trade policies.

NRAs for the main agricultural commodities

In this subsection, we focus on the distortions faced by farmers in China between 1981 and 2005. We first chart the NRAs on output (at the wholesale and farm levels) for each of the 11 commodities. Because input subsidies were generally small during most of our sample period, we do not discuss these measures in this subsection. Each NRA is computed at adjusted exchange rates (see above). The resulting NRAs are summarized in table 3.4 as five-year averages, and annual prices and NRAs are provided in numerous additional tables and figures in Huang et al. (2007).

Table 3.4. NRAs for Covered Agricultural Products, China, 1981–2005

(percent)

Indicator, product	1981–84	1985–89	1990–94	1995–99	2000–05
Exportables[a,b]	−58.1	−46.3	−22.0	−0.8	−0.2
Rice	−55.7	−34.0	−30.4	−6.6	−7.2
Fruit	−28.5	−9.4	−4.0	0.0	0.0
Vegetables	−41.9	−57.5	−22.3	0.0	0.0
Poultry	25.1	−27.1	−2.7	0.0	0.0
Pig meat	−78.6	−48.8	−14.9	0.0	0.0
Import-competing products[a,b]	−12.0	19.1	1.6	19.3	9.8
Wheat	1.9	22.3	11.3	30.2	4.0
Soybeans	0.6	1.3	4.7	29.5	16.3
Sugar	43.7	44.7	11.7	26.6	29.4
Milk	128.7	58.3	−4.3	18.3	24.8
Mixed trade status[a]					
Maize	−35.2	−16.1	−25.1	5.3	12.6
Cotton	−33.7	−34.6	−26.2	−3.6	0.7
All covered products[a]	−50.8	−40.6	−18.9	2.3	0.9
Distortions					
Domestic input price distortions	0.3	0.3	0.2	0.7	0.5
Domestic output price distortions	−12.6	−6.3	−6.2	−1.1	−1.4
Border distortions	−38.5	−34.6	−12.9	2.7	1.8
Dispersion, covered products[c]	74.3	52.3	20.7	18.4	15.5
Coverage, at undistorted prices	85	89	85	80	66

Sources: Huang et al. 2007; data compiled by the authors.

a. Weighted averages; the weights are based on the unassisted value of production.

b. Depending upon their trade status during a particular year, products of mixed trade status are included among exportable products or import-competing products.

c. Dispersion is a simple five-year average of the annual standard deviation around the weighted mean of the NRAs of covered products.

Distortions in the grain economy before 1995. The distortions in the rice economy of China in the 1980s and early 1990s were characterized by two important features. First, the NRA for rice, an exportable commodity, was negative every year between 1981 and 1995. Ranging between around −60 and −10 percent, the negative NRA, together with the fact that China was able to export rice, suggests that the country was highly competitive in international rice markets during these years. Nonetheless, trade policy kept exporters from shipping large quantities of rice onto world markets and kept the free-market price of rice in China's port cities below the world price. This shows the government's commitment to keeping domestic market prices low. Even if there had been no other distortions in the rice economy, producers would have faced prices below world market prices.

The second feature demonstrates that domestic marketing and procurement represented an additional tax on farmers and would have insulated the domestic price of rice from the world market price even if there had been no trade restriction at the border. Because of this marketing policy, which lasted to the mid-1990s, the artificially low government procurement price kept the average price received for rice by farmers systematically below the free-market price.

Together, these two features meant that the producer tax on rice ranged between −66 in 1981 and −33 in 1991, making rice producers among the most heavily taxed farmers in China (Huang et al. 2007).

Our NRA estimates show that, unlike the case of rice, trade policy offered some protection to wheat between 1981 and the mid-1990s (table 3.4). During this period, the free-market price of wheat in China's port cities ranged between 27 and 64 percent higher than the international price of wheat and averaged about 45 percent higher. This alone suggests that wheat producers in China—who are known to produce at a higher cost than producers in many other countries (Huang and Ma 2000)—received significant protection through trade policy. However, domestic marketing policies were having an impact in the opposite direction. The NRA results show how the wheat quotas reduced the potential benefits to farmers from the high rates of protection at the country's borders. Although protection averaged 15 percent for wheat farmers in most years between 1981 and 1995, the rates were zero or even slightly negative in 5 of the 15 years during this period (1981–82, 1990, and 1992–93).

The case of maize is a mix of the case of rice and the case of wheat (table 3.4). In some years, trade policy provided positive protection for maize (1983–87, 1989, and 1994), while, in other years, the domestic price of maize was lower than the world market price. On average, trade policy protected maize only marginally between 1981 and 1995. As with rice and wheat, procurement policy depressed the price of maize among farmers. Indeed, except for 1985 and 1994, the net effect of international trade and domestic marketing policy from the 1980s to the early 1990s was to tax maize producers.

Distortions to the grain economy after 1995. Our analysis shows that the government's international trade and domestic marketing policies changed strikingly after 1995 (table 3.4). The procurement policies that had been taxing rice, wheat, and maize farmers either by adding to the tax imposed by export policy, as in the case of rice, or by reducing protection, as in the case of wheat, were finally eliminated from domestic marketing policy. The elimination of the procurement quota contributed significantly to a reduction in the tax burden shouldered by farmers (Huang, Rozelle, and Wang 2006).

The liberalization of domestic markets in the mid-1990s was accompanied by a liberalization in trade policy at least in the case of the country's major food grains. After 1995, the taxation and subsidization of rice and wheat were clearly being phased out: the NRAs for rice were rising steadily (they were becoming less negative), and the NRAs for wheat were falling. Probably partly in preparation for the country's accession to the WTO, the government liberalized trade in the main food grains so extensively that, between 1995 and 2001, most of the protection for these crops was phased out. In 2001–05, the NRAs for both rice and wheat were almost zero.

The case of maize is a bit different from the situation among other crops. The NRAs for maize have been positive in some of the years since 2000. This protection for maize producers may be partly the result of lobbying by Jilin Province in seeking national support for its most important crop (Rozelle and Huang 2004).

Edible oils and cotton. The biggest difference in the analysis of the distortions affecting grain staples and the analysis of the distortions affecting cash crops (at least for soybeans and cotton) is the smaller historical role played by domestic marketing policy among the cash crops. Although procurement delivery quotas aimed at soybean producers existed in some counties, they were not as widespread as the quotas for grains; in many counties, soybeans were not a target of the government procurement system. In addition, the implicit tax on soybeans in places where the soybean quotas were collected was lower than the implicit tax on staple grain crops. There is thus little difference between the NRAs on output at the wholesale and farm levels. The same is true of cotton, although the free-market procurement of cotton by private traders was not allowed until the mid-1990s. When reform finally came to the cotton industry, policy makers chose not to adopt a two-tier pricing system. Instead, they opted for both private trade and private procurement through commercialized government cotton procurement stations. As a result, the NRA measures of distortion on cotton output are nearly the same at the wholesale and farm levels. This is true of all other commodities as well (livestock, horticultural commodities, milk, and sugar). For this reason, the discussion in the rest of this subsection—on the 1980s, the 1990s, and the post-2000 period—focuses only on trade policy.

Our analysis shows that, before 1995, soybeans were sometimes taxed and sometimes protected (table 3.4). Although the average level of protection was close to zero, it ranged from −20 percent to +40 percent. Rozelle and Huang (2005) show that much of this fluctuation was caused by domestic production policy, which encouraged soybean production before discouraging it, and then encouraging it again, although the trade regime permitted little trade. However, trends in the NRAs indicate that there has been some movement toward trade liberalization in soybeans. Beginning in the late 1990s and continuing through to 2005, the protection rate for soybeans fell from around 30 percent to less than half that amount. This should not be a surprise given the gradual integration of China into world soybean markets and the monotonic rise in imports (which exceeded 25 million tons in 2005). The situation in soybeans stands in sharp contrast to the case of maize, which enjoyed increasing protection. Maize and soybeans compete for land and other resources; it appears that, when the level of protection began to rise for maize, soybean production was significantly liberalized.

The NRAs suggest that cotton and rice share similarities. The combination of trade and monopoly procurement policy kept domestic cotton prices lower than world market prices in the 1980s and early 1990s. It appears that planners were taxing cotton farmers to supply the country's emerging textile industry with relatively inexpensive raw materials. The high implicit tax on cotton, along with ravages caused by insects, undoubtedly contributed to the stagnant and sometimes falling share of cotton in the total planted area in many regions (data of the National Bureau of Statistics).

Since 1995, however, (mostly) because of the liberalization in domestic markets and (somewhat) because of trade liberalization, there has been a clear shift in the level of the distortions faced by cotton producers. Although there were fluctuations (protection was high in 2000, but cotton was implicitly taxed in 1999 and 2001), the average NRA since the mid-1990s has been close to zero (if, in choosing the border price, one takes into account the trade status during each year). Recently, in most years, despite their authority to impose tariff rate quotas on cotton after a threshold amount has been imported, trade officials have essentially allowed the level of imports to be determined by the market.

Livestock, sugar, and horticultural commodities.   With the exception of fruit for several years in the late 1980s and early 1990s and of poultry before 1985, the patterns of distortion in the livestock and horticultural subsectors are remarkably similar (table 3.4). In all cases during the early reform period, there was heavy implicit taxation on livestock and horticultural commodities. As noted by Huang, Rozelle, and Chang (2004), this situation was created partly by the government's grain-first policy. Although China can be competitive in livestock and horticultural products, producers were not encouraged to produce or export these commodities on a large scale. Another part of the problem was the country's own barriers, such as the quotas on exports to Hong Kong, China.

Since the late 1990s, the gaps between the domestic and the world prices received by livestock and horticultural producers have narrowed. NRAs have risen toward zero for all these commodities, including pig meat, poultry, vegetables, and fruit. The relaxation in grain-first policies (often called structural adjustment policies) has allowed producers to expand livestock and horticultural production significantly. The main reason for the expansion is the rising demand inside the country (Rosen, Huang, and Rozelle 2004). Nonetheless, China's accession to the WTO and the emergence of a large export-oriented livestock and horticultural segment in the sector have increased the interest and feasibility of participation in international markets.

The situation for milk and sugar contrasts with the situation for livestock and horticultural commodities. During the 1980s, the NRAs for milk and sugar were positive and large (table 3.4). The NRAs for milk ranged from 40 to 160 percent between 1980 and 1987. They fell through the early 1990s, but rose again in the late 1990s before falling back somewhat thereafter.

The aggregate picture. After aggregating the 11 commodities in our study, we notice a striking pattern in our results (table 3.4 and figure 3.3). In the 1980s and

Figure 3.3. NRAs for Exportable, Import-Competing, and All Agricultural Products, China, 1981–2004

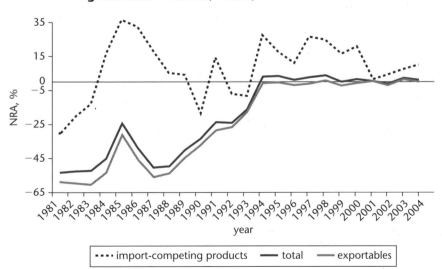

Source: Huang et al. 2007.

Note: A total NRA may be above or below the exportable and import-competing averages because the assistance to nontradables and non-product-specific assistance are also included.

through to the mid-1990s, import-competing products such as wheat, soybeans, milk, and sugar were only slightly taxed, on average, at the farm level. This conclusion takes into account the effect of input subsidies and domestic output price distortions, as well as distortions at the border, the average contributions of which are shown towards the bottom of table 3.4. The rate of protection varied considerably across the 11 commodities. It also varied inversely with international price movements, suggesting that the government was seeking to insulate the domestic market a little from world price fluctuations. Exported commodities such as rice, livestock, and horticultural products were subject to substantial rates of taxation, averaging 37 percent in 1981–95, though the variations from year to year were large and included nominal rates of taxation of more than 50 percent in several years. Since exported agricultural products accounted for a greater part of the economy than import-competing agricultural products during the early reform period, the agricultural distortions were negative, on average. In other words, for most of the reform period, the government was taxing farmers through international trade and domestic marketing policies.

One of the main findings of our study is evident in figure 3.3. After 1995, the NRAs of import-competing products fell from around 20 percent to less than 10 percent. During this period, the average NRA for exportables rose (or the implicit taxes on them fell) from about −40 percent to around −15 percent.

Taken together, the distortions in agriculture fell to less than 10 percent. In many years, the overall protection was between 0 and −5 percent. Clearly, the combination of domestic marketing reforms and international trade liberalization generated an agricultural economy that, on average, was neither taxed nor assisted. This does not mean, however, that all distortions were eliminated. In 2000–05, there was still wide dispersion in the NRAs across commodities, several of which continued to show relatively high rates of protection (figure 3.4). For example, the NRAs for sugar and milk were above 20 percent, and the NRAs for soybeans and maize were nontrivial, at more than 10 percent, while the NRAs of the fruit, vegetable, pig meat, and poultry exportable categories were close to zero. The dispersion is much less than in earlier decades, however. This is indicated in the decline in the standard deviation in the NRAs across our 11 commodities, but also in the (anti)trade bias index (tables 3.4 and 3.5).

The elimination of distortions has affected food consumers as well. In the 1980s and early 1990s, consumers were being taxed because of the positive protection on import-competing farm products, but, at the same time, they were gaining from being able to consume exportables that were implicitly subsidized by marketing and export-restricting policies. Some consumers of rice, wheat, and maize were also receiving additional consumer subsidies. The net effect of these interventions is that, until the late 1990s, consumers were enjoying a large, implicit

Figure 3.4. Average NRAs for Producers of Major Commodities, China, 2000–05

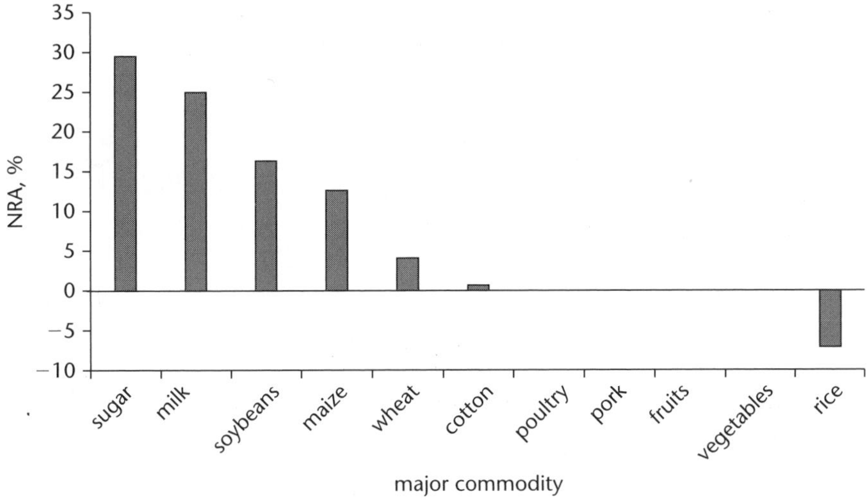

Source: Huang et al. 2007.

subsidy, which was reflected in the negative average CTEs in the 1980s (around −40 percent) and early 1990s (around −15 percent). After the mid-1990s, as the distortions against producers declined and markets became the main mechanism for food flows, those households that were net food buyers saw their implicit subsidy fall to close to zero overall even though the average CTE for import-competing products was still well above the average for exportables (similar to the NRA: compare tables 3.4 and 3.6).

Comparisons with the results of other studies

Three recent studies provide information on protection rates for agricultural products in China that may be compared with the estimates in our study. Two of the studies have been conducted by the OECD (2005, 2007); the other study was carried out by the International Food Policy Research Institute (Orden et al. 2007). These studies use a similar methodology, although they differ from our study in covering a much shorter time period, in the specific series used for price comparisons, and in the details of the methodology, including the treatment of exchange rates. The OECD studies cover 1993–2005, while the International Food Policy Research Institute study provides estimates for most commodities from 1995 to 2001 (compare with our coverage, which begins in 1981).

Table 3.5. NRAs in Agriculture Relative to Nonagricultural Industries, China, 1981–2005

(percent)

Indicator	1981–84	1985–89	1990–94	1995–99	2000–05
Covered products[a]	−50.8	−40.6	−18.9	2.3	0.9
Noncovered products[b]	−29.1	−15.4	−7.3	7.8	4.2
All agricultural products[a]	−47.6	−37.9	−17.2	3.5	2.0
Non-product-specific assistance	2.4	2.4	2.9	3.1	4.0
Total agricultural NRA[c]	−45.2	−35.5	−14.3	6.6	6.0
Trade bias index[d]	−0.50	−0.55	−0.23	−0.15	−0.07
NRA, all agricultural tradables[e]	−45.2	−35.5	−14.3	6.6	6.0
NRA, all nonagricultural tradables	41.6	28.3	24.9	9.9	4.7
RRA[f]	−60.6	−49.9	−31.1	−3.0	1.3
Memorandum items: ignoring exchange rate distortions[g]					
NRA, all agricultural products	−34.9	−27.1	−11.6	3.5	2.0
Trade bias index	−0.33	−0.38	−0.13	−0.15	−0.07
RRA	−52.2	−41.0	−26.5	−3.0	1.3

Sources: Huang et al. 2007; data compiled by the authors.

a. Including product-specific input subsidies.
b. Noncovered import-competing products are assumed to be protected at 75 percent of the rate applying to covered products. Noncovered exportables are assumed to be protected or taxed at 80 percent of the rate applying to covered products.
c. Including product-specific input subsidies and non-product-specific assistance. The total assistance to primary factors and intermediate inputs, divided by the total value of primary agriculture production at undistorted prices.
d. The trade bias index is defined as $(1 + NRAag_x/100)/(1 + NRAag_m/100) - 1$, where $NRAag_m$ and $NRAag_x$ are the average percentage NRAs for the import-competing and exportable parts of the agricultural sector, respectively.
e. Assuming all agricultural production is tradable and including product- and non-product-specific subsidies.
f. The RRA is defined as $100*[(100 + NRAag^t)/(100 + NRAnonag^t) - 1]$, where $NRAag^t$ and $NRAnonag^t$ are the percentage NRAs for the tradables parts of the agricultural and nonagricultural sectors, respectively.
g. The average values of the indicators, as captured by our methodology, if we ignore the distortions in the foreign exchange market, (see Anderson et al. 2008 and appendix A).

Broadly comparable estimates for six commodities—rice, wheat, maize, sugar, soybeans, and cotton—in 1995–2001 may be obtained from the three studies.[3] In addition, it is possible to compare the OECD and World Bank results for milk over this period. The estimated average protection rates for 1995–2001 are shown in figure 3.5. It is evident from the figure that most of the estimates are similar, and the estimates are close for rice and maize, two extremely important commodities. The estimates for wheat are noticeably different. Our study suggests that wheat was protected, while the other studies suggest it was taxed. Our estimates for

Table 3.6. CTEs for Covered Agricultural Products, China, 1981–2005

(percent)

Product	1981–84	1985–89	1990–94	1995–99	2000–05
Exportables[a,b]	−52.0	−47.7	−19.2	−0.6	0.1
Rice	−35.7	−28.8	−22.3	−4.2	0.1
Fruit	−29.8	−11.8	−6.3	0.0	0.0
Vegetables	−42.4	−57.9	−22.5	0.0	0.0
Poultry	26.7	−26.1	−1.9	0.0	0.0
Pig meat	−75.1	−46.8	−14.9	0.0	0.0
Import-competing products[a,b]	16.5	43.6	32.9	25.7	7.4
Wheat	27.5	49.1	43.3	29.0	1.2
Soybeans	4.5	10.3	10.2	26.3	19.2
Sugar	89.1	36.2	32.6	43.0	60.4
Milk	127.2	57.5	−4.8	17.7	22.3
Mixed trade status[a]					
Maize	−13.2	10.9	−13.4	8.4	14.9
Cotton	−36.4	−37.5	−29.0	−8.6	−6.6
All covered products[a]	−44.5	−41.7	−15.8	1.7	0.7

Source: Huang et al. 2007.

a. Weighted averages; weights are based on the undistorted value of consumption.
b. Depending upon their trade status during a particular year, products of mixed trade status are included among exportable products or import-competing products.

sugar, soybeans, and cotton are broadly comparable with the results of the International Food Policy Research Institute study, but quite different from the OECD estimates. Finally, our estimate of protection for the dairy industry is much lower than the OECD estimate.

Careful examination reveals that the differences between our estimates for wheat and the OECD estimates have arisen because of separate assumptions about the quality differentials in domestic and imported wheat. While our study uses a quality adjustment coefficient of −40 percent for domestic wheat relative to imported wheat that is based on Huang, Rozelle, and Chang (2004), the OECD study uses an adjustment coefficient of −15 percent. The much lower OECD estimate of the protection for soybeans over this period appears to result primarily from the OECD's use of a Heilongjiang price (a carefully considered decision based on the fact that producers in Heilongjiang Province produce commercially and compete with imports) rather than a national price for soybeans. We find our higher rate of protection in 1993–2001 more plausible given the rapid expansion in imports when the protection subsequently fell. However, the two sets of estimates are reassuringly comparable for 2003–05.

Figure 3.5. NRA Estimates in Other Studies, by Product, China, 1995–2001

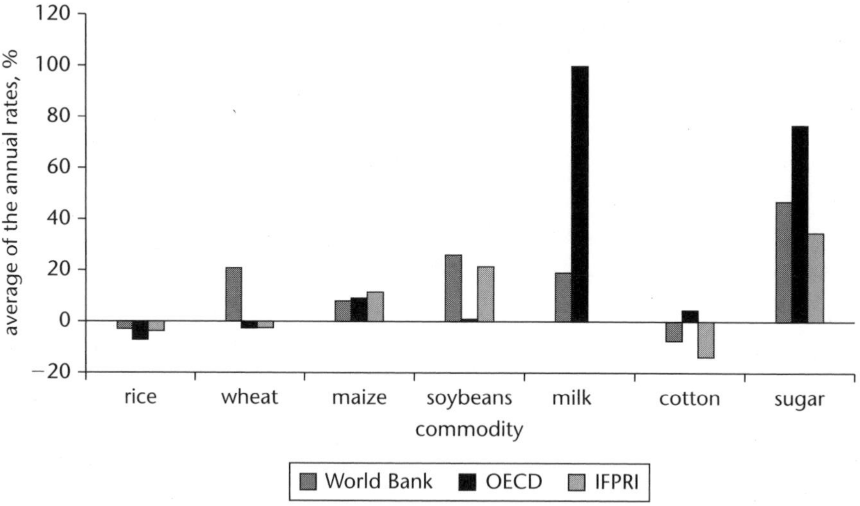

Source: Huang et al. 2007.

Note: IFPRI = International Food Policy Research Institute.

Our analysis of the distortions on milk uses the New Zealand price for milk as the reference price, plus a transport margin, while the OECD uses measures based on the international trade in processed milk products considered on a milk-equivalent basis. Our reference price is notably higher over the period covered, resulting in our lower estimate of the rate of protection. The sizable difference in the two estimates for sugar arises largely because of differences between the farm and wholesale levels in the assumed marketing and handling costs for sugar. Whereas we have assumed that these costs were around 15 percent of the total, the OECD has assumed costs at around 60 percent of the farmgate price.

These comparisons of estimates for particular products over a specific period highlight the differences, without emphasizing the important similarities in most of the estimated values, particularly the similarities in the trends over time. However, they do emphasize the importance of examining and reexamining the effect of particular assumptions on NRA estimates.

Agricultural Versus Nonagricultural Protection

The rate of assistance to a particular sector is an incomplete measure of the implications of the trade regime for outcomes in that sector. The protection in other tradable sectors competing for the same mobile resources such as labor and capital also matters. In a simple model with only two traded-goods sectors, agriculture and nonagriculture, a broad idea of the total effect of the prevailing distortions may be obtained using information only on the magnitude of two NRA measures. The distortion in the price of agricultural goods relative to nonagricultural goods provides the signal needed to guide the transfer of resources between the two sets of trading activities. For any given level of world prices, this price signal is given by the ratio:

$$(1 + NRAag^t)/(1 + NRAnonag^t). \tag{3.1}$$

This may be converted into an RRA, as follows:

$$RRA = 100^*[(100 + NRAag^t)/(100 + NRAnonag^t) - 1]. \tag{3.2}$$

The estimates of NRAnonag[t] are provided in Huang et al. (2007). These estimates take into account the effects of the trade planning mechanism, tariffs, the exchange rate overvaluation prior to 1994, and nontariff measures such as licensing and quotas. While extremely simple, we believe that these estimates supply a realistic indication of the broad pattern of incentives in nonagricultural tradables for our sample period.

The average rates of assistance to agriculture and to nonagriculture are presented in table 3.5 and figure 3.6. The data show that the agricultural sector was subject to

Figure 3.6. NRAs for Agricultural and Nonagricultural Tradables and the RRA, China, 1981–2004

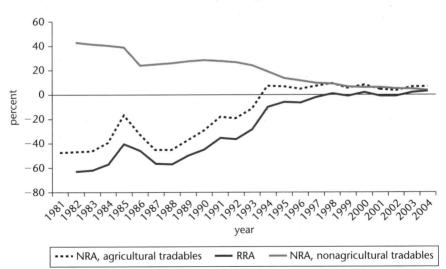

Source: Huang et al. 2007.

Note: For the definition of the RRA, see the text and table 3.5, note f.

two strong and reinforcing sets of tax measures in the early years of our sample, one direct and the other indirect. The direct taxation through border measures and the procurement system resulted in a negative NRA of 45 percent in 1981–84. The negative NRA was only slightly lower, at 36 percent, in 1985–89. The indirect taxation of this sector, through support for nonagricultural activities, was similar in magnitude (42 and 28 percent) to the direct taxation during the two periods.

The first major change in the incentive environment in the agricultural sector appears to have occurred in the mid-1980s when the rate of protection for nonagricultural sectors declined. A sharp reduction in the taxation of manufacturing exportables resulted from the widespread availability of duty exemptions for the imported goods used in the production of exports. Protection in the nonagricultural sectors appears to have risen slightly during several years in the late 1980s. Increases in tariff rates and in the exchange rate distortions outweighed the reductions in the effects of trade planning and nontariff barriers. However, the protection for nonagricultural sectors declined steadily beginning in 1990. The decline in the direct taxation of the agricultural sector began only later; a sharp fall in the early 1990s occurred, in large part, because of a reduction in the domestic taxation of the agricultural sector via the procurement pricing system (see above).

The declines in both the negative protection for agriculture and the positive protection for nonagricultural tradables since the 1990s have dramatically changed the distortions in agricultural incentives. Instead of facing an RRA of close to -50 percent as in the 1980s, farmers are now receiving slightly positive assistance, with an average RRA of 1 percent in 2000–05. Clearly, this phasing out of farmer disincentives has been a major achievement in the government's policy of reform and opening up.

Conclusions and Implications

The main finding of this study is that the nature and extent of government policy intervention in agriculture in China have changed dramatically over the past 25 years. An agricultural sector characterized by significant distortions has been transformed into a relatively liberal sector. Distortions in external and domestic policies during the early reform period—the 1980s and early 1990s—isolated domestic producers and consumers from international markets. The prices that domestic farmers and consumers faced were nearly independent of trade policy. Domestic pricing and marketing policies forced farmers to sell much of their surplus to the government at an artificially lower price even in the case of exportable commodities such as rice (the free-market price of which was close to the international price). Hence, although there was little trade taxation at the border, domestic policies levied a tax on farmers. Similar dynamics characterized the situation among importable commodities such as wheat and soybeans. Despite fairly high rates of protection through trade policies, producers were receiving much less protection than they would have received had there been a free domestic market for the importables. This occurred even though consumers were implicitly taxed.

In contrast, after the late 1980s and early 1990s, the liberalization of domestic markets reduced the distortions deriving from domestic policies. The market has gradually replaced the state as the primary mechanism for allocating resources and has become the basis for the production and marketing decisions of farmers. Especially in the case of importable commodities, trade policy has also become more liberalized, and the distortions arising from border measures have fallen substantially.

Thus, we find that China's agriculture has become much less distorted in recent years in two ways. First, the differences between international and domestic market prices have narrowed considerably for many commodities because of trade policy liberalization. Second, the elimination of domestic policy distortions means that, as trade liberalization allows more imports or exports of agricultural commodities, prices in the domestic market change, and farmers are therefore more directly affected.

There are still plenty of distortions to agricultural incentives in China. In some cases, the remaining distortions have arisen from tariffs on importable commodities (for example, wheat and soybeans). In the case of other importable commodities (for example, maize), the use of implicit export subsidies (permitted under WTO rules as domestic marketing, transport, and storage subsidies) represents a wedge between the domestic price and the international price. Thus, some dispersion of NRAs among farm products remained in 2005, but much less than in the 1980s.

Notes

1. These findings are based on intensive interviews and surveys conducted by the Center for Chinese Agricultural Policy among a wide range of agricultural ministry personnel, research administrators, research staff, and others involved in the agricultural research system.

2. Raw data on the official exchange rate and the several measures of the secondary-market rate are presented in Huang et al. (2007), together with estimated foreign exchange retention rates, calculated measures of the exchange rates applying, at the margin, to exporters and importers during the period, and estimated equilibrium rates.

3. We thank Andrzej Kwiecinski of the OECD for thoughtful comments that helped us understand the differences between the sets of estimates.

References

Anderson, K., J. Huang, and E. Ianchovichina. 2004. "Will China's WTO Accession Worsen Farm Household Incomes?" *China Economic Review* 15 (4): 443–56.

Anderson, K., M. Kurzweil, W. Martin, D. Sandri, and E. Valenzuela. 2008. "Measuring Distortions to Agricultural Incentives, Revisited." *World Trade Review* 7 (4): 675–704.

Ashton, B., K. Hill, A. Piazza, and R. Zeitz. 1984. "Famine in China, 1958–1961." *Population and Development Review* 10 (4): 613–45.

Center for Price Monitoring. various years. "National Major Commodity (Service) Price Monitoring Data Compilation." Unpublished data compilation, Center for Price Monitoring, National Development and Reform Commission, Beijing.

Chang, G., and G. Wen. 1997. "Communal Dining and the Chinese Famine of 1958–1961." *Economic Development and Cultural Change* 46 (1): 1–34.

China Customs. various years. "Import and Export Statistics." Statistics compilations, Customs Administration, Beijing.

deBrauw, A., J. Huang, and S. Rozelle. 2004. "The Sequencing of Reforms in China's Agricultural Transition." *Economics of Transition* 12 (3): 427–66.

deBrauw, A., J. Huang, S. Rozelle, L. Zhang, and Y. Zhang. 2002. "The Evolution of China's Rural Labor Markets during the Reforms." *Journal of Comparative Economics* 30 (2): 329–53.

de Gorter, H., D. Just, and J. Kropp. 2008. "Cross-Subsidization Due to Infra-marginal Support in Agriculture: A General Theory and Empirical Evidence." *American Journal of Agricultural Economics* 90 (1): 42–54.

Dong, X., and G. Dow. 1993. "Monitoring Costs in Chinese Agricultural Teams." *Journal of Political Economy* 101 (3): 539–53.

Fan, S. 1991. "Effects of Technological Change and Institutional Reform on Production Growth in Chinese Agriculture." *American Journal of Agricultural Economics* 73 (2): 266–75.

———. 1997. "Production and Productivity Growth in Chinese Agriculture: New Measurement and Evidence." *Food Policy* 22 (3): 213–28.

Fan, S., and P. Pardey. 1997. "Research Productivity and Output Growth in Chinese Agriculture." *Journal of Development Economics* 53 (1): 115–37.

Fisman, R., and S. Wei. 2004. "Tax Rates and Tax Evasion: Evidence from 'Missing Imports' in China." *Journal of Political Economy* 112 (2): 471–96.

Gale, F. 2006. "Trends in Chinese Food Demand and Trade Patterns." Paper presented at the U.S. Department of Agriculture Agricultural Outlook Forum 2006, "Prospering in Rural America," Arlington, VA, February 16–17.

Honma, M., and Y. Hayami. 2008. "Distortions to Agricultural Incentives in Japan, Korea, and Taiwan." Agricultural Distortions Working Paper 35, World Bank, Washington, DC.

Hu, R., and J. Huang. 2001. "Investment in Agro-Technology Extension and Its Effect in China." *Strategy and Management* 3: 25–31.

Huang, J., and H. Bouis. 1996. "Structural Changes in Demand for Food in Asia." Food, Agriculture, and the Environment Discussion Paper 11, International Food Policy Research Institute, Washington, DC.

Huang, J., and C. Chen. 1999a. "Effects of Trade Liberalization on Agriculture in China: Institutional and Structural Aspects." CGPRT Centre Working Paper 42, Regional Co-ordination Center for Research and Development of Coarse Grains, Pulses, Roots, and Tuber Crops in the Humid Tropics of Asia and the Pacific, United Nations Economic and Social Commission for Asia and the Pacific, Bogor, Indonesia.

———. 1999b. "Effects of Trade Liberalization on Agriculture in China: Commodity Aspects." CGPRT Centre Working Paper 43, Regional Co-ordination Center for Research and Development of Coarse Grains, Pulses, Roots, and Tuber Crops in the Humid Tropics of Asia and the Pacific, United Nations Economic and Social Commission for Asia and the Pacific, Bogor, Indonesia.

Huang, J., and H. Ma. 2000. "International Comparison of Agricultural Prices." *International Trade* 10: 20–24.

Huang, J., and S. Rozelle. 1996. "Technological Change: Rediscovering the Engine of Productivity Growth in China's Rural Economy." *Journal of Development Economics* 49 (2): 337–69.

———. 2002. "China's Accession to WTO and Likely Shifts in the Agriculture Policy." Working paper, Center for Chinese Agricultural Policy, Chinese Academy of Sciences, Beijing.

Huang, J., S. Rozelle, and M. Chang. 2004. "The Nature of Distortions to Agricultural Incentives in China and Implications of WTO Accession." *World Bank Economic Review* 18 (1): 59–84.

Huang, J., S. Rozelle, W. Martin, and Y. Liu. 2007. "Distortions to Agricultural Incentives in China." Agricultural Distortions Working Paper 29, World Bank, Washington, DC.

Huang, J., S. Rozelle, and H. Wang. 2006. "Fostering or Stripping Rural China: Modernizing Agriculture and Rural to Urban Capital Flows." *Developing Economies* 44 (1): 1–26.

Jin, S., J. Huang, R. Hu, and S. Rozelle. 2002. "The Creation and Spread of Technology and Total Factor Productivity in China's Agriculture." *American Journal of Agricultural Economics* 84 (4): 916–39.

Kiguel, M., and S. O'Connell. 1995. "Parallel Exchange Rates in Developing Countries." *World Bank Research Observer* 10 (1): 21–52.

Lardy, N. R. 1983. *Agriculture in China's Modern Economic Development.* Cambridge: Cambridge University Press.

———. 1992. *Foreign Trade and Economic Reform in China, 1978–90.* Cambridge: Cambridge University Press.

———. 2001. *Integrating China into the Global Economy.* Washington, DC: Brookings Institution.

Lin, J. 1991. "Prohibitions of Factor Market Exchanges and Technological Choice in Chinese Agriculture." *Journal of Development Studies* 27 (4): 1–15.

———. 1992. "Rural Reforms and Agricultural Growth in China." *American Economic Review* 82 (1): 34–51.

Lin, J., F. Cai, and Z. Li. 1996. *The China Miracle: Development Strategy and Economic Reform.* Hong Kong, China: Chinese University Press.

Lin, J., and D. Yang. 2000. "Food Availability, Entitlement and the Chinese Famine of 1959–61." *Economic Journal* 110 (460): 136–58.

Lyons, T. 1987. *Economic Integration and Planning in Maoist China.* New York: Columbia University Press.

Martin, W. 2002. "Implications of Reform and WTO Accession for China's Agricultural Policies." *Economics of Transition* 9 (3): 717–42.

McMillan, J., J. Whalley, and L. Zhu. 1989. "The Impact of China's Economic Reforms on Agricultural Productivity Growth." *Journal of Political Economy* 97 (4): 781–807.

Ministry of Agriculture. various years. *China Agricultural Yearbook.* Beijing: China Agricultural Press.

———. various years. *China Agricultural Development Report.* Beijing: China Agricultural Press.

Ministry of Commerce. various years. *China Foreign Trade Yearbook.* Beijing: China Foreign Economic and Trade Press.

National Bureau of Statistics of China. various years. *China Rural Statistical Yearbook.* Beijing: China Statistics Press.

———. various years. *China Yearbook of Agricultural Price Survey.* Beijing: China Statistics Press.

———. various years. *Statistical Yearbook of China.* Beijing: China Statistics Press.

National Development and Reform Commission. various years. *Agricultural Production Cost and Revenue Materials Compilation.* Beijing: China Statistics Press.

Nickum, J. 1998. "Is China Living on the Water Margin?" *China Quarterly* 156 (December): 880–98.

Nyberg, A., and S. Rozelle. 1999. *Accelerating China's Rural Transformation.* Washington, DC: World Bank.

OECD (Organisation for Economic Co-operation and Development). 2005. *OECD Review of Agricultural Policies: China.* Paris: OECD.

———. 2007. *Agricultural Policies in Non-OECD Countries: Monitoring and Evaluation 2007.* Paris: OECD.

OECD PSE-CSE Database (Producer and Consumer Support Estimates, OECD Database 1986–2005). Organisation for Economic Co-operation and Development. http://www.oecd.org/document/55/0,3343,en_2649_33727_36956855_1_1_1_1,00.html (accessed December 2007).

Office of Tariff Regulation of the State Council. 1998. *Import and Export Tariff Regulation of the People's Republic of China, 1996, 1997 and 1998.* Beijing: Law Press.

————. 2005. *Import Tariff and Export Tariff Rebate Compilation 2005.* Beijing: Economic and Scientific Press.

Orden, D., F. Cheng, H. Nguyen, U. Grote, M. Thomas, K. Mullen, and D. Sun. 2007. *Agricultural Producer Support Estimates for Developing Countries: Measurement Issues and Evidence from India, Indonesia, China, and Vietnam.* Research Report 152. Washington, DC: International Food Policy Research Institute.

Park, A., H. Jin, S. Rozelle, and J. Huang. 2002. "Market Emergence and Transition: Arbitrage, Transition Costs, and Autarky in China's Grain Market." *American Journal of Agricultural Economics* 84 (1): 67–82.

Putterman, L. 1993. *Continuity and Change in China's Rural Development.* New York: Oxford University Press.

Rosen, D., J. Huang, and S. Rozelle. 2004. *Roots of Competitiveness: China's Evolving Agriculture Interests.* Washington, DC: Institute for International Economics.

Rozelle, S., and J. Huang. 2004. "China's Maize Economy: Supply, Demand and Trade." Report, U.S. Grains Council, Beijing.

————. 2005. "China's Soybean Economy: Supply, Demand, and Trade." Report, American Soybean Association, Beijing.

Rozelle, S., J. Huang, and D. Sumner. 2006. "Supply, Demand and Trade for Horticultural Commodities in China." Working paper, Department of Agricultural and Resource Economics, University of California Davis, Davis, CA.

Rozelle, S., A. Park, J. Huang, and H. Jin. 2000. "Bureaucrat to Entrepreneur: The Changing Role of the State in China's Transitional Commodity Economy." *Economic Development and Cultural Change* 48 (2): 227–52.

Rozelle, S., and J. Swinnen. 2004. "Success and Failure of Reform: Insights from the Transition of Agriculture." *Journal of Economic Literature* 42 (2): 404–56.

Shan, W. 1989. "Reforms of China's Foreign Trade System: Experiences and Prospects." *China Economic Review* 1 (1): 33–55.

Sicular, T. 1988a. "Agricultural Planning and Pricing in the Post-Mao Period." *China Quarterly* 116 (December): 671–705.

————. 1988b. "Plan and Market in China's Agricultural Commerce." *Journal of Political Economy* 96 (2): 283–307.

————. 1995. "Redefining State, Plan, and Market: China's Reforms in Agricultural Commerce." *China Quarterly* 144 (December): 1020–46.

Stone, B. 1988. "Developments in Agricultural Technology." *China Quarterly* 116 (December): 767–822.

Stone, B., and S. Rozelle. 1995. *Foodcrop Production Variability in China, 1931–1985.* Research Notes and Studies, vol. 9. London: School of Oriental and African Studies, University of London.

Timmer, C. P. 1998. "The Agricultural Transformation." In *International Agricultural Development,* 3rd ed., ed. C. Eicher and J. Staatz, 113–35. Baltimore: Johns Hopkins University Press.

UNCTAD (United Nations Conference on Trade and Development). 1994. *Monitoring Import Regimes.* Part 1 of *Directory of Import Regimes.* New York: United Nations.

Wang, D., S. Rozelle, and J. Huang. 1999. "The Impact of Procurement Quota on Agricultural Production in China's Agriculture." Working paper, Center for Chinese Agricultural Policy, Chinese Academy of Agricultural Sciences, Beijing.

Wang, H., X. Dong, J., Huang, S. Rozelle, and T. Reardon. 2006. "Producing and Procuring Horticultural Crops with Chinese Characteristics: A Case Study in the Greater Beijing Area." Working paper, Center for Chinese Agricultural Policy, Chinese Academy of Sciences, Beijing.

Wang, J., J. Huang, and S. Rozelle. 2005. "Evolution of Tubewell Ownership and Production in the North China Plain." *Australian Journal of Agricultural and Resource Economics* 49 (2): 177–95.

Wang, J., Z. Xu, J. Huang, and S. Rozelle. 2005. "Incentives in Water Management Reform: Assessing the Effect on Water Use, Productivity, and Poverty in the Yellow River Basin." *Environment and Development Economics* 10 (6): 769–99.

Watson, A. 1994. "China's Agricultural Reforms: Experiences and Achievements of the Agricultural Sector in the Market Reform Process." Working Paper 94/4, Chinese Economic Research Unit, University of Adelaide, Adelaide, Australia.

Wen, G. 1993. "Total Factor Productivity Change in China's Farming Sector: 1952–1989." *Economic Development and Cultural Change* 42 (1): 1–41.

World Bank. 1985. *World Development Report 1985: International Capital and Economic Development.* New York: Oxford University Press; Washington, DC: World Bank.

———. 1994. *China: Foreign Trade Reform.* World Bank Country Study. Washington, DC: World Bank.

Yao, S. 1994. *Agricultural Reforms and Grain Production in China.* London: Macmillan.

Zhang, L., Q. Li, and S. Rozelle. 2005. "Fertilizer Demand in China: What is Causing Farmers to Use So Much Fertilizer?" Working paper, Center for Chinese Agricultural Policy, Chinese Academy of Sciences, Beijing.

PART III

SOUTHEAST ASIA

4

INDONESIA

George Fane and Peter Warr

In Indonesia, agricultural trade policy is a politically charged subject. Rice, the staple food, is a net import, and this one commodity has been a central focus of the government's food policy throughout the postindependence period. Self-sufficiency in rice, meaning the elimination of rice imports, has been a cherished goal of agricultural policy for all this time. It is an emotive subject, closely linked in the public imagination to Indonesian nationalism. When asked to name his proudest single achievement, Soeharto, the president of Indonesia for 32 years, until 1998, cited the country's self-sufficiency in rice.[1] The dominance by rice is evident in this study, which documents the changing structure of agricultural protection in Indonesia and attempts to explain the forces that have driven the changes.

Our four central themes may be summarized as follows. First, the variations in distortion by sector have been driven by the government's wish to (a) be self-sufficient in food, (b) stabilize food prices at acceptable levels, and (c) promote manufacturing. (Food processing has been an important component of manufacturing; it was even more important in the 1970s and 1980s than it is now.) These aims led to taxes on unprocessed exports and to subsidies for processing. Two import-competing industries—sugar and rice—have been significantly protected, and the rates of this protection have increased in recent years. The rate of protection of the sugar industry is particularly high. Growers of rice have also received protection, but, until around 2000, this occurred mainly through input subsidies

The authors gratefully acknowledge the excellent research assistance of Arief Ramayandi; the helpful comments and data assistance of Neil McCulloch, Rina Oktaviani, Peter Rosner, and Peter Timmer; the useful comments of workshop participants; and the significant work with spreadsheets undertaken by Marianne Kurzweil and Ernesto Valenzuela.

rather than through the price for the product. This protection may be explained through our hypotheses both as the main element in food self-sufficiency and as a result of the effect rice prices have on manufacturing wages through the cost of living. Since 2000, the rice industry has become more tightly protected; rice imports have been banned.

Second, during the long presidency of Soeharto, the country could afford aims (a) to (c) under good fiscal conditions, but not under bad fiscal conditions. So, good fiscal conditions meant more protection and bad trade policies, while bad fiscal conditions meant less protection and good trade policies.

Third, growing evidence from around the world convinced policy makers in Indonesia and most other East Asian countries to rely more on markets and less on government intervention. This evidence was based on theoretical arguments, statistical studies, and simple two-country comparisons such as Myanmar and Thailand, the German Democratic Republic and the Federal Republic of Germany, Austria and Hungary, and the Democratic People's Republic of Korea and the Republic of Korea. The resulting policy shift was influenced by the collapse of the communist system and the victory of capitalism in the Cold War. This may have contributed to the long-term shift worldwide toward less manufacturing protection and less agricultural export taxation beginning around the mid-1980s.

Fourth, following the democratic reforms that occurred in the wake of the Asian financial crisis of the late 1990s, agricultural protectionism increased somewhat in Indonesia. Aggregate measures of protection indicate that these changes, along with reduced protection in manufacturing, caused a switch in the agricultural sector from net taxation to net subsidization (by a narrow margin) relative to manufacturing. However, these aggregate measures mask the fact that agricultural protection is concentrated in only two crucial industries: sugar and rice.

The next section describes the changing structure of the Indonesian economy, with an emphasis on the agricultural sector. The subsequent two sections provide overviews on government economic policy in general and on government policies toward agriculture during the period since independence. In the following sections, we attempt to supply a political econometric explanation for the changing structure and pattern in agricultural distortions over the last three decades, estimates of which we provide for individual farm industries and for agriculture as a whole. The final section concludes.

Economic Growth and Structural Change

From 1968 to 2005, Indonesia's gross domestic product (GDP) grew in real terms at an average annual rate of 6.3 percent. The broad characteristics of this growth are summarized in table 4.1. For ease of comparison with other Asian economies,

Table 4.1. Real GDP Growth and Its Sectoral Components, Indonesia, 1968–2005
(annual average percent)

Sector	Preboom, 1968–86	Boom, 1987–96	Crisis, 1997–99	Recovery, 2000–05	Total, 1968–2005
Total GDP	7.4	7.7	−2.5	4.6	6.3
Agriculture	4.4	3.4	0.6	3.5	3.7
Industry, including mining	10.6	9.8	−2.3	4.2	8.5
Services	7.8	7.9	−4.0	5.7	6.6

Source: Author calculations based on World Development Indicators Database 2008.

the table distinguishes between the preboom period prior to 1987 and the 10 boom years that preceded the Asian crisis of the late 1990s. During the precrisis decade of 1987–96, many Asian countries witnessed growth that was far more rapid than the growth in preceding decades. Indonesia also grew rapidly during this decade, but, as the table shows, the growth was only marginally more rapid than the growth during the previous two preboom decades. The country's economic growth had been sustained over several decades. Output contracted during the crisis years, and, during the subsequent recovery period, growth averaged a more moderate 4.6 percent (see Fane and Warr 2007 for additional evidence on points discussed in this section).

As typically occurs in rapidly growing economies, agricultural output expanded more slowly than GDP, implying that there was a declining share of agriculture in aggregate output. The agricultural sector accounted for 56 percent of GDP in 1965. By 2004, this share had declined to 15 percent. Over the same period, the GDP share of manufacturing and other industry rose from 13 to 44 percent, and the share of services rose from 31 to 41 percent. For a more detailed study of the changing composition of the agricultural sector, one may conveniently use the BPS input-output tables that are available on Indonesia for 1971, 1980, 1990, and 2000. As incomes rise, the share of spending on starchy staples usually falls, while the share of spending on meat, fruits, and vegetables usually rises. The Indonesian experience fits this common pattern.

The output growth within agriculture was achieved despite a rapidly diminishing share of the supply of labor and capital. Furthermore, while agriculture grew more slowly than other sectors during boom periods, the growth rate also declined less during the crisis years than the corresponding rates of growth in other sectors. The agricultural sector has acted as a shock absorber; this was particularly important during the crisis, when agricultural employment absorbed the large numbers of people laid off in urban centers. Although GDP grew much

Table 4.2. Subsector Shares of Agricultural Value Added, Indonesia, 1971–2000

(percent)

Subsector	1971	1980	1990	2000
Paddy	46.1	38.0	37.5	30.8
Maize	3.1	3.7	4.1	5.9
Root crops	7.2	6.8	7.6	8.9
Fruits and vegetables	14.1	14.5	21.7	21.8
Other food crops	3.3	4.4	6.4	3.9
Rubber	5.5	5.2	2.0	5.5
Sugarcane	2.2	2.4	2.1	2.5
Coconut	5.2	4.3	3.3	3.7
Palm oil	2.9	2.1	2.4	2.3
Tobacco	2.5	1.7	0.7	0.3
Coffee	2.6	4.3	1.5	0.9
Tea	1.4	1.9	0.5	0.3
Cloves	1.4	3.0	1.6	0.9
Other agriculture	1.8	1.7	3.5	7.3
Livestock	0.6	6.0	5.0	4.9
Total	100.0	100.0	100.0	100.0

Source: BPS 1971, 1980, 1990, 2000.

more slowly during the recovery in 2000–05 than it had during the boom decade, agricultural growth did not fall with respect to the boom years.

Table 4.2 summarizes the changing composition of the value added in agriculture since 1971 based on data from the input-output tables. The output of paddy (unmilled rice produced at the farm level) contracted from 46 to 31 percent of agricultural value added, while the share of fruits and vegetables increased from 14 to 22 percent and the share of livestock rose from 0.6 to 5 percent.

It is somewhat surprising that the shares of intermediate inputs used in agriculture actually contracted. The apparent reason is that fertilizer and pesticide usage was subsidized from the late 1960s until the late 1980s under a government rice-intensification program called Bimas (discussed below). When the subsidies were phased out, fertilizer and pesticide use contracted markedly, especially in rice production. Most intermediate goods used in agriculture are domestically produced. Between 1980 and 2000, the annual share of imported intermediate goods in total intermediate goods used in the country increased from 3.8 to 10.2 percent.

In 1971, sales of paddy by farmers to intermediate users (rice millers) accounted for 56 percent of the total value of paddy output, implying that almost half of the output was being milled by individual households. By 2000, sales to

Table 4.3. Export Sales in Total Sales and Imports in Total Usage, Indonesia, 1971–2000

(percent)

Subsector	Export share 1971	1980	1990	2000	Import share 1971	1980	1990	2000
Paddy[a]	0.0	0.0	0.0	0.0	0.0	0.0	0.0	0.0
Maize	11.4	0.3	1.8	0.3	0.0	1.1	0.2	11.3
Root crops	4.7	3.7	0.7	0.3	0.0	0.1	0.0	0.1
Fruits and vegetables	0.1	0.2	0.2	0.3	0.6	1.1	0.9	4.9
Other food crops	4.3	0.3	1.9	0.4	0.0	22.7	18.1	47.7
Rubber	57.5	58.4	6.5	0.6	0.1	0.0	0.1	0.7
Sugarcane	0.0	0.0	0.0	0.0	0.0	0.0	0.0	0.0
Coconut	6.6	1.2	0.3	1.5	0.0	0.0	0.0	0.1
Palm oil	2.3	33.5	29.5	0.2	0.0	0.0	0.1	0.2
Tobacco	7.4	12.3	7.6	0.0	1.6	7.3	15.6	0.0
Coffee	21.5	58.7	13.7	0.0	0.0	0.0	0.0	0.0
Tea	24.5	18.5	32.5	0.0	0.0	0.0	3.9	0.0
Cloves	0.0	0.0	0.1	3.0	47.4	12.7	0.0	24.5
Other agriculture	40.5	15.9	26.7	21.2	24.1	43.8	1.4	30.3
Livestock	1.2	0.0	1.8	2.1	0.0	0.5	0.9	8.4
Total Agriculture	7.5	9.3	2.8	2.6	1.3	2.8	2.0	8.7
Milled rice[a]	0.0	0.8	0.0	0.0	13.5	12.5	0.2	3.9
Fertilizers and pesticides	0.0	4.4	14.6	22.9	66.0	18.1	9.6	23.3

Source: BPS 1971, 1980, 1990, 2000.

a. The input-output tables classify paddy (unmilled rice) as an output of the agricultural sector and milled rice as an output of the manufacturing sector

intermediate users accounted for 98 percent of the total value of the output. Similar trends occurred in maize, rubber, sugarcane, palm oil, coffee, and tea.

The international trading position of the major agricultural commodities is summarized in table 4.3. The most important import-competing agricultural products are rice, sugar, maize, and soybeans. Major export-competing products include coffee, rubber, tobacco, tea, palm oil, copra, shrimps, and spices. Paddy is neither exported nor imported, but milled rice has historically been a major import item. Since 2002, rice imports have been officially banned, but some imports have still occurred. Cassava is mainly nontraded, although there are exports of its derivatives, manioc and tapioca. Much of the livestock subsector is also nontraded, although chickens are exported, while beef and dairy products compete with imports.

Over time, some sectors have shifted from one trade category to the other (import-competing or exportable). The key example is sugar, which was the most important export during the colonial era, but has become one of the most highly protected import-competing products in the postindependence period. Another example is maize, which switched from net export status to net import status during the 1990s. Fruits and vegetables have become major net imports, as have soybeans (which are included in the government's input-output tables as "other food crops").

Policy Evolution

Indonesia obtained its independence from the Netherlands in 1949. The next two decades were chaotic. The postindependence government of President Soekarno pursued a nationalistic, quasi-socialist economic policy that produced hyperinflation and economic stagnation. In 1966, Soekarno was displaced amid economic chaos by one of his generals, Soeharto, whose regime, called the New Order, lasted until the macroeconomic crisis of 1998. Soeharto pursued more market-oriented economic policies than his predecessor had. On assuming power, Soeharto speedily introduced a macroeconomic stabilization program and then began liberalizing trade and investment policies. In 1967, foreign investors were guaranteed the right to repatriate both capital and profit, and, beginning in 1970, the capital account was almost completely open. As we see below, trade policy under Soeharto's government was much less open. It was characterized by the taxation of exports, especially nonfood agricultural exports, and the protection of imports, including some food imports.

In the wake of the commodity boom of 1972–73 and the oil price shocks of 1973–74 and 1979–80, trade policy became increasingly inward-looking. These external events tripled the ratio of Indonesia's export prices to its import prices. Between the early 1970s and the mid-1980s, the government taxed or banned some traditional exports, pursued self-sufficiency in rice, and used part of the burgeoning oil revenues to establish import-substituting manufacturing industries, which it then protected. In the early to mid-1980s, several traditional export industries were subjected to quantitative trade restrictions. The restrictions included a ban on log exports that conferred high rates of effective protection on the plywood manufacturing industry, for which raw timber is the principal input. Licensing systems were introduced for exports of vegetable oils, several spices, coffee, and some grades of rubber. In the case of palm oil, domestic refiners were protected by a tax on exports and a requirement that growers supply these refiners with part of their output at low, controlled prices.

In 1982, the price of petroleum began to decline. By the mid-1980s it had fallen from US$28 to US$10 per barrel. Many oil-exporting countries, including Nigeria and República Bolivariana de Venezuela, were unable to adjust to these external changes without devastating domestic consequences, but Indonesia responded quickly by cutting public spending and devaluing its currency, partly to promote non-oil exports. In addition, a value added tax was introduced between 1983 and 1986. At first, trade policy became increasingly oriented toward import substitution, and the system of import licensing was extended. After this initial protectionist response to lower petroleum export revenues, however, trade policy was significantly liberalized starting in 1985.

With the stated goal of promoting non-oil exports, the government introduced a series of reforms that reduced tariffs and nontariff barriers (NTBs). Following tariff cuts in 1985, the government transferred most customs functions from the Indonesian Customs Service to an international inspection company, SGS of Switzerland. The role of SGS was phased out by 1995. NTBs on imports were progressively relaxed beginning in 1986, and the system of providing exporters with duty-free inputs was extended.

According to the estimates in table 4.4, the effective rate of protection in agriculture declined from 24 to 12 percent between 1987 and 1995, while, in manufacturing, it declined much farther, from 86 to 24 percent, over the same period. Since there was probably more water (unused protection) in the tariffs in 1987 than in 1995, the true reductions in protection were probably somewhat smaller than these numbers indicate, but the decline was still substantial. Meanwhile, many NTBs were replaced by tariffs. The coverage of restrictive NTBs

Table 4.4. Estimated Effective Rates of Protection, Indonesia, 1987, 1995, and 2003

(percent)

Sector, indicator	1987	1995	2003
Agriculture	24	12	9
Manufacturing, excluding oil and gas	86	24	16
Manufacturing, including oil and gas	48	20	13
All tradable sectors	18	8	4
Antitrade bias[a]	52	28	20

Source: 1987–95: Fane and Condon 1996; 2003: author estimates (Fane).

Note: The estimates for 1987 and 1995 measure the rates shortly before the reform package of December 1987 and shortly after the reform package of May 1995. The estimates for 2003 apply the same methodology, but using the tariff cuts announced in the May 1995 package for implementation by 2003. With relatively minor exceptions, the plans announced in 1995 were implemented. The projections of the rates for agriculture in 2003 make no allowance for the increased protection of rice and sugar that occurred beginning in 2000.

a. The antitrade bias (ATB) is defined as: $1 + ATB = (1 + g^m)/(1 + g^e)$, where g^m and g^e denote the average rate in, respectively, all import-competing sectors and all export-competing sectors.

declined from 44 percent of total value added in all traded industries in 1986 to 23 percent in 1995. This switch from NTBs to tariffs was more extensive in manufacturing than in agriculture, where the coverage of NTBs declined from 67 to 48 percent. In the wake of the financial crisis of 1997–98, the government was obliged to allow free imports of both rice and sugar as a condition for borrowing from the International Monetary Fund (IMF). However, since the end of the IMF program, imports of rice and sugar have again been restricted by both tariffs and NTBs.

Agricultural Protection by Subsector

The distinction between import-competing products and export products is not always entirely clear-cut, but it is nevertheless crucial to any discussion of Indonesian agricultural policies. Whereas import-competing production has generally been protected by government policies, export-competing production has generally been taxed. For centuries, the country's major staple food crops have been net imports. Both the Dutch colonial government and the government of Indonesia after independence generally tried to control the price of rice and other important food crops to balance the competing interests of domestic producers and consumers. Except when the world prices of food crops have been unusually high, imports have been directly restricted, or subject to tariffs, or both. On the rare occasions when world prices have been so high that growers would have had an incentive to export food crops such as rice, they have usually been prevented from doing so by nontax measures, including outright export bans.

In contrast, export crops have been seen by successive governments over the last two centuries as a useful source of tax revenue. Under the cultivation system (*cultuurstelsel*) introduced by the Dutch in 1830, the production of cash crops for export was stimulated by imposing taxes on villagers that could be most easily paid in kind by handing over crops that the Dutch East India Company then processed and exported. By far the most important of these exports was sugar; other important exports in the 19th century were coffee, tea, indigo, and cinnamon. Booth (1988) reports that, in the late 1830s, 40 percent of the total income of the government of the Netherlands was derived from the cultivation system in the Indonesian colonies.

Since independence, the Indonesian government's revenue from export crops has been obtained through export taxes that have tended to depress the domestic production and the exports of the relevant crops. The main reason for raising export revenue in this quite different way has presumably been the government's desire, since independence, to promote the development of the manufacturing sector, of which food processing is an important part. Rice, sugar, and soybeans have been protected from import competition by NTBs. The remainder of import-competing agriculture has been protected by tariffs and tariff surcharges. (Rice, sugar, and soybeans, along with maize, are discussed in the next four subsections. Import-competing and export agriculture are discussed in the subsequent subsections.)

Rice

The most important and most enduring NTBs have been those on rice and sugar. Chart a in figure 4.1 shows estimates of the domestic wholesale prices and border prices for rice.[2] (All the price series in figures 4.1–4.4 are in rupiah per kilogram, divided by the GDP deflator indexed at 1 in 2005. The nominal rate of protection [NRP] from import competition is the percentage by which the domestic price exceeds the border price.) While there have been enormous nominal increases in rice and sugar prices since the early 1970s, figures 4.1 and 4.2 show that any trends in the real prices of these products have been relatively small.

It is clear from chart a in figure 4.1 that the domestic wholesale price of rice has fluctuated much less than the border price and that domestic prices have not differed greatly, on average, from the trend level of border prices. Price stabilization was achieved by giving the government's food logistics agency, Bulog (*Badan Urusan Logistik*), a monopoly over international trade in rice and directing the agency to build up buffer stocks to smooth out fluctuations in domestic supply. It is significant that this stabilization of domestic prices was achieved while keeping the trend value of domestic prices roughly in line with the trend in world prices. Average rates of protection in the output market were low, but input markets were another matter.

Beginning in the 1970s, the Soeharto government used part of its new oil wealth to promote self-sufficiency in rice by subsidizing the adoption of high-yielding varieties that had been made available through the Green Revolution. These new varieties required greatly increased use of irrigation, fertilizers, and pesticides, which the government helped to finance. An important motivation for this policy was the fear of a repetition of the riots precipitated by high food prices in 1965.

Under the Bimas (*bimbingan masal* or massive guidance) program, which was introduced with the explicit goal of rice self-sufficiency, farmers received agricultural extension services and subsidized credit, seeds, fertilizers, and pesticides. The government also upgraded irrigation facilities and expanded irrigation coverage. The resulting rise in the profitability of rice growing, together with some coercion among farmers who were reluctant to extend the area of rice cultivation, led to a 17 percent increase in gross harvested area in the decade to 1985.[3] The increase in

Figure 4.1. Border and Domestic Prices of Import-Competing Products Relative to the GDP Deflator, Rice and Urea Fertilizer, Indonesia, 1975–2005

a. Rice

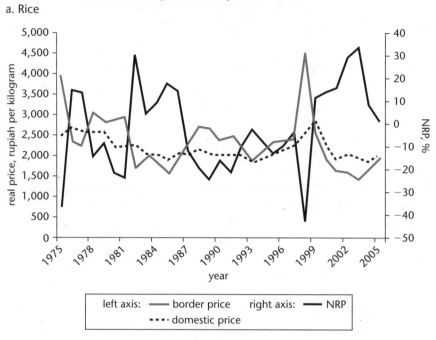

b. Urea fertilizer

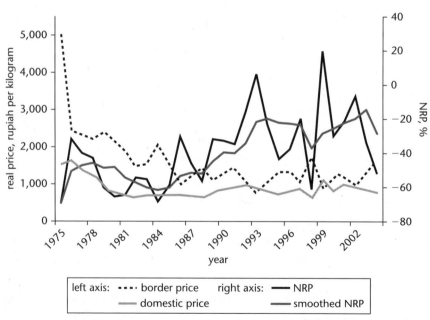

Source: Fane and Warr 2007.

cultivated area, together with a 50 percent rise in average yields during the same period, allowed Bulog to reduce domestic rice prices relative to the consumer price index between the late 1970s and 1985, while gradually phasing out imports and then halting imports altogether in 1985.

Lower world oil prices and advice from the World Bank contributed to the reduction in agricultural input subsidies in the late 1980s and early 1990s. Graph b in figure 4.1 indicates the fall in the real price of urea from the late 1970s to the early 1980s and the subsequent rise in the domestic wholesale price of urea relative both to the consumer price index and to the border price in the late 1980s and early 1990s. Under an export licensing scheme, exports of urea require special approval from the Ministry of Trade. The year-to-year determination of the magnitude of the licensed exports is not transparent, but the ministry tends to place priority on ensuring that domestic supplies are stable at a price lower than the world market price. This results in the negative rates of protection from import competition shown in figure 4.1, graph b.

In the late 1980s, the strict policy of zero imports of rice was replaced by a policy involving borrowing rice from Vietnam in times of shortage and repaying the rice loans in times of surplus. These loans were conducted in bilateral government-to-government deals in which Bulog represented the Indonesian government. In the early 1990s, it gradually became apparent that Indonesia was unable to maintain rice self-sufficiency even on average over a period of years. To satisfy domestic demand at acceptable prices, Bulog was obliged to undertake substantial net imports.

When the Asian crisis forced the government to borrow from the IMF in 1997, one of the loan conditions to which the government agreed was the removal of Bulog's monopoly on rice imports. Until 1999, there was also no import duties on rice, but the IMF's aim of free trade in rice proved illusory because the financial crisis briefly converted rice into a potential export and the government banned exports to reduce pressure on domestic prices. Graph a in figure 4.1 shows that border prices, converted to rupiah at the devalued exchange rate, were far above domestic prices in 1998. This occurred because the massive depreciation of the exchange rate between mid-1997 and mid-1998 initially outweighed the much more gradual rise in domestic prices. This episode clearly demonstrates that the government's policy has always been to stabilize food prices at acceptable levels rather than simply to protect growers.

The general increase in domestic prices in 1998–99 and the stabilization of the exchange rate after mid-1998 removed the incentive to export rice. Bulog's monopoly on imports was not immediately reimposed, but a 20 percent tariff on rice imports was introduced in 1999. Problems with underinvoicing by importers resulted in this tariff being converted to a specific tariff at Rp 430 per kilogram. In

2002, Bulog's monopoly over imports was restored, and, since 2004, rice imports have officially been banned, although Bulog has occasionally been issued with special import permits.

Sugar

The Indonesian sugar industry is dominated by the state-owned mills, mainly on Java, that were acquired through the nationalization of the formerly Dutch-owned sugar estates in 1957. Investment and technical progress in this sector have been extremely sluggish, and the industry has languished behind protective barriers. The finished product of the antiquated factories—known as mill white or plantation white—is not precisely comparable to the refined sugar or the raw sugar traded on the world market. Plantation white contains more impurities, mainly molasses, than internationally traded raw sugar, but has already undergone some of the bleaching processes that separate refined sugar from raw sugar in more technologically advanced sugar industries. Most firms in the food and beverage subsectors are unable to use plantation white because of its relatively high level of impurities; their needs are mainly met by imports of raw sugar, although a small amount of raw sugar is produced domestically.

As in the case of rice, the main motive behind government policy on sugar appears to be the desire to stabilize the domestic price at an acceptable level. In addition, in the case of sugar, the government has tried to protect the sugar factories that it owns. This may explain why, at least since 1957, the sugar industry has been more tightly regulated than any other agricultural sector: the government has monopolized not only imports, but also domestic marketing. Government ownership likewise helps to explain newspaper reports that, in the 1970s, farmers in traditional sugar-growing areas were regularly forced to grow sugar to supply local factories because of threats that their other crops would be burned.

Figure 4.2 compares the border price of raw sugar (after allowing for margins between the free on board price and the domestic wholesale price) with the domestic wholesale price of plantation white. The figure shows that, for much of the period since 1970, the domestic price was about twice the border price, implying an NRP of about 100 percent. However, in 2006, this gap was narrowed appreciably because of the abrupt rise in world prices.

Our estimates of the NRP for sugar ignore two factors, the first of which indicates that our estimates tend to understate the true NRP, while the second goes in the opposite direction. The first factor is that our estimates make no adjustment for the relatively low polarity (high level of impurities) of plantation white. The offsetting factor is the neglect of the cost of bleaching to obtain plantation white. Sugar industry experts have suggested that the low polarity

Figure 4.2. Border and Domestic Prices of Import-Competing Products Relative to the GDP Deflator, Sugar, Indonesia, 1971–2005

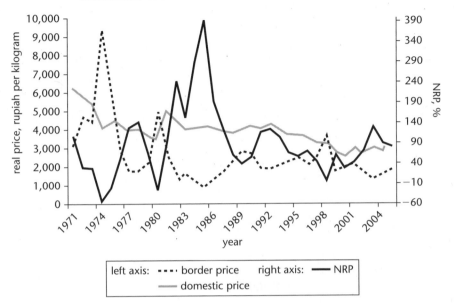

Source: Fane and Warr 2007.

effect is probably more important than the effects of bleaching, but that the difference is small.

Soybeans

Until 1996, the government protected soybean growers by assigning Bulog a monopoly on imports. Since 1996, soybean imports have been unrestricted, and the tariff is currently zero (figure 4.3). The excess of the domestic price of soybeans over the border price was reduced in 1988, when a local soybean crushing plant run by PT Sarpindo Industri began to operate. However, Bulog prevented the domestic price of beans from falling as rapidly as the world price in 1988–94; and Sarpindo was protected by a local-content scheme that required domestic feed mills to source at least 20 percent of their total usage of soybean meal from local supplies, which meant Sarpindo, the only local supplier of soybean meal. The high cost of feed inhibited the growth of the increasingly powerful poultry industry. In 1996, the local-content scheme was abandoned, and Sarpindo was allowed to go out of business.

Figure 4.3. Border and Domestic Prices of Import-Competing Products Relative to the GDP Deflator, Soybeans, Indonesia, 1970–2005

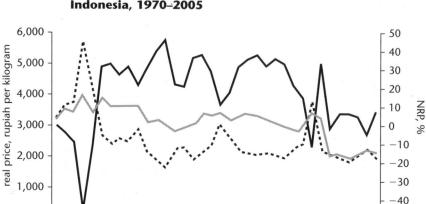

Source: Fane and Warr 2007.

Maize

Maize was a substantial net export industry in the 1970s, but maize subsequently became a net import item. This transition coincided with a movement from negative protection during the export phase to a small amount of positive protection since the early 1980s (figure 4.4). The tariff on imports of processed maize in the form of pellets and flour is currently only 5 percent, but, during the presidency of Megawati Sukarnoputri (2001–04), Rini Suwandi, the minister of trade (supported by Bulog), created import licenses that restricted imports, raising average NRPs well above 5 percent. The rents created by this measure accrue to members of the maize importers association.

Other import-competing agriculture: tariffs and tariff surcharges

The growth in protection during the 1970s and early 1980s and the reduction in protection in the late 1980s and 1990s were mainly achieved by changing the rates of import tariff surcharges (*bea masuk terbahan*) rather than the rates of the

Figure 4.4. Border and Domestic Prices of Import-Competing Products Relative to the GDP Deflator, Maize, Indonesia, 1969–2005

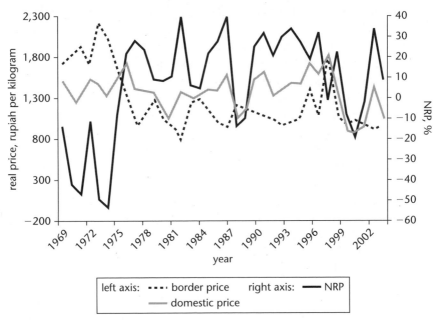

Source: Fane and Warr 2007.

import tariff (*bea masuk*).[4] In terms of their economic effects, the surcharges were equivalent to tariffs, but, unlike tariffs, the rates of the surcharges could be changed by administrative decree without the need to amend the law. The rates of import duty shown in appendix table A4 in Fane and Warr (2007) are the combined rates of tariffs, plus tariff surcharges. A comparison of the changes in the tariffs and the changes in the tariff surcharges in appendix tables A5 and A6 in Fane and Warr (2007) shows that much of the growth of protection in 1974–79 and almost all of the much larger increases in protection in 1979–85 were achieved by raising tariff surcharges rather than tariffs. When protection was reduced in 1985–89, about half the reduction was obtained by largely eliminating tariff surcharges, which were negligible by 1989, but had been an important part of total import duties in 1985. By 1994, tariff surcharges had been totally abolished, and, since then, there has been no need to distinguish between tariffs and total import duties.

The import duties on food processing have always been higher than those on agriculture. In every year, the average import tax rate on food processing alone

(Harmonized Commodity Description and Coding System, 15–24) is higher than the corresponding average rate on the entire agriculture and food processing products category (1–24). Vegetables and flowers, particularly orchids, have always been the most highly protected of the industries within agricultural categories 1–14.

Among the more traditional agricultural subsectors, livestock and estate crops have always received relatively significant protection from imports. However, whereas livestock is mainly import-competing (but also partly nontraded), many estate crops are mainly export-competing. In these cases, of which coffee, tea, and spices are major examples, there is a great deal of water in the tariffs. In the 1970s, the total import tax rates on tea, coffee, vanilla, cinnamon, nutmeg, and ginger were 70 percent; by 1985, this rate had increased to 100 percent. However, by 1989, the total import duty rates on all these products had been reduced to 30 percent, and, by the mid-1990s, they had fallen to 5 percent.

The import duty rates on food crops have generally been relatively low, at least in the period before 2000. However, these rates understate the extent of the protection for food crops for two reasons: food crop producers have received input subsidies, and food crops have also been protected by NTBs; hence, their separate treatment above.

Estate crops: rubber, copra, coffee, and tea

Rubber, copra, coffee, and tea are all produced by perennial plants and, in Indonesia, tend to be produced on large estates, although copra is also produced by smallholders. All have been export crops and all have been taxed, but at varying rates. The export volumes of all these commodities have declined since the 1980s. The high rates of export taxation are a significant part of the explanation. Figure 4.5 shows the calculations of the NRPs for each of these four commodities. For rubber, the export tax rate has been low, but the data show high rates of export taxation for copra and tea. For coffee, the rate has declined from the high rates prior to the 1990s.

The Political Economy of Protection: Do Good Times Produce Bad Policy, and Bad Times, Good Policy?

Key characteristics of Indonesia's political environment provide background on the attempts to explain the changes in trade policy summarized above. First, the confidence of the country's elite was boosted because of the economic successes achieved elsewhere in East and Southeast Asia starting in the 1970s. There seemed

Figure 4.5. Border and Domestic Prices of Export Crops Relative to the GDP Deflator, Indonesia, 1967–2005

a. Rubber

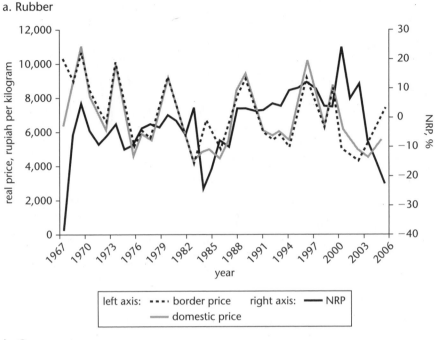

b. Copra

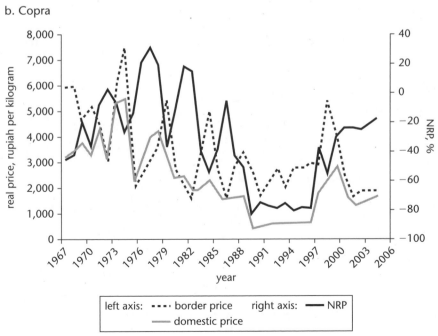

(Figure continues on the following page.)

Figure 4.5. Border and Domestic Prices of Export Crops Relative to the GDP Deflator, Indonesia, 1967–2005 (*continued*)

c. Coffee

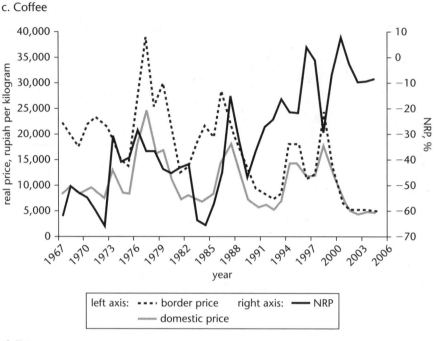

d. Tea

Source: Fane and Warr 2007.

no fundamental reason why Indonesia should not succeed as well. This confidence meant that bolder strategies could be contemplated. This may be contrasted with the timidity and the skepticism with regard to the international trading system that characterized most of South Asia at the time. Second, Soeharto's political authority within Indonesia was unchallenged until the end of his regime. Even policies that were unpopular, at least initially, could be contemplated if Soeharto considered them necessary.

Observers of economic reform in Indonesia have coined the phrase "good times produce bad policy, and bad times produce good policy," where good times means favorable external conditions, and good policies means deregulation and lower barriers to international trade and investment. The phrase describes much of the history of economic reform in Indonesia. The oil price booms of the 1970s were followed by a series of trade-restricting import-substitution policies aimed at protecting at least some of the traded goods industries that could potentially be harmed by the "Dutch disease" effect of the petroleum booms, that is, the decline in the domestic competitiveness of the traded goods industries caused by a rise in the prices of nontraded goods and services relative to traded goods and services (see Corden 1984; Warr 1986). Trade liberalization followed the adverse terms of trade effect of the decline in petroleum prices beginning in the early 1980s. But, while good times-bad policy, bad times-good policy *describes* the Indonesian experience, it does not provide an *explanation*. Why have good times produced bad policy, and bad times, good policy in Indonesia?

Observers of policy formation under Soeharto have reported on a contest for Soeharto's attention between the technocrats and the nationalists (Hill 2000). At various times, either of these groups might have had ascendancy, which meant that Soeharto was heeding their messages. The technocrats, many of whom were professional economists trained in the United States, favored a market-oriented economy, a strong emphasis on macroeconomic stability, and a relatively open trade policy. This group dominated the Ministry of Finance and Bappenas, the National Development Planning Agency, and had considerable influence on the Bank of Indonesia. The World Bank used its influence directly in support of the technocrats, and the Bank's resources and technical expertise also assisted the technocrats in making their case more convincing.

The economic nationalists were more diverse. They included, in particular, the engineers, led by the minister for research and technology, B. J. Habibie, a German-trained engineer with a strong preference for crash-through economic programs based on advanced technology. This group promoted large-scale, capital-intensive projects in aeronautics, shipbuilding, steel, fertilizers, petrochemicals, and other industries. To ensure the profitability of these projects, high rates of protection were advocated on infant industry grounds. This group was influential within

Dr. Habibie's own department, as well as at the state-owned petroleum company, Pertamina. A second group of nationalists was represented by the advocates of self-sufficiency in food, particularly rice. This group dominated the Ministry of Agriculture and Bulog (for example, see Warr 1992; Timmer 1996). More general support for policies based on import substitution was concentrated at the Ministry of Industry.

During bad economic times, the technocrats tended to gain Soeharto's attention. During good times, he listened to the nationalists. The central dynamic derived from the role of the external shocks to the Indonesian economy that operated through petroleum prices. During the Soeharto period, petroleum was both a principal source of foreign exchange, through direct oil exports, and a major source of government revenue, through the royalties received by the government on the exports. Reduced oil prices implied both balance of payments and budgetary stresses. In addition, the majority of the country's foreign debt was public debt. When the price of oil fell, the fiscal burden of debt servicing became more painful. This increased the influence of the World Bank, whose willingness to extend concessional loans to the country was important directly and also as a signal to other potential foreign lenders. At such times, the government needed these loans to balance its budget. The only alternative was inflationary financing, the consequences of which had been experienced under Soeharto. The increased influence of the World Bank meant greater influence for the technocrats and the policies they advocated. In addition, reduced oil prices meant a reduction in the influence of Pertamina because they lowered Pertamina's contribution to government revenue. It also meant greater influence for the Ministry of Finance, which implemented the tax reforms—designed by technocrats and like-minded foreign advisors—that helped make up for the lost oil revenues.

In other countries, a deterioration in the terms of trade might be met by exchange controls, import licensing, and other import-substitution policies. In Indonesia, a protectionist response also occurred briefly after the oil price declines of the early 1980s. But it did not last long because it did not address the simultaneous fiscal problem. An example of the tax reforms that emerged from this dynamic was the introduction of a value added tax in 1986 and, at the same time, a reduction in import duties. An import duty (tariff) is equivalent to both a tax on consumption and a subsidy on production set at the same ad valorem rate. The tariff raises positive net revenue because the volume of consumption of an import commodity exceeds the volume of production of that commodity. A value added tax is a tax on consumption alone. Moreover, it is able to raise the same amount of revenue as a tariff, but at a lower rate of tax. This is so because it does not expend revenue to subsidize production. Similarly, the switch from NTBs to tariffs generates revenue. NTBs may be thought of as privately levied tariffs that make no contribution to government revenue. A final example is the phasing out of the Bimas scheme that was designed to help rice growers achieve self-sufficiency. The budgetary cost of the fertilizer and pesticide subsidies and subsidized lending involved in Bimas became serious because of the fiscal deterioration of the 1980s.

During times of reduced petroleum prices, such as the early to mid-1980s, illiberal trade policies were unaffordable in fiscal terms, and this reinforced the argument that trade liberalization would promote improved foreign exchange earnings from non-oil exports. The technocrats then held sway. In contrast, during the euphoria of the 1970s that was induced by high petroleum revenues, the import-substitution schemes advocated by the nationalists seemed affordable and were politically attractive. Then, the nationalists captured Soeharto's attention.

The Asian financial crisis of 1997–98 was the worst of times, and it produced the best of economic policies, given that best is being used here to mean that the policies more closely conformed to the laissez-faire advice of neoclassical economists. The Asian crisis also provides the clearest illustration of the causal link between bad times and laissez-faire policies: the reforms that the government introduced in the wake of the crisis were explicitly adopted to meet IMF loan conditions when all other sources of external lending had dried up.

Since Soeharto's political demise in 1998 and the subsequent shift to a more democratic form of government, the president no longer holds absolute authority, and policies are therefore no longer determined simply by a contest between the technocrats and nationalists to influence the president. The parliament, a token institution under Soeharto, now has teeth, and the president cannot ignore its will. Populist economic nationalism has tended to dominate in parliament; and this has reduced, but not eliminated, the influence of the technocrats. In addition, the conspicuous reluctance of the major industrialized countries to lower the protection for their own agricultural sectors has weakened the influence of the technocrats who argue against Indonesian restrictions on trade. The greater protection for the rice and sugar subsectors that followed the end of the IMF program was a direct consequence of these political changes. Rice self-sufficiency and protection for farmers are both politically attractive goals in Indonesia, and, in the public imagination, both are strongly associated with the national interest. Protection for the rice industry is supported by all major political parties. Because of democracy, rice and sugar farmers therefore now receive more protection from imports than they did under Soeharto.

Imputed Protection at the Farm Level

The discussion above about protection rates has focused on the effects of policy interventions at the wholesale market level. In this section, we extend the analysis to the way protection (or its opposite) at the wholesale level produces price effects at the farm level.

Theory

One of the intentions of agricultural protection policy is to influence prices at the farm level. But the goods produced directly by farmers seldom enter international trade. The raw commodities produced by farmers are generally nontraded, whereas the commodities that enter international trade are the processed or partially processed versions of these raw products. Between the nontraded raw product produced by the farmer and the traded processed commodity that enters international trade, there may be several steps: transport, storage, milling, processing, repackaging, and so on.

   The significance of this is that border protection policy operates directly on the goods that actually enter international trade either as exports or imports, not on the raw commodities produced by farmers. Protection at the farm level is therefore a derived effect. It depends on the extent to which policies applied to trade in processed agricultural goods induce changes in prices that are then transmitted to the prices actually faced by farmers. The question thus arises: to what extent do price changes at the wholesale level that are induced by protection policy affect the prices actually received by farmers for the raw products they sell.

   We construct a simple econometric model to investigate this issue. We use the notational convention that uppercase roman letters (such as X) denote levels in the values of variables and lowercase roman letters (such as x) denote the natural logarithms of the variables, thus: $x = \ln X$. Protection at the wholesale level is therefore defined as:

$$P_{it}^W = P_{it}^*(1 + T_{it}^W), \tag{4.1}$$

where P_{it}^W denotes the level of the wholesale price of commodity i at time t; P_{it}^* is the corresponding border price expressed in the domestic currency and adjusted for the handling costs that, in the case of an import, must be taken into account in shifting the cost, insurance, and freight price of the commodity to the domestic wholesale price or, in the case of an export, in shifting the wholesale price of the commodity to the free on board price. The NRP at wholesale is given as T_{it}^W. In this discussion, both the border price and the NRP are treated as exogenous variables. The border price is determined by world markets, and the country involved is presumed to be a price taker, that is, the country is presumed to be unable to influence the international price. The NRP is determined by the government's protection policy.

The farmgate price of a raw material is denoted by P_{it}^F, and its logarithm, p_{it}^F, is related to the logarithm of the wholesale price by:

$$p_{it}^F = a_i + b_i p_{it}^W + u_{it}, \qquad (4.2)$$

where a_i and b_i are coefficients, and u_{it} is a random error term. The coefficient b_i is the pass-through or transmission elasticity. The estimated values of the coefficients a_i and b_i are denoted by $\hat{a}_i$ and $\hat{b}_i$, respectively. The econometric estimation of these parameters is discussed below.

The estimated coefficients are used as follows. We estimate the logarithm of the farm price that would obtain in the *absence* of any protection as:

$$\hat{p}_{it}^{F*} = \hat{a}_i + \hat{b}_i p_{it}^{W*}, \qquad (4.3)$$

where p_{it}^{W*} is the estimated value of the wholesale price that would obtain in the absence of protection, $p_{it}^{W*} = \ln P_{it}^{W*}$. This is then compared with the estimated value of the wholesale price in the *presence* of protection:

$$\hat{p}_{it}^F = \hat{a}_i + \hat{b}_i p_{it}^W. \qquad (4.4)$$

We denote the antilogs of $\hat{p}_{it}^F$ and $\hat{p}_{it}^{F*}$ by $\hat{P}_{it}^F$ and $\hat{P}_{it}^F$, respectively, and then estimate the NRP at the farm level as:

$$\hat{T}_{it}^F = (\hat{P}_{it}^F - \hat{P}_{it}^{F*})/\hat{P}_{it}^F. \qquad (4.5)$$

It is important to observe that the value of the protection-inclusive farm price used in these calculations is the level estimated in the econometric model (equation 4.4) rather than the actual price given by the raw data. This is because our intention is to use the model to estimate the *change* in the farmgate price caused by protection at the wholesale level. Thus, both the protection-inclusive price and the protection-exclusive price used in equation (4.5) are the predicted values obtained from the model.

The implied NRP at the farm level may be related to the NRP at the wholesale level as follows. Substituting $\hat{P}_{it}^F = \hat{A}_i(P_{it}^W)^{\hat{b}_i}$ and $\hat{P}_{it}^{F*} = \hat{A}_i(P_{it}^{W*})^{\hat{b}_i}$ into equation (4.5), where $\hat{A}_i$ is the antilog of $\hat{a}_i$, then rearranging, and using equation (4.1), we obtain the simple expression:

$$\hat{T}_{it}^F = (1 + T_{it}^W)^{\hat{b}_i} - 1. \qquad (4.6)$$

Obviously, if $T_{it}^W = 0$, then $\hat{T}_{it}^F = 0$ regardless of the value of $\hat{b}_i$. Similarly, if $\hat{b}_i = 0$, then $\hat{T}_{it}^F = 0$ regardless of the value of T_{it}^W. Also, if $\hat{b}_i = 1$, then $\hat{T}_{it}^F = T_{it}^W$. It may readily be seen that, if $T_{it}^W > 0$, then $\hat{T}^F \geq T_{it}^W$ as $\hat{b}_i \geq 1$, but if $T_{it}^W < 0$, $\hat{T}^F \leq T_{it}^W$ as $\hat{b}_i \leq 1$. If $T_{it}^W < 0$, then $\hat{T}^F \leq T_{it}^W$ as $\hat{b}_i \geq 1$, but $\hat{T}^F \geq T_{it}^W$ as $\hat{b}_i \leq 1$.

Econometric application

The purpose of the econometric analysis is to estimate the parameter $\hat{b}_i$ for each commodity.[5] For each commodity, we conduct the analysis using time series price data in which each variable is expressed in logarithms, and each is deflated by the GDP deflator for Indonesia: the farmgate price (LFP), the wholesale price (LWP), and the log of the international price, adjusted by the nominal exchange rate and transport and handling costs (LIP). The data extend from 1976 to 2001. The seven commodities for which these data are available are rice, maize, soybeans, sugar, rubber, coffee, and tea.

We first tested each of the series (each deflated by the GDP deflator) for the existence of a unit root. For rice, the null hypothesis of a unit root was rejected for all three price series (recalling that they are real, not nominal, price series using the GDP deflator) at the 10 percent level of significance. The price series are thus considered stationary. For other commodities, the results are more mixed. For maize, the null hypothesis of a unit root could not be rejected for farm prices (LFP), but was strongly rejected for the other two price series. For soybeans, the null hypothesis of a unit root could not be rejected for the wholesale price series (LWP), but was rejected at the 10 percent level for the other two series. For sugar, the null hypothesis of a unit root could not be rejected for any of the three series, especially the farm price series (LFP). For rubber, coffee, and tea, the results were similar: the null hypothesis of a unit root marginally failed to be rejected for the farm price series (LFP), but was rejected for the other two series.

We first produced ordinary least squares estimates of equation (4.2). In most cases, autocorrelation was a problem, and an AR(1) correction term was included to eliminate it, which was accomplished effectively. The ordinary least squares estimates assume that LFP is endogenous and LWP is exogenous. These assumptions were tested using Hausman's endogeneity test, although the test has low power when the number of data points is small, as in this case. For each commodity, the null hypothesis that LWP was (weakly) exogenous to LFP failed to be rejected, confirming the validity of the ordinary least squares estimates. Reverse Hausman's tests were also conducted, and the null hypothesis that LFP was exogenous to LWP was rejected in the cases of maize, sugar, rubber, coffee, and tea. This hypothesis marginally failed to be rejected for rice and soybeans. The results roughly support the validity of the use of the ordinary least squares framework to estimate the transmission elasticity from LWP to LFP, while treating LWP as exogenous.

Usable estimates were produced for five commodities: rice, soybeans, sugar, rubber, and tea. The estimated elasticity had the expected positive sign and was significantly different from zero, and the estimated equation performed well.

Table 4.5. Estimates of Transmission Elasticities from Wholesale to Farm Prices, Indonesia

Commodity	Estimated elasticity	t-statistic
Rice	0.73	(5.24)
Soybeans	0.53	(3.17)
Sugar	0.61	(2.29)
Rubber	0.44	(2.60)
Tea	0.26	(2.65)

Source: Author calculations.

Note: The table has been created using the data and methodology discussed in the text. The estimates shown relate to the parameter b_i in equation (4.2).

Table 4.5 summarizes the estimates. For maize and coffee, the estimated elasticity was not significantly different from zero, and the estimated equation performed poorly. It is often asserted that the commodity price changes that, because of protection or international price movements, arise at the wholesale level are prevented by middlemen from being transmitted to farmers. This hypothesis is rejected by the Indonesian data, at least for the five commodities listed above. The transmission elasticities are not zero. Economists often assume that the transmission elasticities are unity. However, the estimated values are generally less than unity and lie between 0.2 and 0.8. The lower values are obtained in the case of rubber and tea, which are perennial crops requiring high processing costs. The other values all exceed 0.5. It is likely that the true transmission elasticities change over time, but the limited data available for this exercise made the assumption necessary that the true values are constant.

Estimation of protection at the farm level

Given the estimated value of the transmission elasticity, equation (4.6) is used, together with the estimated NRPs at wholesale discussed above, to produce estimates of imputed NRPs at the farm level. Because usable estimates of the transmission elasticity could not be obtained for three commodities (maize, coffee, and copra), the estimated values for rice, tea, and rubber, respectively, were used as proxies for the true elasticities of these commodities. The imputed farm NRPs are somewhat lower in absolute value than the NRPs at wholesale because the transmission elasticities lie between zero and unity, but, given the assumption of constant transmission elasticities, they track the pattern of the wholesale results closely.

Aggregate Measures of Assistance

In this section, we calculate aggregate measures of rates of protection using the information assembled from the preceding analysis and following, as much as possible, the methodology outlined in Anderson et al. (2008) and appendix A. The annual calculations reported fluctuate somewhat from year to year because international and domestic price changes alter the protective effects of all instruments of protection except ad valorem tariffs. In addition, the time taken for domestic prices to adjust to international price changes means that annual data on price differences indicate some variation from one year to the next.

The calculations of NRPs at the wholesale and farm levels described in the previous section are used to calculate nominal rates of assistance (NRAs) at the farm level that take account of the assistance for fertilizer input use, in addition to output price distortions. Thus, the NRA for a particular commodity is calculated as the NRA on the output of the commodity, plus the product of the cost share of fertilizers in the production of the commodity and the nominal rate of subsidy for fertilizer use (which was up to two-thirds of the price of fertilizer in the early 1970s, but which has declined since then and, in recent years, has been only one-fifth of this price). The aggregate NRA therefore exceeds the NRAs on output for each commodity that uses fertilizer as an input.

The calculations of the NRAs confirm that, in 2000–04, import-competing commodities were significantly protected, notably rice and especially sugar (table 4.6). The rates of assistance for these two commodities have increased significantly relative to the rates in the 1990s, whereas the assistance for maize and soybean producers has fallen. Tea is still moderately taxed, but export commodities such as rubber, copra, and coffee are either only lightly taxed or only slightly assisted today, having been taxed—sometimes significantly—prior to the late 1990s. The average NRA for import-competing farm products is always above the average NRA for exportables, and the extent of this antitrade bias within the agricultural sector has not diminished over time (figure 4.6 and table 4.7). Nor has the dispersion of the NRAs of covered products declined as measured by the annual standard deviation around the weighted mean (table 4.6), which means that the inefficiency of the use of resources across industries within the sector remains nontrivial.

Finally, the relative rate of assistance (RRA) to agriculture is a function of the difference between the NRA in tradable agriculture and the NRA in nonagricultural tradables such as manufactures, but also nonfarm primary fishing, forestry, and mining products.[6] Our RRA estimates show that, before the Asian crisis of the late 1990s, agriculture was effectively taxed by between one-quarter and one-third, but, shortly after the crisis, it was a slightly net subsidized sector (table 4.7 and figure 4.7). Because we have erred on the side of understating rates of manufacturing

Table 4.6. NRAs for Covered Agricultural Products, Including Fertilizer Use Subsidies, Indonesia, 1970–2004

(percent)

Indicator, product	1970–74	1975–79	1980–84	1985–89	1990–94	1995–99	2000–04
Exportables[a]	−3.3	−0.3	−7.0	−16.5	−24.6	−17.2	−3.0
Coffee	−7.1	−3.7	−8.6	−2.2	−0.5	2.3	3.0
Tea	−6.3	−1.9	1.8	−2.3	−2.5	−13.9	−15.5
Coconuts	−5.9	2.2	−6.1	−22.0	−45.6	−29.4	−8.1
Rubber	15.2	−3.4	−16.2	−20.5	−31.9	37.0	16.7
Palm oil	−14.5	−9.2	22.2	−1.1	11.9	−18.3	−3.8
Import-competing products[a]	−3.6	16.5	19.5	5.1	−0.7	−5.8	24.7
Rice	—	13.9	7.5	−0.9	−8.7	−13.0	18.7
Maize	−15.4	10.2	18.6	21.9	22.5	24.6	10.8
Soybeans	−5.9	31.8	49.0	17.0	17.7	17.5	1.2
Sugar	2.1	23.5	53.8	8.5	3.9	11.3	49.4
Poultry[b]	72.8	144.3	147.5	86.8	94.9	87.9	99.8
All covered products[a]	−3.9	11.1	12.2	−0.3	−5.5	−9.1	16.4
Dispersion, covered products[c]	27.6	49.4	53.6	35.0	40.5	49.0	36.3
Coverage, at undistorted prices	65	68	64	61	64	63	59

Source: Fane and Warr 2007.

Note: The output-subsidy equivalent of the subsidy for fertilizer input is incorporated in the NRA for each crop. It is estimated by multiplying the input subsidy by the share of fertilizer in the cost of production of each product and adding it to the output NRA. — = no data are available.

a. Weighted averages; the weights are based on the unassisted value of production.

b. The first and last periods refer to 1971–74 and 2000–03, respectively.

c. Dispersion is a simple five-year average of the annual standard deviation around the weighted mean of the NRAs of covered products.

Figure 4.6. NRAs for Exportable, Import-Competing, and All Agricultural Products, Indonesia, 1970–2004

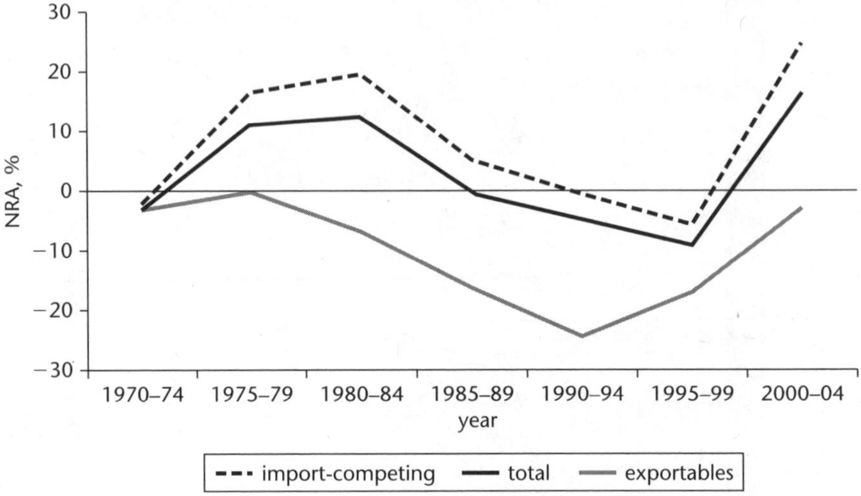

Source: Fane and Warr 2007.

protection prior to 1987, better estimates of manufacturing protection during this period would show *larger* negative RRAs prior to the 1990s and would thereby reinforce rather than undermine the above finding.

Conclusions and the Prospects for Reform

Having previously taxed agriculture relative to the nonfarm sectors during the postindependence period, Indonesia's trade policies have, on average, not taxed agriculture since around 2000. This change occurred following the Asian crisis of the late 1990s. The switch took the form of (a) increases in the protection of the import-competing commodities sugar and rice; (b) declines in the taxation of agricultural exports, especially rubber and copra; and (c) declines in manufacturing protection. The transition to a more democratic form of government has weakened the influence of the country's technocrats, who have generally favored liberalized trade policies. Greater protection among some key agricultural commodities has been a consequence.

Assistance for agriculture primarily takes the form of protection for the import-competing sugar and rice subsectors. Other output subsectors receive virtually no direct assistance. Subsidies for fertilizers and other inputs were once an indirect source of assistance for agriculture, but the nominal rates of these subsidies have declined.

Table 4.7. NRAs in Agriculture Relative to Nonagricultural Industries, Indonesia, 1970–2004
(percent)

Indicator	1970–74	1975–79	1980–84	1985–89	1990–94	1995–99	2000–04
Covered products[a]	−3.9	11.1	12.2	−0.3	−5.5	−9.1	16.4
Noncovered products	−2.3	5.4	4.2	−3.8	−8.4	−7.7	7.1
All agricultural products[a]	−3.4	9.3	9.2	−1.7	−6.6	−8.6	12.0
Non-product-specific assistance	0.0	0.0	0.0	0.0	0.0	0.0	0.0
Total agricultural NRA[b]	−3.4	9.3	9.2	−1.7	−6.6	−8.6	12.0
Trade bias index[c]	0.03	−0.14	−0.21	−0.20	−0.24	−0.12	−0.22
NRA, all agricultural tradables	−3.8	10.4	10.5	−1.9	−7.5	−9.7	13.9
NRA, all nonagricultural tradables	27.7	27.7	27.7	26.5	17.6	10.6	8.1
RRA[d]	−24.7	−13.6	−13.5	−22.5	−21.3	−18.3	5.4

Source: Fane and Warr 2007.

a. Including product-specific input subsidies.
b. Including product-specific input subsidies and non-product-specific assistance. Represents total assistance to primary factors and intermediate inputs, divided by the total value of primary agriculture production at undistorted prices.
c. The trade bias index is defined as $(1 + NRAag_x/100)/(1 + NRAag_m/100) - 1$, where $NRAag_m$ and $NRAag_x$ are the average percentage NRAs for the import-competing and exportable parts of the agricultural sector, respectively.
d. The RRA is defined as $100*[(100 + NRAag^t)/(100 + NRAnonag^t) - 1]$, where $NRAag^t$ and $NRAnonag^t$ are the percentage NRAs for the tradables parts of the agricultural and nonagricultural sectors, respectively.

Figure 4.7. NRAs for Agricultural and Nonagricultural Tradables and the RRA, Indonesia, 1970–2004

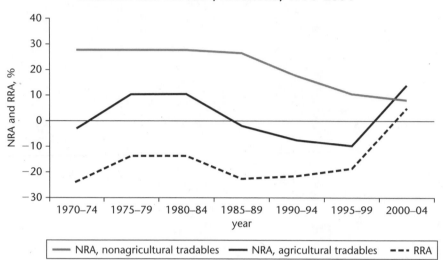

Source: Fane and Warr 2007.

Note: For the definition of the RRA, see table 4.7, note d.

The political explanations for the protection of sugar and the protection of rice are quite different. The protection of sugar is a consequence of the political power of the highly concentrated refining industry, including the state-owned component of this industry, which is closely linked with large-scale sugar plantations.

In contrast, the farm production of rice (paddy) is dominated by small-scale farm producers. The rice milling industry is much more concentrated and much more well organized, however, and this is relevant because rice imports compete with milled rice rather than the raw, unmilled product (paddy) produced by the farmers. The political power of rice millers has been an important source of support for the protection of the rice industry. The enhanced political power of the Indonesian parliament since the upheavals induced by the Asian crisis, together with the economic nationalism that dominates among members of parliament, has strengthened the support for the protection of the rice industry. Since 2004, rice imports have officially been banned. In part, this policy has reflected the mistaken claim, advanced by supporters of rice industry protection, that restricting rice imports reduces poverty. A general equilibrium analysis presented in Warr (2005) shows that the policy is more likely to have increased poverty within both rural and urban areas because the poverty-increasing effects of raising the consumer price of rice far exceed the poverty-reducing effects of raising the producer price.

Given the politics at work, trade liberalization in the country's sugar and rice industries seems unlikely in the foreseeable future. Indeed, rising protectionism seems a more likely outcome, and this might conceivably extend to industries other than sugar and rice.

Notes

1. Soeharto's New Order began in March 1966, although Soekarno, Soeharto's predecessor, remained nominal president for 12 more months. The statement about rice self-sufficiency was reportedly made during Soeharto's visit to the headquarters, in Rome, of the Food and Agriculture Organization of the United Nations, in 1985, when Indonesia's rice imports stood (briefly) at zero.

2. The border price of rice in chart a, figure 4.1 has been converted to make it as nearly comparable as possible to the wholesale price. The free on board price was adjusted to the cost, insurance, and freight level by adding freight and insurance costs; the resulting price was then adjusted to the wholesale level by adding margins to allow for the estimated handling, warehousing, and interest costs.

3. Gross indicates that each hectare that is harvested twice in a single year is counted as 2 hectares.

4. The term tariff surcharge is a misnomer in the sense that the base to which the rates of the tariff surcharge applied was not the tariff, but the border value (cost, insurance, and freight) of the imports subject to the tariff surcharge. For example, in 1985, in the case of live animals (other than pure bred), the tariff was 30 percent, and the tariff surcharge was 15 percent, giving a total import duty of 45 percent of the border value (cost, insurance, and freight).

5. The results are summarized here. Details of the econometric analysis are available upon request.

6. The NRAs for nonagricultural tradables are estimated mainly on the basis of the effective rates of protection for manufacturing in Fane and Condon (1996), who estimated these rates for 1987 and 1995 at 48 and 20 percent, respectively. These authors also projected the corresponding effective rate for 2003 at 13 percent based on the May 1995 tariff reduction package, which was to be implemented by 2003 and which was, in fact, largely implemented. For all years before 1987, we have used the 1987 values even though some tariff reduction occurred during the few years before 1987. For 1987–95 and 1995–2003, we have interpolated linearly. For 2004, we have used the 2003 value. (As noted above, the focus of this discussion is the identification of broad long-run trends in the structure of protection rather than annual fluctuations.)

References

Anderson, K., M. Kurzweil, W. Martin, D. Sandri, and E. Valenzuela. 2008. "Measuring Distortions to Agricultural Incentives, Revisited." *World Trade Review* 7 (4): 675–704.

Booth, A. 1988. *Agricultural Development in Indonesia*. Sydney: Allen and Unwin.

BPS (Badan Pusat Statistik, Statistics Indonesia). 1971. *Input-Output Tables, Indonesia*. Jakarta: BPS.

———. 1980. *Input-Output Tables of Indonesia*. Jakarta: BPS.

———. 1990. *Input-Output Tables of Indonesia*. Jakarta: BPS.

———. 2000. *Input-Output Tables of Indonesia*. Jakarta: BPS.

Corden, W. M. 1984. "Booming Sector and Dutch Disease Economics: A Survey." *Oxford Economic Papers* 36 (3): 359–80.

Fane, G., and T. Condon. 1996. "Trade Reform in Indonesia, 1987–1995." *Bulletin of Indonesian Economic Studies* 32 (3): 33–54.

Fane, G., and P. Warr. 2007. "Distortions to Agricultural Incentives in Indonesia." Agricultural Distortions Working Paper 24, World Bank, Washington, DC.

Hill, H. 2000. *The Indonesian Economy*. 2nd ed. Cambridge: Cambridge University Press.

Timmer, C. P. 1996. "Does Bulog Stabilize Rice Prices in Indonesia? Should it Try?" *Bulletin of Indonesian Economic Studies* 32 (2): 45–74.

Warr, P. G. 1986. "Indonesia's Other Dutch Disease: Economic Effects of the Petroleum Boom." In *Natural Resources and the Macroeconomy,* ed. J. P. Neary and S. van Wijnbergen, 288–320. Oxford: Basil Blackwell.

———. 1992. "Comparative Advantage and Protection in Indonesia 1." *Bulletin of Indonesian Economic Studies* 28 (3): 41–70.

———. 2005. "Food Policy and Poverty in Indonesia: A General Equilibrium Analysis." *Australian Journal of Agricultural and Resource Economics* 49 (4): 429–51.

World Development Indicators Database. World Bank. http://go.worldbank.org/B53SONGPA0 (accessed May 2008).

5

MALAYSIA

Prema-Chandra Athukorala
and Wai-Heng Loke

Malaysia is notable among developing countries for its long-standing commitment to the maintenance of a relatively open trade policy regime. It has never relied heavily on quantitative restrictions or other forms of nontariff protection, and its tariffs on domestic manufacturing and agriculture have been low relative to similar tariffs in other developing countries. In the first half of the 1980s—as part of a government-led strategy of heavy industrialization—and in the immediate aftermath of the 1997–98 economic crisis, tariffs on some manufactured goods were substantially increased, and some goods were brought under quantitative restrictions to support selected domestic industries in the face of a massive domestic economic contraction. However, these measures were eventually reversed, and additional tariff cuts were undertaken in the ensuing years.

Unlike its counterparts in other countries, the Malaysian government has consistently avoided exerting direct influence on export prices or the direct procurement of agricultural output through government marketing boards. Export duties on the two major primary commodities, rubber and palm oil, were a major source of government revenue until the mid-1980s. However, export taxes were periodically adjusted in line with world price trends to keep producer prices relatively stable. The government also plowed a significant share of this revenue into well-designed and efficiently implemented replanting schemes and productivity-enhancing research in these industries. Over the past two decades, export duties on rubber and palm oil have decreased drastically. However, these traditional export industries have been under persistent domestic cost pressure, which has arisen from the rapid structural transformation of the economy through successful global integration.

The production of paddy rice—the staple food of the country and the principal domestic food crop—stands out as the single most heavily assisted economic activity. During the immediate postwar years, assistance for this crop was introduced by the colonial government on the grounds of food security. After independence, particularly after the launch, in 1970, of the New Economic Policy (*Dasar Ekonomi Baru*), a sweeping affirmative action policy package aimed at increasing the share of certain ethnic groups in the economy, rice became an increasingly sensitive political crop. While the achievement of food self-sufficiency has continued to represent a moving target in successive development plans, protection for rice farmers, who are concentrated in relatively economically backward states, remains the overwhelmingly predominant reason behind protection. Producers of subsidiary crops, horticultural products, livestock, and fishing products have been operating under a virtually free trade regime throughout, with the exception of quantitative restrictions on the importation of round cabbages. High-value (processed) food products have emerged as an important dynamic export product over the past two decades.

This chapter has two main purposes: first, to provide an analytical narrative of the nature and evolution of trade in Malaysia and the related and accompanying policies that have had an impact on domestic agriculture (with a focus on the underlying political economy) and, second, to examine the degree of and changing patterns in the policy distortions affecting the incentives in domestic agriculture, including both direct (sector-specific) incentives and indirect incentives emanating from economy-wide policies. We also aim to inform the debate in Malaysia on the future direction of national development policy as it relates to domestic agriculture. The analysis is undertaken against the backdrop of the ongoing process of rapid structural transformation of the country's economy over the past three decades. As an integral part of the analysis, we attempt to delineate the implications—over and above the implications of policy-induced incentives—of the process of structural transformation for the long-term viability of traditional plantation crops and the new opportunities for agricultural output expansion in the subsidiary food-crop subsector.

Our study covers the period from 1960 (the earliest year for which reliable data are available after independence in 1957) to 2004. We emphasize four major products: rubber, palm oil, cocoa, and rice. The first three are exportable products, while the fourth, the main food staple, is an import-competing product. Together, the four products accounted for three-fifths to four-fifths of the value of total agricultural gross domestic product (GDP) over the period. Because of the paucity of data, we are unable to cover other commodities, but virtually all other agricultural products have been facing free trade conditions throughout the period we study.

The structure of the chapter is as follows. The next section provides an overview of growth and structural change in the economy during the postindependence era (since 1957), with an emphasis on the relative importance of the agricultural sector and the trends and compositional shifts in agricultural output and trade. This is followed by a survey of the evolution of agricultural trade policy during the era since 1957 against the backdrop of overall national development strategy and macroeconomic policy. We pay particular attention to the political economy considerations that underpin policy directions. In the subsequent section, we provide estimates of the extent of and patterns in the direct and indirect distortions in the incentives faced by domestic agriculture. The estimates are based on indicators that have been specifically constructed for our study. The final section contains a summary of the key findings and policy inferences.

Agriculture in the Malaysian Economy

To aid an understanding of the policy environment in Malaysia, we explain the growth trends in the economy and the patterns of structural change intersectorally and within the agricultural sector.

Economic growth trends

At independence in 1957, Malaysia was a classic agrarian economy in which agriculture and the mineral industry were concentrated in primary production for export (Levin 1960). Natural rubber directly accounted for 25 percent of GDP, while the second largest export, tin, accounted for 5 percent (Meerman 1979). In addition, a host of service activities that embraced trade, transport, and finance was dependent on the export sector. Production patterns exhibited only limited changes until about the mid-1970s. The structural changes since then have been dramatic, however. In particular, beginning in the late 1980s, there has been an expansion in export-oriented manufacturing and related activities in the modern sector. The share of agriculture in GDP had declined to 19 percent by the late 1980s and then plummeted to 8.5 percent in 2005 (table 5.1 and figure 5.1).

In the early 1970s, agriculture directly absorbed about half the total labor employed in the country. This share had declined to 13.7 percent by 2005. The contraction in the relative importance of agriculture in total labor absorption was particularly marked over the two decades before 2005 (table 5.1). Despite this dramatic structural transition, the promotion of employment opportunities in the rural economy, which is roughly equivalent to the agricultural sector, has continued to be an important focus of the government's successive 10-year development plans. This is so particularly because of the delicate ethnic dimension involved: over

Table 5.1. Agriculture in the Economy, Malaysia, 1970–2005
(percent)

Year	Real annual average growth		Share of agriculture	
	In GDP	In agriculture	In GDP	In employment
1970–74	2.3	3.4	25.5	50.9
1975–79	7.3	5.2	23.3	46.4
1980–84	6.6	3.4	20.4	39.5
1985–89	4.8	4.3	19.1	32.4
1990–94	9.3	0.2	15.3	26.9
1995–99	5.2	0.1	10.1	17.9
2000–04	5.2	3.8	8.7	15.0
2005	5.3	2.1	8.5	13.7

Source: Ministry of Finance, various.

Figure 5.1. Commodity Composition of Agricultural GDP, Malaysia, 1965–2005

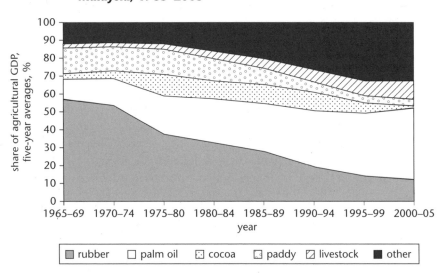

Sources: Author compilation based on data of the Economic Planning Unit; Athukorala and Loke 2007.

Note: The figure excludes forestry and forestry products.

90 percent of the agricultural labor force belongs to the Malay community. The incidence of poverty in the rural economy is still high. The poverty rate was 11 percent in the rural economy in 2003, while it was only 2.2 percent in the urban sector and 6 percent, on average, at the national level (Economic Planning Unit 2006).

Over the past three decades or so, the agricultural sector has been under constant pressure because of the resource-pull effects of the rapid structural changes in the economy (Barlow and Jayasuriya 1987; Athukorala and Manning 1999). Widening urban-rural wage differentials and an aversion among younger people to engagement in agricultural pursuits has increased rural-to-urban labor migration. This has caused widespread labor shortages in the rural economy and added to the stress on agricultural wages. The area under traditional plantation crops has shrunk in semiurban areas because of the dispersion of industrial centers across Peninsular Malaysia and the resulting higher demand for land for residential and industrial expansion. In the face of severe shortages of local labor, agricultural producers—at first, plantation enterprises and, more recently, smallholder producers of cash crops and paddy—began to rely increasingly on foreign workers. The estimated foreign labor force in Malaysia increased from around 500,000 in the mid-1980s to 1.8 million (23 percent of the total labor force) by 2003; about half of these workers were in the agricultural sector (Athukorala 2006a). The dependence on foreign labor is particularly high in the rubber industry because of the relatively high labor intensity of cultivation and harvesting. However, the relatively more capital-intensive palm oil industry also began to depend more on foreign workers because fresh fruit bunch-harvesting is conducted manually. According to a recent Malayan Agricultural Producers Association survey, 37 percent of the total labor force on private sector plantations in Peninsular Malaysia are foreign workers, while the share is as high as 80 percent in East Malaysia (Khoo and Chandramohan 2002).

Structural changes: plantation (cash) crops

Beginning in the 1890s, rubber was the preferred crop of the foreign-owned estate sector during the colonial period (Barlow 1978). Oil palms were first commercially planted in 1917 (although palm oil remained a relatively minor crop until the mid-1950s). During the ensuing three decades, palm oil proved to be more profitable than rubber and expanded in the plantation subsector at the expense of rubber. The government policy emphasis in the plantation subsector shifted dramatically from rubber to palm oil, and the support for the expansion of palm oil production increased when rubber replanting grants—grants to plant oil palms on land still under rubber—began to be distributed. The government played a vigorous role in the expansion of palm oil production by embarking on a large resettlement effort (especially though the Federal Land Development Authority) under which palm oil was the crop of choice (Pletcher 1991).[1] The country's success in promoting palm oil exports was aided by the inappropriate agricultural and economy-wide policies of the traditional palm oil exporting countries in

Africa (MacBean 1989; Athukorala 1991). Cocoa gained importance as an alternative crop in the plantation subsector starting around the beginning of the 1970s. However, about the mid-1980s, producers began to contract the area under cocoa cultivation sharply because of the persistently low world prices for cocoa beans.

Around the late 1980s, the plantation subsector came under severe strain because of the resource-pull effects of the rapid structural changes in the economy (see elsewhere above). These effects were felt more acutely in the rubber and cocoa industries, where the cultivation and harvesting processes were more labor intensive relative to the palm oil industry. Moreover, the world prices for the two former products were unfavorable relative to the world price of palm oil. At the end of the crop cycle, many plantation enterprises and smallholders replanted some of the land given over to rubber with less labor-intensive crops, particularly oil palms, or used the land for residential and industrial expansion.

Many rubber estate companies were facing hard times. They began employing foreign workers to overcome labor shortages, and then they used their technology and their management expertise to invest in neighboring countries (particularly Indonesia and the Philippines) in which wages and land cost less. Smallholders also continued to tap rubber using hired migrant labor, although the higher price elasticity of supply among the smallholders resulted in declining output when output prices fell in the early 1990s (Barlow 1997). In recent years, despite the natural cushion provided by the relative capital intensity of production and the relatively favorable price trend, the palm oil subsector has also felt the pinch of the resource-pull effects. Many large plantation enterprises have shifted their investments to neighboring land- and labor-abundant countries.

The three main plantation crops are rubber, palm oil, and cocoa. The area under rubber increased from 1.7 million hectares in the early 1960s to 2.0 million hectares in the late 1970s and early 1980s. However, it has declined steadily since then, reaching 1.3 million hectares in 2000–04. The area under oil palm cultivation rose from less than 100,000 hectares in 1960–64 to 3.8 million hectares in 2000–04. The expansion in output was more rapid in both rubber and palm oil than the expansion in area under cultivation. This reflects the widespread use of new high-yielding varieties and improved cultivation practices.

Since the late 1990s, the rubber and palm oil industries have benefited from increased world demand, especially growing demand in China, and the resulting favorable price trends. The palm oil industry has benefited additionally in recent years from the tight world supply of edible oils and fats and the expanding demand for biodiesel fuel, which has pushed up palm oil prices.

In the case of rubber, the supply response to favorable prices took the form of greater cropping intensity in the context of the persistent decline in cultivated area. In contrast, the area under oil palm cultivation showed some mild positive response to favorable prices. In cocoa, both the output and the area under cultivation have declined steadily since the early 1990s.

Meanwhile, the yield per hectare in palm oil rose throughout. In rubber, the yield increased notably in the 1960s and 1970s, but this was followed by virtual stagnation. The stability of rubber yields in the face of the decline in the total output of rubber occurred largely because of a contraction in the area under cultivation, which suggests that marginal plantations showing poor yields were being abandoned (Athukorala and Loke 2007).

The smallholder share of the land under rubber cultivation has always been high. In 1960–2004, it grew from 50 to 93 percent. The relatively capital-intensive palm oil industry was initially dominated by large plantations, although the smallholder share rose from 16 percent in 1970 to around 40 percent after 1990 (Athukorala and Loke 2007).[2] The dominance of estate cultivation is an unusual feature of the palm oil industry in Malaysia (and in Indonesia) because the smallholder production of palm oil is much more important in other parts of the world (Pletcher 1991).

Structural changes: food crops

Rice farming, nearly all wet paddy farming, is the major source of income for rural households in the states of the north and east in Peninsular Malaysia and parts of East Malaysia. At independence, about three-quarters of the native peasant producers (predominantly rice growers and fishermen) were Malays; about 90 percent of the rice growers were Malays; and about one-third of the economically active Malay male population represented the peasant sector (Meerman 1979). This ethnic dimension of rice farming persisted during the ensuing years, making rice a highly sensitive political crop.

Nearly half of all peasant cultivators grow some rice. The area under paddy cultivation rose from 490,000 hectares in 1960–64 to 750,000 hectares in 1970–74 and has remained near this level since then. Paddy production rose steadily from the early 1960s to the mid-1990s, however, because of increases in yield per hectare starting in the 1970s. Paddy producers were aided significantly by government policies such as sponsored irrigation schemes that permitted double cropping, the introduction of high-yielding varieties, the consolidation of paddy smallholdings through group farming in the eight granary areas, and direct assistance to farmers through price supports and credit and fertilizer subsidies (see below). By the end of the eighth plan period in 2005, almost all farming operations in major paddy growing areas had been fully mechanized. As a result, the labor input per hectare declined from 47 to 15 worker days in 1995–2000 (Economic Planning Unit 2001). At independence in 1957, about 45 percent of all rice consumed in

Malaysia was imported, but, since the mid-1970s, around 90 percent of the rice consumed has been produced in the country.

Beginning in the mid-1990s, rice production stagnated. This has been followed by a mild, but steady decline in recent years despite the constant rise in yields per hectare (Athukorala and Loke 2007). As in the case of plantation crops, paddy farming has been under pressure because of labor shortages arising from rural-to-urban labor migration and the aging of the farming community (Ahmad and Tawang 1999). It seems that massive government support has been insufficient to maintain paddy farming in the context of the enormous pressure emanating from the ongoing structural adjustment in the economy at large.

A noteworthy development in nonplantation agriculture over the past 15 years has been the rise in the output of subsidiary food products, such as fruits, vegetables, fish, and livestock, which has been growing at a more rapid rate than paddy output (Economic Planning Unit 2006). While there has been some increase in the exports of these high-value food products, the expansion in production has so far gone predominantly to satisfying domestic demand. This is because of the rapid income growth in the modern sector of the economy and the high income elasticity of demand for high-value food products relative to rice. The importance of the subsidiary food subsector is bound to rise rapidly in years to come.

Figure 5.1 provides data on the composition of the value added by agricultural production in the economy. The dominance of the plantation crop subsector in agriculture declined steadily, from 73 percent in the early 1970s to 53 percent in 2000–05. Within this subsector, there has been a noticeable shift in the composition of output from rubber toward palm oil. Cocoa accounted for around 10 percent of total agricultural GDP from the mid-1970s to the early 1990s, but this share declined thereafter, reaching negligible levels by the end of the 1990s. The combined share of food crops, which remained around 28 percent in the 1960s and 1970s, rose sharply during the ensuing years, reaching 47 percent in 2000–05. Within this subsector, the relative importance of paddy has declined appreciably over the past two decades. This reflects the compositional shift toward livestock, fish, and other subsidiary food crops, mainly fruits and vegetables.

Agricultural trade

The dramatic shifts in the structure of domestic production were closely mirrored in the patterns of export. The combined share of agricultural products in total merchandise exports declined from 39 percent in 1970–74 to 8 percent in 2000–04 (table 5.2). (The respective shares are 58 and 10 percent if timber and wood exports are included.) Among agricultural products (excluding timber and wood), the share of rubber declined from 62 to slightly less than 10 percent over the same years; this was offset by an increase in the share of palm oil from 24 to 42 percent.

Table 5.2. Product Shares, Agricultural Exports, Malaysia, 1970–2004

(percent)

Indicator	1970–74	1975–79	1985–89	1995–99	2000–04
Agriculture in merchandise exports					
Total	58	54	36	13	10
Excluding timber and wood	39	38	24	11	8
Composition, agricultural exports[a]					
Rubber	62.4	52.9	33.7	12.9	9.7
Palm oil	23.9	27.5	31.9	44.1	41.6
Cocoa	2.1	2.3	6.4	2.5	2.6
Spices	2.2	2.1	1.5	1.1	0.8
Processed food	8.7	8.5	15.6	26.2	31.6
World market share					
Rubber	62	57	37	20	19
Palm oil	70	77	75	64	55
Cocoa	3	3	11	4	4

Sources: Ministry of Finance, various; Bank Negara Malaysia, various.

a. Excluding timber and wood.

The share of Malaysia in the total world exports of natural rubber fell from 62 to around 20 percent between the late 1970s and 2004, when Malaysia was the third most important exporter of rubber in the world after Thailand and Indonesia (Athukorala and Loke 2007). In world crude palm oil exports, Malaysia was the largest exporter until recently, accounting for a share between 65 and 80 percent from the mid-1970s to the late 1990s. Indonesia has since become the world's largest exporter; it now accounts for over 50 percent of total world exports (not shown in table 5.2). This is the result of massive investment in relocation by Malaysian plantation companies in the face of mounting domestic cost pressures.

A noteworthy development in the structure of exports over the past two decades has been the emergence of processed food as a dynamic export line. The average annual growth rate of processed food exports rose from 5 to 19 percent between 1985–99 and 2000–04. The share of processed food in total agricultural exports increased from 9 percent in 1970–74 to 16 percent in 1985–89 and 32 percent in 2000–04 (table 5.2). The rapid expansion of processed food compared with traditional food products (coffee, tea, sugar, cocoa, and so on) has been a universal phenomenon in world trade over the past two decades (Athukorala and Jayasuriya 2003).[3] The recent performance of Malaysia in this lucrative growth area, while impressive relative to past performance, has lagged behind that of many other counties (particularly Thailand) with similar agricultural resource endowments (Athukorala 2006a). An interesting issue that deserves more analysis revolves around whether the country's highly interventionist paddy sector support policy has constrained a shift in agricultural resources to these new, more dynamic product lines.

Policy Context

The development prospects of Malaysia (then the Federation of Malaya) at independence in 1957 were mixed at best.[4] On the positive side, the country's per capita income was on a par with incomes in Hong Kong, China and Taiwan, China and higher than incomes elsewhere in East Asia, save Japan. Although the rate of population growth was already rapid, the highly favorable ratio of land and other natural resources to total population offered great potential to raise per capita incomes. Moreover, the colonial inheritance included well-developed infrastructure, efficient administrative mechanisms, and a thriving primary export sector with considerable potential for expansion.

The mobilization of this development potential to build the economy of the newly independent Malaysia had to be accomplished in the face of challenges posed by a pluralistic society inherited from the colonial past. At the time, ethnic Malays, who accounted for 52 percent of the population, dominated in politics, but were relatively poor and were involved mostly in low-productivity agricultural activities. Ethnic Chinese (37 percent of the population) enjoyed greater economic power and dominated in the modern sector, but they did not match the ethnic solidarity or political power of the Malays.[5] Ethnic divisions weakened the national fabric; the machinery of government was fragile, and the democratic political leadership remained untested. In this context, there was not much room for optimism regarding the development policies that might be expected from the newly elected government (World Bank 1955). The development challenges faced by the country were generally considered more problematic than the challenges being faced in other countries that had also newly emerged from a colonial past, particularly Ghana, India, Kenya, Myanmar, and Pakistan.[6]

From independence to the mid-1960s, national development policy was generally in line with traditional liberal notions of the limited state. The public command of economic resources in these early years was narrow, and prevailing economic policies were conservative. The policy thrust basically involved continuing the colonial open-door policy stance relating to trade and industry, while attempting to redress ethnic and regional economic imbalances through rural development schemes and the provision of social and physical infrastructure (Snodgrass 1980).

As in many other developing countries, industrialization through import substitution was a key part of the Malaysian development strategy during this period. However, Malaysian policy makers, unlike their counterparts in other countries, did not seek forced industrialization through direct import restrictions and the establishment of state-owned industrial enterprises (Lim 1992).[7] Moderate tariff protection was, by and large, the key instrument used to encourage new investment in manufacturing. The average tariff rate in 1965 has been estimated at a mere 13 percent, and few industries enjoyed nominal tariffs above 30 percent. Nontariff barriers were almost nonexistent (Power 1971; Lin 1984).

The race riots in Kuala Lumpur in 1969 generated a dramatic shift in development policy along ethnic lines. The leadership of the ruling National Front concluded that severe discrepancies in wealth had to be rapidly eliminated, partly though public sector activity, if the country was to evolve into an integrated community. The basic goals of the leadership were the eradication of poverty through a rise in incomes and the creation of more opportunities for all Malaysians irrespective of race, as well as a rapid transformation of society to correct economic imbalances and reduce and eventually eliminate the association between race and economic role (Government of Malaysia 1971). However, in the language of the New Economic Policy, a larger share of gross national product among Malays was not to be provided at the expense of the citizens in other ethnic groups. Given the delicate ethnic composition of the ruling coalition, economic equality was to be fostered primarily by raising employment and establishing a mechanism to ensure that a greater share of any newly generated assets would accrue to Malays. The redistribution of existing assets was anathema. Nationalization, land reform, and local or foreign expropriation were not considered in the New Economic Policy (Ness 1967; Snodgrass 1980; Ganguly 2003).

Because of the crucial role played by foreign-owned companies in the production and marketing of plantation crops, the government took care to pursue favorable and unambiguous policies toward direct foreign investment. Transferring a progressively larger share of foreign-owned companies to local ownership was a declared policy objective, but the government consistently declared that the transfer of ownership would occur through formal share trading rather than through arbitrary expropriation (Myint 1984; Pletcher 1991).

In the first half of the 1980s, the promotion of heavy industries through direct government involvement was emphasized as part of the Look East policy of Mahathir bin Mohamad, who became prime minister in 1981. The symbol of the selective industrial policy that resulted was the Proton, the Malaysian national car project, a joint venture of DRB-HICOM and the Mitsubishi Corporation, Japan. By 1987, there were 867 public corporate enterprises in the country, more than one-third of which were manufacturing enterprises. Tariffs on a wide range of manufactured goods were substantially increased in the first half of the 1980s as part of the shift toward heavy industrialization. However, there was no significant reliance on quantitative import restrictions (Athukorala and Menon 1999).

The economic crisis of 1985–87—caused by a combination of adverse price trends among the country's major export products and the budget deficits arising from the shift toward heavy industrialization—put an end to the government-led push toward heavy industrialization. The policy package assembled to manage the crisis placed greater emphasis on the role of the private sector and fostered more favorable conditions for export-oriented industrialization through the greater participation of foreign direct investment. The structural adjustment reform package that was subsequently introduced sought the gradual privatization and restructuring of publicly owned enterprises. The reforms of the late 1980s also involved significant tariff reductions and the removal of quantitative import restrictions. Some of the tariff increases introduced in the first half of the 1980s were reversed, and additional tariff cuts were implemented as part of the market-oriented reforms. By the early 1990s, public sector ownership in manufacturing was limited to a modest number of politically sensitive ventures in automobile manufacturing (the Proton project) and in the cement, petrochemical, and iron and steel industries.

The policy response to the 1997–98 Asian financial crisis involved a departure from the persistent trade liberalization of the previous decade (Athukorala 2002). The 1998 budget relied on higher import duties on automobiles, vans, and motor-cycles. The duties rose from 30–200 to 40–300 percent for completely assembled motor vehicles, from 4–42 to 30–80 percent for unassembled motor vehicles, and from 0–35 to 5–50 percent for construction equipment. In addition, other products were brought under nonautomatic import licensing. This included heavy equipment, construction equipment, hot-, cold-, and flat-rolled products of iron or nonalloy steel, ephedrine and ephedrine salts, chemical products, and selected household electrical appliances. The declared purpose of these measures was to bring down the current account deficit; but cushioning local producers, including the national car producer, Proton, against contractions in domestic demand was also a key motivating factor. However, there was no notable retreat from the long-standing commitment to a highly open trade regime.

Despite recent tariff increases, the average applied import duty rate—total duty collection as a percentage of total merchandise exports—has declined steadily (Athukorala and Loke 2007). The underlying tariff structure is far from uniform, however. The domestic automobile market is heavily protected through tariff and nontariff measures. At the two-digit level of the Harmonized Commodity Description and Coding System, the average nominal tariff on automobiles is 30 percent, while all the other tariff rates are around or below 20 percent.[8] The overall tariff structure cascades: the tariffs on final goods are generally higher than the tariffs on production inputs (intermediate and capital goods) (Athukorala 2005).

As part of its World Trade Organization commitments, Malaysia has bound 65 percent of its tariff lines. The bound rates are much higher than the applied most favored nation rates (Athukorala 2002).[9] This feature of the tariff structure has given the government scope to raise applied tariffs (in 1998), thereby imparting a degree of uncertainty to these tariffs. There are no import quotas in Malaysia, and import prohibitions are limited to the prohibitions implemented for national security reasons. By the mid-1990s, only 4.5 percent of all tariff lines involved tariffs that were not ad valorem. This share had declined to 0.7 percent by 2002 because of the additional rationalization of the tariff structure following the Uruguay Round agreement in 1995. There are no tariff quotas or variable import levies (Athukorala 2002). By 2000, the coverage ratio (unweighted) of nontariff barriers in import trade amounted to 2.3 percent, down from the 3.7 percent of the mid-1990s.[10] Despite recent tariff increases, the average tariff rate is relatively low by regional standards in terms of both the simple average and the import-weighted average. However, measured by the coefficient of variation, the degree of dispersion among tariff rates is relatively high because of high tariffs for a few product lines, especially motor vehicles (Athukorala 2005).

Agricultural trade policy: plantation crops

Duties on the two major primary export commodities, rubber and palm oil, were a major source of government revenue until the mid-1980s. Subsequently, duty rates were adjusted in line with world price trends to maintain stable producer prices. Export duties were reduced sharply beginning in the mid-1980s when the viability of some industries was under severe strain because of labor shortages and rising wages, which were propelled by dramatic structural changes in the economy that were driven by export-led industrialization (Ariff and Semudram 1990). The reduction of export duties was aided by tax buoyancy in a rapidly growing economy and by increasing government revenue from petroleum exports.

The import duty rates on rubber and palm oil, which increased steadily in the 1960s and 1970s, have declined over the past two decades. In 2000–04, the average annual duty rate was 4.7 percent on rubber and 1.1 percent on palm oil. The higher duty rate on rubber was generated by the additional duty (cess) that continued to be levied to finance the rubber replanting scheme. Duties ranging from 5 to 10 percent are levied on specific grades of crude palm oil to promote domestic processing. By 2000, only a few other primary products, such as selected forest products and crude oil, were subject to export duties. Export duties contributed a mere 2 percent to total government revenue (Ministry of Finance 2006).

Conventional trade policy and direct government support through funding for research and replanting schemes by and large lost their relevance when the structural changes in the economy began severely to impede the long-term viability of plantation crops. Consequently, in recent years, the focus of policy has shifted toward new issues such as forging links between the agricultural sector and the rapidly growing manufacturing sectors, improving the productivity and efficiency of certain agricultural subsectors, and assisting plantation enterprises in relocating to other countries where factor market conditions enable profitable production. Relaxing restrictions on labor imports both formally and informally (that is, by turning a blind eye to illicit immigration) has also become an important short-tem measure for reducing labor market pressures (Athukorala 2006a).

Agricultural trade policy: food crops

Rice is the single most highly assisted crop since the guaranteed price scheme was introduced by the colonial government in 1949 (Ness 1967; Meerman 1979; Pletcher 1989; Zubaidi 1992; Rudner 1994). The emphasis on assistance for paddy farmers gained impetus after independence, particularly as part of the New Economic Policy.

The government has assisted rice producers through an all-encompassing guaranteed minimum price scheme, a price subsidy scheme, and a fertilizer subsidy. In 1998 (the latest year for which data are available), the total government expenditure on the three schemes amounted to RM 547 million (US$150 million) or about 3 percent of the total value added for this crop. The guaranteed minimum price scheme was first introduced in 1949, and the minimum price was subsequently adjusted in 1973, 1974, 1979, 1980, 1984, and 1997. Under the scheme, Bernas (a government trading company) undertakes to buy paddy from farmers at no less than the guaranteed minimum price (since 2000, RM 5.49 per kilogram). Bernas procures paddy from farmers and mills rice as a business operation. It competes with private millers in the procurement of paddy and the marketing of milled rice. It purchases about 45 percent of the marketable surplus paddy available. Only Bernas is permitted to import rice (at zero duty) into the country. It undertakes to import rice and implement the rice price subsidy program under a long-term contract with the government. The import volume is determined by Bernas according to the shortfall in production over consumption. Rice millers are required to produce 30 percent of their output at standard and premium quality. Bernas is free to determine the price for its superior quality rice, and the profits realized on this rice are used to cross-subsidize the minimum production required in standard- and medium-quality rice.

A cash subsidy for every ton of paddy sold was introduced in 1980 and was increased in 1984 and 1990. Under this scheme, the government makes a fixed payment to farmers (currently RM 2.48 per kilogram) for the paddy sold by them to any commercial rice mills. The subsidy is provided in addition to the guaranteed minimum price received by farmers. The fertilizer subsidy scheme has been in operation since 1985. There was also a subsidy credit scheme for paddy farmers, but this was terminated in 1996. In 2004, the total government outlay on the price subsidy and the fertilizer subsidy was RM 477 million (about 2 percent of the value added in the paddy subsector). The government also assists paddy farmers by providing drainage and irrigation facilities and management and extension services. The total outlay on these support measures accounted for around 1.5 percent of the total value added in the paddy subsector in 2004 (WTO 2006).

Accompanying policies

Despite instances of policy slippage, government macroeconomic policy was generally sound over the period under analysis. It supported growth and structural transition in the real sectors of the economy. Budget deficits were mostly kept within prudent limits, while the use of borrowed funds was minimized. The government continued to adhere strictly to the colonial policy of avoiding loans from the central bank for budgetary purposes. Overall deficits arose occasionally, but they were financed through noninflationary domestic sources, particularly the private savings accumulated in the Employee's Provident Fund. Moreover, the broadening of the tax base when the economy boomed, coupled with greater efficiency in tax collection, brought about a rapid increase in government revenues. For the first time in the history of the country, the government achieved a balanced budget in 1993, and budget balance was maintained in subsequent years. Relative to 1986–89, the public sector was a net saver in 1990–96. Fiscal balance as a share of GDP shifted from an annual average deficit of 2.5 percent to a surplus of 1.5 percent between these two periods. Deficit financing reemerged, however, as part of the policy response to the 1997–98 financial crisis. The budget deficit as a share of GDP rose from 1.8 to 5.2 percent in 1998–2002. The share fell thereafter, reaching 3.5 percent in 2006.

By developing countrywide standards, Bank Negara Malaysia (the central bank) has maintained an impressive track record in maintaining domestic price stability and averting real exchange rate misalignment (Corden 1996; Athukorala 2001). As part of the macroeconomic adjustment package launched in 1986, greater flexibility was introduced to the basket peg. The policy of Bank Negara Malaysia involved allowing the exchange rate to reflect underlying trends in the economy, while intervening in the foreign exchange market to smooth the excessive fluctuation in exchange rate movements that was caused by fluctuations in short-term capital inflows. This policy was successful in achieving significant depreciation in the overall real exchange rate from 1987 to about 1993. There was a mild appreciation of the real exchange rate in the three years leading up to the financial crisis in 1997. This reflected macroeconomic imbalances in the booming economy. The crisis was instrumental in reversing the appreciation. By 2000, although the exchange rate of the ringgit had been fixed against the U.S. dollar (at RM 3.8 per dollar) in September 1998 and despite the deficit financing that had been undertaken as part of the crisis management package, the real exchange rate had depreciated by almost 20 percent against precrisis levels.[11] It has remained virtually unchanged since then.

Athukorala and Loke (2007) show that, over the past three decades, the real exchange rate in the export crop subsector has been behaving quite differently from the overall real exchange rate. Notwithstanding periodic depreciations triggered by increases in world commodity prices, the exchange rate in the export crop subsector has appreciated steadily over the past 25 years. This contrast reflects the ongoing structural transformation of the economy that has resulted in a deterioration in the relative profitability of the traditional plantation crop subsector.

Trends and Patterns in Distortions in Agricultural Incentives

In this section, we provide an analysis of the changing scope of and patterns in direct and indirect distortions in the incentives faced by domestic agriculture in Malaysia. We use the methodology developed by Anderson et al. (2008) and described in appendix A. The main focus of the methodology in our study is government-imposed distortions that create a gap between domestic prices and prices as they would be under free-market conditions. Since it is not possible to understand the characteristics of agricultural development through a sectoral view alone, we estimate not only the effects of direct agricultural policy measures, but also, for comparative evaluation, the distortions in nonagricultural tradables. Specifically, we compare the nominal rates of assistance (NRAs) for tradable farm products with the NRAs for nonagricultural tradables by calculating indicators of the relative rate of assistance (RRA). In our calculations, we assume that the agricultural products that we do not cover have an average NRA of zero, and we assume that the shares of noncovered farm production are one-third each for exportables, importables, and nontradables.

We have been unable to avoid two important limitations in our estimates because of a lack of data. First, in the case of the three plantation (cash) crops, rubber, palm oil, and cocoa, we ignore the potential differences between border (reference) prices and domestic prices that arise because of quality differences. This may infuse an underestimation bias into our calculations. Second, in all cases, we have assumed that there is a complete pass-through to farmgate prices of any change in wholesale prices. This may introduce an upward bias into our estimates. These limitations are only important, however, in comparisons among the effects on incentives among products or across countries at a given moment. They are unlikely to distort inferences based on intertemporal comparisons (changes in incentives over time) because the magnitude of the bias is less liable to vary over time. It is also important to note that, because of our estimation method, our RRA estimates do not fully capture the distortions in agricultural incentives arising from changes in the tariffs on tradable inputs. Given the cascading nature of Malaysia's tariff structure, this is a potentially important source of downward bias in the RRA estimates (Athukorala 2006b).

Our estimates of the direct distortions in the incentives for covered products are reported as five-year averages in table 5.3, and they are shown as annual averages in summary form in figure 5.2. The average NRAs for all covered products were negative from 1960 to 1984, but the magnitude of the NRAs declined during the period. The five-year average fluctuated between 0 and 3 percent starting in the mid-1980s. However, this aggregate picture conceals the significant assistance provided to paddy farmers.

NRA estimates for individual commodities point to broadly similar patterns in the changes in the incentives faced by the two most important plantation products, rubber and palm oil (table 5.3). In both cases, the NRAs were negative throughout, but the absolute magnitude declined sharply over the two most recent decades. This reflected cuts in export duties. However, with the exception of some of the earlier years, the negative incentives in the palm oil industry were much lower in magnitude relative to the incentives in the rubber industry. For the entire period of 1960–2004, the annual average NRA for palm oil was −7.5, compared with −11.5 for rubber. Given that the fortunes of both products have been predominantly determined by domestic resource-pull effects that have arisen because of rapid structural adjustment in the wider economy, the generally high negative assistance to rubber relative to palm oil remains a puzzling feature of the structure of the incentives. Cocoa was never taxed heavily because it was always considered a minor export crop. The NRA for this product varied between 0 and −3 percent over the period.

Among the four products under study, paddy rice is notable for a persistently high rate of assistance. The average NRA for paddy and rice in the 1960s and early 1970s was 8.5 percent, although there was a high degree of annual fluctuation. The average rice NRA was nearly 40 percent in 1975–79 following an upward adjustment in the guaranteed minimum price. It then reached a peak average of

Table 5.3. NRAs for Covered Agricultural Products, Malaysia, 1960–2004
(percent)

Indicator, product	1960–64	1965–69	1970–74	1975–79	1980–84	1985–89	1990–94	1995–99	2000–04
Exportables[a]	−12.1	−9.6	−13.4	−20.0	−12.8	−5.6	−4.7	−3.6	−1.6
Palm oil	−11.4	−10.6	−15.2	−15.0	−5.8	−3.2	−3.1	−3.0	−1.1
Cocoa	0.0	−1.2	−2.8	−1.7	−1.5	−1.4	−2.3	−2.1	0.0
Rubber	−12.1	−9.5	−12.8	−22.5	−18.2	−8.7	−8.1	−6.8	−4.7
Import-competing products[a]	19.1	−1.9	3.1	39.2	93.8	158.0	127.2	57.4	71.0
Rice	19.1	−1.9	3.1	39.2	93.8	158.0	127.2	57.4	71.0
All covered products[a]	−8.4	−8.7	−10.5	−15.3	−5.7	1.8	3.4	−0.3	2.4
Dispersion, covered products[b]	30.6	18.5	21.1	43.8	53.4	65.8	57.3	36.7	43.2
Coverage, at undistorted prices	86	86	86	85	80	75	67	59	57

Source: Athukorala and Loke 2007.

a. Weighted averages; the weights are based on the unassisted value of production.
b. Dispersion is a simple five-year average of the annual standard deviation around the weighted mean of the NRAs of covered products.

Figure 5.2. NRAs for Exportable, Import-Competing, and All Agricultural Products, Malaysia, 1960–2004

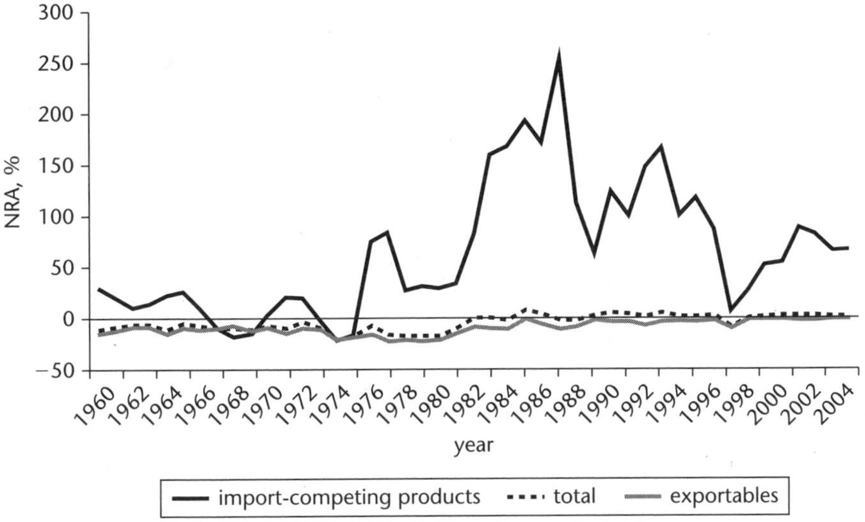

Source: Athukorala and Loke 2007.

158 percent during the five years from 1985 to 1989 following the introduction of a price subsidy (over and above the guaranteed minimum price). But, during the two decades following the macroeconomic crisis in 1985–87, the NRAs for paddy more than halved, although, in 2000–04, it was still above 70 percent. The disaggregated data show that the farmgate price of paddy continued to be high and that there were only periodic upward shifts resulting from increases in the guaranteed minimum price and the price subsidy (Athukorala and Loke 2007). In this context, the year-to-year variations in the NRAs arose mostly because of changes in the reference (border) price. For instance, the dramatic decline in NRAs from 127 percent in 1990–94 to 57 percent in 1995–99 was brought about by a sharp decline in world rice prices between these two periods. The NRAs then increased to 71 percent, which reflected the recovery in world prices.

Finally, a comparison of the weighted average NRAs for the exportables (rubber, palm oil, and cocoa) and the importables (which, in our case, is limited solely to paddy) points to a persistent bias in agricultural incentives in favor of import-competing production relative to export-oriented production (see the trade bias index shown in table 5.4). Based on similar estimates for 1960–82, Jenkins and Lai (1991) inferred that the excessive protection accorded to paddy farmers had a negative effect on the expansion of export agriculture. This inference does not seem

Table 5.4. NRAs in Agriculture Relative to Nonagricultural Industries, Malaysia, 1960–2004
(*percent*)

Indicator	1960–64	1965–69	1970–74	1975–79	1980–84	1985–89	1990–94	1995–99	2000–04
Covered products[a]	-8.4	-8.7	-10.5	-15.3	-5.7	1.8	3.4	-0.3	2.4
Noncovered products	0.0	0.0	0.0	0.0	0.0	0.0	0.0	0.0	0.0
All agricultural products[a]	-7.2	-7.5	-9.0	-13.0	-4.6	1.3	2.3	-0.2	1.3
Non-product-specific assistance	0.0	0.0	0.0	0.0	0.0	0.0	0.0	0.0	0.0
Total agricultural NRA[b]	-7.2	-7.5	-9.0	-13.0	-4.6	1.3	2.3	-0.2	1.3
Trade bias index[c]	-0.22	-0.06	-0.14	-0.31	-0.35	-0.33	-0.28	-0.12	-0.12
NRA, all agricultural tradables	-7.6	-7.9	-9.4	-13.7	-4.9	1.4	2.6	-0.2	1.5
NRA, all nonagricultural tradables	7.4	7.0	7.1	6.5	5.2	3.9	2.8	2.0	0.9
RRA[d]	-14.0	-13.9	-15.5	-18.9	-9.6	-2.4	-0.3	-2.2	0.6

Source: Athukorala and Loke 2007.

a. Including product-specific input subsidies.

b. Including product-specific input subsidies and non-product-specific assistance. The total assistance to primary factors and intermediate inputs, divided by the total value of primary agriculture production at undistorted prices.

c. The trade bias index is defined as $(1 + NRAag_x/100)/(1 + NRAag_m/100) - 1$, where $NRAag_m$ and $NRAag_x$ are the average percentage NRAs for the import-competing and exportable parts of the agricultural sector, respectively.

d. The RRA is defined as $100*[(100 + NRAag^t)/(100 + NRAnonag^t) - 1]$, where $NRAag^t$ and $NRAnonag^t$ are the percentage NRAs for the tradables parts of the agricultural and nonagricultural sectors, respectively.

Figure 5.3. NRAs for Agricultural and Nonagricultural Tradables and the RRA, Malaysia, 1960–2004

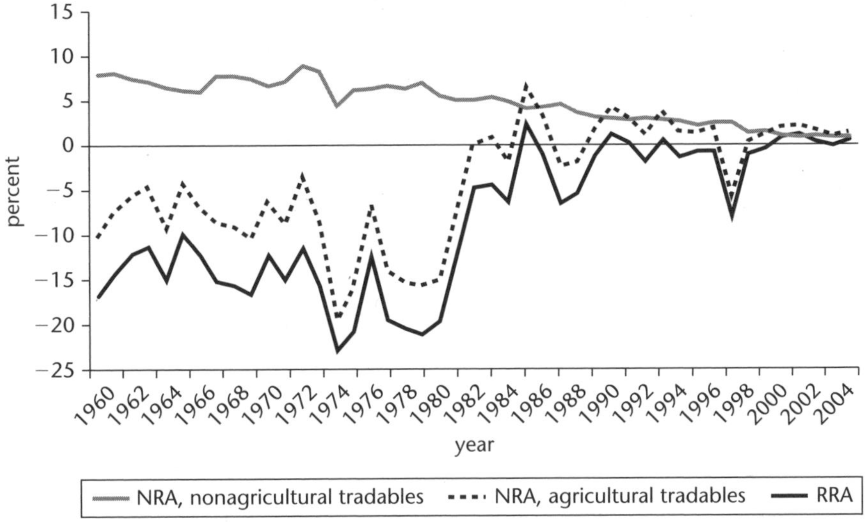

Source: Athukorala and Loke 2007.

Note: For the calculation of the RRA, see table 5.4, note d.

valid for the period starting around the late 1980s. The steady deterioration in the profitability of export-oriented agriculture, as well as paddy production, was rooted mainly in the ongoing process of structural transformation in the wider economy. Nonetheless, the significant assistance for paddy producers was presumably a major source of the distortions within the food-crop subsector. These distortions constrained resource reallocation from the structurally weak paddy subsector to high-value food production for the domestic and export markets.

The NRAs for nonagricultural tradables, which recorded a mild decline in the 1960s and 1970s, plummeted thereafter and had reached almost zero by around 2000 (figure 5.3). Direct tariff cuts and the rapid expansion in export-oriented manufacturing, which enjoys duty-free status for all imported inputs in the production process, contributed to this decline. Disaggregated data (for brevity, not reported here) show that the rapid expansion in export-oriented manufacturing continued to act as a more powerful force than the direct tariff cuts.

As a consequence of these changes in agricultural and nonagricultural assistance, average RRAs gradually shifted from larger negative levels in the earlier decades to almost zero (table 5.4). However, this does not mean that there would be no economic gains from additional policy reform. Indeed, as shown at the bottom of table 5.3, the dispersion of NRAs within the farm sector has not declined much over time; so, there is still scope for improved resource reallocation if the assistance for paddy production is phased out.

Concluding Remarks

Malaysia stands out among developing countries because of the government's long-standing commitment to the maintenance of a relatively open trade and investment policy regime. The government has persistently avoided heavy reliance on quantitative restrictions and other forms of nontariff protection. Tariffs on domestic manufacturing and agriculture continue to be low relative to the corresponding tariffs in other developing countries. Export taxes, which were important sources of government revenue until about the mid-1980s, were reduced when the plantation subsector experienced severe cost pressure because of rapid growth and structural change under export-led industrialization. The average level of import tariffs also declined significantly, notwithstanding the periodic upward adjustment in some tariffs and the special case of the heavy protection in the automotive industry. The government's record of commitment to openness is particularly remarkable in that it reflects unilateral and voluntary policy choices rather than pressure from major trading partners or from conditions imposed by multilateral donor agencies or resulting from negotiations under the auspices of the World Trade Organization.

Nonetheless, there are notable anomalies in the incentive structure in Malaysia that encourage the channeling of resources into inefficient activities. In particular, the tariff structure is characterized by a dualistic pattern whereby export-oriented production occurs within a virtual free trade regime, side-by-side with production predominantly oriented toward the domestic market in manufacturing and agriculture and assisted through tariff protection. The tariff rate structure is also characterized by a high degree of dispersion because of high tariff peaks on a few product lines and growing reliance on nonautomatic import licensing to regulate the imports of a significant number of products that directly compete with the domestic production carried out by public sector enterprises. This substantial departure from neutrality implies that there is ample room for policy discretion, as opposed to pure economic policy, in the effort to influence resource allocation in the economy.

The excessive assistance for paddy farmers remains a major distortion in agricultural incentives. In addition to the obvious welfare implications, this anomaly presumably hinders the diversification of domestic agriculture toward new dynamic product lines. Given the ongoing process of dramatic structural transformation in the economy that has ushered in an era of massive urban-to-rural labor migration and generates cost pressures on traditional agriculture, the case for protecting paddy farmers on self-sufficiency grounds has lost relevance. The outright dismantling of assistance is a nonoption because of political economy considerations. Nonetheless, there is a strong case for replacing the existing complicated and costly incentives with direct income support for farmers. The fiscal burden of this support is unlikely to be high because the agricultural labor force has been rapidly depleting, and the incidence of rural poverty, though relatively high by national standards, has been declining. This issue deserves additional systematic analysis.

Notes

1. By 1984, the Federal Land Development Authority accounted for 28 percent of the 1.3 million hectares under oil palms.

2. The bulk of the land classified as smallholding in these data involves farmers who participate in large government-run plantation schemes. Smallholders who do not participate in these schemes account for only 8 percent of the planted area measured in hectares.

3. Powerful forces on both the demand side and the supply side have underpinned this structural shift. On the demand side, the internationalization of food habits—the growing significance of imported processed items in consumption patterns in developed countries, as well as among large sections of populations in many developing countries—appears to have played a key role. Factors such as international migration, the communications revolution, and tourism have contributed to the phenomenon. This significant demand-side impetus seems to have been supported by important supply-side developments such as improvements in food technology, refrigeration facilities, and transportation that have fostered international trade in various processed food products that are generally highly perishable. Indonesia is more well placed than Malaysia to benefit from this structural shift in world food trade given its rich agricultural resource base and greater availability of labor (food processing and food packaging for export are highly labor intensive).

4. The Federation of Malaya, comprising 11 states in the Malay Peninsula, secured independence from Britain on August 31, 1957. Sabah, Sarawak, and Singapore joined Malaya to form Malaysia on September 16, 1963. Singapore left the federation in August 1965.

5. The emergence of three identifiable and mutually exclusive ethnic groups as distinct, self-conscious groups (Chinese, Indian, and Malay) stemmed in substantial part from the needs and priorities of British colonial policy (Ganguly 2003).

6. In the Rosentein-Rodan (1961) growth trajectory up to 1976 for 66 countries considered developing countries at the time, Malaysia was classified in the low-growth category, together with Indonesia; the Republic of Korea; Singapore; Taiwan, China; and Thailand.

7. In a recent comprehensive study of the patterns and chronology of trade policy reforms, Sachs and Warner (1995) identify Malaysia as one of eight developing countries in which trade regimes remained open throughout the post–World War II period.

8. Unless otherwise noted, we have taken the tariff rates reported in this chapter from the latest (2003) tariff schedule available in the APEC Tariff Database.

9. In 2002, the simple average bound, unbound, and applied tariff rates were 19, 35, and 9.2 percent, respectively. All agricultural tariff lines were bound, but at much higher average levels than the manufacturing tariff lines.

10. Calculated as a percent share in total imports of the import value of the Harmonized Commodity Description and Coding System 6 tariff lines affected by nontariff barriers.

11. The ringgit peg to the U.S. dollar was eventually abandoned in favor of a managed float system. The system went into effect on July 21, 2005.

References

Ahmad, T. M. A. T., and A. Tawang. 1999. "Effects of Trade Liberalization on Agriculture in Malaysia: Commodity Aspects." CGPRT Centre Working Paper 46, Regional Co-ordination Center for Research and Development of Coarse Grains, Pulses, Roots, and Tuber Crops in the Humid Tropics of Asia and the Pacific, United Nations Economic and Social Commission for Asia and the Pacific, Bogor, Indonesia.

Anderson, K., M. Kurzweil, W. Martin, D. Sandri, and E. Valenzuela. 2008. "Measuring Distortions to Agricultural Incentives, Revisited." *World Trade Review* 7 (4): 675–704.

APEC Tariff Database (Asia Pacific Economic Cooperation Tariff Database). Asia-Pacific Economic Cooperation. http://www.apectariff.org/ (accessed May 2008).

Ariff, M., and M. Semudram. 1990. "Malaysia." In *Trade, Finance, and Developing Countries: Strategies and Constraints in the 1990s*, ed. S. Page, 23–55. London: Harvester Wheatsheaf.

Athukorala, P.-C. 1991. "An Analysis of Demand and Supply Factors in Agricultural Exports from Developing Asian Countries." *Weltwirtschaftliches Archiv* 127 (4): 764–91.

———. 2001. *Crisis and Recovery in Malaysia: The Role of Capital Controls*. Cheltenham, UK: Edward Elgar.

———. 2002. "Malaysian Trade Policy and the WTO Trade Policy Review 2001." *World Economy* 25 (9): 1299–1317.

———. 2005. "Trade Policy in Malaysia: Liberalization Process, Structure of Protection, and Reform Agenda." *ASEAN Economic Bulletin* 22 (1): 19–34.

———. 2006a. "International Labour Migration in East Asia: Trends, Patterns, and Policy Issues." *Asian-Pacific Economic Literature* 20 (1): 18–39.

———. 2006b. "Post-Crisis Export Performance: The Indonesian Experience in Regional Perspective." *Bulletin of Indonesian Economic Studies* 42 (2): 177–211.

Athukorala, P.-C., and S. K. Jayasuriya. 2003. "Food Safety Issues, Trade, and WTO Rules: A Developing Country Perspective." *World Economy* 26 (9): 141–62.

Athukorala, P.-C., and W.-H. Loke. 2007. "Distortions to Agricultural Incentives in Malaysia." Agricultural Distortions Working Paper 27, World Bank, Washington, DC.

Athukorala, P.-C., and C. Manning. 1999. *Structural Change and International Migration in East Asia: Adjusting to Labour Scarcity*. Melbourne: Oxford University Press.

Athukorala, P.-C., and J. Menon. 1999. "Outward Orientation and Economic Performance: The Malaysian Experience." *World Economy* 22 (8): 1119–39.

Bank Negara Malaysia. various issues. *Monthly Bulletin of Statistics*. Kuala Lumpur: Bank Negara Malaysia.

Barlow, C. 1978. *The Natural Rubber Industry: Its Development, Technology, and Economy in Malaysia*. Kuala Lumpur: Oxford University Press.

———. 1997. "Growth, Structural Change, and Plantation Tree Crops: The Case of Rubber." *World Development* 25 (10): 1589–1607.

Barlow, C., and S. Jayasuriya. 1987. "Structural Change and Its Impact on Traditional Agricultural Sectors of Rapidly Developing Countries: The Case of Natural Rubber." *Agricultural Economics* 1 (2): 159–74.

Corden, W. M. 1996. *Pragmatic Orthodoxy: Macroeconomic Policies in Seven East Asian Economies*. San Francisco: International Center for Economic Growth.

Economic Planning Unit. 2001. *Eighth Malaysia Plan*. Putrajaya, Malaysia: Economic Planning Unit, Prime Minister's Department.

———. 2006. *Ninth Malaysia Plan*. Putrajaya, Malaysia: Economic Planning Unit, Prime Minister's Department.

Ganguly, S. 2003. "Ethnic Policies and Political Quiescence in Malaysia and Singapore." In *Government Policies and Ethnic Relations in Asia and the Pacific*, ed. M. E. Brown and S. Ganguly, 233–72. Cambridge, MA: MIT Press.

Government of Malaysia. 1971. *Second Malaysia Plan, 1971–1975*. Kuala Lumpur: Government Printers.

Jenkins, G. P., and A. Lai. 1989. *Trade, Exchange Rate, and Agricultural Policies in Malaysia*. World Bank Comparative Study. Washington, DC: World Bank.

———. 1991. "Malaysia." In *Asia*. Vol. 2 of *The Political Economy of Agricultural Pricing Policy,* ed. A. O. Krueger, M. Schiff, and A. Valdés, 67–106. World Bank Comparative Study. Baltimore: Johns Hopkins University Press; Washington, DC: World Bank.

Khoo, K. M., and D. Chandramohan. 2002. "Malaysian Palm Oil Industry at Crossroads and Its Future Direction. *Oil Palm Industry Economic Journal* 2 (2): 10–15.

Levin, J. V. 1960. *The Export Economies*. New Haven, CT: Yale University Press.

Lim, D. 1992. "The Dynamics of Economic Policy-Making: A Study of Malaysian Trade Policies and Performance." In *The Dynamics of Economic Policy Reforms in South-East Asia and the South-West Pacific,* ed. A. J. MacIntyre and K. Jayasuriya, 94–114. Singapore: Oxford University Press.

Lin, T. Y. 1984. "Inter-ethnic Restructuring in Malaysia, 1970–80: The Employment Perspective." In *From Independence to Statehood: Managing Ethnic Conflict in Five African and Asian States*, ed. R. B. Goldman and J. Jayaratnam Wilson, 44–61. London: Frances Printer.

MacBean, A. I. 1989. "Agricultural Exports of Developing Countries: Market Conditions and National Policies." In *The Balance between Industry and Agriculture in Economic Development,* ed. N. Islam, 129–64. London: Macmillan.

Meerman, J. 1979. *Public Expenditure in Malaysia: Who Benefits and Why?* New York: Oxford University Press.

Ministry of Agriculture. 1997. *Third National Agricultural Policy, 1998–2010*. Kuala Lumpur: Ministry of Agriculture.

Ministry of Finance. 2005. *Economic Report 2005/2006*. Kuala Lumpur: Ministry of Finance.

———. 2006. *Economic Report 2006/2007*. Kuala Lumpur: Ministry of Finance.

———. various issues. *Economic Report*. Kuala Lumpur: Ministry of Finance.

Myint, H. 1984. "Inward and Outward-Looking Countries Revisited: The Case of Indonesia." *Bulletin of Indonesian Economic Studies* 20 (2): 39–52.

Ness, G. D. 1967. *Bureaucracy and Rural Development in Malaysia*. Berkeley, CA: University of California Press.

Pletcher, J. 1989. "Rice and Padi Market Management in West Malaysia, 1957–86." *Journal of Developing Areas* 23 (April): 363–84.

———. 1991. "Regulation with Growth: The Political Economy of Palm Oil in Malaysia." *World Development* 19 (6): 623–36.

Power, J. H. 1971. "Structure of Protection in West Malaysia." In *The Structure of Protection in Developing Countries*, ed. B. Balassa, 203–22. Baltimore: Johns Hopkins University Press; Washington, DC: World Bank.

Rosentein-Rodan, P. 1961. "International Aid for Underdeveloped Countries." *Review of Economics and Statistics* 43 (2): 107–38.

Rudner, M. 1994. *Malaysian Development: A Retrospective*. Ottawa: Carleton University Press.

Sachs, J. D., and A. Warner. 1995. "Economic Reforms and the Process of Global Integration." *Brookings Papers on Economic Activity* 26 (1): 1–118.

Snodgrass, D. R. 1980. *Inequality and Economic Development in Malaysia*. Kuala Lumpur: Oxford University Press.

World Bank. 1955. *The Economic Development of Malaya*. Baltimore: Johns Hopkins University Press.

WTO (World Trade Organization). 2006. *Trade Policy Review: Malaysia*. Geneva: WTO.

Zubaidi, A. 1992. "The Welfare Cost of Malaysian Rice Policy under Alternative Regimes." *Malaysian Journal of Economic Studies* 29 (2): 1–12.

6

THE PHILIPPINES

Cristina David, Ponciano Intal, and Arsenio M. Balisacan

The economic performance of the Philippines has lagged behind that of most other developing countries in Asia. Whereas the Philippine economy and agricultural sector performed moderately well in the 1960s and 1970s because of the early advent of the Green Revolution in rice and the world commodity boom, the country has shown the lowest average growth rates in South and Southeast Asia in gross domestic product (GDP), gross value added (GVA) in agriculture, and agricultural exports over the past two decades (table 6.1).

Previous studies have argued that the country's poor agricultural performance has been caused largely by weaknesses in the policies and institutional framework governing the sector and less by real domestic and external market factors (David 2003; Balisacan, Fuwa, and Debuque 2004). Government price and trade policies have distorted economic incentives, and the choice of policy instruments has promoted rent seeking and raised the economic cost of government intervention. The lack of market infrastructure, underinvestment in agricultural research, distortions in land markets because of the agrarian reform program, and other weaknesses in governance have all contributed to the poor performance in the sector.

The declining trend in tariff protection since the 1980s through a series of unilateral tariff reform programs and multilateral and regional trade agreements are well documented (Manasan and Pineda 1999; Aldaba 2005a, 2005b; Pasadilla 2006). Ex ante assessments of the welfare impacts of trade liberalization that rely on computable general equilibrium models consistently report positive effects (Clarete 1991; Cororaton 2000; Habito and Cororaton 2000). International

The authors are grateful to Ernesto Valenzuela for computational assistance.

Table 6.1. Agriculture in the Economy, Growth Rates, the Philippines and Other Asian Countries, 1960–2004
(percent)

Country	1960–80			1980–2004		
	GDP	Agriculture, GVA	Agriculture, exports	GDP	Agriculture, GVA	Agriculture, exports
Philippines	5.3	4.1	12.0	2.7	2.0	1.6
Bangladesh	2.6	1.6	3.1	4.3	2.7	1.3
China	5.5	4.3	15.0	9.5	4.2	6.6
India	3.6	2.2	9.0	5.4	3.4	5.8
Indonesia[a]	7.9	4.6	11.6	5.4	2.9	7.2
Malaysia[b]	7.2	4.8	12.7	6.6	2.2	5.7
Pakistan	5.8	3.6	14.2	4.7	3.7	7.2
Thailand	7.5	4.8	13.5	6.0	2.7	6.7
Vietnam[c]	—	—	—	6.6	3.7	18.2

Source: Author compilation based on data in World Development Indicators Database 2008; FAOSTAT Database 2008.

Note: Growth rates have been estimated through the regression method. — = no data are available.

a. 1960–80: GDP and GVA data refer to 1970–80.
b. 1960–80: GVA data refer to 1970–80.
c. 1980–2004: GVA data refer to 1985–2004.

Table 6.2. Changes in Agricultural Structure and Trade Openness, the Philippines, 1960–2004

(percent)

Indicator	1960	1970	1980	1990	2000	2004
Share of agriculture						
GDP	30	28	24	22	20	14
Employment	61	52	48	45	37	37
Imports[a]	19	14	8	10	9	8
Exports	64	44	35	15	5	6
Indicators of trade openness						
Share of agricultural imports in the GVA[a]	6 [9]	10 [16]	9 [23]	13 [27]	22 [45]	26 [51]
Share of agricultural exports in the GVA	33 [9]	44 [15]	26 [17]	14 [19]	15 [51]	19 [46]
Total agricultural imports and exports in the GVA	38 [18]	54 [36]	35 [43]	28 [48]	37 [96]	45 [97]

Sources: Compiled based on data of the National Statistical Coordination Board; the Bureau of Labor and Employment Statistics, Department of Labor and Employment; and the National Statistics Office.

Note: The numbers in square brackets refer to the corresponding indicators of trade openness in the entire economy.

a. For 2004: if agricultural inputs are included, the ratio of agricultural imports to the GVA in agriculture would be significantly higher, reaching 39 percent; the ratio of agricultural inputs to total imports based on this broader definition would be 11 percent.

studies, mostly using the Global Trade Analysis Project model, likewise generally show that the results of trade reform are favorable. Yet, after more than two decades of effort at trade liberalization, the country has not enhanced its economic performance significantly. Per capita income continues to stagnate; domestic employment opportunities remain limited; and poverty reduction lag relative to the progress being accomplished in most of the country's Asian neighbors.

Although the economy appears to have become more open if one considers the substantial rise in the ratio of the traded value of imports and exports to GDP (table 6.2), the rise in this ratio has not been accompanied by growth in GDP. The improvement in the indicators of trade openness has been achieved primarily through rapid export growth in semiconductors and electronic components that exhibit high shares of imported content and low shares of value added. The growth rate in food and agricultural exports continue to drop, and the country's dependence on agricultural imports has risen sharply (table 6.2).[1]

Several complex factors may help explain why the predicted impacts of trade liberalization have not been realized. One explanation, at least with respect to the agricultural sector, may be that the rate of trade liberalization measured according to the trends in average tariffs (typically used as indicators by local and international analysts) does not accurately reflect the extent or the direction of change in agricultural protection during recent decades.

The objective of our study is to quantify trends and patterns in agricultural distortions from the early 1960s to 2004 and explain changes in these trends and patterns over time. In the next section, historical patterns in agricultural performance and structural change are briefly described. The subsequent section examines the evolution of economy-wide and agriculture-specific policies that have distorted price incentives in the sector. In the following section, we discuss the estimated impact of these policies on agricultural incentives. The penultimate section analyzes the reasons behind policy choices, including the role of multilateral and regional trade agreements in the changes observed in recent years. Finally, we draw out the prospects for national policy reform, including the likely versus the desirable policy direction through to 2020, the implications for the choice of policy instruments and for the trend level in the distortions in agricultural incentives, and the policy lessons for other developing and transition economies.

Agricultural Performance and Structural Change

Despite the relatively slow growth of the Philippine economy, the structural transformations that have occurred in the course of economic development have not been unusual. The decline in the contribution of agriculture to GDP was rather slow from 1960 to 1980 (from 30 to 24 percent), but has become more rapid in recent years (14 percent by 2004). The decline was accompanied by a steady drop in the share of the sector in total employment from 61 to 37 percent from 1960 to 2000. The share has remained constant since then (table 6.2).

Unlike the rapid industrialization that characterized economic growth among the Asian tigers, however, the share of industry in the Philippines rose from 31 to 39 percent in 1960–80, but then fell, reaching around 30 percent by 2004. Food manufacturing accounts for about 40 percent of the industrial sector. Half of this share consists of light processing of rice, maize, sugar, coconuts, livestock, and poultry. Services have accounted for the largest contribution to GDP and total employment. While the growth in services has been driven primarily by domestic demand for logistics, trading, and financial services, the rapid expansion in business process outsourcing has been changing the nature and the prospects for growth of the sector in recent years.

Growth rate and composition

Average annual growth rates in the GVA of major agricultural commodities have been quite erratic. The crop subsector grew rapidly prior to 1980 because of the

Table 6.3. GVA Growth Rates, Major Agricultural Commodities, the Philippines, 1960–2004
(at constant 1985 prices, percent)

Product	1960–70	1970–80	1980–90	1990–2004
Crops	4.3	6.2	1.1	1.9
Rice	—	4.3	2.9	3.6
Maize	—	5.2	3.1	1.9
Coconuts, including copra	—	7.8	−3.9	1.1
Sugar	—	5.2	−1.8	4.1
Bananas	—	13.9	−1.8	4.0
Other crops	—	8.1	2.2	0.8
Livestock and poultry	3.1	3.1	5.7	4.4
Livestock	—	0.8	4.8	3.5
Poultry	—	8.5	7.5	5.7

Source: Compiled based on data of the National Statistical Coordination Board.

Note: — = no data are available.

Green Revolution in rice production and the world commodity boom, but it performed poorly thereafter, when the average growth rate was far below the growth rate of the population. The general slowdown may be observed across commodities (table 6.3).

Rice is the main staple and the single most important crop. While the growth rate in rice production declined beginning in 1970, it was higher than the population growth rate. Rice continues to receive the bulk of public expenditure in the crop subsector, and it has also benefited from increasing price protection (see below). Rice imports as a share of the total supply of rice have risen since the 1980s, reflecting the effect of rising incomes and a shift away from maize as a food staple. Maize production experienced declining growth rates despite rising price protection and a rapid expansion in the demand for maize as feed in the pig meat and poultry industries.

The poorest performers are the traditional export crops such as coconuts, sugar, abaca, and tobacco, each of which showed a decreasing growth rate. In contrast, nontraditional export crops such as bananas, pineapples, and mangoes showed high growth rates. However, crop diversification, particularly toward high-value horticultural crops that raised the growth rates of the agricultural sectors in Chile, Thailand, and other developing countries, was not as pronounced in the case of the Philippines.

The growth rate in livestock production accelerated after 1980. The contribution of livestock to the GVA rose from 18 to nearly 25 percent within only 25 years. This remarkable performance was generated by increasing domestic demand, as well as productivity gains resulting from the shift to larger-scale operations and the adoption of the new technologies embedded in imported breeds, veterinary medicines, and feed ingredients.

Agricultural trade and trade openness

Agriculture has historically been a net earner of foreign exchange. In the 1960s, agricultural exports accounted for nearly two-thirds of total exports, while agricultural imports accounted for less than 20 percent of total imports (table 6.2). The share of the sector in total exports began dropping sharply in the 1990s. By 2004, the sector had ceased to be a net earner of foreign exchange; the ratio of agricultural imports to agricultural exports rose from about one to three in the 1960s and 1970s to around four to three in 2004. The relatively high growth rate of agricultural exports in the 1970s arose mainly because of the world commodity boom and the expansion of nontraditional commodities (bananas, pineapples, and fishery products). However, world commodity prices fell sharply in the 1980s and have remained low until recently. Meanwhile, the growth in nontraditional agricultural exports had leveled off by the 1990s. In stark contrast, neighboring countries experienced a major export boom in cash crops during the same period. Thus, Thailand showed dramatic success in rubber, Malaysia in palm oil, and Indonesia in palm oil and cocoa.

The composition of agricultural exports has been changing in the Philippines. Coconut products has continued to be the top earner of foreign exchange, although their share in agricultural exports has decreased from nearly 70 percent in 1970 to less than 30 percent recently. The contribution of sugar to agricultural exports, which was second only to coconuts in the 1970s (30 percent), is now only 3 percent. The export value of bananas has been about twice that of sugar; and this has been exceeded by the export value of pineapples since the 1990s. Fruits and vegetables now account for nearly 30 percent of agricultural exports.[2]

The rapid growth in agricultural imports relative to agricultural exports has stemmed from several factors. First, economic development has increased the demand for food products exhibiting higher income elasticities. The Philippines does not have a comparative advantage in many of these products, including wheat, beef, milk, and other dairy products. Second, livestock and poultry require agricultural inputs, such as soybean meal, maize, fishmeal, and other feed ingredients, that are cheaper to import than to produce domestically. Third, agricultural modernization has led to greater reliance on modern manufactured inputs that are mostly imported, such as fertilizers, agricultural chemicals, farm and agroprocessing machinery, and veterinary medicines. Fourth, trade liberalization has generated more imports of once highly protected agricultural commodities such as fruits and beef.

If one measures trade openness by imports and exports as a share of the GVA, then there has been a decline in agriculture's trade openness (table 6.2). While agriculture was more open relative to the rest of the economy up to the 1970s, the reverse has been true since then. This shift has been caused not so much by the reduction in the ratio of imports to the GVA (because these have increased in both the agricultural and nonagricultural sectors), but rather by the declining export ratios in agriculture in contrast to the steadily rising trend in the rest of the economy. The declining trend in the trade openness of agriculture in the 1970s and 1980s gradually reversed in the 1990s, but the rate of the rise in import ratios continued to be higher than the rate of the rise in export ratios.

Comparative advantage and trends in productivity

The growth of agriculture has occurred more slowly in the Philippines than in other developing Asian economies. The stagnation in agricultural exports from the Philippines suggests that the country has been losing its comparative advantage in the sector. Indeed, measures of revealed comparative advantage show a sharp drop for Philippine agriculture as a whole, as well as for all major Philippine agricultural exports (table 6.4). For example, the country's share of the world market in coconut products has fallen, and sugar is now also imported. (Exports

Table 6.4. Revealed Comparative Advantage, Major Agricultural Commodities, the Philippines, 1960–2004

(percent)

Product	1960	1970	1980	1990	2000	2004
All agriculture[a]	3.0	2.6	2.9	1.6	0.6	0.8
Coconuts	116	145	224	212	71	97
Sugar[b]	18	21	12	4	1	1
Bananas	—	—	3	23	11	14
Pineapples						
Canned	—	—	82	70	27	29
Fresh	—	—	49	55	10	8

Source: Compiled based on data in FAOSTAT Database 2008.

Note: Comparative advantage is calculated as the ratio of the share of a commodity group in the total exports of a country to the share of the same commodity group in total worldwide exports. Except for 1960 and 2004, the data represent three-year averages centered on the year shown. — = no data are available.

a. Including fisheries.

b. Sugar has historically been exported to the United States at a preferential price (that is, at higher than world prices). Hence, a value greater than unity in this case does not reveal comparative advantage. The sharp declining trend may nonetheless be interpreted as an indicator of a rapid deterioration in comparative advantage.

have been limited to shipments to the high-priced U.S. market where they have benefited from preferential access.) Even among nontraditional exports, such as bananas and pineapples, the shares of Philippine products on world markets have been declining since the mid-1980s.

The apparent loss in comparative advantage in agriculture is consistent with trends reported in the indicators of labor and land productivity (David 2003). Labor productivity and land productivity both increased up to the late 1970s, particularly during the Green Revolution in rice production. Whereas labor productivity in agriculture as a whole recovered after a sharp drop in the early 1980s, labor productivity in the crop subsector has stagnated since then. Land productivity in the crop subsector has grown slowly, particularly recently; yields per hectare among traditional exports have generally remained constant or have declined. Higher growth in yields may be observed in rice, maize, and nontraditional exports such as bananas, pineapples, and mangoes. However, productivity growth appears to have occurred in the livestock subsector, where international technology transfers, the greater scale of operations, and other management-related innovations have increased production efficiencies significantly.

The Historical Evolution of Price Intervention Policies

It is helpful to describe policy trends since the 1960s. We begin with economy-wide policies and then turn to policies specific to agriculture.

Economy-wide policies

An import-substitution industrialization strategy dominated Philippine economic policies up to the late 1970s. The groundwork for the strategy involved comprehensive foreign exchange and import controls that were established in response to the severe balance of payments crisis that occurred in the late 1940s, shortly after the country's political independence from the United States. The government's use of essentiality criteria in allocating foreign exchange and import licenses during the 1950s encouraged domestic production at the final stages of the production of primarily nonessential and semiessential consumer goods rather than backward integration in the production of raw materials and intermediate and capital goods. These policies defended an overvalued peso and thus clearly penalized exports and agriculture.

A tariff system was instituted as a decontrol measure in 1957. However, the system largely preserved the bias in the incentive structure: tariffs depended on essentiality criteria. Import duties were higher for semifinished products than for raw materials and capital goods and even higher for finished products. Moreover, quantitative trade restrictions continued to be implemented on a substantial number of agricultural and nonagricultural products. Indeed, the balance of payments problem encountered in the early 1960s rendered tariff protection redundant; import and foreign exchange controls were predominant. The adoption of a multiple exchange rate system added to the penalization of traditional agricultural exports.

In the early 1970s, a balance of payments crisis resulted in a major devaluation of the peso. By then, the high economic cost of the import-substitution industrialization strategy and the detrimental effects of the strategy on export potential were becoming well recognized. Nonetheless, the policy response was to provide industrial incentives directly to selected firms, including exporting enterprises, through tax holidays and the like (Bautista and Tecson 2003). No attempt was made to modify the highly protective tariff system. In fact, tariff protection was raised on many import-competing products, such as primary and processed food and agricultural products, chemical products, metal manufactures, electrical appliances, machinery, and transport equipment. During this period, the Philippines had the highest average tariff rate in Southeast Asia (Intal and Power 1991). In addition, the share of imported products (based on the seven-digit Philippine Standard Industrial Classification) subject to quantitative restrictions rose from 26 percent in 1970 to 52 percent in 1980 (Bautista and Tecson 2003).

In the early 1980s, the government adopted various structural adjustment and stabilization measures to correct fundamental distortions in economic incentives and imbalances in the external and public sector accounts. These measures included the liberalization of the foreign exchange market, as well as trade policy reforms to remove quantitative trade restrictions and reduce the level and dispersion of tariffs. The tariff reform program—the first of the unilateral trade liberalization programs—was instituted in 1981 to respond to a condition for a World Bank structural adjustment loan package. Under the program, the dispersion of tariff rates was to be reduced by lowering the peak tariff rates of 100 and 70 percent to 50 percent in two stages, while the low tariff rates were to be raised to at least 10 percent by 1985. Overall, the average tariff dropped substantially, from 43 percent in 1980 to 28 percent in 1985. To complement the tariff reform program, import licensing was also to be relaxed gradually. The plan was to remove selected nontariff barriers over three years. From the original list of 1,300 import items banned or requiring prior approval by the Central Bank of the Philippines and other government agencies, 264 items were to be removed in 1981, another 610 in early 1982, and the remainder by the end of 1983 (Bautista and Tecson 2003).

However, the balance of payments crisis of 1983, following Benigno Aquino's assassination, stalled these initiatives. The government again adopted comprehensive import and foreign exchange controls, rendering the tariff reductions ineffective. Commercial banks were required to turn over their foreign exchange receipts to the central bank so that priority imports and other payments could be facilitated. A 5 percent general import tax was imposed in November 1983 to generate government revenue and discourage imports; the rate was raised to 8 percent in April 1984 and then to 10 percent two months later. Additional export duties ranging from 2 to 5 percent were levied on traditional export products from November 1983 to December 1984, and an economic stabilization tax of 30 percent was levied on all exports briefly in 1984.

To curtail imports and capital outflows, the peso was devalued on successive occasions, and, in late 1984, the exchange rate was allowed to float. Tax reforms in 1983–85 gradually unified the sales tax on imports and import substitutes, removing one source of import protection. The markup rate (which increases the tax base for imports) on essential and semiessential goods was reduced to a uniform 25 percent in 1985 and removed altogether in 1986.

Under the new government of Corazon Aquino, the trade liberalization program was revived in 1986. Export taxes on all commodities except logs were abolished. The process of lifting import licensing was accelerated: 951 import items were liberalized in 1986, 170 in 1987, and another 209 in 1988. Of the remaining 673 restricted import items, those on list A were scheduled for immediate liberalization, and 94 had been liberalized by the end of 1989; those on list B were scheduled for review. However, those on list C (114 items) continued to be restricted for national security or health reasons.

The second tariff reform program was launched in July 1991 through an executive order. This was intended to reduce the range of tariff rates to 30 percent over a five-year period. Although about 10 percent of all commodity lines were still subject to tariffs outside the target range, the average tariff rate had declined from 33 percent in 1990 to 27 percent by the end of 1995.

As part of the second tariff reform program, an executive order was also issued to convert the quantitative restrictions on 153 agricultural products into tariff equivalents and realign the tariffs on 48 commodities. However, the order was soon reversed based on the Magna Carta of Small Farmers, which was passed in 1991 and, among other provisions, allowed the government blanket authority to restrict agricultural imports that competed with domestic production.

The price and trade protection supplied for most major import-competing agricultural products were largely untouched by the series of unilateral trade liberalization measures introduced beginning in the late 1980s, however. Despite World Trade Organization (WTO) and regional trade agreements, nontariff trade barriers continue to distort the prices of some of the most important commodities.

Agriculture-specific policies up to the mid-1980s

Although they may be generally levied on all agricultural products and inputs, import tariffs are more commonly applied only on agricultural inputs and agricultural products that are not locally produced in any significant quantity. Such products include milk, wheat, and soybeans. Tariff protection for nontraded commodities and for exportable products that are competitive in world markets is redundant because of prohibitive transport and other marketing costs.

Over the period under study, a wide variety of policy instruments that influence price incentives were applied to major agricultural commodities. These included government monopoly control over international trade and domestic marketing operations, import bans, quantitative trade restrictions, import licensing, export taxes, and export bans.[3] Furthermore, despite serious efforts at unilateral trade liberalization, some of the policy instruments applicable to the more important import-competing agricultural products were kept largely intact. Indeed, some of the interventions had a long history going back to the U.S. Commonwealth period that began in 1935. During the martial law era under Marcos, which began in late 1972, the government had considerably more leeway in intervening in setting prices and in marketing in agriculture, and it exercised this power. In the following discussion, we therefore distinguish between the evolution of agricultural price intervention policies before and after 1986, when the Corazon Aquino administration took over the reins of government.

Rice and maize

When bad weather caused a drastic shortfall in staple food grains in 1936, the National Rice and Corn Administration was established to ensure low, stable prices for consumers and adequate price incentives for farmers. To achieve these conflicting objectives, the agency was granted monopoly control over the imports and exports of rice and maize, as well as budgetary support and a credit line to undertake domestic market operations to defend price floors and retail ceilings and narrow the geographical and seasonal dispersion of prices.

Because of high world commodity prices in the early 1970s, the government monopoly control over food commodities through this agency, which had been renamed the National Food Authority, was expanded beyond rice and maize to allow the tariff-free importation of wheat, soybeans, soybean meal, ruminant livestock, and beef.

Sugar

The sugar industry has historically been assisted more than any other industry. This is because of the preferential access assigned to Philippine sugar in the U.S. market beginning in 1902 and the authority entrusted to the Philippine government to administer its sugar export quota to the United States through the Jones-Costigan Act passed by the U.S. Congress in 1934.

Initially, the domestic quota system was established for the orderly distribution of the U.S. quota among sugar producers. In the 1960s, the quota system was also charged with reducing the burden on domestic consumers of the higher export prices resulting from the 1962 devaluation and the greater U.S. quota allocation arising because of the Cuban missile crisis (given Cuba's role as a major producer). Under this system, which is still in force, producers are paid a composite price derived as an average of the export price, a lower domestic wholesale price, and a reserve price weighted by the quantity allocations targeted for U.S. exports, the domestic market, and as a reserve.

When the Laurel-Langley Agreement—a trade agreement between the United States and the Philippines—expired in 1974, sugar trading was effectively nationalized, first under Philippine Exchange Inc. and subsequently under the National Sugar Trading Corporation. The latter was the sole Philippine wholesale buyer and seller of sugar in both the domestic and international markets until the end of the Marcos administration in early 1986. It also established new refineries, operated sugar market outlets, and acquired leading enterprises involved in the transport, storage, and handling of sugar for export.

Export commodities

Except in the aftermath of the 1970 devaluation and the sharp increases in world commodity prices in the mid-1970s, there have been few attempts to intervene in the production and trade of exportable agricultural products. Initially, as part of stabilization measures, export taxes from 4 to 6 percent were imposed on major agricultural exports and other primary exports; to generate revenue, these taxes remained in place until the mid-1980s. The higher rate of 6 percent was imposed on traditional exports of coconuts (copra) and centrifugal sugar to promote more processing of agricultural exports. The lower rate of 4 percent was applied to coconut oil, desiccated coconuts, coconut cake and meal, molasses, abaca, bananas, and pineapple products.[4]

In 1974, because of the world commodity boom, additional premium duties were briefly imposed on exports. The duties ranged from 20 to 30 percent of the difference between the ruling export price and a February 1974 base price. Windfall gains from the devaluation and the commodity boom were thus partially siphoned off from the producers of these agricultural and primary exportable commodities.

The Coconut Consumers Stabilization Fund implemented an additional levy on the coconut industry in 1973 (commonly known as the coco levy). The levy was aimed partly at protecting domestic consumers from a sharp rise in the price for coconut oil on the world market and partly at raising funds for the development of the coconut industry.[5] There was also a belief that taxing or restricting coconut exports might be beneficial because the Philippines was thought to possess some monopoly power on the world market. (While the Philippines accounted for a high share of total world coconut and coconut oil exports, any monopoly power was curtailed by the fact that coconut oil comprises only about 7 percent of the world lauric oil market.) Some of the revenue from this levy was used to buy up 80 percent of the coconut oil milling industry, which was then reorganized under a newly created and privately owned company, United Coconut Oil Mills. This company eventually acted as a monopsonist buyer of coconut in the farm sector. When the world prices of coconut oil fell in 1982, the levy was lifted, only to be replaced by a ban on coconut exports to protect coconut oil mills.

Agriculture-specific policies after 1986

World commodity prices began to fall in the late 1970s. However, the policies and institutions established to cope with high world prices persisted because they proved to be a convenient means of raising revenues. The related measures heavily taxed farmers so as to support private interests and cover bureaucratic inefficiencies (David 1983). In 1986, under the new Corazon Aquino government, several of the direct government price and market regulations were finally dismantled.

The reforms under Corazon Aquino

Export taxes, including the coconut export ban, were abolished, and the National Food Authority's monopolistic controls over international trade in wheat, soybeans, soybean meal, and meat were removed, limiting the authority's functions to rice and maize (also the case prior to martial law). The authority's domestic marketing operations were also effectively reduced because financial support had to be provided mostly through annual budgetary allocations rather than profits from imports.

The National Sugar Trading Corporation was eventually replaced by the Sugar Regulatory Administration, which functioned primarily as a market regulator. It mainly allocated U.S. sugar quotas, determined the allowable quantities of imports, the importers, the amounts to be sold in the domestic market, and the amounts to be kept in reserve. It also performed developmental functions, such as research and extension, but it has ceased to engage in direct market operations.

Quantitative trade restrictions on fertilizers were removed, and tariffs on major agricultural inputs were lowered substantially. However, the monopsonist control exercised by United Coconut Oil Mills over the coconut market has continued; the government's attempts to wrest ownership of this entity have been bogged down in court proceedings.

Despite efforts at trade liberalization in the late 1980s, most major importable agricultural commodities that are also produced in significant volumes in the Philippines are still subject to quantitative import restrictions, particularly those commodities protected by laws passed by Congress. Efforts to remove the quantitative restrictions were preempted by the passage of the Magna Carta of Small Farmers in 1991, which provided blanket authority to restrict agricultural imports that competed with domestic production. In addition, the Seed Law was passed to regulate imports of seeds and other planting materials.

The Uruguay Round Agreement on Agriculture

The country's ratification of the Uruguay Round Agreement on Agriculture in the mid-1990s promised to set a decisive path toward trade liberalization in the sector. It aimed to replace all quantitative restrictions by tariffs, impose a ceiling on tariff rates, and reduce tariff protection. Unfortunately, the specific agreements and the manner of implementation did not live up to the promise (David 1994, 2003).

First, one of the most heavily regulated commodities, rice, was exempted from tariffication until 2004, which is similar to the situation in Japan and the Republic of Korea.[6]

Second, the quantitative trade restrictions lifted by executive order in April 1996 were replaced by tariff rate quotas that initially raised out-of-quota tariffs to the maximum (bound) tariffs allowed under the WTO commitments, while the in-quota tariffs were set mostly at the levels existing in 1995. The initial out-of-quota tariffs of 100 percent were typically higher than the nominal protection rates implied by the quantitative restrictions in 1990–94. They were also higher than the book tariff rates under the executive order that set out the unilateral tariff reductions on a wide range of agricultural and industrial goods. Despite the reductions in the out-of-quota tariffs scheduled for no later than 2004, the tariff rates are still equal to or higher than the tariff rates in 1995, and they are higher than the government's target average tariff of 5 percent.

Furthermore, whereas the quantitative restrictions on primary and lightly processed products were supposed to be lifted, the tariffs were raised on a number of imported agricultural products that are considered substitutes for other commodities (for example, feed wheat and barley as substitutes for maize). Tariffs were also increased to this same level on more heavily processed products using these commodities as main raw materials (for example, preserved and canned meat products, milled rice and maize, and roasted coffee).

Third, the manner in which the minimum access volume provision or the tariff rate quota system of the Uruguay Round Agreement on Agriculture was administered for major import-competing commodities simply perpetuated quantitative trade restrictions. The quantities that may be imported at the lower in-quota tariffs were sometimes changed to prevent domestic prices from rising sharply whenever production shortfalls occurred. Thus, in effect, the tariffs were no different than quantitative restrictions. For certain commodities, the right to import was assigned mostly to domestic producers of the same products (for example, pork and poultry), and these producers have often chosen not to utilize their import allocation so as to protect their domestic production. Moreover, because most of the minimum access volumes were lower than the demand for imports at the in-quota tariff rate and because the right to import the minimum access volumes was not auctioned, large quota rents accrued to those entities given access to the minimum access volume allocation, at least during the early period of implementation.

Finally, the agreement's lack of provision for the market operations of parastatals allowed the Sugar Regulatory Administration to continue exercising its regulatory authority over import levels and the market destinations of domestic sugar production. In fact, the domestic market operations of the National Food Authority in support of producer prices were expanded in the late 1990s to include sugar.[7]

Regional trade agreements

In 1992, the six member countries of the Association of Southeast Asian Nations at the time (Brunei Darussalam, Indonesia, Malaysia, the Philippines, Singapore, and Thailand) agreed to form a free trade area. The aim was to reduce tariffs to between 0 and 5 percent and to abolish quantitative trade restrictions and other nontariff trade barriers by 2010. Under the related Common Effective Preferential Tariff Scheme, unprocessed agricultural products were commonly included in a sensitive products list that allows trade liberalization to begin later (between 2001 and 2003), though the 0 to 5 percent tariff targets are still to be reached by 2010. A recent study has indicated, however, that the effective protection rates in agriculture have been largely unaffected by the scheme thus far (Pimentel 2006).

Unlike other free trade areas, which usually delay or totally exclude trade liberalization in agriculture, the agreement signed between China and the free trade area of the Association of Southeast Asian Nations in 2002 specifically covered a significant portion of all agricultural products through the Early Harvest Program. The agreement called for the elimination of tariffs on live animals, meat and edible meat offals, fish, dairy products, other animal products, live trees, vegetables, fruits and nuts, and a few commodities in other categories of the Harmonized Commodity Description and Coding System. The changes were to be implemented starting in January 2004 and were to be in full operation no later than January 2006 in the free trade area, although exceptions were allowed in some cases depending upon negotiations with China.

The Philippines signed an Early Harvest Program Agreement with China in early 2006. The agreement covered proportionately fewer commodities than the agreements reached by other countries of the Association of Southeast Asian Nations, suggesting that there is less interest in the Philippines in engaging with China in more open agricultural trade (Pasadilla 2006). In general, consumers will benefit from lower prices on covered commodities, while producers of exportable bananas, pineapples, mangoes, other tropical fruits, and coconut and coconut oil are expected to gain from greater access to the vast Chinese market. However, producers of vegetables, leguminous crops, and pig meat, together with producers of fruits for local markets, will be hurt, at least initially, by the entry of relatively cheap frozen meat and other meat products, potatoes, carrots, onions, garlic, peanuts, pears, apples, oranges, and other fruits and vegetables from China.

Estimates of Nominal and Relative Rates of Assistance

Measuring the distortions in incentives caused by price and trade policies has had a long history in the Philippines. The first effort was undertaken by Power (1971) in a study on the situation in 1965. This was followed by studies conducted by Norma Tan (1979), on 1974; Elizabeth Tan (1994), on the 1980s; Manasan and Pineda (1999), on the 1990s; and Aldaba (2005a, 2005b), on recent years. These studies estimated the effective protection rates in all industries, both agricultural and nonagricultural. However, the main interest and analysis were concentrated on the manufacturing sector.

The first studies on agricultural protection were conducted by David (1983), Intal and Power (1991), and, more recently, David (2003). Unlike the industrial protection studies that quantified the effects of tariffs and indirect sales taxes, these agricultural protection studies were based on domestic and border price comparisons. This enabled the effects of nontariff trade barriers to be measured and redundancy in the tariffs, if any, to be taken into account. The indirect impacts of industrial protection and other economy-wide factors on agricultural incentives (through effects on the exchange rate) were also analyzed.

Methodology

In this study, we estimate nominal rates of assistance (NRAs) in industries. The main focus of our study's methodology is government-imposed distortions that create a gap between domestic prices and the prices that would emerge under free

Figure 6.1. Value Shares of the Primary Production of Covered and Noncovered Commodities, the Philippines, 1966–2004

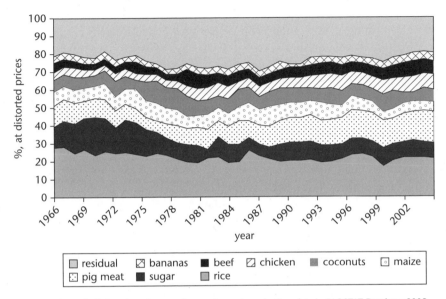

Source: Author calculations based on producer price and production data in FAOSTAT Database 2008.

market conditions. (For a detailed description of the methodology, see Anderson et al. 2008 and appendix A.) Since it is not possible to understand the characteristics of agricultural development through a sectoral view alone, our project's methodology not only estimates the effects of direct agricultural policy measures, but, for comparative evaluation, also generates estimates of the distortions in nonagricultural sectors.

More specifically, our study computes NRAs for producers of the main farm products (figure 6.1). It also generates NRAs for nonagricultural tradables for comparison with the NRAs for agricultural tradables via the calculation of a relative rate of assistance (RRA). This approach provides a consistent time series measure of distortions over more than four decades using the values of production as weights to compute sectoral and subsectoral averages. This contrasts with the previous studies, which, except for Manasan and Pineda (1999), computed sectoral averages using trade volumes as weights.

We assume that the Philippine economy is small and open and, thus, that the country's level of trade does not affect world prices.[8] Border prices are estimated based on world price series reported by the World Bank. For importables, these data are adjusted to values that include cost, insurance, and freight by assuming the cost of transport and insurance at a constant 20 percent of free on board world prices. We have not chosen the country's officially recorded unit values for imports or exports because foreign exchange controls, export taxes, and other taxes mean that the export unit data are significantly undervalued, particularly up to the mid-1980s. For rice, maize, and sugar, the import unit data may be either overvalued (in the case of imports by the National Food Authority) or undervalued (because private importers seek to lower their tariff payments by underinvoicing). There were also no imports of some importable products during various periods.

Rice, maize, sugar, pig meat, beef, and poultry are consistently classified as importables even though there were no imports of these products during some years. In the case of sugar, the first imports occurred only in the 1990s, but, even in the 1960s and 1970s, exports of sugar were confined to the high-priced U.S. market, where the Philippines has had preferential access, and were not competitive at the free-market world price. Sugar is thus also treated as an importable.

In the absence of detailed time series data on marketing costs, we define the domestic price as the wholesale price that is the closest to the same point of the border price in the marketing chain.

For most of the agricultural commodities for which we compare the domestic and border prices, we rely on the data for the commodity that is internationally traded and is lightly processed rather than the data on the primary product sold at the farmgate. Thus, we take milled rice versus paddy; raw or refined sugar versus sugarcane; frozen pig meat, beef, or poultry versus hog, cattle, or chicken birds. In the case of sugar, the rates of the protection received by farmers and millers are the same because the revenues derived from the sale of raw and refined sugar in both the domestic and U.S. markets are shared proportionately between the two at the ratio of 70 to 30.[9] The ratio of the farm price of paddy to the retail price of rice did not change significantly, suggesting that farmers and rice millers, together with traders, share proportionately in the protection accorded the rice industry. For rice, maize, pig meat, beef, and poultry, we assume that the NRAs of the processed products and the farm products are equivalent. Indeed, the import tariffs on the farm products are generally the same as the tariffs on the lightly processed varieties.

Aside from the major agricultural commodities specified above, we have estimated the NRAs for other, noncovered crops within the sector. Since price comparisons are more difficult to perform in the case of noncovered exportables, including pineapples, mangoes, abaca, and tobacco, we have assumed that the relevant average NRAs are zero or equal to the export tax whenever this applies. For products that are nontraded because of prohibitive marketing costs, such as roots and tuber crops, we have assigned zero NRA values.[10] For the many import-competing vegetables, fruits, and other minor crops, we assume that the NRAs for the group are the same as the average NRAs for covered importable products.[11]

We also assume that the weights are one-third each for exportables, importables, and nontradables in the noncovered part of farm production (which, in aggregate, amounts to around one-fifth of the agricultural sector's value of production at undistorted prices).

For importable nonagricultural products, the NRAs are generally based on book tariff rates, apart from the case of lightly processed food manufacturing industries in which the NRAs are based on price comparisons, including rice and maize milling, sugar milling and refining, coconut oil production and refining, and so on.[12] For a number of nonagricultural primary products in fishing, forestry, and mining, we use the export taxes that applied from 1970 to 1985. The definitions we use for a product's tradability and for industry weights are the same for the agricultural and nonagricultural sectors.

NRAs in agriculture

Our estimates of the NRAs for agricultural commodities from 1962 to 2004 are summarized in table 6.5. Although the estimated NRAs are highly variable over time (see the annual estimates in David, Intal, and Balisacan 2007), several general patterns emerge from the five-year averages shown in the table.

First, import-competing products have enjoyed much more assistance than exportables. Coconut production has been penalized by negative NRAs over the entire period of our study, averaging around −20 to −25 percent from the 1970s to the mid-1980s. Besides the multiple exchange rate policy prior to 1970 (not measured here), this was caused by the imposition of several measures, including the export tax, the coconut levy, and the coconut export ban that were aimed at siphoning off windfall gains from the 1970 devaluation; the subsequent world commodity boom·of 1973–74 that was incompletely transmitted to the domestic market; and the lower raw material costs for the coconut oil milling industry. Despite the abolition of these policy instruments in 1986, however, coconut farmers continued to be implicitly taxed, albeit at a lower rate of around 15 percent of border prices. Evidently, the government's failure to dismantle the ownership of 70 to 80 percent of the coconut oil milling industry by United Coconut Oil Mills has allowed this entity to maintain its monopsonist power over the domestic price for coconuts even now.

Second, among import-competing commodities, the level of the NRAs has differed significantly, and the differences have widened between two groups of import-competing products: the NRAs for the most important commodities—rice, maize, and sugar—have increased, while those for the many more minor, but higher-valued commodities have declined. Each of these commodities is considered in detail below.

Table 6.5. NRAs for Covered Agricultural Products, the Philippines, 1962–2004
(percent)

Indicator, product	1962–64	1965–69	1970–74	1975–79	1980–84	1985–89	1990–94	1995–99	2000–04
Exportables[a]	−9.0	−7.6	−14.3	−14.6	−22.6	−16.5	−11.4	−5.4	−8.7
Coconuts	−24.4	−20.2	−25.3	−16.7	−27.1	−20.6	−15.3	−7.8	−14.1
Bananas	0.0	0.0	−4.0	−4.0	−4.0	−0.8	0.0	0.0	0.0
Import-competing products[a]	−1.1	17.4	−5.6	−5.8	2.2	30.2	25.1	48.1	31.4
Rice	−3.4	−1.4	−9.7	−17.9	−16.3	14.5	20.9	52.7	50.7
Maize	0.5	38.4	14.0	24.3	20.1	59.8	62.6	78.5	54.5
Sugar	−8.2	120.7	−11.7	−1.7	59.5	123.2	49.3	97.2	79.3
Beef	15.0	15.0	12.0	10.0	5.0	17.0	28.0	28.0	10.0
Pigs	−30.0	13.6	3.2	−5.5	35.8	51.0	25.1	20.6	−8.3
Chicken	8.9	67.1	28.9	28.1	38.4	42.9	56.5	42.2	52.1
All covered products[a]	−1.9	15.3	−6.5	−8.1	−5.1	16.1	17.5	37.9	24.9
Dispersion, covered products[b]	17.1	29.6	25.2	22.3	28.6	29.9	27.5	27.9	30.4
Coverage, at undistorted prices	78	79	79	74	73	73	77	77	80

Source: David, Intal, and Balisacan 2007.

a. Weighted averages; the weights are based on the unassisted value of production.
b. Dispersion is a simple five-year average of the annual standard deviation around the weighted mean of the NRAs of covered products.

Third, the increasingly higher NRAs observed since the 1980s may be partly caused by the government's efforts to reduce the burden of the adjustment of the agricultural sector to a long-term decline in world commodity prices. This declining trend is visible in real domestic prices relative to real world prices for several commodities noted in David, Intal, and Balisacan (2007).

Fourth, the dispersion of NRAs among agricultural products within the farm sector (measured according to the standard deviation of these NRAs and reported in table 6.5) has not diminished. The trade bias index has not diminished either (table 6.6), indicating that the NRAs for importable farm products have persistently remained above the NRAs for exportables. Both of these indicators imply that the efficiency of resource use within the farm sector has been substantially compromised by agricultural policies.

Fifth, the NRAs have fluctuated from year to year, mostly in response to world price changes and sometimes in response to exchange rate adjustments (see figure 6.2). For example, the NRAs for import-competing agricultural products were below the trend in 1973–74 and 1980, when international prices were high, but above the trend in the mid-1980s, when international prices were low. This suggests that domestic price stabilization has been an important objective of agricultural price and trade policy. Table 6.7 shows that the estimated coefficients of the variation in domestic prices tended to be considerably lower than the corresponding coefficients in world prices, particularly among major import-competing commodities.

Rice

The trends in the NRAs for rice reflect the inability of the National Food Authority to attain simultaneously its inherently conflicting objectives of providing low prices to consumers and remunerative incentives to farmers. Prior to the late 1980s, the domestic price of rice was, on average, about equal to the long-term level of the border price. The negative protection from the 1970s to the early 1980s was caused by the unusually high world prices during this period. This did not discourage farmers, however, because the Green Revolution in rice and the land reform in rice farming were transforming tenant farmers to owner-operators.[13]

Because of the drop in the world price of rice, a sharp fall in irrigation investments, and stagnation in the yield potential of newer modern varieties, growth in the demand for rice increased more rapidly than rice production beginning in the late 1980s. The NRAs for rice became positive; they had risen to about 50 percent by the early 2000s. This occurred despite the most significant rice imports ever, which reflected the country's rising comparative disadvantage in rice production.

Table 6.6. NRAs in Agriculture Relative to Nonagricultural Industries, the Philippines, 1962–2004
(percent)

Indicator	1962–64	1965–69	1970–74	1975–79	1980–84	1985–89	1990–94	1995–99	2000–04
Covered products[a]	–1.9	15.3	–6.5	–8.1	–5.1	16.1	17.5	37.9	24.9
Noncovered products	–0.4	5.8	–2.3	–2.4	0.3	10.0	8.4	16.0	12.3
All agricultural products[a]	–1.6	13.3	–5.6	–6.6	–3.6	14.4	15.4	33.0	26.0
Non-product-specific assistance	0.0	0.0	0.0	0.0	0.0	0.0	0.0	0.0	0.0
Total agricultural NRA[b]	–1.6	13.3	–5.6	–6.6	–3.6	14.4	15.4	33.0	26.0
Trade bias index[c]	–0.03	–0.18	0.04	–0.03	–0.15	–0.31	–0.26	–0.34	–0.31
NRA, all agricultural tradables	–1.7	14.3	–6.0	–7.2	–4.0	15.8	16.7	35.7	27.9
NRA, all nonagricultural tradables	19.0	20.3	16.3	16.3	12.9	11.0	9.9	8.6	7.3
RRA[d]	–17.4	–5.0	–19.8	–20.3	–14.9	4.3	6.1	24.9	19.1

Source: David, Intal, and Balisacan 2007.

a. Including product-specific input subsidies.
b. Including product-specific input subsidies and non-product-specific assistance. The total assistance to primary factors and intermediate inputs, divided by the total value of primary agriculture production at undistorted prices.
c. The trade bias index is defined as $(1 + NRAag_x/100)/(1 + NRAag_m/100) - 1$, where $NRAag_m$ and $NRAag_x$ are the average percentage NRAs for the import-competing and exportable parts of the agricultural sector, respectively.
d. The RRA is defined as $100*[(100 + NRAag^t)/(100 + NRAnonag^t) - 1]$, where $NRAag^t$ and $NRAnonag^t$ are the percentage NRAs for the tradables parts of the agricultural and nonagricultural sectors, respectively.

**Figure 6.2. NRAs for Exportable, Import-Competing, and All
Agricultural Products, the Philippines, 1962–2004**

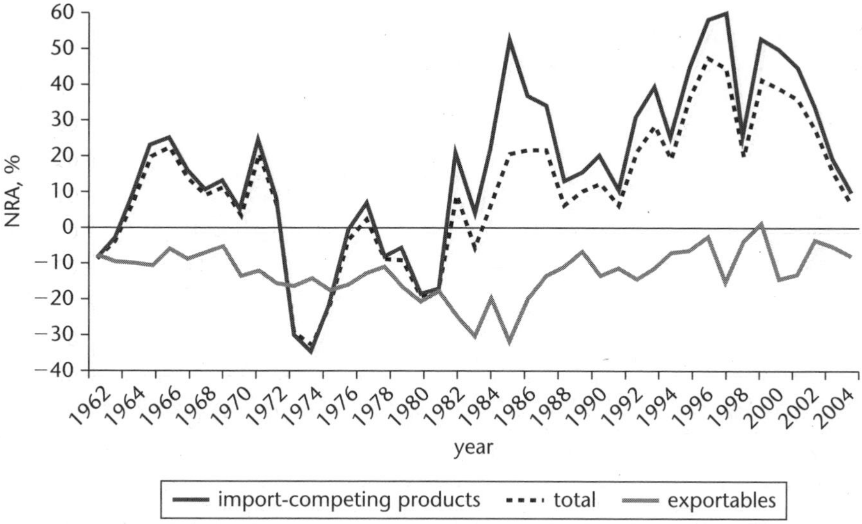

Source: David, Intal, and Balisacan 2007.

Maize

Maize is a food staple for 10 to 15 percent of the population and a major feed
ingredient for livestock. In contrast to rice, however, domestic production in
maize has been consistently protected. The NRAs for maize grew steadily from
about 25 percent in the late 1970s and early 1980s to nearly 80 percent in the late
1990s. Unlike rice, there is less political pressure to lower maize prices for poor
consumers because maize is mostly a subsistence crop among upland farmers in
the southern part of the country.

Sugar

If sugar is categorized as an importable and the world price of sugar—not the unit
value of exports to the premium U.S. market—is used as the border price in the calculation of NRAs, then the domestic sugar industry is clearly the most highly protected industry throughout the period we study. U.S. consumers paid for a large
share of the income transfers to the sector in the 1960s and early 1970s when nearly
all domestic production was exported. However, the burden shifted to consumers
and food processors in the Philippines when the Laurel-Langley Agreement expired
in 1974. At that time, the U.S. sugar quota dropped sharply. Exports, which continue
to be confined to the protected U.S. market, now account for only around 10 percent
of domestic production. Yet, because of import restrictions, the average NRA in the
sugar industry has increased, averaging around 90 percent during the past decade.[14]

Table 6.7. Coefficients of Variation in Real International Prices and Philippine Wholesale Prices, Major Agricultural Commodities, 1960–2004

Product	1960–2004	1960–80	1980–2004
Rice			
World	47	32	34
Domestic	19	12	11
Maize			
World	38	17	27
Domestic	23	17	14
Coconuts			
World	49	27	40
Domestic	45	31	36
Coconut oil			
World	50	27	43
Domestic	43	32	33
Sugar			
World	80	71	60
Domestic	19	14	18
Beef			
World	33	21	23
Domestic	28	35	17
Pig meat			
EUV Sing	46	44	23
Domestic	13	12	14
Poultry			
EUV Sing	37	33	14
Domestic	29	17	15

Source: Author estimates based on data in David, Intal, and Balisacan 2007.

Poultry and other livestock products

Poultry producers benefited from a high level of protection. A slightly rising trend in the NRAs has been discernable, from about 40 percent prior to 1985, when the high tariff protection (70 percent) was redundant to a significant extent, to about 50 percent thereafter.

The tariff protection for the pig meat industry has been significant, although it has generally been lower than the protection for poultry. Beginning in 1995, the government adopted the same level of high in- and out-of-quota tariffs for both poultry and pig meat under the Uruguay Round Agreement on Agriculture. However, the low tariff was largely redundant up to the 1980s, as were the relatively high tariffs after 1995.

The tariff protection for beef has been historically less than that for pig meat. The NRAs for beef averaged around 10 percent until the late 1980s. Beef was not included among the sensitive products on which tariffs were raised following the WTO agreement. Nonetheless, an upward trend in the estimated NRAs for beef may also be observed for the 1990s. It appears that the government's attempt to promote activities aimed at fattening cattle, which relied on allowing duty-free imports of young cattle from Australia, was accompanied by more restrictive non-tariff trade barriers on beef to increase incentives. The expansion of the cattle fattening business was short-lived, however; tariffs on beef were reduced in the late 1990s, and import restrictions became untenable.[15] That beef benefited from less protection than poultry may be explained by the prevalence of large-scale integration farming operations that produced poultry through contract farming, in contrast to the beef industry, which is dominated by backyard producers. However, the pig meat industry is also dominated by backyard producers, and this subsector benefited from relatively high protection rates.

Agricultural inputs

To infer the effect of price interventions on value added, David, Intal, and Balisacan (2007) report on trends in the NRAs for the major intermediate inputs commonly used in agricultural production. Until the mid-1980s, the government's policies on industrial promotion raised the domestic prices for manufactured inputs in agriculture significantly. The consumer tax equivalent of the import protection provided for agricultural inputs such as fertilizers, agricultural chemicals, farm machinery, and even water pumps was generally higher than the NRAs for agricultural outputs, aside from the case of sugar in some years. With the exception of subsidies for gravity irrigation in rice, there was no significant offsetting input assistance in agriculture. Indeed, despite price controls, tax free imports, and direct subsidies for fertilizer companies before the mid-1980s, the consumer tax equivalent on farm inputs was negative only during 1970–74 (because of the fourfold jump in world oil prices). These data are not incorporated in the aggregate NRAs for crop agriculture; but, if they had been incorporated in the manner described in Anderson et al. (2008) and appendix A, they would have lowered the estimated NRAs for crops by a few percentage points, especially in the earlier decades of the period we study. The estimated NRAs for livestock would also be lower if the impact on the prices of feedmix deriving from the import restrictions on maize had been taken into account.

NRAs for nonagriculture and RRAs for agriculture

Agricultural incentives are affected indirectly by rates of assistance to nonagriculture. Mobile resources move across sectors or industries according to the relative incentives. Figure 6.3 and table 6.7 show the trends in the average NRAs of the agricultural and nonagricultural sectors, as well as the RRAs for agriculture.

Figure 6.3. NRAs for Agricultural and Nonagricultural Tradables and the RRA, the Philippines, 1962–2004

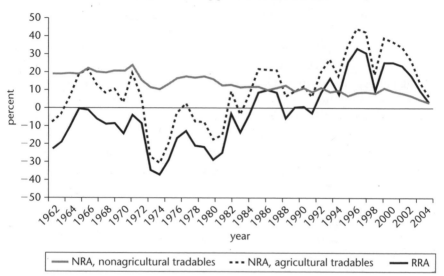

Source: David, Intal, and Balisacan 2007.

The contrast in the trends between the two sectors is striking. Whereas the average NRAs for agriculture were lower than the average NRAs for nonagriculture prior to the mid-1980s, they have risen to more than 30 percent in the past 10 years or so. Meanwhile, because of unilateral trade liberalization measures, the NRAs in nonagriculture declined steadily from nearly 20 percent in the 1960s and 1970s to only 7 percent by the early 2000s.

As a consequence, the assistance to agriculture is now much greater than the assistance to nonagriculture; thus, RRAs have risen from an average of around −15 percent prior to the mid-1980s to an average of more than 20 percent in recent years. This trend indicates that the efficiency of resource use in farming relative to the production of nonagricultural tradables first increased as RRAs became less negative and then decreased as RRAs became more positive. This indicates that there were too few resources in the agricultural sector up to the mid-1980s, but that, since then, there have been too many resources, on average (especially in import-competing agriculture).

Explaining the Patterns in the Distortions in Agricultural Incentives

In general, countries have shifted from taxing to subsidizing agriculture in the course of economic development primarily because of political economy factors (Anderson and Hayami 1986; Lindert 1991; Anderson 1995). In any country that would be self-sufficient in food in a world of free agricultural trade, this shift is expected to occur when the country's per capita income reaches 2.6 times the global average (Tyers and Anderson 1992). In a country that would be only 65 percent self-sufficient in food under free trade, the shift would occur when the per capita income reaches the global average (US$4,300 in 1992). In the case of the Philippines, the shift from taxing to assisting agriculture directly through price interventions occurred at a level of economic development that was lower than predicted by earlier studies: per capita income in the Philippines was only about US$1,200 even in the late 1990s.

Why did the switch toward higher agricultural protection occur early in the Philippines? The explanation lies in unique historical events, political economy factors, the local political system, and the strong nationalist sentiment for food self-sufficiency, especially in rice. The country's highly skewed distribution of landownership and dualistic agrarian structure that arose'from colonial land policies and agroecological conditions meant that there were large landowners and plantation operators who were able to lobby effectively for their own interests. The farm producers in these groups provided the major political leaders in Congress and in the executive branch of government at all levels. Landed oligarchs also represented the business elite, which successfully pushed for an industrial protection policy that biased incentives against the agricultural sector (Hara 1994). As the international pressure for trade liberalization has mounted during the past two decades, it has become easier to resist the opening of domestic markets for food staples by playing up the national sentiment for food self-sufficiency. Political pressure to raise agricultural protection has been strengthened by expanded lobbying efforts undertaken by farmer organizations, large landowners, and agribusiness firms such as livestock and poultry producers, millers; seed companies, and input suppliers.

There has been little resistance to the high prices for white maize as food because white maize is primarily a subsistence crop. Livestock producers (including poultry producers) and feed millers who use mostly yellow maize have chosen to lobby for greater protection for livestock output to offset the high maize prices rather than lobby for a more rational policy in maize and livestock. The objections to the highly restrictive policy on maize imports have been addressed by providing import allocations at lower tariffs for the large, more well organized, and more vocal feed, poultry, and pig meat industries. The larger feed mills and livestock producers also own flour mills and are thus able to substitute low-grade wheat, which is subject to only a 10 percent tariff, for the artificially high-priced maize. This policy structure provides large-scale feed and livestock producers with a cost advantage over smaller producers who must rely on the domestic market for maize supplies.

Aside from the large size of farms and mills, the sugar subsector has historically had strong political power because of its close relationship and common interest with the government in lobbying to protect the country's preferential market access to the U.S. sugar market. In contrast, the share of sugar in direct household expenditure is small, and consumers have therefore generally tolerated or been unaware of the high sugar prices. Resistance from the food processing subsector against high sugar prices was mitigated by granting larger, more vocal food processors the privilege to import sugar free of tariffs.

Concluding Remarks

Price intervention policies became more favorable in the agricultural sector beginning in the mid-1980s. The protection for major import-competing commodities was increased, and unilateral trade liberalization measures lowered the implicit tariffs on inputs and the protection of nonagricultural sectors. Thus, improvements in agricultural incentives occurred at the cost of the inefficiencies in resource allocation arising from widening distortions in prices within agriculture and between agriculture and nonagriculture.

Artificially raising the profitability of major import-competing commodities directly increased the cost of land for the production of other crops. It also indirectly reduced the competitive advantage of exportable agricultural products in world markets. The high-price maize policy also lowered the international competitiveness of the pig meat industry, in which the Philippines may well have a comparative advantage. The significant protection for sugar hurts not only consumers, but also the food processing industry, which accounts for over 20 percent of manufacturing employment and value added. The excessive protection for major staple food commodities reduces the welfare of rural landless and urban poor households and puts pressure on wages, rendering labor-intensive manufacturing industries less competitive relative to low-wage, low-cost food economies such as China and Vietnam.

The economic waste caused by price intervention policies is magnified by the continued use of quantitative trade restrictions instead of tariffs. In particular, the government's monopoly on rice imports and domestic marketing operations through the National Food Authority has been extremely costly, and it has also failed to achieve the basic and conflicting objectives of lowering food prices for consumers, raising producer prices, and stabilizing both sets of prices. The use of quantitative restrictions promotes rent seeking, reduces government revenues, incurs significant bureaucratic costs, and aggravates price uncertainties.

Unfortunately, recent policy changes in response to the WTO agreement on agriculture seem to have exacerbated rather than mitigated such problems; the nominal protection rates for major import-competing commodities have not only been raised, but the scope of the operations of the National Food Authority has also been inadvertently expanded. Rice market interventions and the use of quantitative restrictions have persisted because the economic costs and even some of the financial costs are not readily apparent to the general public. Meanwhile, the bureaucracy is being corrupted through commissions, bribes, and the other rents typically involved in government procurement and import licensing, making it even more difficult to effect trade liberalization.

There are no indications that the government will move toward greater trade liberalization in agriculture in the near future. In the current negotiations under the Doha Round, efforts are being made to retain the relatively high level of tariff protection for major import-competing agricultural commodities. Furthermore, the government is not taking any steps to dismantle the institutions and other policy instruments that regulate the imports of rice, sugar, and other commodities. Because of the sharp rise in world grain prices in recent years, the government will be politically compelled to continue its food self-sufficiency strategy rather than rely on open international markets to achieve food security.

Notes

1. Because there was an acceleration in overseas labor migration, real wages did not decline. Migration boosted foreign exchange earnings, and remittances began to account for at least a 10 percent share in gross national product.

2. Fishery products, led by tuna and shrimps, have become major agricultural exports. They now account for about 20 percent of total agricultural exports.

3. Even for relatively minor crops, specific laws were passed prohibiting imports. This affected, for example, onions, garlic, potatoes, and cabbages in 1955, coffee in 1960, and cigarettes and tobacco, except for blending purposes, in 1964.

4. Export taxes were also imposed on logs at 10 percent; copper ore at 6 percent; and other metal ores, shrimps, prawns, lumber, plywood, and veneer at 4 percent.

5. About 20 percent of the revenues from the tax briefly supported the direct subsidy on the domestic consumption of coconut oil products. The remainder was supposed to be used to finance development programs in the coconut industry such as replanting, vertical integration, and scholarships. Subsequent research showed that little benefit, if any, accrued to farmers from these expenditures (Clarete and Roumasset 1990).

6. The Philippines is still negotiating in the WTO's Doha Round to keep government monopoly control over rice imports.

7. The government also occasionally used the WTO-sanctioned safeguard mechanism when additional tariffs were imposed on poultry.

8. The country is a significant trader only in coconut products, in which it has been the world's largest producer and exporter for most of the period we study. However, to a large extent, competing products such as palm oil and soybean oil may be substituted for coconut products. Coconut oil, the most important coconut product, constitutes only a small (7 percent) share of the world trade in vegetable oils.

9. According to Borrell et al. (1994), the quedan system, which allocates products to the various markets in fixed proportions, reduces the incentive to increase production and invest in yield-increasing technology. This is because higher production cuts into gross revenues. Also, because export allocation to the United States occurs at a fixed ratio, there is no incentive to improve milling quality for export so as to increase net returns. Meanwhile, the sugar-sharing arrangement—whereby 60 to

70 percent goes to growers, and 30 to 40 percent goes to millers (depending on the recovery rate)—that was instituted by law to provide millers a share of the benefits from price protection also happens to reduce the incentive of growers and millers to raise productivity. Thus, growers receive only 60 to 70 percent of the benefits of productivity-enhancing investments, while millers receive only 30 to 40 percent of these benefits.

10. As described in Anderson et al (2008) and appendix A, a commodity is considered nontradable if the proportion of imports and exports in the total value of production is less than 5 percent. If a commodity or commodity group is both exported and imported in significant amounts (that is, more than 2.5 percent of the total value of output), we estimate the NRA as the average of the NRA of the commodity as an exportable and the NRA of the commodity as an importable, weighted by the respective proportions of the export and import values to the total traded value.

11. Despite the supposed removal of quantitative trade restrictions on all agricultural commodities except rice, nontariff barriers appear to be significant in the case of many commodities, such as vegetables, fruits, and meat. Price comparisons are difficult to perform for many of these products because of the lack of consistent world price series, difficulties in making adjustments for quality differences, and the complexity of measuring the effect the increased imports of a commodity that may not be grown in the country may have on the price of a highly substitutable product that is produced domestically. One clear indication of this effect, however, is the substantial smuggling of vegetables, fruits, and nuts from China. The exports of these commodities to the Philippines reported in Chinese trade statistics have been up to 10 times more substantial than the corresponding imports of these commodity groups reported in official Philippine trade statistics despite the already low tariffs on these smuggled products (mostly 3 percent, but, in some cases, up to 10 percent since the late 1990s).

12. To the tariffs in the computation of NRAs, we have added the differences between the indirect tax on domestically produced goods and the indirect tax on imported products imposed from 1960 to the early 1980s. While the tax rates on imports and the tax rate on exports were the same in most cases, the taxes were effectively greater in the case of imports because the tax base for imports was the tariff-inclusive price, augmented by a percentage markup. In 1974, the weighted average nominal tariff rate was 22 percent for manufacturing products, but the nominal rate of protection would nonetheless be significantly higher, 31 percent, if one takes into account the effect of the difference in the tax base (Tan 1979).

13. New seed fertilizer technologies and the accompanying expansion in irrigation increased the country's comparative advantage in rice production, briefly turning the Philippines from a net rice importer to rice self-sufficiency and, by the late 1970s, reducing the domestic price of rice in real terms.

14. Even the large margins conferred on sugar importers as a result of the high level of nominal protection have been received mostly by sugarcane growers, who receive the major part of the import rights dispensed by the Sugar Regulatory Administration.

15. During this period, annual imports of live cattle averaged more than 200,000 head. The number declined significantly thereafter, and the cattle fattening business is now limited to Del Monte and San Miguel Corporation–Monterey Foods, which use by-products of their other businesses, that is, pineapple canning and beer manufacturing, respectively, as main cattle feed ingredients. Previously, live cattle were mostly imported for almost immediate slaughter, and the government's policy was thus aimed at promoting the slaughtering business rather than cattle production.

References

Aldaba, R. M. 2005a. "Policy Reversals, Lobby Groups and Economic Distortions." Discussion Paper 2005–04, Philippine Institute for Development Studies, Makati City, the Philippines.

———. 2005b. "The Impact of Market Reforms on Competition, Structure and Performance of the Philippine Economy." Discussion Paper 2005–24, Philippine Institute for Development Studies, Makati City, the Philippines.

Anderson, K. 1995. "Lobbying Incentives and the Pattern of Protection in Rich and Poor Countries." *Economic Development and Cultural Change* 43 (2): 401–23.

Anderson, K., and Y. Hayami, eds. 1986. *The Political Economy of Agricultural Protection: East Asia in International Perspective.* London: Allen and Unwin.

Anderson, K., M. Kurzweil, W. Martin, D. Sandri, and E. Valenzuela. 2008. "Measuring Distortions to Agricultural Incentives, Revisited." *World Trade Review* 7 (4): 675–704.

Balisacan, A. M., N. Fuwa, and M. H. Debuque. 2004. "The Political Economy of Philippine Rural Development since the 1960s." In *Rural Development and Agricultural Growth in Indonesia, the Philippines, and Thailand,* ed. T. Akiyama and D. F. Larson, 214–93. Canberra: Asia Pacific Press.

Bautista, R. M., and G. R. Tecson. 2003. "International Dimensions." In *The Philippine Economy: Development, Policies, and Challenges,* ed. A. M. Balisacan and H. Hill, 136–71. New York: Oxford University Press.

Borrell, B., D. Quirke, B. de la Pena, and L. Noveno. 1994. *Philippine Sugar: An Industry Finding Its Feet.* Canberra: Center for International Economics.

Clarete, R. L. 1991. "E.O. 470: The Economic Effects of the 1991 Tariff Policy Reform." Unpublished report, United States Agency for International Development–Philippines, Manila.

Clarete, R. L., and J. A. Roumasset. 1990. "The Relative Welfare Cost of Industrial and Agricultural Policy Distortions: A Philippine Illustration." *Oxford Economic Papers* 42 (2): 462–72.

Cororaton, C. B. 2000. "Philippine Tariff Reform: A CGE Analysis." Discussion Paper 2000–35, Philippine Institute for Development Studies, Makati City, the Philippines.

David, C. C. 1983. "Economic Policies and Philippine Agriculture." Working Paper 83–02, Philippine Institute for Development Studies, Makati City, the Philippines.

———. 1994. "GATT-UR and Philippine Agriculture: Facts and Fallacies." *Journal of Philippine Development* 21 (1–2): 141–78.

———. 2003. "Agriculture." In *The Philippine Economy: Development, Policies, and Challenges,* ed. A. M. Balisacan and H. Hill, 175–218. New York: Oxford University Press.

David, C. C., P. Intal, and A. M. Balisacan. 2007. "Distortions to Agricultural Incentives in the Philippines." Agricultural Distortions Working Paper 28, World Bank, Washington, DC.

FAOSTAT Database. Food and Agriculture Organization of the United Nations. http://faostat.fao.org/default.aspx (accessed May 2008).

GTAP Database (Global Trade Analysis Project Database). Center for Global Trade Analysis, Department of Agricultural Economics, Purdue University. https://www.gtap.agecon.purdue.edu/databases/v6/default.asp (version 6).

Habito, C. F., and C. B. Cororaton. 2000. "WTO and the Philippine Economy: An Empirical and Analytical Assessment of Post-WTO Trade Reforms in the Philippines." Unpublished report, Agile Program, United States Agency for International Development–Philippines, Manila.

Hara, Y. 1994. *Tonan ajia shokoku no keizai hatten* (*The Economic Development of Southeast Asian Countries*). Tokyo: Institute of Oriental Culture, University of Tokyo.

Intal, P. S., and J. H. Power. 1991. "The Philippines." In *Asia.* Vol. 2 of *The Political Economy of Agricultural Pricing Policy,* ed. A. O. Krueger, M. Schiff, and A. Valdés, 149–94. World Bank Comparative Study. Baltimore: Johns Hopkins University Press; Washington, DC: World Bank.

Lindert, P. 1991. "Historical Patterns of Agricultural Policy." In *Agriculture and the State: Growth, Employment, and Poverty in Developing Countries,* ed. C. P. Timmer, 29–83. Ithaca, NY: Cornell University Press.

Manasan, R. G., and V. S. Pineda. 1999. "Assessment of Philippine Tariff Reform: A 1998 Update." Unpublished working paper, Philippine Institute for Development Studies, Makati City, the Philippines.

Pasadilla, G. O. 2006. "Preferential Trading Agreements and Agricultural Liberalization in East and Southeast Asia." Working Paper 11, Asia-Pacific Research and Training Network on Trade, Trade and Investment Division, United Nations Economic and Social Commission for Asia and the Pacific, Bogor, Indonesia.

Pimentel, A. 2006. "A Study on the Impact of the Philippine Tariff Reform Program: An Input-Output Model." Unpublished working paper, Southeast Asia Research Center for Agriculture, Los Banos, the Philippines.

Power, J. H. 1971. "The Structure of Protection in the Philippines." In *The Structure of Protection in Developing Countries,* ed. B. Balassa, 271–80. Baltimore: Johns Hopkins University Press; Washington, DC: World Bank.

Tan, E. S. 1994. "Trade Policy Reforms in the 1990s: Effects of EO 470 and the Import Liberalization Program." Research Paper 94–11, Philippine Institute for Development Studies, Makati City, the Philippines.

Tan, N. A. 1979. "The Structure of Protection and Resource Flows in the Philippines." In *Industrial Promotion Policies in the Philippines,* ed. R. M. Bautista and J. H. Power, 122–67. Makati City, the Philippines: Philippine Institute for Development Studies.

Tyers, R., and K. Anderson. 1992. *Disarray in World Food Markets: A Quantitative Assessment.* New York: Cambridge University Press.

World Development Indicators Database. World Bank. http://go.worldbank.org/B53SONGPA0 (accessed May 2008).

THAILAND

Peter Warr and Archanun Kohpaiboon

Thailand is a major net agricultural exporter, and its agricultural trade policy is dominated by this fact. The list of agricultural exports includes many of the most important agricultural products produced and consumed within the country, including the staple food, rice (exports of which account for between 30 and 50 percent of the total output of the product), and also cassava, sugar, rubber, and poultry products. The list of imported agricultural commodities is much shorter. Maize has been a net export in most years, but it was also a net import during some years in the 1990s. Soybeans were a net export for several decades, but, since the early 1990s, have been a net import. Palm oil has fluctuated between a net import and a net export, but, since the late 1990s, it has been a net export.

Historically, Thailand's large agricultural surplus has always led to a degree of policy complacency regarding the agricultural sector. Agricultural importing countries are typically concerned about food security and raising agricultural productivity to reduce import dependence. In Thailand, these matters have not been a significant concern, although stabilizing food prices for consumers has been a recurrent theme of agricultural pricing policy. Until the 1980s, agricultural exports were viewed as a source of government revenue. Unlike manufacturing, traditional agriculture was not seen as a dynamic sector of the economy that might contribute to rapid growth. Because the price elasticity of supply for most agricultural products was low, at least in the short run, it was felt that the

The authors gratefully acknowledge the excellent research assistance of Arief Ramayandi and the helpful comments and assistance with data of the following colleagues: Ammar Siamwalla, Chalongphob Sussangkarn, and Wisarn Pupphavesa of the Thailand Development Research Institute; Isra Sarntisart of Chulalongkorn University; and Nipon Poapongsakorn, Prayong Netayarak, and Somboon Siriprachai of Thammasat University. They are also grateful for the helpful comments of workshop participants and the intensive assistance with spreadsheets by Marianne Kurzweil and Ernesto Valenzuela.

production of these products could be taxed heavily without creating a significant contraction in output. Moreover, most agricultural producers were impoverished, poorly educated, and politically unorganized. This was particularly the case among rice producers; so, taxing agriculture, especially rice, was politically attractive, and rice exports were taxed until 1986 (Siamwalla, Setboonsarng, and Patamasiriwat 1993).

Because of greatly increased income per person, rapid urbanization, and the swing toward more democratic political institutions, policy has shifted from taxing agriculture to more neutral trade policies. This change has almost certainly owed more to politics—the political necessity of finding ways to attract the support of the huge rural electorate and the desire of the urban electorate to establish better economic conditions for the farm population—than to a desire to liberalize agricultural trade for the efficiency reasons that economists emphasize. However, the transition away from taxing agriculture has not progressed much in the direction of subsidizing agriculture. The key reason is that many important agricultural commodities are net export items, and this has made subsidizing agriculture problematic. Had the commodities farmers produce been competing with imports and thus amenable to the imposition of tariffs, there might have been more political pressure to protect farmers.

Thailand is an active member of the Cairns Group of agricultural exporting countries within the membership of the World Trade Organization. Nonetheless, while its agricultural trade is relatively liberal, the country cannot be described as a free trader with regard to agricultural commodities. Within Thailand, opposition to agricultural import liberalization is strong in the case of soybeans, palm oil, rubber, rice, and sugar. The protective measures include nontariff instruments that permit substantial discretion by government officials. The import controls include import prohibitions, strict licensing arrangements, local content rules, and a requirement for special case-by-case approval of imports. The commodities for which these restrictions are applied include the five above, plus onions, garlic, potatoes, pepper, tea, raw silk, maize, coconut products, and coffee.

The inclusion of rice in this list of protected commodities may seem strange. Thailand is the world's largest exporter of rice and is undoubtedly one of the world's most efficient rice producers. Why should the rice industry require protection from imports? Imports of rice are, in fact, *prohibited* unless they are specifically approved by the Ministry of Commerce. The Ministry of Agriculture and Cooperatives vigorously opposes any liberalization commitments with regard to rice. The reasons apparently relate to the ministry's wish to keep its options open with respect to rice policy in the event market conditions should change unexpectedly. Sudden changes in the price of rice can have far-reaching political consequences. The domestic rice market operates almost entirely without government intervention, but the instruments for intervention are ever ready.

A lesser reason for the import controls on rice is that, as with most agricultural commodities, rice is a highly differentiated commodity. Not all grades of rice are produced efficiently within Thailand, and the government wishes to protect domestic producers from imports of the grades of rice that are closer substitutes for local grades on the consumption side than they are on the production side. The lower grades of rice produced in Vietnam, but not in Thailand, are an important example.

Thailand's general exclusion list applies to agreements in the free trade area of the Association of Southeast Asian Nations and includes several agricultural industries, among which are rice, sugar, and palm oil (both crude and refined). Within government circles, discussions about problems in the agricultural sector revolve overwhelmingly around the treatment of Thai exports by other countries. Thailand's own agricultural import policy is a closed question. Problems have been encountered with a number of trading partners about environmental issues and sanitary and phytosanitary issues with Thailand's agricultural exports. These problems have included a well-publicized dispute with the United States over shrimps (environmental issues) and another with Australia over precooked frozen chicken (sanitary and phytosanitary issues).

Poverty in the country is heavily concentrated in rural areas, and public opinion favors government support for the rural poor. Since the economic crisis of 1997–98 and especially during the government of Prime Minister Thaksin Shinawatra in 2001–06, a wide range of income support programs, cash grants to villages, and subsidized credit schemes have been introduced. Support for these schemes was a significant component of the populist economic policy agenda of the Thaksin government. However, the operations of few of these schemes, if any, depended on the prices faced by agricultural producers. Because they were not linked directly to the production of agricultural commodities, it seems that they were not distorting resource allocations. The results of our study make an assessment possible of whether the price incentives facing agricultural producers were, indeed, distorted relative to international prices during the period of populist government.

The following section of the chapter briefly describes the changing structure of the Thai economy, especially the agricultural sector. The core of the analysis, contained in the section thereafter, relies on comparisons between the domestic prices and the international prices for major agricultural commodities and fertilizer and relates the price comparisons to tariff and nontariff barriers on the same products. It focuses on whether the relative prices for traded commodities at wholesale have differed from the relative border prices, adjusted for transport and handling costs. The subsequent section extends this analysis to the farm level. The raw commodities produced by farmers generally do not enter international trade directly. These raw commodities are inputs into the production of the processed commodities that actually enter international trade. For example, rice produced at the farm level (paddy) must be milled before it can be traded internationally. Rice milling, transport, packaging, and storage are all costly activities, and several steps in the marketing chain intervene between farmers and the international market. This raises the controversial issue of the effect exerted on the prices actually received by farmers for their output, such as paddy, by the protection of processed commodities, such as milled rice, that is observed at the wholesale level and captured by the price comparisons. In the penultimate section, we analyze this issue econometrically using price data, and, from this analysis, we derive the imputed rates of protection for farm-produced commodities. The final section concludes with a discussion of the future prospects for agricultural trade policy in Thailand.

Economic Growth and Structural Change

Over almost four decades, from 1968 to 2005, Thailand's economic output grew in real terms at an average annual rate of 6.5 percent. The broad characteristics of this growth are summarized in table 7.1. For ease of comparison with other Asian economies, the table distinguishes between the two-decade preboom period ending in 1986 and the following boom decade that preceded the Asian crisis of 1997–98. As the table shows, the growth rate of gross domestic product (GDP) during the boom decade was 9.5 percent, which was the most rapid GDP growth in the world and almost half again as rapid as the GDP growth during the two preboom decades. Output contracted during the crisis years of 1997–98. During the subsequent recovery, growth averaged a moderate 5.1 percent.

In Thailand, as in many other rapidly growing economies, agricultural output increased more slowly than GDP, implying that agriculture had a declining share in aggregate output. The agricultural sector accounted for 32 percent of GDP in 1965. By 2004, this share had declined to 10 percent. Over the same period, the GDP share of industry rose from 23 to 43 percent, and the share of services

Table 7.1. Real GDP Growth and Its Sectoral Components, Thailand, 1968–2005

(average annual percent)

Sector	Pre-boom, 1968–86	Boom, 1987–96	Crisis, 1997–99	Recovery, 2000–05	All years, 1968–2005
Total	6.7	9.5	−2.5	5.1	6.5
Agriculture	4.5	2.6	0.1	3.6	3.5
Industry	8.5	12.8	−1.7	6.3	8.5
Services	6.8	9.0	−3.6	4.2	6.2

Source: Author calculations based on data in World Development Indicators Database 2008.

Table 7.2. Subsector Shares of Agricultural Value Added, Thailand, 1975–2000

(percent)

Subsector	1975	1980	1985	1990	1995	2000
Paddy	38.0	30.3	34.7	24.9	26.9	26.1
Maize	6.4	4.3	4.2	3.7	3.7	3.4
Other cereals	0.5	0.6	0.5	0.2	0.1	0.2
Cassava	4.2	7.6	5.5	6.6	5.2	2.5
Beans and nuts	2.4	2.5	3.7	3.0	2.1	1.7
Vegetables	11.7	10.4	9.1	12.7	9.9	10.6
Fruits	11.4	15.0	10.5	10.9	11.1	15.8
Sugarcane	5.9	5.4	3.2	6.7	5.2	5.3
Coconuts	1.4	1.7	1.8	1.2	0.9	0.7
Palm nuts and palm oil	0.0	0.1	0.6	1.2	1.2	1.4
Rubber	2.2	4.6	8.4	10.2	17.5	12.4
Other crops	5.7	5.2	5.3	4.3	4.3	4.3
Cattle and buffalo	2.5	3.3	5.3	6.3	3.9	4.8
Swine	3.2	3.0	1.6	1.9	1.7	1.5
Poultry	1.1	2.0	4.0	3.6	3.9	6.6
Other livestock	3.6	4.0	1.9	2.7	2.1	2.9
Total	100	100	100	100	100	100

Source: Author calculations based on data in NESDB, various.

grew from 45 to 47 percent. Part of this long-term contraction is explained by the declining terms of trade for the country's agricultural exports (Warr and Kohpaiboon 2007).

For a more detailed study of the changing composition of the agricultural sector, one may use input-output tables, which are available at five-year intervals from 1975 to 2000 (NESDB, various). Over this period, the value added in paddy production (unmilled rice produced at the farm level) declined from 38 to 26 percent of total agricultural value added (table 7.2). Changes in the distribution of expenditure as incomes increased explain most of this change. As incomes rise, the expenditure on starchy staples typically declines as a share of total expenditures. The shares of maize and cassava similarly declined, but the shares of fruit, poultry, cattle, and rubber rose.

For almost all agricultural commodities, the share of intermediate inputs in the value of total output increased significantly over 1975–2000 (Warr and Kohpaiboon 2007). In paddy production, for example, the share rose from 14 to 30 percent. For the entire agricultural sector, this cost share rose from 21 to 37 percent over the same period. Most intermediate goods used in agriculture are domestically produced, but the share of imports in total intermediate input use increased from 10 to 17 percent (Warr and Kohpaiboon 2007).

There have been substantial changes in the pattern of sales among agricultural products. In 1975, sales of agricultural products to intermediate users (millers and processors) accounted for 57 percent of total sales, but, by 2000, these sales had risen to 70 percent. Almost all paddy is milled into edible rice commercially rather than on-farm. Paddy is not exported or imported, but milled rice has historically been an important export item, as has refined sugar. Cassava is similarly exported in the form of processed animal feed. Rubber exports have become increasingly significant since the 1990s. Soybeans have become a major net import and are used for processed foods and for animal feed (Warr and Kohpaiboon 2007).[1]

The Changing Structure of Assistance at the Wholesale Level

In their definitive studies of agricultural price policy in Thailand up to the mid-1980s, Siamwalla and Setboonsarng (1989, 1991) make the point that policies on the various agricultural commodities were determined individually in response to circumstances that varied depending on the commodity rather than forming part of a single, integrated agricultural policy approach. For this reason, they argue, it is best to consider the main commodities one at a time, which they then do for rice, sugar, maize, and rubber. The discussion that follows will also rely on this strategy, except that the range of commodities includes cassava, soybeans, and palm oil, in addition to the four reviewed by Siamwalla and Setboonsarng. Our analysis also considers a major input, urea fertilizer. Following this commodity-specific review, we address common themes, if any, that may run through agricultural policy as a whole.

The main focus of our study's methodology is government-imposed distortions that create a gap between domestic prices and the prices that would emerge under free market conditions. (For a detailed description of the methodology, see Anderson et al. 2008 and appendix A.) Since it is not possible to understand the characteristics of agricultural development through a sectoral view alone, the methodology not only estimates the effects of direct agricultural policy measures, but, for comparative evaluation, it also includes estimates of distortions in nonagricultural tradable sectors. Specifically, we compute nominal rates of assistance (NRAs) for farmers, including an adjustment for direct interventions on tradable inputs such as fertilizer.[2] We also calculate NRAs for nonagricultural tradables for use with the NRAs for agricultural tradables to generate relative rates of assistance (RRAs).

We conduct our analysis at the wholesale level; so, in what follows, the domestic price means the domestic wholesale price. In the calculation of the NRAs, the border prices are amended by the transport and handling costs involved in adjusting the price of imports from the cost, insurance, and freight level to the domestic wholesale level and in adjusting the price of exports from the domestic wholesale level to the free on board level. (The relevant transport and handling costs are summarized in Warr and Kohpaiboon 2007.) These adjustments are required to obtain prices that are comparable with domestic wholesale prices. The border prices adjusted for transport and handling costs may then be interpreted as an indication of domestic wholesale prices as they would be in the absence of protection.

Rice

From the end of World War II to 1986, the Thai government taxed rice exports. There were four individual instruments of export taxation, each with distinct legal foundations, and each under the control of different parts of the government bureaucracy. The revenues these various instruments generated were directed toward separate parts of the government. Siamwalla and Setboonsarng (1989, 1991) describe these independent tax streams and point out that their combined effect was a rate of export taxation of around 40 percent from the late 1950s to the early 1970s. The rate increased to around 60 percent during the commodity price boom of 1972–74, but subsequently diminished quickly to about 20 percent. There was another peak, at about 40 percent, at the time of the second Organization of the Petroleum Exporting Countries oil price shock in 1979–80 and then a steady decline until all four forms of tax were suspended in 1986. Rice exports have remained untaxed for the two decades since then.[3]

The implications of these events for actual prices are summarized in figure 7.1, which is based on the data assembled in Warr and Kohpaiboon (2007). As with each similar figure presented thereafter on another agricultural commodity, figure 7.1 compares domestic wholesale prices with border prices for rice of comparable quality. Since rice is a net export, border price in the figure means export price, adjusted for transport and handling costs between the wholesale level and the export level. The calculations of the nominal rates of protection (NRPs) that emerge are similar to those that would be inferred from the rates of taxation described above, except that the NRPs after 1986 are not zero, but average around −6 percent. It is possible that the transport and handling costs between the wholesale and free on board locations are not fully accounted for in the data in Warr and Kohpaiboon (2007). For rice, the data in figure 7.1 support the view that the domestic market has received zero protection and zero subsidies; moreover, rice is also no longer taxed.

Figure 7.1. Price Comparisons and NRPs at Wholesale, Rice, Thailand, 1968–2005

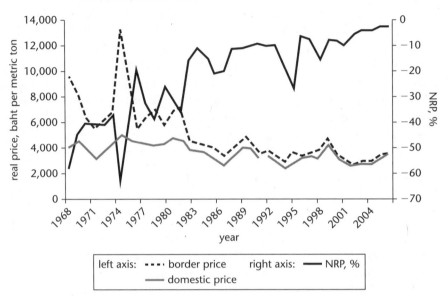

Source: Warr and Kohpaiboon 2007.

Note: NRP = 100*(domestic price − border price)/border price.

Maize

Maize was a net Thai export item until the 1990s. In 1992 and 1995–2000, imports dominated. Maize subsequently reverted and is now a net export good once more. In 1965–81, the government intervened in the export market to preserve the exports to Japan and Taiwan, China, where they were used primarily for animal feed. In both markets, season-long stability in supply was an import requirement. To ensure the fulfillment of the domestic contracts needed to ensure this stability, the government imposed quota restrictions on exports to markets other than the markets of these two economies. The effects of this policy included an increase in the price volatility passed on to domestic producers and average producer earnings that were somewhat reduced. Meanwhile, Malaysia, Singapore, and other countries closer to Thailand had developed their own livestock industries. The Japanese and Taiwan, China markets therefore seemed less crucial, and, by 1981, the export controls on maize were removed. The data in figure 7.2 indicate that there was roughly zero protection for the maize industry. Whether maize was a net import product or a net export product, this outcome does not seem to have varied in any systematic way.

Figure 7.2. Price Comparisons and NRPs at Wholesale, Maize, Thailand, 1968–2005

Source: Warr and Kohpaiboon 2007.

Note: NRP = 100*(domestic price − border price)/border price.

Cassava

Thailand's cassava exports developed for the supply of animal feed to European and some Asian markets, including Taiwan, China. Because of the quota restrictions of the European Union, rents were attached to export quotas from Thailand, which, in turn, led to corruption in the allocation of the quotas. The rents associated with the quotas are analogous to a privately collected export tax. As a result of the rents, the export price exceeded the domestic price by amounts averaging around 10 percent (figure 7.3).

Soybeans

Soybeans were a net export item from 1960 until 1988. By 1992, they were a net import item. During the export period, exports were taxed, but, beginning in 1995, the trade regime shifted nominally to tariff quotas. The operation of the tariff quotas is described in Warr and Kohpaiboon (2007). Within the import quota volume permitted, soybeans could be imported at low or zero tariffs. Beyond the quota, the applied tariff was set at the maximum amount permitted by World Trade Organization obligations, which varied between 80 and 90 percent.

Figure 7.3. Price Comparisons and NRPs at Wholesale, Cassava, Thailand, 1969–2004

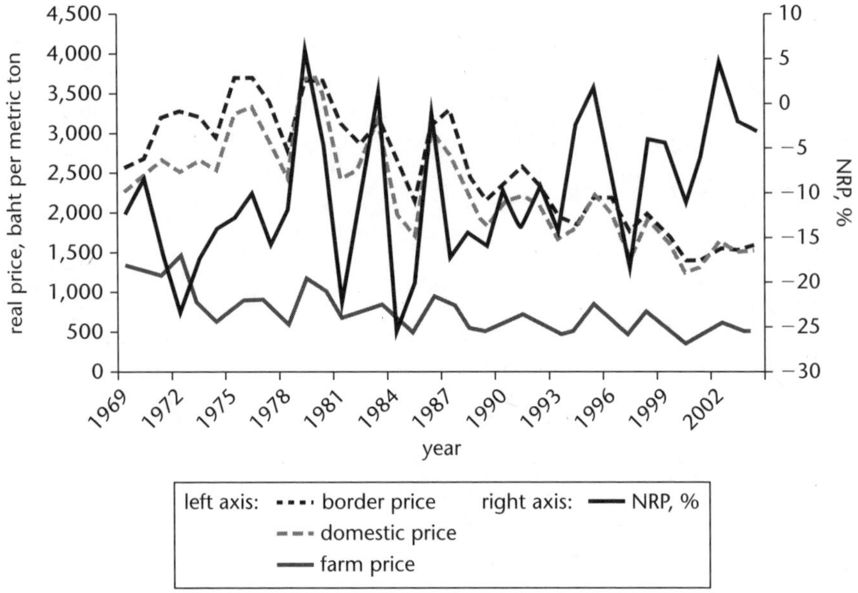

Source: Warr and Kohpaiboon 2007.

Note: NRP = 100*(domestic price − border price)/border price.

Figure 7.4 indicates that the transition of soybeans from a net export to a net import in 1992 coincided with a shift from negative NRPs of around −20 percent to positive NRPs of 30–40 percent.

Sugar

In discussions on agricultural economics, the sugar industry is often considered an outlier in the treatment it receives from trade policy. Thailand is no exception. Sugar was an imported item until the late 1950s, but has been a net export item since then. Nonetheless, it receives protection through a home price scheme. This type of scheme involves taxing consumers and using the proceeds to subsidize exports. A scheme of this sort was practiced in the Australian sugar and dairy industries in the 1950s and 1960s (Sieper 1982). It is said that a Thai economics student at an Australian university learned about the scheme and brought the idea to Thailand, where the scheme was applied in the sugar industry long after it had been abandoned in Australia.

A home price scheme drives up the domestic consumer and producer prices of the product to subsidize producers at the expense of consumers. The scheme

Figure 7.4. Price Comparisons and NRPs at Wholesale, Soybeans, Thailand, 1984–2005

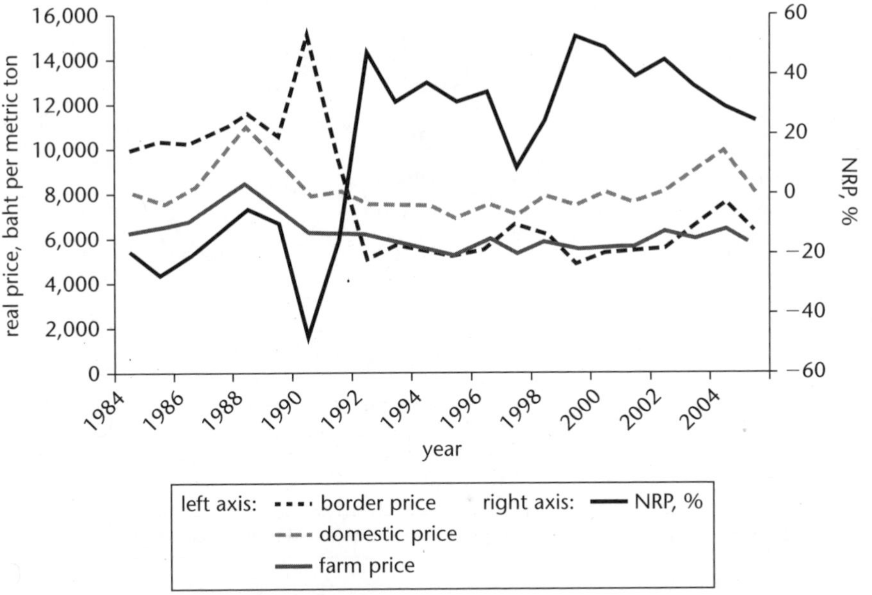

Source: Warr and Kohpaiboon 2007.

Note: NRP = 100*(domestic price − border price)/border price.

requires that leakage be prevented from the export market to the more profitable domestic market. In most industries, this is difficult. Reimporting for domestic consumption must also be restricted, and, as Corden (1974) points out, this may be achieved through a restrictive tariff. Because the scheme is self-financing, it is attractive for finance ministries. However, the scheme is a protectionist device, and has a notable limitation: the capacity of the consumption tax to subsidize exports is reduced if the volume of exports comes to represent a substantial share of total output (exports, plus domestic consumption). This has been an issue in the case of the sugar industry in Thailand.

Siamwalla and Setboonsarng (1989, 1991) attribute the political power of the Thai sugar industry to technological changes in milling that call for large mills and the precise scheduling of sugar deliveries to the mills. Milling is highly capital intensive, and, during the sugar processing season, processing plants must be fully utilized. Growers and millers have bickered over prices, but they have been able to combine their efforts to lobby the government for intervention on their behalf; other agricultural export industries in Thailand have been unable to achieve this success. Sugar growers and millers are highly organized. The technological

Figure 7.5. Ratios, Consumer Prices to Border Prices and Miller Prices to Grower Prices, Sugar, Thailand, 1968–2005

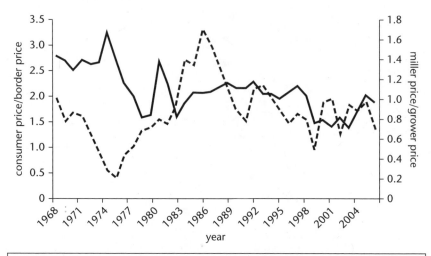

left axis: ---- consumer price/border price   right axis: —— miller price/grower price

Source: Warr and Kohpaiboon 2007.

changes in sugar milling have also helped restrict leakage from the export market to home consumption because the mills are large and few in number.

The scheme has stabilized consumer prices relative to export prices. Figure 7.5 shows two series: the ratio of consumer prices to border prices (left axis) and the ratio of miller prices to grower prices (right axis). The peak export prices of the early 1970s were not transmitted to consumers or producers, and the NRPs for sugar (calculated as the percent deviation of the grower price from the export price) were negative at the time (figure 7.6). However, during most of the period of the operation of the scheme, consumer and producer prices were well above export prices. Since the mid-1980s, the NRPs have averaged over 60 percent. Although it is exported, sugar is the most heavily protected agricultural subsector by far.

Palm oil

Palm oil has sometimes been a net import item and sometimes a net export item. Although the palm oil industry has been a net exporter since 1998, a system of import quotas remains in place (see Warr and Kohpaiboon 2007). Figure 7.7 shows the NRPs for palm oil at wholesale.

Figure 7.6. Price Comparisons and NRPs at Wholesale, Sugar, Thailand, 1968–2005

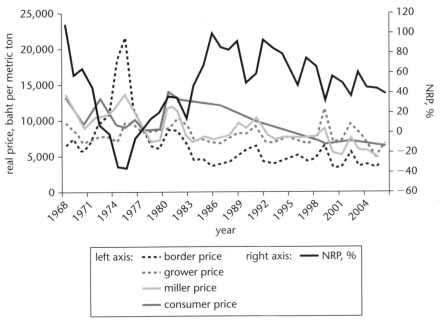

Source: Warr and Kohpaiboon 2007.

Note: NRP = 100*(domestic price − border price)/border price.

Figure 7.7. Price Comparisons and NRPs at Wholesale, Palm Oil, Thailand, 1995–2004

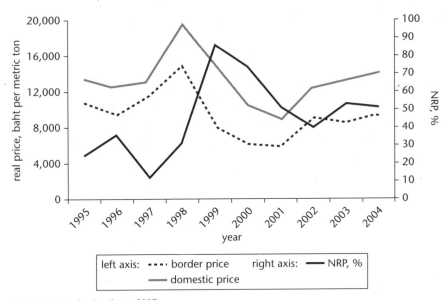

Source: Warr and Kohpaiboon 2007.

Note: NRP = 100*(domestic price − border price)/border price.

Figure 7.8. Price Comparisons and NRPs at Wholesale, Rubber, Thailand, 1968–2005

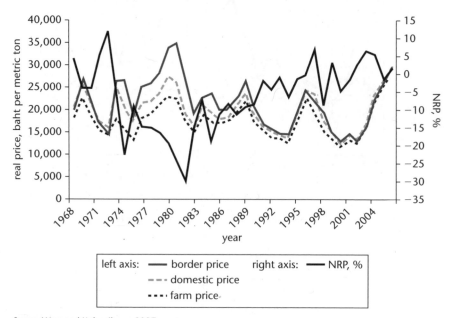

Source: Warr and Kohpaiboon 2007.

Note: NRP = 100*(domestic price − border price)/border price.

Rubber

Rubber is a net export item, and the rubber industry was subject to an export tax for many years. The manner of calculating the tax meant that the rate drifted upwards along with inflation, and, because of the inflation in the 1970s, the export tax rate on rubber had reached 26 percent by the early 1980s. Pressure from members of Parliament representing rubber production areas in the southern parts of the country led to a revision of the method of calculating the tax. This generated a return to the lower tax rates that had been in place in the 1960s. Figure 7.8 confirms that, since 1990, the tax rate on rubber has been close to zero.

Fertilizer

Urea is imported for use as fertilizer, the rates of tariff protection for these imports have been declining. The import taxation implies that there is disprotection (taxation) for the agricultural industries using this input. The decline in tariff rates began in the early 1990s, and, by the early 2000s, the rates were negligible. This policy change is confirmed by the price comparisons reported in figure 7.9. NRPs

Figure 7.9. Price Comparisons and NRPs at Wholesale, Urea Fertilizer, Thailand, 1984–2005

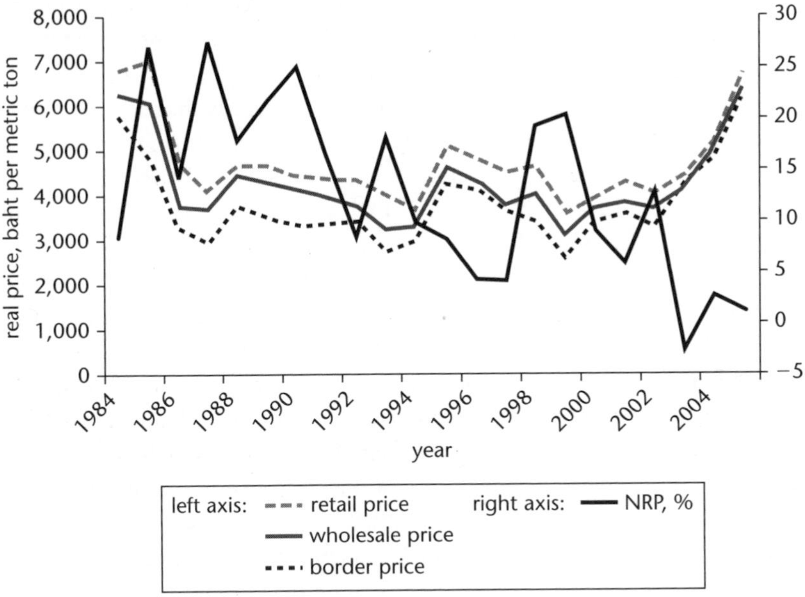

Source: Warr and Kohpaiboon 2007.

Note: NRP = 100*(domestic price − border price)/border price.

have declined steadily and are currently close to zero. This treatment of fertilizer—steadily declining rates of taxation—contrasts with the treatment in several neighboring countries, where fertilizer use has tended to be subsidized as part of a general program of agricultural subsidization.

Imputed Assistance at the Farm Level

Our discussion of protection rates has focused so far on the effects that policy interventions have on the wholesale market. In this section, we extend the analysis to consider the way protection (or its opposite) in the wholesale market produces price effects at the farm level.

Theory

One of the aims of agricultural protection policy is to influence prices at the farm-gate. However, the goods produced by farmers seldom enter international trade directly. The raw commodities produced by farmers are generally nontraded, whereas the commodities that enter international trade are the processed or partially processed versions of these raw products. Between the nontraded raw product produced by the farmer and the traded processed commodity that enters international trade, there may be several other steps, including transport, storage, milling, processing, and repackaging.

However, border protection policy operates on the goods that enter international trade either as exports or as imports. It does not operate on the raw commodities produced by farmers. Protection at the farm level is therefore a derived effect. It depends on the extent to which the policies applied to the trade in processed agricultural goods induce changes in the prices of these goods and then transmit the changes to the prices faced by farmers. An issue thus arises about the degree to which price changes at wholesale that are induced by protection policy affect the prices received by farmers for the raw products they sell.

We construct a simple econometric model to investigate this issue. We use the notational convention that uppercase roman letters (such as X) denote the level of the values of variables and that lowercase roman letters (such as x) denote the natural logarithms of these values. Thus, $x = ln\ X$. Protection at the wholesale level is therefore defined as:

$$P_{it}^W = P_{it}^*(1 + T_{it}^W), \qquad (7.1)$$

where P_{it}^W denotes the level of the wholesale price of commodity i at time t; P_{it}^* is the corresponding border price expressed in the domestic currency and adjusted for the handling costs involved in transferring the commodity from the cost, insurance, and freight price level to the domestic wholesale price level in the case of an import or in transferring the commodity from the wholesale price level to the free on board price level in the case of an export. The NRP at the wholesale level is given by T_{it}^W. In this discussion, both the border price and the NRP are treated as exogenous variables. The border price is determined by world markets, and we presume that the country under discussion is a price taker. The NRP is determined by the government's protection policy.

The farmgate price of the raw material is denoted by P_{it}^F, and its logarithm, p_{it}^F, is related to the logarithm of the wholesale price as follows:

$$p_{it}^F = a_i + b_i p_{it}^W + u_{it}, \qquad (7.2)$$

where a_i and b_i are coefficients, and u_{it} is a random error term. The coefficient b_i is the pass-through or transmission elasticity. The estimated values of the coefficients a_i and b_i are denoted by $\hat{a}_i$ and $\hat{b}_i$, respectively. The econometric estimation of these parameters is discussed below.

The estimated coefficients are used as follows. We estimate the logarithm of the farm price that would obtain in the *absence* of any protection as:

$$\hat{p}_{it}^{F*} = \hat{a}_i + \hat{b}_i p_{it}^{W*}, \qquad (7.3)$$

where p_{it}^{W*} is the estimated value of the wholesale price that would obtain in the absence of protection so that $p_{it}^{W*} = \ln P_{it}^{W*}$. This is then compared with the estimated value of the wholesale price in the *presence* of protection, as follows:

$$\hat{p}_{it}^F = \hat{a}_i + \hat{b}_i p_{it}^W. \tag{7.4}$$

We denote the antilogs of $\hat{p}_{it}^F$ and $\hat{p}_{it}^{F*}$ by $\hat{P}_{it}^F$ and $\hat{P}_{it}^{F*}$, respectively, and then estimate the NRP at the farm level as:

$$\hat{T}_{it}^F = (\hat{P}_{it}^F - \hat{P}_{it}^{F*})/\hat{P}_{it}^F. \tag{7.5}$$

It is important to observe that the value of the protection-inclusive farmgate price we use in these calculations is the price we have estimated using the econometric model (equation 7.4) rather than the actual price given by the raw data. We do this because our intention is to use the model to estimate the *change* in the farmgate price generated by the protection at the wholesale level. Thus, both the protection-inclusive and the protection-exclusive prices used in (7.5) are the predicted values obtained through the model.

The implied NRP at the farmgate can be related to the NRP at wholesale, as follows. Substituting $\hat{P}_{it}^F = \hat{A}_i(P_{it}^W)^{\hat{b}_i}$ and $\hat{P}_{it}^{F*} = \hat{A}_i(P_{it}^{W*})^{\hat{b}_i}$ into equation (7.5), where $\hat{A}_i$ is the antilog of $\hat{a}_i$, rearranging, and using equation (7.1), we obtain the simple expression:

$$\hat{T}_{it}^F = (1 + T_{it}^W)^{\hat{b}_i} - 1. \tag{7.6}$$

Obviously, if $T_{it}^W = 0$, then $\hat{T}_{it}^F = 0$, regardless of the value of $\hat{b}_i$. Similarly, if $\hat{b}_i = 0$, then $\hat{T}_{it}^F = 0$, regardless of the value of T_{it}^W. Also, if $\hat{b}_i = 1$, then $\hat{T}_{it}^F = T_{it}^W$. It may be readily seen that, if $T_{it}^W > 0$, then $\hat{T}^F \geq T_{it}^W$ as $\hat{b}_i \geq 1$ and $\hat{T}^F \leq T_{it}^W$ as $\hat{b}_i \leq 1$. If $T_{it}^W < 0$, then $\hat{T}^F \leq T_{it}^W$ as $\hat{b}_i \geq 1$, but $\hat{T}^F \geq T_{it}^W$ as $\hat{b}_i \leq 1$.

Econometric application

The purpose of the econometric analysis is to estimate the parameter $\hat{b}_i$ for each commodity.[4] We conduct the analysis for each commodity by relying on time series price data in which each variable is expressed in logarithms, and each is deflated by the GDP deflator for Thailand: the farmgate price (LFP), the wholesale price (LWP), and the log of the international price, adjusted by the nominal exchange rate and transport and handling costs (LIP).

We first test each of the series for the existence of a unit root. The null hypothesis of a unit root was rejected for all price series for all commodities except soybeans. (One should recall that the price series, relying on the GDP deflator, are real, not nominal.) However, in the case of soybeans (the two price series for which the null hypothesis of a unit root could not be rejected), the series were not cointegrated. For all commodities except soybeans, the price series were thus considered stationary.

First, we produced ordinary least squares estimates of equation (7.2). In most cases, autocorrelation was a problem, and an AR(1) correction term was included to eliminate it. The correction term accomplished this task effectively. The ordinary least squares estimates assume that LFP is endogenous and LWP is exogenous. These assumptions were tested using Hausman's endogeneity test. In the case of each commodity, the null hypothesis that LWP was (weakly) exogenous to LFP failed to be rejected, confirming the validity of the estimates. Reverse Hausman's tests were also conducted, and the null hypothesis that LFP was exogenous to LWP was rejected in every case. These results support the validity of the use of the ordinary least squares framework to estimate the transmission elasticity from LWP to LFP, treating LWP as exogenous. For completeness, instrumental variable estimates were produced for each commodity using LIP as the instrument for LWP. The resulting estimates of $\hat{b}_i$ differed from the ordinary least squares estimates (some larger, some smaller), but not by much.

Table 7.3 summarizes the estimates. All the ordinary least squares estimates of transmission elasticity were significantly different from zero and showed the expected positive signs. This is an important point. It is often asserted that the commodity price changes arising at the wholesale level (because of protection or international price movements) are prevented by middlemen from being transmitted to farmers. This hypothesis is strongly rejected by the Thai data. The transmission elasticities are not zero. Economists often assume that the transmission elasticities are unity. However, the estimated values are generally less than unity;

Table 7.3. Estimates of Transmission Elasticities from Wholesale to Farm Prices, Thailand

Commodity	Estimated elasticity	t-statistic
Rice	0.76	(7.30)
Maize	0.81	(14.38)
Cassava	1.07	(8.20)
Soybeans	0.80	(11.23)
Sugar	0.53	(3.93)
Palm oil[a]	[0.90]	(19.97)
Rubber	0.90	(19.97)
Fertilizer	0.89	(17.70)

Source: Author calculations.

Note: The table has been created using the data and methodology discussed in the text. The estimates shown relate to the parameter b_i in equation (7.2).

a. An estimate for palm oil has not been possible because of insufficient data points. The estimated value for rubber has been used instead.

most are between 0.7 and 0.9. In one case (sugar), the estimate is somewhat lower (0.53), and, in another (cassava), the estimated value slightly exceeds unity, but is not significantly different from unity.[5] It is likely that the true transmission elasticities change over time, but the limited data available for this exercise have made it necessary to assume that the true values remain constant.

Estimation of assistance at the farm level

Given the estimated value of the transmission elasticity, we use equation (7.6), together with the estimated NRPs at the wholesale level discussed above, to produce estimates of the imputed NRAs at the farm level. These are shown in Warr and Kohpaiboon (2007). Because the estimated values of the transmission elasticity are between zero and unity (except for the case of cassava), the imputed NRAs at the farmgate are somewhat lower in absolute value than the NRAs at the wholesale level, but, because of the assumption of constant transmission elasticities over time, they closely track the pattern of the results at the wholesale level.

Aggregate Measures of Agricultural Assistance

In this section, we calculate aggregate measures of rates of assistance using the information assembled from the preceding analysis and following, as much as possible, the methodology outlined in Anderson et al. (2008) and appendix A. The annual calculations reported in this section fluctuate somewhat from year to year. International and domestic price changes from year to year alter the protective effects of all instruments of protection except ad valorem tariffs. In addition, the time required for domestic prices to adjust to international price changes means that the annual data on price differences produce some spurious variations from one year to the next. Our interest is in broad trends rather than in these annual fluctuations.

Table 7.4 reports estimates of the NRAs at the farmgate for all commodities. These estimates take account of the assistance for fertilizer inputs. The NRAs are calculated as the corresponding NRPs (discussed above), minus the product of the cost share of fertilizer in the production of the relevant commodity and the consumer tax equivalent of the import protection for the fertilizer industry. The consumer tax equivalent for fertilizer is positive every year but one, although the rates of taxation have declined since the mid-1980s. The NRAs for covered products at wholesale are therefore below the NRAs at the farmgate for every commodity for which fertilizer is an input in production. The broad pattern in the NRAs for farmers is otherwise similar to the pattern in the NRAs discussed above.

The NRAs are negative in all years for rice and in most years for maize, cassava, and rubber. For these commodities, the absolute magnitudes of these negative

Table 7.4. NRAs for Covered Agricultural Products, Thailand, 1970–2004
(percent)

Indicator, product	1970–74	1975–79	1980–84	1985–89	1990–94	1995–99	2000–04
Exportables[a]	−26.7	−19.4	−11.1	−11.7	−9.2	−3.8	−0.6
Soybeans[b]	—	—	—	−19.9	n.a.	n.a.	n.a.
Rice	−30.1	−28.3	−18.0	−15.0	−16.2	−11.0	−7.6
Maize	−2.2	−2.6	−2.2	−7.6	−4.5	−11.5	−0.3
Cassava	−23.1	−0.8	−9.0	−16.6	−10.8	−13.8	−10.0
Sugar	12.6	−3.2	12.7	36.8	34.0	22.4	12.6
Rubber	−0.5	−8.7	−17.9	−13.3	−4.4	−1.1	0.2
Poultry	−32.9	16.1	26.8	−7.1	−11.0	17.8	20.4
Palm oil	—	—	n.a.	n.a.	n.a.	−12.6	−18.3
Import-competing products[a]	−4.8	1.9	45.3	22.0	6.4	34.4	4.7
Soybeans[b]	n.a.	n.a.	n.a.	n.a.	27.5	21.5	30.0
Pig meat	−4.8	1.9	51.7	20.8	1.5	36.5	−1.8
Palm oil	—	—	−25.7	32.2	26.5	n.a.	n.a.
All covered products[a]	−25.8	−18.4	−8.4	−9.7	−7.7	−1.1	−0.6
Dispersion, covered products[c]	25.0	20.8	28.5	29.3	25.1	22.9	16.7
Coverage, at undistorted prices	65	65	68	71	71	75	78

Source: Warr and Kohpaiboon 2007.

Note: — = no data are available. n.a. = not applicable.

a. Weighted averages; the weights are based on the unassisted value of production.

b. For exportables, 1985–89 refers to 1984–91. For import-competing products, 1990–94 refers to 1992–94, and 2000–04 refers to 2000–03.

c. Dispersion is a simple five-year average of the annual standard deviation around the weighted mean of the NRAs of covered products.

rates have declined over time. For soybeans, the nominal rate was negative until soybeans became a net import item in the early 1990s. Since then, soybeans have been significantly protected. Sugar has been a protected commodity in almost all years. The weighted average for all covered products was more than −25 percent before the later 1970s, but the mean rate of taxation has since fallen to virtually zero. The dispersion of rates for individual commodities around this mean has not fallen much though, suggesting that there is still considerable scope for policy reform to reduce distortions within the farm sector (bottom of table 7.4).

We have calculated the RRAs in agriculture to take into account not only the NRAs in agriculture, but also the NRAs in manufacturing and other nonfarm tradable sectors. We estimate the average NRAs for import-competing manufacturing based on data in Nicita and Olarreaga (2006), while we assume that the average NRAs for other nonfarm tradable sectors are zero.[6] The weighted average of these two sets of NRAs is then calculated using weights from the input-output tables of the National Economic and Social Development Board (NESDB, various). The estimated RRAs are negative every year, but have declined in absolute value from more than −30 percent in the early 1970s to around −7 percent in recent years (table 7.5 and figure 7.10). These estimates suggest that, over the past four decades, agriculture has undergone a shift from a severely taxed sector to a mildly taxed sector (both net).

Conclusions and Prospects for Future Reform

As Thailand has industrialized, successive governments have become more interested in intervening on behalf of agricultural producers. Nonetheless, because the country is a major agricultural exporter, the scope for a policy of protection as a means of influencing domestic commodity prices has been limited. This chapter has used comparisons of the prices of agricultural commodities in domestic markets and in international markets as a means of examining the magnitude of the government's interventions.

The direct taxation of agricultural exports has been gradually eliminated. This has been important in the case of rice, on which the high rates of export taxation before the mid-1980s have been abolished. Rubber exports, taxed prior to 1990, have been untaxed since then. Cassava exports have continued to be taxed to a minor extent through the system of export quotas. Fertilizer is a major input into agricultural production, and the effective taxation of fertilizer use has been steadily eliminated since the early 1990s. Maize exports have been consistently untaxed, as have chicken exports. Most of this evolution in taxation and protection has involved eliminating the price distortions that once disfavored agricultural export industries.

Table 7.5. NRAs in Agriculture Relative to Nonagricultural Industries, Thailand, 1970–2004

(percent)

Indicator	1970–74	1975–79	1980–84	1985–89	1990–94	1995–99	2000–04
Covered products[a]	−25.8	−18.4	−8.4	−9.7	−7.7	−1.1	−0.6
Noncovered products	−10.4	−5.8	11.3	3.4	−0.9	10.1	1.4
All agricultural products[a]	−20.3	−14.0	−2.0	−6.2	−5.7	1.7	−0.2
Non-product-specific assistance	0.0	0.0	0.0	0.0	0.0	0.0	0.0
Total agricultural NRA[b]	−20.3	−14.0	−2.0	−6.2	−5.7	1.7	−0.2
Trade bias index[c]	−0.18	−0.20	−0.37	−0.24	−0.14	−0.27	−0.03
NRA, agricultural tradables	−23.1	−15.9	−2.3	−6.9	−6.4	1.8	−0.2
NRA, nonagricultural tradables	16.1	16.0	14.2	11.1	10.0	8.9	7.8
RRA[d]	−33.7	−27.5	−14.4	−16.3	−14.9	−6.5	−7.4

Source: Warr and Kohpaiboon 2007.

a. Including product-specific input subsidies.

b. Including product-specific input subsidies and non-product-specific assistance. Represents total assistance to primary factors and intermediate inputs, divided by the total value of primary agriculture production at undistorted prices.

c. The trade bias index is defined as $(1 + NRAag_x/100)/(1 + NRAag_m/100) - 1$, where $NRAag_m$ and $NRAag_x$ are the average percentage NRAs for the import-competing and exportable parts of the agricultural sector, respectively.

d. The RRA is defined as $100*[(100 + NRAag^t)/(100 + NRAnonag^t) - 1]$, where $NRAag^t$ and $NRAnonag^t$ are the percentage NRAs for the tradables parts of the agricultural and nonagricultural sectors, respectively.

**Figure 7.10. NRAs for Agricultural and Nonagricultural
Tradables and the RRA, Thailand, 1970–2004**

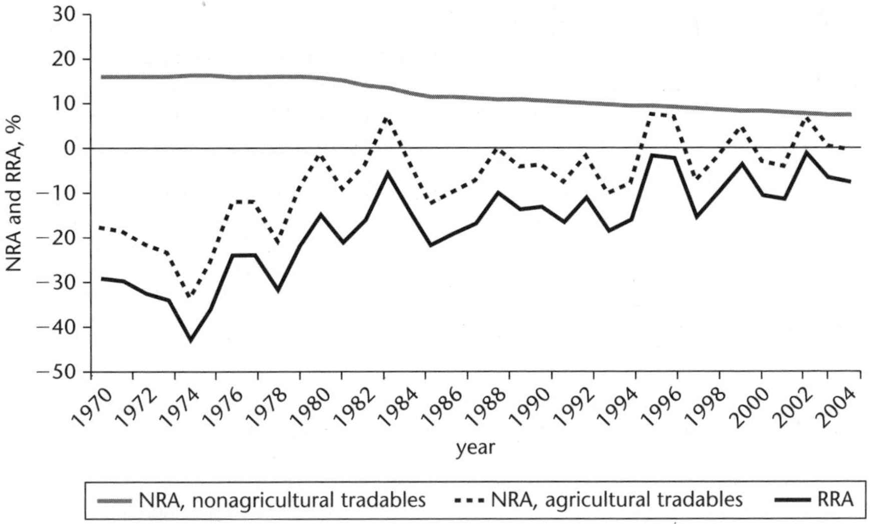

Source: Warr and Kohpaiboon 2007.

Note: For the definition of the RRA, see table 7.5, note d.

Three commodities depart from this general liberalization in agricultural markets. Soybeans were an export before 1992 and have been a net import item since then. The imports have been subject to quota restrictions. The shift from a net export item to a net import item coincided with a switch from negative to positive NRPs. Since the early 1990s, the domestic soybean industry has benefited from an NRP of around 30–40 percent. Sugar is an export commodity, but the domestic sugar industry is protected by a system that taxes domestic consumers and transfers the revenue to producers. NRPs have averaged over 60 percent. The political power of the highly capital-intensive sugar milling industry is behind this pattern of protection. The case of palm oil is qualitatively similar to sugar, but the rates of protection are somewhat lower.

Government interventions on behalf of rural people have been important, but they have generally not taken the form of interventions in agricultural commodity markets. Cash transfers to village organizations, subsidized loan schemes not linked to agricultural production, and a generally good system of public infrastructure have been the main instruments. The prospects for more trade liberalization are not encouraging unless this occurs through bilateral preferential trading arrangements such as the scheme proposed with the United States.[7]

Notes

1. A full description of the trading position of the major agricultural commodities is provided in the appendix tables in Warr and Kohpaiboon (2007).

2. The price variables and the formula used in these NRA calculations are summarized in the appendix tables in Warr and Kohpaiboon (2007). Annual price data are also included in those tables.

3. The economic effects of the rice export taxes, including the distributional effects, are explored in Warr (2001). See also the analyses of Pinthong (1976, 1984); Wong (1978); Meenaphant (1981); Barker and Herdt (1985); Roumasset and Setboonsarng (1988); Somporn and Poapongsakorn (1995); Warr and Wollmer (1997); and Choeun, Godo, and Hayami (2006).

4. The results are summarized here. Details of the econometric analysis are available upon request.

5. There is no theoretical reason to suppose that the true value of the transmission elasticity is necessarily below unity. For example, if all margins between the farmgate and the wholesale level remain constant in nominal terms as the wholesale price changes, the percent change in the derived farmgate price would necessarily exceed the percent change in the wholesale price. The transmission elasticity would therefore exceed unity.

6. Because the Nicita and Olarreaga (2006) data are incomplete, we have assumed that the NRAs for manufacturing before 1982 and after 2002 are the same as the respective 1982 and 2002 NRAs calculated by Nicita and Olarreaga. This undoubtedly understates rates of manufacturing protection in the 1970s and overstates them post-2002. More complete estimates for manufacturing would therefore reinforce our broad conclusions rather than undermine them.

7. A bilateral trade arrangement with the United States was under negotiation up to February 2006, but the negotiations were suspended thereafter. The protection of the soybean industry was expected to be an important issue in these negotiations.

References

Anderson, K., M. Kurzweil, W. Martin, D. Sandri, and E. Valenzuela. 2008. "Measuring Distortions to Agricultural Incentives, Revisited." *World Trade Review* 7 (4): 675–704.

Barker, R., and R. W. Herdt. 1985. *The Rice Economy of Asia*. With Beth Rose. Washington, DC: Resources for the Future.

Choeun, H., Y. Godo, and Y. Hayami. 2006. "The Economics and Politics of Rice Export Taxation in Thailand: A Historical Simulation Analysis, 1950–1985." *Journal of Asian Economics* 17 (1): 103–25.

Corden, W. M. 1974. *Trade Policy and Economic Welfare*. Oxford: Clarendon Press.

Meenaphant, S. 1981. "An Economic Analysis of Thailand's Rice Trade." PhD dissertation, Rice University, Houston.

NESDB (National Economic and Social Development Board). various years. "Input-Output Table of Thailand." Spreadsheet, NESDB, Bangkok.

Nicita, A., and M. Olarreaga. 2006. "Trade, Production, and Protection, 1976–2004." *World Bank Economic Review* 21 (1): 165–71.

Pinthong, C. 1976. "A Price Analysis of the Thai Rice Marketing System." PhD dissertation, Stanford University, Palo Alto, CA.

———. 1984. "Distribution of Benefit of Government Rice Procurement Policy in Thailand." [in Thai] *Thammasat University Journal* 13 (2): 166–87.

Roumasset, J. A., and S. Setboonsarng. 1988. "Second-Best Agricultural Policy: Getting the Price of Thai Rice Right." *Journal of Development Economics* 28 (3): 323–40.

Siamwalla, A., and S. Setboonsarng. 1989. *Trade, Exchange Rate, and Agricultural Pricing Policies in Thailand*. Washington, DC: World Bank.

———. 1991. "Thailand." In *Asia*. Vol. 2 of *The Political Economy of Agricultural Pricing Policy*, ed. A. O. Krueger, M. Schiff, and A. Valdés, 236–80. World Bank Comparative Study. Baltimore: Johns Hopkins University Press; Washington, DC: World Bank.

Siamwalla, A., S. Setboonsarng, and D. Patamasiriwat. 1993. "Agriculture." In *The Thai Economy in Transition,* ed. P. G. Warr, 81–117. Cambridge: Cambridge University Press.

Sieper, E. 1982. *Rationalizing Rustic Regulation.* Sydney: Center for Independent Studies.

Somporn, I., and N. Poapongsakorn. 1995. "Rice Supply and Demand in Thailand: The Future Outlook." Paper presented to the Sectoral Economic Program, Thailand Development Research Institute, Bangkok.

Warr, P. G. 2001. "Welfare Effects of an Export Tax: Thailand's Rice Premium." *American Journal of Agricultural Economics* 83 (4): 903–20.

Warr, P. G., and A. Kohpaiboon. 2007. "Distortions to Agricultural Incentives in Thailand." Agricultural Distortions Working Paper 25, World Bank, Washington, DC.

Warr, P. G., and F. Wollmer. 1997. "Testing the Small Country Assumption: Thailand's Rice Exports." *Journal of the Asia Pacific Economy* 2 (2): 133–43.

Wong, C. M. 1978. "A Model for Evaluating the Effects of Thai Government Taxation of Rice Exports on Trade and Welfare." *American Journal of Agricultural Economics* 60 (1): 65–73.

World Development Indicators Database. World Bank. http://go.worldbank.org/B53SONGPA0 (accessed May 2008).

8

VIETNAM

Prema-Chandra Athukorala, Pham Lan Huong, and Vo Tri Thanh

Since the late 1980s, Vietnam has been making remarkable progress in its transition from a closed command economy toward an open market economy and integration in the world economy. The initial progress was slow and hesitant following the announcement of the *doi moi* (renovation) policy in 1986, but more significant reforms were undertaken in the first half of the 1990s. The process lost momentum in 1996–98, perhaps reflecting complacency after the success of the first reforms, but also the economic uncertainty created by the 1997–98 Asian financial crisis. Since about 1999, there has been a renewed emphasis on completing the unfinished reform agenda.

The key reform measures have included widespread agricultural reforms involving a transition from the collective regime to a system in which farmers possess more freedom in making production decisions and in marketing their produce. Quantitative import restrictions have been dismantled in all cases except sugar and petroleum products. Significant tariff reforms have led to notable reductions in the level and dispersion of effective rates of protection. Public sector enterprises have been exposed to greater market discipline. Restrictions have been relaxed on foreign direct investment, particularly in export-oriented projects, and they have been lifted on private sector participation in foreign trade and the establishment of business ventures by private individuals and companies. These initiatives have been accompanied by sweeping macroeconomic policy reforms, including the unification and realignment of the exchange rate, the liberalization of agricultural prices, the relaxation of exchange controls, and a firm commitment to fiscal prudence.

The purpose of this chapter is to examine the implications of the market-oriented policy reforms in Vietnam for the incentives faced by farmers in the context of the changes in the overall structure of the incentives for private sector activities in the economy. We undertake the analysis against the backdrop of a narrative on the evolution of agricultural policy and the key policy trends dating back to the era of the command economy. The empirical analysis of agricultural incentives covers six major products—rice, sugar, pig meat, poultry, rubber, and coffee—using data from 1986 (the earliest postreform year for which the required data are available) to 2004. The six covered products accounted for more than two-thirds of the total value of agricultural production in Vietnam during the period. Our aim is to contribute to the contemporary policy debate on reforming the structure of incentives for domestic agriculture as an integral part of the endeavor to accelerate the country's economic integration into the world economy.

The study has four main parts. The next section presents an overview of the growth and structural changes during the postreform era (since the mid-1980s). It emphasizes the relative importance of the agricultural sector and the trends and compositional shifts in agricultural output and trade. The subsequent section provides an overview of the origins, key elements, and achievements of the effort to meet reform commitments. It highlights the political economy of the related policy making. The penultimate section—the analytical core of the chapter—examines trends and patterns in the incentives in domestic agriculture by relying on a set of indicators based on the methodology described in Anderson et al. (2008) and appendix A. The final section summarizes the key findings and policy implications.

Agriculture in the Vietnamese Economy

We first document the extraordinary economic growth performance of this transforming economy and then review the structural changes that have accompanied this success.

Growth trends

During the era of central planning (from the mid-1950s in the north of the country and, in the south, beginning in 1975 following unification), the economy was not subject to forced industrialization to the same degree as the centrally planned economies of China and the Soviet bloc. The prolonged military conflict with the regime in the south and with the United States caused industrial transformation to be limited to the establishment of industries that met the priorities of the war economy. Thus, agriculture—broadly defined to include farming, fisheries, and forestry—remained the dominant sector of the economy up to the 1980s. During the period from 1955 to 1985, the share of agriculture in gross domestic product (GDP) fluctuated from around 38 to 52 percent without showing any clear trend (GSO 2001). By the mid-1980s, over 72 percent of the total labor force was engaged in agricultural pursuits (Riedel 1993).

The process of the collectivization of agriculture in the northern part of the country had been completed by the early 1960s. The forced replacement of a semisubsistent peasant commodity production system by a regular plan ushered in an era of suppressed growth, if not stagnation, in agriculture. During most of the ensuing three decades, agricultural output in the north was only barely sufficient to meet domestic consumption requirements in that part of Vietnam. Attempts to replicate the collectivized system in the south following the administrative unification of the country in 1976 resulted in a severe disruption in agricultural production there. Piecemeal reforms implemented in 1979–80 to loosen the structures of central planning had only limited impact in containing output contraction. By the mid-1980s, large areas of the country were experiencing near-famine conditions, and food shortages were resulting in widespread suffering. National food security became a leading preoccupation (White 1985; Riedel and Comer 1997; Pritchett 2003).

The response of agriculture to the market-oriented policy reforms launched in the late 1980s was remarkably swift. Between 1988 and 1992, GDP increased by 27 percent; nearly 30 percent of this increase arose directly from agriculture. In addition, rapid agricultural growth contributed to an expansion in rural nonagricultural services, input supply, and food processing. During the ensuing years, the growth turned out to be broadly based, and industry and services developed at a pace that was more rapid than the pace of development in agriculture. Nonetheless, the growth rate in agriculture remained impressive (3.0 to 5.2 percent per year) relative to the precrisis experience in Vietnam and the average performance in other low-income and transition economies. Despite the notable structural changes over the past 15–20 years, agriculture still has a substantial weight in the Vietnamese economy, contributing about 20 percent of GDP (figure 8.1) and absorbing 57 percent of the total labor force in 2005. Slightly more than two-thirds of households in the lowest income quintile were occupied in agriculture in 2004, and almost three-fifths of the incomes among households in that quintile was generated by agricultural activities (compared with less than one-fourth of the incomes in the highest income quintile).

The impressive agricultural growth, especially the surge in paddy production, played a key role in winning political support for more reforms by ensuring national food security, a source of much political anxiety in the 1980s. Agricultural growth was also at the heart of the success in the rapid reduction in rural

Figure 8.1. Agriculture, GDP, and Value Added, Vietnam, 1985–2005

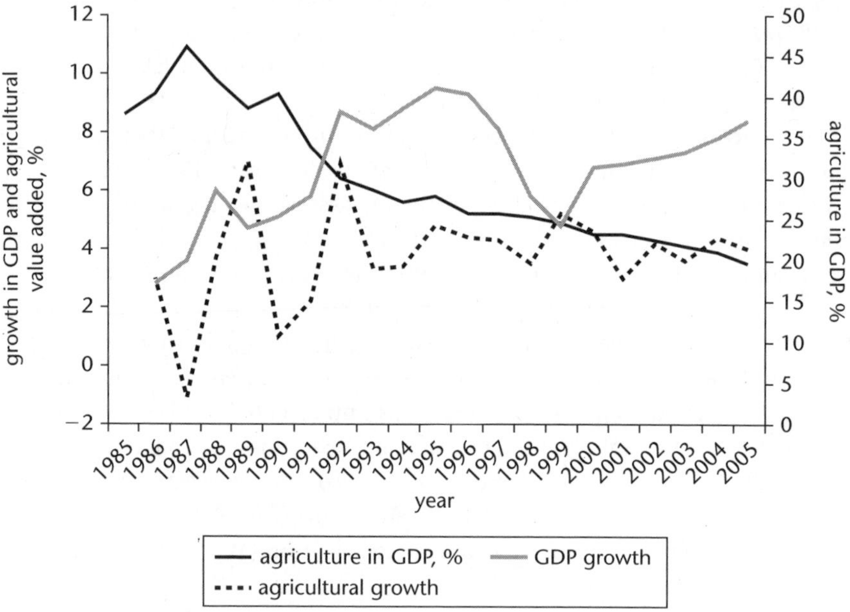

Source: Compiled from data in GSO, "Statistical Yearbook," various.

poverty. The increase in rural incomes supported the economic transition by reducing the pressure for migration from rural to urban areas despite the widening gap between rural and urban incomes. In contrast to China, internal migration in Vietnam has occurred as much from one rural area to another as from the countryside to the city. This has limited the demand for substantial expenditure on urban development (Minot and Goletti 2000; Van Arkadie and Mallon 2003).

The production of major commodities

Paddy and rice were the prime movers of agricultural growth during the immediate postreform period. Since the mid-1990s, agricultural production has been diversifying significantly into other food crops (maize, peanuts, and soybeans), cash crops (particularly rubber, coffee, tea, cashews, pepper, and cinnamon), fruits and vegetables, marine and aquaculture products (shrimps, fish, cuttlefish, and crabs), and animal husbandry (pig meat and poultry). In cash crops such as coffee, cashews, and pepper, there has been a shift from negligible production to sufficient production to make the country a major player in the relevant world markets. The initial expansion in the production of some cash crops (especially rubber) reflected returns to government investment in state farms in the 1980s,

Table 8.1. Structure of the Agricultural Economy, Vietnam, 1986–2004

(percent)

Indicator, product	1986–89	1990–94	1995–99	2000–04
Agriculture in GDP	42	34	26	23
Composition of agricultural output	—	100.0	100.0	100.0
Rice	—	46.6	45.4	35.7
Rubber	—	1.6	2.0	2.3
Coffee	—	2.1	5.2	3.8
Sugar	—	3.5	4.4	3.4
Pig meat	—	6.4	7.3	9.9
Other	—	39.7	35.8	45.0

Source: Compiled from data in GSO, "Statistical Yearbook," various.

Note: The estimates have been calculated by applying value added shares, at current prices, from the input-output tables in 2000 to gross output data. — = no data are available.

but the growth in agricultural production during the postreform era has arisen predominantly from smallholder production in the private sector.

Rice, the staple food of the country, accounts for three-quarters of the calorie intake among the population and is the dominant agriculture product. In 2004, paddy accounted for 57 percent of total cultivated area and 36 percent of total agricultural output (tables 8.1 and 8.2 and figure 8.2). The Red River Delta and the Mekong River Delta account for around one-third and more than half of the total national production of paddy, respectively, although paddy, the primary food crop, is also grown widely in all other parts of the country. Paddy production increased steadily from 19.2 million tons in 1990 to 36.1 million tons in 2005. The impressive annual compound growth rate of 4.2 percent was generated largely because of an improvement in yield per hectare, while the area under paddy remained virtually unchanged (Athukorala, Huong, and Thanh 2007). Paddy yields rose from 2.8 tons to 4.9 tons per hectare between 1986 and 2005.

Coffee, rubber, and sugarcane are the three most important cash crops. In 2004, coffee accounted for 3.8 percent of agricultural output, while sugarcane and rubber accounted for 3.4 and 2.3 percent, respectively. Coffee and rubber production is largely aimed at export markets; the sugar industry generally meets only domestic demand. Coffee and sugar are predominantly smallholder crops. Rubber is mainly produced on farms owned by state-owned enterprises at the provincial level or by the General Rubber Corporation, a state-owned enterprise at the national level. The area of cultivation under rubber and coffee and the yield and overall output levels of these two products have recorded impressive growth since the early 1990s (Athukorala, Huong, and Thanh 2007). Sugar production jumped

Table 8.2. Share of Planted Area by Crop, Vietnam, 1990–2004
(percent)

Crop	1990	1995	2000	2004
Paddy	66.8	64.5	60.6	56.6
Maize	4.8	5.3	5.8	7.5
Sugar	1.4	2.1	2.4	2.2
Groundnuts	2.2	2.5	1.9	2.0
Soybeans	1.2	1.2	1.0	1.4
Tea	0.7	0.6	0.7	0.9
Coffee	1.3	1.8	4.4	3.8
Rubber	2.5	2.7	3.3	3.4
Pepper	0.1	0.1	0.2	0.4
Coconuts	2.3	1.6	1.3	1.0
Total	100.0	100.0	100.0	100.0
Total area, hectares, 1,000s	9,040	10,497	12,644	13,150

Source: Compiled from data in GSO, "Statistical Handbook," various.

Figure 8.2. Commodity Shares in Agricultural Production, Vietnam, 1991–2002

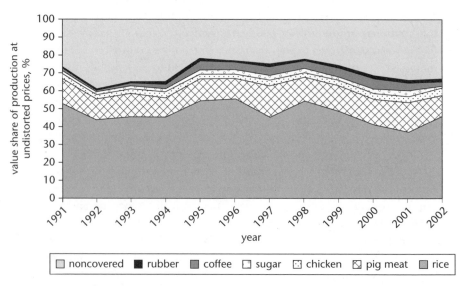

Source: Compiled from data in GSO, "Statistical Yearbook," various.

Note: The figure is based on estimates relying on data in the input-output tables in 2000.

in 1995 following the launch of the One Million Tons of Sugar Program and continued to increase up to 1999. However, a mild downward trend characterized by significant annual fluctuations has been evident since then. Sugar yields rose from 396 to 553 quintals per hectare in 1986–2005. The area under sugarcane cultivation has declined in recent years because of a shift by farmers to other crops, mostly subsidiary food crops. Despite its relatively poor performance (or because of it), sugarcane production remains the most well assisted agricultural activity (see below). In 1995, the government launched the One Million Tons of Sugar Program, which was aimed at achieving sugar self-sufficiency by 2000 and creating employment in the rural economy (Nguyen et al. 2006).

The other cash crops that have shown impressive growth during the postreform era include cashews, groundnuts, tea, and pepper. Vietnam is the world's largest producer of pepper, the third largest producer of cashew nuts, the fifth largest producer of tea, and the tenth largest producer of groundnuts. However, the combined share of these products in the total agricultural GDP of the country remains small, at less than 3 percent.

Livestock production has expanded rapidly since the early 1990s. It accounted for about 14 percent of agricultural value added in 2000 (IAPP 2001). Pig meat is the most important livestock product (60 percent), followed by poultry (15 percent) and beef (8 percent). The share of pig meat in agricultural value added rose from 6 percent in 1990–94 to 10 percent in 2000–04 (table 8.1). Currently, over 90 percent of total pig meat production is consumed domestically, although exports (mainly to China) have been increasing rapidly in recent years.

Agricultural exports

Primary products accounted for nearly half of non-oil merchandise exports in the mid-1980s. The share rose in the early years of the postreform period when the first positive response to the reforms was registered in agricultural products, especially rice. In 1998, Vietnam became self-sufficient in rice and then a net exporter. In 2005, rice exports peaked at 5.3 million tons, making the country the third largest rice exporter in the world (after the United States and Thailand). The composition of agricultural exports has become increasingly diversified; pepper, cashews, rubber, coffee, and fish products have shown impressive growth. Since the late 1990s, manufacturing exports have been growing more rapidly, resulting in a notable shift in the composition of exports away from primary products. However, agricultural products still accounted for over one-quarter of total non-oil merchandise exports in 2004 (table 8.3).[1]

Until about the mid-1990s, rapid volume expansion and favorable price trends were contributing to the growth in agricultural export earnings (figure 8.3). Prices

Table 8.3. Composition of Agricultural Exports by Value, Vietnam, 1990–2004

(percent)

Indicator, product	1990	1995	2000	2004
Agricultural exports in total non-oil exports	80	46	25	22
Composition of agricultural exports	100.0	100.0	100.0	100.0
Groundnuts	—	3.7	2.3	0.9
Rubber	4.7	12.0	9.4	20.5
Coffee	7.3	37.4	28.4	22.0
Tea	0.6	0.8	4.0	3.3
Rice	80.2	40.7	37.8	32.7
Cashews	3.8	9.8	9.5	15.0
Black pepper	3.5	4.5	8.3	5.2
Cinnamon	—	—	0.3	0.3

Source: Compiled from data in GSO, "Statistical Yearbook," various.

Note: — = no data are available.

Figure 8.3. Volume, Value, and Price Indexes, Agricultural Exports, Vietnam, 1990–2004

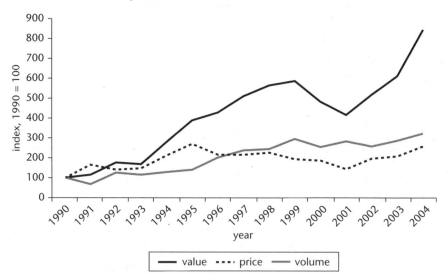

Source: Athukorala, Huong, and Thanh 2007.

continued to decline thereafter; the rate of decline has intensified in recent years. Rapid volume expansion compensated for the price decline until about 1998, generating mild, but positive growth in export earnings. However, the rate of growth in agricultural export earnings has steadily slowed over the past five years or so; this mostly reflects declining prices.

The Reform Process: From Plan to Market

Under the collective system of agriculture instituted in the north in the early 1960s, cooperatives were the key link between agricultural households and the national economic plan. As the prime institution in the effort to replace the market by the plan, the agricultural cooperatives were responsible for organizing the deployment of the agricultural labor force, undertaking production according to plans approved by the central authorities, selling surplus production to the state at state-controlled prices, and implementing obligatory procurement quotas introduced from time to time for sales to the state of selected essential commodities (White 1981).

After the defeat of the government in the south in 1975 and the formal administrative reunification of the economy in 1976, replacing the market by the plan in the south presented a formidable challenge. Immediately after reunification, the attempt to bring southern agriculture into the collective system was fairly cautious. However, the rapid growth in private trade, combined with concerns about the political resistance to socialist transformation among southern farmers and the southern business community, which was dominated by ethnic Chinese, led to an attempt to accelerate the process. The Second Party Plenum, in July 1977, set ambitious targets to speed the collectivization of individual farm households. The resistance among farmers to the introduction of the collective system, coupled with uncertainty about the future direction of reform, resulted in declines in agricultural output. The process of collectivization in the south was slowed. Agreements were then reached on the need to decentralize decision making and provide better incentives for increasing production though private household initiatives (Duiker 1989; Fforde and de Vylder 1996; Naughton 1996).

Reforms in 1979–80 introduced production contracts under which cooperatives subcontracted land to households and allowed households greater latitude in decision making on production issues. Under this new system, which was similar to the household responsibility system in China, households were allowed to keep or to sell on the free market any surplus above the amount stipulated for delivery to cooperatives under the contracts. In effect, the cooperatives were limited to the subsidiary role of allocating land, supplying inputs, and providing technical assistance (Woodside 1989).

These reforms had an immediate and dramatic effect: in 1994 prices, total agricultural production rose from D 37 trillion in 1979 to D 46 trillion in 1982 (GSO 2001). However, rather than responding to improved production by amplifying reforms, as the Chinese government did, the Vietnamese government backpedaled for most of the rest of the decade. The emergence in the early 1980s of severe macroeconomic imbalances, which were reflected in high and rising inflation, undermined the reform movement. The macroeconomic problems were interpreted as a symptom of the failure of the reforms, and they also created dissatisfaction because they led to a reduction in real wages in the civil service. Thus, the influence of hard-liners within the Communist Party of Vietnam had gained strength by the mid-1980s, and this added to the pressure to enforce the collectivization of agriculture in the south (Riedel and Comer 1997).

By the mid-1980s, the economy was stagnating because of hyperinflation and a chronically poor balance of payments situation. Furthermore, it was clear by 1988 that Soviet aid would soon decline. In the face of these problems, a more concerted push toward reform was announced at the Sixth Congress of the Communist Party of Vietnam in December 1986 (CPV 1994). The implementation of this program of reform, referred to as *doi moi,* did not, however, gain much momentum until the collapse of the Soviet Union, which put an end to Soviet aid. Massive contraction in agricultural output in 1988, which brought near-famine conditions in many parts of the country, also played a role in reducing the resistance to reform. The focus of early reform was mainly on unshackling agriculture. Initially, the reform process largely ignored the private sector except in agriculture, and the process of establishing the institutions needed to support private sector activity outside agriculture was undertaken only in the early 1990s after emerging signs of unrest.

Unshackling agriculture

The transition to a more decentralized, market-oriented system of agricultural production was launched through the adoption of a decree by the Communist Party of Vietnam in 1988. The decree recognized the peasant household rather than the cooperative as the basic unit in the agrarian structure. It recognized the right of households to the conditional use of private land for a period of 10–15 years; to own draft animals, farm tools, and other equipment; to barter output for inputs; and to retain the income earned through production once they had paid a modest tax. However, cooperatives continued to have ultimate control over land and water resources; and the sale of output, at prices set by the government, remained restricted to sales within the same district. Additional measures introduced in 1989 reduced the direct involvement of the government in the allocation of inputs. In July 1993, the duration of tenure rights over agricultural land was extended to 20 years, and farmers were permitted to sell, lease, exchange, mortgage, and bequeath land. Cooperatives were still meant to provide a focus for various rural activities sponsored by the government, but, in the majority of communes, they were reduced to only a minor role. They were to act as local tax collectors, the holders of residual property rights, and a component of the formal state structure (Riedel 1993; Sachs and Woo 1994; Riedel and Comer 1997).

Land tenure reforms were accompanied by sweeping domestic market price reforms. In 1987–88, the rationing system was abolished for many commodities, and the official prices of nonessential goods were raised to a level close to free-market prices. Administered prices on most consumer goods and a large number of agricultural and industrial inputs were abolished. In June 1990, the procurement of farm products by the government, usually at prices below free-market prices, formally came to an end, allowing farmers to sell their produce at market prices. By 1990, commodity prices were largely determined by domestic market conditions, and direct subsidies had been eliminated. The sellers market was replaced because of the shift toward market-clearing prices. The weakening of the state trading system at the local level permitted private traders to develop local markets, while many state trading enterprises became more responsive to market opportunities. Starting in 1989, the international trade in agricultural products was also liberalized in phases, and this eventually allowed private sector participation.

Trade policy reforms

Foreign trade and investment regimes were liberalized in stages in conjunction with the domestic market price reforms. The law on import and export duties introduced in January 1988 marked the launch of the new trade tax system. The original import tariff schedule was replaced in 1992 by a detailed, consolidated schedule based on the Harmonized Commodity Description and Coding System of tariff nomenclature. During the rest of the 1990s, the tariff structure was fine-tuned to mirror a policy trend toward selective protection in the case of consumer goods (cosmetics and several categories of food products), activities upstream of the textile and garment industry (silk, cotton, and some fiber production), and some intermediate goods (metal products, cement, and glass). In the early and mid-2000s, following Vietnam's accession to the free trade area of the Association of Southeast Asian Nations in 1995 and in preparation for the country's accession to the World Trade Organization (WTO), the government took steps to reorganize and rationalize the tariff structure (Thanh 2006).

After more than 15 years of reform, tariffs are now the major instruments used in regulating import trade. The average (import-weighted) import duty rate declined from 22 percent in 1999 to 13.6 percent in 2004 (figure 8.4). The maximum tariff rate (at the six-digit level of the Harmonized Commodity Description and Coding System) declined from 200 percent in 1997 to 120 percent in 2001 and then 113 percent in 2004. By October 2005, of all tariff lines, less than 1 percent (accounting for around 4 percent of total import value) were subject to tariff rates above 50 percent. The tariff on about one-third of the tariff lines was zero. Despite

Figure 8.4. Weighted Average Import Duties, Vietnam, 1990–2004

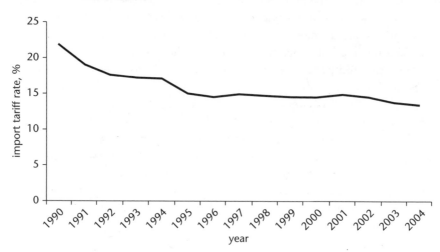

Source: Nicita and Olarreaga 2006; CIE 1998.

notable efforts to rationalize the tariff structure, tariffs are still relatively high and nonuniform according to regional standards (Athukorala 2006).[2]

The tariff rates are generally higher for manufacturing products than for agricultural products and other primary products. By mid-2003, the weighted average duty rate on manufacturing imports was 29 percent, while the corresponding rates were 11 percent on agricultural products and 3.6 percent on mineral products. Within manufacturing, the tariff rates are particularly high for processed foods and some consumer goods, notably garments, footwear, ceramic products, and leather goods (Athukorala 2006; Athukorala, Huong, and Thanh 2007).

By 2004, only two products, sugar and petroleum, remained subject to quantitative restrictions (import licensing). As part of its trade reform commitments under the WTO accession agreement, the government offered to replace import licensing on sugar by a WTO-consistent tariff trade quota system. Imports of two products—poultry eggs and raw tobacco—were already subject to tariff rate quotas. The list of prohibited imports included military equipment, toxic chemicals, antiquities, narcotics, firecrackers, toxic toys, used consumer goods, and right-hand-drive automobiles. In addition, a considerable number of import items (such as pharmaceuticals, some chemicals, some food items, fertilizer, and recording and broadcasting equipment) required approval from the relevant ministries. In 2000, in value terms, around 10 percent of imports were subject to this form of regulation. As in many other countries, these regulations are generally maintained in Vietnam for heath and security reasons, and they do not appear to distort trade patterns substantially.

Among the early market-oriented reforms, the government introduced duties on a number of export items. The duties were justified at the time by the need to raise revenue, protect the environment, conserve natural resources, and retain inputs for domestic production. Most of the duties were subsequently eliminated. By 1998, only a few export products—iron ore, crude oil, scrap metal, and raw cashews—were subject to duties. Export prohibitions now apply only to environmentally sensitive items such as agroforestry products, round wood and saw wood cut from domestic natural forests, firewood and charcoal obtained from natural-growth domestic forestry wood, and rare wild animals.

When the country began exporting rice in 1989, the exports were subject to licensing to ensure adequate domestic supplies and reduce the price volatility in the domestic market. Export quotas were issued only to a few state-owned enterprises. During the next years, the number of enterprises affected ranged from 15 to 40. The intense lobbying by these enterprises to share in the export quotas during the early years of the rice exports suggests that the quotas were binding and ensured that the domestic price was below the relevant border price. However, starting in about 1998, the quotas became ineffective because of the rapid expansion in rice production and, thus, in the marketable surplus. In April 2001, the rice export quota allocation mechanism, together with the import quota system for fertilizer, was abolished by a prime ministerial decision. Enterprises were thenceforth permitted to export rice, provided they had obtained general business licenses to trade in rice or other agricultural products. For rice exports to countries with which the government has bilateral trade agreements, the Ministry of Trade assigns export rights to selected enterprises in consultation with the Vietnam Food Association. However, this trade is too small to have a significant impact on domestic rice markets.

Other reforms

The reforms in agriculture and foreign trade were accompanied by significant macroeconomic policy reforms (Dollar 1992; Dollar and Ljunggren 1997). To fight inflation, interest rates were raised to high levels. The government also tried to curb deficit financing, which required a large fiscal adjustment that led, for example, to the release of 500,000 soldiers from the military and sharp cuts in the subsidies to state-owned enterprises. These policy measures, combined with revenue windfalls from petroleum operations that had come on line, brought the budget deficit down from 11.4 to below 4 percent of GDP in 1989–92. Fiscal adjustment and monetary

Figure 8.5. Index, Real Exchange Rate, Vietnam, 1988–2005

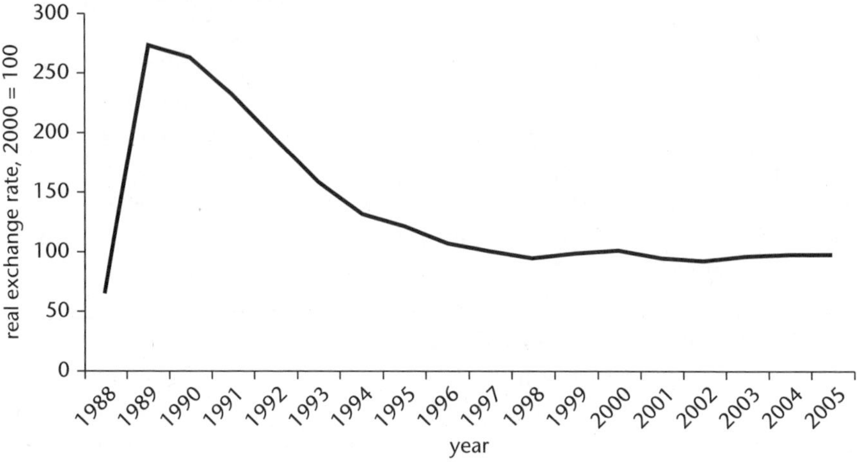

Source: Athukorala, Huong, and Thanh 2007.

restraint were successful in reducing the inflation rate from over 160 percent a year in 1988 to less than 10 percent a year by the mid-1990s.

Exchange rates were unified, and the new rate was sharply devalued in 1989. The real exchange rate devaluation amounted to 72.5 percent according to the International Monetary Fund (Dollar 1992). Since then, the Vietnamese dong (D) has been on a managed floating exchange rate regime whereby the State Bank of Vietnam (the central bank) determines the unified rate according to foreign exchange market trading. In 1990–98, the gap between the official exchange rate and the exchange rate in the interbank market varied from 5 to 10 percent. Since then, the approach of the state bank to exchange rate management has become more flexible, and the gap between the two rates has been reduced to around 0.1 percent on any given business day. The black market premium on the U.S. dollar, which stood at over 50 percent in 1988–95, had fallen to less than 5 percent by 2004 (Athukorala, Huong, and Thanh 2007). Because of successful macroeconomic stabilization and exchange rate management, the real exchange rate has remained stable since the mid-1990s (figure 8.5).

Trends and Patterns in Agricultural Incentives

In this section, we provide an analysis of the changing scope of and patterns in the direct and indirect distortions in the incentives faced by domestic agriculture in

Vietnam. We rely on the methodology developed by Anderson et al. (2008) and described in appendix A. The main focus of our use of the methodology is government-imposed distortions that create a gap between domestic prices and the prices that would emerge under free market conditions. We estimate the effects of direct agricultural policy measures, but, for comparative evaluation and because it is not possible to understand the characteristics of agricultural development through a sectoral view alone, we also estimate the distortions in nonagricultural tradables. Specifically, we compute nominal rates of assistance (NRAs) for farm producers of the six products we cover. We also calculate a relative rate of assistance (RRA) based on the NRAs for nonagricultural tradables and the NRAs for agricultural tradables. We assume that the NRAs for noncovered agricultural exportable products are the same as the average NRAs for covered exportables, and we assume that the average NRA for noncovered import-competing products is 10 percent of the NRAs for sugar. We also assume that the average NRA for nontradables is zero and that the share of nontradables in noncovered farm production is 68 percent, while the exportable share is 25 percent.

We have estimated the NRAs for nonagricultural tradables by assuming that the implicit duty rate on nonagricultural importables (the total tariff revenue generated from nonagricultural imports, divided by the value of nonagricultural imports) is the rate of distortion in this component of nonagricultural tradables and that nonagricultural exportables (the share of which is three-quarters as large as the share of import-competing products) are not subject to any export taxes or subsidies.

One should bear in mind two important caveats that arise from the paucity of data. First, we have ignored potential differences between border (reference) prices and domestic prices that arise from quality differences. This might have infused an underestimation bias into our calculations. Second, we have assumed that there is a complete pass-through of the changes in producer (wholesale) prices to farmgate prices. This may result in an upward bias in the estimates. However, these limitations are important only in comparisons of the levels of distortion in the incentives among products or across countries at a given time. They are unlikely to distort inferences based on intertemporal comparisons (changes in incentives over time) because the magnitude of the bias is less liable to vary over time. Given the nature of the estimation method, our RRA estimates also do not fully capture the indirect distortions that arise in agricultural incentives from changes in the tariffs on tradable inputs. The tariff structure in Vietnam is cascading. This may be an important source of downward bias in our RRA estimates (Athukorala 2006). We have also not captured the distortions caused by nontariff import restrictions.

Table 8.4. NRAs for Covered Agricultural Products, Vietnam, 1986–2004

(percent)

Indicator, product	1986–89	1990–94	1995–99	2000–04
Exportables[a]	−13.2	−27.2	−2.1	16.9
Rice	−2.8	−26.6	−0.4	22.9
Rubber	—	21.2	18.6	16.8
Coffee	−49.4	−21.1	−7.1	−12.0
Pig meat	−41.8	−37.5	−6.1	8.9
Poultry	−3.1	−3.6	3.7	1.6
Import-competing products[a]	—	49.6	112.9	160.2
Sugar	—	49.6	112.9	160.2
All covered products[a]	−13.2	−27.2	−0.2	20.6
Dispersion, covered products[b]	28.8	46.1	157.7	221.3
Coverage, at undistorted prices	70	67	76	63

Source: Athukorala, Huong, and Thanh 2007.

Note: — = no data are available.

a. Weighted averages; the weights are based on the unassisted value of production.
b. Dispersion is a simple five-year average of the annual standard deviation around the weighted mean of the NRAs of covered products.

Our estimated distortion rates are summarized in five-year averages in tables 8.4 and 8.5 and are plotted in figure 8.6. Detailed annual estimates, the estimated NRA series for each of the covered products, and the related domestic and border price series are reported by Athukorala, Huong, and Thanh (2007). In the late 1980s and the first half of the 1990s, the policy regime was characterized by a significant bias against agriculture. The RRA averaged −20 percent in 1990–94. The direct negative assistance to agriculture (as measured by the NRAs for agriculture) underpinned this high degree of distortion in agricultural incentives. The main factors that kept domestic prices artificially suppressed relative to border prices were the continued dominance of state-owned enterprises in the trading and processing of agricultural commodities; a stringent export licensing system in the rice trade; other trade restrictions; administered prices, which were usually maintained below border prices; and, perhaps, a lack of experience among the emerging private traders who were operating in the newly competitive trading environment.

Until the mid-1990s, four exportable agricultural products—rice, coffee, pig meat, and poultry—faced significant negative assistance (table 8.4). Rubber is unique among the five exportables because it has enjoyed positive assistance over the last two decades. This reflects production subsidies for the state-owned plantation companies that account for the bulk of rubber production. In the

Table 8.5. NRAs in Agriculture Relative to Nonagricultural Industries, Vietnam, 1986–2004

(percent)

Indicator	1986–89	1990–94	1995–99	2000–04
Covered products[a]	−13.2	−27.2	−0.2	20.6
Noncovered products	−14.5	−25.0	0.3	22.3
All agricultural products[a]	−14.0	−26.5	−0.1	21.2
Non-product-specific assistance	0.0	0.0	0.0	0.0
Total agricultural NRA[b]	−14.0	−26.5	−0.1	21.2
Trade bias index[c]	−0.19	−0.17	−0.01	0.00
NRA, agricultural tradables	−16.1	−26.4	0.0	20.7
NRA, nonagricultural tradables	4.3	−11.2	1.5	20.8
RRA[d]	−19.4	−17.4	−1.3	0.0

Source: Athukorala, Huong, and Thanh 2007.

a. Including product-specific input subsidies.
b. Including product-specific input subsidies and non-product-specific assistance. Represents total assistance to primary factors and intermediate inputs, divided by the total value of primary agriculture production at undistorted prices.
c. The trade bias index is defined as $(1 + NRAag_x/100)/(1 + NRAag_m/100) - 1$, where $NRAag_m$ and $NRAag_x$ are the average percentage NRAs for the import-competing and exportable parts of the agricultural sector, respectively.
d. The RRA is defined as $100*[(100 + NRAag^t)/(100 + NRAnonag^t) - 1]$, where $NRAag^t$ and $NRAnonag^t$ are the percentage NRAs for the tradables parts of the agricultural and nonagricultural sectors, respectively.

mid-1990s, after the liberalization of the export trade and the removal of direct price interventions and some export duties, the incentives for rice, pig meat, and poultry were significantly improved. Even though coffee production remained disprotected (taxed), the overall NRA index for exportable agriculture rose steadily in the ensuing years from around −27 percent in 1990–94 to around 17 percent in 2000–04.

Sugar, the only import-competing product covered in our study, occupies a singular position because of the trend in assistance. Sugarcane producers enjoyed NRAs that were exceptionally high relative to the NRAs among producers of other products, and the measured level of assistance increased steadily. In 2000–04, the NRA for sugarcane was 160 percent, while the weighted average was 20 percent for all covered products. This points to the stringency of the licensing regime governing sugar imports. The government's policy of protecting sugar has been systematically analyzed in several recent studies (for instance, see CIE 2001; Nguyen et al. 2006). These studies conclude that the government's sugar industry development strategy, which is enshrined in the One Million Tons of Sugar Program launched in 1995, has been a dismal failure and that a competitive, economically viable

Figure 8.6. NRAs for Agricultural and Nonagricultural Tradables and the RRA, Vietnam, 1986–2004

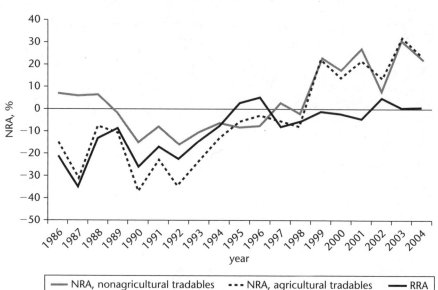

Source: Athukorala, Huong, and Thanh 2007.

Note: For the definition of the RRA, see table 8.5, note d.

sugar industry cannot be developed through isolation from world market conditions. The substantial protection provided to the sugar industry is a major constraint on the diversification of scarce land resources to more dynamic, export-oriented crops. Moreover, the high domestic sugar prices not only tax domestic consumers, but also hamper the competitiveness of the domestic confectionary, food, and beverage industries.

Improvement in the NRAs for exportable agriculture, coupled with the maintenance of the high NRAs enjoyed by sugarcane producers, have generated an improvement in the RRAs for agriculture over the past 10 years. Moreover, this improvement in the relative incentives in agriculture has taken place against the backdrop of a steady rise in the NRAs for nonagricultural sectors over time (table 8.5 and figure 8.6). Clearly, the elimination of various direct price interventions in domestic trade, the removal of export duties on almost all agricultural products, the liberalization in import trade, and the exchange rate reforms have been instrumental in redressing the antiagricultural bias in the incentive structure within the economy.

A comparison of the weighted average NRAs for the covered exportables (rice, rubber, coffee, pig meat, and poultry) with the corresponding NRAs for sugar (an import-competing product) points to a persistent bias in agricultural incentives in favor of import-competing production in agriculture (table 8.4). However, this comparison needs to be qualified: the NRAs for import-competing products refer only to the protection for sugar, which is an outlier relative to other import-competing agricultural products in Vietnam that are not covered in this study.

Concluding Remarks

Over the past two decades, Vietnam has made significant progress in market-oriented reforms. The foreign trade regime has become more liberalized; there has been a palpable transition from quantitative restraints to tariffs as the main instrument in regulating imports. Export taxes on all significant products have been eliminated. In domestic trade, the dominance of state-owned enterprises in most areas has ended, and price controls and restrictions on production and the movement of goods no longer exist.

The reform process is far from complete, however. The structure of trade protection is still out of step with the level and the dispersion of nominal and effective protection rates among Vietnam's major trading partners in the region. Stringent quantitative import restrictions on sugar and high import duties on agricultural products in which the country has a clear comparative advantage, particularly rice, coffee, and tea, are major anomalies. The tariff rates are excessive on crucial agricultural inputs and other intermediate goods that are produced locally by state-owned enterprises. Had information on these rates been available to us in our analysis, our NRA estimates in agriculture would have been lower. The licensing scheme for rice exports, although seemingly nonbinding for some time now, remains an important source of uncertainty among private sector traders.

The attempt to unshackle domestic agriculture accounted for the first of the market-oriented reforms, and the reforms in this area have been more wide-ranging than the reforms in other areas. The predominance of agriculture in the prereform economy—its importance in determining the fortunes of the economy and ensuring the livelihoods of a majority of the population—made the sweeping agricultural reforms politically palatable. Because the vast potential of agriculture was untapped under the command economy, the response of agriculture to the reforms was swift. The impressive outcome played a pivotal role in sustaining the momentum of the reforms and supporting market-oriented programs.

Our empirical analysis of trends and patterns in the incentives in agriculture has yielded several important findings. In the first half of the 1990s, the policy regime was characterized by a significant bias against agriculture. This bias dissipated because of the gradual removal of the privileges enjoyed by state-owned enterprises in procuring, processing, and trading agricultural products; the opening of domestic and foreign trade to the private sector; and the emergence of the nascent private sector in a competitive trade environment. By 2000–04, the NRAs in agriculture and the degree of antiagricultural bias embodied in the overall policies affecting tradables represented evidence that the bias had been reversed. The improvement in the relative incentives for agriculture was generated predominantly, if not solely, by direct reforms in agriculture. This is demonstrated by the small size of the increase in the NRAs for nonagricultural tradables. In this context, the implementation of the tariff reform commitments undertaken during the accession to the WTO may play a vital role in consolidating the reform effort and reducing the remaining sectoral policy bias.

According to our commodity-level estimates, the excessive assistance provided to sugar producers, mainly though stringent quantitative restrictions on sugar imports, is the major irregularity in the incentive structure. The NRAs have continued to be high in recent years despite a steady decline in border prices; this reflects the severity of the existing quantitative restrictions. The significant protection provided to this industry is a major constraint on the diversification of agriculture into dynamic export-oriented crops. High domestic sugar prices tax domestic consumers, but also hamper the competitiveness of the domestic confectionary, food, and beverage industries. Redressing this anomaly in the incentive structure remains a formidable challenge because sugarcane has long been a choice crop in the government's rural development and agricultural diversification programs. Unfortunately, the government has missed the opportunity to make use of the WTO accession process to face down the political resistance to reform. Instead, it has chosen the soft option of replacing the sugar import licensing scheme by WTO-consistent tariff rate quotas during 2008.

Notes

1. Export shares are estimated in gross terms, that is, on the basis of published trade data without adjusting for import content. This tends to understate the balance of payments implications of agricultural exports, particularly because most of the newly emerging manufactured exports greatly depend on imported inputs.

2. By mid-2003, the average unweighted tariff rate, 16.7 percent, was aa little lower than the average rates in China (17.5 percent) and Thailand (18.5 percent), but much higher than the rates in Indonesia (8.4 percent), Malaysia (10.2 percent), and the Philippines (7.6 percent). The degree of dispersion in the tariff rates—measured through the coefficient of variation—is much higher in Vietnam than in China, the Philippines, and Thailand, but lower in Vietnam than in Indonesia and Malaysia.

References

Anderson, K., M. Kurzweil, W. Martin, D. Sandri, and E. Valenzuela. 2008. "Measuring Distortions to Agricultural Incentives, Revisited." *World Trade Review* 7 (4): 675–704.

Athukorala, P.-C. 2006. "Trade Policy Reforms and the Structure of Protection in Vietnam." *World Economy* 29 (2): 161–87.

Athukorala, P.-C., P. L. Huong, and V. T. Thanh. 2007. "Distortions to Agricultural Incentives in Vietnam." Agricultural Distortions Working Paper 26, World Bank, Washington, DC.

CIE (Center for International Economics). 1998. *Vietnam's Trade Policies 1998.* Canberra: CIE.

———. 2001. *Vietnam Sugar Program: Where Next?* Canberra: CIE.

CPV (Communist Party of Vietnam). 1994. "Political Report of the Central Committee to the Midterm Party Conference." Report, CPV, Hanoi. Cited in Dollar and Ljunggren 1997, 464.

Dollar, D. 1992. "Vietnam: Successes and Failures of Macroeconomic Stabilization." In *The Challenge of Reform in Indochina*, ed. B. Ljunggren, 207–31. Cambridge, MA: Harvard University Press.

Dollar, D., and B. Ljunggren. 1997. "Vietnam." In *Going Global: Transition from Plan to Market in the World Economy*, ed. P. Desai, 439–71. Cambridge, MA: MIT Press.

Duiker, W. J. 1989. *Vietnam since the Fall of Saigon.* 3rd ed. Athens, OH: Ohio University Press.

Fforde, A., and S. de Vylder. 1996. *From Plan to Market: The Economic Transition in Vietnam.* Boulder, CO: Westview Press.

GSO (General Statistics Office). 2000. *Statistical Data of Vietnam Agriculture, Forestry, and Fishery, 1975–2000.* Hanoi: Statistical Publishing House.

———. 2001. *Vietnamese Economy during the Years of Renovation in Aggregated Economic Indicators of the System of National Accounts.* Hanoi: Statistical Publishing House.

———. various years. *Statistical Yearbook of Vietnam.* Hanoi: Statistical Publishing House.

———. various years. *Statistical Handbook of Vietnam.* Hanoi: Statistical Publishing House.

IAPP (Institute for Agricultural Planning and Projecting). 2001. "Report on Strategy for Developing the Livestock Sector in Vietnam until 2010." Unpublished study, IAPP, Hanoi. Cited in Nguyen and Grote 2004, 13.

Minot, N., and F. Goletti. 2000. "Rice Market Liberalization and Poverty in Viet Nam." Research Report 114, International Food Policy Research Institute, Washington, DC.

Naughton, B. 1996. "Distinctive Features of Economic Reform in China and Vietnam." In *Reforming Asian Socialism: The Growth of Market Institutions*, ed. J. McMillan and B. Naughton, 273–96. Ann Arbor, MI: University of Michigan Press.

Nguyen, Hoa, and Ulrike Grote. 2004. "Agricultural Policies in Vietnam: Producer Support Estimates, 1986–2002." MTID Discussion Paper 79, Markets, Trade, and Institutions Division, International Food Policy Research Institute, Washington, DC.

Nguyen M. T., D. Harris, T. Chong Thang, and N. Q. Nguyen. 2006. "Building a Roadmap for the International Integration of Vietnam's Sugar Industry." Unpublished study, Ministry of Agriculture and Rural Development and Australian Agency for International Development, Hanoi.

Nicita, A., and M. Olarreaga. 2006. "Trade, Production, and Protection, 1976–2004." *World Bank Economic Review* 21 (1): 165–71.

Pritchett, L. 2003. "A Toy Collection, a Socialist Star, and a Democratic Dud?" In *In Search of Prosperity: Analytic Narratives on Economic Growth*, ed. D. Rodrik, 123–51. Princeton, NJ: Princeton University Press.

Riedel, J. 1993. "Vietnam: On the Trails of the Tigers." *World Economy* 16 (4): 401–22.

Riedel, J., and B. Comer. 1997. "Transition to a Market Economy in Vietnam." In *Economies in Transition: Comparing Asia and Eastern Europe*, ed. W. T. Woo, S. Parker, and J. D. Sachs, 189–213. Cambridge, MA: MIT Press.

Sachs, J. D., and W. T. Woo. 1994. "Experiences in the Transition to a Market Economy." *Journal of Comparative Economics* 18 (3): 271–75.

Thanh, V. T. 2006. "Vietnam's Trade Liberalization and International Economic Integration: Evolution, Problems and Challenges." *ASEAN Economic Bulletin* 22 (1): 75–91.

Van Arkadie, B., and R. Mallon. 2003. *Vietnam: A Transition Tiger?* Canberra: Asia Pacific Press.

White, C. 1981. "Agrarian Reform and National Liberation in the Vietnamese Revolution, 1920–1957." PhD dissertation, Cornell University, Ithaca, NY.

———. 1985. "Agricultural Planning, Pricing Policy and Co-operatives in Vietnam." *World Development* 13 (1): 97–114.

Woodside, A. 1989. "Peasants and the State in the Aftermath of the Vietnamese Revolution." *Journal of Peasant Studies* 16 (4): 283–97.

PART IV

SOUTH ASIA

9

BANGLADESH

Nazneen Ahmed, Zaid Bakht,
Paul A. Dorosh, and Quazi Shahabuddin

The government of Bangladesh has substantially liberalized its trade and agricultural pricing policies since the country's independence in 1971. The government had removed most of the distortions in agricultural incentives by the mid-1990s. Although it has raised the level of trade protection for some agricultural and industrial products sharply since 1998, the total distortions in agriculture remain small. In particular, relative to India and Pakistan, domestic and international trade policies for the major staples—rice and wheat—are substantially more liberal in Bangladesh.

In the early 1970s, the government pursued highly restrictive trade and exchange rate policies through import regulations, high import tariffs, export taxes, pervasive quantitative restrictions, and an overvalued exchange rate. These polices were similar to the policies implemented in the 1960s when Bangladesh was part of Pakistan. The policy regime in the 1970s was especially restrictive in the agricultural sector. The government had a monopoly on the imports of most agricultural commodities and placed stiff export restrictions on raw jute, the major agricultural export. Because of these distortions, agricultural price incentives were substantially reduced during the period (Rahman 1994).

Under pressure from donors and disenchanted by the slow economic growth and continued balance of payments problems despite the policies, the government initiated reforms in the early 1980s. Broad liberalization was not undertaken until the early 1990s, however. The liberalization was accompanied by agricultural trade and pricing reforms. By the mid-1990s, distortions in the output prices for rice and wheat had been virtually eliminated, and the total distortions were minimal. The government raised the import tariffs on rice in response to subsidized exports by India in 2001, but domestic rates of assistance calculated relative to international market prices indicate that there have been only small overall agricultural price distortions since around 2000.

In the next section, we describe growth and structural change in the economy of Bangladesh. We focus on the agricultural sector. In the subsequent section, we offer an overview of the evolution of agricultural policies since independence. We then report our time series estimates of nominal rates of assistance (NRAs) for selected agricultural products. In the penultimate section, we discuss the changing political economy of agricultural price and trade policies. We follow with some concluding observations.

Economic Growth and Structural Change

The growth of gross domestic product (GDP) has accelerated steadily in Bangladesh since the early 1980s. The average growth rate rose from 3.2 percent in 1980–84 to 5.3 percent in 2000–04.[1] The acceleration in per capita income growth has been even greater, mainly because the population growth rate has declined from 2.2 to 1.5 percent per year over the last 25 years. Several features of the policy context during this period of growth are noteworthy, including the stable macroeconomic environment and the emphasis on the private sector as the engine of economic growth, on economic liberalization and outward orientation, and on agriculture and rural development.

At only 2.8 percent in 1980–2004, the growth rate in the agricultural sector (including forestry and fishing) has been considerably slower than overall GDP growth. It was also uneven. It averaged only 1.7 percent a year during the first half of the 1990s, when growth in the crop subsector declined slightly. During the second half of the 1990s, growth in the crop subsector surged to an average 3.8 percent a year, while total agriculture grew at 4.8 percent a year. Growth in the fishing subsector was even more rapid in the 1990s, averaging 8.1 percent a year, but then slowed substantially to 1.7 percent after 2000 (Ahmed et al. 2007).

Thus, as in most other countries, sustained economic growth in Bangladesh has been accompanied by a structural transformation that has involved a declining share of agriculture despite positive agricultural GDP growth. The GDP share of agriculture declined from 32 percent in 1980–84 to 23 percent in 2000–04. About 7 percentage points of the growth throughout this period was accounted for by forestry and fishing. Meanwhile, the share of industry in GDP rose from 18 to 28 percent, and the share of services was steady at around 50 percent. Exports of ready-made garments have boomed in the past two decades, causing agriculture's share in total exports to fall from more than 33 percent in the 1970s and 1980s to less than 8 percent after 2000. Nonetheless, more than 60 percent of the country's labor force continues to be employed in agriculture at least part time. Moreover, because agricultural production provides critical links for development in the rest of the economy, its performance has an important bearing on employment generation, food security, and poverty reduction. For these reasons, agricultural growth is still a development priority.

Field crops and horticulture are the dominant activities in agriculture, accounting for four times as much agricultural value added as livestock activities since the early 1980s (Ahmed et al. 2007). Cropping is dominated by the production of cereals, especially rice, in which technological progress, supported by the development of irrigation infrastructure, has been the main engine of growth. Rice represented about 70 percent of the value added arising from crop production in 1973 and about 80 percent in 1999. The rapid expansion of rice production has been achieved in part at the expense of pulses and oilseeds, which remain important sources of protein and micronutrients. Apart from rice and wheat, the only crops showing rapid growth over the past two decades are maize, potatoes, and vegetables.

Domestic demand factors have contributed to this structural change in the agricultural economy. They include income growth in aggregate, plus the acceleration in the growth in per capita income generated by the slowdown in population growth. Population growth was the dominant factor behind the growth in domestic demand for food in the 1970s, when per capita incomes were basically stagnant. In the 1990s, income growth and the varying income elasticity of demand for different food items became major factors behind the pattern of growth in domestic demand. Farmers have now started to respond to market signals by reallocating resources to activities that are showing strong market growth (Hossain 2001).

Agricultural exports

In 1973, exports of agricultural commodities stood at slightly more than 80 percent of total exports. Their value grew at a modest trend rate of 4.2 percent in nominal terms and 1.4 percent in real terms over the subsequent three decades. Most of the growth was recorded by fishing (shrimps). In contrast, overall exports grew at a trend rate of nearly 11 percent (8.4 percent in real terms), which largely reflected rapid growth in ready-made garments. The share of ready-made garments in total exports had risen to nearly 75 percent by 2004–05, while the share of agriculture in total exports had declined from 37 to 7 percent (Ahmed et al. 2007).

The composition of agricultural exports has also undergone significant change during the last three decades. In the 1970s, the average share of exports of raw jute in total agricultural exports was 70 percent, while the corresponding share of exports of tea and shrimps were 17 and 9 percent, respectively. However, exports of raw jute began facing stiff competition from synthetic substitutes, and the real value of raw jute exports declined by about two-thirds from the 1970s to the early 1990s before stabilizing, although the share of the exports in total agricultural export earnings continued to fall as exports of shrimps and vegetables expanded. By 2004, the share of jute exports was only 15 percent (and of tea exports, less than 3 percent) compared with 65 percent for shrimps and 6 percent for vegetables (from zero in the 1970s). The rising demand for vegetables by expatriate Bangladeshis and various policy measures, particularly the provision of cash incentives and subsidized freight charges, facilitated the rapid growth in vegetable exports.

Agricultural imports

Similar to the case of agricultural exports, the share of major agricultural imports in total imports has declined since the 1970s. The share of these imports—wheat, raw cotton, edible oil, rice, sugar, milk and cream, pulses, spices, oilseeds, and tobacco—declined from an average of 33 percent in the 1970s to 24 percent in the 1980s and only 16 percent in 2000–04 (Ahmed et al. 2007). The total real value of major agricultural imports nonetheless increased over this period by an average of 2.1 percent a year. This is more rapid than the increase in the value of agricultural exports (1.4 percent a year), but slower than the increase in the value of total imports (4.9 percent a year). In 2004, raw cotton, edible oil, wheat, rice, sugar, and milk powder accounted (in decreasing order) for most agricultural imports.

However, the above figures cover recorded imports only. Studies have shown that illegal imports from India constitute nearly 20 percent of Bangladesh's total recorded imports (Bakht 1999). Of these illegal imports, two-thirds consist of only six agricultural goods: cattle (42 percent), sugar (7 percent), pulses (6 percent), milk powder (3 percent), spices (3 percent), and rice (2 percent).

Historically, food aid has constituted an important component of the wheat imports of Bangladesh. During the 1980s and 1990s, food aid in wheat accounted for about two-thirds of total wheat imports; thus, average wheat food aid was about 1.0 million tons a year, and average total wheat imports were 1.5 million tons a year. Government commercial imports accounted for the remainder of total imports. Domestic wheat procurement, food aid, private commercial imports (since the trade liberalization in the early 1990s), and government commercial imports have contributed wheat to the public food distribution system. The amount of food aid has dropped substantially since 1999 following large gains in domestic grain production. Food aid never provided more than 0.5 percent of rice supplies, however. Before 1992–93, the public sector accounted for all commercial imports of rice; but, in response to market incentives, private sector imports have increased since then to supplement domestic production and government imports.

In most years since 2000, raw cotton has surpassed rice and wheat, combined, as the major agricultural import. The growth in the real value of raw cotton imports has been especially rapid since the early 1990s, when the government started offering a 25 percent cash subsidy for exports of ready-made garments produced using domestic fabric, a policy that encouraged a surge in investment in textile spinning and composite mills (Bakht 2001a). Growth in the real value of raw cotton imports averaged 12 percent a year in the 1990s and 15 percent a year in 1999–2004.

The real value of imports of edible oil rose by 3.2 percent a year from the early 1970s to 2004, so that the share of edible oil in total agricultural imports remained close to one-fifth over the period. Recorded sugar imports (not including sugar smuggled from India) increased even more rapidly, rising from 1.4 percent of the value of agricultural imports in the early 1970s to 7 percent in 1999–2004. Between 1973 and 2003, the domestic production of sugar increased by only about 100,000 metric tons, raising the output level from 90,000 tons in 1973 to around 190,000 tons in 2003. In contrast, domestic demand for sugar increased by nearly 700,000 tons during this period. As a result, imports of sugar increased from about 12,000 tons in 1973 to nearly 600,000 tons in 2003.

Exchange Rate and Trade Policies

The government followed inward-oriented, import-substituting trade policies beginning at independence in 1971 until major reforms were instituted in the 1980s and especially the 1990s. This section provides a brief history of the policies and the reforms during these years.

The 1970s: Inward-oriented policies

Faced with an imminent balance of payments crisis in 1971, the first independence government continued the highly restrictive trade and exchange rate policies that had been in place when Bangladesh had been part of Pakistan. Quantitative restrictions on imports, high tariff rates, and a fixed, overvalued exchange rate were used to control imports, conserve scarce foreign exchange, and provide protection for domestic industry. However, in line with the political philosophy of the government, the protectionist trade regime was maintained even after the possibility of a balance of payments crisis had decreased substantially in the mid-1970s following a recovery in export earnings, an increase in foreign aid, a decline in world prices for grains and other commodities, and the 70 percent devaluation of the taka (Tk) in 1975 from Tk 8.9 to Tk 15.1 per U.S. dollar.

Initially, under the fixed exchange rate system, all foreign exchange accrued to the government and was then allocated for competing uses through a discretionary and cumbersome mechanism of import licensing. However, in the early 1970s, in response to a crisis in foreign exchange, the government instituted a system, eventually known as the wage earner scheme, that allowed foreign exchange earned by Bangladeshis abroad—worker remittances—to be used to import particular categories of goods. At the same time, under the export performance license system, certain exporters were given a specified proportion of their export earnings in the form of import entitlement certificates. The certificates could be used to import particular categories of goods, or they could be sold at a premium so that other traders could import such goods. There was thus a de facto dual exchange rate, whereby the export performance license premium reflected the market price of foreign exchange to some extent. In 1977, wage earners were allowed to sell their foreign exchange earnings directly in a market that came to be known as the *secondary exchange market*. A special foreign exchange rate, called the *wage earner scheme rate*, was available to them on this market.

During the early years of restrictive trade policy, most agricultural commodities were on lists of restricted or banned imports. These lists were aimed at protecting producers from external competition by ensuring that producers received remunerative prices. There were also restrictions on agricultural exports, and some agricultural products were subject to export duties. The goal was to ensure that adequate stocks of agricultural commodities were available in the domestic market. However, fiscal incentives were also established to promote exports of nontraditional items. According to an export policy order issued in 1976, earnings from exports of nontraditional items were doubled from 15–20 to 30–40 percent.[2] Duty drawback schemes were undertaken to promote exports of textile products manufactured using imported raw materials.

The outcome of these autarkic trade and exchange rate policies was disappointing with regard to export development, the balance of payments situation, and overall economic growth, particularly considering the rapid growth achieved by East Asian economies that followed a more outward-oriented development strategy. Disenchanted with the import-substitution strategy (and encouraged by donor conditionalities), policy makers in Bangladesh and other South Asian countries began to adopt more open economic policies in the late 1970s. This shift was facilitated by a change in government in 1975; the new government had a more positive view on the development of a mixed economy and favored a more open trade regime. However, the export promotion measures that were introduced in the late 1970s were limited in scope and were implemented only gradually. Overall trade policies continued to be inward looking, and the economy, particularly the external sector, remained overregulated.

The 1980s: Initial policy reforms

The new government that came to power in March 1982 initiated a wide-ranging policy reform package, the New Industrial Policy, to liberalize the economy. A large number of nationalized companies, especially in the jute and textile subsectors, were privatized within a few years, and measures to increase foreign and domestic investment were adopted. However, only limited trade liberalization occurred under the New Industrial Policy or its successor, the Revised Industrial Policy, introduced in 1986. A cash compensatory scheme administered by Bangladesh Bank was also introduced in 1986, providing cash equal to 15 percent of free on board export values for exports manufactured using local fabrics.[3]

Ultimately, the progress in trade liberalization was slow in the 1980s, especially in the reduction in import tariffs (Bakht 2001b). However, some liberalization in agricultural exports did occur. Export duties on raw jute and tea were withdrawn in 1981, and the duties on exports of dried fruit, fresh fruit, oil cakes, coriander seed, dry chilies, dry ginger, black pepper, turmeric, tobacco, vegetables, and potatoes were withdrawn in 1986. Restrictions on exports of jute seed, wheat, pulses, shrimps other than frozen, frogs (dead or alive) and frog legs, and onions were maintained even after 1995. Export restrictions on rice, wheat bran, and molasses were removed only in 1998.

There were major reforms in exchange rate policy. In mid-1979, Bangladesh adopted a flexible policy, fixing the taka to a basket of the currencies of the country's major trading partners.[4] Then, in 1986, the export performance license system was simplified substantially through the introduction of an export performance benefit. Exporters could directly cash any benefit entitlements at their banks at the existing wage earner scheme rate. During the 1980s, these policies, particularly the export performance benefit, contributed to rapid growth in nontraditional exports. They also contributed to rapid expansion in the secondary (wage earner scheme) market. A wide range of agricultural commodities were favored by the export performance benefit incentives (Ahmed et al. 2007). However, exports of raw jute were not included in this benefit scheme and thus suffered directly from the overvalued exchange rate.

Meanwhile, imports financed at the official exchange rate were quickly reduced, and an increasing share of imports became subject to the secondary exchange market, including a portion of the foreign exchange received through commodity aid. By 1991, 41 percent of all imports were financed through this means, while the share of the secondary exchange market in nonaid imports was nearly 70 percent. The enhanced role of the secondary exchange market helped narrow the gap between the official exchange rate and the wage earner scheme rate. The two rates were finally unified in 1992, and this marked the end of the export performance benefit arrangement (Rahman 1992).

1990s: Major trade liberalization

After a decade of half-hearted attempts at trade liberalization, the democratic government that came to power in 1991 sought boldly to reform the trade regime. The reforms included tariff reductions and rationalization, the establishment of a less-complicated import tax structure, the gradual elimination of nontariff import restrictions, and promotion for exports through income tax exemptions, bonded warehousing, and flexible exchange rate management.[5]

Until the 1990s, the government relied heavily on quantitative restrictions to control imports, especially in agricultural commodities. About 37 percent of the tariff lines for agricultural products (21 percent of all products) were either banned or restricted in 1987 (World Bank 1994). By 1984, all quantitative restrictions on agricultural products had been removed, and only 2 percent of the tariff lines of all products were still facing quantitative restrictions. In particular, private sector imports of rice and wheat were legalized in the early 1990s, ending the government's monopoly on food grain imports. The ban on exports of fine quality rice (but not on ordinary coarse rice) was also lifted.

Trade liberalization in the early 1990s brought tariff rates down sharply. Total protective import duty rates, both customs duties and para-tariff measures (surcharges, license fees, regulatory duties, value added taxes, and supplementary duties), declined from 74 to 32 percent between 1991 and 1995 (measured according to the unweighted average of all tariff lines). Likewise, import tariffs and the total tax incidence on the imports of major agricultural commodities declined rapidly during the early 1990s (table 9.1).[6] Refined edible oil, sugar, milk powder, and spices were subject to relatively high duty rates, while raw cotton, wheat, rapeseeds, and lentils enjoyed lower duty rates (table 9.2).

Trade reforms have stalled in recent years, however. Although customs duties declined from 29 percent in 1995 to 19 percent in 2003, the effect of para-tariff measures rose sharply, mainly because of a steep increase in supplementary duties. Average total protective import duty rates have thus remained essentially unchanged since the mid-1990s. For some products that were already protected, including processed fruits, cement, soap, cotton shirts and sheets, selected ceramic and steel products, batteries, bicycles, and toys, total protection rates rose by more than 30 percent between 1997 and 2003 (World Bank 2004).

Table 9.1. Tariff Rates on Imports, Bangladesh, 1991–2003
(*unweighted average,* %)

Year	All tariff lines			Industry tariff lines			Agricultural tariff lines		
	Customs duties	Para-tariffs	Total rate	Customs duties	Para-tariffs	Total rate	Customs duties	Para-tariffs	Total rate
1991	71	3	74	70	3	73	77	0	77
1992	58	3	61	57	3	60	62	0	62
1993	43	2	46	43	3	46	46	0	45
1994	34	3	38	34	4	37	37	2	40
1995	29	3	32	28	3	32	30	2	32
1996	28	3	32	28	4	31	30	2	33
1997	27	6	33	27	6	33	29	5	35
1998	27	6	32	26	6	32	28	5	34
1990	22	7	29	22	7	29	25	5	30
2000	21	7	29	20	8	28	25	5	30
2001	21	8	29	20	8	29	25	8	33
2002	20	7	26	19	7	26	24	5	29
2003	19	10	29	18	9	27	23	17	40

Source: World Bank 2004.

Table 9.2. Total Taxes on Agricultural Commodity Imports, Bangladesh, 1992 and 2002

(percent)

Commodity	1992	2002
Milk powder	72	74
Refined soybean oil	101	59
Refined palm oil	87	59
Sugar	135	47
Spices	80	39
Crude soybean oil	66	39
Tobacco	—	39
Rice	89	29
Lentils	20	14
Rapeseeds	20	14
Wheat	8	14
Raw cotton	8	7

Source: World Bank 2004.

Note: — = no data are available.

Impacts of Agricultural Price and Trade Policies on NRAs

In this section, we consider the distortionary policies on several key crop products: rice, wheat, sugar, and potatoes, plus jute and tea, the traditional export crops. Together, these products account for around three-quarters of the value of agricultural production at distorted prices (figure 9.1). In line with the methodology of our project (see Anderson et al. 2008 and appendix A), we estimate NRAs for the output of each of these products. Through careful comparisons of domestic prices and border prices or international reference prices (adjusted for quality differences, marketing margins, and the dual exchange rate system), these measures capture the proportional extent to which government-imposed distortions create a gap between domestic prices and prices as they would be under free market conditions.[7] Since it is not possible to understand the characteristics of agricultural development through a sectoral view alone, we use our project's methodology to estimate the effects of direct agricultural policy measures (including distortions in the foreign exchange market), but, for comparative evaluation, we also generate estimates of the distortions in nonagricultural sectors. More specifically, we compute NRAs for the key products of farm producers. The NRAs include adjustments for direct interventions on farm inputs such as fertilizer. We also generate NRAs for nonagricultural tradables for comparison with the

Figure 9.1. Commodity Shares in Agricultural Production, Bangladesh, 1971–2003

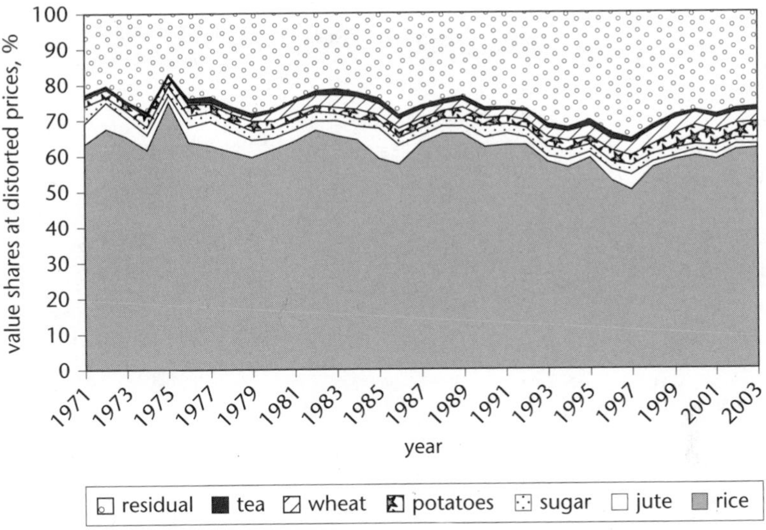

Source: Author calculations based on producer price and production data in FAOSTAT Database 2008.

NRAs for agricultural tradables so as to calculate relative rates of assistance (RRAs) (see Anderson et al. 2008 and appendix A).[8]

Rice

The impact of trade policy on agricultural incentives is largely determined by the price and trade policies for rice because of this commodity's predominance in the agricultural sector. Bangladesh has always been a net importer of rice, although only small quantities were imported in some years. From independence until 1992, private sector rice imports were banned, and government commercial imports accounted for almost all rice imports. (Rice was insignificant as an item in food aid.) Since 1993, when rice imports were liberalized, the private sector has accounted for most rice imports.

Since 1980, the average annual volume of wheat imports has been about three times the corresponding volume of rice imports (about 1.6 million tons and 0.6 million tons, respectively) (table 9.3). The higher share of wheat in total food grain imports partly reflects inflows of food aid in wheat and partly reflects government policy that tended to favor the use of lower-cost wheat in the public food distribution system. Although rice accounted for about one-third of the grain

Table 9.3. Production and Imports, Rice and Wheat, Bangladesh, 1973–2004

Indicator, year	Rice	Wheat	Total
Production, 1,000 tons			
1973–78	12,255	259	12,514
1979–88	14,501	1,085	15,586
1989–98	18,230	1,305	19,534
1999–2004	24,822	1,476	26,298
Imports, 1,000 tons			
1973–78	216	1,292	1,507
1979–88	308	1,655	1,963
1989–98	660	1,363	2,022
1999–2004	795	1,680	2,475
Imports/net availability,[a] %			
1973–78	2.5	81.7	12.7
1979–88	1.9	60.6	11.1
1989–98	3.6	52.1	9.9
1999–2004	3.4	59.7	9.5

Sources: Ministry of Finance 2005; BBS, various.

a. Net availability is estimated as production, less a 10 percent adjustment for seed, feed, and wastage, plus imports. Variations in public stocks are not counted.

distributed through the system (the other two-thirds was wheat), rice distribution represented only 4 percent of the total net availability of rice from the 1970s through the 1990s. This is about the same as the corresponding share in East Pakistan in the 1950s and 1960s (see Ahmed, Nuruddin, Chowdhury, and Haggblade 2000). Total rice imports averaged about 3 percent of net rice availability over 1980–2004 (calculated without consideration of changes in public stocks). In contrast, wheat imports—largely food aid until the late 1990s—accounted for about two-thirds of total wheat availability during the period. In total, however, imports as a share of availability steadily declined, from an average of 17 percent in the 1980s to 14 percent in the 1990s and only 11 percent in 2000–04.

From the early 1970s to 2005, the wholesale price of rice averaged close to the import parity price (calculated on the basis of the average price of rice imports). This masks wide fluctuations from year to year, however. This is so particularly during the period when the public sector held a monopoly on imports, and there was thus no direct link between international and domestic prices.

The country experienced a famine in 1974 in the wake of the damage and destruction to transport infrastructure during the war in 1971 and the shortfall in rice production in 1974. The government lacked sufficient foreign exchange to

Figure 9.2. NRAs and Border Prices, Rice, Bangladesh, 1974–2004

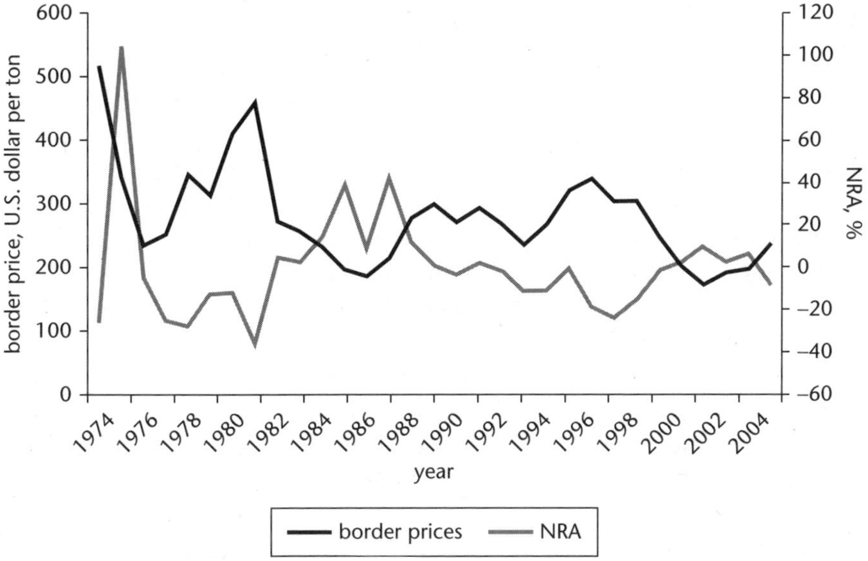

Source: Ahmed et al. 2007.

Note: The Pearson correlation coefficient between the two series shown is −0.41.

make up the deficit by purchasing rice imports at the high prevailing international price.[9] The domestic price for rice rose substantially in the 1974/75 season, but was still below the international price. After this crisis and the 61 percent devaluation in the taka relative to the U.S. dollar in May 1975, the domestic wholesale price for rice was double the import parity price, but it went below this level again during the subsequent six years (figure 9.2).

Rice and wheat imports represented 10 percent of the total food grain supply, but, because wheat was not a close substitute for rice in domestic consumption, the effect of wheat imports (mainly food aid) on the market price for rice was likely to have been small. Nonetheless, in the absence of wheat imports, domestic rice prices would have been somewhat higher during this period.[10]

In the early 1980s, rapid increases in the domestic production of rice led to greater availability and lower real wholesale prices. International rice prices were falling even more rapidly, however, so that, over the five-year period 1983–87, the average domestic price was 21 percent above the import parity price. The government monopoly on imports thus had an effect on rice tariffs similar to the effect of an import tariff under a liberalized trade environment that favors net sellers of rice relative to net buyers. A surge in domestic rice production (mainly of winter rice [boro]) following major floods in 1987 and 1988 led to another drop in real wholesale rice prices in 1989, and this brought domestic prices close to par with border prices and eliminated the implicit protection for producers. This price-stabilizing role of government has tended to generate a negative correlation between NRAs and border prices, the extent of which is evident in figure 9.2.

Trade liberalization in the early 1990s created a possible direct link between domestic and border prices for rice, particularly during periods following poor domestic rice harvests. Throughout the 1980s and early 1990s, Thailand was the major source of rice imports to Bangladesh. However, the 1994 liberalization that permitted private sector imports in Bangladesh coincided with rice trade liberalization and the buildup of public rice stocks in India, which made private sector rice imports from India legal and feasible.[11] Because of lower transport costs, reduced delivery times (for private sector imports), and the possibility of smaller contracts for the delivery of imports by truck, India rapidly replaced Thailand as the major source of rice imports in Bangladesh in the mid-1990s. Large-scale rice imports from India supplemented domestic supplies during crop shortfalls in Bangladesh in 1994, 1997, and 1998.[12] In 1997 and 1998, 92 percent of rice imports came from India. However, during periods following normal or above-average rice harvests (most of 1996 and 1997, in 2000, and in the first half of 2001), domestic rice prices in Bangladesh were below import parity levels, eliminating any incentives for private sector imports (figure 9.2).[13] Average domestic wholesale prices were 5 and 12 percent below average import parity prices in 1990–94 and 1995–99, respectively, although there were few trade barriers during these years. The negative NRAs reflect periods when rice came close to being a nontradable because of good domestic harvests.

Beginning in 2000, the government of India adopted increasingly aggressive measures to promote exports to reduce a massive public stock buildup. The measures included subsidies for rice exports that involved the provision of grain from government stocks to exporters at prices that were below cost.[14] Because domestic rice prices in Bangladesh were approximately equal to the full-cost import parity prices, including taxes, for below-poverty-line rice made in India, small amounts of low-quality rice were imported into Bangladesh in 2000.[15] However, when the Indian government lowered its above-poverty-line sales price for fine rice from Rs 11.3 per kilogram to only Rs 8.3 per kilogram in July 2001, the government of Bangladesh increased rice import tariffs and taxes from 5 to 37.5 percent.[16] This raised the below-poverty-line import parity price, plus taxes, to 33 percent above the domestic price in Bangladesh, thereby essentially cutting off the incentive for private sector rice trade with India (figure 9.3).[17] However, in mid-2002, the domestic price again rose toward the import parity price, including taxes, leading to relatively large-scale private sector trade with India once more. Until early 2006, domestic prices were at or near below-poverty-line import parity prices,

Figure 9.3. Prices and Private Sector Imports, Rice, Bangladesh, 1997–2007

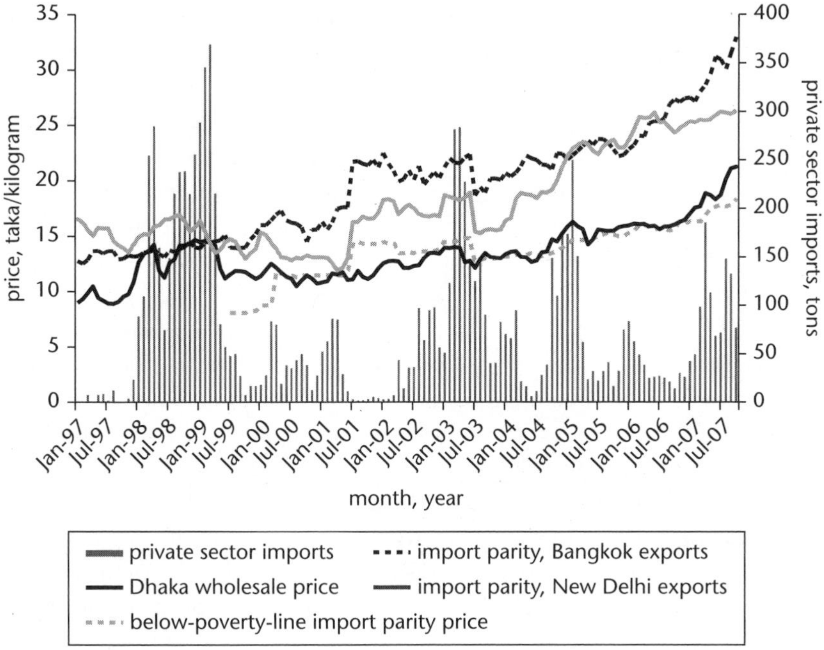

Source: Ahmed et al. 2007.

Note: Import parity prices include taxes.

including taxes, suggesting that the former were essentially being determined by the latter during this period.[18]

In 2002–04, the average wholesale price in Bangladesh was only 1 percent below the below-poverty-line import parity price, including taxes. Import tariffs raised the domestic price relative to the import parity price, without taxes, for subsidized Indian below-poverty-line rice by an average of 10 percent. However, the domestic price in Bangladesh was 28 percent below the import parity price based on the wholesale price in New Delhi and 15 percent below the import parity price based on Bangkok exports. In the absence of these subsidized imports, the net domestic supply of rice, without government intervention, would have been 5 percent less over 2002–04, and the domestic rice price would have been about 15–25 percent higher. The lower value assumes an own-price elasticity of rice demand of −0.3, and the higher value assumes an own-price elasticity of rice demand of −0.2. Thus, under the first assumption, the domestic price would have risen close to the import parity price based on Bangkok exports, and net imports would have been near zero.

Wheat

Wheat was a minor crop in Bangladesh in the 1960s, prior to independence. Wheat production increased rapidly thereafter, from an average of about 0.1 million tons a year in 1969–74 to more than 1.8 million tons a year in 1997–99. This rise was associated with a sevenfold expansion in the area cultivated in wheat and a twofold expansion in wheat yields per hectare. Wheat production growth was especially rapid in the 1970s, increasing by an average 37 percent a year as the area under wheat expanded by 19 percent a year, and yields per hectare rose by 15 percent a year. In 1998–2003, the area under wheat declined from a peak of 967,000 hectares to 704,000 hectares, while the area planted in maize, potatoes, and winter rice expanded (Dorosh 2006).

Because of the government monopoly on external trade, there was no explicit link between the international price of wheat and the domestic price from the 1970s to the early 1990s. Because food aid and government commercial imports accounted for over half of the total supply, government policy on the net distribution of wheat (there was limited domestic procurement of wheat) was the dominant factor determining the domestic market price.

Partly because of food aid conditionality among donors stipulating that food aid should not generate price disincentives for domestic production, the average domestic price on wheat was close to the import parity price throughout this period. After the devaluation in 1975, the estimated NRAs on output averaged only 3 percent until 1993 (table 9.4).

After the liberalization of wheat imports in 1992, the import parity price of wheat provided a price ceiling for wheat in the same way the import parity price of rice accomplished this for rice. In most years, domestic prices were close to this ceiling, so that the average NRA on output was less than 4 percent after 1994. Only during a period when international wheat prices were high (around 1996) were domestic prices substantially below border prices (NRAs of −14 percent).

From the mid-1990s until 2000, most commercial wheat imports involved high-gluten wheat for baking that was imported from major international wheat exporters such as Australia, the European Union, and the United States. This wheat accounted for about 10 percent of total wheat use in Bangladesh, and it did not directly compete with soft, lower-gluten domestic wheat, which is used mostly for traditional breads (for example, *roti* and *chapati*). However, in 2000 and in several years since then, subsidized wheat exports from India were found on markets in Bangladesh.

Because of the rapid increases in rice production and rice supply and the lower real price of rice, which tended to reduce the demand for wheat, the significant food aid beginning in 1999, if it had been maintained, would likely have reduced

Table 9.4. NRAs for Covered Agricultural Products, Bangladesh, 1974–2004

(percent)

Indicator, product	1974	1975–79	1980–84	1985–89	1990–94	1995–99	2000–04
Exportables[a]	−28.7	−34.6	−26.2	−32.4	−33.0	−9.9	−33.2
Jute	−30.0	−37.1	−29.3	−35.4	−38.4	−5.6	−38.7
Tea	1.4	−14.5	−10.7	−19.9	−11.9	−20.5	−20.4
Import-competing products[a]	−20.6	6.5	−1.9	24.4	−0.1	−7.9	6.1
Rice[b]	−25.7	6.5	−5.2	20.4	−5.3	−12.0	2.6
Wheat	38.9	30.3	−5.8	11.3	4.5	2.6	−0.3
Sugar	73.7	92.1	137.0	436.0	166.1	138.8	223.9
Nontradables[a]							
Potatoes	1.3	1.5	1.3	1.7	2.2	2.7	1.8
All covered products[a]	−20.8	2.8	−3.8	16.8	−2.2	−7.6	3.9
Dispersion, covered products[c]	52.1	71.4	67.6	190.7	77.5	67.9	101.2
Coverage, at undistorted prices	77	77	78	72	72	70	72

Source: Ahmed et al. 2007.

a. Weighted averages; the weights are based on the unassisted value of production.

b. Calculated based on the average cost of rice imports.

c. Dispersion is a simple five-year average of the annual standard deviation around the weighted mean of the NRAs of covered products.

the domestic price of wheat below the import parity price (del Ninno and Dorosh 2003). However, donors substantially reduced food aid after 2001. There were three reasons for this reduction: the government had achieved its domestic food production target of 454 grams per person per day, thus eliminating the notional food gap; the European Union was reducing its use of in-kind food aid; and the United States and other countries were shifting their deliveries of food aid resources to other parts of the world. Nonetheless, wheat production has declined since 2000. This has largely been the result of growing competition from maize, including hybrid varieties that have been profitable and have been satisfying a domestic market for poultry feed.

Jute

After the onset of the boom in the production of ready-made garments in Bangladesh in the early 1980s, jute lost its prominent share in total export earnings. Nonetheless, it is still an important farm export commodity. Bangladesh remains the leading exporter of raw jute in the world, and a significant number of farm households continue to depend on jute cultivation for their livelihoods.

International jute prices have been declining steadily, however, and the world demand for jute has been shrinking in the face of synthetic substitutes. The nominal U.S. dollar export price of jute fell by an average 1.5 percent a year from 1973 to 2004. The decline in real prices has been an even steeper −4.2 percent per year (measured using the U.S. wholesale price index as a deflator for the dollar price series). As a result, the real 2004–05 dollar price of jute fell by two-thirds between the late 1970s and the early 2000s. Because the quantity of raw jute exports remained rather flat over the period, export earnings fell dramatically (Ahmed et al. 2007).

The domestic price of jute has been consistently below the export parity price partly because of an effort to encourage the domestic processing of jute products for export.[19] In the 1970s and 1980s, the average domestic wholesale price of jute was more than 30 percent below the export parity price.[20] Following the trade liberalization of the early 1990s, the NRAs on jute output averaged only 6 percent. However, after the closing of public sector jute mills, the domestic price of raw jute again fell significantly below the export parity price, perhaps reflecting the disruption in marketing channels and the greater differential between the quality of raw jute for export and jute for the domestic market (table 9.4).

Tea

Like jute, tea was once a major export of East Pakistan and then Bangladesh. Between 1973 and 1983, the value of tea exports rose in nominal dollar terms mainly because of an increase in the international price of tea. However, from the peak value of exports, at US$69 million in 1983, export earnings from tea declined steadily to only US$16 million in 2004. One factor in the decline in exports was the rise in the domestic demand for tea. During the last three decades, tea production has expanded at a trend rate of 2 percent, while domestic tea consumption increased at a trend rate of 7.5 percent, leaving a smaller exportable surplus.

The domestic price of tea, which is based on the auction at Chittagong, has been consistently 10 to 20 percent below the export parity price, which is equivalent to the average export price in Chittagong. This may reflect handling costs at the port. Rahman (1994) uses a border price based on the London auction price, discounted by 30 percent, less marketing and processing costs to cover the transfers to Chittagong port from the tea gardens in Sylhet in northeastern Bangladesh. He finds little difference between the domestic price and the border price in most years between 1974 and 1987 except when the border price spiked in 1976, 1983, and 1984. The gaps between the average export price and the Chittagong auction price or the London auction price may largely reflect quality differences rather than trade and domestic pricing policy distortions.

Sugar

Bangladesh produces less than 20 percent of the sugar it consumes. The remainder is provided by official sugar imports (nearly 50 percent of consumption) and sugar smuggled from neighboring India.[21] The country's sugar industry is highly protected through import tariffs. Imports have been controlled through licensing (before 1992), a government monopoly (1992–2001), and a combination of parastatals and private traders (since June 2002). As a result, the domestic price of sugar is substantially higher than the world price. Farmers do not reap all the benefits of this policy, however, since sugarcane prices are fixed by the government, and sugar mills retain a monopsony on sugarcane purchases within designated sugarcane areas near each mill.[22]

Official trade has generally faced high import tariffs. For example, tariffs on sugar imports were 135 percent in 1992 before major trade liberalization, but still 47 percent in 2002 after the liberalization. These high tariffs on sugar have greatly reduced imports of sugar through official channels, but have also provided major incentives for sugar smuggling.

Our NRA estimates for output vary substantially over time largely because of fluctuations in the world price of sugar, but also because milling, transport, and marketing costs are subtracted from the border price for sugar to determine the sugarcane price at the farmgate. Our NRAs on output average more than 150 percent for the 1980s and 1990s and even more since 2000 (table 9.4).

Distortions in input prices

Modern agricultural technology was introduced in East Pakistan in the early 1960s. There was eventually heavy public sector involvement in the procurement and distribution of modern agricultural inputs and in investments for the development of water resources. A parastatal, the East Pakistan Agricultural Development Corporation, later known as the Bangladesh Agricultural Development Corporation, was established in 1963. The corporation held a virtual monopoly over the procurement and distribution of fertilizers, seeds, pesticides, and small irrigation equipment, although it had to conform to pricing policies and related policies that the government formulated from time to time.[23]

Major reforms in the markets for fertilizer and irrigation equipment were launched in the late 1970s (Ahmed et al. 2007). Under the new marketing system established in 1978, private sector trade in fertilizer was liberalized, leading to a substantial expansion in the number of wholesalers and retailers operating in the fertilizer market.[24] The share of private trade climbed to 75 percent in 1989 and nearly 100 percent in 1992, when the ban on private sector fertilizer imports was removed and the deregulation of fertilizer marketing was completed. Between December 1994 and March 1995, however, a serious shortage in the supply of urea led to a crisis in the market. The government partially reversed the reform process by initiating controls on wholesale markets, regulating pricing at the factory gate, and imposing restrictions on domestic traders who were selling outside the districts in which they had been registered (Ahmed 2001).[25]

Subsidies for the domestic production of nitrogenous fertilizer have been responsible for the greatest distortion in agricultural input prices. By 1983, fertilizer prices at the farmgate had been deregulated throughout the country and direct subsidies to farmers for the production of urea had been eliminated. However, subsidies continued through 1991 for imports of other fertilizers—namely, triple superphosphate and muriate of potash—that were designed to improve the balance of chemical nutrients. Subsidies for imported fertilizers such as these were reintroduced in January 2005 at the rate of 35 percent.

Government controls on urea and on the volume of urea imports and exports have helped maintain the domestic wholesale price for urea consistently below the import parity border price and generally above the export parity price, despite the liberalization in marketing.[26] The average domestic price for urea was 37–50 percent below the import parity price in the 1970s and 1980s and 50 percent below the import parity price in the 1990s and 2000s. (The average domestic price for urea was about 40 percent above the average export parity price from 1990–91 to 2004–05.) However, the average domestic price of triple superphosphate has been only 18 percent below the import parity price since 1990, though it had been 47 percent below the import parity price in the 1970s and 1980s (Ahmed et al. 2007).

Given that the cost of fertilizer accounts for an average of only 5 percent of the total cost of paddy and even less for most other crops, the fertilizer subsidy has not had a major effect on the overall NRAs in agriculture in recent years. Indeed, it has added only 1 or 2 percent during most years. This also applies to the main non-tradable food, potatoes, which would otherwise show NRAs of zero.

The total assistance to agriculture

For the agricultural sector as a whole, including both tradable and nontradable goods, average NRAs since the mid-1970s have been low. Since 1975, the five-year average NRAs for the six products we cover have ranged from −8 percent in the mid-1990s, when international prices were high, to 17 percent in the later 1980s, when international prices were low (table 9.4). Three key factors have driven this result. First, since rice accounts for two-thirds of covered product output, the NRAs for rice largely determine the total NRAs for tradable agriculture. The product exhibiting the greatest price distortions, sugarcane, accounts for only 1 or 2 percent of the total value of domestic agricultural production in most years and so has little influence on the sector's average NRAs.

Second, the implicit taxation of agricultural exports (jute and tea) partially offsets the protection for importables in our total NRA estimates. However, jute and tea account for only a small weight in the average NRA (less than 5 percent since the late 1980s).

Third, while the share of potatoes, the nontradable good shown in table 9.4, has a somewhat larger weight in the average, up to 7 percent in recent years, the only measured assistance involved arises from the assistance for fertilizer, and, so, the NRA for potatoes is small.

Our NRA estimates suggest that, relative to import-competing agricultural products, agricultural exports are discouraged. This is illustrated in figure 9.4. Our estimates also suggest that the dispersion of the NRAs for our covered products around the mean value each year is wide and has not declined over the past 30 years. One measure of this phenomenon, shown near the bottom of table 9.4, is the standard deviation in these NRAs: it was around 70 percent or more. This lack of convergence in NRAs implies that the allocation of land and other farm resources among our covered industries continues to be inefficient.

Virtually all noncovered products, including fruits, vegetables, and meat products, receive little assistance; we therefore assume that the corresponding NRAs are zero. We also assume that they are nontradable over the period we study. Including these

Figure 9.4. NRAs for Exportable, Import-Competing, and All Agricultural Products, Bangladesh, 1974–2004

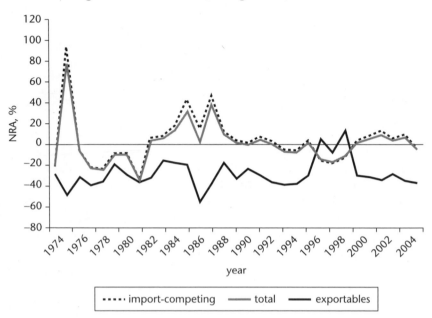

Source: Ahmed et al. 2007.

goods, which account for about one-quarter of the total value of agricultural production, the weighted average NRAs for total agriculture are closer to zero relative to the weighted average of the covered products alone (upper portion of table 9.5).

The assistance provided by government policies to nonagricultural tradable sectors is also important for the competitiveness of agriculture within the economy and the ability of agriculture to contribute to the economy. The effect of import tariffs and import quotas on the domestic prices of nonfarm import-competing goods may be expressed as an implicit tariff rate. This rate is defined as the ratio of domestic prices (measured at the border) to import prices. In the absence of detailed data on domestic and import prices, we have calculated estimates of this implicit tariff. Our calculations provide NRAs for the import-competing parts of the nonfarm sector. We combine these with an assumed NRA of zero for the exportable part of the same sector to generate production-weighted average NRAs for nonagricultural tradables. Though this method may be crude, it provides a reasonable measure that may be compared with the NRAs for tradable agriculture so as to derive RRAs. The RRAs indicate the extent to which the prices received by farmers are depressed relative to the prices faced by the producers of other tradables in the economy (table 9.5, note d.).

Table 9.5. NRAs in Agriculture Relative to Nonagricultural Industries, Bangladesh, 1974–2004

(percent)

Indicator	1974	1975–79	1980–84	1985–89	1990–94	1995–99	2000–04
Covered products[a]	−20.8	2.8	−3.8	16.8	−2.2	−7.6	3.9
Noncovered products	0.0	0.0	0.0	0.0	0.0	0.0	0.0
All agricultural products[a]	−16.0	1.4	−3.3	11.7	−1.5	−5.2	2.7
Non-product-specific assistance	0.0	0.0	0.0	0.0	0.0	0.0	0.0
Total agricultural NRA[b]	−16.0	1.4	−3.3	11.7	−1.5	−5.2	2.7
Trade bias index[c]	−0.10	−0.30	−0.23	−0.45	−0.33	0.00	−0.37
NRA, all agricultural tradables	−21.6	3.1	−3.9	17.5	−2.4	−8.0	4.0
NRA, all nonagricultural tradables	45.9	28.4	22.4	28.5	33.3	29.0	23.4
RRA[d]	−46.3	−19.7	−21.5	−8.6	−26.7	−28.6	−15.8

Source: Ahmed et al. 2007.

a. Including product-specific input subsidies.

b. Including product-specific input subsidies and non-product-specific assistance. Represents total assistance to primary factors and intermediate inputs, divided by the total value of primary agriculture production at undistorted prices.

c. The trade bias index is defined as $(1 + NRAag_x/100)/(1 + NRAag_m/100) - 1$, where $NRAag_m$ and $NRAag_x$ are the average percentage NRAs for the import-competing and exportable parts of the agricultural sector, respectively.

d. The RRA is defined as $100*[(100 + NRAag^t)/(100 + NRAnonag^t) - 1]$, where $NRAag^t$ and $NRAnonag^t$ are the percentage NRAs for the tradables parts of the agricultural and nonagricultural sectors, respectively.

Figure 9.5. NRAs for Agricultural and Nonagricultural Tradables and the RRA, Bangladesh, 1974–2004

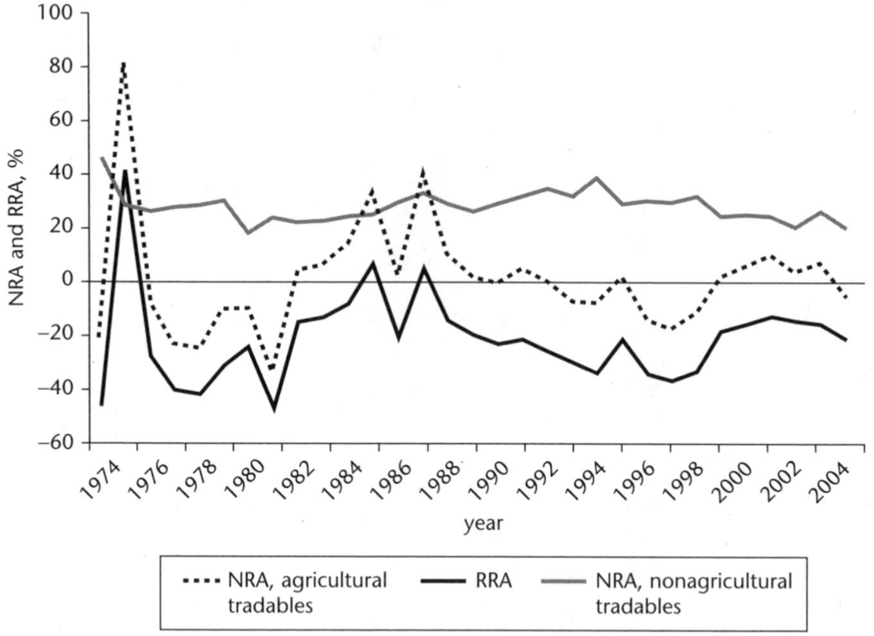

Source: Ahmed et al. 2007.

Note: For the definition of the RRA, see table 9.5, note d.

In table 9.5, we summarize the RRA findings on the basis of annual estimates reported in Ahmed et al. (2007). These estimates reveal that, although the NRAs for agricultural tradables were positive in some years, they were always well below the NRAs for nonagricultural tradables. Hence, the RRA estimates are quite negative; they suggest that the relative prices of farm products have been depressed by more than one-fifth since independence. The value of the RRAs in the first half of the present decade is considerably higher than the value of the RRAs for the 1990s, however (at an average −16 percent compared with −27 percent). Additional reform in the nonfarm sectors will be needed to eliminate the distortions in resource allocation among the sectors that produce tradables (figure 9.5).

The Political Economy of Agricultural Policies

There was a progressive shift in government agricultural policies toward privatization, deregulation, and a reduction in input subsidies. The shift began in the mid-1970s and continued in stages up to the early 1990s. There are still government controls on fertilizers, sugar production, and the wholesale trade, but these are of relatively minor economic significance.

The successive government administrations that formulated and implemented these policies, like all governments, balanced a variety of objectives against a range of constraints. In the policy-making process, pressures and counterpressures are exerted on governments by various interest groups, and the responses of the governments are usually conditioned by interests held in common by the pressure groups and government leaders. Sometimes, if effective pressure groups have not emerged or if they may be successfully set against one another, the government might then pursue its own agenda, which may be predatory, altruistic, or a blend of the two (Grindle 1991). Even if reform proposals are sound on the economics, the reforms will not be successful and sustainable unless they find acceptance according to minimum social and political criteria. If they do not find such acceptance, the government may be forced to backtrack and adopt policies that are less satisfactory on economic grounds.[27]

In Bangladesh, several factors have been especially important in determining the influence of various interest groups on agricultural policies and reforms since independence. These include the relative political strengths of farmers versus urban groups, academic and political views on socialism and capitalism, debates within government ministries, and the reach of donors.

One of the most important facets of the political economy is the relative weakness of farmers and the rural poor in lobbying the government. These groups include a large number of households, but their geographical dispersion, internal differences, ideological orientations, and poor resource base render them largely ineffective politically. In contrast, the working class in the urban formal sector, the bureaucracy as a pressure group within the government apparatus, and private entrepreneurs constitute organized and powerful interest groups that few governments can afford to antagonize.[28]

The weak political position of farmers and smallholders explains why conflicts of interest between agriculture and industry have consistently been resolved in favor of industry. Thus, for example, in the case of agricultural-based industrial raw materials such as jute, the policy has focused on keeping the price of the input low so that the relevant industrial product is competitive. Export taxes and restrictions on agricultural commodity exports contributed to the discrimination against agriculture. The weak representation of the interests of the peasantry within the major political parties and the predominance of trading and industrial interests led to an excessively protected economic regime and shaped the political economy so that government policies continued to discriminate against agriculture. Even in the case of policy measures such as input subsidies, farmers failed to derive much benefit because the subsidies were largely usurped by rent-seeking public officials who were in collusion with middlemen. Any residual benefits to farmers were often more than offset by depressed farm output prices.

Another important factor shaping agricultural and economic policies more generally is the wide divergence of views among social scientists and other professionals on the issue of reform. The views of some critics of market mechanisms were initially shaped by colonialism, which these critics consider a form of exploitation by world capitalism. These critics once pointed to the apparent successes of China and the Soviet Union in economic transformation and to certain blatant examples of market failure, such as the Bengal famine in 1943. The strides taken in China toward the market economy and the disintegration of the Soviet Union have, more recently, disillusioned many of these critics regarding the virtues of central planning. Nonetheless, an articulate antimarket lobby still persists among intellectuals that effectively counters the sweeping and sometimes simplistic claims for the market made by votaries.

The policy process is also complicated by the fact that policy makers and implementers often hold divergent views on the appropriateness of particular reform measures. Sometimes, this occurs because of differences in the social and political orientation of these actors. Rivalry among ministries and the unwillingness of the bureaucracy to relinquish the levers of control even in cases in which political leaders are committed to deregulation may also lead to such outcomes. For example, a ministry of commerce may obstruct liberalization measures proposed by a ministry of finance.

Finally, donors have had a major effect on government policy in Bangladesh in part because of the importance of foreign aid in the development budget and in balance of payments support. Within agriculture, donor support in the funding for agricultural research, rural infrastructure, and food aid was especially important in the 1970s and 1980s, and this contributed to the weight of donor views in the policy process. In particular, the Asian Development Bank, the United States Agency for International Development, and the World Bank exerted substantial influence during the formulation and implementation of agricultural policy by tying program loans and import credits to the policy reform agenda.

Major Reforms in Agricultural Pricing

The major reforms in agricultural policy in the 1980s were swayed by the policy perspectives of the dominant donor agencies as outlined in papers on agricultural and food policy and pricing prepared by the World Bank and the United States Agency for International Development. The World Bank (1979) argued that the net effect of policy interventions in developing countries was to discourage agricultural production, that higher price incentives might be an important instrument in increasing food production, and that input subsidies had proved an inefficient means of protecting agriculture. The World Bank also highlighted the complexities in the effects of food prices on various groups and advocated a gradual rise in food prices to avoid the hardships resulting from abrupt price increases. The United States Agency for International Development (USAID 1982) likewise argued that government interventions in agricultural markets tended to reduce efficiency in the allocation of resources, inhibited gains in productivity, and often did little for the groups they were supposed to help. The U.S. aid agency advocated policies that did not suppress producer prices, that did not attempt to regulate consumer access to food, and that led to a speedy withdrawal of subsidies for agricultural inputs, including credit. Government interventions were to be limited to agricultural research, the construction of large-scale irrigation systems, and special feeding programs to combat malnutrition.

Thus, donors generally advocated a market-oriented agricultural policy, though they also suggested that a central role should be reserved for output price supports to promote self-sufficiency in food grains.[29] This objective was ultimately achieved in 2000 (Osmani and Quasem 1990).[30]

Reforms in agricultural input markets, particularly those related to fertilizer prices, generally faced more opposition. In 1973, the First Five-Year Plan of Bangladesh (1973–78) underscored the need for the eventual removal of agricultural input subsidies and emphasized that the inputs should be sold at a profit. Indeed, urea prices were raised substantially in 1973. Sections of the bureaucracy were opposed to the elimination of input subsidies and to the privatization of the distribution of fertilizer and irrigation equipment. This resistance was partly caused by the bureaucracy's reluctance to accept a curtailment in its power over market controls and distribution. A misplaced concern about equity also contributed to the opposition of bureaucrats to the proposed reforms. Donor pressure to carry out the reforms swiftly played a major role in quelling this opposition.

Fertilizer markets were liberalized again in the early 1990s. The country witnessed a major crisis in the fertilizer market in 1994–95. This led to a partial reversal of the reform in the fertilizer market. Indeed, farmers agitated so militantly that there were incidents involving police gunfire and several deaths. This was in sharp contrast to the 1974 famine, which caused little uproar in rural Bangladesh, and to the fertilizer shortage in 1993 when farmers were paying high fertilizer prices without much protest (Abdullah 1996). The unmet expectations about the lower prices that were supposed to be generated by policy reforms and a perception that there had been injustices may explain the outrage of farmers in the mid-1990s.[31]

The 1974 famine had a different dynamic in the sense that it affected mainly landless laborers. In contrast, the fertilizer shortage in 1993 mainly affected mid-level farmers, who are known to be more militant and among whom marketed rice surpluses are not usually sufficiently large to offset higher urea prices (Wolf 1971). Because national elections were pending, the political parties in opposition also tried to reap dividends from the crisis by mobilizing the peasantry.

Not all reforms in agricultural input markets have been opposed by farmers. Some policy reforms seem to have benefited a majority of farmers. For example, the elimination of the standards requirement in irrigation equipment has been popular. This policy faced opposition from public sector employees, particularly those active in exercising government market controls and government authority over imports (especially the Bangladesh Agricultural Development Corporation). However, this opposition did not prove to be a major roadblock. The issue was never politicized, and the government and its development partners handled the matter tactfully, but also with firmness (Abdullah and Shahabuddin 1993).

Concluding Observations

Agriculture has undergone major structural changes and achieved major successes in Bangladesh over the last four decades. Despite the many problems and constraints, a quiet agricultural revolution has taken place that has enabled the country to achieve its national food security targets in the production of food grains. Agriculture continues to evolve in response to numerous factors, including natural calamities, sociopolitical changes, population growth, urbanization, new technology, opportunities in the rural nonfarm sector, and commercialization. Government macroeconomic, trade, and agricultural pricing policies have played a major role in shaping price incentives in production and consumption and will continue to be important determinants of agricultural growth.

For over 30 years, a central objective of government agricultural policy was self-sufficiency in food grains. To achieve this objective, the government attempted to maintain sufficient incentives for the expansion of domestic rice and wheat production through the maintenance of remunerative output prices and fertilizer subsidies. Investments in agricultural research and technology that permitted large gains in productivity and a substantial increase in irrigation in the area under rice cultivation were also crucial. Meanwhile, government policy was also designed to protect poor consumers through the subsidized sale of rice (until the early 1990s) and extensive safety nets involving food for work programs and food transfers, particularly wheat.

Although trade liberalization has faced substantial opposition, the government nonetheless undertook major reforms in trade policy, including reducing tariffs on industrial products in the 1980s and the early 1990s and liberalizing private sector trade in rice and wheat in the 1990s. As a result, the domestic output price for wheat and rice (the main agricultural products in value) has been close to the border price in most years since the early 1990s. Thus, price distortions in agriculture have averaged less than 5 percent of the value of domestic production since 1990 despite the ongoing price distortions on a few products (notably, sugarcane) and inputs (chemical fertilizers). The country has reaped great benefit from trade liberalization through enhanced food security because private sector imports have helped stabilize markets following significant production shortfalls. Keeping the domestic prices of most agricultural commodities close to the respective border prices has also generated overall efficiency gains in the agricultural sector.

Reducing the remaining disincentives for agricultural production—caused by the protection for nonagricultural producers—will be a necessary part of any future strategy aimed at agricultural growth and rural poverty reduction. Even a liberalized trade policy would not guarantee higher incomes among farmers. For example, in the early part of this decade, the upward trend in the ratio of fertilizer prices to paddy prices that was partly driven by movements in world prices eventually reduced the price incentive for paddy production and contributed to lower returns to farmers. In 2007–08, the world prices for fertilizer and rice rose substantially and, combined with the limits imposed by India on rice exports to Bangladesh, contributed to large increases in the domestic prices for fertilizer and rice in Bangladesh in early 2008. Policies aimed at increasing production and stabilizing prices need not rely mainly on price subsidies or substantial increases in public stocks, however. Indeed, productivity-enhancing investments in agricultural research and extension, improvements in postharvest management and agroprocessing, and investments in market infrastructure can complement agricultural price and trade policies and enable rapid agricultural growth and higher farmer incomes even in a context of shifting world prices.

Notes

1. Throughout this chapter, crop or fiscal years are indicated by the second of the two calendar years. For example, 2004 here refers to the year 2003/04 in official statistics.

2. By 1995, exporters were also enjoying income tax exemptions on 50 percent of their export earnings.

3. Other measures included the export policy order issued in 1986, which provided special inducement and promotional freight rates by the national flag carriers, Biman Bangladesh Airlines and Bangladesh Shipping Corporation, for exports of fruits, vegetables, and ornamental plants.

4. Initially, the reference currency was the U.K. pound sterling; but this was changed to the U.S. dollar in early 1983 because of the large weight of the United States in the total trade of Bangladesh.

5. In 1996, the government accepted the conditions of article VIII of the Articles of Agreement of the International Monetary Fund by making the taka fully convertible for international current account transactions. Under this arrangement, exporters may freely utilize their export earnings to pay for imports.

6. For details on the duty structure affecting imports of major agricultural commodities in 1991–2003, see Ahmed et al. 2007.

7. Our NRAs for tradables include an estimate of the trade tax effect of the overvalued exchange rate. For this estimate, we rely on the black market exchange rate premium (see Global Development Network Growth Database). We also assume that only half of the foreign exchange rate earnings of exporters is sold to the government at the official rate. For details on this methodology, see Anderson et al. (2008) and appendix A.

8. Throughout this section, the term *agricultural sector* refers only to crop and livestock production and excludes fishing and forestry.

9. See Ravallion (1990) and del Ninno, Dorosh, and Islam (2002) for detailed discussions of markets and government policy during this period.

10. To analyze this policy fully would require a multimarket model (see Dorosh and Haggblade 1997).

11. Other factors also contributed to the increase in rice exports from India, including a 27 percent depreciation of the Indian rupee in real terms (see Dorosh 2001).

12. Several successive rice harvests were poor in Bangladesh: wet season rice (*aman*) in 1994, 1995, and 1997; winter rice in 1995; and severe losses in autumn (*aus*) rice and wet season rice following the mid-1998 flood. See Dorosh et al. (2004) for a discussion of government trade and pricing policies in food grains following the 1998 flood.

13. Small amounts of nonparboiled rice were imported in 2000, mainly from Vietnam. Higher-quality (noncoarse) rice imports likely accounted for much of the rest (Dorosh 2001).

14. For example, in the targeted public distribution system in India, wheat and rice were distributed at a special, highly subsidized rate to consumers certified as living below the poverty line; in 2000, state trading parastatals in India could buy wheat at these below-poverty-line prices and then export the wheat (USDA 2001; see also Dorosh and Shahabuddin 2005 and chapter 10, on India, in this volume).

15. Bangladesh imported 281,000 tons of rice across the land borders with India during 2000. This was about the same as the 286,000 tons imported in 1999. A breakdown of the rice by quality is not available, but a 9 percent decline in the average price of imports from India—from Tk 12.1 per kilogram in 1999 to Tk 11.1 per kilogram in 2000—suggests that the average quality of imports may have declined over the two years.

16. The total tariffs and fees were raised from 10.5 to 43.0 percent if one includes an advanced income tax of 3 percent and a license fee of 2.5 percent.

17. The increase in import taxes raised the above-poverty-line import parity price, including taxes, to 71 percent above the domestic price.

18. Our NRA estimates on output using the average cost of imports suggest that these NRAs were around zero, perhaps because shipments of high-quality rice raised the average import price above the import parity price for below-poverty-line rice.

19. For example, from 1995–96 through 2002–03, the value of manufactured jute products was more than three times the value of raw jute exports (calculated based on data in World Bank 2005).

20. The jute export tax equivalent in East Pakistan during the 10 years leading up to the independence of Bangladesh from Pakistan in 1971 was at least as severe as and probably more severe than the jute export tax equivalent during the rest of the 1970s.

21. Pursell's estimates (2005) for 2002 are domestic production at 177,000 tons, official imports from India at 349,000 tons, official imports from other countries at 93,000 tons, and sugar smuggled from India at 400,000 tons.

22. Until June 2002, the Trading Corporation of Bangladesh and the Bangladesh Sugar and Food Industries Corporation, a public enterprise, shared a monopoly on sugar imports (Pursell 2005).

23. Another parastatal, the Bangladesh Water Development Board, was established in the early 1960s to implement large-scale projects in surface water irrigation, flood control, and drainage. The initiatives were based on recommendations contained in a master plan prepared in the aftermath of disastrous floods in the mid-1950s.

24. Despite privatization in the distribution of fertilizers, the public sector continued to account for most urea production.

25. Like fertilizer, irrigation water was also heavily subsidized in the early years of the expansion in irrigation. There was a rapid reduction in subsidies in the late 1970s when irrigation equipment previously owned by the public sector was privatized. Since 1988, the government has eliminated all restrictions on imports of irrigation equipment by the private sector, cancelled import duties on agricultural machinery, and removed restrictions aimed at standardization and quality control in the production of agricultural machinery. These policy changes have had a significant impact on the use of low-end irrigation equipment, especially shallow tube wells, and they have led to a rapid expansion in the total area under irrigation in the country (Ahmed 2001).

26. In most years, the country has produced urea from domestic natural gas. Net exports of urea on a large scale began in 1988 (Renfro 1992).

27. For an analysis of the oscillation of postcolonial governments between technocratic and populist policies, see Huntington and Nelson (1976).

28. In reforming the grain procurement and ration shop system in the early 1990s, the government was able to avoid direct conflict with consumer groups by only gradually reducing the price subsidy on ration shop grain. Without the support of consumer groups, which no longer reaped significant benefit from the ration shop system, millers lacked the political clout to resist the call to end the millgate procurement system (Chowdhury and Haggblade 2000).

29. Various studies of the comparative advantage of Bangladesh in agriculture demonstrate that the attainment of self-sufficiency in rice production is an important sociopolitical objective and also an eminently sensible goal strictly from the point of view of economics (see Mahmud, Rahman, and Zohir 2000; Shahabuddin 2000; Shahabuddin and Dorosh 2004).

30. Government interventions through domestic procurements were largely ineffective in maintaining floor prices for producers. A number of factors contributed to the failure of domestic procurement, including an inadequate coverage of production areas by procurement centers, cumbersome payment procedures that raised the transaction costs for small farmers, the lack of financial resources in the public food distribution system, and collusion between traders and officials that enabled traders to capture the margin between the market price and the procurement price (Shahabuddin 1996).

31. When the issue price of fertilizer was reduced in the 1994 budget, farmers expected that they would be the major beneficiaries. So, their notion of a just price was outraged when they were required to pay prices that were nearly double (and sometimes more) the prices the middlemen paid to the factories.

References

Abdullah, A. 1996. "Urea Market in Bangladesh, 1994–95: The Anatomy of a Crisis." In *State, Market and Development: Essays in Honour of Rehman Sobhan,* ed. A. Abdullah and A. R. Khan, chap. 12. Dhaka, Bangladesh: University Press.

Abdullah, A., and Q. Shahabuddin. 1993. "Critical Issues in Bangladesh Agriculture: Policy Response and Unfinished Agenda." Paper presented at the Asian Development Bank and Academy for Planning and Development conference, "Bangladesh Economy in Transition," Dhaka, Bangladesh.

Ahmed, A. W. Nuruddin, L. H. Chowdhury, and S. Haggblade. 2000. "History of Public Food Interventions in Bangladesh." In *Out of the Shadow of Famine: Evolving Food Markets and Food Policy in Bangladesh,* ed. R. Ahmed, S. Haggblade, and T.-E. Chowdhury, 121–36. Baltimore: Johns Hopkins University Press; Washington, DC: International Food Policy Research Institute.

Ahmed, N., Z. Bakht, P. A. Dorosh, and Q. Shahabuddin. 2007. "Distortions to Agricultural Incentives in Bangladesh." Agricultural Distortions Working Paper 32, World Bank, Washington, DC.

Ahmed, R. 2001. *Retrospect and Prospects of the Rice Economy of Bangladesh.* Dhaka, Bangladesh: University Press.

Ahmed, R., S. Haggblade, and T.-E. Chowdhury, eds. 2000. *Out of the Shadow of Famine: Evolving Food Markets and Food Policy in Bangladesh.* Baltimore: Johns Hopkins University Press; Washington, DC: International Food Policy Research Institute.

Anderson, K., M. Kurzweil, W. Martin, D. Sandri, and E. Valenzuela. 2008. "Measuring Distortions to Agricultural Incentives, Revisited." *World Trade Review* 7 (4): 675–704.

Bakht, Z. 1999. "Impact of SAFTA on the Official and Unofficial Trade of Bangladesh." Unpublished working paper, Bangladesh Institute of Development Studies, Dhaka, Bangladesh.

———. 2001a. "Preparation of the Sixth Five-Year Plan: Background Paper on Industry." Unpublished working paper, Bangladesh Institute of Development Studies, Dhaka, Bangladesh.

———. 2001b. "Trade Liberalization, Exports and Growth of Manufacturing Industries in Bangladesh." In *Strategies for Industrialization: The Case of Bangladesh*, ed. M. M. Huq and J. Love, chap. 5. Dhaka, Bangladesh: University Press.

BBS (Bangladesh Bureau of Statistics). various years. *Statistical Yearbook of Bangladesh*. Dhaka, Bangladesh: BBS.

Chowdhury, T.-E., and S. Haggblade. 2000. "Dynamics and Politics of Policy Change." In *Out of the Shadow of Famine: Evolving Food Markets and Food Policy in Bangladesh*, ed. R. Ahmed, S. Haggblade, and T.-E. Chowdhury, 165–88. Baltimore: Johns Hopkins University Press; Washington, DC: International Food Policy Research Institute.

del Ninno, C., and P. A. Dorosh. 2003. "Impacts of In-Kind Transfers on Household Food Consumption: Evidence from Targeted Food Programs in Bangladesh." *Journal of Development Studies* 40 (1): 48–78.

del Ninno, C., P. A. Dorosh, and N. Islam. 2002. "Reducing Vulnerability to Natural Disasters: Lessons from the 1998 Floods in Bangladesh." *IDS Bulletin* 33 (4): 98–107.

Dorosh, P. A. 2001. "Trade Liberalization and National Food Security: Rice Trade between Bangladesh and India." *World Development* 29 (4): 673–89.

———. 2006. "Accelerating Income Growth in Rural Bangladesh." Background report, World Bank, Washington, DC.

Dorosh, P. A., N. Farid, R. Amin, and M. A. Aziz. 2004. "Policy Response to Production Shocks: The 1997/98 Aman Shortfall and the 1998 Flood." In *The 1998 Floods and Beyond: Towards Comprehensive Food Security in Bangladesh*, ed. P. A. Dorosh, C. del Ninno, and Q. Shahabuddin, 155–80. Dhaka, Bangladesh: University Press; Washington, DC: International Food Policy Research Institute.

Dorosh, P. A., and S. Haggblade. 1997. "Shifting Sands: The Changing Case for Monetizing Project Food Aid in Bangladesh." *World Development* 25 (12): 2093–104.

Dorosh, P. A., and Q. Shahabuddin. 2005. "Trade Liberalization and Food Security in Bangladesh." In *Economic Reforms and Food Security: The Impact of Trade and Technology in South Asia*, ed. S. C. Babu and A. Gulati, 141–62. New York: Haworth Press; Washington, DC: International Food Policy Research Institute.

FAOSTAT Database. Food and Agriculture Organization of the United Nations. http://faostat.fao.org/default.aspx (accessed May 2008).

Global Development Network Growth Database. Development Research Institute, New York University. http://www.nyu.edu/fas/institute/dri/global%20development%20network%20growth%20database.htm (accessed June 2007).

Grindle, M. S. 1991. "The New Political Economy: Positive Economics and Negative Politics." In *Politics and Policy Making in Developing Countries: Perspectives on the New Political Economy*, ed. G. M. Meier, 41–68. Richmond, CA: ICS Press.

Hossain, M. 2001. "Recent Development and Structural Changes in Bangladesh Agriculture: Issues for Reviewing Strategies and Policies." In *Changes and Challenges: A Review of Bangladesh's Development 2000*, ed. R. Sobhan, chap. 3. Dhaka, Bangladesh: University Press and Center for Policy Dialogue.

Huntington, S., and J. Nelson. 1976. *No Easy Choice*, Cambridge MA: Harvard University Press.

Mahmud, W., S. H. Rahman, and S. Zohir. 2000. "Agricultural Diversification: A Strategic Factor for Growth." In *Out of the Shadow of Famine: Evolving Food Markets and Food Policy in Bangladesh*, ed. R. Ahmed, S. Haggblade, and T.-E. Chowdhury, 232–60. Baltimore: Johns Hopkins University Press; Washington, DC: International Food Policy Research Institute.

Ministry of Finance. 2005. *Bangladesh Economic Review*. Dhaka, Bangladesh: Ministry of Finance.

Osmani, S. R., and A. Quasem. 1990. "Pricing and Subsidy Policies for Bangladesh Agriculture." Unpublished working paper, Bangladesh Institute of Development Studies, Dhaka, Bangladesh.

Pursell, G. 2005. "Free Trade between India and Bangladesh: A Case Study of the Sugar Industry." Unpublished report, World Bank, Washington, DC.

Rahman, S. H. 1992. "Trade Policies and Industrialization in Bangladesh: An Assessment." Unpublished working paper, Bangladesh Institute of Development Studies, Dhaka, Bangladesh.

———. 1994. "The Impact of Trade and Exchange Rate Policies on Economic Incentives in Bangladesh Agriculture." Working Papers on Food Policy in Bangladesh 8, International Food Policy Research Institute, Washington, DC.

Ravallion, M. 1990. *Markets and Famines*. Dhaka, Bangladesh: University Press.

Renfro, R. Z. 1992. "Fertilizer Price and Subsidy Policies in Bangladesh." *World Development* 20 (3):437–55.

Shahabuddin, Q. 1996. "Public Interventions in Food Grain Markets in Bangladesh: An Appraisal." In *State, Market and Development: Essays in Honour of Rehman Sobhan*, ed. A. Abdullah and A. R. Khan, chap. 13. Dhaka, Bangladesh: University Press.

———. 2000. "Comparative Advantage in Bangladesh Agriculture." *Bangladesh Development Studies* 26 (1): 37–68.

Shahabuddin, Q., and P. A. Dorosh. 2004. "Diversification of Agricultural Production: Comparative Advantage in Crops and Implications of the World Trade Organization." In *The 1998 Floods and Beyond: Towards Comprehensive Food Security in Bangladesh,* ed. P. A. Dorosh, C. del Ninno, and Q. Shahabuddin, 313–34. Dhaka, Bangladesh: University Press; Washington, DC: International Food Policy Research Institute.

USAID (United States Agency for International Development) 1982. "Pricing, Subsidies and Related Policies in Food and Agriculture." Policy Paper, USAID, Washington, DC.

USDA (United States Department of Agriculture). 2001. "India: Grain and Feed Annual Report 2001." Report, Foreign Agricultural Service, USDA, Washington, DC.

Wolf, E. 1971. "Peasant Wars of the Twentieth Century." London: Faber and Faber.

World Bank. 1979. *Bangladesh Food Policy Issues*. Report 2761-BD. Washington, DC: World Bank.

———. 1994. *Bangladesh: From Stabilization to Growth*. Report 12724-BD. Washington, DC: World Bank.

———. 2004. *An Overview*. Vol. 2 of *Trade Policies in South Asia: An Overview*. Report 29949. Washington, DC: World Bank.

———. 2005. *Bangladesh: Growth and Export Competitiveness*. Report 31394-BD. Washington, DC: World Bank.

10

INDIA

*Garry Pursell, Ashok Gulati,
and Kanupriya Gupta*

This chapter analyzes the impacts on price incentives in India's agricultural sector that have resulted from government price, trade, and exchange rate policies. Previous studies have established that, from the 1970s to 1995, the incentive system strongly favored manufacturing and services over the principal agricultural crops, although the extent of the antiagricultural bias had diminished considerably by the mid-1990s (Pursell 1999).[1] Our study updates these earlier estimates to 2005 and incorporates estimates for agriculture going back to 1965. In addition, we extend the previous work by considering policies affecting the incentives for the production of fresh fruits and vegetables and for dairying, which account for large shares of the rural economy as measured by the respective contributions to gross domestic product (GDP). We also briefly discuss policies affecting food processing.

The chapter is organized as follows. In the next section, we provide overviews of economic growth and structural change in the Indian economy and the evolution of trade policies since independence, including the effects of current government policies on agricultural trade with the country's neighbors in South Asia. In the subsequent section, we discuss the exchange rate and its interaction with trade policies, especially during the massive rupee devaluation of 1985–93. We then offer quantitative evidence on nominal rates of assistance (NRAs) in various agricultural subsectors, including subsidies for electricity and fertilizer inputs. We also estimate the distortions in the incentives for farmers relative to the incentives for

The authors thank the members of the central project team (especially Marianne Kurzweil and Ernesto Valenzuela) for their contributions and technical help with the data spreadsheets from which several of our tables and figures have been generated.

producers of nonagricultural tradables. We use this evidence to show that the initial, notable antiagricultural bias of government policies gradually gave way to a slight bias in favor of agriculture. Finally, we discuss the political economy forces that are likely to influence the direction of government policies, including the possibility that a strong proagricultural bias may emerge as has occurred in more-advanced, densely populated economies in East Asia and elsewhere.

Economic Growth and Structural Change

Agriculture accounted for slightly more than 50 percent of GDP in 1950, but its share is now less than 20 percent.[2] Most of this decline occurred in crop agriculture. In contrast, the livestock subsector (mainly dairying) grew more rapidly than the rest of the economy. The GDP share of this subsector rose from 2 percent in the early 1980s to 4.4 percent in 2005. Forestry was important after independence, but, in 2003, it provided only around 1 percent of GDP, as did fishing, despite fairly speedy growth over a long period, mainly impelled by fish farm development. Meanwhile, mining's contribution grew from less than 1 percent in the 1950s to 2.8 percent in 2005. The steep decline in agriculture's contribution to the economy since independence has been generated principally by the more rapid growth in the services sector, from barely 30 percent of GDP in 1950 to 63 percent in 2003. The growth of the services sector has been especially brisk since the early 1990s, and it accelerated during the late 1990s and early years of the next decade because of swift advances in information technology and export outsourcing. The share of manufacturing in the economy also increased, but not nearly as quickly as it did in many other developing countries. The share of manufacturing in GDP in 2005 was 16 percent (much lower than in East Asian economies). This compares with 10 percent in 1950, shortly after independence (table 10.1).

The contribution of the rural sector to GDP has declined by almost 70 percent since independence. However, the sector still accounted for around 60 percent of national employment in 2003, and this share had been declining only slowly since the early 1990s (partly because of slow growth in manufacturing employment).

International trade in agricultural products has always been tiny relative to the size of the agricultural sector. In 2005, agricultural imports were equivalent to only 0.8 percent of the value of agricultural production (or 2.1 percent if edible oil imports are included), while exports were 6.4 percent of production. Even during earlier periods, when agriculture represented a major share of total trade (for example, 27 and 44 percent of total imports and exports, respectively, in 1960), imports and exports still only accounted for a little more than 3 percent of agricultural production (table 10.2).

The most important primary agricultural import initially was wheat, followed by cotton and powdered milk. Beginning around the mid-1970s, the need for

Table 10.1. Sectoral Share of GDP and Employment, India, 1950–2005
(percent)

Sector	1950	1960	1970	1980	1990	2000	2003	2004	2005
All agriculture[a]	56.9	46.7	46.1	38.9	31.3	23.4	20.9	18.8	18.3
Livestock	—	—	—	1.9	4.7	5.4	4.6	4.8	4.4
Crops	—	—	—	33.7	23.8	15.8	14.4	12.2	12.1
Forestry and logging	3.0	2.2	2.1	2.5	1.8	1.0	0.9	0.8	0.7
Fishing	0.4	0.5	0.6	0.7	1.0	1.1	1.1	1.0	1.1
Mining and quarrying	0.8	1.1	1.1	1.7	2.7	2.4	2.5	3.0	2.8
Manufacturing	10.6	13.8	13.8	16.3	17.1	15.6	15.2	15.9	16.0
Services	31.8	38.4	39.1	43.1	48.8	58.7	61.3	62.4	62.9
Agriculture's share in employment	—	—	—	—	69	62	60	—	—

Sources: Author computations based on Ministry of Finance, various; CGA Database 2008.

Note: — = no data are available.

a. Agriculture includes crop agriculture, horticulture, livestock activities, inland and ocean fisheries, and forestry activities.

Table 10.2. Profile of Agricultural and Manufacturing Imports and Exports, India, 1960–2005
(percent)

Indicator	1960	1970	1980	1990	2000	2004	2005
Share in total imports							
Primary agricultural, fishing, and forest products	27.2	23.7	3.5	1.9	0.7	0.9	0.8
Edible oils	0.3	2.4	5.6	0.8	2.6	2.2	1.4
Manufactured products	66.1	61.3	42.9	56.9	51.9	46.2	47.1
Share in total exports							
Primary agricultural, fishing, and forest products	44.3	30.7	30.2	17.8	12.8	9.8	9.6
Manufactured products	45.3	53.6	59.2	72.3	77.7	73.0	70.3
Imports as a share of production							
Primary agricultural, fishing, and forest products	3.4	1.7	0.7	0.4	0.3	0.8	0.8
Edible oils	0.0	0.2	1.2	0.2	1.2	1.8	1.3
Manufactured products[a]	9.5	4.2	5.6	6.3	8.6	11.6	13.3
Exports as a share of production							
Primary agricultural, fishing, and forest products	3.2	2.1	3.3	3.2	5.1	5.9	6.4
Manufactured products	3.7	3.4	4.1	6.1	11.4	13.8	14.3

Sources: Author computations based on Ministry of Finance, various; CGA Database 2008.

a. Excludes petroleum, oils, lubricants, and nonmetallic mineral manufactures, which consist mainly of rough diamonds.

these and other agricultural imports were eliminated because of growing domestic production, and, since then, they have accounted for only a small share of total imports even when they were imported during poor crop seasons, for example, in wheat and sugar.

The largest consistent imports of processed food have involved edible oils. Imports of these products expanded rapidly during the 1970s and early 1980s, triggering a major government program to replace the imports through domestic production. For a while, edible oil imports declined, but, despite high tariffs (an 80 percent tariff on palm oil in 2006, for instance), import growth resumed in the 1990s, and, by 2005, imports accounted for about 40 percent of the domestic consumption of these products.

During the 1950s and 1960s, agricultural products represented slightly less than half of the country's total merchandise exports, but the share has steadily declined since then and is now around 10 percent. A diverse range of agricultural products are regularly exported, including fish and fish preparations, oil cakes, cashew kernels, tea, coffee, tobacco, spices, fruits, vegetables, pulses, basmati rice, and, periodically, large quantities of sugar and common rice (more than 4 million tons of rice in 2004/05, for example). Except for cashew kernels, the share of exports in the total domestic production of these individual products is small.

Since the late 1980s, manufactured exports have usually accounted for 70–80 percent of total merchandise exports, compared with 40–50 percent in the 1950s and 1960s. Manufactured exports have also increased in relation to total manufacturing production, especially since the late 1980s, growing about twice as quickly, at 20–30 percent a year, in 2000–05. However, relative to many other developing countries, these exports still constitute a small share of manufacturing sector output (around 15 percent in 2005).

Service sector exports have also been growing rapidly in recent years, at about 25 percent annually. In 2004, net invisible exports represented 4.9 percent of GDP, compared with the negative net balances before 1990. The most dynamic components of this trade are software exports, other exports related to information technology, and the outsourcing of services.

The share of food expenditure in household budgets is high in India, amounting to 54 percent and 42 percent of total per capita consumption expenditure in rural and urban areas, respectively. The shares of food in the budgets of the poorest 10 percent of households is even higher, averaging 62 percent in rural areas and 58 percent in urban areas in 2003. Because of these high shares of food in household budgets (the shares have been declining only slowly), it is not surprising that food prices and food availability are regular news items in the local and national press and other media, and that food prices, especially sudden increases such as in 2008, are highly sensitive politically. One of the most prominent objectives of the independence movement in India was to establish institutions and policies that would permanently eliminate catastrophic famines, such as those that occurred during the colonial period, and that would also ensure that basic food items would be available to the entire population at affordable prices.

To achieve these food policy goals, the government has intervened in food grain markets since the late 1940s. In 1958, it established the current public distribution system, which sells basic foods at subsidized prices through fair price shops. (There are currently about 460,000 of these shops.) For most of its history, the system has distributed wheat, rice, sugar, and edible oils on the basis of ration cards that entitle the bearers to specified quantities of food items at announced low prices. In June 1997, the system was changed by distinguishing, according to fixed criteria, between below-poverty-line and above-poverty-line buyers. The former group was eligible to benefit from especially low prices, while the latter group was eligible to buy the food items at prices that were slightly below free-market prices. In 2001, edible oils were removed from the system, and, in 2002, the role of sugar was drastically reduced by allowing subsidized sales only to below-poverty-line households. The principal government food subsidy activity today is the sale of rice and wheat through the fair price shops to below-poverty-line households and distribution as part of other antipoverty programs. In 2003, the total government food subsidy was estimated at Rs 258 billion (about US$5.7 billion, or 0.83 percent of GDP); this subsidy was defined as the Food Corporation of India's total procurement handling and distribution costs, less the subsidized sales value.

Trade and Exchange Rate Policies since Independence

During the second half of the 1800s and until about 1921, the British rulers of India followed free trade policies that imposed few restrictions or taxes on exports or imports.[3] These free trade policies began to change in the early 1920s following the collapse of the post–World War I boom, and protective tariffs continued to be introduced during the 1920s and 1930s. Then, in 1940, general controls were imposed on all imports and exports to deal with scarcities in goods, shipping, and foreign exchange and to address wartime priorities. The general rule was that imports would only be allowed if they were essential and could not be supplied by local industries.

After independence in August 1947, the government relaxed wartime import controls by expanding the scope of lists of goods that could be imported without obtaining a license (the open general license) and by raising tariffs to take pressure off the import licensing system. However, the start of the Second Five-Year Plan in 1956 coincided with a severe foreign exchange crisis, and, until 1966, the comprehensive administration of the import licensing system was tight. These foreign trade policies were an extension of more general economic policies under which the commanding heights of the industrial economy (which excluded farming) were dominated by state enterprises, and the private sector (including agriculture) was subject to extensive controls. Collectively, these controls came to be known as the license *Raj* (the Hindi word for reign or rule).

In June 1966, the rupee was devalued. This was accompanied by a brief episode of liberalization during which import licensing was relaxed, tariffs were cut, and export subsidies were abolished or reduced. However, the import licensing system remained intact, and, by 1968, most liberalizing initiatives had been reversed and tight import and domestic controls had been reinstated. This remained the situation until the end of the 1970s, when a new phase of slow, partial liberalization commenced.

The slow liberalization trend of the late 1970s and early 1980s included the relaxation of industrial licensing rules, regular additions of intermediate products and capital goods to open general license lists, and tariff increases that succeeded in capturing some of the economic rents inherent in the import licensing system. Liberalization gained momentum during the Rajiv Gandhi government administration (1985–89) when the economic growth rate accelerated above the slow average rate that had characterized the previous 40 years. The boom culminated in a severe foreign exchange crisis in 1991. The government reacted by implementing a sharp devaluation. The devaluation was accompanied by sweeping liberalizing measures that removed many of the key domestic controls over manufacturing, nearly all the import licensing system for intermediate and capital goods, and a key export subsidy program. The initiatives also included a four-year program of tariff reductions. These reductions continued into the 1990s and brought tariffs down far below the extremely high and prohibitive rates of the 1980s (when they averaged more than 100 percent), though the tariffs were still high by international standards.

Domestic policies and trade policies that affected the rural sector were basically untouched by the 1991 reforms. In particular, government enterprises continued to dominate the domestic and international trade in cereals (notably the Food Corporation of India, which periodically imported wheat to meet domestic shortages), and agricultural products remained subject to the import licensing system that applied to all consumer goods. With some important exceptions, import licenses were not issued for agricultural products. The system thus amounted to an import ban on agriculture. The exceptions in agriculture included a few products for which imports had been open even during the most restrictive periods (pulses, for example) and other products, such as cotton and wool, for which unrestricted low-tariff imports of important inputs had been successfully negotiated by influential industrial lobbyists. Edible oils were also imported on a large scale (despite efforts undertaken to replace the imports through domestic production), first, by state trading firms holding import monopoly rights and, later, by the private sector. However, the edible oil imports were subject to high tariffs.

It has been estimated that, in the mid-1990s, five years after the 1991 reforms, about two-thirds of tradable GDP was still protected by explicit nontariff barriers (about 36 percent in manufacturing, 84 percent in agriculture, and 40 percent in mining). During the second half of the 1990s, this situation began to change, in large measure in response to international pressures linked to the Uruguay Round agreements and the negotiations associated with them. Starting in 1998, the general import licensing system began gradually to be dismantled, and, on April 1, 2001, the last 715 of 2,714 tariff lines (including nearly all the agricultural tariff lines) were removed, and the system itself was abolished.

Understandably, after almost 50 years of de facto autarchy, the lifting of these controls generated considerable apprehension over the ability of domestic producers of manufactured consumer goods and agricultural products to compete with imports. A war room was created at the Ministry of Commerce, and a list of 300 sensitive products was drawn up so that imports of these products could be monitored to ensure that prompt action would be taken to preempt or minimize disruptions in local production. More substantively, during and following the Uruguay Round negotiations, the government sought to protect or subsidize domestic producers by marshaling all the techniques not explicitly forbidden by the World Trade Organization agreements. They included techniques of uncertain legality that the government believed might be used without attracting serious complaints from trading partners.[4]

It became apparent soon after the final abandonment of import licensing in April 2001 that the war room psychology had greatly exaggerated the danger represented by rapidly expanding imports. During the next couple of years, existing tariffs and the other measures that had been introduced proved more than adequate in keeping out competing manufacturing and agricultural imports. Eventually, without a formal announcement, the sensitive products lists quietly disappeared from official publications and public discussion. At the same time, manufactured exports entered a new phase of rapid expansion that continued into 2007 (at around 20–25 percent annually). This was supplemented by similarly rapid growth in exports in services. Together with greater capital inflows, these developments helped create a strong balance of payments and historically high foreign exchange reserves, and they were accompanied by brisk economic growth.

Responding to the new confidence that these changes created, the government commenced a program of drastic reductions in industrial tariffs in April 2003 that, over the next four years, lowered the average tariff by approximately

Figure 10.1. Import Tariffs, Agricultural and Nonagricultural Products, India, 2002–06

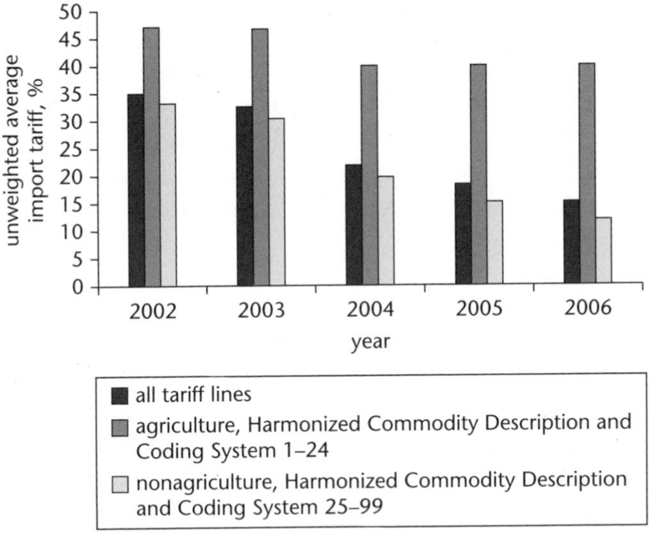

Source: Author computation based on data in Goyal, various.

Note: 2002/03 (2003) and 2003/04 (2004) include para-tariffs that were abolished in 2004/05 (2005). The averages reflect ad valorem tariffs only. They do not take account of specific components in compound duties.

two-thirds, from over 33 percent to about 12 percent (figure 10.1).[5] This was followed by another tariff reduction in the 2007 budget. Because of these cuts, India became one of the world's low-protection countries (measured according to average ad valorem industrial tariffs) after having been one of the world's most protected countries.[6] The average industrial tariffs are now slightly higher than the corresponding average in China and the Republic of Korea and about the same as the average in Sri Lanka, which has traditionally been considered the sole low-protection economy in South Asia. Moreover, because of the top-down reduction process, the industrial tariff structure is uniform. Thus, in 2007, over 80 percent of the industrial tariff lines were at or below the new general maximum of 10 percent; this limited the scope for high effective protection through escalated tariff structures.

However, from the beginning, agriculture and processed foods were not covered by the new tariff reduction program (figure 10.1). In 2006, the unweighted average tariffs protecting these industries (Harmonized Commodity Description and Coding System, 1–24) were about 40 percent, almost four times the average industrial tariffs and among the highest in the world. Moreover, these tariffs are highly dispersed; about 15 percent of the tariffs are in the 50–100 percent range. These high tariffs have been maintained despite substantial tariff redundancy among most agricultural commodities (see elsewhere below). The domestic prices for many commodities are not only lower than duty-inclusive import prices, but are also frequently lower than duty-exclusive import prices. This special treatment provided through agricultural trade policies reflects the pressure exerted by many farmer and processor interest groups and mediated through and supported by the Ministry of Agriculture.

Regional trade agreements

As a by-product of the country's highly protective agricultural trade policies, the trade in primary and processed agricultural and livestock products between India and its South Asian neighbors has been seriously hindered.[7] Ironically, the main victim has likely been Indian exports to these countries rather than Indian imports from the region. Indian domestic prices are low, and, even under a free trade regime, the products of neighboring countries would face difficulties competing there. Meanwhile, India's high tariffs and other barriers to imports have reinforced and helped justify domestically the reluctance of other South Asian countries to reduce their own barriers to agricultural trade either multilaterally or as part of regional and bilateral preferential trade arrangements.

Thus, for many years, the South Asian Preferential Trade Agreement had only limited relevance in regional agricultural trade because all agricultural imports to India were subject to that country's discretionary import licensing system. Import licensing was lifted among members of the South Asian Preferential Trade Agreement in 1998, three years before it was finally phased out by this group with respect to the rest of the world. Nonetheless, since then, the combination of high redundant tariffs, low domestic prices for most agricultural products, and the continuing role of state trading enterprises has meant that it is impossible for these countries to compete in the majority of India's domestic markets. Except for Bhutan and Nepal, the government of India has provided few tariff preferences for agricultural products under its bilateral trade agreements, notably, in its bilateral free trade agreement with the government of Sri Lanka. Under the South Asia Free Trade Agreement, most agricultural tariff lines, including the lines for processed foods, are on the government of India's sensitive list of the products for which it has made no commitments.

The reluctance of the government to provide tariff preferences partly reflects a desire to prevent imports from third countries through preference-receiving countries. Reciprocally, Bangladesh, Pakistan, and Sri Lanka have been unwilling to provide tariff preferences for agricultural products under the South Asian Preferential Trade Agreement and have also placed most agricultural products that they produce on their own South Asia Free Trade Agreement sensitive products lists. This is largely a reaction to the Indian position because, even though these agreements, in principle, involve a number of countries, the potential regional trade that really matters is, in practice, the bilateral trade with India. However, in Bangladesh and Sri Lanka, the reciprocity also reflects a realistic assessment that agricultural free trade with India would generate more agricultural imports from India than exports to India, in the process threatening the viability of some of the more highly protected agricultural industries of these countries, such as sugar, various fresh fruits, vegetables, and a wide range of processed foods in Bangladesh, and, in Sri Lanka, rice, potatoes, and onions.[8]

If it were opened up, India-Pakistan bilateral agricultural trade would probably be more balanced. Recent studies suggest that there is considerable potential for welfare-improving bilateral trade in wheat and sugar. The direction and timing of this trade would vary with weather and other seasonal factors and, compared to trade through the ports with countries outside the South Asia region, would benefit from large transport cost savings, especially trade between the Indian northwest states and Pakistan Punjab. It is also likely that the poultry and other livestock products of Pakistan could be profitably exported to India. However, bilateral trade between India and Pakistan is hostage to the difficult political relationship of the two countries, which is reflected in Pakistan's positive list of products that may be legally imported from India. This list includes almost no agricultural products. Moreover, rules enforced in both countries (with a few minor exceptions) do not allow trade over the land border.

The exchange rate regime and trade policies

Trade policies must be understood in the context of exchange rate policies.[9] The rupee was pegged to the pound sterling before independence in 1947, and this continued until September 1975. In June 1966, the fixed rupee-pound rate was devalued by 57.5 percent and by the same proportion to the U.S. dollar, to Rs 7.50. In line with the fixed link with the pound, the rupee-dollar rate floated down slightly between 1966 and 1975. In September 1975, the peg to the pound sterling was removed, and, until 1992, the rate was fixed by the Reserve Bank of India. In 1992, this system was replaced by a managed floating rate, whereby the Reserve Bank of India allowed the rupee to move in relation to a basket of currencies.

A prolonged period of nominal devaluation began in 1982. The devaluation rate was rapid at first. It slowed for three years in the mid-1980s and then accelerated between 1989 and 1991. This process culminated in a major devaluation to deal with the July 1991 foreign exchange crisis, and the nominal rupee-dollar rate fell by approximately 70 percent between 1991 and 1993. During the next 10 years, the exchange rate was devalued at a modest pace that approximately offset domestic inflation in relation to inflation among India's principal trading partners. From 2003 to mid-2008, the nominal rupee-dollar rate appreciated because of a new export boom and the buildup of large foreign exchange reserves.

The economic significance of the trends in the country's nominal exchange rates becomes clearer if one takes account of the nominal rates in relation to the currencies of India's principal trading partners (not only the U.S. dollar) and of the inflation rate in India relative to the inflation rates in these countries. These effects are systematically captured in real effective exchange rate series. Comprehensive real effective exchange rate indexes are available for India since 1980. Figure 10.2 illustrates an index for this period weighted by India's total trade with 25 countries, and this index has been linked to earlier estimates of the World Bank and others to produce a series starting in 1965. Based on this series, the interaction between India's exchange rate history and the country's trade policies may be

Figure 10.2. Index, Real Effective Exchange Rate, India, 1965–2004

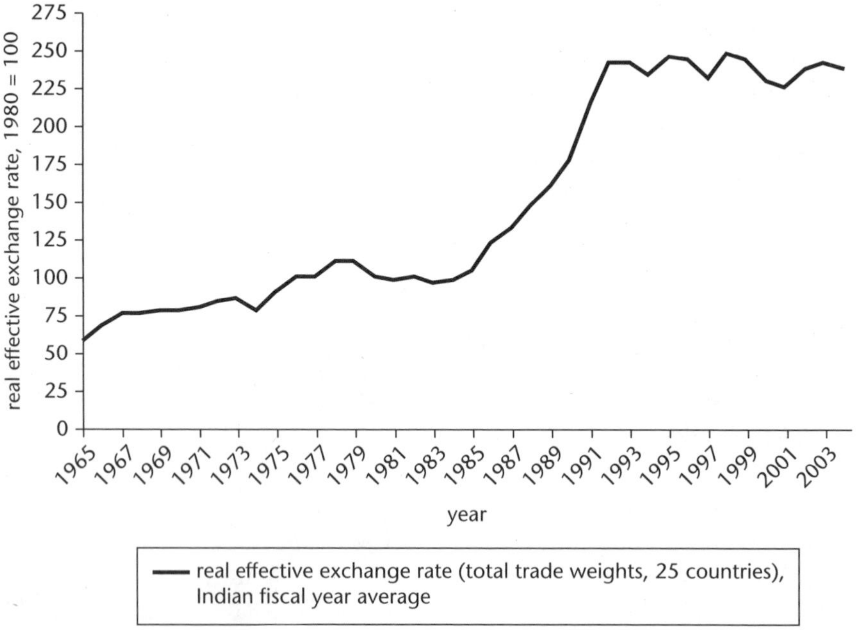

real effective exchange rate (total trade weights, 25 countries), Indian fiscal year average

Source: Author calculations based on RBI Database 2008.

Note: Rising numbers indicate devaluation; falling numbers indicate appreciation.

divided into four periods. Details of the changes in the exchange rate and the related changes in sectoral trade policies during these periods are provided below following our discussion of the period from independence to the mid-1960s.

From 1947 to the 1966 devaluation

By 1956, inflation had begun to erode the effects of the devaluation in 1949. The inflation accelerated during the 10 years to the mid-1960s. In effect, this amounted to a substantial real appreciation of the rupee in relation to the rates fixed to the pound sterling and the U.S. dollar. For most of the period from independence to the mid-1960s, agricultural trade policies were characterized by stringent export controls, and, when exports were allowed, by high export taxes that affected, for example, jute and jute products, oil cakes, cotton, tea, and black pepper. Despite these restrictions and taxes, agricultural and mineral products (the latter also subject to export taxes) accounted for about half the foreign exchange earnings from exports, and, because foreign exchange was becoming increasingly scarce after 1956, the export taxes were steadily reduced and almost eliminated prior to the 1966 devaluation. On the import side, agricultural imports by the private sector were effectively banned, and substantial cereal imports, mostly of wheat under the U.S. Public Law 480 food aid program, were managed by the government.

Before and immediately after independence, nearly all imports in manufacturing were subject to discretionary import licensing or were canalized through government monopoly trading organizations. After 1956, import licensing was regularly tightened in response to the steadily worsening foreign exchange situation. Meanwhile, tariffs were increased and had reached high levels by early 1966. These steps caused large, highly variable gaps to appear between the domestic and international prices of manufactured products. The other principal reaction to the increasingly overvalued exchange rate was the government's attempt to offset the resulting antiexport bias by providing substantial subsidies for manufactured exports, mainly by allowing exporters to import otherwise restricted raw materials, components, and machines free of duties; the exporters then could sell in the domestic market for premiums that reflected scarcity values.

No studies have tried to measure the effects of these policies on the relative incentives in agriculture and manufacturing during these years. However, it is clear from the literature of the period that the economic policy thrust favored manufacturing. The period was therefore likely characterized by a marked antiagricultural bias. This probably expanded along with the increasing overvaluation of the exchange rate and the countermeasures that concentrated on providing higher incentives to manufacturers in the domestic market and in exports, while attempting to keep agricultural prices low and stable.

From the 1966 devaluation to 1978

The nominal devaluation in June 1966 was 57.5 percent in relation to the pound sterling and the U.S. dollar, but, owing to high domestic inflation, it has been estimated at about 30 percent in real terms. In subsequent years, inflation was gradually brought down to much lower levels, and, by 1980, the real effective exchange rate had declined by another 46 percent (figure 10.2). The 1966 devaluation helped clean up some crisis-induced trade policies, but such policies were otherwise highly restrictive and interventionist.

In agriculture, one of the outcomes of the devaluation and, more importantly, of the suspension of U.S. Public Law 480 grain supplies from the United States during the first India-Pakistan war was to reinforce the government's determination to make India self-sufficient in food grains and other basic agricultural products. This coincided with the development and distribution of new seeds and techniques that were instrumental in practically eliminating once substantial cereal imports by the end of 1970s and that were behind the program launched in 1971 to make India self-sufficient in dairy products. To support these objectives, earlier policies were continued. With few exceptions, these allowed imports only of bulk agricultural commodity products, such as wheat, that were brought into the country by parastatals according to need. In the interests of domestic availability and low consumer prices, exports of most food products were not allowed although the domestic prices for some food products, notably rice, were usually well below farm-level export parity prices. Immediately after the devaluation, export taxes on nonessential exported commodities (jute, coffee, tea, cotton, oil cakes, spices) were sharply increased; the apparent purpose was to absorb some of the windfall gains accruing to exporters. However, because of slow export growth during the 1970s, these taxes were steadily reduced and had practically disappeared by the early 1980s.

In manufacturing, the 1966 devaluation was accompanied by tariff reductions, a relaxation in import licensing, and the abolition or reduction of some export subsidies. However, by 1968, tight import licensing had been reinstated, and imports of nearly all consumer goods, including textiles, were effectively banned; the only imports allowed were intermediate materials, components, and capital equipment as long as the actual users could demonstrate that the goods were essential and not otherwise locally available. Tariffs, which remained at about the same level during the 1970s, were still being used mostly to transfer some import licensing rents to the government and were irrelevant as protective instruments except to the extent they influenced the cost of imported intermediates and equipment that was not locally produced.

Empirical evidence suggests that trade policies during this period led to terms of trade that were more highly unfavorable for agriculture relative to manufacturing in the domestic economy than the terms of trade prevailing in world markets (see elsewhere below).

From 1978 to 1993

The government averted a balance of payments crisis in 1980–81 with the help of a loan from the International Monetary Fund, while maintaining the real value of the rupee. However, beginning in the spring of 1985, a new policy was implemented that led to the steady devaluation of the currency in real terms. This devaluation continued without a break for the next six years, almost on a monthly basis, until the sharp devaluation in July 1991, which was followed by additional depreciation until September 1992. The real rupee devaluation was large during the second half of the 1980s, about 62 percent between 1985 and 1990, and it was around 145 percent over the whole period to 1993. Among other effects, this radically changed the environment of agricultural and manufacturing trade policies.

In agriculture, the rupee depreciation after 1985 partly offset a major decline in world agricultural prices that had started in 1981 and continued until 1987. World prices recovered thereafter, and the continuing rupee depreciation translated these world price changes into much larger increases in the border prices for some of the country's major agricultural commodities. However, owing to the traditional isolation of the domestic market, the domestic prices for most of these commodities were unaffected and continued to shift independently of the changes in the border prices. The principal exceptions were cotton, pulses, oil cakes, and the main export-oriented agricultural commodities that are sold in auction markets in which exporters and domestic traders compete, especially tea, coffee, spices, and tobacco. Despite many complex trade policy interventions and other interventions and owing to the influence of textile producers who were acting with the support of the Ministry of Textiles, domestic cotton prices broadly tracked border prices, and pulses were (and still are) the sole major primary food product that could be imported at low or moderate tariffs without import licensing or other interventions. The country has consistently possessed excess supplies of oil cakes (produced in fixed proportions by the edible oil industry in conjunction with the oilseed crushing process) because of low demand by the livestock subsector that is, in turn, associated with the vegetarian diets of a large proportion of the country's population. However, these products account for only a small share of total agricultural production, around 14 percent, and about 10 percent of total rural production if livestock, fishing, and forestry products are included. During this period, the rest (about 90 percent of total rural production) was essentially nontraded owing to government import monopolies, import licensing, export controls, and other non-tariff interventions, as well as prohibitive tariffs in some cases.

In manufacturing, during the 1980s, domestic prices were similarly delinked from international prices by the import licensing system and high tariffs that averaged over 100 percent. In addition, manufactured exports, although they were growing more rapidly than domestic production, were limited relative to total manufacturing output; the export share was only about 7 percent in the mid-1980s. Hence, overall, the massive rupee devaluation did not pass through directly to domestic industrial prices. It affected them indirectly in a minor way through increases in export prices and in the prices of intermediate and capital goods that were allowed to be imported, which increased manufacturing costs. The devaluation generated big increases in border prices, which led to a steep decline in average implicit manufacturing protection as measured by the excess in domestic ex-factory prices relative to border prices. This had important repercussions in manufacturing trade policies. First, it made the liberalization program that was undertaken in 1991 quite painless, including, especially, the abolition of nearly all import licensing for manufactured intermediate goods, machinery, and equipment, the removal of a major export subsidy, and the tariff reduction program that continued into the mid-1990s.

Second, many manufacturing firms that had been vulnerable to import competition found that, now, following the correction of the exchange rate overvaluation, they could not only easily compete with imports, but could outcompete with foreign manufacturers in export markets. Combined with the new, sweeping domestic deregulation of manufacturing that accompanied the trade policy program, this created fresh momentum in investment, productivity improvements, and output expansion in the manufacturing sector.

The devaluation's repercussions in agriculture and manufacturing led to the end of most of the systematic antiagricultural bias in the incentive system as measured by relative rates of assistance (RRAs). However, it did not translate into a noticeable improvement in the domestic terms of trade in agriculture because nearly all agricultural prices and a large proportion of manufacturing prices, including prices on all consumer goods, remained delinked from world prices by the import licensing system and other nontariff barriers and were still mainly determined by domestic conditions and government policies. This situation did not begin to change until after the import licensing system was finally removed in 2001.

From 1993 to 2007

From 1993 until mid-2007, the exchange rate was managed by regular adjustments in the nominal rates that stabilized the real effective exchange rate index at the postdevaluation level within a narrow range of about 10 percent (figure 10.2). The size of the devaluation up to 1993 probably overshot the decline needed to reestablish the balance in foreign exchange and support the 1991 trade policy reforms. However, by being maintained at this level for the next 14 years (by far the longest period of real exchange rate stability in the independent economic history of India), it also proved adequate in supporting the removal of the import licensing system between 1998 and 2001 and the post-2003 tariff reduction program in manufacturing.

In agriculture, however, highly protectionist trade policies continued throughout the 1990s and were still in place in mid-2007. On the import side, high to prohibitive tariffs, plus technical standards and sanitary and phytosanitary controls, played the role previously played by import licensing and import monopolies among state trading enterprises.[10] With some exceptions, the predominant view is that international agricultural markets are unreliable and unstable and should only have a residual role in agricultural policies, in particular, by providing extra supplies in times of domestic shortages and as a means of disposing of excess stocks in times of domestic surpluses. Consistent with this view, agricultural trade policies on some major commodities, especially cereals and sugar, are highly opportunistic and involve frequent and significant changes, especially in tariffs and export subsidies.[11] For other products, tariffs appear to be deliberately prohibitive. For example, 100 percent tariffs apply to tea and coffee, both of which are exported on a large scale. The domestic prices for these two products are set in auction markets in which exporters and domestic traders operate, suggesting that the domestic prices are about equivalent to international prices after allowing for quality differences.

In manufacturing, after the 1991 reforms, producers of intermediate and capital goods were no longer protected by import licensing, and manufacturing tariffs declined. Nonetheless, the devalued exchange rate, plus manufacturing tariffs (mostly in the 30–40 percent range) and other measures (notably antidumping initiatives), removed most competitive pressures on the import side. In addition, manufactured consumer goods, including the entire textile and garment subsector, were still protected by import licensing until the gradual removal of the system was initiated in the late 1990s. Hence, during the 1990s and up to about 2004, most manufacturing remained insulated from import competition, and the impact of world market conditions occurred mainly through manufactured exports, which, however, began to expand at a rate that was more rapid than the overall growth rate in manufacturing. This partial orientation toward world markets only changed in about 2004 following the end of import licensing in 2001 and the implementation of the first stages of the post-2003 manufacturing tariff reduction program. Since then, most of the manufacturing sector has been opened to world markets either through exports or through actual or potential imports at relatively low tariffs.

The 1985–93 devaluations removed most of the long-standing antiagricultural bias in the incentive system as measured by RRAs. However, high formal protection rates and substantial tariff redundancy in manufacturing and agriculture allowed plenty of scope for the domestic terms of trade between the two sectors to shift substantially in either direction. However, all this changed in the mid-2000s. Since then, tariffs have been a real constraint on the domestic prices for manufactured goods. The ongoing high formal protection of agriculture, combined with substantial input subsidies, has nonetheless offered considerable scope for the bias of the system against agriculture to become a bias in favor of agriculture.

The Measurement of Distortions in Agricultural Incentives

The main focus of our study is the extent of the distortions in agricultural prices and the government-imposed policy measures that create a gap between actual domestic prices and prices as they would emerge under free market conditions.[12] Since it is not possible to understand the characteristics of agricultural development through a sectoral view alone, we provide estimates of the effects of direct agricultural policy measures, including distortions in the foreign exchange market, and we also report estimates of distortions in the prices faced by the producers of nonagricultural products, especially manufactures. Specifically, we compute NRAs for farmers that include an adjustment for direct interventions directed at inputs, such as subsidies for fertilizers and electricity. For comparative purposes, we also generate aggregate NRAs for nonagricultural tradables and for agricultural tradables so as to calculate RRAs (see Anderson et al. 2008 and appendix A).

We examine 12 products, plus the collective of fruits and vegetables. Milk is classified as an import-competing product. The other 11 commodities—rice, wheat, maize, sorghum, groundnuts, rapeseeds, soybeans, sunflower seeds, sugar, cotton, and chickpeas—have mixed trade status, which means they are exportables or nontradables in some years and import-competing products in other years.[13] Over the period we analyze, these primary agricultural commodities account altogether for nearly 70 percent of the value of agricultural production in India. The 11 crops have made up approximately half this share in recent years; fruits and vegetables, one-quarter; and dairying, another one-quarter (table 10.3).

Our study builds on a considerable body of earlier work, and we use the project methodology to provide a consistent and internationally comparable set of estimates back to 1964 (or, in the case of milk, 1975). The earlier work includes producer support estimates for the major crops in India in 1984–2001 that have been made available by the International Food Policy Research Institute, estimates for

Table 10.3. Structure of the Agricultural Economy, India, 1964–2004

(percent)

Product	1964–72	1973–79	1980–86	1987–96	1997–2004
Rice, including basmati	19.8	19.4	15.1	14.6	11.7
Wheat	4.5	6.0	9.5	9.2	9.5
Maize	1.2	1.1	1.2	1.0	1.3
Sorghum (jowar)	2.1	1.9	1.9	1.3	0.9
Soybeans	0.0	0.1	0.3	1.0	1.6
Rapeseeds, mustard seeds	0.7	0.7	1.1	1.4	1.3
Sunflower seeds	0.0	0.0	0.2	0.3	0.2
Chickpeas (gram)	2.4	2.8	1.9	1.6	1.4
Groundnuts	3.6	3.4	2.6	2.5	2.1
Seed cotton (kapas)	2.3	2.5	2.5	2.4	2.1
Sugarcane	1.5	2.7	2.3	3.3	2.7
Fresh fruits and vegetables	12.7	13.6	14.8	14.4	18.3
Dairying	9.6	11.7	13.5	15.8	17.5
All covered products	60.4	66.0	67.0	69.0	70.7
Noncovered products	39.6	34.0	33.0	31.0	29.3

Source: Author estimates based on the farmgate value of production at domestic prices reported in CGA Database 2008.

Note: Values are at distorted prices.

fruits and vegetables in a recent World Bank study of the horticultural subsector in India, and NRA estimates for raw milk based on a study of the dairy sector (see Gulati and Kelley 1999; Mullen, Orden, and Gulati 2005; Rakotoarisoa and Gulati 2006; Orden et al. 2007; Mattoo, Mishra, and Narain 2007).

In considering our NRA estimates, one should bear in mind that, for most products in most of the years we cover, there were no exports or imports, or exports and imports were much too limited or specialized to provide reliable indications of the likely border prices of most domestic products. Consequently, domestic prices are compared with various international reference prices and then adjusted for delivery and selling terms, specification and quality differences, freight and insurance to or from the Indian border, Indian port costs, domestic transport costs and margins, and so on. Domestic and international transport and handling costs have been sufficiently high to make the major products nontradable an average 40 percent of the time. The NRAs for fresh fruits and vegetables are especially sensitive to transport and handling costs because of the need for special packaging and transport and storage facilities, including refrigeration, to minimize spoilage and maximize shelf life at final wholesale and retail markets. Even for food grains, it is necessary to take into account domestic transport and trading margins from the inland growing regions to the large port cities before comparing farmgate prices and the estimated prices of equivalent imported products landed at the ports. These and numerous other complexities in estimating NRAs in India are discussed in Pursell, Gulati, and Gupta (forthcoming). Data sources and various data on the products are summarized in appendix B.

Other studies that have estimated NRAs or incentive indicators such as ours rely on the official exchange rate to express border prices in rupees (free on board or cost, freight, and insurance). During the years before the 1991 devaluation when the black market premium was substantial, almost all agricultural exports and imports were managed by parastatal monopolies under the direct supervision of the central bank (see Pursell, Gulati, and Gupta 2007). In manufacturing, there are reports that underinvoicing occurred in exports to accumulate unrecorded foreign exchange abroad; however, underinvoicing was limited because of the benefits available to exporters through various export facilitation schemes and export subsidies that were based on declared, free on board values. The main suppliers of foreign exchange in the parallel market for foreign exchange were Indian worker remittances from abroad and people in India who obtained foreign exchange to transfer black money out of the country. Since the 1991 devaluation, when the main export subsidy was removed and the foreign exchange controls of the Reserve Bank of India were relaxed, the parallel market premium has been negligible or nonexistent.

Table 10.4. Structure of Fertilizer and Electricity Subsidies, Key Crops, India, 2004

(percent)

Crop	Share in total subsidy	Share in gross value of production	
		At domestic prices	At reference prices
Rice	37.1	18.3	15.4
Wheat	35.2	27.2	18.9
Maize	2.1	9.3	8.8
Sorghum	1.8	12.4	11.5
Chickpeas	2.7	11.4	10.9
Groundnuts	2.7	8.4	5.7
Rapeseeds, mustard seeds	4.5	11.7	18.0
Soybeans	1.1	4.3	2.9
Sunflower seeds	0.5	8.8	8.6
Sugar	6.6	12.5	15.4
Cotton	5.6	13.2	12.3
Total	100.0	16.9	13.0

Source: Pursell, Gulati, and Gupta 2007.

Note: The total value of the input subsidies for the 11 crops in 2004 was US$7.8 billion: US$1.9 billion for fertilizer and US$5.9 billion for electricity.

Assistance in agriculture

We have calculated NRA estimates for India for crops beginning in 1964 and for dairying (raw milk) beginning in 1975. The NRAs account for output price distortions, as well as for the output price equivalents of input subsidies. (The latter estimates begin in 1983.) The NRAs are expressed as a percent share of the corresponding undistorted prices (for example, the import reference prices of comparable products). Relevant input subsidies have been allocated to the various crops in the manner summarized in table 10.4.[14]

Our NRA estimates exhibit several striking features. First, the average NRAs across covered products show only a slight upward trend over the 41 years we survey (figure 10.3 and table 10.5).

Second, figure 10.3 and table 10.5 also show that the average NRAs for import-competing products were well above the average NRAs for exportables, although the difference narrowed after the reforms were launched in the early 1990s. Specifically, the average NRAs for import-competing products were 62 percent in the 25 years to the end of the 1980s, but only 32 percent over the subsequent 15 years,

Figure 10.3. NRAs for Exportable, Import-Competing, and All Agricultural Products, India, 1965–2004

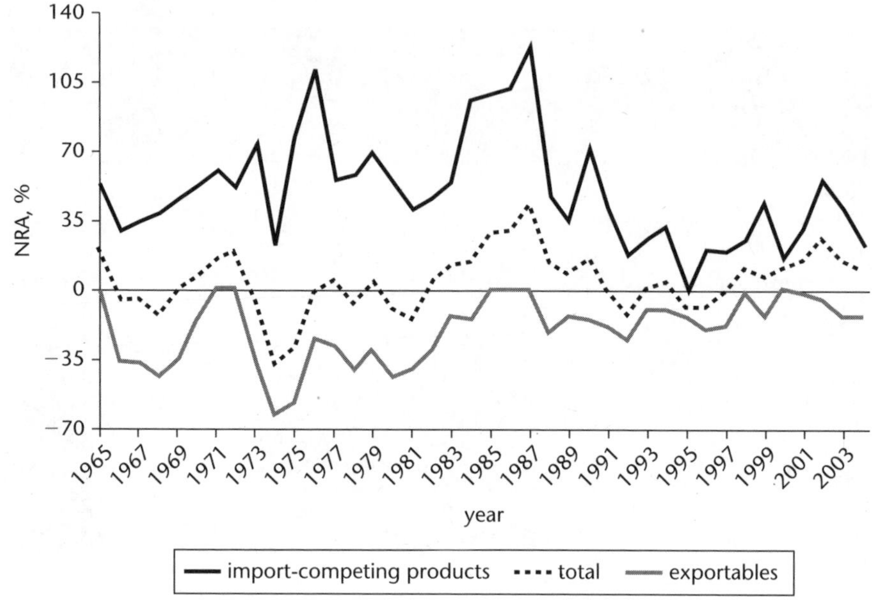

Source: Pursell, Gulati, and Gupta 2007.

while the corresponding NRAs for exportables were −25 and −11 percent, respectively. This is captured in the average trade bias index, which was −0.53 during the period before 1990 and −0.32 thereafter (table 10.6).

Third, the NRAs fluctuate widely around the trend values. Even if the NRAs are averaged over all import-competing products or all exportables, it is clear from figure 10.3 that there is significant movement in the NRAs from year to year. This is partly because the trade status of products often changed, but there is also a clear systematic element in this finding. Before the reforms of the 1990s, the average NRAs for import-competing products and exportables were lowest in 1974, when international food prices were at record highs, and highest around 1987, when international food prices were at record lows in real terms. More generally, there is little year-to-year correlation between the domestic prices and the border prices of major food products. This reflects the success of the government's policy effort to stabilize domestic prices and insulate domestic markets from fluctuations in world prices.

Table 10.5. NRAs for Covered Agricultural Products, India, 1965–2004
(percent)

Product, indicator	1965–69	1970–74	1975–79	1980–84	1985–89	1990–94	1995–99	2000–04
Milk	—	—	152.6	113.5	136.8	40.5	22.1	32.3
Rice	-30.0	-23.4	-39.2	-31.0	-3.8	-21.1	-13.0	20.8
Wheat	31.4	30.3	2.8	1.6	9.2	10.5	14.2	38.4
Maize	63.8	49.2	2.5	-1.2	26.5	3.1	2.6	11.9
Sorghum	41.7	55.0	11.6	6.5	35.7	7.2	21.2	15.7
Groundnuts	23.4	1.6	-17.0	21.7	61.6	17.7	7.9	12.9
Fruits and vegetables	0.0	0.0	0.0	0.0	0.0	-15.7	-13.4	-8.9
Rapeseeds, mustard seeds	62.9	38.8	16.6	38.2	74.8	64.8	37.0	64.8
Soybeans[a]	—	0.0	-14.8	-1.3	19.1	3.1	2.9	2.9
Sunflower seeds	—	—	0.0	7.8	56.1	17.9	13.3	14.6
Sugar	158.4	17.7	-9.4	9.5	56.0	7.2	12.6	39.3
Cotton	17.5	78.3	8.9	0.4	33.6	22.6	6.2	12.0
Chickpeas	24.5	1.3	0.0	7.7	12.2	9.2	15.0	18.7
Import-competing products[b]	41.2	52.6	74.4	59.0	81.5	38.3	22.6	34.2
Exportables[b]	-30.0	-22.3	-35.8	-27.8	-6.8	-15.4	-12.4	-6.1
Nontradables	0.0	0.0	0.0	0.7	4.0	6.8	16.1	22.6
All covered products[c]	-0.2	0.2	-5.5	1.9	24.9	1.8	0.6	15.8
Input subsidies	—	—	—	—	4.6	5.8	7.6	9.7
Dispersion, covered products[d]	42.8	17.8	6.5	18.8	49.0	46.6	12.5	24.1
Coverage, at undistorted prices	59	62	68	66	68	69	72	70

Source: Pursell, Gulati, and Gupta 2007.

Note: — = no data are available.

a. 1970–74 refers to 1973–74.
b. Products of mixed trade status are included among exportables or import-competing products depending on the trade status each year.
c. Weighted averages; the weights are based on the unassisted value of production.
d. Dispersion is a simple five-year average of the annual standard deviation around the weighted mean of the NRAs of covered products.

361

Table 10.6. NRAs in Agriculture Relative to Nonagricultural Industries, India, 1965–2004

(percent)

Indicator	1965–69	1970–74	1975–79	1980–84	1985–89	1990–94	1995–99	2000–04
Covered products[a]	−0.2	0.2	−5.5	1.9	24.9	1.8	0.6	15.8
Noncovered products[b]	−0.2	0.2	−5.5	1.9	24.9	1.8	0.6	15.8
All agricultural products[a]	−0.2	0.2	−5.5	1.9	24.9	1.8	0.6	15.8
Trade bias index[c]	−0.51	−0.50	−0.63	−0.55	−0.48	−0.38	−0.28	−0.29
NRA, all agricultural tradables	−7.0	12.6	−7.4	4.1	67.5	2.0	−2.3	15.4
NRA, all nonagricultural tradables	113.0	83.1	64.8	59.3	48.6	15.9	12.6	5.2
RRA[d]	−56.3	−38.3	−43.8	−33.5	11.7	−12.1	−12.9	12.5

Source: Pursell, Gulati, and Gupta 2007.

a. Including product-specific input subsidies and non-product-specific assistance (see table 10.5). Represents total assistance to primary factors and intermediate inputs, divided by the total value of primary agriculture production at undistorted prices.

b. Noncovered products—30 percent of the sector's value of production in 2000–04—are assumed to have the same average NRAs as covered products, as well as the same shares of production in the import-competing, exportable, and nontradable categories.

c. The trade bias index is defined as $(1 + NRAag_x/100)/(1 + NRAag_m/100) - 1$, where $NRAag_m$ and $NRAag_x$ are the average percentage NRAs for the import-competing and exportable parts of the agricultural sector, respectively.

d. The RRA is defined as $100*[(100 + NRAag^t)/(100 + NRAnonag^t) - 1]$, where $NRAag^t$ and $NRAnonag^t$ are the percentage NRAs for the tradables parts of the agricultural and nonagricultural sectors, respectively. $NRAnonag$ in 1965–69 is an author guesstimate.

Figure 10.4. Real Domestic Producer Prices and International Reference Prices, Rice, India, 1965–2004

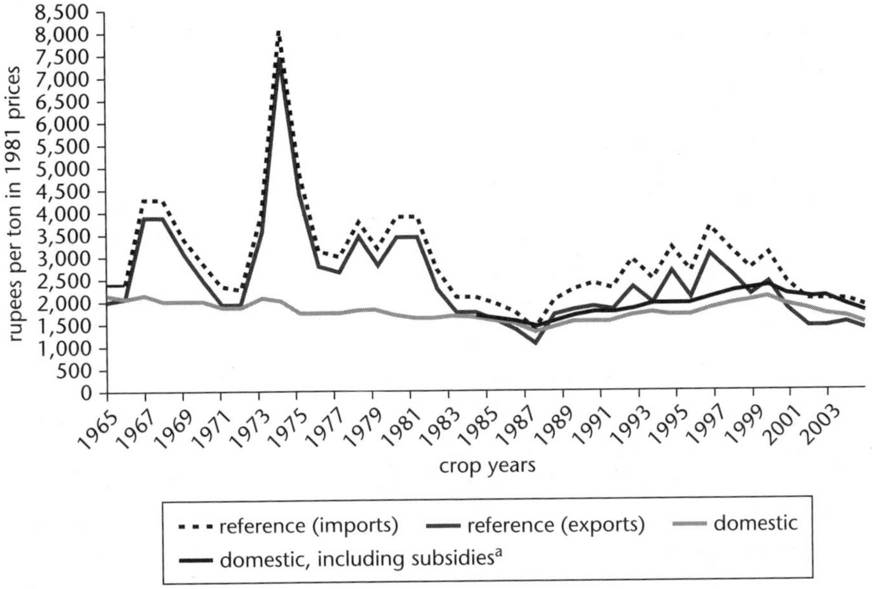

Source: Pursell, Gulati, and Gupta 2007.

Note: To remove the effects of inflation from the analysis, rupee prices are expressed in constant 1981 rupees using the wholesale price index.

a. No data prior to 1984.

This insulating role of policy measures is especially clear in the country's main food staple, rice. The domestic price of rice has been kept stable in real terms over the past four decades (figure 10.4). For most of these years, export restrictions have generated an implicit export tax on rice that has varied substantially as international prices have changed. For example, in the 1990s, the annual average implicit export tax varied from zero to 31 percent to keep the real consumer price from fluctuating (Pursell, Gulati, and Gupta 2007). Figure 10.4 also shows that this insulating policy generated positive NRAs for rice in 2000–04. Had the data been available for more recent years, they would have revealed that, with the boost in the international price for rice in 2007–08, the country again imposed restrictions on rice exports, thereby implicitly taxing net sellers of rice for the benefit of net buyers of rice.

Sugar is another example. As in many other countries, sugar is still subject to sporadic government interventions in India, especially through trade policies. In 2007, for example, the relevant trade policies included de facto nontariff import controls, a 60 percent import tariff, the availability of export subsidies, and a complex initiative that allowed sugar mills with excess capacity to import unrefined sugar duty-free for refining and then resell in the domestic market. These measures were implemented to insulate the domestic market from wide swings in international sugar prices, but also to help address domestic disequilbriums resulting from weather conditions and from production cycles imposed by the highly politicized minimum sugarcane prices mandated by state governments. Likewise, in 2000–02, export subsidies were used to help dispose of large excess sugar stocks, whereas, in some years during the 1990s, imports were allowed duty-free to meet temporary domestic shortages.[15] Similar to the case of rice, domestic sugar prices have been kept quite stable for long periods, but have steadily declined in real terms over time. Thus, between 1965 and 1982, they declined by about one-third, and, between 1981 and 2004, by one-quarter.

Fourth, the dispersion of NRAs across the products we cover has been wide, although it has narrowed considerably since the reforms began in the early 1990s. Shortly before then, the average annual standard deviation around the weighted mean NRA was 45, whereas, since 1990, the average has been less than half that (see near the bottom of table 10.5).

Fifth, the contribution of farm input subsidies in the NRAs for covered products have been steadily increasing, particularly fertilizers and electricity, which is used mainly in pumping irrigation water. In the later 1980s, input subsidies contributed 4 percentage points to the average NRA of 25 percent (data have not been compiled for earlier years), but, by 2000–05, they were contributing almost 10 percentage points (see near the bottom of table 10.5).[16] Without input subsidies, the average NRA would have been negative in the 1990s, mainly because of the restrictions on exports of rice. (The weight of rice has been between around one-eighth and one-third over the past four decades; see Pursell, Gulati, and Gupta 2007.) Input subsidies helped reduce the gap between the benefits to rice producers and the export price of rice in the 1990s (figure 10.4).

Sixth, while the trade status of each crop product we cover has tended to change frequently over the past four decades, self-sufficiency in each product nonetheless remains close to 100 percent (table 10.7). Thus, in so far as government policies on food pricing and trade have been aimed at reducing the country's dependence on food imports, they have achieved their objective.

Assistance to producers of agricultural tradables relative to other tradables

In the absence of precise information, we have assumed that the average NRAs for covered products are the same as the corresponding NRAs for noncovered farm products, which accounted for 30 percent of total agricultural production in 2000–04. The incentives among farmers depend not only on agricultural NRAs,

Table 10.7. Self-Sufficiency Ratios, Selected Food Products, India, 1961–2004
(percent)

Product	1961–64	1965–69	1970–74	1975–79	1980–84	1985–89	1990–94	1995–99	2000–04
Milk	1.00	1.00	1.00	1.00	1.00	1.00	1.00	1.00	1.00
Rice	0.99	0.98	0.97	1.04	1.05	1.04	1.04	1.05	1.02
Wheat	0.72	0.71	0.91	1.02	0.99	0.96	1.00	1.02	1.02
Maize	0.97	0.97	1.00	1.00	1.00	0.99	1.00	1.00	1.01
Sorghum	1.00	0.92	0.96	0.99	1.00	1.00	1.00	1.00	1.00
Groundnuts	1.01	0.99	1.02	1.03	1.02	1.02	1.02	1.04	1.02
Soybeans	0.96	0.89	1.02	1.03	1.07	0.95	0.98	1.15	0.94
Sunflower seeds	—	—	1.00	1.00	1.00	1.00	1.00	1.00	1.04

Sources: Author computation based on data in FAO Agricultural Trade Database 2008; FAOSTAT Database 2008; FAO SUA-FBS Database 2008.

Note: The table shows production as a proportion of consumption. — = no data are available.

Figure 10.5. NRAs for Agricultural and Nonagricultural Tradables and the RRA, India, 1965–2004

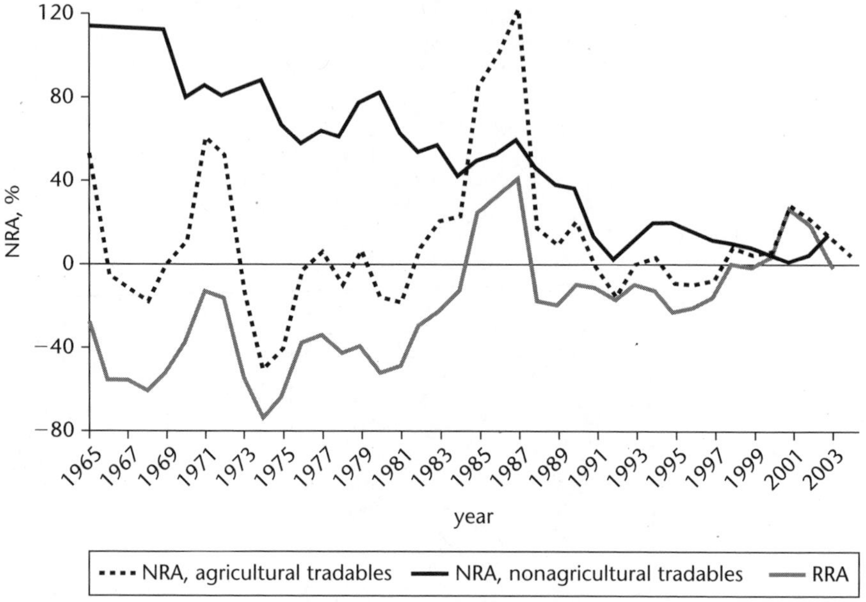

Source: Pursell, Gulati, and Gupta 2007.

Note: For the definition of the RRA, see table 10.6, note d.

however. They also depend on the way trade and other price-distorting policies affect the incentives among producers of other tradables. To help one understand the evolution of relative incentives, we compare, in figure 10.5 and table 10.6, the NRAs for agricultural tradables with estimates of the NRAs for nonagricultural tradables. We also indicate our estimates of RRAs (see table 10.6, note d). The NRAs for nonfarm activities are weighted averages of the estimated NRAs for the tradable parts of manufacturing and mining. In these NRAs, we thus assume that the services sector is nontradable, which has been a reasonable assumption until recently; even today, the tradables part of the services sector is small relative to the size of the goods sectors.

Until about 2004, average tariffs were not helpful indicators of the protection in the manufacturing sector. We have therefore used the results of a recent study by Pursell, Kishor, and Gupta (2007) on the implicit protection in manufacturing that covers 1970–2004. The study provides a time series that compares the annual weighted averages of the ex-factory prices of manufactured goods and the import prices of the same or similar goods.[17] This measure plausibly describes the economic history of the period. First, the extremely high implicit nominal protection of between 80 and 100 percent from the 1970s to the mid-1980s is consistent with what we know about the restrictive import licensing system of that period. Second, the steep decline in implicit nominal protection, from around 70 percent in 1987 to almost zero in 1992, is consistent with the real rupee devaluation of approximately 80 percent during the same period (see figure 10.2). The decreasing value of the rupee during these years pushed up the border prices of importable manufactured goods expressed in rupees, and these increases were far greater than the corresponding increases in the prices for domestically produced manufactured goods, which mirrored domestic inflation and other factors. Consequently, the average excess of the prices for domestically manufactured goods over the rupee border prices for the same goods consistently declined, and it seemed nearly to disappear altogether in 1992. After 1992, it increased for a while (between 1995 and 1997, though this may have reflected the low international prices associated with the Asian financial crisis), but, in most years, it was well below 20 percent; the average rate was only 12 percent between 1992 and 2004 (the latest year for which estimates are available). Until 2002, the apparent implicit protection rates were far below unweighted average industrial tariffs, for example, 45 percent in 1990 versus average tariffs of 129 percent, 9 percent in 1999 versus average tariffs of 39 percent, and 5 percent in 2002 versus average tariffs of 33 percent. This gap narrowed sharply in 2003, however, and the possibility that domestic prices would exceed international prices was reduced by the cuts in manufacturing tariffs in the March 2007 budget, which decreased the average tariff to below 10 percent.

The most important group of nonfarm tradable products other than manufactures are minerals, especially coal, iron ore, crude oil, and natural gas. These industries account for about 2.5 percent of GDP. The tariffs on these items are currently low (in 2007, mostly zero, 2 percent, 5 percent, or 10 percent, respectively); except for crude oil and petroleum products, there are no major quantitative restrictions on imports or exports. Trade in these products is considerable; there are substantial imports (for example, coal) and exports (for instance, iron ore). We have constructed for this study an NRA series that begins with an assessment of the situation in 2004. For coal, which accounted for about 62 percent of domestic mineral subsector output in 1970 and about 38 percent in 2004, these estimates assume that domestic prices were about equal to import reference prices in 2004 (NRA = 0); we have generated NRA estimates for earlier years using the coal wholesale price index for India and an index of coal export prices for Australia.[18] The NRAs for coal are low in many earlier years, which is consistent with the depression of domestic coal prices, coal production, and, potentially, coal exports by Coal India, the parastatal monopoly that controls the industry. This changed during the late 1990s, when accelerating demand for coal pushed up domestic prices to about the level of import prices. This eventually led to the current situation, wherein coal is being imported in large quantities, mostly at zero tariffs. The other principal components of the mining sector are petroleum, natural gas, and a catch-all category that includes all other minerals. In the absence of any recent studies on protection in these subsectors, we have assumed, based on limited information and other analysis, that the NRAs of these components were zero over the whole period. Based on this assumption and our estimates for coal, we have derived a weighted average NRA series for mining. The series comprises low NRAs up to about the mid-1980s, followed by NRAs in the vicinity of zero, indicating that average domestic mineral prices were about equal to world prices from 1985 to 2004.

In figure 10.5 and table 10.6, we do not show the NRAs for mining separately, but combine these with the NRAs for manufacturing to provide a series of weighted average NRAs for manufacturing and mining together, wherein the value added at distorted prices is used as weights.[19] Our estimates for manufacturing and mining go back only to 1970. The average NRAs for 1965–69 (113 percent) are guesstimates based on the belief that, in those years, the average NRAs would have been somewhat higher than the average NRAs in 1970–74. NRAs at about the level of our estimates seem plausible in light of the economic situation during this period. (See our discussion elsewhere above on manufacturing trade policies prior to and following the 1966 devaluation.) For the rest of the years we cover and for which we give estimates, the share of the mineral subsector in combined value added ranged from 7 to 14 percent and averaged around 12–13 percent. The implicit taxation of the mining subsector during the 1970s and early 1980s pulled the combined weighted average NRAs below the corresponding NRAs for manufacturing alone. However, the combined rate, though declining, remained high during these years. Beginning in about 1993, however, and following the steep decline in the implicit protection for manufacturing that accompanied the 1985–93 rupee devaluations, the two series merged at much lower levels, leading to historically low assistance levels in these sectors in 2001–05.

It is clear from figure 10.5 and table 10.6 that, from the mid-1960s to the mid-1980s, the assistance going to producers of nonagricultural tradables far exceeded the assistance going to farmers. This is reflected in our calculations of the RRA, which is an indicator of the distortion to farm prices relative to nonfarm prices for tradables. In the 1960s and 1970s, the RRAs suggest, farmers effectively received less than half (average RRAs of −51 percent) the relative price for their products that they would have received under free markets. Because of the drop in international food prices in the mid-1980s, the extent of the implicit export tax on rice and other exportable farm goods fell markedly, generating a rise in the NRAs for farm and nonfarm tradables to the same level so that RRAs were above zero in

1985–87. After the return to trend international food prices in the 1990s, the agricultural NRAs fell to close to zero so that, even though the NRAs for nonfarm industries were reduced by more than half, the RRAs returned to negative values (averaging −13 percent during the decade). Although protection in manufacturing fell dramatically during the 1985–93 devaluations, the devaluations also pushed up agricultural reference prices and reduced agricultural NRAs. Hence, following the devaluations and associated reforms, the antiagricultural bias in the system continued, but it was now far less marked. Then, beginning around 2000, more reductions in the protection for manufacturing, combined with a rise in agricultural input subsidies, boosted agricultural NRAs above the NRAs for nonfarm tradables once more.

Where Are Indian Policies Heading?

Protection levels in most Indian manufacturing and also in the mining subsector are now constrained by low tariffs. Even in a few of the industries protected by high tariffs, such as textile fabrics, garments, and auto assembly, expanding exports and domestic competition suggest that prices are unlikely to rise much above world prices in the foreseeable future. In contrast, most tariffs and other formal instruments protecting the agricultural sector are much higher than the implicit protection rates, and, if they are maintained at current levels, they will not stop domestic prices from rising well above world prices.

Is it probable that the government will follow a high-protection, high-subsidy path in agriculture as the Indian economy develops? The political economy of this issue is complex. Some forces and some arguments appear to make it likely that a high-protection path in agriculture will be followed, while others argue against this outcome.

The politically important considerations favoring protection over open trade policies are as follows: the high share of employment in the rural sector (still around 60 percent), the desire to insulate farmers from the large price fluctuations that occur in world agricultural markets, and the feeling that the country should be self-sufficient or nearly self-sufficient in the production of basic foods and other agricultural commodities. (The last argument is based on the notion that demand is too substantial to rely on world markets for supplies in the event of serious crop failures or other disruptions to supplies.) These general arguments for protection reinforce the economic interests of farmer groups that are highly organized and politically effective at lobbying with the states and the central government. Within the central government, the Ministry of Agriculture represents farmer interests and ensures that these views are heard in policy discussions. These are the basic reasons for the exclusion of agriculture and the food processing industries from the liberalizing trade policy reforms in 1991, for fixing high tariff bindings during the Uruguay Round multilateral negotiations, and for leaving agriculture out of the unilateral tariff reduction program that started in 2003. They also explain the currently high agricultural tariffs, which have been deliberately set at prohibitive levels to keep out imports in case there is a dip in world prices or the opening of a niche market opportunity for imports.

In contrast, because of the high share of food in household budgets in India, there is strong pressure to keep agricultural prices down. For many years, this goal dominated agricultural policies and was compatible with expanding agricultural production and national self-sufficiency largely because of the successful adoption of Green Revolution technologies in crop agriculture, in conjunction with large-scale government investment in irrigation and other rural infrastructure. Between 1965 and 1988, domestic rice and wheat prices declined by 44 and 52 percent in real terms, respectively. Because of steadily increasing farm productivity, this major long-term benefit to consumers was compatible with rising farmer prosperity, especially in northwestern India. There were also additional benefits arising among low-income households from subsidized rice and wheat supplied through the public distribution system. Moreover, the trade policy regime of the period kept the prices of the principal food grains low—directly through export restrictions and indirectly through the exchange rate overvaluations that were generated by the high-protection import-substitution policies in place in manufacturing. In the case of rice, an export ban was in force in 1965–88, and average domestic rice prices were about 23 percent below export parity prices and were lower still in relation to export prices under counterfactual simulations of the exchange rate under free trade.[20] In these ways, food consumers benefited at the expense of farmers during the license Raj, although they lost as consumers of manufactured goods and, much more importantly, as a consequence of the missed opportunities for more rapid overall economic growth that was forgone because of these policies.

There are no organized groups representing the interests of food consumers. Nonetheless, politicians and bureaucrats are sensitive to consumer concerns over food prices, which are a major topic in public debates, especially debates on the efficacy of the supply of below-poverty-line groups with subsidized wheat, rice, and sugar through the public distribution system. In these ways, consumer interests remain important counterforces to the producer lobbyists pressing for higher agricultural prices, usually through increases in support prices.

However, a number of factors limit the extent to which public concerns over consumer welfare constrain lobbying groups in favor of farmers and other producers.

First, politicians and government bureaucrats are mainly sensitive to increases in the retail prices of mass consumption staple foods, including wheat, rice, sugar, edible oils, milk, pulses, and selected vegetables such as onions. They are less concerned about the prices for other food products, especially fresh fruits, other vegetables, and spices because consumers have long been accustomed to fluctuating prices in retail and wholesale markets for these products.

Second, as in other countries, producer lobbying groups can be at least partially placated through increases in input subsidies without incurring the political pain that may follow output price increases. This explains the rapid rise in fertilizer and electricity subsidies since 1985, the long-term decline in canal irrigation fees for water, and subsidized credit for farmers supplied through government banks. It also explains the government's reaction to the 2007–08 boom in world agricultural and fertilizer prices, which included a ban on rice exports that was aimed at protecting domestic consumers, but also raised subsidies to keep domestic fertilizer prices below world prices; the latter was aimed at placating farmers. However, there were limits to increases in these subsidies. For example, no additional subsidy was possible if electricity was being supplied free of charge, which was the case in a number of Indian states. The subsidies had other consequences, notably, the effects of the farm electricity subsidies on state government budgets and the viability and operating efficiency of state electricity boards and the effects of the fertilizer subsidies on the central government budget (Gulati and Narayanan 2003). Until around 2005, there were signs that these limits and consequences may have checked the rate of growth in farm subsidies.

Third, the objective of national food self-sufficiency sometimes trumped the concerns about consumer welfare. The clearest example is the unsuccessful attempt to replace palm oil imports by domestic production through import restrictions initially and through high tariffs currently (85 percent). Over long periods, dairy import policies also involved high consumer prices without generating much debate on behalf of consumers. In both cases, the interests pushing for the import-substitution policies dominated public discussions, and there seems to have been little, if any, public awareness that lower prices were a realistic alternative.

Fourth, the political concern about the prices for staple foods was mainly an issue of price stability, rather than about price level. If prices unexpectedly decline, producers become worried; consumers worry if prices unexpectedly increase. Although organized commodity markets and trade associations were reporting on international commodity prices, there was little public interest in the divergence between domestic prices and world prices. Thus, as long as there are no sudden large price changes in the current context of high redundant tariffs, it is quite plausible that domestic food prices might steadily rise and diverge from international prices, especially if general inflation is low and the exchange rate appreciates.

Fifth, producers have discovered they can be effective in blocking imports without attracting much opposition if they act quickly and early before the imports achieve much domestic market penetration. There is minimal established importer and consumer interest to overcome if this is the approach. If imports are blocked early, there is no or little subsequent consumer and political awareness of imports as a lower-cost alternative to domestic production. Increases in tariffs on chicken parts and garlic (from 35 to 108 percent in 2001 and in 2003, respectively) are recent examples of this strategy, and the same strategy might be applied to other products if imports threaten to overcome the already comprehensive protective barriers.

This all suggests that the political interest in low consumer prices is unlikely to represent an obstacle to increases in agricultural protection, while domestic and external conditions could conceivably create strong producer pressure for agricultural protection. Medium- or long-term scenarios that would favor a boost in protection might include a loss in the ability of the domestic production of major crops such as rice and wheat to respond to domestic demand, leading to pressure for increases in prices or in input subsidies to maintain self-sufficiency; a fall in world prices in a context of stable or slowly rising domestic prices in real terms; a real exchange rate appreciation that reduces rupee border prices, while domestic prices remain about the same or only slowly increase; or limited progress in achieving a reduction in agricultural protection in developed countries through negotiations at the World Trade Organization. This last would reinforce the already strong resistance to liberalization in the government's agricultural trade policies on the argument, first, that tariff concessions should be held in reserve as a bargaining chip to exchange for substantial concessions by developed countries and, second, that continuing the isolation of the domestic markets in developed countries perpetuates price instability in world markets, and the government's trade policies should therefore continue to insulate domestic markets in India from world market conditions.[21]

Scenarios that might ease the pressures for greater protection include stable world prices in a long-run rising trend; productivity increases, especially in yields and in transport, storage, and marketing, that might partially or fully offset other factors tending to raise domestic prices relative to border prices; productivity and production increases that lead to exportable surpluses and growing pressure to cut production if export subsidies are needed to profitably export surpluses; successful negotiations with the World Trade Organization on reductions in the protection and the subsidies (especially export subsidies) in developed countries; greater willingness in India to implement more open agricultural trade policies; and successful negotiations through the World Trade Organization to close or tighten loopholes permitting export subsidies and more active enforcement by other countries so as to facilitate the Indian government's no-export-subsidy commitment under the Uruguay Round Agreement on Agriculture.[22]

A distinction needs to be made between changes in implicit protection and changes in the formal protective instruments such as tariffs. Under a scenario of greater protection, domestic prices would rise relative to world prices. However, because of the considerable redundancy in the level of formal protection, big increases could occur without a boost in tariffs or tighter protection. If tariffs and other formal protective instruments are to be reduced, the initiative must come through the World Trade Organization; there appears to be little or no domestic pressure to achieve such a reduction.

Notes

1. Unless otherwise indicated, throughout the paper, the years are Indian financial years. For example, 1996 is 1996/97, that is, the financial year from April 1, 1996 to March 31, 1997. This includes the various time series, except for some series that are based on crop years (for example, sugar and sugarcane).

2. Agriculture is used here and in other places in the chapter in a broad sense to include crop agriculture, horticulture, livestock activities, inland and ocean fisheries, and forestry activities. This broad use of the term should be apparent from the context. However, our computations of rates of assistance in agriculture include livestock, but not fisheries or forestry, which is consistent with the usage throughout the volumes in this World Bank research project.

3. In this and the following section, the discussion of policies before 1990 relies to a large extent on Pursell (1992). More information on the earlier years, especially the 1960s and 1970s, may be found in the references cited there.

4. The techniques included modest general tariff increases through the use of para-tariff measures and customs duties in 1997–2001; prohibitively high tariff bindings that, under the Uruguay Round Agreement on Agriculture, may be applied to products freely within a wide range (100, 150, or 300 percent); specific tariffs on most textile fabrics and garments that were implemented beginning in 2001 and that are sufficiently severe to discourage any imports of these products from entering the domestic market; local-content rules in the auto industry that were introduced in 1995 and dropped in 2002 following objections by other World Trade Organization members; the widespread use of antidumping measures that were undertaken in the early 1990s and have been applied mainly to manufactured intermediates; the use of state trading enterprises to control imports of cereals, fertilizers, and petroleum products; the use of tariff rate quotas to protect local producers of edible oils and powdered milk; new rules on technical standards introduced in 2000 within the administration of the Bureau of Indian Standards; new sanitary and phytosanitary rules applicable to imports of nearly all agricultural, livestock, and food products under the general supervision of the Ministry of Agriculture; ad hoc export subsidies that are used periodically to dispose of agricultural surpluses (for example, in wheat and sugar) and that are certainly inconsistent with the spirit and, possibly, also with the letter of the government's no-export subsidy commitments under the Uruguay Round Agreement on Agriculture; and, starting in 2005, a subsidy scheme for exports of fruits, vegetables, dairy products, and poultry (NIAM, various). Within India, the predominant view appears to be that technical barriers to trade rules and sanitary and phytosanitary measures, in addition to the legitimate roles sanctioned by the World Trade Organization, are instruments that may be activated or withdrawn according to whether individual industries are in need of nontariff protection against imports.

5. The information has been calculated from data on tariffs and other import taxes published annually in Goyal (various). These publications also provide detailed information on quantitative import restrictions, sanitary and phytosanitary measures, rules on technical barriers to trade, bilateral and regional trade agreements, and other trade policy instruments. Additional reductions in industrial tariffs appeared in the 2008 budget.

6. The main exceptions to the low industrial tariffs are specific duties on most textile fabrics and garments and a 60 percent tariff protecting the auto industry. However, there is evidence of considerable tariff redundancy in these industries, whereby typical domestic ex-factory prices are about equal to or even below the import prices. There are also nontariff barriers protecting domestic urea producers, and the domestic prices for products derived from some of these plants are high relative to world prices.

7. Two exceptions are the rice imports of Bangladesh from India and India's imports of raw jute from Bangladesh, both of which are subject to low tariffs.

8. A World Bank study (2006) of the likely consequences of a free trade agreement between Bangladesh and India finds that the prices for many agricultural products and processed foods are higher in Bangladesh than in India. It concludes that, under a bilateral free trade agreement, there appear to be few possibilities for expanded agricultural and processed food exports from Bangladesh to India, but considerable potential for increased Indian agricultural exports to Bangladesh. The latter would involve trade diversion costs for Bangladesh, including lost customs revenue, resulting from the replacement of duty-paying imports from the rest of the world by duty-free imports from India.

9. A comprehensive account of the Indian government's macroeconomic policies, including exchange rate policies, between 1964 and 1991 is offered by Joshi and Little (1994).

10. One major role of state trading enterprises in import and domestic policies was eliminated in June 2006, when it was announced that cereal imports would no longer be a monopoly of the Food Corporation of India. It was also announced that this entity would no longer buy wheat and rice at procurement prices, but, instead, would rely on competitive wholesale markets to purchase the supplies needed for the public distribution system and general food security stocks. However, in 2006, wheat and rice tariffs, at 50 and 70–80 percent, respectively, were prohibitive.

11. Reductions in agricultural tariffs are often undertaken through special partial or complete exemptions on a particular occasion or for a particular importing organization, while the most-favored-nation tariff is formally left unchanged. Between 2001 and 2005, substantial export subsidies were paid to make it worthwhile for private traders to help dispose of large excess wheat stocks. In February 2006, it was announced that, in view of the inadequate stocks, the Food Corporation of India would import 0.5 million tons of wheat at zero duty. Sugar trade policies have been especially opportunistic. There have been significant changes in sugar tariffs over the last 15 years or so, and, between 2001 and 2004, when about 4.3 million tons were exported, export subsidies were used extensively (Pursell 2007).

12. For the reasons discussed in appendix A, tariffs have been irrelevant as indicators of the actual differences between domestic and prevailing world prices for nearly all primary and processed agricultural products. Our estimates of the actual rates of assistance must therefore rely on painstaking direct product-by-product comparisons of domestic prices and border prices, adjusted by port, handling, and domestic transport costs and supplemented by information on the subsidies and rates of protection for inputs.

13. The trade status of each product in a given year is endogenously determined in the analysis depending on whether the domestic price was greater than the import reference price (import-competing), less than the export reference price (exportable), or between these two (nontradable). The import reference price (also often called the *import parity price*) is the cost, insurance, and freight price, plus port, handling, transport, and other charges. The export reference price (also known as the *export parity price*) is the free on board price, minus transport, handling, and other charges incurred in getting the product to the free on board stage. The trade status is the same in at least two-thirds of all years for only 3 of the 13 product groups Pursell, Gulati, and Gupta (2007) cover in their analysis (see their appendix table A4).

14. On the complexities of calculating input subsidies in the Indian context, see Gulati and Narayanan (2003). There are implicit taxes on other tradable farm inputs because of import licensing and tariffs, but, in the second half of the 1980s, these taxes were quite small relative to fertilizer and electricity subsidies (Gulati, Hanson, and Pursell 1990; Pursell and Gupta 1998; Gulati and Kelley 1999). The implicit taxes declined, along with the decline in protection in manufacturing, during the rupee devaluations in 1985–93. By 2007, most tariffs on nearly all manufactured farm inputs and also

on trucks and specialized handling, storage, and agroprocessing equipment had declined to 7.5 percent. Hence, excluding these generates an upward bias in the estimated contribution of input subsidies in crop NRAs probably by less than 1 percentage point.

Indian farmers also benefit from subsidized credit and are exempt from income taxes, but these subsidies are small relative to fertilizer and electricity subsidies. More importantly, farmers receive subsidized water through canal irrigation schemes that charge fees well below the costs of operation and maintenance. Moreover, farmers do not contribute to the capital costs of the dams, canals, and other public infrastructure from which they are the principal beneficiaries. The resource allocation consequences of the canal irrigation subsidies are especially problematic because the water supplied through canal irrigation is rationed. Thus, an increase in water fees would only transfer economic rents from farmers to the recipients of the fees (mainly state governments) without directly affecting the production of the irrigated crops. For this reason, we do not cover canal irrigation subsidies in our study.

15. Over long periods, sugar prices in India have been much lower than sugar prices in Bangladesh, where prices have been well supported, through quantitative restrictions initially and, later, through customs duties and various para-tariff measures. The price differences in the two countries have generated a regular legal export trade from India to Bangladesh, as well as substantial unrecorded smuggling in exports across the porous land border to Bangladesh (Pursell 2007; see also chapter 9 in this volume). However, the quantities exported, though constituting large shares of the market in Bangladesh, have not been sufficient to have much impact on domestic prices in India. If the government of Bangladesh were to remove or substantially reduce sugar tariffs, a principal initial impact would probably be to divert a considerable portion of the smuggled imports from India into legal channels. Sugar prices in Pakistan are at about the same general level as Indian prices, and there is considerable potential for welfare-improving trade in both directions (especially across the land border) that would help reduce seasonal and cyclical disturbances. However, except for the occasional ad hoc relaxation of restrictions, the highly restrictive bilateral trade relationship between the two countries prevents this from happening.

16. The total input subsidy and subsidy rate appeared to have reached a plateau in 2001–05, but, since 2007, there have been large increases in the fertilizer subsidy; the government thus partially insulated farmers from steep rises in world fertilizer prices.

17. We have used only import reference prices in measuring the rates of assistance in manufacturing and aggregating them across manufacturing subsectors. Export reference prices have not been considered directly partly because manufactured exports have constituted a small share of total manufacturing production in India, but principally because the gaps between free on board and cost, insurance, and freight prices and export-import reference prices are generally quite small in the case of the prices for manufactured goods.

18. We cross-checked the resulting NRA series by applying the same price indexes to estimates of the coal protection rates in 1982 derived from an early study. The resulting series was broadly similar, although the NRAs were somewhat lower.

19. We use GDP-share value added weights because they provide a better indication of the relative size of the manufacturing and mining sectors than do output weights. Ideally, to take account of input-output relationships, especially in manufacturing, the effective protection of the two sectors should be averaged in a calculation that relies on the value added in world prices as weights. However, there is only one known estimate of aggregate effective protection in manufacturing (for 1986/87), but there is no time series, and no estimates or time series exist for the mineral subsectors. In our judgment, the use of this procedure—if it were possible to use it—would probably not change the general level or trend of the nonagricultural NRA series much. On the one hand, the average would be reduced, especially for the 1970s and 1980s, owing to the increased weight of the mineral subsectors, but, on the other hand, it would be increased owing to the likely excess of effective protection rates over nominal rates of protection in the manufacturing sector.

20. This does not mean that domestic rice prices would have been an average 23 percent higher without the export ban. This is so because Indian supply would have depressed world prices.

21. It has been suggested that one reason the government set such high agricultural tariffs was the proposal of the United States that applied tariffs rather than tariff bindings should be the starting point for negotiations on tariff reductions (Gulati 2004).

22. Some export subsidies in India have been justified under the World Trade Organization rule that allows developing countries to subsidize the transport and marketing costs of agricultural exports.

References

Anderson, K., M. Kurzweil, W. Martin, D. Sandri, and E. Valenzuela. 2008. "Measuring Distortions to Agricultural Incentives, Revisited." *World Trade Review* 7 (4): 675–704.

CGA Database (Database of the Controller General of Accounts). Controller General of Accounts, Department of Expenditure, Ministry of Finance. http://cga.nic.in/ (accessed May 2008).

FAO Agricultural Trade Database (FAOSTAT). Food and Agriculture Organization of the United Nations. http://faostat.fao.org/site/342/default.aspx (accessed May 2008).

FAOSTAT Database. Food and Agriculture Organization of the United Nations. http://faostat.fao.org/default.aspx (accessed May 2008).

FAO SUA-FBS Database (Supply Utilization Accounts and Food Balance Sheets Database, FAOSTAT). Food and Agriculture Organization of the United Nations. http://faostat.fao.org/site/354/default.aspx (accessed May 2008).

Goyal, A., ed. various years. *BIG's Easy Reference Customs Tariff*. New Delhi: Academy of Business Studies.

Gulati, A. 2004. "Trade Policies, Incentives and Institutions in Indian Agriculture." Unpublished paper, International Food Policy Research Institute, Washington, DC.

Gulati, A., J. Hanson, and G. Pursell. 1990. "Effective Incentives in India's Agriculture: Cotton, Groundnuts, Wheat, and Rice." Policy, Planning, and Research Working Paper WPS 332, World Bank, Washington, DC.

Gulati, A., and T. Kelley. 1999. *Trade Liberalization and Indian Agriculture*. New Delhi: Oxford University Press.

Gulati, A., and S. Narayanan. 2003. *Subsidy Syndrome in Indian Agriculture*. New Delhi: Oxford University Press.

Joshi, V. J., and I. M. D. Little. 1994. *India: Macroeconomics and Political Economy 1964–1991*. New Delhi: Oxford University Press.

Mattoo, A., D. Mishra, and A. Narain. 2007. *From Competition at Home to Competing Abroad: A Case Study of India's Horticulture*. Oxford: Oxford University Press; Washington, DC: World Bank.

Ministry of Finance. 2005. *Economic Survey 2004–2005*. New Delhi: Ministry of Finance. http://indiabudget.nic.in.

———. Various years. *Economic Survey*. New Delhi: Ministry of Finance. http://indiabudget.nic.in.

Mullen, K., D. Orden, and A. Gulati. 2005. "Agricultural Policies in India: Producer Support Estimates 1985–2002." MTID Discussion Paper 82, Markets, Trade, and Institutions Division, International Food Policy Research Institute, Washington, DC.

NIAM (National Institute of Agricultural Marketing). various issues. *WATS, World Agro Trade Scanner*. Fortnightly newsletter, NIAM, Jaipur, India.

Orden, D., F. Cheng, H. Nguyen, U. Grote, M. Thomas, K. Mullen, and D. Sun. 2007. *Agricultural Producer Support Estimates for Developing Countries: Measurement Issues and Evidence from India, Indonesia, China, and Vietnam*. Research Report 152. Washington, DC: International Food Policy Research Institute.

Pursell, G. 1992. "Trade Policies in India." In *National Trade Policies*, ed. D. Salvatore, 423–58. Handbook of Comparative Economic Policies 2. Westport, CT: Greenwood Press.

————. 1999. "Some Aspects of the Liberalization of South Asian Agricultural Policies: How Can the WTO Help?" In *Implications of the Uruguay Round Agreement for South Asia: The Case of Agriculture,* ed. B. Blarel, G. Pursell, and A. Valdés, 29–46. New Delhi: Allied Publishers; Washington, DC: World Bank.

————. 2007. "Smuggling and the Economic Consequences of an FTA: A Case Study of India-Bangladesh Trade in Sugar." ASARC Working Paper 2007/5, Australia South Asia Research Center, Australian National University, Canberra.

Pursell, G., A. Gulati, and K. Gupta. 2007. "Distortions to Agricultural Incentives in India." Agricultural Distortions Working Paper 34, World Bank, Washington, DC.

————. Forthcoming. *Agricultural Trade Policies in India.* Washington, DC: World Bank.

Pursell, G., and A. Gupta. 1998. "Trade Policies and Incentives in Indian Agriculture: Methodology, Background Statistics and Protection and Incentive Indicators, 1965–95; Background Paper 1, Sugar and Sugarcane." Policy Research Working Paper 1953, World Bank, Washington, DC.

Pursell, G., N. Kishor, and K. Gupta. 2007. "Manufacturing Protection in India since Independence." ASARC Working Paper 2007/7, Australia South Asia Research Center, Australian National University, Canberra.

Rakotoarisoa, M., and A. Gulati. 2006. "Competitiveness and Trade Potential of the Dairy Sector in India." *Food Policy* 31 (3): 216–27.

RBI Database (Reserve Bank of India Database on the Indian Economy). Reserve Bank of India. http://www.rbi.org.in/scripts/Statistics.aspx (accessed May 2008).

World Bank. 2006. *Studies on India-Bangladesh Trade: Trade Policies and Potential FTA.* 2 vols. Report 37863-BD. Washington, DC: World Bank.

11

PAKISTAN

Paul A. Dorosh and Abdul Salam

Trade and agricultural pricing policies, along with public investments in irrigation and agricultural research and extension, have played a crucial role in the agricultural development of Pakistan.[1] From the 1960s to the mid-1980s, trade policies, controls on foreign exchange, and major government interventions in domestic agricultural markets created large distortions in agricultural prices. In general, the overall effect of these policies, including the indirect effects of trade policy distortions on real exchange rates, was to lower the real prices of tradable agricultural products (Dorosh and Valdès 1990; Hamid, Nabi, and Nasim 1990). Despite price disincentives, however, agricultural output rose rapidly because of the adoption of the Green Revolution package of inputs (improved seeds, fertilizers, irrigation) and the resulting increase in productivity (Ali and Byerlee 2002). Major investments in land and, most important in the context of Pakistan, in water supply (particularly through tube wells) also allowed increases in the net area sown.

Substantial liberalization took place from the mid-1980s to the early 1990s, however, greatly reducing explicit tariffs and taxes, as well as government direct interventions in markets for most agricultural products (Nabi 1997; Salam 2001; Ahmad 2003). Nonetheless, the government continues to intervene heavily in domestic wheat markets, and significant tariffs still exist for vegetable oils and milk products. This chapter describes these interventions and presents internally consistent estimates of nominal rates of assistance (NRAs), as well as estimates of broader trade policy effects through real exchange rate distortions.

The authors are grateful to Marika Krausova for excellent research support and Garry Pursell for helpful comments.

In the next section, we present a brief overview of agriculture in Pakistan that highlights growth rates in the area under cultivation, yields, and production in various crops. In the subsequent section, we describe key trade and pricing policies for major crops and measures of policy distortions (the NRAs) over time. Then, we present broader trade and exchange rate policies and estimates of the indirect effects of the distortions on the relative prices faced by agricultural producers. The final section concludes with a discussion of the political economy of the country's agricultural policies.

The Agricultural Sector

Although agriculture is the primary sector of employment for nearly 50 percent of the national workforce, it contributes barely 20 percent of national gross domestic product and only around 12–13 percent of exports, even if processed foods are included. The decline in the relative importance of agriculture has been less rapid on Pakistan than in other South Asian countries except in exports, the share of which was more than 50 percent prior to the 1970s (table 11.1). Agricultural earnings still account for about 70 percent of rural household incomes.

Four crops—wheat, cotton, sugarcane, and basmati and coarse rice—account for around two-thirds of the total cropped area and the gross domestic product in crop agriculture and over one-third of total agricultural gross domestic product. Much of the focus of agricultural policy, research, and extension has been on these crops. The adoption of Green Revolution technology to improve seeds and the greater use of fertilizers and irrigation, especially private tube wells that provided more effective control over water, contributed to substantial increases in the yields and the volume

Table 11.1. Agriculture in the Economy, Pakistan, 1965–2004
(percent)

Indicator	1965–69	1975–79	1985–89	2000–04
Agriculture in employment				
Pakistan	55	53	49	45
All South Asia	74	70	65	57
Agriculture in gross domestic product				
Pakistan	35	29	24	22
All South Asia	43	36	29	21
Agriculture in exports				
Pakistan	53	38	30	12
All South Asia	46	40	26	13

Sources: Sandri, Valenzuela, and Anderson 2007; World Development Indicators Database 2008.

Figure 11.1. Commodity Shares in Agricultural Production, Pakistan, 1965–2005

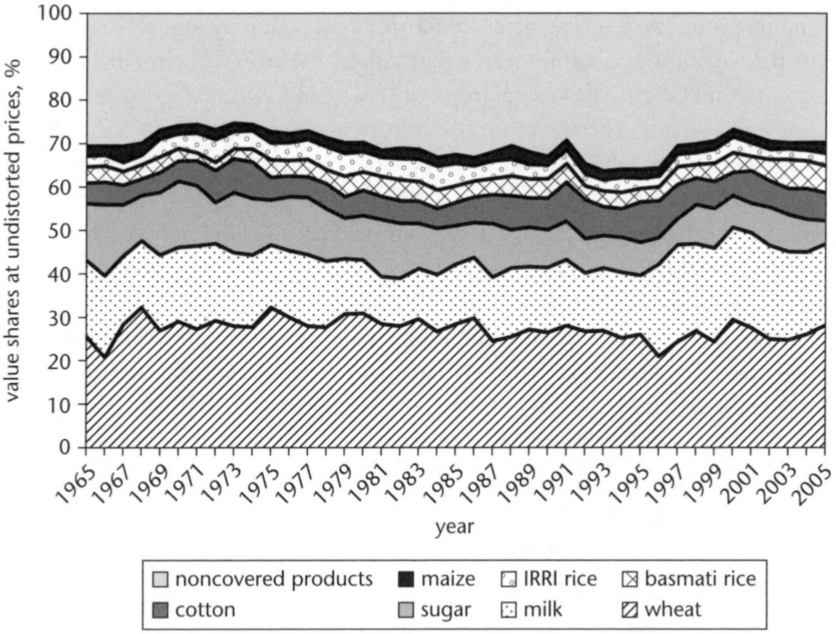

Source: Dorosh and Salam 2007.

Note: Basmati rice is long grained and aromatic. IRRI rice, so-called after the International Rice Research Institute, is ordinary coarse rice.

of wheat and rice production in the 1970s and 1980s. Livestock—mainly dairy, but also poultry, sheep, and goats—accounts for nearly half of agricultural gross domestic product. The shares of the gross value of agricultural production (at undistorted prices) attributable to the products we cover are shown in figure 11.1.

Nearly 80 percent of the total cropped area is irrigated, and agriculture is the dominant single user of water in the country, consuming an average of about 95 percent of all water resources. The increase in the water available for irrigation and expansion in the area under irrigation have played a central role in agricultural growth since the 1960s. Between 1960 and 2005, the total irrigated area rose from 10 million to 19 million hectares. This advance was generated mainly by an expansion in tube well irrigation. In 2004, 41 percent of all irrigated land was irrigated by canal water and tube well water, 37 percent solely by canal water, and 18 percent solely by tube well water.[2]

Annual agricultural growth averaged 3.7 percent from 1959 to 2001 though there were wide year-to-year variations. Apart from a period of slow growth in the first half of the 1970s, average agricultural growth exceeded 3.2 percent per year in each five-year period from 1960 to 2000, largely because of significant growth in the crop sector in the 1970s and 1980s that is attributable to Green Revolution technology (improved seeds, increased fertilizer use, and irrigation). However, the performance of the agriculture sector, particularly the crop subsector, has suffered in recent years because of severe droughts, rising soil salinity, and deteriorating groundwater quality. The agricultural sector grew at a modest rate of only 2.6 percent per year from 1999 to 2005, however (0.5 percent per year on a per capita basis). Real value added in the four major crops—wheat, cotton, sugarcane, and basmati and other rice—rose by 2.6 percent per year over the period. There have been substantial fluctuations in recent years. Value added in the livestock subsector increased somewhat more rapidly, at 3.5 percent.

Most of the increase in production in the major crops since the early 1990s has been generated by higher yields. For example, from 1990 to 2005, the average annual growth in the area under wheat or basmati rice was 0.2 and 2.5 percent, respectively, while yields expanded by 2.2 and 3.6 percent, respectively (table 11.2). Cotton yields, in contrast, stagnated over this period, increasing by only 0.8 percent per year (although the 2004 crop was a bumper crop). Yields in sugarcane rose by only 0.9 percent per year. Maize enjoyed a large expansion in yields (4.7 percent per year) and production (5.8 percent per year) over the same period.

Trade and Exchange Rate Policies

Pakistan operated a fixed nominal exchange rate regime. Only the rate relative to the U.S. dollar changed between the year of independence and the early 1980s.[3] In the 1960s, the government operated various export bonus schemes that substantially raised the rupee price of foreign exchange for exporters. The official nominal exchange rate remained fixed throughout the 1960s. A major devaluation in 1971–72 halved the rupee in U.S. dollar terms. Domestic inflation, coupled with a fixed nominal exchange rate, steadily eroded export incentives (a real exchange rate appreciation) in the late 1970s and early 1980s, however. To restore the incentives for export growth, the Zia government undertook a succession of nominal devaluations of the rupee (totaling 73 percent), from PRs 9.90 to PRs 17.2 to the U.S. dollar, between fiscal years 1981 and 1987 that achieved a real exchange rate depreciation of 65 percent.[4]

There was little subsequent change in real exchange rates until 1996, when the nominal exchange rate was allowed to depreciate more rapidly. Between fiscal years 1996 and 2001, the nominal exchange rate depreciated by 74 percent, from PRs 33.6 to PRs 58.4 to the U.S. dollar, although, because of relatively high domestic inflation, the real exchange rate depreciated by only 11 percent.

Table 11.2. Structure of the Agricultural Economy, Major Crops, Pakistan, 2004–06
(annual average)

Crop	Area		Yield		Production	
	hectares, millions	% growth[a]	tons per hectare	% growth	tons, millions	% growth
Wheat	8,292	0.19	2.52	2.19	20,937	2.39
Rice[b]	2,534	1.33	2.03	1.92	5,140	3.28
Basmati	1,539	2.51	1.65	3.60	2,538	6.20
Other Rice	951	−0.52	2.52	1.45	2,398	0.93
Maize	984	1.01	2.80	4.74	2,751	5.80
Other food grains[c]	850	−1.37	0.60	0.55	514	−0.68
Pulses (gram)	1,047	−0.38	0.64	2.08	669	1.70
Sugarcane	982	0.71	49.19	0.92	48,325	1.64
Oilseeds[d]	315	−0.84	0.74	0.80	234	0.22
Cotton	3,093	0.77	0.67	0.79	2,086	1.56
Tobacco	51	−0.09	2.01	1.05	102	0.96
Other crops[e]	4,506	−0.66	n.a.	n.a.	n.a.	n.a.
Total	22,653	0.15	n.a.	n.a.	n.a.	n.a.

Sources: Author calculations; Ministry of Finance 2006.

Note: n.a. = not applicable.
a. Average annual growth rate, 1990/91–2005/06.
b. Basmati and other rice refer to 2004–05.
c. Pearl millet (*bajra*), sorghum (*jowar*), and barley.
d. Oilseeds include rapeseeds, mustard, and sesame.
e. Other crops include fruits, other vegetables, and all other crops. Data for 2005/06 are preliminary.

Large inflows of foreign capital (both public and private) began in late 2001. These were related to post–September 11 shifts in donor policies and the repatriation of private sector capital to Pakistan. They contributed to an 8 percent appreciation in the real exchange rate from September 2001 to October 2002. The capital inflows also helped the government avoid a pending balance of payments crisis and increase public spending. Careful macromanagement, including repayment of international debt, combined with a surge in public and private sector imports, resulted in a depreciation of the real exchange rate in 2003 and 2004. More recent trends suggest that expansionary monetary and fiscal policies may have adversely affected the incentives for tradable goods relative to nontradables because the real exchange rate appreciated by 14 percent between December 2004 and November 2005.

Prior to major reforms in 1991 and 1997, the government generally followed an import-substitution trade policy aimed at promoting the industrial sector. Trade taxes were also a major source of government revenue. Under the first Nawaz Sharif government (November 1990 to July 1993), tariff rates were cut sharply in 1991 and, as a result, net tariff revenues as a share of imports fell from 34 percent in 1990 to 27 percent in 1991. Unweighted average tariff rates fell from 77 percent in 1988 to only 45 percent in 1994. The number of items subject to quantitative restrictions was also reduced, from 1,361 in 1988 to only 970 in 1993, although nearly 10 percent of all commodities were still subject to quantitative restrictions in 1993 (Nabi 1997). This trade reform was accompanied by a liberalization in foreign exchange markets in 1992, including allowing foreign currency bank deposits (Hasan 1998).

Six years later, in March 1997, under the second Nawaz Sharif government (February 1997 to October 1999), the maximum tariff rate was reduced from 65 to 45 percent; the number of tariff slabs was reduced from 13 to 5; and there was a sharp reduction in the tariff rates on smuggling-prone items to between 10 and 25 percent (Hasan 1998).

These changes in trade policy were reflected in net customs duties, which fell from an average 34 percent in 1985–89 to 22 percent in 1990–96, 12 percent in 1997–2000, and 9 percent in 2001–03. The decline in the total taxes on imports was far less dramatic, however, because, as customs duties were lowered, sales taxes on imports were raised. Thus, total taxes on imports declined by only 10 percentage points between 1990 and 2000, from 34 to 24 percent.[5] The average statutory tariff rates were similar for agriculture and for industrial products: 21.8 and 20.2 percent, respectively, in 2001 (World Bank 2004).

Along with a reduction in tariff rates, trade liberalization in the 1990s included a gradual reduction in the number of products subject to quantitative restrictions.

By 1997, only 2.7 percent of all product lines were subject to traditional quantitative restrictions. The subsequent reforms begun in 1997 led to the elimination of essentially all remaining traditional quantitative restrictions and parastatal import monopolies by 2003, with the important exceptions of a ban on imports of the products not included in a positive list of 677 items and local-content programs in the automobile industry (World Bank 2004).

The combined effect of import tariffs and quotas on domestic prices may be expressed as an implicit tariff rate defined as the ratio of domestic prices (measured at the border) to import prices. In the absence of detailed data on domestic and import prices, we have calculated estimates of the implicit tariff, thereby extending an earlier series by Dorosh and Valdès (1990) using the average percentage change in actual average tariff rates. The calculations suggest that the trade liberalization in Pakistan reduced implicit tariffs sharply over time, from an average of 53 percent in 1985–89 to an average of only 15 percent in 2001–03. Likewise, the effects of trade policy distortions on the real exchange rate have diminished over time (figure 11.2).[6]

Figure 11.2. Import Tariffs and the Real Exchange Rate, Pakistan, 1985–2004

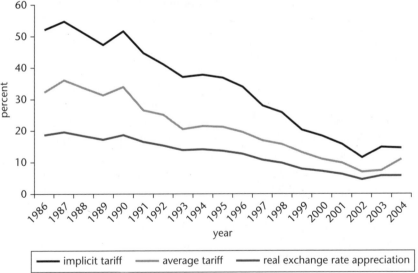

Source: Author calculations.

Impacts of Agricultural Price and Trade Policies on NRAs

We consider in this section distortionary policies on milk and several key crop products, including wheat, cotton, sugar, maize, and rice (basmati rice and IRRI rice; see the note to figure 11.1). Together, these products account for around 70 percent of the value of agricultural production (figure 11.1). In line with our project methodology, we estimate NRAs on output for each of those products. (For details on the methodology, see Anderson et al. 2008 and appendix A). Through careful comparisons of domestic prices and prices at the border or international reference prices, which we have adjusted for quality differences, marketing margins, and the dual exchange rate system, we capture in these measures the proportional extent to which government-imposed distortions create a gap between domestic prices and prices as they would be under free market conditions.[7]

Wheat

Wheat is Pakistan's main staple food, accounting for an average 1,040 calories per person per day in 2001, which represents 42 percent of total caloric consumption (FAO SUA-FBS Database 2007).[8] The adoption of Green Revolution technology enabled the country to more than double wheat production from the early 1970s to the late 1990s, and the production has risen by an additional one-quarter since then (table 11.3).[9] Nonetheless, in most years since 1960, Pakistan has been a net wheat importer.

Government wheat policy

Through its wheat policy, the government attempts to balance the competing interests of producers and consumers. On the production side, the policy is aimed at increasing wheat productivity (yields) and output, as well as supporting farmer incomes. Increased wheat production is also considered part of an overall national food security strategy of reducing dependence on food imports. On the consumption side, the government has attempted to enhance household food security, particularly by ensuring the availability of wheat flour at affordable prices and by maintaining price stability. The food policy options are limited, however, by overall fiscal constraints and by a desire to minimize the fiscal subsidies on food. Moreover, the wheat procurement price has been viewed as a major determinant of overall inflation because of its role as a wage good and an indicator of overall government price policy. Thus, wheat policy is to some degree constrained also by inflation targets and inflation policy.

To achieve the policy objectives, the federal and provincial governments have employed various instruments. Domestic procurement quantities and prices are

Table 11.3. Production and Trade, Wheat, Pakistan, 1972–2005

Consumption year	Production	Imports[a]	Exports	Domestic procurement	Releases	Net injections[b] (NI)	Net availability (NA)	NI/NA, %	Closing stocks
1972–79	8,223	1,188	0	1,452	2,456	1,004	8,405	12	225
1980–89	12,167	944	0	3,534	3,925	391	11,341	3	1,290
1990–99	16,305	2,418	0	3,655	5,752	2,097	16,771	12	787
2000–05	19,771	326	578	4,580	4,124	–456	17,504	–3	1,337
2001–02	20,051	174	606	6,308	4,457	–1,851	16,195	–12	2,193
2003–04	18,970	537	752	3,645	4,574	929	18,002	52	509
2005	21,612	0	0	3,930	2,107	–1,823	18,627	–10	2,110

Sources: Author calculations; Ministry of Finance, various.

Note: All data are expressed in thousands of tons except NI/NA, which is expressed in percent. The years are fiscal years. For production, the data refer to the previous fiscal year.

a. Government imports.
b. Net injections in 2005 include an estimated 1.0 million tons of private imports.

387

the major instruments for spurring domestic production and improving farmer incomes.[10] The targets for the national support price and procurement quantities are set at the federal level, in consultation with provincial governments, although the implementation of procurement policy is the responsibility of provincial governments and the Pakistan Agricultural Storage and Services Corporation.[11] Likewise, sales of government wheat, almost exclusively to flour mills on a quota basis, are largely the responsibility of provincial governments.[12]

Provincial governments have generally set procurement targets aimed at securing enough grain for planned distribution and stock buildup. Restrictions on the transport of wheat were widely used until the mid-1990s to help ensure that the district officials of provincial food departments were able to meet procurement targets. The marketing of wheat was subsequently liberalized, but, in 2004, the Punjab government reimposed restrictions on the transport of wheat in an effort to meet procurement targets. It removed these restrictions once again in 2005. Imports of wheat undertaken by the federal government have been used to supplement provincial food stocks and enable sufficient wheat sales to keep domestic prices from rising too high. The government (along with private sector contractors) also exported wheat in the 2000–03 May to April marketing years following record levels of production and procurement in 2000.[13]

Effects of government policy on domestic wheat prices

Despite the objective of boosting wheat production and reaching self-sufficiency, the government's trade and pricing policies have consistently taxed wheat producers and subsidized consumers relative to world prices. The mechanisms and levels of taxation have changed over time. In the 1960s, average wheat procurement prices were two-thirds higher than border prices measured using the official exchange rate.[14] If we take into account the distortions in the foreign exchange market generated by the two-tiered exchange rate system, however, we find that average NRAs among wheat producers were below zero in 1962–69. Thus, during this period, exchange rate policy fully offset the impact of high nominal domestic procurement policies, although the offset in the later 1960s was less than the offset in the early 1960s (table 11.4).

During the 1970s, average domestic prices were maintained almost 20 percent below border prices (measured at equilibrium exchange rates) through large-scale government imports; net injections (releases, minus domestic procurement) averaged 12 percent of total net availability (see table 11.3).[15] Nonetheless, nominal rates of protection fluctuated widely from year to year during this period. Massive distortions in the foreign exchange market (and high NRAs for wheat) continued until a sharp devaluation in late 1972 following the secession of Bangladesh (East Pakistan) the previous year. During 1972–74, when the

Table 11.4. NRAs for Covered Agricultural Products, Pakistan, 1962–2005

(percent)

Product, indicator	1962–64	1965–69	1970–74	1975–79	1980–84	1985–89	1990–94	1995–99	2000–05
Exportables[a]	−33.3	−35.3	−20.1	−33.5	−29.1	−32.1	−16.7	−4.4	−6.9
Basmati rice	−51.0	−41.1	−37.3	−46.6	−49.5	−56.2	−17.9	−1.7	−25.3
IRRI rice	−42.8	−46.0	−18.8	−33.8	−24.6	−20.2	−0.5	8.1	12.5
Cotton	−18.8	−17.5	−6.3	−5.1	3.1	−6.1	−19.9	−7.9	7.0
Import-competing products[a]	9.2	45.0	19.2	−4.3	−1.9	5.4	−7.9	−1.9	3.4
Wheat[b]	−13.2	11.4	−16.2	−21.2	−22.3	−21.7	−27.1	−20.2	−13.9
Maize	−19.9	−9.8	−19.4	−13.0	−5.9	1.2	−2.2	−1.9	−10.6
Sugar	137.0	234.2	113.4	33.6	72.4	123.7	52.1	54.3	86.5
Milk	—	70.4	123.8	54.6	47.5	54.5	25.4	16.9	19.7
All covered products[a]	−1.0	21.7	9.3	−11.8	−9.3	−5.9	−10.2	−2.6	1.0
Dispersion, covered products[c]	62.1	105.6	74.5	43.2	49.6	65.2	32.2	27.7	39.5
Coverage, at undistorted prices	69	70	74	72	69	68	66	68	71

Source: Dorosh and Salam 2007.

Note: The nominal rates of protection for maize, milk, rice, and sugar are calculated at the farmgate. — = no data are available. All other rates are calculated at the wholesale market level. All other rates are calculated at the farmgate. — = no data are available.

a. Weighted averages; the weights are based on the unassisted value of production.

b. The wheat import parity price calculations assume that Karachi is the central market for imported wheat.

c. Dispersion is a simple five-year average of the annual standard deviation around the weighted mean of the NRAs of covered products.

world prices of wheat and other grains rose sharply, the government effectively insulated the domestic wheat market from the shock through government imports and subsidized sales. The implicit tax on wheat farmers peaked at 70 percent in 1973, but, during the remainder of the 1970s, as world prices fell and the government's wheat policy maintained real domestic wheat prices at approximately constant levels, the NRAs became much less negative (Dorosh and Salam 2007).

Government net injections in wheat markets were substantially smaller in the 1980s, averaging only 2.7 percent of net availability. During that decade, wheat NRAs averaged −22 percent. Policy reforms during the 1990s reduced exchange rate distortions to a low level, but net government market interventions rose again to an average of one-eighth of net availability. The NRAs averaged −24 percent, meaning that domestic prices had become somewhat lower relative to border prices.

The country briefly became a net exporter of wheat following a bumper harvest in early 2000. Because world market prices were lower than domestic prices, these exports required government subsidies. Government domestic procurement was greater than sales by 3 million and 660,000 tons in 2000 and 2001, respectively. Without these government interventions, domestic prices would have been about 10 percent lower in 2000 and 2001. From 2002 through 2004, net government injections averaged 929,000 tons a year, about 5.2 percent of net availability and about half the share of net availability in the 1990s. Similar to the situation during most of the 1990s, prices were again below import parity levels (by 23 percent).

In 2005, the government allowed private wheat imports, which totaled around 1 million tons for the year and kept wholesale prices in Karachi close to import parity prices. Because the release prices of wheat were about the same or higher than the market prices in parts of Punjab and Sindh in late 2005 and early 2006, total government sales to flour mills were lower than normal, resulting in a buildup of year-end stocks and net market withdrawals of about 1.8 million tons (10 percent of net availability), which was similar to the average levels of 2000 and 2001 (Dorosh and Salam 2008).

Thus, government wheat policy has helped stabilize prices, albeit well below border prices, although wheat is an import-competing product. Policy interventions have also adjusted to changing market conditions. Large-scale subsidized import sales reduced prices during years of high world prices, particularly the early 1970s and much of the 1990s, thereby benefiting consumers. In years of good harvests (a less frequent occurrence: several years in the 1980s and 2000–01), net market withdrawals kept domestic prices from falling steeply, thereby protecting farmer incomes.

Cotton

Cotton, the largest cash crop in Pakistan, is second only to wheat in area sown. The area under cotton has averaged around 3 million hectares, accounting for 15 percent of the total cropped area annually and about 25 percent of the value added in key crops. Domestic cotton is also a major input into textiles. The cotton subsector likewise contributes to export earnings indirectly in that various cotton products (cotton lint, yarn, cloth, and garments) account for about two-thirds of the value of merchandise exports.[16]

As the textile industry has expanded, exports of raw cotton have declined, and an increasingly large proportion of cotton is processed domestically into yarn. Raw cotton (lint) exports dropped from an annual average of 414,000 tons in the 1980s to only 161 tons in the 1990s and 72 tons in 2000–05. Meanwhile, the country has imported substantial volumes of lint cotton; net exports in lint cotton declined from an annual average 408,000 tons in the 1980s to −205,000 tons (net imports) during 2001–05 (table 11.5). Imports of cotton lint are mainly high-grade longer-staple cottons.

To help ensure adequate incomes among cotton farmers, the government began announcing support prices for cotton lint and seed cotton (*phutti*) in 1975. The mechanisms by which the government attempted to influence market prices changed substantially during this period, however. Thus, support prices for cotton lint were discontinued after 1995.

From 1974 through 1986, the Cotton Export Corporation, which had been established in the early 1970s, had a monopoly on cotton (lint) exports. By restricting the volume of exports, the corporation depressed the domestic price of cotton below the world price. At the official exchange rate, the NRAs on cotton lint averaged −12 and −9 percent in the 1970s and 1980s, respectively. Cotton

Table 11.5. Production and Trade, Cotton, Pakistan, 1960–2005

Year	Production, tons, 1,000s	Exports net of imports, tons, 1,000s	Domestic use, tons, 1,000s	Net exports in total production, %
1960–69	427	114	307	27
1970–79	584	132	447	21
1980–89	1,068	408	616	36
1990–99	1,627	96	1,487	5
2000–05	1,925	−205	2,108	−11

Source: PSD Online Database 2008.

Note: The data refer to the subsequent cotton marketing year. For example, the cotton harvest of October–December 2004 is indicated as 2005.

producers nonetheless benefited from the trade protection for vegetable oils that boosted the domestic price of cottonseed, which averaged approximately one-quarter of the value of seed cotton in 2000–04. Including the protection on cottonseed, the total NRAs for cotton farmers were less negative. However, if the dual exchange rate system is taken into account, the average NRAs for cotton become −18 percent in the 1960s, −6 percent in the 1970s, and −2 percent in the 1980s (see table 11.4).

Beginning in 1986 and continuing through 1993, export taxes on cotton were calculated as a fixed percentage of the margin between the benchmark price (the target ex-gin price of lint, plus export incidentals) and the minimum export price, which is fixed daily by the Interagency Committee and announced by the State Bank of Pakistan. That minimum export price is based on the international prices of lint, the domestic prices of yarn and lint, the domestic requirements of the industry, and the global and local supply situation.[17] The tax rate on this margin and the benchmark price were adjusted frequently, however, because the government was attempting to maximize export tax receipts and ensure low prices for the domestic yarn and textile industries.[18] This system of variable export taxes effectively insulated the domestic market from movements in international prices. Nonetheless, the underinvoicing of cotton exports continued through the shipment of grades higher than the declared grades.

Poor domestic cotton harvests in 1993 and 1994 caused the country to become a net importer of cotton; imports were around 100,000 tons each year. The increasing cotton imports and the dwindling availability of cotton for export brought into focus the demerits of the benchmark system, which heavily taxed cotton farmers, but provided cheap raw materials for the textile industry and encouraged inefficiency in the textile subsector. There was great resentment and opposition against the system among farmers, who demanded the elimination of the system. The export duty on cotton was thus abolished in 1994, and, since the 1994 cotton season, domestic prices have been in line with or higher than international prices.

Since 1994, the demand for lint in the textile subsector has outpaced supply, and the country has become a net importer of cotton lint. Gross imports averaged 259,000 tons per year during 2000–04. Moreover, despite the expiration of the Multifiber Agreement at the end of 2004, the country's textile subsector has flourished. The imports of lint in 2005 approximated the levels in each of the previous two years, about 400,000 tons.

Export and import duties on cotton have been low since the mid-1990s, and direct market interventions have likewise been minimal, except in 2004, when the Trading Corporation of Pakistan bought 270,000 tons of cotton (11 percent of production) in an effort to boost domestic prices.[19] However, annual price movements suggest that the domestic price of seed cotton is determined essentially by the world price of cotton lint and the domestic price of cottonseed (Orden et al. 2005). If this is the case, attempts to stabilize prices through procurement are unlikely to have a major effect on prices unless external trade is restricted.

Thus, trade policy distortions in domestic markets for cotton lint are minimal, though seed cotton enjoys some protection because of import tariffs on vegetable oils that boost the price of cottonseed oil. Using the domestic price of cottonseed in our calculations, we estimate the average nominal rate of protection for seed cotton in 2000–05 at only 4 percent at export parity.[20] The protection provided for cottonseed oil, however, raises the nominal rate of protection for seed cotton by about 3 percentage points, to a total of 7 percent at export parity for lint in the same period (table 11.4).

Basmati and IRRI rice

Rice is the country's third largest crop after wheat and cotton. It accounts for 19 percent of the area planted in food grains, and the average production is around 5 million tons. Two major varieties of rice are produced: basmati rice and IRRI rice. Both varieties are exported. Basmati rice exports have accounted for about 35 percent or 780,000 tons per year of total rice exports of 2.2 million tons per year in recent years.

Substantial quantities of basmati rice were exported following the large increase in world oil prices in the early 1970s and the consequent boost in Middle East demand for rice imports. The Bhutto government, which nationalized many domestic industries, including rice milling in 1976, set up the Rice Export Corporation as a state monopoly.[21] On the assumption that the elasticities of domestic supply and international demand were low, the government set a low procurement price. To keep domestic consumption low and export volumes high, the government also instituted a monopoly procurement scheme with only limited domestic sales. NRA estimates for basmati paddy suggest that, during the 1960s and 1970s, farmers received barely half the price they would have received under free market conditions (table 11.4).[22]

Following the coup by General Zia in July 1977, rice mills were returned to the private sector, and basmati rice marketing was gradually liberalized. From 1977 to 1987, provincial food departments retained considerable influence in domestic markets through the annual Monopoly Procurement Scheme for basmati rice. The scheme set licensing rules, restrictions on the movement of rice across district boundaries, and quotas among dealers for sales in domestic markets. Traders were allowed to sell 20 percent of the amount delivered to procurement centers in the domestic market; the remainder was exported. Because of these restrictions on domestic supply, consumer prices were substantially above procurement prices. Compulsory procurement was abandoned during the 1986 harvest season. Limited private sector exports were allowed, and procurement prices were raised. The system of voluntary procurement at the announced support price of paddy continued to 2001.

Over 60 percent of the IRRI rice produced in the country is produced in Sindh, where it is also a staple food. Government policies on IRRI rice included announced support prices and domestic procurement, although, in the 1970s and 1980s, the Rice Export Corporation did not procure IRRI rice in Punjab because the higher transport costs relative to Sindh, the center of procurement, made exports of Punjab rice unprofitable. The NRAs for IRRI rice, calculated on the basis of world rice prices, show that producer taxation in the 1980s was slightly more than 20 percent, but that the taxation has gradually disappeared since then.[23] In 2003, the government began announcing indicative prices for paddy, but procurement has been minimal. Currently, no export tax is levied on rice, and imports are subject to a 10 percent customs duty. This is reflected in the IRRI rice NRAs of 12.5 percent in 2000–05 (table 11.4).

Sugarcane

Sugarcane, which is cultivated exclusively on irrigated land in Pakistan, accounts for 4 or 5 percent of the 22 million cropped hectares per year in the country. About half the area under sugarcane is represented by farms operating on less than 5 hectares. The geographical distribution of sugarcane production follows a pattern that is similar to the pattern in other irrigated crops, that is, two-thirds of the crop is cultivated in Punjab, and about one-fourth in Sindh. The area planted in sugarcane rose by 61 percent between 1979 and 1999. This was accompanied by a rise in the number of sugar mills, from 32 in 1980 to 79 in 2005, all of which are now in the private sector. Crop production is highly variable because of changing price incentives and fluctuations in water availability that influence the area under cultivation and the yields. Sugarcane production in Punjab ranged from 19 million to 34 million tons and, in Sindh, from 9 million to 17 million tons in 1979–2005. To stabilize prices despite the variations in production, the government frequently adjusts import tariffs (set at 15 percent in 2005) and the related taxes on sugar; it has also applied export bans.

The domestic marketing and processing of sugarcane were highly regulated until the mid-1980s. The zoning of sugar mills, whereby each farmer was required to sell 80 percent of the farm's sugarcane output to mills located in the local zone, was abolished in 1987, freeing farmers to sell their sugarcane to the mills they preferred. Until 2000, the government announced a support price for sugarcane each year; since then, support prices have been determined by provincial governments. However, there is no institutional arrangement for the public sector procurement of sugarcane if sugar mills do not pay farmers the full support price.[24]

Because of the wide variations in domestic production and in world prices, domestic sugar prices and the measured NRAs have also fluctuated greatly. In general, though, sugarcane and refined sugar production have been highly protected. The NRAs averaged over 100 percent in the 1960s, the early 1970s, and the later 1980s, when the international prices fell again. Since then, the NRAs have remained above 50 percent (table 11.4).

Maize

Maize is counted as a major crop, although it is sown in a total area of less than 1 million hectares (one-eighth of the area given over to wheat). Production averaged 2.1 million tons per year in 2002–04, which represented 8 percent of total grain production. Maize is cultivated on irrigated and nonirrigated land mainly in North West Frontier Province (57 percent of the area under maize) and Punjab (41 percent of the maize area). The area under cultivation expanded by an average 1.0 percent per year from 1989 to 2005, and the adoption of hybrid maize planted in the spring on irrigated land contributed to a 4.7 percent growth in yields per year. Most maize is used as livestock and poultry feed, and this application has expanded rapidly along with the growth in the domestic demand for poultry products.

Apart from import duties, which have ranged from 10 to 25 percent since the mid-1990s, the government has not intervened in maize production and marketing. Maize has often been a nontradable since the 1980s because domestic prices have been below the import parity prices (even without import tariffs), but above export parity prices. Thus, the protection from import competition provided by tariffs has had little effect on domestic prices, and maize NRAs have been close to zero (table 11.4).

Milk

To protect the domestic dairy industry, the government has consistently levied tariffs on imported milk powder. The NRAs arising from these tariffs averaged above 70 percent in the 1960s and 1970s.[25] The tariff rates for milk powder were lowered in the early 1990s and have ranged from 20 to 45 percent since the mid-1990s. The NRAs averaged 40 percent in the 1990s and 20 percent from 2000 through 2005. The contrast between this high level of assistance for dairying and for sugar and the much lower, usually negative NRAs for the other covered products is evident in figure 11.3.

Figure 11.3. NRAs for Major Covered Products, Pakistan, 1962–2005

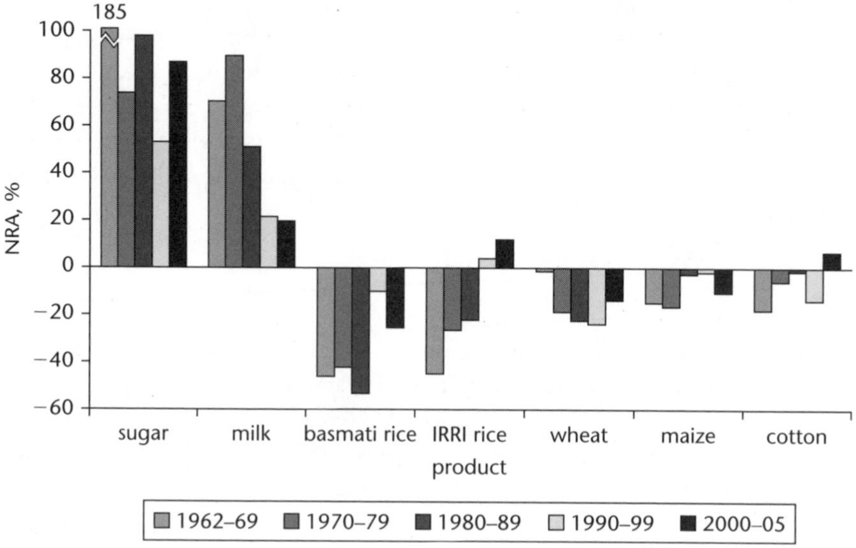

Source: Dorosh and Salam 2007.

Edible oils and oilseeds

The country meets over two-thirds of its edible oil requirements through imports, which rose from 1.1 million tons in 2000 to 1.6 million tons in 2004. In value terms, imports of edible oils more than doubled, from US$326 million to US$758 million during this period. Traditional sources of domestic edible oil production have been cottonseed (a by-product of cotton farming), rapeseeds, and mustard.[26] The area under rapeseed and mustard, sown in winter, has averaged 273,000 hectares in recent years. Sunflowers and soybeans were introduced in the 1980s and promoted through various development schemes and policy measures, including attractive support prices to encourage production and procurement by public sector agencies and facilitate marketing. The area planted in sunflowers increased rapidly, especially in southern Punjab and lower Sindh, from 108,000 hectares in 2002 to 264,000 hectares in 2004.[27]

There was little direct taxation of imported vegetable oils in the 1970s and 1980s. Exchange rate distortions led to an implicit subsidy on imports (and taxation of domestic producers) of only 3 percent in the 1970s and zero in the 1980s. Since the early 1990s, however, vegetable oils have been consistently taxed. For example, from 2000 through 2005, import tariffs on soybean oil were PRs 9,050 per ton, which was equivalent to an average 32 percent of the import value (using the average price of imports for each year). Import tariffs on palm oil were equivalent to about 40 percent of the import value. Likewise, except for three years in which world prices were relatively high (1994, 1995, and 1997), the domestic prices of sunflower seeds have been substantially higher than the estimated border prices. We have not calculated NRAs for these products, however, because edible oils as a group constitute a tiny fraction of the value of the country's agricultural production.

Distortions in input prices

The major distortion in nonfactor input prices in agriculture has been the subsidy for nitrogenous fertilizer.[28] The domestic producer prices of nitrogenous fertilizers, mainly urea, have been kept consistently below import parity border prices. This has been achieved by using domestic natural gas inputs in domestic fertilizer production and passing on some of the savings to farmers through a discounted price. Since the early 1990s, there has been little or no subsidy for diammonium phosphate and other major fertilizers that are generally not produced domestically and therefore must be imported. In the later 1970s and the 1980s, the domestic prices of urea and diammonium phosphate averaged between 30 and 45 percent less than the import parity prices. From 1990 to 2005, however, the domestic price of diammonium phosphate was an average of only 4 percent less than the import parity price, while the price of urea was 38 percent less than the border price.

The cost of urea and the cost of diammonium phosphate represented 8 and 10 percent, respectively, of the value of wheat production according to estimates of the Agricultural Prices Commission for 2002. This implicit subsidy on fertilizer was equivalent to about 3 percent ($0.08 * 0.38$) of the value of wheat production from 1990 to 2005. Thus, the NRAs for wheat in this period should be inflated by about 3 percentage points. For the late 1970s and the 1980s, when diammonium phosphate was subsidized as well, the NRAs for wheat should be about 7 percentage points ($0.18 * 0.40$) higher. The NRAs for paddy, cotton, and sugarcane are also understated by similar amounts in the two periods. These calculations are rather imprecise. They do not include water subsidies, but we nonetheless add them to the NRA time series for the various crops for completeness and because they are nontrivial.

Assistance for Agricultural Tradables Relative to Nonagricultural Tradables

Using the values of production at undistorted prices as weights, we have obtained a weighted average of the above NRA estimates. This information is provided in table 11.4, along with separate averages for the import-competing and exportable

Figure 11.4. NRAs for Exportable, Import-Competing, and All Agricultural Products, Pakistan, 1973–2005

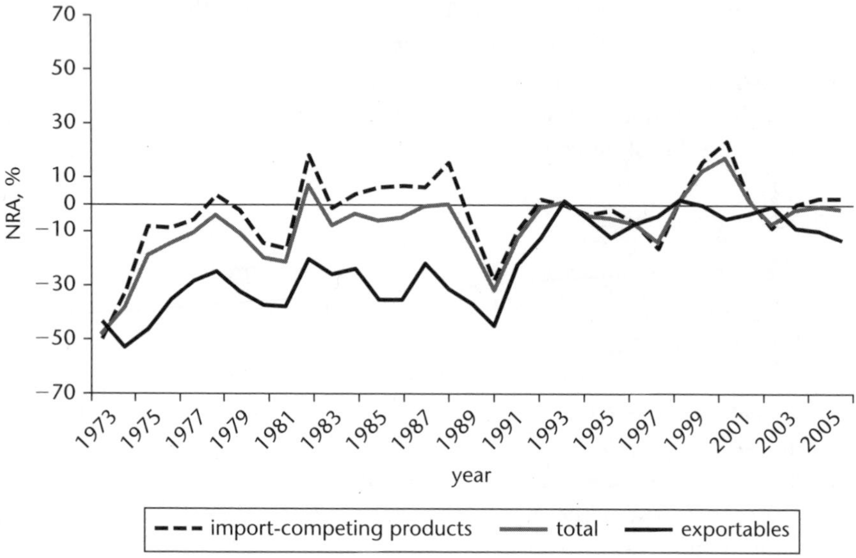

Source: Dorosh and Salam 2007.

subsectors. These averages show that, prior to the devaluation in 1972, the nominal assistance provided to import-competing farmers more than outweighed the implicit taxation on exporters. In the following 20-plus years, however, import subsidies for wheat and less import protection for sugar meant that the NRAs for the import-competing subsector fell to near zero. Thus, because exportables were still being implicitly taxed by between 20 and 30 percent, the NRAs for all covered products averaged slightly below zero. Over the past dozen years, they have averaged close to zero (table 11.4 and figure 11.4).

Another consequence of the changes in the NRAs has been a considerable decline in the dispersion of product NRAs around the mean value each year. One measure of this, shown near the bottom of table 11.4, is the dispersion or standard deviation of these NRAs, which fell from more than 100 percent in the later 1960s to less than 60 percent in the 1970s and 1980s and to closer to 30 percent since 1990. This convergence in NRAs, which may be seen in figure 11.3, suggests that the allocation of land and other farm resources among our covered industries is more efficient now than it was in earlier decades.

Our covered products account for as much as 70 percent of the value of the country's agricultural output at undistorted prices. Most of the country's other farm products are nontradable or are not subject to interventions that significantly affect price incentives. We therefore assume that the average NRAs for these products are zero. This assumption lowers the weighted average total agricultural NRAs, bringing them closer to zero relative to the corresponding NRAs for our covered products. This is shown in table 11.6, row 5, which assumes that the average rate of non-product-specific assistance to farmers is zero.

The trade bias index shown in table 11.6, row 6 captures the extent to which the NRA averages differ in the import-competing and exporting subsectors of agriculture. This indicator makes clear that the considerable degree of antitrade bias in the industry pattern of assistance has been greatly diminished over the past 15 years notwithstanding the implicit import subsidies for wheat. Given that trade openness tends to enhance productivity growth, this trend enhances the prospect that agriculture will contribute more to the country's prosperity.

The extent to which nonagricultural tradable sectors are assisted by government policies is also important for agriculture's competitiveness and ability to contribute to the national economy. The combined effect of import tariffs and import quotas on the domestic prices of nonfarm goods may be expressed as an implicit tariff rate, which is defined as the ratio of domestic prices (measured at the border) to import prices. In the absence of detailed data on domestic and import prices, we have calculated estimates of this implicit tariff by extending an earlier series by Dorosh and Valdès (1990) backward and forward and using the average percentage changes in actual average tariff-equivalent rates.[29] Our calculations provide NRAs for the import-competing parts of the nonfarm sector. We have combined these with an assumed NRA of zero for the exportable parts of the nonfarm sector to generate production-weighted average NRAs for nonagricultural tradables. Crude though this method is, it represents a reasonable measure that we compare with the NRAs for tradable agriculture using the relative rate of assistance (RRA) concept (see table 11.6, note d). The RRAs show the extent to which the prices received by farmers are depressed relative to the prices faced by producers of other tradables in the country.

In the middle rows of table 11.6, we summarize our RRA findings using annual estimates reported in Dorosh and Salam (2007). The NRAs for nonfarm sectors are clearly large in the highly overvalued pre-1972 currency. The dual exchange rate system generated significant levels of protection for import-competing manufacturing. These NRAs declined sharply following the devaluation in 1972 and then remained reasonably steady for more than a decade. Beginning in the late 1980s, they dropped steadily and, in recent years, have averaged less than 10 percent. Thus, although agriculture enjoyed high positive NRAs before 1972, these NRAs were substantially smaller than the average NRAs for nonfarm activities. Clearly, resources were being attracted away from farming. Relative to the prices for nonfarm goods, the prices for farm goods averaged almost 60 percent less than the prices as they would have been under free market conditions. Following the

Table 11.6. NRAs in Agriculture Relative to Nonagricultural Industries, Pakistan, 1962–2005
(percent)

Indicator	1962–64	1965–69	1970–74	1975–79	1980–84	1985–89	1990–94	1995–99	2000–05
Covered products[a]	−1.0	21.7	9.3	−11.8	−9.3	−5.9	−10.2	−2.6	1.0
Noncovered products	0.0	0.0	0.0	0.0	0.0	0.0	0.0	0.0	0.0
All agricultural products[a]	−0.7	15.3	6.8	−8.5	−6.4	−4.0	−6.9	−1.6	0.8
Non-product-specific assistance	0.0	0.0	0.0	0.0	0.0	0.0	0.0	0.0	0.0
Total agricultural NRA[b]	−0.7	15.3	6.8	−8.5	−6.4	−4.0	−6.9	−1.6	0.8
Trade bias index[c]	−0.38	−0.55	−0.27	−0.31	−0.28	−0.35	−0.10	−0.02	−0.09
NRA, all agricultural tradables	−1.0	21.7	9.3	−11.8	−9.3	−5.9	−10.2	−2.6	1.0
NRA, all nonagricultural tradables	174.9	224.5	146.7	44.0	48.3	45.1	39.3	27.0	14.5
Relative rate of assistance[d]	−63.8	−62.4	−55.9	−38.6	−38.6	−35.1	−35.2	−23.0	−11.9
Memorandum items: ignoring exchange rate distortions									
NRA, all agricultural products	−3.6	1.4	−15.7	−15.7	−15.4	−6.6	−9.0	−3.7	−1.6
Agricultural trade bias index	−0.51	−0.55	−0.26	−0.31	−0.28	−0.35	−0.10	−0.02	−0.08
Relative rate of assistance[d]	−69.6	−68.5	−67.2	−45.7	−47.4	−37.8	−37.5	−25.3	−14.7

Source: Dorosh and Salam 2007.

a. Including product-specific input subsidies.
b. Including product-specific input subsidies and non-product-specific assistance. The total assistance to primary factors and intermediate inputs, divided by the total value of primary agriculture production at undistorted prices.
c. The trade bias index is defined as $(1 + NRAag_x/100)/(1 + NRAag_m/100) − 1$, where $NRAag_m$ and $NRAag_x$ are the average percentage NRAs for the import-competing and exportable parts of the agricultural sector, respectively.
d. The relative rate of assistance (RRA) is defined as $100*[(100 + NRAag^t)/(100 + NRAnonag^t) − 1]$, where $NRAag^t$ and $NRAnonag^t$ are the percentage NRAs for the tradables parts of the agricultural and nonagricultural sectors, respectively.

Figure 11.5. NRAs for Agricultural and Nonagricultural Tradables and the RRA, Pakistan, 1973–2005

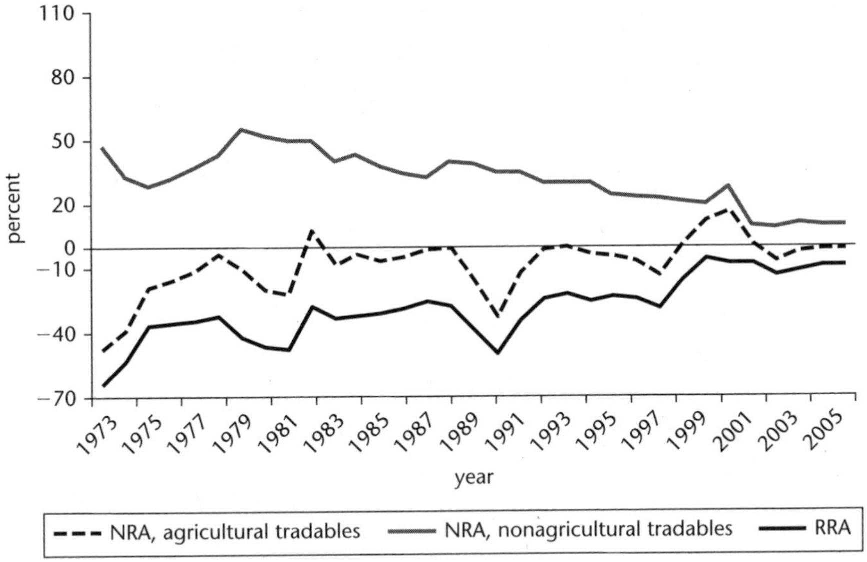

Source: Dorosh and Salam 2007.

Note: For the definition of the RRA, see table 11.6, note d.

1972 devaluation, the degree of antiagricultural bias diminished somewhat, but the RRAs still averaged around −35 percent until the early 1990s. The RRAs began to rise significantly then, and, since the late 1990s, they have averaged less than −10 percent (figure 11.5). So, an antiagricultural bias remains, but it is small relative to the corresponding bias that prevailed during 1970s and 1980s and, especially, during the decades before the secession of Bangladesh (East Pakistan) from Pakistan in the early 1970s.

In table 11.6, we also report how the estimated NRAs, RRAs, and trade bias index for agriculture would differ if we had not taken into account the dual exchange rate, which added to the antitrade bias. A comparison of the two sets of numbers suggests that, if we had not used the dual exchange rate, we would have overstated the degree of direct and indirect taxation of agriculture, especially in the later 1960s and early 1970s before the devaluation.

Political Economy and Conclusions

The government of Pakistan has a long history of intervening in agricultural product markets to influence prices, production, and total supply. In major food commodities, particularly wheat, consumer interests have tended to outweigh producer interests in determining policy, and domestic prices have generally been kept below free trade levels. In cotton, industrialists in the spinning, weaving, and clothing industries benefited from policies to keep the domestic price of the raw materials low. Producers of rice, a major export, were taxed until the mid-1990s through restrictions on sales or through explicit export taxes and controls. Among major commodities, only producers of milk and vegetable oils have consistently gained from government trade and pricing policies (mainly import tariffs). Off-setting the negative effects on output prices to some extent, however, have been the implicit subsidies on canal water (irrigation fees have been lower than the canal maintenance costs), electricity, fuel for pumps, fertilizers, and credit for the purchase of tractors.

Competing interests and the relative strengths of various groups of stakeholders help explain the diversity in policies. In the case of wheat, for example, farmers, par-ticularly farmers achieving net sales, benefit from increases in procurement prices and quantities.[30] Flour millers are able to gain from low issue (sales) prices for wheat that are typically below open market prices. Low market prices for wheat and wheat flour benefit the net buyers of this staple, who account for about 80 percent of the country's population. Provincial food departments make a great effort to achieve domestic procurement targets that provide most of the grain for subsequent distri-bution. Large-scale procurement and subsidized sales create the possibility for sub-stantial economic rents. Sales of grain (at the issue price) from the surplus provinces—typically, Punjab—to other provincial food departments involve an implicit cross-subsidization to the receiving provinces because issue prices do not cover the full cost of procurement, storage, and distribution. The provincial and fed-eral governments are also concerned to minimize fiscal subsidies and overall infla-tion. Donors have generally pushed for reductions in food subsidies and an increased role for the private sector in wheat marketing.

In cotton and sugarcane, agricultural processors have an even stronger influ-ence on policies. Industrialists in the spinning, weaving, and clothing industries have a dominant voice in cotton policy debates because of the importance of these subsectors in terms of value added, employment, and foreign exchange earnings. The position of sugar millers is stronger than the position of the processors of most other crops because the high transport costs and the perishability of the input (the yield of sugar—the *rendement*—produced from harvested sugarcane drops sharply within days of the harvest) limit the competition among sugar mills. Consequently, relations between farmers and sugar mills have been tenuous at best, and this has adversely affected the development of sugarcane and related subsectors. However, despite the opposing interests of processors and consumers (see above), farmers in Pakistan have more political power to defend their inter-ests than do farmers in many developing countries with more equal distribution of land. This is because the presence of many large farmers gives the agricultural sector a stronger voice in political debates.

Nonetheless, macroeconomic considerations, the demonstration effect of broad trade liberalization in other countries, and pressure from donors have resulted in a general reduction in the level of government interventions and the extent of policy-induced agricultural price distortions since the 1970s despite the competing interests of producers and consumers. During the 1970s, the Bhutto government nationalized major industries and set up agricultural marketing institutions that played a major role in the agricultural markets for wheat, cotton, rice, and sugarcane. Broad trade and macropolicy reforms in the mid-1980s reduced overall import protection both directly and through exchange rate distortions. Price distortions were substantially reduced, but the agricultural marketing institutions of the 1970s were left in place. Reforms in the 1990s were deeper in the sense that government direct interventions in markets (the buying and selling of commodities) were dramatically reduced in cotton and rice; the Rice Export Corporation of Pakistan and the Cotton Export Corporation were abolished; and private sector involvement in external trade was generally encouraged. Distortions were reduced in trade overall and in the trade for agricultural products. Since 2000, the price distortions in agricultural markets have remained relatively small. However, the government continues to intervene heavily in wheat markets in ways that incur significant costs, but that have generally had little effect on market prices, although the purchasing following the bumper wheat harvest of 2000 is an exception. The government also reentered the cotton market following the bumper cotton crop in 2004.

The government's agricultural and trade policies are far more liberalized now than they were 30 years ago, and price distortions across sectors are generally small. Nonetheless, the pressure exerted by various stakeholders continues to influence government policy decisions to intervene directly in the markets for the main farm products, particularly in years of bumper harvests that threaten dramatically to reduce producer prices or in situations of supply shortfalls in key consumer goods (for example, wheat and sugar). Maintaining consistent and transparent policies is thus crucial for improvements in market efficiency. Overall, price distortions are no longer a major constraint on agricultural growth and the real incomes of farmers, but the sector could contribute more to economic prosperity if the dispersion in NRAs among farm products were reduced.

Notes

1. Throughout the chapter, the data and policy analysis refer to the current territory of Pakistan, which, prior to 1971, was West Pakistan. In that year, East Pakistan became the independent country of Bangladesh.

2. Throughout this chapter, crop or fiscal years are indicated by the second of the two calendar years; for example, 2005 refers to the 2004/05 crop or fiscal year.

3. See Hamid, Nabi, and Nasim (1990) for a detailed discussion of the government's trade and exchange rate policies from the 1960s to the mid-1980s.

4. According to economic theory, nominal devaluations alone do not cause real exchange rate changes. However, because of import quotas, the nominal devaluations in Pakistan also directly reduced the implicit tariff on imports, a policy shift that does affect relative prices.

5. Note that, to the extent domestic goods also pay sales taxes, these import sales taxes do not represent a trade policy distortion if they are applied in lieu of sales taxes on imported products.

6. If we utilize a value of -0.41 for the omega parameter, we find that the implicit appreciation of the rupee because of trade policy fell from an average 15 percent in 1985-89 to only 5 percent in 2001–03. The omega parameter is defined as the percentage change in the real exchange rate, divided by the percentage change in trade policy, which is measured as 1, plus the equivalent tariff adjusted for export taxes. The value of the omega parameter derives from an ordinary least squares estimate using monthly price and trade data from 1972 to 1987 (Dorosh and Valdès 1990). Cointegration techniques were not utilized in the Dorosh and Valdès report, but a regression based on first differences of variables resulted in an omega value of -0.54. Note that black market premiums are small in Pakistan after 1985, averaging 6.4 percent from 1985 to 1993 and 12.0 percent from 1996 to 1999. The real exchange rate appreciation caused by trade policy, however, is conceptually different from a black market premium, which largely reflects controls on foreign exchange rather than explicit trade policies. See Anderson et al. (2008) and appendix A for a discussion of this issue in the context of our project.

7. Our NRAs for tradables include an estimate of the trade tax effect of the overvalued exchange rate. For this estimate, we rely on the black market exchange rate premium (see Global Development Network Growth Database). We also assume that only half the foreign exchange rate earnings of exporters is sold to the government at the official rate. For details on this methodology, see Anderson et al. (2008) and appendix A.

8. Data of the Household Integrated Economic Survey of 2000–01 (FBS 2001) show a slightly higher absolute figure (1,052 calories per person per day), but a much higher caloric share (58 percent of 1,819 calories per person per day). Rural consumption per capita is 42 percent higher than urban consumption per capita, at 10.3 versus 7.2 kilograms per month.

9. Most wheat is harvested in March and April, which is toward the end of the fiscal year (July to June). In our discussion here, fiscal years are used unless otherwise noted, and we rely on data on production in the previous fiscal year in calculating net availability for the current fiscal year.

10. Provincial governments, particularly the government of Punjab (the largest province), intervene heavily in wheat markets. Government procurement averaged 4.0 million tons per year in 2002 and 2003, more than 20 percent of production in those years. Punjab alone accounted for almost 90 percent of this procurement, equivalent to 27 percent of its wheat production.

11. The corporation supplies wheat to food-deficit provinces, the Northern Areas, Azad Jammu and Kashmir, and the defense establishment.

12. Substantial wheat market liberalization took place in the late 1980s through the abolition of wheat ration shops and the liberalization of private wheat imports (subsequently disallowed).

13. There are major fiscal subsidies and economic rents involved in the sale of wheat to flour mills at below market rates. Wheat issue prices (the price of wheat sales to flour mills) do not cover the full cost of procurement (domestic or imported), storage, and handling. Provincial food subsidies in 2002 reached PRs 6.8 billion. The subsidies were 12 percent greater than the total Public Sector Development Program budget for the Health Division in 2004 (PRs 6.1 billion). Subsidies on the sale of imported wheat accounted for another PRs 1.2 billion that year. See Dorosh and Salam (2008).

14. Nominal rates of protection are calculated assuming that Karachi serves as the central market for wheat, that is, in the absence of distortions, wheat imports would not reach northern Pakistan (Punjab). See appendix A for details on the calculation of border prices.

15. These calculations assume that private sector imports and exports were zero except in 2005; this includes an estimated 1.0 million tons of private sector imports. The data on wheat availability in table 11.3 indicate an excess of net imports over net injections. This gap, equal to 453,000 tons per year in 1981–90, 321,000 tons per year in 1991–2000, and 204,000 tons per year in 2001–06, reflects net private sector imports, storage losses, and public stock changes (as well as possible discrepancies across data sources).

16. However, the country also imports some cotton and synthetic yarn, cloth, and garments.

17. This system was designed to correct a problem of underinvoicing that had lowered export tax receipts.

18. Private sector exports were allowed again beginning in 1987, but cotton lint had to be purchased initially from the Cotton Export Corporation. In 1988, exporters were allowed to buy cotton from ginners directly.

19. The Trading Corporation of Pakistan also procured 35,000 tons (2 percent of production) in 2001 to support prices.

20. The import parity price is calculated on the basis of Liverpool Cotton Price Index B; the export parity price relies on Pakistan's actual average export price of lint.

21. This history of the rice sector through 1987 is based on Hamid, Nabi, and Nasim (1990).

22. The calculations of the border price by the Agricultural Prices Commission set a high cost for transport and processing for basmati rice from Punjab to Karachi (the export port) of PRs 4,650 per ton, about twice the total cost of the import incidentals and transport for wheat from Karachi to the procurement center in Punjab (PRs 2,542 per ton) or the cost to export IRRI rice (PRs 2,300 per ton). Because of these high marketing margins, the border price calculated by the Agricultural Prices Commission for basmati rice at the farmgate is the market price.

23. For the world rice price, we use the free on board Bangkok price for white milled 5 percent broken rice (IFS 57876n7M81) and a 0.71 quality adjustment factor that is equal to the average ratio of the average price of Pakistan rice exports (except basmati rice) to the free on board Bangkok price during 1974–79.

24. In some years, provincial sugarcane commissioners must exert pressure on mills to pay farmers the full support price.

25. We have estimated these rates using the unit import value of dry skim milk, which we have adjusted through a conversion ratio of 1 to 8 and a quality factor of 90 percent (following Dorosh and Valdès 1990).

26. Other minor oilseed crops include groundnuts, safflower, sesame, canola (an improved cultivar of rapeseeds and mustard), and linseed.

27. Soybeans are a minor crop. The area under soybeans has been steady at around 220 hectares.

28. Surface irrigation water is also implicitly subsidized because the water charges (*abiana*) are insufficient to cover the cost of the maintenance of dams, canals, and other water channels. The measurement of the economic value of these subsidies would involve an assessment of overall investment and maintenance costs and of the distribution of these costs among the various crops. We have not attempted such a measurement in our study.

29. Dorosh and Valdès (1990) estimate an equivalent tariff of 47 percent in 1986 based on changes in relative price indexes and a base estimate of the equivalent tariff in 1980 of 55.0 percent computed by Naqvi and Kemal (1983). The calculations rely on changes in tariff rates as an index of the overall implicit change in tariffs, instead of price indexes, to extend the $(1 + t_m)/(1 - t_x)$ series reported in Dorosh and Valdès (1990) because t_x was zero that year.

30. Data of the *Household Integrated Economic Survey, 2001–02* (FBS 2002) also indicate that wheat sales are highly concentrated. The wheat farmers who are in the top 10 percent in sales account for 47

percent of total wheat sales; the top 20 percent of wheat farmers in sales (only 5 percent of the country's households) account for 67 percent of total wheat sales. Overall, only 20 percent of households have a surplus in wheat production over home consumption, while 23 percent of wheat farmers are net wheat purchasers. (Net purchases are calculated on the basis of household production and an assumed per capita consumption of 140 kilograms per person per year.)

References

Ahmad, M. 2003. "Agricultural Product Markets in Pakistan." Unpublished background paper, World Bank, Washington, DC.

Ali, M., and D. Byerlee. 2002. "Productivity Growth and Resource Degradation in Pakistan's Punjab: A Decomposition Analysis." *Economic Development and Cultural Change* 50 (4): 839–63.

Anderson, K., M. Kurzweil, W. Martin, D. Sandri, and E. Valenzuela. 2008. "Measuring Distortions to Agricultural Incentives, Revisited." *World Trade Review* 7 (4): 675–704.

Dorosh, P. A., and A. Salam. 2007. "Distortions to Agricultural Incentives in Pakistan." Agricultural Distortions Working Paper 33, World Bank, Washington, DC.

———. 2008. "Wheat Markets and Price Stabilization in Pakistan: An Analysis of Policy Options." *Pakistan Development Review* 44 (1): 71–88.

Dorosh, P. A., and A. Valdès. 1990. *Effects of Exchange Rate and Trade Policies on Agriculture in Pakistan.* Research Report 84, International Food Policy Research Institute, Washington, DC.

FAO SUA-FBS Database (Supply Utilization Accounts and Food Balance Sheets Database, FAOSTAT). Food and Agriculture Organization of the United Nations. http://faostat.fao.org/site/354/default.aspx (accessed December 2007).

FBS (Federal Bureau of Statistics). 2001. *Household Integrated Economic Survey, 2000–01.* Islamabad: FBS.

———. 2002. *Household Integrated Economic Survey, 2001–02.* Islamabad: FBS.

Global Development Network Growth Database. Development Research Institute, New York University. http://www.nyu.edu/fas/institute/dri/global%20development%20network%20growth%20database.htm (accessed June 2007).

Hamid, N., I. Nabi, and A. Nasim. 1990. *Trade, Exchange Rate, and Agricultural Pricing Policies in Pakistan.* Washington, DC: World Bank.

Hasan, P. 1998. *Pakistan's Economy at the Crossroads: Past Policies and Present Imperatives.* Islamabad: Oxford University Press.

IFS Database (International Financial Statistics Online). International Monetary Fund. http://www.imfstatistics.org/imf/ (accessed May 2008).

Ministry of Finance. 2006. *Pakistan Economic Survey, 2005–2006,* Islamabad: Ministry of Finance.

———. various years. *Pakistan Economic Survey.* Islamabad: Ministry of Finance.

Nabi, I. 1997. "Outward Orientation of the Economy: A Review of Pakistan's Evolving Trade and Exchange Rate Policy." *Journal of Asian Economics* 8 (1): 143–63.

Naqvi, Syed N. H., and A. R. Kemal. 1983. *The Structure of Protection in Pakistan: 1980–81.* Islamabad: Pakistan Institute of Development Economics.

Orden, D., A. Salam, R. Dewina, H. Nazli, and N. Minot. 2005. "The Impact of Global Cotton Markets on Rural Poverty in Pakistan." Pakistan Poverty Assessment Update, Background Paper Series, Asian Development Bank, Islamabad.

PSD Online Database (Production, Supply, and Distribution Online). Foreign Agricultural Service, U.S. Department of Agriculture. http://www.fas.usda.gov/psdonline/psdHome.aspx (accessed January 2008).

Salam, A. 2001. "Support Price Policy in Pakistan: Rationale, Practice and Future Options." APCom Series 196, Agricultural Prices Commission, Islamabad.

Sandri, D., E. Valenzuela, and K. Anderson. 2007. "Economic and Trade Indicators for Asia, 1960 to 2004." Agricultural Distortions Working Paper 20, Washington, DC, World Bank.

World Bank. 2004. *An Overview*. Vol. 2 of *Trade Policies in South Asia: An Overview*. Report 29949. Washington, DC: World Bank.

World Development Indicators Database. World Bank. http://go.worldbank.org/B53SONGPA0 (accessed May 2008).

12

SRI LANKA

Jayatilleke Bandara
and Sisira Jayasuriya

In Sri Lanka, the government's agricultural policies since independence from colonial rule in 1948 have reflected changes in overall development strategy, as well as the interplay of conflicting domestic political considerations, including the need to balance producer and consumer interests, government revenue needs, and ethnic and regional factors.

The country possessed a relatively affluent open agricultural economy in 1948. It had one of the highest levels of per capita income in Asia, a vibrant democracy, and health and education indicators that rivaled the corresponding human development indicators in many developed industrial economies. It was an oasis of peace, stability, and order in a turbulent region (de Silva 1981). The opportunities for rapid economic development appeared rosy. To many observers, Sri Lanka seemed the country with the best prospects for development in Asia (Athukorala and Jayasuriya 1994). However, five decades later, the country has clearly failed to live up to its early promise. Sri Lanka remains a low-income economy; it has slipped well below the high-performing East Asian economies in per capita income and is mired in violent, intractable ethnic and social conflicts.

Since independence, government administrations have experimented with a wide variety of policy regimes. They have switched from noninterventionist, open free-market policies (up to 1959) to dirigiste import-substituting industrialization (1960–77) and export-oriented liberalization (after 1977). Although the country's economic growth performance since the late 1970s has been satisfactory relative to the performance of many similar developing countries, its agricultural sector performance—nearly stagnant per capita agricultural output—has been

409

disappointing and has hampered poverty reduction. Government agricultural policies have reflected the changes in the thrust and direction of the government's broader development strategy. However, there have also been enduring elements in agricultural policy throughout this period.[1]

The agricultural sector has two main parts: the import-competing food-crop subsector, which is dominated by rice and includes a range of subsidiary food crops, and the export crop subsector, which is dominated by tea—Sri Lanka is the world's largest tea exporter—and includes rubber, coconuts, and several minor export crops such as cinnamon and spices.[2] Fruits, vegetables, livestock, and dairy are mostly import-competing products and are generally protected although small quantities of specific commodities are exported.

Agricultural policy until well into the 1980s taxed export agriculture, while providing various input subsidies—irrigation, fertilizers, research and development, and extension—for protected import-competing food agriculture, particularly rice. Beginning in the late 1950s, the shift to inward-oriented development strategies that protected import-substituting industries and the accompanying real exchange overvaluation (leading to exchange controls and a discriminatory dual exchange rate regime) exacerbated the burden on export crops. Despite the assistance and protection for import-competing food agriculture, the policy regime during this period probably had an overall antiagricultural bias.

The process of policy liberalization beginning in the late 1970s eroded the overall antiagricultural bias. The direct taxation of export crops was sharply reduced in the 1980s and largely eliminated by the early 1990s, and manufacturing trade liberalization drastically lowered the indirect agricultural burden flowing from industrial protectionism. However, policy reforms have been limited and selective in the import-competing parts of the agricultural sector. Many import-competing agricultural industries, including rice, but also several other commodities such as sugar, potatoes, and dairy, have continued to enjoy direct input subsidies and, to a varying degree, protection through the trade regime. Thus, overall policies—now generally far more liberal than at any time since the late 1950s—tend to show a proagricutural bias because of the reduction in the taxes on agricultural exports.

Protection from import competition and direct assistance for food agriculture failed to achieve the stated goals of encouraging the adequate production of staples and reducing the growing gap between rural and urban household incomes. Domestic rice production increased substantially, but overall food production nearly stagnated (growing less than half as quickly in Sri Lanka relative to other developing countries over the 1990s), such that food self-sufficiency has continued to decline and rural poverty reduction has been slow. A comprehensive reassessment of agricultural policies should be a priority issue on the government's agenda.

Economic Growth and Structural Change

In Sri Lanka since independence in 1948, there has been a regular change in government, and each government has had a distinct economic policy orientation. Government administrations have experimented with a wide variety of economic policy regimes. Nonetheless, since 1977, the fundamental direction of policy has not changed, although there have been differences in the pace and scope of liberalization measures under different administrations. Figure 12.1 indicates growth rates in real gross domestic product (GDP) and the changing policy regimes.[3]

The relatively slow per capita growth during the 1950s and 1960s was followed by a particularly traumatic period in 1970–77, when the policy responses to the impacts of the first oil shock of 1973 and to a youth rebellion led to severe import compression and shortages in essential goods. This generated widespread popular discontent against import-substituting industrialization and extensive government economic intervention. As a result, there was massive popular support for a shift that brought into power a new United National Party government in 1977 that pledged to adopt open economy policies. A major liberalization effort was launched in 1977, marking a decisive break with the previous policy regime.

Figure 12.1. Real GDP Growth, Political Episodes, and Policy Regimes, Sri Lanka, 1951–2005

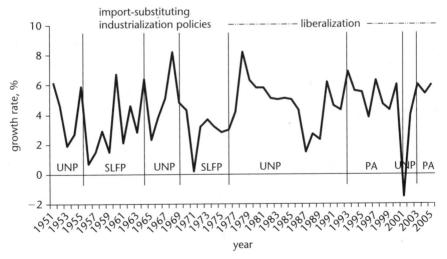

Source: Author compilation.

Note: UNP = United National Party, which has traditionally been right of center. SLFP = Sri Lanka Freedom Party, which is left of center. Both parties have frequently formed coalition governments with other parties. PA = Peoples Alliance, a coalition dominated by the Sri Lanka Freedom Party.

Because of the progressive promarket reforms in 1977 and thereafter, Sri Lanka became the most open economy in South Asia, a distinction it probably still holds. Since 1977, the country has had a reasonably healthy real average annual GDP growth rate of 4.8 percent (3.5 percent per capita). An average per capita income of US$1,200 at the official exchange rate and over US$4,000 in purchasing power parity dollars was reached in 2006. Despite ongoing ethnic and social conflicts that have plagued the country for nearly two decades, the growth rate is higher than the rates achieved since the mid-1970s by most countries at similar per capita incomes; only Botswana has recorded more rapid growth.

Performance across a wide range of human development indicators has been above average in Sri Lanka since the early years of independence, when the good performance was achieved through investments in health and education that were financed by taxes on plantation crop exports. Life expectancy at birth among men and women, for example, has averaged 72 and 76 years, respectively, which is higher than the average among middle-income countries. The literacy rate is over 90 percent. Nonetheless, the country's overall developmental performance is disappointing relative to the case of the high-performing East Asian economies, particularly because real incomes and human capital endowments were comparable or relatively higher in Sri Lanka in the 1950s and early 1960s. The poor performance of Sri Lanka is at least partly the fault of the ongoing civil war and ethnic conflicts, which have caused enormous damage to the economy and the wider sociopolitical environment.[4]

The overall position of agriculture within the national economy is outlined in table 12.1. The shares of the agricultural sector in GDP, employment, and exports have declined progressively since the 1950s, although the sector represents a major source of income and employment among a large proportion of the population and a significant source of national export earnings (see table 12.1, note a). In contrast to agriculture's share in GDP, which shrank gradually, the fall in agriculture's share in exports was sharp in the 1970s and 1980s (figure 12.2). Until the late 1960s, agricultural commodities had accounted for more than 90 percent of exports, but, since the early 1990s, their share has been below 20 percent, and manufacturing, particularly the garment subsector, has emerged as the major export category.[5]

The share of various agricultural products in the value of agricultural production is shown in figure 12.3. Paddy accounted for around 25 percent of agricultural and fisheries output in the early 1980s, but its share is now barely half that much. Likewise, the share of rice in household spending has declined by half during the same period and is currently around 10 percent.

The agricultural sector is widely considered to have contributed to the poor performance of the economy: "In terms of sectoral contributions to growth,

Table 12.1. Agriculture in the Economy, Sri Lanka, 1950–2005
(percent)

Sector, subsector	1950–51	1960–61	1970–71	1980–81	1990–91	2000–02	2005
GDP, share							
Agriculture	44.5	34.6	35.1	33.7	26.3	21.9	18.9
Plantation agriculture	26.3	17.8	15.8	13.9	8.1	5.2	4.4
Tea	7.7	6.5	3.2	2.6	2.4	1.4	1.2
Rubber	5.5	2.3	1.8	1.4	0.6	0.4	0.4
Coconut	7.1	4.8	4.0	3.8	2.4	1.4	1.1
Processing[a]	6.5	4.2	6.8	6.1	2.7	2.0	1.7
Nonplantation agriculture	14.6	14.5	16.7	15.0	14.8	12.1	11.5
Paddy	1.5	5.7	7.2	6.1	4.9	3.1	3.0
Other	13.1	8.8	9.4	8.9	9.9	9.0	8.5
Forestry	1.9	1.4	1.4	2.0	1.6	1.9	1.7
Fishing	1.2	0.9	1.2	2.7	1.8	2.7	1.3
Manufacturing	8	9	14	18	23	26	27
Services	53	55	51	48	51	52	55
Exports, share							
Agriculture[a]	>90	>90	94.6	61.6	36.3	19.3	18.2
Tea	>50	>50	55.5	35.1	24.9	14.3	12.8
Rubber	>20	>20	22.0	14.7	3.9	0.5	0.7
Coconut	>15	>15	14.5	7.0	3.5	1.7	1.8
Other	—	—	3.1	4.8	4.0	2.8	2.9
Manufacturing	<2	<2	1.7	31.2	56.6	77.1	80.3
Unclassified	—	—	3.9	2.7	7.1	1.0	1.5
Employment, share	1953	1963	1971	1981	1991	2001	2005
Agriculture	53	53	50	45	42	33	31
Manufacturing	12	12	12	15	20	22	24
Services	35	35	38	40	38	45	45

Source: CBSL, "Economic and Social Statistics," various.

Note: — = no data are available.

a. To indicate the overall contribution of the agricultural sector to the economy, the processing of tea, rubber, and coconut products, which is usually included under manufacturing, is included in agriculture under GDP and export shares (but not under employment shares).

agriculture has been a continual drag," and "the long-term average growth rate in agriculture has barely exceeded the rate of population growth, which has contributed to the persistence of poverty (the headcount ratio stood at 23 percent in 2002, which is relatively high for Sri Lanka's per capita income)" (IMF 2005, 5).

Figure 12.2. Agriculture in GDP and Exports, Sri Lanka, 1950–2005

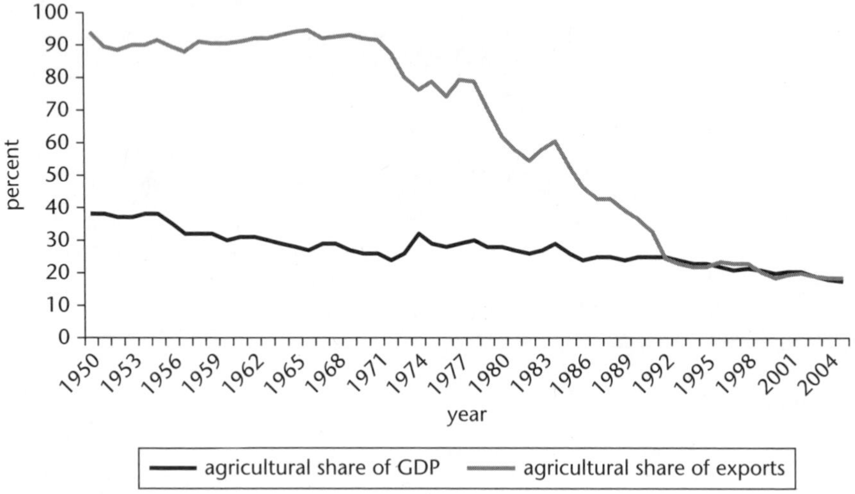

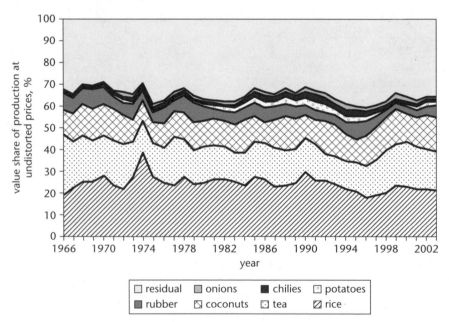

Source: CBSL, "Annual Report," various.

**Figure 12.3. Commodity Shares in Agricultural Production,
Sri Lanka, 1966–2004**

Sources: Author calculations; Bandara and Jayasuriya 2007; FAOSTAT Database 2008.

Within agriculture, the output of most crops has stagnated or declined since the 1980s (Bandara and Jayasuriya 2007). Tea is the sole important exception. Tea output expanded from around 200 million kilograms per year in the early 1980s to around 300 million kilograms in 2000. An increase in the area under cultivation (primarily from an increase in smallholder cultivation in low-altitude regions) and the use of new, higher-yielding cultivars were stimulated by the higher prices for the stronger teas produced in lower altitudes. The production of rice and coconuts—the two crops that dominate smallholder agriculture—has stagnated, while the output of rubber, minor crops, and subsidiary food crops, including income-elastic horticultural crops, has fallen significantly. This has meant that agricultural exports (except tea) have fallen, while food imports have grown. Overall, per capita food production has dropped by over 12 percent since 1980, compared with an average rise of 48 percent in other developing countries (World Bank 2003). This raises a question about the extent of the contribution of policy distortions to the relatively poor performance.

Policy Evolution

At independence, three plantation crops—tea, rubber, and coconuts—dominated exports, while significant quantities of rice, wheat, and other food products were imported. This basic distinction between exportable and import-competing agricultural products is critical to understanding the government's agricultural policy. Export dependence varies greatly, however. For example, more than 80 percent of the coconut crop is domestically consumed, and coconuts and coconut oil are essential parts of the local diet. The share of domestic consumption is quite low in the case of tea (less than 15 percent), while, for rubber, it is around 35 percent thanks to an expansion in rubber-based manufacturing industries.

The tea and rubber subsectors had a pronounced dualistic structure. Large foreign-owned plantations contributed a substantial share of output during the immediate postindependence period, but these were taken over by the government in 1974. Then, beginning in the early 1990s, they were progressively handed back to the private sector, including foreign companies. Meanwhile, the share of large plantations in output has been in gradual decline. In contrast, import-competing food crops, as well as coconuts, have always been dominated by smallholders, although a substantial portion of the coconut industry was located among large plantations until the land reforms of the early 1970s.

Export taxes on agricultural crops (tea, rubber, and coconut products) were initially a major source of government revenue, accounting for around 30 percent of all government tax revenue during the 1950s. They helped finance expenditures on public education, health care, and food subsidies. Levies on exports also financed agricultural research, extension, and replanting programs in plantation crops. The structure of export taxes reduced average producer revenues, but also had the effect of greatly lowering the gains from any price increases. If domestic prices rose because of world price increases or currency devaluations, government tax revenues siphoned off the bulk of the price increases. This meant that, while producers had to bear the cost of increases linked to domestic inflation, they were largely deprived of the benefit of any exchange rate adjustments that were made to restore the international competitiveness of tradables, for instance, on several occasions beginning in the late 1960s.

In common with governments in many developing countries, the government of Sri Lanka followed a food self-sufficiency policy that, more narrowly interpreted, encouraged rice self-sufficiency. On the production side, the policy involved major investments in irrigation (irrigation water was supplied at no cost to farmers), fertilizer subsidies, and the provision of rice and other agricultural research and extension services. There was also a public distribution system for the procurement and marketing of paddy and other commodities. The system was aimed at making rice more affordable for consumers. Prices for food staples were heavily regulated until the 1977 liberalization, and many of these staples remain subject to strong government interventions, including the regulation of import volumes, that are aimed at maintaining price stability.

Beginning in the late 1950s, the structure of incentives became additionally biased against export crops through the adoption of import restrictions and foreign exchange controls. These were implemented in response to growing balance of payments problems partly caused by a secular downward movement in the country's international terms of trade. The measures, rather than a currency devaluation, led to real exchange rate overvaluation. The import restrictions (tariff measures and, increasingly, nontariff measures) and exchange controls were subsequently strengthened after the ideological shift to an import-substituting industrialization development strategy. The result was high manufacturing protection; severe import compression; pervasive state controls in trade, marketing and distribution; persistent exchange rate overvaluation; exchange controls; and a formal dual exchange rate system between 1968 and 1977.[6] The dual exchange rate system included a basic official rate and the rate of the Foreign Exchange Entitlement Certificate Scheme, which, initially in 1968, was set at 44 percent higher (more depreciated) than the basic rate, but adjusted to 55 percent in 1969 and then 65 percent in 1972. Exporters of the main plantation crops—the traditional exports of tea, rubber, and coconuts—had to convert export earnings at the less favorable official exchange rate, while producers of nontraditional exports were eligible for the rate available through the entitlement certificate scheme.[7] The highly overvalued official exchange rate, rather than the somewhat more realistic certificate rate, was also applied on some imports of major agricultural products such as rice, wheat, and sugar. However, these imports were heavily regulated and were also under direct government control. Hence, rice producers were still shielded from import competition. The high premium in black market rates of exchange and other evidence indicate that substantial real exchange overvaluation discriminated against exportable industries and favored import-competing products in agriculture and elsewhere.

The rice subsector was granted special incentives, and other import-competing agricultural products also gained significant protection through the import-substitution strategy. Nonetheless, Bhalla (1991) and others conclude that there was an overall bias against agriculture because of the severity of the impact of the overvalued currency on exports, the large weight of exports in farm output, and the high protection granted to manufacturing. This started to change only in 1977 because of the policy shift away from import-substituting industrialization and toward more liberal promarket policies.

After the 1977 policy liberalization, consumer food subsidies were sharply reduced, and the emphasis on food self-sufficiency was enhanced.[8] Public investments in major irrigation systems were expanded, for example. The government implemented a huge irrigation-cum-hydropower scheme, the Accelerated Mahaweli Development Project, with substantial foreign assistance. Around one-third of all government capital expenditure was devoted to this single project for several years beginning in 1979. The project was explicitly rationalized as a major step toward rice self-sufficiency, a coveted national goal. It thereby appealed to the popular imagination, and this partially blunted the political impact of cuts in food subsidies.[9]

The 1977 reforms also reduced trade protection in the manufacturing sector, and explicit export taxes on plantation crops were largely eliminated in the 1980s. There were fiscal pressures and political imperatives driving the reduction of export taxes on plantation crops. Thus, large foreign-owned plantations were nationalized and transferred to state ownership beginning in the mid-1970s, while the land reforms of the early 1970s had broadened the ownership base, largely among Sinhalese smallholders (Moore 1985).

Trade liberalization was not uniform, however. It extended to some import-competing agricultural products, but excluded others. Crops that were widely cultivated in the north (for example, red onions, chilies, grapes) were subject to liberalization, while protection for other crops (such as potatoes) was maintained or increased.

After the initial economic growth stimulus following the liberalization of 1977 and the huge public sector investment boom (assisted by a massive flow of foreign aid), growth started to slacken, although the economy was cushioned for a while by a tea price boom in the early 1980s. Simmering ethnic tensions erupted into a secessionist war following anti-Tamil riots in 1983, and social tensions in the south led to a highly disruptive rural youth rebellion in the late 1980s. Economic and political conditions worsened, and the economy lost steam. In 1990–91, responding to an emerging balance of payments crisis, the government devalued the currency and initiated a second wave of liberalization (Dunham and Kelegama 1997).

Liberalization proceeded unevenly following the initial measures. Export duties on plantation crops, already reduced substantially in the mid-1980s, were eliminated in 1992, while the high rates of nominal (and effective) protection for import-competing agriculture were maintained (Edwards 1993; World Bank 1995). By manipulating licensing and variable tariffs, the government frequently used regulatory controls on imports to achieve not only protection, but also price stability. The latter was particularly important in the case of politically sensitive commodities such as rice and, sometimes, coconuts. Tariffs on agricultural imports were gradually reduced until 1993, and, in January 1995, as part of the Uruguay Round Agreement on Agriculture, the government bound all its tariffs on agricultural goods at a uniform rate of 50 percent, although this was well above the applied tariffs. Subsequently, the government removed quantitative restrictions on all agricultural imports except wheat and wheat flour. In fact, some of the most important changes after the early 1990s involved not so much the level of the restrictions, but the shift from various forms of nontariff barriers, including regulatory interventions, to more transparent tariff-based import restrictions. The various indicators of assistance described hereafter confirm that the policy regime in recent years has generally provided assistance to import-competing agriculture and that it has done this at rates similar to the rates of assistance in manufacturing.[10]

Despite periods of slow progress and occasional backsliding, the trend in overall policy has been toward progressive liberalization, and the country now has perhaps the most open trade regime in South Asia. The evolution of the overall structure of incentives may be seen by looking at changes in the manufacturing sector and the two main parts of the agricultural sector. During the reforms in 1977, the implicit rates of protection for manufacturing and for many import-competing agricultural commodities were extremely high. Even after the major reforms, in 1979, the estimated effective rate of protection in the manufacturing sector was 137 percent (Cuthbertson and Athukorala 1990). This had fallen to 90 percent in 1981, and was estimated at 77 percent in 1991 and 43 percent in 1994 (World Bank 2004). By 2005, liberalization had progressed in the manufacturing sector.

There was also an important effort toward liberalizing import competition in the food industry. Wheat imports were liberalized by ending a government-granted long-term monopoly in flour milling to Prima, a company based in

Singapore, that had also given the company a virtual monopoly on the supply of animal feed. Government trading enterprises play a role in domestic distribution and in international trade, but it is minor.

Trade policy continues to protect rice and several other import-competing food crops, such as potatoes, through tariffs and specific duties that vary seasonally. The interventions respond to domestic conditions in price and supply. Furthermore, despite the shrinking share of agriculture in GDP and employment, agricultural producer subsidies remain important, and the government experiences intense pressure to maintain and even expand these subsidies. For example, a fertilizer subsidy is still used that is targeted largely, though not solely, toward import-competing crops, particularly those cultivated by smallholders. Periodically, a fertilizer subsidy has been a component of government assistance in agriculture, and populist governments have used the subsidy to appeal to the politically important farming community. Until recently, the aggregate assistance effect of the subsidy would have not been large, but the amount of the subsidy was doubled in 2005–06, and the cost of the subsidy may have risen by an additional one-third, to SLRs 11 billion (around $100 million) or more in 2007 (figure 12.4). There are also frequent ad hoc changes in import policies, particularly in the case of subsidiary food crops such as potatoes and onions, over which small—but politically powerful—farm groups exercise much political clout.

Thus, the broad contours of agricultural policies in Sri Lanka appear to resemble today some aspects of the early agricultural policy evolution in more

Figure 12.4. Fertilizer Subsidy, Sri Lanka, 1962–2007

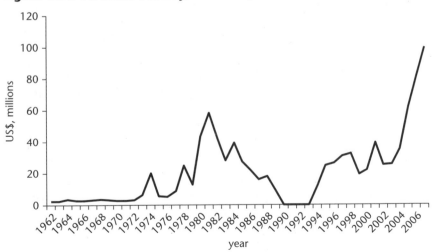

Source: CBSL, "Economic and Social Statistics," various.

well-developed East Asian economies: overall, the trade regime is relatively liberal, but it grants significant protection to particular import-competing agricultural industries. In the next section, we present our estimates of a number of indicators of the incentives for major agricultural products and various categories of commodities, such as exportables and import-competing products. We also attempt to explain the changing patterns in agricultural taxation and assistance since independence that have led to the current outcome.

Direct and Indirect Distortions in Incentives

The main focus of our study's methodology for estimating the extent of distortions to agricultural incentives is on government-imposed measures that create a gap between actual domestic prices and these prices as they would be under free market conditions. (For details on the methodology, see appendix A and Anderson et al. 2008.) Because it is not possible to understand the characteristics of agricultural development through a sectoral view alone, our methodology estimates the effects of direct agricultural policy measures, including distortions in the foreign exchange market, but also distortions in nonagricultural sectors that compete with farmers for mobile resources such as labor and capital. More specifically, our study computes nominal rates of assistance (NRAs) for farmers. We also generate NRAs for nonagricultural tradables for comparison with NRAs for agricultural tradables through the calculation of relative rates of assistance (RRAs).

We present, in table 12.2 our estimates of the temporal patterns in the distortions to agricultural incentives for seven major commodities from 1955 to 2004: three exportables (rubber, coconuts, and tea) and four import-competing products (rice, potatoes, onions, and chilies).[11] In table 12.3, we show our guesstimates of the NRAs for noncovered farm products, which account for around one-third of the overall value of agricultural production. The guesstimates assume that the noncovered products are equally divided among exportables, nontradables, and import-competing products (one-third each of the residual value of farm production). They also assume that the NRAs are zero for nontradables and, for exportables and importables, are equal to the estimated NRAs for the two subsets of covered products (all of which are tradable). Farm input assistance was minor before 2005, and, so, we include no estimate for such non-product-specific assistance. The NRAs for nonagricultural tradables are based on the import duty collection rate for import-competing manufacturing and our assumption that the direct assistance to nonagricultural exportables is zero.[12] This method may substantially underestimate the actual rate of manufacturing protection because high tariffs or binding nontariff barriers may lead to lower import volumes and therefore lower collection rates on import duties. We believe the nonagricultural NRAs before

Table 12.2. NRAs for Covered Agricultural Products, Sri Lanka, 1955–2004
(five-year averages, %)

Product, indicator	1955–59	1960–64	1965–69	1970–74	1975–79	1980–84	1985–89	1990–94	1995–99	2000–04
Exportables[a]	−22.8	−40.0	−38.6	−41.1	−45.2	−31.1	−21.4	−24.2	−2.0	5.9
Rubber	−15.8	−51.5	−48.9	−56.2	−59.6	−51.4	−37.7	−21.8	−4.4	−0.2
Coconuts	−28.6	−29.6	−24.9	−32.8	−36.5	−19.6	−5.1	−34.6	−1.3	16.7
Tea	−22.3	−39.4	−39.1	−36.8	−37.4	−30.4	−25.6	−12.6	−1.5	−1.2
Importables[a]	62.5	11.9	−5.9	9.0	−3.7	−0.6	−2.1	22.4	31.8	12.8
Rice	62.5	11.9	−5.9	9.0	−7.7	−5.8	0.1	8.6	19.2	3.7
Potatoes	—	—	—	—	77.6	43.3	32.6	157.7	124.8	205.8
Onions	—	—	—	—	−11.6	28.7	−12.6	43.7	79.3	53.4
Chilies	—	—	—	—	52.6	33.4	6.9	62.1	76.9	67.2
All covered products[a]	−10.3	−29.9	−30.0	−20.3	−31.9	−19.2	−12.6	−1.7	11.5	8.6
Dispersion, covered products[b]	44.2	28.7	20.9	31.9	26.2	22.8	22.4	25.0	20.8	12.6
Coverage, at undistorted prices	66	66	67	65	64	63	67	65	62	64

Source: Bandara and Jayasuriya 2007.

Note: — = no data are available.

a. Weighted averages; the weights are based on the unassisted value of production.
b. Dispersion is a simple five-year average of the annual standard deviation around the weighted mean of the NRAs of covered products.

Table 12.3. NRAs in Agriculture Relative to Nonagricultural Industries, Sri Lanka, 1955–2004
(percent)

Indicator	1955–59	1960–64	1965–69	1970–74	1975–79	1980–84	1985–89	1990–94	1995–99	2000–04
Covered products[a]	−10.3	−29.9	−30.0	−20.3	−31.9	−19.2	−12.6	−1.7	11.5	8.6
Noncovered products	13.2	−9.3	−14.8	−10.7	−16.3	−10.6	−7.8	−0.6	9.9	6.2
All agricultural products[a]	−2.4	−23.0	−24.9	−16.9	−26.4	−16.0	−11.1	−1.4	10.9	7.7
Non-product-specific assistance	0.0	0.2	0.4	0.6	0.8	2.4	1.1	0.1	1.3	1.7
Total agricultural NRA[b]	−2.4	−22.8	−24.5	−16.3	−25.5	−13.5	−9.9	−1.2	12.2	9.5
Trade bias index[c]	−0.52	−0.45	−0.35	−0.45	−0.43	−0.31	−0.18	−0.38	−0.25	−0.05
NRA, all agricultural tradables	−2.7	−25.7	−27.6	−18.5	−29.0	−15.4	−11.2	−1.3	14.0	10.8
NRA, all nonagricultural tradables	104.9	124.6	138.4	70.7	52.9	57.1	59.0	47.1	36.4	22.9
RRA[d]	−52.5	−66.6	−68.0	−51.6	−53.5	−46.2	−44.3	−32.9	−16.3	−9.8
Memorandum items: ignoring exchange rate distortions[d]										
NRA, all agricultural products	−2.4	−12.9	−15.2	−11.0	−19.7	−11.0	−8.0	−0.9	11.7	9.5
Agricultural trade bias index	−0.52	−0.21	−0.06	−0.23	−0.23	−0.22	−0.09	−0.34	−0.24	−0.05
Relative rate of assistance	−52.5	−61.7	−63.9	−48.0	−49.2	−44.3	−42.9	−32.6	−16.8	−9.8

Source: Bandara and Jayasuriya 2007.

a. Including product-specific input subsidies.

b. Including product-specific input subsidies and non-product-specific assistance. Represents total assistance to primary factors and intermediate inputs, divided by the total value of primary agriculture production at undistorted prices.

c. The trade bias index is defined as $(1 + NRAag_x/100)/(1 + NRAag_m/100) - 1$, where $NRAag_m$ and $NRAag_x$ are the average percentage NRAs for the import-competing and exportable parts of the agricultural sector, respectively.

d. The RRA is defined as $100*[(100 + NRAag^t)/(100 + NRAnonag^t) - 1]$, where $NRAag^t$ and $NRAnonag^t$ are the percentage NRAs for the tradables parts of the agricultural and nonagricultural sectors, respectively.

liberalization in 1977–78 would be significantly higher than the NRAs indicated by these data. We also believe that the RRAs may therefore correspondingly underestimate the policy bias against agriculture. (Annual time series NRAs and the shares of various commodities in the value of production are tabulated in appendix B.)

Export crops

We first focus on export crops and then import-competing products. We refer especially to our five-year average NRA estimates in table 12.2 and our annual estimates in figures 12.5–12.8.

Tea

The annual NRA estimates for tea, which are based on the ratio of the domestic Colombo Auction price and the average free on board export price of bulk leaf tea, suggest that the tea industry was taxed by more than 30 percent until the mid-1980s (figure 12.5). Thereafter, the estimated rate of taxation declined sharply as export taxes were progressively lowered and then largely abolished by the early 1990s. The NRAs fluctuated around this trend primarily because the export tax rate was on a sliding scale such that taxation was higher during periods of high international prices. There was thus a steep increase in taxes in the immediate

Figure 12.5. NRAs for Tea, Sri Lanka, 1955–2004

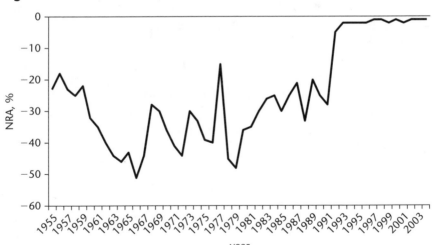

Source: Bandara and Jayasuriya 2007.

aftermath of the 1977 reforms that was associated with the exchange rate depreciation accompanying the liberalization (which increased the domestic currency price on which the tax was based), as well as with the international tea price increase of the early 1980s. There is no evidence for the existence of significant market imperfections within the domestic market for tea production, processing, and wholesale marketing through the auction. The Colombo Tea Auction is considered quite competitive, though there has been criticism of the system. Hence, the rate of export taxes and cesses provides a reasonable estimate of the NRAs. It is not possible to use domestic and border price data to compute NRAs directly because of the growth in the importance of value added teas (tea bags and so on) for which reliable border prices are not available.

Not reflected in figure 12.5 is the fact that tea imports have been effectively subject to a near total ban until recently, ostensibly to ensure that inexpensive foreign teas are not reexported as quality Ceylon tea. There has been some relaxation in the ban, but a prohibitive tariff has nonetheless effectively ensured that tea imports are negligible. As a result, the country has lost the chance to develop a tea blending industry, and Dubai has emerged as the center of this lucrative industry, which relies on significant quantities of Sri Lankan tea and imported Sri Lankan labor (Ganewatta 2002).

Rubber
The annual NRAs for sheet rubber are based on the percentage gap between the average domestic Colombo Auction price for sheet rubber and the average free on board price of rubber. They suggest that the tax on this industry was over 50 percent higher than the tax on the tea industry until the early 1980s. Since then, the rate of taxation has declined fairly rapidly (figure 12.6). Reflecting the virtual elimination of export taxes, the NRA estimates have averaged close to zero in recent years. They have fluctuated around the trend primarily because the export tax rate was on a sliding scale such that taxation was higher during periods of high international prices. Similar to the situation in tea, the rate of export taxes and cesses provides a reasonable estimate of NRAs in recent years given that it is difficult to compute reliable NRAs from available price data because of the changes in the composition of exported rubber.

Coconuts
Coconut products (copra, oil, fiber and coir products, and so on) were a major export product category at the time of independence. Export volumes have since fallen. Because of the importance of coconuts as a food crop and in the production of coconut oil for household consumption (coconut oil is the most widely used cooking oil), coconuts have attracted significant direct price and nonprice

Figure 12.6. NRAs for Rubber, Sri Lanka, 1955–2004

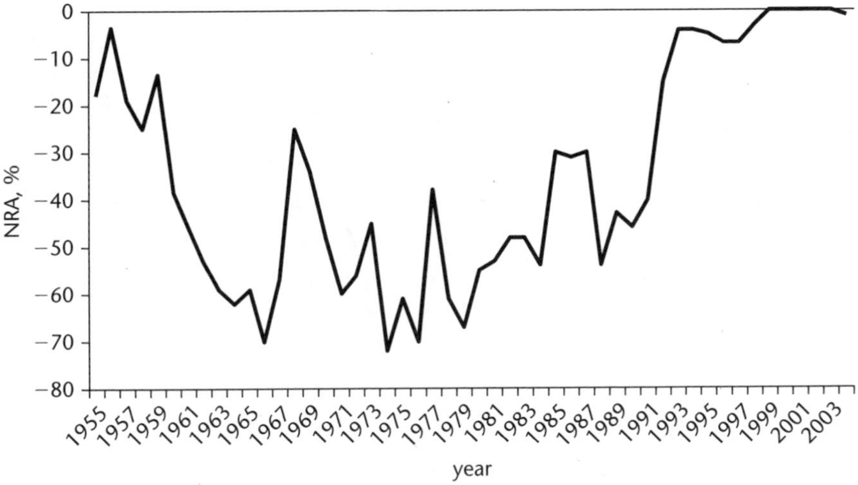

Source: Bandara and Jayasuriya 2007.

interventions by the government, which has thereby sought to stabilize domestic prices, while maintaining reasonable producer prices (de Silva 1979). However, imported palm oil has emerged as a viable substitute for coconut oil in many domestic uses. Thus, in more recent years, coconut oil has come to be considered an import-competing product. Up to the early 1980s, the NRA estimates suggest that the tax on the coconut industry was similar to the tax on tea (hence, less than the tax on rubber), but, thereafter, the taxation averaged closer to zero (figure 12.7). In the late 1990s and early 2000s, the industry enjoyed positive NRAs. This reflects the fact that imported palm oil has become a viable substitute for coconut oil in many uses, and protection from this competition raised the domestic price of coconuts above the price as it would have been without the palm oil import restrictions. In the case of coconuts, the reductions in export taxes did not generate corresponding reductions in the NRAs because of the trade restrictions (such as export bans) imposed on coconuts and coconut products to maintain low consumer prices and reasonable producer prices.

Import-competing farm products

Rice
The patterns in the NRAs for rice reflect the fluctuating impacts of direct government interventions in response to changes in domestic supplies and international

Figure 12.7. NRAs for Coconuts, Sri Lanka, 1955–2004

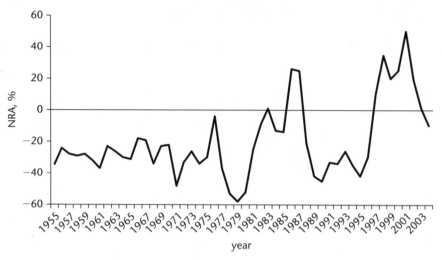

Source: Bandara and Jayasuriya 2007.

Figure 12.8. NRAs for Rice, Sri Lanka, 1955–2004

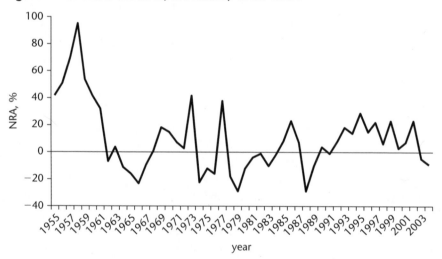

Source: Bandara and Jayasuriya 2007.

prices. Apart from the 1980s, the average NRAs during each decade have been positive, which is consistent with the fact that average domestic consumer and producer rice prices have usually been above the average import cost, insurance, and freight prices (table 12.2 and figure 12.8).[13]

Pressure for assistance emerges if domestic prices fall whether because of a bumper harvest at home or a fall in the price of imports. Rather than increase domestic prices through direct purchases, the response to such political pressures from the rice farming lobby has usually involved raising import barriers and expanding input subsidies for fertilizer, research and development, and so on. The ad hoc policy shifts in rice import tariffs since 1995 are outlined in Bandara and Jayasuriya (2007), while figure 12.4 indicates the dramatic increase in the fertilizer subsidy in recent years.

To obtain a fuller picture of rice policy, one should place the policy in the context of the wider policies on cereal staples, particularly wheat, which is the closest substitute for rice in consumption although it is not produced domestically. Rice consumption averages around 100 kilograms per capita per year, but wheat consumption has increased, along with urbanization, from less than 25 kilograms per capita during the 1950s to nearly 50 kilograms now. For wheat flour, the consumer tax equivalent of import measures was low and sometimes even negative until the early 1980s, but it then increased significantly and has since fluctuated widely around an average value of more than 50 percent.

Chilies, onions, and potatoes

High rates of import protection were enjoyed by producers of chilies and onions in the protectionist period before liberalization, but the level of protection declined after the liberalization in 1977/78. In contrast, the protection for potatoes increased sharply in the postliberalization period, particularly in the 1990s. Although imports were briefly liberalized around 1996, potatoes, which are produced by only a few thousand farmers, have continued to enjoy a preeminent position among protected crops.[14]

Sugar

NRAs are not provided for sugar because sugar is predominantly imported, and the amount of domestic production is quite small, although sugar has been heavily protected. The level of protection has declined since the 1980s, but remains quite high. During the period up to the late 1970s, when consumer food subsidies were not uncommon, sugar was an exception. The high tariff on sugar brought in government revenue that helped maintain other food subsidy expenditures.

Agricultural versus nonagricultural assistance

The products covered in table 12.2 account for about two-thirds of the overall value of agricultural production. The weighted average NRAs for these products were around −30 percent in the 1960s and 1970s, but, following the reforms of the late 1970s, they rose to around −15 percent in the 1980s, −2 percent in the

Figure 12.9. NRAs for Exportable, Import-Competing, and All Agricultural Products, Sri Lanka, 1955–2004

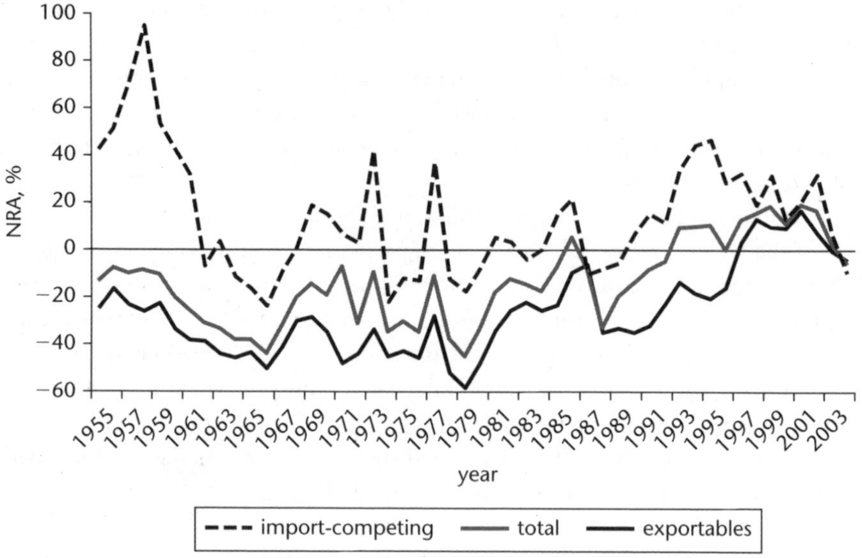

Source: Bandara and Jayasuriya 2007.

first half of the 1990s, and an average of around 10 percent thereafter. The picture does not change much if our assumptions about the NRAs for noncovered products are included (top of table 12.3). This allows us to conclude that the direct taxing of the agricultural sector has been gradually phased out over the past three decades. We do not mean to indicate that the sector is without price distortions given that there is still some dispersion in the product NRAs; in particular, the NRAs for exportables remain below the NRAs for importables. However, these indicators of dispersion are now well below the levels of earlier decades. This is depicted in figure 12.9 and is also captured in the trade bias index shown in the middle of table 12.3.

Also important for intersectoral resource allocation is the extent to which nonagricultural tradables have been assisted by government policy. Prior to the 1977 reforms, the protection for import-competing manufacturing was extremely high. Even if we take account of the lower assistance to producers of other tradables, the NRAs for all nonagricultural tradable sectors were well over 100 percent prior to the 1970s. By the late 1970s, they had fallen to below 60 percent. Since the early 1990s, they have fallen more and are now below 25 percent. If we combine these estimates with the estimates for agriculture to generate the RRAs, the full

Figure 12.10. NRAs for Agricultural and Nonagricultural Tradables and the RRA, Sri Lanka, 1955–2004

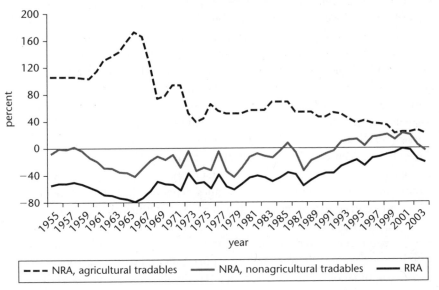

Source: Bandara and Jayasuriya 2007.

Note: For the definition of the RRA, see table 12.3, note d.

extent of the discrimination against farmers becomes evident. As shown in the middle rows of table 12.3, the RRA values suggest that, during the 1960s, farmers received only one-third of the prices they would have received had markets for both farm and nonfarm goods been free (the RRA average of −67 percent). In the 1970s, the extent of discrimination was not much less (the RRA average of −53 percent). The average RRA continued to fall, to around −45 percent in the 1980s, −25 percent in the 1990s, and to slightly less than −10 percent in recent years. As is clear from figure 12.10, the decline in the protection for manufacturing did more to reduce the distortions harming farmers then did the changes in direct agricultural policies. Likewise, exchange rate distortions were not a major contributor to this trend in average NRA and RRA values, but they did affect the antitrade bias of past policies substantially (see the bottom rows of table 12.3).

The Political Economy of Agricultural Policies

What were the political forces behind the government's agricultural policy choices? We consider the export subsector first and, then, the import-competing subsector.

Export crops

At independence, relatively large-scale, foreign-owned companies dominated in tea and, to a lesser extent, in rubber. Even the coconut subsector, though largely smallholder based, still relied on a significant number of large estates. There was little political sympathy for the plantation subsector from the left of center coalitions that ruled the country from 1956 to 1965 (with a brief interruption in 1960) and then again in 1970–77. The foreign plantations were under threat of nationalization beginning in 1956, and they were finally nationalized in the mid-1970s when all large holdings were subjected to land reform. The majority of the initial workers on the large plantations had migrated from southern India beginning in the mid-19th century, and plantation workers were politically marginalized through disenfranchisement during the first postindependence government. Most importantly perhaps, government revenues depended heavily on foreign trade taxes, and export duties alone contributed nearly one-third of all government revenues during the first decade after independence. Because of slow economic growth, governments were continually under fiscal pressure and had little scope, even if they desired to do so, to reduce export taxes on plantation crops.

The combination of high taxes, secular falls in real world prices, and threats of nationalization led to slow, but steady decline in the plantation subsector, particularly the large plantations. The subsector became based more on smallholders, a process that accelerated after the land reforms. Large foreign-owned firms passed into state ownership. The 1977 liberalization did not have an immediate positive impact on these industries, however. The exchange rate reforms, which involved a significant nominal devaluation, failed to have much of a positive impact on the subsector. This was because the structure of the progressive export taxes, which including a sliding tax scale, effectively taxed away most of the gains of devaluation and the periodic relative price improvements.

The plantation crop subsector and its role within the economy had changed in quite fundamental ways by the mid-1980s. The subsector's share of the national economy had shrunk, and new investments in replantings and factory modernization were clearly essential if the decline of the subsector was to be arrested. The political tensions that emerged in the aftermath of the 1977 liberalization made the government more sensitive to the political importance of plantation crop cultivators. Plantation crops were cultivated almost entirely in the wetter central, western, and southern regions of the country, and the cultivators were predominantly members of the majority Sinhalese community, the support of which was critical if the governing political parties were to stay in power. Also, the export taxes on plantation crops directly reduced the revenues of large state-owned plantations. These factors combined to erode the economic and political incentives for maintaining the traditional regime of high export taxes.

Import-competing crops

We have seen that government policies toward import-competing crops have not been uniform. Furthermore, in the case of key staple food crops and, most importantly, in the case of rice, there has been tension between the twin objectives of producer support and maintenance of low consumer prices. The enduring theme of import-competing agricultural policy in the postindependence period is this difficult balancing act between producers and consumers in staple food crops. This is well illustrated if we examine policies in the rice sector.

Rice policy

Rice is the most sensitive political commodity. Aided by proceeds from high commodity prices during the Korean War, immediate postindependence governments were able to maintain or expand the policy of providing inexpensive subsidized rice to consumers through a universal rice ration that they had inherited from British colonial rulers. Rationing formed a central component in a wider political strategy that aimed at undercutting the potential threat from a Marxist political left that had strong roots within trade unions. An attempt to reduce the rice subsidy in 1953 brought the country to the verge of revolution. Subsequent attempts to reduce the subsidy almost invariably led to the downfall or political humiliation of the government administration. Subsidized rice distributed through the ration system became a symbol of the political power of powerful left-wing parties.

Rice has enormous symbolism and emotive power in Sri Lanka. Rice self-sufficiency has been a slogan that has found appeal in deep-seated nationalist aspirations, particularly among the Sinhalese, whose history has included an ancient civilization based on irrigated rice cultivation and who were stirred by the vision, irrespective of historical precision, of a golden age when Sri Lanka had exported rice to other parts of Asia and was the granary of the East. At a more mundane level, landed rice cultivators and powerful rice millers exert much clout in garnering electoral support for particular political parties. In Sri Lanka, the drive to attain rice self-sufficiency was not only a means of achieving a Green Revolution on existing rice lands. Beginning already in the 1930s, the promotion of rice cultivation through land settlement schemes or colonization schemes was linked to the restoration of the ancient glory of the Sinhalese in the sparsely populated dry zone, which had been the cradle of the ancient hydraulic empire. The restoration of old irrigation systems that was initiated by the British during colonial times and the construction of new, grandiose irrigation systems were seen as a vehicle for new Sinhalese farmer settlements in those parts of the country that had been largely abandoned.[15] As Bruton (1992, 82) points out, "the paddy society was almost entirely Sinhalese."

Thus, the rice self-sufficiency drive became associated with the rising Sinhala nationalism of the postindependence era.

In addition to the free or subsidized provision of irrigation water, fertilizers, seeds, research, extension, and other assistance for producers, the government purchased paddy from farmers at a guaranteed price through a state trading entity. It distributed varying quantities of rice rations to consumers at subsidized prices until the late 1970s, including a period when some rationed rice was distributed free of charge (1966–78). Farmers also sold rice to private buyers, who milled it themselves or sold it to millers, who sold it on the open market. In 1972, facing rising international prices and seeking to increase domestic supplies at lower prices, the government granted monopoly procurement rights to the state-owned Paddy Marketing Board. However, the monopoly could not be enforced and was abolished in 1975.[16] The government has continued to regulate international trade and supplies to maintain stable consumer prices. This remains a central goal of food policy.[17]

The nonuniform pattern of trade liberalization beginning in 1977 may only be understood if we recognize the central political role of rice in consumption and in production. The reform government of 1977 was led by J. R. Jayewardene, who was a lifelong opponent of the left, was strongly pro-Western in foreign policy, and had tried and failed once to dismantle the rice subsidy scheme. The Accelerated Mahaweli Development Project now played a critical political role by providing the crucial popular political support that enabled the Jayewardene government to dismantle the rice subsidy scheme and crush the traditional political left, while implementing major liberalization measures.

However, the end of the rice subsidy scheme did not mean that the domestic prices for rice were left to the market so that rice producers would be exposed to the pressure of cheap imports. Post-1977 government policies continued to aim at consumer price stabilization around a reasonable price, while assisting producers through input subsidies and import protection. The NRAs in rice also reflect the impact of changes in the international price and weather-related domestic supply. Because nontariff barriers insulate domestic markets from international markets, changes in domestic supply change domestic prices and, even in the absence of any change in the policy regime, change estimated NRAs. Hence, good harvests depress domestic prices and generate pressures for assistance and increased protection.

Its signature of the Uruguay Round Agreement on Agriculture in 1994 did not constrain the government from exercising a high degree of discretion in changing tariffs because the applied tariffs were significantly lower than the bound tariffs. The government has frequently chosen to alter import tariffs in response to domestic pressures. For example, beginning in 1995, rice imports were subject to a tariff of 35 percent. An import licensing requirement was also imposed in

July 2000. In July 2001, when the domestic price for rice rose because of a production shortfall, the government allowed the state-run Cooperative Wholesale Establishment, as well as private traders, to import rice duty-free, waiving the 35 percent tariff. Then, in January 2002, a specific duty, SLRs 7 per kilogram, replaced the tariff, although the Cooperative Wholesale Establishment was allowed to import rice at a special duty of SLRs 4 per kilogram. In March 2002, the licensing requirement was removed, and the special duty was raised to SLRs 5 per kilogram. The special duty was raised again, to SLRs 7, in March 2003, SLRs 9 in August 2003, and SLRs 20 in January 2006 (see IPS 2003; WTO 2004; Bandara and Jayasuriya 2007).

These policy gyrations reflect the political power of the large rice producers and processors, but also the sensitivity of governments to consumer opposition to increases in the price of the main staple food. The policy liberalization in 1977 clearly reduced the high levels of protection, but protection has not been trending downward since then. Sri Lanka is considered a high-cost rice producer at the fringe; so, the sector would come under considerable pressure, particularly in marginal areas, if trade were fully liberalized.[18] It would be a mistake to assume that the negative NRAs for rice observed in 2003 and 2004, for example, represent a permanent policy shift. The difficult balancing act between serving producer and consumer interests will continue. The policy responses will be most sensitive to domestic price movements. High domestic prices will tend to induce import liberalization, while low domestic prices will tend to induce import restrictions or input subsidies (constrained, of course, by the need to control fiscal deficits).

Wheat and sugar import policies

The changes in government policies toward wheat have been closely linked to government rice policies. During the 1950s and 1960s, when the government was providing a subsidized rice ration for consumers, a significant proportion of the ration rice had to be imported because domestic procurement was inadequate. The government had an incentive to encourage the substitution of wheat for rice in consumption to reduce the fiscal burden of the rice subsidy because wheat was relatively less expensive than rice in international markets. Meanwhile, some wheat was also provided through United States government aid. With the phase-out of the subsidized rice ration scheme starting in 1979, the incentives changed. Thus, beginning in the early 1980s, rice was implicitly protected through tougher restrictions on wheat imports.[19]

Sugar imports were heavily taxed before liberalization. Tax levels have declined since 1977, but are still high. There is a simple explanation for the heavy taxation before liberalization: almost all sugar was imported; there was little domestic production; and import taxes contributed to reducing the fiscal burden imposed by other food subsidies. The prevailing domestic price for sugar was accepted by consumers although it was much higher than the international price. So long as domestic prices were not increased too much, there was little political opposition to the maintenance of this implicit protection. The high protection of the sugar industry in recent years has not been maintained so much to raise government revenue, but, rather, to honor an agreement signed in the early 1980s by the government and a foreign private enterprise.[20]

Chilies and onions

The liberalization of 1977 involved import liberalization that was selective and discriminatory. The agricultural subsectors chosen for liberalization or ongoing protection had a clear regional dimension that also overlapped with ethnicity. The protectionist policies before liberalization had benefited subsidiary food crops such as chilies and red onions, as well as crops such as grapes. Protection had encouraged the expansion of these crops in particular regions, such as the Jaffna Peninsula. Jaffna District produced two-thirds of the country's entire production of red onions. The dependency of local farmers on these high-value crops was such that, by 1977/78, red onions and chilies accounted for around 75 percent of the total area devoted to nonrice (minor food crop) cultivation in Jaffna District (DCS 1979). It was also the only dry zone district that was in a rice deficit. The 1977 liberalization produced a sharp fall in protection. Despite the negative income effects on producers, the opposition of producers to the reform was ineffective. The ability of Jaffna farmers to obtain any response to their demands was constrained by the "marginality of the Sri Lankan Tamils to the electoral system as a whole" (Moore 1985, 109).

Even so, this issue played an important role in Jaffna in the 1982 presidential elections. The escalation of ethnic tensions into a full-scale secessionist war beginning in 1983 has had devastating effects on the agricultural economy in the northern and eastern provinces. During the past two decades, commercial ties with the rest of the country have been massively disrupted. As an upshot of these developments, farmers in the southern regions have expanded their production of minor food crops, and this has changed the political dynamics behind government policies in minor crops. This is most clear in the policies toward potatoes, for example. A small group of producers was able to gather significant political clout, and the consumer resistance to high prices could be largely ignored. Despite occasional declines, the protection for potatoes has tended to increase over time, and this has also been accompanied by increases, though to a lesser degree, in crops such as red onions and chilies (see table 12.2). From many viewpoints, a strong case can be made for removing the assistance for potato production, particularly given its destructive impact on the country's fragile ecosystems, including the most important river catchments and repositories of significant sources of biodiversity. As Bruton (1992, 170) points out, "the strong commitment to the Sinhalese culture made it difficult to design an economic policy that was equally appropriate for both major ethnic groups." There can be little doubt that the pattern of liberalization in 1977/78 is suggestive of a strong ethnic bias. However, the near-complete marginalization of Tamil farmers in the north and east from mainstream political life and the collapse of the agricultural economy in these regions beginning in the mid-1980s because of war have meant that the role of ethnicity has diminished in agricultural policy formulation. Tensions between producer and consumer interests have thereby become the dominant political economy issue.

Future Prospects

Our discussion of the political economy of agricultural policies has pointed to a range of factors that have influenced policy formation in agricultural crops. The broad sweep of trade liberalization since the late 1970s has not passed the agricultural sector by. More progress in liberalization is likely if many smaller import-competing subsectors are unable to withstand the pressure for reform and liberalization. Liberalization will be difficult in the case of rice, the most politically sensitive industry. The history of agricultural policy in Sri Lanka and the experience of other countries in Asia suggest that this will remain the strongest bastion of protectionist pressures in the country. Even recently, whenever the rice industry has been put under stress because of falling prices, the government has faced pressure to placate the industry. Almost invariably the government has ceded to the pressure and maintained the historical pattern of special treatment for rice. Arguably, the course of future agricultural trade liberalization will depend on the extent to which rice producers are able to retain their political influence. Nonetheless, as long as rice and wheat are major items in the consumption basket, the level of direct price protection will be constrained by the need to satisfy consumer interests, particularly if international prices spike at high levels as they did in 2008. Fiscal pressures will also place a limit on the ability of the government to provide assistance through input subsidies. One wonders if the government will be able to maintain the level and type of protection now being offered to the livestock, chicken, and dairy industries, the data on which have not been adequate for inclusion in this study.

Notes

1. For reviews of the government's agricultural policy in Sri Lanka, see Thorbecke and Svejnar (1987); Bhalla (1991); World Bank (1995); Athukorala and Kelegama (1998); Anderson (2002); Sanderatne (2004).

2. The minor export crops are often referred to as nontraditional agricultural exports to distinguish them from the traditional exports of tea, rubber, and coconuts although many of these crops have been exported for thousands of years, while tea and rubber were introduced in the country only in the late 19th century.

3. For more on policy regimes and the growth experience, see Athukorala and Jayasuriya (1994); Athukorala and Rajapatirana (2000); Kelegama (2004); Weerakoon (2004); World Bank (2004).

4. The cost of the war between 1983 and 2000 has been conservatively estimated at twice the value of the country's GDP in 1996 (Arunatilaka, Jayasuriya, and Kelegama 2001).

5. Agriculture's contribution to net exports is greater than implied by these gross export data because the garment exports that dominate manufactured exports have a large import content (Athukorala and Bandara 1989).

6. See Athukorala and Jayasuriya (1994) for a description of these developments. Athukorala and Rajapatirana (2000) provide an analysis of developments in the manufacturing sector.

7. The large plantation crop subsector also suffered from investor uncertainty beginning in the mid-1950s and faced the threat of nationalization until the producers were finally taken over by the government in the mid-1970s (Ministry of Plantation Industries, various issues).

8. To reduce the fiscal burden of the consumer rice subsidy, the government had previously encouraged wheat consumption over rice consumption.

9. An appeal to extend the irrigation system to Tamil farming areas was rejected, and the newly irrigated lands were settled largely by members of the majority Sinhalese community. The project was thus resented by sections of the minority Tamil community. This has been highlighted in numerous studies. For example, a study for the Development Assistance Committee pointed out how the project exacerbated ethnic tensions. The study found that the conspicuous absence of consideration of the project's possible negative impact on simmering tensions was striking, considering that the project had glaring ethno-political implications: (a) there was an ethnic overlay to the geographical areas which would benefit (or not) from the project; and (b) the government decision to resettle displaced Sinhalese villagers in traditionally Tamil regions. The decision by the Jayawardene government to compress and accelerate the 30-year program into 6 years further exacerbated ethnic tensions. The original version of the program had included irrigation projects in the Tamil-majority Northern Province; but this was removed from the accelerated program with the argument that it would be too expensive and problematic technically.

These facts, reported by Bush (1999), are well known, extensively documented, and not contested by any serious scholar of Sri Lanka:

> Since the 1930s and especially the 1940s resettlement projects have been implemented in Sri Lanka to alleviate the growing shortage of land in the south-west, where the population is largely Sinhalese. Sri Lanka's Tamils have opposed these projects because they threaten to change the ethnic majority in the provinces concerned to the disadvantage of the Tamils and Muslims. With the Mahaweli project, which has been planned since the 1960s and consists of a large number of subsidiary energy generation projects, the country's largest scheme was launched, the aim being to use at least 74 percent of the settled area—where Tamils previously formed the majority of the population—for Sinhalese. The Sinhalese settlement projects became one of the decisive motivating factors in the Tamils' resistance. This is not least evident from the many attacks on colonies of new Sinhalese settlers during the civil war. (Klingebiel 2001, 10)

According to another study, the scheme was redesigned in a way that excluded the largely Tamil-populated Northern Province (also see Moore 1985):

> The choice of projects to be developed also reflects the focus on Sinhalese settlement. Under the Water Resources Development Plan, systems J, K, and L and part of system I fell within the Northern Province and were to irrigate 232,000 acres by a Northern Central Province canal. None of these systems were included in the accelerated program. (Peebles 1990, 43)

The World Bank, a major donor, subsequently acknowledged the problems related to the project's perceived ethnic bias: "Donors may have missed a significant opportunity to promote equitable participation through the huge Mahaweli power, irrigation, and resettlement scheme" (Kreimer at al. 1998, 22).

10. Athukorala and Kelegama (1998) suggest that the level of protection for manufacturing tended to be overestimated given the use of gazetted tariff rates, which were often higher than actual tariffs because of various loopholes and exemptions. However, the same may be true of earlier estimates of the effective assistance to agriculture. For example, the World Bank (1995) produced estimates that attempted to take into account the provision of free or subsidized inputs such as the irrigation water used for many import-competing crops grown under irrigated conditions, including rice. We believe the approach used to derive the implicit subsidy associated with free irrigation water tended to overestimate the subsidy.

11. Some commodities, such as livestock and dairying, are not included in this exercise because of the severe data limitations. In the livestock subsector, for example, consistent time series data on the domestic prices of meat products are not available, and the international prices for meat products of comparable quality are also not available. The quality differences between domestic products and world market products, except perhaps in the case of chickens, are sufficiently large to make comparisons untenable.

12. Our NRAs for tradables include estimates of the trade tax effect of the overvalued exchange rate. For these estimates, we rely on the black market exchange rate premium (see Global Development Network Growth Database). We also assume that only half the foreign exchange rate earnings of exporters is sold to the government at the official rate. For details on this methodology, see Anderson et al. (2008) and appendix A.

13. For readers familiar with the long history of the government's provision of subsidized rice to consumers, this may seem puzzling. However, the subsidies that are implemented through ration shops apply only to a small fraction of national consumption, such that the weighted average of the (low) price of government-provided rice rations and the open market consumer price is close to the latter.

14. Tobacco also enjoys a high level of protection. According to the World Trade Organization (2004), the average tariff for the tobacco subsector was 149 percent in 1998 and 153 percent in 2003. These rates are well above the bound rate of 50 percent that was applied on most agricultural products.

15. The president and other government leaders were quite explicit about the goal of land settlement. For example, the minister responsible for the Accelerated Mahaweli Development Project, Gamini Dissanayake, wrote that the project represented "a return of the people to the ancient homeland . . . in the Rajarata" (Dissanayake 1983, 6, cited in Tennekoon 1988). Rajarata is the popular name for the area, largely in North Central Province, that was the heartland of the ancient Sinhalese kingdoms.

Nimal Sanderatne, former director of economic research at the Central Bank of Sri Lanka, writes:

Colonization had another political significance in pluralist Sri Lanka. It gave the majority ethnic community the opportunity to resettle Sinhalese in the ancient historical capitals and ancient kingdoms and thereby confirm the area as a Sinhalese rather than a Tamil region. The land settlement issue has been a most controversial issue and was an underlying cause for the ethnic conflict (Sanderatne 2004, 211).

Moore (1985, 96) adds:

Dry Zone development has been explicitly viewed as a means of increasing the Sinhalese population in the historic heartland of Sinhalese civilization. . . . Between 1946 and 1971 the Sinhalese proportion of the population of the five "frontier" districts—Amparai, Batticaloa, Polonnaruwa, Trincomalee, and Anuradhapura—increased from 33 to 51 percent. The main cause was the migration of Sinhalese settlers during new irrigation schemes.

16. The monopoly measures included procurement price increases and prohibitions on the storage and transportation of paddy in bulk. Because of high open-market prices and the activity of private

traders in procuring rice despite the restrictions, the state agency was unable to procure the quantities expected.

17. For a recent comprehensive discussion of the paddy-rice subsector, see Weerahewa (2004). Note that numerous categories of consumer and producer prices have existed for rice and that there are many varieties of rice. This complicates the problem of estimating average prices.

18. The extent of the country's comparative advantage in rice production, if any, has been the subject of studies and much debate. See Abeyratne et al. (1990); Shilpi (1995); Rafeek and Samaratunga (2000); Kikuchi et al. (2000, 2001); Weerahewa, Gunatilake, and Pitigala (2003); Thibbotuwawa (2004).

19. The state monopoly on wheat imports and the distribution of wheat that prevailed until 2001 (through the Cooperative Wholesale Establishment) enabled the government to influence domestic grain prices. Prima, a Singapore-based company, was granted a monopoly on wheat milling in 1980 under a 20-year agreement signed by the government (and extended for five more years in 2000). The Cooperative Wholesale Establishment supplied wheat to this monopoly miller until 2001, when Prima was granted the right to import wheat. Prima also gained a virtual monopoly in the animal feed sector because it was allowed to retain the wheat bran and other milling by-products and because it had bought out the only viable competitor (a state agency that had been privatized). During the contract period, Prima could import wheat grain and mill-related equipment duty-free; it also enjoyed exemptions on income taxes. Prima's monopoly in wheat imports ended in 2006, but this step is being challenged in the courts. The official justification for the agreement with Prima is that the agreement helped attract a wheat miller to Sri Lanka. This has certainly come at a large cost to the country. Clearly, the special privileges offered to a foreign-owned entity impose a burden on consumers, while not providing any benefits to producers—no wheat is produced in the country—or in government revenues. We refrain from speculating on the reason the government supplied these special privileges to a large foreign firm with no obvious compensating benefits for the country. For a fuller discussion, see Athukorala and Kelegama (1998).

20. The agreement is strikingly similar to the Prima wheat agreement. The sugar agreement imposes a huge cost on domestic consumers, while delivering substantial profits to the subsidiary of a giant sugar producer based in the United States. As in the case of Prima, this agreement has been justified by the government on the grounds that it attracted a foreign investor. Other explanations are also possible. Issues that have been raised by the sugar agreement include good governance, complicity, rent extraction, and rent sharing.

References

Abeyratne, F., E. Neville, W. G. Somaratne, and P. Wickramaarachchi. 1990. "Efficiency of Rice Production and Issues Relating to Protection." *Sri Lankan Journal of Agricultural Economics* 1 (1): 16–25.

Anderson, K. 2002. "Agricultural Development and Trade Reform: Their Contributions to Economic Growth, Poverty Alleviation, and Food Security in Sri Lanka." Background paper, World Bank, Washington, DC.

Anderson, K., M. Kurzweil, W. Martin, D. Sandri, and E. Valenzuela. 2008. "Measuring Distortions to Agricultural Incentives, Revisited." *World Trade Review* 7 (4): 675–704.

Arunatilake, N., S. Jayasuriya, and S. Kelegama. 2001. "The Economic Cost of the War in Sri Lanka." *World Development* 29 (9): 1483–1500.

Athukorala, P.-C., and J. S. Bandara. 1989. "Growth of Manufactured Exports, Primary Commodity Dependence, and Net Export Earnings: Sri Lanka." *World Development* 17 (8): 897–903.

Athukorala, P.-C., and S. Jayasuriya. 1994. *Macroeconomic Policies, Crises, and Growth in Sri Lanka, 1969–90*. Washington, DC: World Bank.

Athukorala, P.-C., and S. Kelegama. 1998. "The Political Economy of Agricultural Trade Policy: Sri Lanka in the Uruguay Round." *Contemporary South Asia* 7 (1): 7–36.

Athukorala, P.-C., and S. Rajapatirana. 2000. *Liberalisation and Industrial Transformation: Sri Lanka in International Perspective*. New Delhi: Oxford University Press.

Bandara, J., and S. Jayasuriya. 2007. "Distortions to Agricultural Incentives in Sri Lanka." Agricultural Distortions Working Paper 31, World Bank, Washington, DC.

Bhalla, S. 1991. "Sri Lanka." In *Asia*. Vol. 2 of *The Political Economy of Agricultural Pricing Policy*, ed. A. O. Krueger, M. Schiff, and A. Valdés, 195–235. World Bank Comparative Study. Baltimore: Johns Hopkins University Press; Washington, DC: World Bank.

Bruton, H. J. 1992. *Sri Lanka and Malaysia: The Political Economy of Poverty, Equity, and Growth*. World Bank Comparative Study. New York: Oxford University Press; Washington, DC: World Bank.

Bush, K. D. 1999. "The Limits and Scope for the Use of Development Assistance Incentives and Disincentives for Influencing Conflict Situations: Case Study, Sri Lanka." Unpublished report, Development Assistance Committee, Organisation for Economic Co-operation and Development, Paris.

CBSL (Central Bank of Sri Lanka). various years. *Annual Report*. Colombo, Sri Lanka: CBSL.

———. various years. *Economic and Social Statistics of Sri Lanka*. Colombo, Sri Lanka: CBSL.

Cuthbertson, A. G., and P.-C. Athukorala. 1990. "Sri Lanka." In *Liberalizing Foreign Trade: Indonesia, Pakistan and Sri Lanka*, ed. D. Papageorgiou, M. Michaely, and A. M. Choksi, 283–411. Oxford: Basil Blackwell.

DCS (Department of Census and Statistics). 1979. *Statistical Abstract of the Democratic Socialist Republic of Sri Lanka, 1979*. Colombo, Sri Lanka: DCS.

de Silva, H. W. S. 1979. "The Coconut Industry in Sri Lanka: An Analysis of Government Intervention Measures." Masters thesis, Australian National University, Canberra.

de Silva, K. M. 1981. *A History of Sri Lanka*. New Delhi: Oxford University Press.

Dissanayake, G. 1983. "Foreword." In *Mahaweli Projects and Programme 1984*, ed. Information Service, 1–6. Colombo, Sri Lanka: Ministry of Lands and Land Development and Ministry of Mahaweli Development.

Dunham, D., and S. Kelegama. 1997. "Does Leadership Matter in the Economic Reform Process? Liberalization and Governance in Sri Lanka, 1989–1993." *World Development* 25 (2): 179–90.

Edwards, C. 1993. "A Report on Protectionism and Trade Policy in Manufacturing and Agriculture in Sri Lanka." Unpublished report, Institute of Policy Studies, Colombo, Sri Lanka.

FAOSTAT Database. Food and Agriculture Organization of the United Nations. http://faostat.fao.org/default.aspx (accessed May 2008).

Ganewatta, G. 2002. *The Market for Value Added Tea Products of Sri Lanka: An Economic Analysis*. PhD thesis, LaTrobe University, Melbourne.

Global Development Network Growth Database. Development Research Institute, New York University. http://www.nyu.edu/fas/institute/dri/global%20development%20network%20growth%20database.htm (accessed June 2007).

IMF (International Monetary Fund). 2005. *Sri Lanka: Selected Issues and Statistical Appendix*. IMF Country Report 05/337. Washington, DC: IMF.

IPS (Institute of Policy Studies). 2003. *Sri Lanka: State of the Economy 2002*. Colombo, Sri Lanka: IPS.

Kelegama, S., ed. 2004. *Economic Policy in Sri Lanka: Issues and Debates*. London: Thousand Oaks.

Kikuchi, M., R. Barker, M. Samad, and P. Weligamage. 2000. "Comparative Advantage of Rice Production in an Ex-rice Importing Country: The Case of Sri Lanka." Paper presented at the III Conference of the Asian Society of Agricultural Economists, Jaipur, Sri Lanka, October 18–20.

———. 2001. "Comparative Advantage of Rice Production in Sri Lanka with Special Reference to Irrigation Costs." Paper presented at the International Rice Research Institute's "International Workshop on Medium- and Long-Term Prospects of Rice Supply and Demand in the 21st Century," Los Baños, Laguna, the Philippines, December 3–5.

Klingebiel, S. 2001. "The OECD, World Bank and International Monetary Fund: Development Activities in the Crisis Prevention and Conflict Management Sphere." Unpublished report, German Development Institute, Bonn.

Kreimer, A., J. Eriksson, R. Muscat, M. Arnold, and C. Scott. 1998. *Experience with Post-Conflict Reconstruction*. World Bank Operations Evaluation Study. Washington, DC: World Bank.

Ministry of Plantation Industries. various issues. *Plantation Sector Pocket Book*. Colombo, Sri Lanka: Ministry of Plantation Industries.

Moore, M. 1985. *The State and Peasant Politics in Sri Lanka.* Cambridge: Cambridge University Press.

Peebles, P. 1990. "Colonization and Ethnic Conflict in the Dry Zone of Sri Lanka." *Journal of Asian Studies* 49 (1): 30–55.

Rafeek, M. I. M., and P. A. Samaratunga. 2000. "Trade Liberalization and Its Impact on the Rice Sector of Sri Lanka." *Sri Lankan Journal of Agricultural Economics* 3 (1): 143–54.

Sanderatne, N. 2004. "Agricultural Development: Controversial Issues." In *Economic Policy in Sri Lanka: Issues and Debates,* ed. S. Kelegama, 195–212. London: Thousand Oaks.

Shilpi, F. 1995. "Policy Incentive, Diversification, and Comparative Advantage of Nonplantation Crops in Sri Lanka." Working paper, World Bank, Washington, DC.

Tennekoon, S. N. 1988. "Rituals of Development: The Accelerated Mahawali Development Program of Sri Lanka." *American Ethnologist* 15 (2): 294–310.

Thibbotuwawa, M. 2004. "Analysis of the Comparative Advantage and Income from Paddy Farming in Anuradhapura, Kurunagala and Gampaha Districts with Special Emphasis on Scale of Cultivation." Unpublished project report, Department of Agricultural Economics and Business Management, Faculty of Agriculture, University of Peradeniya, Peradeniya, Sri Lanka.

Thorbecke, E., and J. Svejnar. 1987. *Economic Policies and Agricultural Performance in Sri Lanka, 1960–1984.* Development Centre Studies. Paris: Organisation for Economic Co-operation and Development.

Weerahewa, J. 2004. "Impacts of Trade Liberalization and Market Reforms on the Paddy/Rice Sector in Sri Lanka." MTID Discussion Paper 70, Markets, Trade, and Institutions Division, International Food Policy Research Institute, Washington, DC.

Weerahewa, J., H. M. Gunatilake, and H. Pitigala. 2003. "Future of Paddy Farming in Sri Lanka: Scale, Comparative Advantage and Rural Poverty." *Sri Lanka Economic Journal* 3 (2): 104–44.

Weerakoon, D. 2004. "The Influence of Development Ideology in Macroeconomic Policy Reform Process." In *Economic Policy in Sri Lanka: Issues and Debates,* ed. S. Kelegama, 54–70. London: Thousand Oaks.

World Bank. 1995. "Sri Lanka: Non-Plantation Crop Sector Policy Alternatives." Report 14564-CE, World Bank, Washington, DC.

———. 2003. *Sri Lanka: Promoting Agricultural and Rural Non-farm Sector Growth.* 2 vols. Report 25387-CE. Washington, DC: World Bank.

———. 2004. *Trade Policies in South Asia: An Overview.* 3 vols. Report 29949. Washington, DC: World Bank.

WTO (World Trade Organization). 2004. *Trade Policy Review: Sri Lanka.* Geneva: WTO.

METHODOLOGY FOR MEASURING DISTORTIONS TO AGRICULTURAL INCENTIVES

Kym Anderson, Marianne Kurzweil, Will Martin,
Damiano Sandri, and Ernesto Valenzuela

This appendix outlines the methodological issues associated with the task of measuring the impact of government policies on incentives faced by farmers and food consumers. The focus is on those border and domestic measures that arise exclusively from government actions, that, as such, may be altered by a political decision, and that have an immediate effect on consumer choices, producer resource allocations, and net farm incomes. Most commonly, these measures include import or export taxes, subsidies, and quantitative restrictions, supplemented by domestic taxes or subsidies for farm outputs or inputs, and consumer subsidies for food staples. The incentives faced by farmers are affected not only by the direct protection or taxation of primary agricultural industries, but also indirectly via policies assisting nonagricultural industries, given that the latter may have an offsetting effect by drawing resources away from farming. This appendix begins by outlining what theory suggests should be measured directly and indirectly. It then outlines the way the theory is put into practice through this study.

Thanks for invaluable comments are due to many project participants, including Bruce Gardner, Tim Josling, Will Masters, Alan Matthews, Johan Swinnen, Alberto Valdés, and Alex Winter-Nelson, plus Ibrahim Elbadawi. The information in this appendix is also available in Anderson et al. 2008a and 2008b.

What, According to Theory, Should Be Measured

The key objective of this study—obtaining a long time series on a wide range of countries that are at different stages of development—requires that the indicators be simple. If the indicators are simple, this also means that it would be easier to update the indicators subsequently for policy monitoring. Throughout, we have followed the concept of Bhagwati (1971) and Corden (1997) whereby a market policy distortion is, by definition, imposed by a government to create a gap between the marginal social return to a seller and the marginal social cost to a buyer in a transaction. The distortion creates an economic cost to society that may be estimated using welfare measurement techniques such as those pioneered by Harberger (1971). As Harberger notes, this focus allows for great simplification in the evaluation of the marginal costs of a set of distortions: changes in economic costs may be evaluated by taking into account the changes in volumes directly affected by the distortions and ignoring all other changes in prices. In the absence of divergences such as externalities, the measure of a distortion is the gap between the price paid and the price received, irrespective of whether the level of these prices is affected by the distortion.

Other developments that change the incentives facing producers and consumers may include flow-on consequences of the distortion, but these should not be confused with the direct price distortion that we aim to estimate. If, for instance, a country is large in world trade for a given commodity, the imposition of an export tax may raise the price in international markets, thereby reducing the adverse impact of the distortion on producers in the taxing country. Another flow-on consequence is the effect of trade distortions on the real exchange rate, which is the price of traded goods relative to nontraded goods. Neither of these flow-on effects is of immediate concern, however, because, if the direct distortions are accurately estimated, they may be incorporated as price wedges into an appropriate country or global economy-wide computable general equilibrium model, which, in turn, will be able to capture the full general equilibrium impacts (inclusive of the real exchange rate effects) of the various direct distortions to producer and consumer prices.

Importantly, the total effect of distortions on the agricultural sector will depend not only on the size of the direct *agricultural* policy measures, but also on the magnitude of distortions generated by direct policy measures that alter the incentives in *nonagricultural* sectors. It is the *relative* prices and, hence, the relative rates of government assistance that affect producer incentives. In a two-sector model, an import tax has the same effect on the export sector as an export tax: this is the Lerner (1936) symmetry theorem. This carries over to a model that has many sectors and is unaffected if there is imperfect competition domestically or internationally or if some of the sectors produce only nontradables (Vousden 1990). The symmetry theorem is therefore also relevant in the consideration of distortions *within* the agricultural sector. In particular, if import-competing farm industries are protected, such as through import tariffs, then this has similar effects on the incentives to produce exportables as does an explicit tax on agricultural exports; and, if both measures are in place, this represents a double imposition on farm exporters.

In what follows, we begin by focusing on direct distortions to agricultural incentives before turning to those distortions affecting the sector indirectly through nonagricultural policies.

Direct agricultural distortions

Consider a small, open, perfectly competitive national economy that encompasses many firms producing a homogeneous farm product with only primary factors. In the absence of externalities, processing, and producer-to-consumer wholesale marketing, plus retail marketing margins, exchange rate distortions, and domestic and international trading costs, such a country would maximize national economic welfare by allowing both the domestic price of the farm product and the consumer price of the farm product to equal E, times P, where E is the domestic currency price of foreign exchange, and P is the foreign currency price of the identical product in the international market. Thus, any government-imposed diversion from this equality, in the absence of any market failures or externalities, would be welfare-reducing in the small economy.

Price-distorting trade measures at the national border

The most common distortion is an ad valorem tax on competing imports (usually called a tariff), t_m. Such a tariff on imports is the equivalent of a production subsidy and a consumption tax, both at rate t_m. If this tariff on the imported primary agricultural product is the only distortion, its effect on producer incentives may be measured as the *nominal rate of assistance* (NRA) to farm output conferred by the border price support, (NRA_{BS}), which is the unit value of production at the distorted price, less its value at the undistorted free-market price expressed as a fraction of the undistorted price, as follows:[1]

$$NRA_{BS} = \frac{E \times P(1 + t_m) - E \times P}{E \times P} = t_m.$$ (A.1)

The effect of this import tariff on consumer incentives in this simple economy is to generate a *consumer tax equivalent* (CTE) on the agricultural product for final consumers:

$$CTE = t_m.$$ (A.2)

The effects of an import subsidy are identical to those in equations (A.1) and (A.2) for an import tax, but t_m would have a negative value in that case.

Governments sometimes also intervene through an export subsidy, s_x (or an export tax, in which case s_x would be negative). If this is the only intervention, then:

$$NRA_{BS} = CTE = s_x. \tag{A.3}$$

If any of these trade taxes or subsidies are specific rather than ad valorem (for example, US\$ per kilogram rather than z percent), the ad valorem equivalent may be calculated using slight modifications of equations (A.1), (A.2), and (A.3).

Domestic producer and consumer price-distorting measures

Governments sometimes intervene through a direct production subsidy for farmers, s_f (or a production tax, in which case s_f is negative, including through informal taxes in kind by local and provincial governments). In that case, if only this distortion is present, the effect on producer incentives may be measured as the NRA to farm output conferred by the domestic price support (NRA_{DS}), which is as above except that s_f replaces t_m or s_x, but the CTE is zero in this case. Similarly, if the government imposes only a consumption tax, c_c, on this product (or a consumption subsidy, in which case c_c is negative), the CTE is as above except that c_c replaces t_m or s_x, but the NRA_{DS} is zero in this case.

The combination of domestic and border price support provides the total rate of assistance to output and domestic consumer tax equivalent:

$$NRA_o = NRA_{BS} + NRA_{DS}, \quad CTE = NRA_{BS} + c_t. \tag{A.4}$$

What if the exchange rate system is also distorting prices?

Should a multitier foreign exchange rate regime be in place, then another policy-induced price wedge exists. A simple two-tier exchange rate system creates a gap between the price received by all exporters and the price paid by all importers for foreign currency, thereby changing both the exchange rate received by exporters and the exchange rate paid by importers relative to the equilibrium rate, E, that would prevail without this distortion in the domestic market for foreign currency (Bhagwati 1978).

Exchange rate overvaluation of the type we consider here requires controls by the government on current account transfers. A common requirement is that exporters surrender their foreign currency earnings to the central bank for exchange to local currency at a low official rate. This is equivalent to a tax on exports to the extent that the official rate is below the level of the exchange rate in a market without government intervention. This implicit tax reduces the incentive of exporters to export and, hence, the supply of foreign currency flowing into the country. With less foreign currency, demanders are willing to bid up the purchase price. This provides a potential rent for the government that may be realized by auctioning off the limited supply of foreign currency extracted from exporters or creating a legal secondary market. Either mechanism will create a gap between the official and parallel rates.

Such a dual exchange rate system is depicted in figure A.1, in which it is assumed that the overall domestic price level is fixed, perhaps by holding the money supply constant (Derviş, de Melo, and Robinson 1981). The supply of foreign exchange is given by the upward sloping schedule, S_{fx}, and demand by D_{fx}, where the official exchange rate facing exporters is E_0 and the secondary market rate facing importers is E_m. At the low rate, E_0, only Q_S units of foreign currency are available domestically, instead of the equilibrium volume Q_E that would result if exporters were able to exchange, at the equilibrium rate, E units of local currency per unit of foreign currency.[2] The gap between the official and the secondary market exchange rates is an indication of the magnitude of the tax imposed on trade by the two-tier exchange rate: relative to the equilibrium rate, E, the price of importables is raised by $e_m \times E$, which is equal to $(E_m - E)$, while the price of exportables is reduced by $E_x \times E$, which is equal to $(E - E_0)$, where e_m and e_x are the fractions by which the two-tier exchange rate system raises the domestic price of an importable and lowers the domestic price of an exportable, respectively. The estimated division of the total foreign exchange distortion between an implicit export tax, e_x, and an implicit import tax, e_m, will depend on the estimated elasticities of supply of exports and of demand for imports.[3] If the demand and supply curves in figure A.1 had the same slope, then $e_m = e_x$ and $(e_m = e_x)$ is the secondary market premium or proportional rent extracted by the government or its agents.[4]

Figure A.1. A Distorted Domestic Market for Foreign Currency

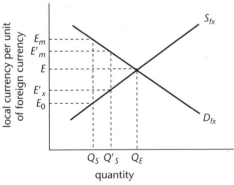

Sources: Martin 1993. See also Derviş, de Melo, and Robinson 1981; Kiguel and O'Connell 1995; Kiguel, Lizondo, and O'Connell 1997; Shatz and Tarr 2000.

If the government chooses to allocate the limited foreign currency to different groups of importers at different rates, this is called a multiple exchange rate system. Some lucky importers may even be able to purchase foreign currency at the low official rate. The more that is allocated and sold to demanders whose marginal valuation is below E_m, the greater the unsatisfied excess demand at E_m, and, hence, the stronger the incentive for an illegal or black market to form and for less-unscrupulous exporters to lobby the government to legalize the secondary market for foreign exchange and to allow exporters to retain some fraction of their exchange rate earnings for sale in the secondary market. Providing a right to exporters to retain and sell a portion of foreign exchange receipts increases their incentives to export and thereby reduces the shortage of foreign exchange and, thus, the secondary market exchange rate (Tarr 1990). In terms of figure A.1, the available supply increases from Q_S to Q'_S, bringing down the secondary rate from E_m to E'_m, such that the weighted average of the official rate and E'_m received by exporters is E'_x; the weights are the retention rate, r, and $(1 - r)$. Again, if the demand and supply curves in figure A.1 had the same slope, then the implicit export tax and import tax resulting from this regime would each be equal to half the secondary market premium.

In the absence of a secondary market and in the presence of multiple rates for importers below E_m and for exporters below E_0, a black market often emerges. The rate for buyers in this market will rise above E, the more the government sells its foreign currency to demanders whose marginal valuation is below E_m, and the more active the government is in catching and punishing exporters selling in the illegal market. If the black market were allowed to operate frictionlessly, there would be no foreign currency sales to the government at the official rate, and the black market rate would fall to the equilibrium rate, E. So, even though, in the latter case, the observed premium would be positive (equal to the proportion by which E is above the nominal official rate E_0), there would be no distortion. For our present purposes, since the black market is not likely to be completely friction-less, it may be considered similar to the system involving a retention scheme. In terms of figure A.1, E'_m would be the black market rate for a proportion of sales, and the weighted average of this and E_0 would be the return going to exporters. Calculating E'_x in this situation (and thereby being able to estimate the implicit export and import taxes associated with this regime) by using the same approach as in the case with no illegal market thus requires not only knowledge about E_0 and the black market premium, but also a guess about the proportion, r, of sales in the black market.

In short, if a country exhibits distortions in its domestic market for foreign currency, the exchange rate relevant for calculating the NRA_o or the CTE for a particular tradable product depends, in the case of a dual exchange rate system, on whether the product is an importable or an exportable, while, in the case of multiple exchange rates, it depends on the specific rate that applies to the product each year.

What about real exchange rate changes?

A change in the real exchange rate alters equally the prices of exportables and importables relative to the prices of nontradable goods and services. Such a change may arise for many different reasons, including changes in the availability of capital inflows, macroeconomic policy adjustments, or changes in the international terms of trade. If the economy receives a windfall, such as a greater inflow of foreign exchange from remittances, foreign aid, or a commodity boom, the community moves to a higher indifference curve (Collier and Gunning 1998). While net imports of tradables may change in response to this inflow of foreign exchange, the domestic supply of and demand for nontradables must balance. The equilibrating mechanism is the price of nontradables. The price of nontradables rises to bring forth the needed increase in the supply of nontradables and to reduce the demand for these products so as to bring the demand into line with supply (Salter 1959).

While this type of alteration in the real exchange rate affects the incentive to produce tradables, it is quite different in two respects from the distortions in the market for foreign currency analyzed above. First, this real exchange rate appreciation reduces the incentives to produce importables and exportables to the same degree. In contrast with the case of the multiple-tier exchange rate, the appreciation does not generate any change in the prices of exportables relative to importables. Second, most such changes do not involve direct economic distortions of the type measurable using tools such as producer surplus or consumer surplus. If the government or the private sector chooses to borrow more from abroad to increase domestic spending, this may raise the real exchange rate, but such an outcome is not obviously a distortion. Moreover, the symmetric treatment of any such overvaluation during periods of high foreign borrowing would require that one take into account exchange rate undervaluation during periods of low foreign borrowing or the repayment of foreign debt. For these reasons, we do not follow Krueger, Schiff, and Valdés (1988) or Orden et al. (2007) in including deviations of real exchange rates from benchmark values unless these deviations arise from direct exchange rate distortions such as multiple-tier exchange rates.[5]

What if trade costs are too high for a product to be traded internationally?

Suppose the transport costs of trading are sufficient to make it unprofitable for a product to be traded internationally, such that the domestic price fluctuates over time within the band created by the cost, insurance, and freight import price and the free on board export price. Then, any trade policy measure (t_m or s_x) or the product-specific exchange rate distortion (for example, e_m or e_x) is redundant. In this case, in the absence of other distortions, $NRA_o = 0$, and the $CTE = 0$. However, in the presence of any domestic producer or consumer tax or subsidy (s_f or t_c), the domestic prices faced by both producers *and* consumers will be affected. The extent of the impact depends on the price elasticities of domestic demand and supply for the nontradable (the standard closed-economy tax incidence issue).

Thus, for example, suppose only a production tax is imposed on farmers producing a particular nontradable, so that $s_f < 0$ and $t_c = 0$. In this case:

$$NRA_{DS} = \frac{s_f}{1 + \dfrac{\varepsilon}{\eta}} \tag{A.5}$$

and

$$CTE = \frac{-s_f}{1 + \dfrac{\eta}{\varepsilon}}, \tag{A.6}$$

where ε is the price elasticity of supply, and η is the (negative of the) price elasticity of demand.[6]

What if farm production involves primary factors, but also intermediate inputs?

Where intermediate inputs are used in farm production, any taxes or subsidies on the production, consumption, or trade of these inputs would alter farm value added and thereby also affect farmer incentives. Sometimes, a government will have directly offsetting measures in place, such as a domestic subsidy for fertilizer use by farmers, but also a tariff on fertilizer imports. In other situations, there will be farm input subsidies, but an export tax on the final product.[7] In principle, all these items might be brought together to calculate an effective rate of direct assistance to farm value added (the effective rate of assistance). The nominal rate of direct assistance to farm output, NRA_o, is a component of this, as is the sum of the nominal rates of direct assistance to all farm inputs, call it NRA_i. In principle, all three rates may be positive or negative.

The participants in this project have not been required to estimate effective rates of assistance because to do so requires a knowledge of each product's value added share of output. Such data are not available for most developing countries for every year in the time series nor even for every few years. And, in most developing countries, distortions to farm inputs are small compared with distortions to farm output prices, and these purchased inputs are a small fraction of the value of output. However, where there are significant distortions to input costs, the ad valorem equivalent is accounted for by summing each input's NRA, multiplying this by the input-output coefficient to obtain the combined NRA_i, and adding this to the farm industry's nominal rate of direct assistance to farm output, NRA_o, to obtain the total NRA in farm production, call it simply NRA.[8]

$$NRA = NRA_o + NRA_i. \tag{A.7}$$

What about postfarmgate costs?

If a state trading corporation is charging excessively for its marketing services, thereby lowering the farmgate price of a product (for example, as a way of raising government revenue in place of an explicit tax), the extent of the excess should be treated as if it were a tax.

Some farm products, including some that are not internationally traded, are inputs into a processing industry that may also be subject to government interventions. In this case, the effect of these interventions on the price received by farmers for the primary product also needs to be taken into account. Before we explain how, it may be helpful first to review the possible role the marketing and distribution margins of the value chain may play in the calculation of distortions in primary agricultural activities so as to ensure that nondistortionary price wedges are not inadvertently included in any distortion calculations.

Nondistortionary price wedges

So far, it has been assumed that there are no divergences among farmer, processor-wholesaler, consumer, and border prices other than those arising because of subsidies or taxes on production, consumption, trade, or foreign currency. In practice, this is not so, and these costly value chain activities need to be explicitly recognized and netted out in using comparisons of domestic and border prices to derive estimates of government policy-induced distortions.[9] Such recognition also offers the opportunity to compare the size of the NRA with wedges associated with, for instance, trade and processing costs (used in trade facilitation and value chain analyses, respectively). It may also expose short-term situations where the profits of importers or exporters are amplified by less-than-complete adjustment by agents in the domestic value chain.

Domestic trading costs

Trading costs may be nontrivial both intra- and internationally, especially in developing countries with poorly developed infrastructure.[10] For example, domestic trading costs are involved in delivering farm products to port or to domestic wholesalers (assuming the latter are at the international border; otherwise, another set of domestic transport costs needs to be added to obtain a relevant price comparison). Suppose, for instance, that domestic transport costs are equal to the fraction T_f of the price received by the farmer.

Processor-wholesaler costs

Domestic processing costs and wholesale and retail distribution margins may represent a large share of the final retail price. Indeed, Reardon and Timmer (2007) argue that these costs and margins are an increasingly important part of the value chain in developing countries because consumers desire more postfarm processing and services added to their farm products, aided by the contribution of the supermarket revolution to globalization.[11] We denote the increases in the consumer price caused by these processing and wholesaling activities, over and above the farmgate price plus domestic trade costs, as m_p and m_u, respectively (or simply m_u above the price of the imported processed product if the processing must be done before the product is internationally tradable), in the absence of market imperfections or government distortions along the value chain.

International trading costs

International trading costs are not an issue in the distortions calculations if the international price used is the cost, insurance, and freight import unit value for an importable or the free on board export unit value for an exportable. But these costs are relevant if there is no trade (because of, say, a prohibitive trade tax on the product) or if the border prices are unrepresentative (because of low trade volumes, for example). In these instances, it is recommended that one select an international indicator price series (such as those of the World Bank or the International Monetary Fund) and account for international trading costs (ocean or air freight, insurance, and so on).[12] We denote T_m as the proportion by which the domestic price of the import-competing product is raised above what it would otherwise be at the country's border, or, equivalently, we denote T_x as the fraction of the free on board price by which the price abroad of the exported product is greater.

Product quality and variety differences

The quality of a product traded internationally is usually considered to differ from the quality of the domestically sold substitute, and consumers typically have a home-country bias.[13] Whenever appropriate, the domestic price should be deflated (inflated) by the extent to which the good imported is deemed by domestic consumers to be inferior (superior) in quality to the domestic product.[14] We denote q_m as the deflating fraction for the adjustment for product quality and variety differences in the case of importables.

The situation is similar for exported goods. Especially if an international indicator price has to be used in lieu of the free on board export unit value (for example, if exports are close to zero and unrepresentative), the international price needs to be deflated (inflated) by the extent to which the good is deemed by foreign consumers to be inferior (superior) in quality relative to the indicator good. We denote q_x as the deflating fraction to adjust for product quality and variety differences in the case of exportables.

Net effect of nondistortionary influences

If one takes into consideration all these influences and so long as the product is still traded internationally, the relationships between the price received by domestic farmers and the international price, in the absence of government-imposed price and trade policies, are described by the following for an importable:

$$E \times P = \frac{P_f(1 + T_f)(1 + m_p)(1 - q_m)}{1 + T_m}, \tag{A.8}$$

and for an exportable it is the following:

$$E \times P = \frac{P_f(1 + T_f)(1 + m_p)(1 + T_x)}{1 - q_x}, \tag{A.9}$$

while the urban consumer price is above the producer price to the following extent:

$$P_c = P_f(1 + T_f)(1 + m_p)(1 + m_u), \tag{A.10}$$

where P_f is the farmgate price.

The impact of distortions in food processing on agricultural NRAs

Some farm products that are not internationally traded in their primary form (for example, raw milk and cane sugar) are tradable once they have been lightly processed, and the downstream processing industry may also be subject to government interventions. In this case, the effect of the latter interventions on the price received by farmers for the primary product also needs to be taken into account, and the primary product should be classified as tradable.

Some analysts have assumed that any protection to processors, if it is passed back fully to primary agriculture (as may be the case with a farmer-owned cooperative processing plant, for example), effectively raises the farmer price by the amount of the rise in the processor price, divided by the proportional contribution of the primary product to the value of the processed product. Another equally extreme, but opposite assumption is that there is zero pass-through by the processor back down the value chain to the farmer. This is likely to be the case if the raw material may be sourced internationally, but seems unlikely if the primary product is nontradable and there is a positive price elasticity of farm supply (since an assisted processor would want to expand). A more neutral assumption is that there is a proportional pass-through by the processor down the value chain to farmers and their transporters or up the value chain to consumers. This would be equivalent to an equal sharing of the benefits along the value chain, which is more likely to be the case, the more equally market power is spread among the players in the chain.

This trio of examples illustrates the importance both of separating primary and processed activities for the purpose of calculating agricultural assistance rates and of being explicit about the extent of pass-through that is occurring in practice and, hence, the consequences for the NRAs in primary agricultural and processing activities.[15]

The above examples involving processors may also be generalized to any participants in the value chain. In particular, state trading enterprises and parastatal marketing boards may intervene significantly, especially if they have been granted monopoly status by the government. Such interventions by domestic institutions may explain the low econometrically estimated degree of transmission of price changes at a border to farmgate domestic prices even following a significant reform of more-explicit price and trade policies (see Baffes and Gardner 2003 and the references cited therein). Where reform has also involved the freeing up of previously controlled parts of the marketing chain, the lowered marketing margin may provide a benchmark against which to compare the prereform margin (as in Uganda beginning in the mid-1990s; see Matthews and Opolot 2006).

The mean and standard deviation of agricultural NRAs

We need to generate a weighted average NRA for covered products in each country because only then will we be able to add the NRA for noncovered products to obtain the NRA for all agriculture. If one wishes to average across countries, each polity is an observation of interest; so, a simple average is meaningful for the purpose of political economy analysis. But, if one wants a sense of the distortions in agriculture in a whole region, a weighted average is needed. The weighted average NRA for covered primary agriculture may be generated by multiplying the value share of each primary industry in production (valued at farmgate equivalent undistorted prices) by the corresponding NRA and then adding across industries.[16] The overall sectoral rate, which we denote as *NRAag*, may be obtained by also adding the actual or assumed information for the commodities not covered and, where it exists, the aggregate value of non-product-specific assistance to agriculture.

A weighted average may be similarly generated for the tradables part of agriculture—including those industries producing products such as milk and sugar that require only light processing before they are traded—by assuming that the share of the non-product-specific assistance goes to producers of tradables. Call this $NRAag^t$.

In addition to the mean, it is important also to provide a measure of the dispersion or variability of the NRA estimates across the covered products. The cost of government policy distortions in incentives in terms of resource misallocation tends to be greater, the greater the degree of substitution in production (Lloyd 1974). In the case of agriculture involving the use of farmland that is sector specific, but transferable among farm activities, the greater the variation of NRAs across industries within the sector, the higher the welfare cost of these market interventions. A simple indicator of dispersion is the standard deviation of industry NRAs within agriculture.[17]

Trade bias in agricultural assistance

A trade bias index also is needed to indicate the extent to which a country's policy regime has an antitrade bias within the agricultural sector. This is important because, as the Lerner (1936) symmetry theorem demonstrates, a tariff that assists import-competing farm industries has an effect on farmer incentives that is the same as the effect of a tax on agricultural exports (see elsewhere above), and, if both measures are in place, this is a double imposition on farm exports. The higher the NRA for import-competing agricultural production ($NRAag_m$) relative to the NRA for exportable farm activities ($NRAag_x$), the more incentive producers in the subsector will have to bid for mobile resources that would otherwise have been employed in export agriculture, all else being equal.

Once each farm industry has been classified as import-competing, as a producer of exportables, or as a producer of a nontradable (the status may sometimes change over the years; see below), it is possible to generate, for each year, the weighted average NRAs for the two different groups of tradable farm industries. These may then be used to generate an agricultural trade bias index, TBI, which is defined as follows:

$$TBI = \left[\frac{1 + NRAag_x}{1 + NRAag_m} - 1 \right], \tag{A.11}$$

where $NRAag_m$ and $NRAag_x$ are the average NRAs, respectively, for the import-competing and exportable parts of the agricultural sector (their weighted average is $NRAag^t$). This index has a value of zero whenever the import-competing and export subsectors are equally assisted, and its lower bound approaches -1 in the most extreme case of an antitrade policy bias.

Indirect agricultural assistance and taxation through nonagricultural distortions

In addition to direct assistance to or taxation of farmers, the Lerner (1936) symmetry theorem also demonstrates that farmer incentives are affected indirectly by government assistance to nonagricultural production in the national economy. The higher the NRA for nonagricultural production (*NRAnonag*), the more incentive producers in other sectors will have to bid up the value of mobile resources that would otherwise have been employed in agriculture, all else being equal. If *NRAag* is below *NRAnonag*, one might expect there to be fewer resources in agriculture than there would be under free-market conditions in the country, notwithstanding any positive direct assistance to farmers, and, conversely, if *NRAag* is greater than *NRAnonag*. A weighted average may be generated for the tradables part of nonagriculture, too; call it *NRAnonag*[^t].

One of the most important negative effects on farmers arises from protections for industrialists from import competition. Tariffs are part of this, but so too (especially in past decades) are nontariff barriers to imports. Other primary sectors (fishing, forestry, and minerals, including the extraction of energy raw materials) tend, on average, to be subject to fewer direct distortions than either agriculture or manufacturing, but there are important exceptions. One example is a ban on logging; however, if such a ban is instituted for genuine reasons of natural resource conservation, it should be ignored. Another example is a resource rent tax on minerals. Unlike an export tax or quantitative restriction on the exports of such raw materials (which are clearly distortive and would need to be included in the NRA for mining), a resource rent tax, like a land tax, may be fairly benign in terms of resource reallocation and, so, may be ignored (see Garnaut and Clunies Ross 1983).

The largest part of most economies is the services sector. This sector produces mostly nontradables, many of which are provided through the public sector. Distortions in service markets have been extraordinarily difficult to measure, and no systematic estimates across countries are available over time or even for a recent period. The only feasible way to generate time series estimates of *NRAnonag* in this project has therefore involved the assumption that all services are nontradable, and that they, along with other nonagricultural nontradables, face no distortions. All the other nonagricultural products may be separated into exportables and import-competing products for purposes of estimating correctly their weighted average NRAs, ideally using production valued at border prices as weights (although, in practice, most of our authors have had to use shares of gross domestic product).

Foreign exchange rate misalignment relative to the value of a country's currency—as suggested by the fundamentals—will be ignored (see elsewhere above). This is because a real appreciation of the general foreign exchange rate uniformly lowers the price of all tradables relative to the price of nontradables; the converse is true for a real devaluation. If a change in the exchange rate has been caused by aid or foreign investment inflows, then the excess of tradables consumption over tradables production leads to a new equilibrium. Certainly, such a new inflow of funds would reduce the incentives among farmers producing tradable products, but this is not a welfare-reducing policy distortion. Thus, it is only the exchange rate distortions caused by a dual or multiple exchange rate system that need to be included in the calculation of the NRAs for the exportable and import-competing parts of the nonagricultural sector and, hence, of $NRAnonag^t$, and this should be accomplished in the same way discussed above for the inclusion of these distortions in the calculation of $NRAag^t$.

Assistance to agricultural production relative to nonagricultural production

Given the calculation of $NRAag^t$ and $NRAnonag^t$ as above, it is possible to reckon a relative rate of assistance (RRA), defined as follows:

$$RRA = \left[\frac{1 + NRAag^t}{1 + NRAnonag^t} - 1 \right]. \qquad (A.12)$$

Since an NRA cannot be less than -1 if producers are to earn anything, then neither can the RRA. The RRA is a useful indicator in undertaking international comparisons over time of the extent to which a country's policy regime has an anti- or proagricultural bias.

The Ways the Theory Is Put into Practice in This Study

Making the theory described above operational in the real world, where data are often scarce, especially over a long time period, is as much an art as a science.[18] Thankfully, for many countries, we have not had to start from scratch. NRAs are available from as early as 1955 in some cases and at least from the mid-1960s to the early or mid-1980s for the 18 countries included in Krueger, Schiff, and Valdés (1988, 1991a) and Anderson and Hayami (1986). Much has been done to provide detailed estimates since 1986 of direct distortions in farmer incentives (though not in food processing) in the high-income countries that are now members of the Organisation for Economic Co-operation and Development (OECD) and, since the early to mid-1990s, in selected European transition economies and Brazil, China, and South Africa (OECD 2007a, 2007b). At least for direct distortions, the Krueger, Schiff, and Valdés measures (1988, 1991a) have been updated to the mid-1990s for some Latin American countries (Valdés 1996) and have also been provided for some countries in Eastern Europe (Valdés 2000), and a new set of estimates of simplified producer support estimates for a few key farm products in China, India, Indonesia, and Vietnam since 1985 is now available from the International Food Policy Research Institute (Orden et al. 2007). The methodology described above is, in some sense, a variation on each of these studies, and the basic price data, at least, as well as the narratives attached to the estimates in these studies, are invaluable springboards for our study.[19]

Time period coverage of the study

For Europe's transition economies, it is difficult to find meaningful data on the situation prior to 1992. For the same reason, estimates are not particularly useful before the 1980s for China and Vietnam. For all other countries, the target start date has been 1955, especially if this date includes years before and after a year of independence so that one might examine the effects of independence, although, for numerous developing countries, the data simply are not available. The target end date has been 2004, but, where available, 2005 data have also been included. In most cases, the most recent few years offer the highest quality data.

Farm product coverage of the study

The agricultural commodity coverage includes all the major food items (rice, wheat, maize or other grains, soybeans or other temperate oilseeds, palm oil or other tropical oils, sugar, beef, sheep and goat meat, pork, chickens and eggs, and milk), plus other key country-specific farm products (for example, other staples, tea, coffee or other tree crop products, tobacco, cotton, wine, and wool). Globally, as of 2001, one-third of the value added in all agriculture and food industries has been highly processed food, beverages, and tobacco (GTAP Database; Dimaranan 2006). We have also addressed these products briefly, in the same cursory way we have addressed nonagricultural products. Fruits and vegetables are another one-sixth; so, the rest constitute the other half. Of that other half, meats are one-third; grains and oilseeds are almost another one-third; dairy products are one-sixth; and sugar, cotton, and other crops account for slightly more than one-fifth. If the high-income countries are excluded, these shares change quite sharply. Then, highly processed food, beverages, and tobacco are only half as important; fruits and vegetables are somewhat more important, and, if these two groups (which together account for 41 percent of the total) are excluded, the residual is equally divided between three groups: meats, grains and oilseeds, and other crops and dairy products. By focusing on all major grain, oilseed, and livestock products, plus any key horticultural and other crop products, the coverage of our project reaches the target of 70 percent of the value added of most countries in agriculture and lightly processed food. Priority has been assigned to the most distorted industries because the residual will then have not only a low weight, but also a low degree of distortion.

If highly processed food, beverages, and tobacco are excluded, then fruits and vegetables account for almost one-quarter of household food expenditure in developing countries. If fruits and vegetables are also excluded, three groups each then account for almost 30 percent of expenditure: pig and poultry products, red meat and dairy products, and grains and oilseed products. All other crops account for the remaining one-eighth. So, from the consumer tax viewpoint, the desired product coverage is the same as the coverage outlined above from a production viewpoint.

Each product is explicitly identified as import-competing, exporting, or nontradable. For many products, this categorization changes over time. In some cases, products move monotonically through these three categories, and, in others, they fluctuate in and out of nontradability. Hence, an indication of a product's net trade status is given for each year rather than for only one categorization for the whole time series. In large-area countries with high internal and coastal shipping costs, some regions may be exporting abroad, even while other regions are net importers from other countries. In such cases, it is necessary to estimate separate NRAs for each region and then generate a national weighted average.

Farm input coverage

The range of input subsidies considered in any particular country study in our project has depended on the degree of distortions in that country's input markets. In addition to fertilizer, the large inputs and distortions are likely to involve electrical or diesel power, pesticides, and credit (including, occasionally, large-scale debt forgiveness, as in Brazil and Russia, although how this is spread out beyond the year of forgiveness is an issue).[20] There are also distortions revolving around water, but the task of measuring water subsidies is especially controversial and complex; so, these distortions have not been included in the NRA calculations. (The OECD has also ignored them in its producer support estimates.) Similarly, distortions in land and labor markets have been excluded, apart from qualitative discussions in the analytical narratives in some of the country case studies.

Trade costs

For the calculation of distortions in international trading costs, T_m and T_x, the free on board–cost, insurance, and freight gap in key bilateral trade in products during years when the products have been traded in significant quantities is used. Both international and domestic trading costs are a function of the quality of hard infrastructure (roads, railways, ports) and soft infrastructure (business regulations and customs clearance procedures at state and national borders), each of which may be affected by government actions. However, because it is difficult to allocate these costs between items that are avoidable and those that are unavoidable, measuring the aggregate size of the distortions involved in a comparable way for a range of countries is beyond the scope of this study.[21]

Classifying farm products as import-competing, exportable, or nontradable

The criteria used in classifying farm industries as import-competing (M), exporting (X), or nontrading (H) are not straightforward. Apart from the complications raised above about whether a product is not traded simply because of trade taxes or nontariff barriers, there will be cases where trade is minimal, or the trade status has been reversed because of policy distortions, or the industry is characterized by significant imports *and* exports. A judgment has to be made for each sector each year as to whether it should be classified as M, X, or H. In the case of the two tradable classifications (that is, leaving out nontradables), this judgment will determine which exchange rate distortion to use. If trade is minimal for reasons of trade cost rather than reasons of trade policy, then a product is classified as nontradable if the share of production exported *and* the share of consumption imported are each less than 2.5 percent, except in situations (for example, rice in China) in which the product is clearly an exportable year after year even though the self-sufficiency rate is rarely above 101 percent. Otherwise, if the share of production exported is substantially above (below) the share of consumption imported, the product is classified as exportable (importable).

In cases in which the trade status has been reversed because of a policy distortion (for instance, an export subsidy, in combination with a prohibitive import tariff, is large enough to encourage sufficient production to generate an export surplus), the product should be given the classification of the trade status that would prevail without the intervention (that is, import-competing). The same applies if tariff preferences reverse a country's trade status with respect to a product. The exports of many countries enjoy preferential access into the protected markets of other countries. In some cases, these arrangements are based on bilateral or plurilateral free trade agreements or customs unions. In other cases, the preferences are unilaterally offered by higher-income countries to developing countries through schemes such as the generalized system of preferences, the Cotonou Agreement (between the Africa, Caribbean, and Pacific group and the

European Union), and the European Union's Everything But Arms Initiative. In the few extreme cases where these preferences are such that they (in combination with a prohibitive import tariff) cause the developing country to become an exporter of a product that would otherwise be import-competing (such as sugar in the Philippines), the product should nonetheless be classified as import-competing because the developing country's import-restrictive policy is allowing the domestic price of the product to equal the price reached in exporting to the preference-providing country.

If there are significant exports *and* imports in a given year, closer scrutiny is required. If, for example, there are high credit or storage costs domestically, a product may be exported immediately following harvest, but imported later in the year to satisfy consumers out of season. The product would be considered an exportable for purposes of calculating the NRA because, even if there are policies restricting out-of-season imports (which would affect the CTE calculation), they would not represent an encouragement for the production earlier in the year in the presence of high credit or storage costs.

If trade or exchange rate distortions are sufficiently large to choke off international trade in a product, then they contribute to the NRA and CTE only to the extent required to drive that trade to zero: any trade taxes that exceed this requirement have an element of redundancy. If there are trade policy distortions, but no trade passes over them (that is, they are prohibitive), there may still be policy effects that need to be measured, but they will differ from those involved in the other cases above. An example would be a prohibitive tariff that is high enough to take the price of imported goods above the autarchy price and thus results in no imports. The NRA would therefore be less than the prohibitive tariff rate. Another common example is an import tariff in a context in which the world price is sufficiently high so that the country is freely exporting the product at issue. In this case, the domestic price would be determined by the world price, less the export trade costs; the import tariff would be irrelevant, and there would be no distortion despite the presence of the import tariff.

Similar conditions apply to exportable goods in a context in which a prohibitive export tax creates a distortion at a level lower than the tax rate. Then, the distortion wedge would be equal to the difference between the autarchy price and the world price, less the export trade costs; if the country were freely importing the good, the export tax would be irrelevant, and there would be no distortion despite the presence of the export tax. The choice of the international price to be compared with domestic prices is therefore not based only on the actual trading status of a country (Byerlee and Morris 1993). Moreover, different prices may be needed for different regions of a large country that simultaneously exports and imports because internal trading costs (including coastal shipping) are so high relative to international trading costs (Koester 1986). In this case, the value of production is split according to the regional production shares in the country. If the only intervention in this sector is a tariff on imports, the tariff rate is the NRA estimate for the import-competing part, and the NRA is zero for the other part of the sector; these different NRAs are then included in the weighted average calculations of the NRAs for the import-competing and exportable subsectors of agriculture.

The transmission of assistance and taxation along the agricultural value chain

A crucial aspect of the NRA calculation for agricultural products is the way any policy measure beyond the farmgate is transmitted back to farmers and forward to consumers. Only a few parameters and exogenous variables are needed to obtain meaningful estimates of an individual agricultural product's NRA and CTE. Specifically, to take account of the pass-through of distortions along the value chain, parameters have been identified as follows (although the default is an equiproportionate pass-through):

- θ_f, the extent to which any distortion to a primary farm product at the wholesale level is passed back to farmers
- θ, the extent to which any distortion to the downstream processed product is passed back to wholesalers of a primary farm product that is nontradable

The CTEs of farm products

Many farm products are processed and are used as ingredients in the additional processing of food products before the food products are purchased by final consumers. (For example, wheat is ground to flour and then mixed with other ingredients before baking, slicing, and packaging for sale as bread.) Other farm products are used as inputs in various farm activities, often after the farm products have undergone some processing. (Thus, soybeans are crushed, and the meal is mixed with maize or other feed grains for use as animal feed, while the oil is sold for cooking.) Because of these many and varied value chain paths and because, in practice, it is difficult anyway to determine the extent to which a change in the primary farm product would be passed along any of these value chains, the OECD expresses its consumer support estimate simply at the level at which a product is first traded (for example, as wheat, or soybeans, or beef). This practice has been adopted here, too, to generate a consistent set of CTEs across countries to use in the analysis in chapter 1 (even though our authors of individual country studies may report CTEs that they have estimated in a more-sophisticated way farther along the value chain). In the absence of any domestic production or consumption taxes or subsidies directly affecting a product, the CTE at the point at which the product is first traded will be the same as the NRA_o. (Also recall that the NRA_o in this case also equals the NRA if NRA_i is zero.)

Key required information

A template spreadsheet has been designed to aid in the management of individual country information and ensure a consistent comparison across regions and periods. The precise ways in which parameters and exogenous variables have entered each country spreadsheet to generate the NRAs and CTEs endogenously are detailed in Anderson et al. (2008a, 2008b). Most are straightforward; the main exception is the treatment of exchange rate distortions that is described below.

The key exogenous variables needed are the agricultural quantities produced and consumed (or imported and exported if the proxy for consumption is production, plus net imports); the wholesale and border prices of primary and lightly processed agricultural goods (along with, where relevant, a quality adjustment to match border prices); agricultural domestic input and output subsidies and taxes (the default is zero); if there are distorted farm input markets, the share of the input in the value of farm output at border prices (and, if there are only farmgate prices rather than wholesale prices for a primary good, the proportion of the farmgate value in the value at the wholesale level measured at the border price); the final domestic food consumer subsidies or taxes (the default is zero); and the official exchange rate (and, where prevalent, the parallel exchange rate and the share of currency going through the secondary or illegal market, plus the product-specific exchange rate if a multiple exchange rate system is in place).

Exchange rate distortions

The treatment of exchange rate distortions is worth spelling out since it differs from the method used by Krueger, Schiff, and Valdés (1988, 1991a).

If there are no exchange rate distortions, the official exchange rate is used. However, in the presence of a parallel market rate (which might be the black market rate if no legal secondary market exists), this is reported, along with an estimate of the proportion of foreign currency that is actually sold by exporters at the parallel market rate. This proportion is the formal retention rate if a formal dual exchange regime is in place; otherwise, it is based on a guesstimate of the proportion traded on the black market. (The black market premiums are provided in Cowitt, various years; Cowitt, Edwards, and Boyce, various years; and the Global Development Network Growth Database). The spreadsheet is then used to compute an estimate for the equilibrium exchange rate for the economy; this is the rate at which international prices are converted into local currency for the computation of each NRA.

Relevant exchange rates for importers and exporters are also then computed endogenously. If they are distorted away from the official exchange rate, the relevant exchange rate for importers and exporters are, respectively, the discounted parallel market rate and the weighted average of the official exchange rate and the discounted parallel rate according to the proportion of the exporter's currency that is sold on the parallel market. However, if a multiple exchange rate system is in place and this system provides for a specific rate for a product that differs from the general rates automatically calculated as above, then the automatically computed relevant exchange rate is replaced by this industry-specific rate.

Guesstimates of NRAs for agricultural products not covered

In the calculation of the weighted average rates of assistance for a subsector or sector, NRAs must be guesstimated for the agricultural products that are not covered (30 percent or so) and for which price comparisons are not calculated. The OECD, in its work on producer support estimates, assumes that the part not measured enjoys the same market price support as the average of the measured part. Another default is the assumption that the rates are zero. Orden et al. (2007) show that these two alternatives produce significantly different results for India. It is therefore preferable to make informed judgments about the import-competing, exportable, and nontradable parts of the residual group of farm products. An average applied import tariff is often the best guess for only the import-competing products among this set if there is no evidence of the existence of explicit production, consumption, or export taxes or subsidies. Even though this approach will miss the nontariff trade barriers affecting these residual products, the bias will be small if the weight is small.

Non-product-specific assistance to agriculture

If, in addition to the product-specific subsidies or taxes, there are non-product-specific forms of agricultural subsidies or taxes that one is unable to allocate among importables, exportables, and nontradables, these are included in the NRAag using the same method (as a percentage of the total value of production) used for these types of interventions in the OECD's calculations of its total support estimate (see OECD 2007a, 2007b).

No attempt is made to estimate the discouraging effects of underinvestment in rural infrastructure or underdevelopment among pertinent institutions. The structure of the related expenditure within the rural sector is also important. This may well be a nontrivial part of the distortions in agricultural incentives, but, unfortunately, it is not captured in the measures of distortions outlined above.

In some higher-income countries, governments also assist farm households through payments that are purported to be decoupled from production incentives. An example is the single farm payment in the European Union. We do not count such payments as part of *NRAag* because the latter refers specifically to measures that alter producer incentives. However, we do include the ad valorem equivalent of these payments in discussing assistance to farmers as a social group so as to be able to compare the order of magnitude of this equivalent with the support provided through measures that alter production incentives.

Assistance to nonagricultural sectors

If nonagricultural sectors are assisted only through import tariffs on manufactures or export taxes on minerals, it is a relatively easy task to estimate a weighted average *NRAnonag* once the shares of import-competing, exporting, and nontradable production have been determined. In practice, however, nontariff trade measures must also be considered among the measures affecting tradables (Dee and Ferrantino 2005; OECD 2005), and most economies have myriad regulations affecting the many service industries. These regulations may be complex (see Findlay and Warren 2000). Because most of the outputs of service industries (including the public sector) are nontradable, the default in this study is to assume that the average rate of government assistance, along with that of nontradable nonagricultural goods, is zero. Then, the task of estimating the *NRAnonag* is reduced to obtaining only the NRAs for the producers of import-competing products and of export-oriented nonagricultural goods, plus the shares of these products and goods in the undistorted value of the production of nonagricultural tradables, so as to derive the weighted average *NRAnonag*[t] to be entered into the RRA calculations.

The use of percentages in the chapters

To simplify the presentation in the chapters, the NRA_o, NRA_i, NRA, CTE, and RRA are expressed there as percentages rather than proportions.

Dollar values of farmer assistance and consumer taxation

For chapter 1, we have taken the country authors' estimate of NRA and multiplied it by the gross value of production at undistorted prices to obtain an estimate in current US dollars of the direct gross subsidy equivalent of assistance to farmers (*GSE*). This can then simply be added up across products for a country and across countries for any or all products to get regional aggregate transfer estimates for the studied countries. To get an aggregate estimate for the rest of the region, we assume the weighted average NRA for nonstudied countries is the same as the weighted average *NRA* for the studied countries, and that the nonstudied countries' share of the region's gross value of farm production at undistorted prices each year is the same as its share of the region's agricultural GDP measured at distorted prices. All current US dollar values are then converted to constant 2000 dollars using the GDP deflator for the United States.

To obtain comparable dollar value estimates of the consumer transfer, we have taken the *CTE* estimate at the point at which a product is first traded and multiplied it by the gross value of consumption at undistorted prices (proxied by production at undistorted prices plus net imports) to obtain an estimate in current US dollars of the tax equivalent to consumers of primary farm products (*TEC*). This too can then be added up across products for a country and across countries for any or all products to get regional aggregate transfer estimates for the studied countries and converted to US dollars again using the GDP deflator. We do not attempt to get an aggregate estimate for noncovered products in the studied countries nor for the region's nonstudied countries.

The *GSE* and *TEC* dollar values can be illustrated in a supply-demand diagram for a distorted domestic market for a farm product (see figure A.2). In the case of an import-competing product subjected to an import tariff t_m plus a production subsidy s_f and a consumption tax c_c, the *GSE* is the rectangle *abcd* and the *TEC* is the rectangle *ahfg*. The *GSE* estimate is an overstatement to the extent of triangle *cdj* and the *TEC* estimate is an understatement to the extent of triangle *efg*, where those triangles are smaller the more price-inelastic are the supply and demand curves S and D, respectively. In the case of an exportable product subjected to an export tax t_x, the *GSE* is the negative of the rectangle *kruv* and the *TEC* is the negative of the rectangle *nquv*.

Figure A.2. Distorted Domestic Markets for Farm Products

(a) An import-competing product subjected to an import tariff t_m plus a production subsidy s_f and a consumption tax c_c

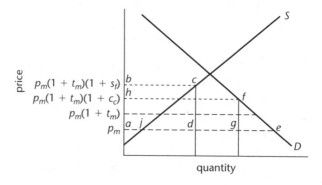

(b) An exportable product subjected to an export tax t_x

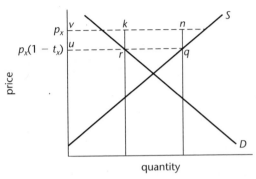

Source: Authors' derivation.

Notes

1. The NRA therefore differs from the producer support estimate calculated by the Organisation for Economic Co-operation and Development (OECD) in that the producer support estimate is expressed as a fraction of the distorted value (see the OECD PSE-CSE Database). It is thus $t_m/(1 + t_m)$, and, so, for a positive t_m, it is smaller than the NRA and is necessarily less than 100 percent.

2. Equilibrium here refers to the situation that would prevail without the distortion in the domestic market for foreign currency. In figure A.1 and in the discussion that follows, the equilibrium exchange rate, E, exactly balances the supply and demand for foreign currency. Taken literally, this implies a zero balance on the current account. The approach here may readily be generalized to accommodate exogenous capital flows and transfers, which would shift the location of Q_E. With constant-elasticity supply and demand curves, all of the results would carry through, and any exogenous change in the capital flows or transfers would imply a shift in the D_{fx} or S_{fx} curves.

3. From the viewpoint of using the NRA_o and CTE estimates later as parameters in a computable general equilibrium model, it does not matter which assumptions are made here about these elasticities because the model's results for real variables will not be affected. What matters for real impacts is the magnitude of the total distortion, not its allocation between an export tax and an import tax; this is the traditional incidence result from tax theory that also applies to trade taxes (Lerner 1936). For an excellent general equilibrium treatment using an early version of the World Bank's 1–2–3 model, see de Melo and Robinson (1989). There, the distinction is drawn between traded and nontraded goods (using the Armington [1969] assumption of differentiation between products sold on the domestic market and products sold on the international market), in contrast to the distinction between tradable and nontradable products made below in the text.

4. Note that this same type of adjustment might be made if the government forces exporters to surrender all foreign currency earnings to the domestic commercial banking system and importers to buy all foreign currency needs from that banking system and if that system is allowed by regulation to charge excessive fees. This apparently occurs in, for example, Brazil, where the spread is reputedly 12 percent. If actual costs in a nondistorted competitive system are only 2 percent (as they are in the less-distorted Chilean economy), the difference of 10 points might be treated as the equivalent of a 5 percent export tax and a 5 percent import tax applying to all tradables (although, as with nontariff barriers, there would be no government tariff revenue, but rather rent, which, in this case, would accrue to commercial banks instead of to the central bank). This is an illustration of the point made by Rajan and Zingales (2004) about the power of financial market reform to expand opportunities.

5. The results of a multicountry research project that has had macropolicy as its focus are reported in Little et al. (1993).

6. As in the case of the two-tier exchange rate, the elasticities are used merely to identify the incidence of these measures; as long as both the NRA_o and the CTE are included in any economic model used to assess the impact of the production tax, the real impacts will depend only on the magnitude of the total distortion, s_f, not on the estimated NRA and CTE.

7. On this general phenomenon of offsetting distortions for outputs and inputs (and even direct payments or taxes), see Rausser (1982).

8. Bear in mind that a fertilizer plant or livestock feed mix plant might be enjoying import tariff protection that raises the domestic price of fertilizer or feed mix to farmers by more than any consumption subsidy (as was the situation with respect to fertilizer in Korea; see Anderson 1983). In such a case, the net contribution of this set of input distortions to the total NRA for agriculture would be negative.

9. This is not to say that there is no interest in comparisons across countries or over time in, for example, the farmgate price as a proportion of the free on board export price, which summarizes the extent to which the producer price is depressed by the sum of internal transport, processing, and marketing costs, plus items such as explicit or implicit production or export taxes. Prominent users of this proportion—which may be less than half in low-income countries even if there is little or no processing—include Bates (1981) and Binswanger and Scandizzo (1983). Users need to be aware, though, that this ratio understates the extent of farmer assistance (that is, it understates the rate of protection or overstates the rate of disprotection to farmers), possibly by a large margin.

10. On the basic economics of trading costs as affected by, for example, infrastructure within the country, at the border (ports, airports), and, in the case of landlocked countries, in transit countries, as well as international freight costs and so on, and their impact on both the aggregate volume and product structure of international trade, see Limão and Venables (2001), Venables and Limão (2002), and Venables (2004). See also the survey by Anderson and van Wincoop (2004), where it is reported that the tax equivalent of trading costs are estimated at more than 170 percent in high-income countries and higher in developing and transition economies, especially those that are small, poor, and remote. By lowering these trading costs (for example, by streamlining customs clearance procedures), trade facilitation may be the result not only of technological changes, but also of government policy choices such as restrictions on the ships that may be used in bilateral trade. For example, Fink, Mattoo, and Neagu (2002) estimate that the policy contribution to the cost of shipping goods from developing countries to the United States is greater than the border import barriers. More generally, on imperfect competition in services markets, including cartelized international shipping, see Francois and Wooten (2001, 2006).

11. The costs of processing and of wholesale and retail distribution, as well as domestic trading costs, change over time not only because of technological advances, but also following policy changes. For example, government investment in rural infrastructure may lower trading costs. Reardon and Timmer (2007) argue that the global supermarket revolution is, in part, driven by the opening of domestic markets following the relaxation of government restrictions on foreign direct investment since the 1980s. These types of government policies are not included in our project's measurement of distortions.

12. Trading costs may be unrelated to the product price (that is, specific rather than ad valorem), in which case the formulas should be adjusted accordingly (for example, if T_f is in dollars per ton). If this were the case with international trading costs, the domestic price of importables (exportables) would change less (more) than proportionally with P. The ad valorem assumption is preferable to the specific one in situations where international price and exchange rate changes are less than those that are fully passed though the domestic value chain to the farmer and consumer because of incomplete market integration caused, for example, by poor infrastructure or weak institutions. Ideally, in such cases, one would estimate econometrically the extent to which the price transmission elasticity is below unity and use this to calculate the margin each year.

Trading costs include the storage costs that would be incurred to hold domestic products until the time in the season when international trade takes place. Any subsidies or taxes on these or any other trading costs should be included in the distortion calculus. On the importance of these domestic trading costs in low-income countries, see Khandker, Balkht, and Koolwal (2006) on Bangladesh; Moser, Barrett, and Minten (2005) on Madagascar; and Diop, Brenton, and Asarkaya (2005) on Rwanda.

13. On the how and the why of the variation by country of origin in the quality and variety of traded goods, see Hummels and Klenow (2005).

14. We assume that the quality difference arises because one good provides more effective units of service than another, so that the relative price is a constant proportion of the value of the first good. If products are simply differentiated, without such a quality dimension (as in Armington 1969), there will be no fixed relationship between the two prices.

15. In using the NRA and the CTE estimates later as parameters in a computable general equilibrium model, as in the case of the incidence of the exchange rate distortion discussed elsewhere above, the assumptions made here about the extent of pass-though along the value chain may not greatly affect the model's results for real variables such as prices, output, and value added.

16. Corden (1971) proposed that free trade volumes be used as weights, but, because these are not observable (and an economy-wide model is needed to estimate them), the common practice is to compromise by using actual distorted volumes, but undistorted unit values or, equivalently, distorted values, divided by $(1 + NRA)$. If estimates of own-and cross-price elasticities of demand and supply are available, a partial equilibrium estimate of the quantity at undistorted values might then be generated, but, if these estimated elasticities are unreliable, this may introduce additional error over and above the error one seeks to correct.

17. The mean and standard deviations might be captured by a single measure, namely, the trade restrictiveness index developed by Anderson and Neary (2005). Calculating this index even in its simplest partial equilibrium mode requires that one know the own-and cross-price elasticities of demand and supply (or, at least, the elasticity of import demand, but this shortcut is only usable if the NRA and CTE are identical).

18. In addition to the methodologies of Krueger, Schiff, and Valdés (1988, 1991a) and the OECD (2007a, 2007b) for estimating agricultural distortion and producer support indicators, see the recent review by Josling and Valdés (2004) of methodologies in earlier studies.

19. Other trade policy studies have also been of great help, particularly studies on trade and exchange rate distortions. These include various multicountry studies such as the one summarized in Bhagwati (1978) and Krueger (1978) and more-recent ones summarized in Bevan, Collier, and Gunning (1989); Michaely, Papageorgiou, and Choksi (1991); Bates and Krueger (1993); and Rodrik (2003).

20. For an analysis of input subsidies in Indian agriculture, see Gulati and Narayanan (2003).

21. That these costs vary hugely across countries and often dwarf trade taxes has now been clearly established. See, for example, World Bank (2006a, 2006b), the Doing Business Database, and the governance and anticorruption indicators in the WGI Database. Also now available is a database on information and communications cost indicators for 144 countries; see the ICT at a Glance Database. In some settings, price bands induced by trading costs arising because of missing or imperfect markets in rural areas lead poor farmers to forgo cash crops to ensure sufficient food production for survival (de Janvry, Fafchamps, and Sadoulet 1991; Fafchamps 1992). This contributes to the low supply responsiveness among poor producers to international price changes for the cash crops.

References

Anderson, James E., and J. Peter Neary. 2005. *Measuring the Restrictiveness of International Trade Policy.* Cambridge, MA: MIT Press.

Anderson, James E., and Eric van Wincoop. 2004. "Trade Costs." *Journal of Economic Literature* 42 (3): 691–751.

Anderson, Kym. 1983. "Fertilizer Policy in Korea." *Journal of Rural Development* 6 (1): 43–57.

Anderson, Kym, and Yujiro Hayami, eds. 1986. *The Political Economy of Agricultural Protection: East Asia in International Perspective.* London: George Allen and Unwin.

Anderson, K., M. Kurzweil, W. Martin, D. Sandri, and E. Valenzuela. 2008. "Measuring Distortions to Agricultural Incentives, Revisited." *World Trade Review* 7 (4): 675–704.

———. 2008b. "Measuring Distortions to Agricultural Incentives, Revisited." *World Trade Review* 7 (4): 675–704.

Anderson, Kym, Will Martin, and Ernesto Valenzuela. 2006. "The Relative Importance of Global Agricultural Subsidies and Market Access." *World Trade Review* 5 (3): 357–76.

Armington, Paul S. 1969. "A Theory of Demand for Products Distinguished by Place of Production." *IMF Staff Papers* 16 (1): 159–78.

Baffes, John, and Bruce L. Gardner. 2003. "The Transmission of World Commodity Prices to Domestic Markets under Policy Reforms in Developing Countries." *Journal of Policy Modeling* 6 (3): 159–80.

Bates, Robert Hinrichs. 1981. *Markets and States in Tropical Africa: The Political Basis of Agricultural Policies.* Berkeley, CA: University of California Press.

Bates, Robert Hinrichs, and Anne O. Krueger, eds. 1993. *Political and Economic Interactions in Economic Policy Reform: Evidence from Eight Countries.* Oxford: Blackwell.

Bevan, David, Paul Collier, and Jan Willem Gunning. 1989. *Peasants and Governments: An Economic Analysis.* With Arne Bigsten and Paul Horsnell. Oxford: Clarendon Press.

Bhagwati, Jagdish N. 1971. "The Generalized Theory of Distortions and Welfare." In *Trade, Balance of Payments and Growth: Papers in International Economics in Honor of Charles P. Kindleberger,* ed. Jagdish N. Bhagwati, Ronald Jones, Robert Mundell, and Jaroslav Vanek, 69–90. Amsterdam: North-Holland.

———. 1978. *Foreign Trade Regimes and Economic Development: Anatomy and Consequences of Exchange Control Regimes.* Cambridge, MA: Ballinger.

Binswanger, Hans P., and Pasquale L. Scandizzo. 1983. "Patterns of Agricultural Protection." ARU Discussion Paper 15, Agricultural Research Unit, Agriculture and Rural Development Department, World Bank, Washington, DC.

Byerlee, Derek, and Michael L. Morris. 1993. "Calculating Levels of Protection: Is it Always Appropriate to Use World Reference Prices Based on Current Trading Status?" *World Development* 21 (5): 805–15.

Collier, Paul, and Jan Willem Gunning. 1998. "Trade Shocks: Theory and Evidence." In *Africa.* Vol. 1 of *Trade Shocks in Developing Countries,* ed. Paul Collier and Jan Willem Gunning, 1–63. With associates. Oxford: Clarendon Press.

Corden, W. Max. 1971. *The Theory of Protection.* Oxford: Clarendon Press.

———. 1997. *Trade Policy and Economic Welfare.* 2nd ed. Oxford: Clarendon Press.

Cowitt, P. P., ed. Various years. *World Currency Yearbook.* Brooklyn: Currency Data and Intelligence, Inc.

Cowitt, P. P., C. A. Edwards, and E. R. Boyce, eds. Various years. *World Currency Yearbook.* Brooklyn: Currency Data and Intelligence, Inc.

Dee, Philippa, and Michael Ferrantino, eds. 2005. *Quantitative Methods for Assessing the Effects of Non-Tariff Measures and Trade Facilitation.* Singapore: World Scientific Publishing; Singapore: Committee on Trade and Investment, Asia-Pacific Economic Cooperation.

de Janvry, Alain, Marcel Fafchamps, and Elisabeth Sadoulet. 1991. "Peasant Household Behaviour with Missing Markets: Some Paradoxes Explained." *Economic Journal* 101 (409): 1400–17.

de Melo, Jaime, and Sherman Robinson. 1989. "Product Differentiation and the Treatment of Foreign Trade in Computable General Equilibrium Models of Small Economies." *Journal of International Economics* 27 (1–2): 47–67.

Derviş, Kemal, Jaime de Melo, and Sherman Robinson. 1981. "A General Equilibrium Analysis of Foreign Exchange Shortages in a Developing Economy." *Economic Journal* 91 (364): 891–906.

Dimaranan, Betina V., ed. 2006. *Global Trade, Assistance, and Production: The GTAP 6 Data Base.* West Lafayette, IN: Center for Global Trade Analysis, Purdue University.

Diop, Ndiame, Paul Brenton, and Yakup Asarkaya. 2005. "Trade Costs, Export Development, and Poverty in Rwanda." Policy Research Working Paper 3784, World Bank, Washington, DC.

Doing Business Database. World Bank and International Finance Corporation. http://www.doingbusiness.org/ (accessed October 2007).

Fafchamps, Marcel. 1992. "Cash Crop Production, Food Price Volatility, and Rural Market Integration in the Third World." *American Journal of Agricultural Economics* 74 (1): 90–99.

Findlay, Christopher, and Tony Warren, eds. 2000. *Impediments to Trade in Services: Measurement and Policy Implications.* Routledge Studies in the Growth Economies of Asia. London and New York: Routledge.

Fink, Carsten, Aaditya Mattoo, and Ileana Cristina Neagu. 2002. "Trade in International Maritime Services: How Much Does Policy Matter?" *World Bank Economic Review* 16 (1): 81–108.

Francois, Joseph F., and Ian Wooton. 2001. "Trade in International Transport Services: The Role of Competition." *Review of International Economics* 9 (2): 249–61.

———. 2006. "Market Structure and Market Access." Draft working paper, Erasmus School of Economics, Erasmus University, Rotterdam.

Garnaut, Ross Gregory, and Anthony I. Clunies Ross. 1983. *The Taxation of Mineral Rents.* Oxford: Clarendon Press.

Global Development Network Growth Database. Development Research Institute, New York University. http://www.nyu.edu/fas/institute/dri/global%20development%20network%20growth%20database .htm (accessed June 2007).

GTAP (Global Trade Analysis Project) Database. Center for Global Trade Analysis, Department of Agricultural Economics, Purdue University. https://www.gtap.agecon.purdue.edu/databases/v6/default.asp (version 6).

Gulati, Ashok, and Sudha Narayanan. 2003. *The Subsidy Syndrome in Indian Agriculture.* New Delhi: Oxford University Press.

Harberger, Arnold C. 1971. "Three Basic Postulates for Applied Welfare Economics: An Interpretative Essay." *Journal of Economic Literature* 9 (3): 785–97.

Hummels, David L., and Peter J. Klenow. 2005. "The Variety and Quality of a Nation's Exports." *American Economic Review* 95 (3): 704–23.

ICT (Information and Communication Technology) at a Glance Database. World Bank. http://go .worldbank.org/FDTYJVBR60 (accessed December 2007).

Industry Commission. 1995. Assistance to Agricultural and Manufacturing Industries. Information Paper. Canberra: Industry Commission, Commonwealth of Australia.

Josling, Timothy E., and Alberto Valdés. 2004. "Agricultural Policy Indicators." ESA Working Paper 04–04, Agricultural and Development Economics Division, Food and Agriculture Organization of the United Nations, Rome.

Kee, Hiau Looi, Alessandro Nicita, and Marcelo Olarreaga. 2006. "Estimating Trade Restrictiveness Indices." Policy Research Working Paper 3840, World Bank, Washington, DC.

Khandker, Shahidur R., Zaid Balkht, and Gayatri B. Koolwal. 2006. "The Poverty Impact of Rural Roads: Evidence from Bangladesh." Policy Research Working Paper 3875, World Bank, Washington, DC.

Kiguel, Miguel A., and Stephen A. O'Connell. 1995. "Parallel Exchange Rates in Developing Countries." *World Bank Research Observer* 10 (1): 21–52.

Kiguel, Miguel A., J. Saul Lizondo, and Stephen A. O'Connell, eds. 1997. *Parallel Exchange Rates in Developing Countries.* Basingstoke, United Kingdom: Macmillan.

Koester, Ulrich. 1986. *Regional Cooperation to Improve Food Security in Southern and Eastern African Countries.* IFPRI Research Report 53. Washington, DC: International Food Policy Research Institute.

Krueger, Anne O. 1978. *Foreign Trade Regimes and Economic Development: Liberalization Attempts and Consequences.* Special Conference Series on Foreign Trade Regimes and Economic Development 10. Cambridge, MA: Ballinger; Cambridge, MA: National Bureau of Economic Research.

Krueger, Anne O., Maurice Schiff, and Alberto Valdés. 1988. "Agricultural Incentives in Developing Countries: Measuring the Effect of Sectoral and Economywide Policies." *World Bank Economic Review* 2 (3): 255–72.

———. 1991a. *Latin America.* Vol. 1 of *The Political Economy of Agricultural Pricing Policy.* Baltimore: Johns Hopkins University Press; Washington, DC: World Bank.

———. 1991b. *Asia.* Vol. 2 of *The Political Economy of Agricultural Pricing Policy.* Baltimore: Johns Hopkins University Press; Washington, DC: World Bank.

————. 1991c. *Africa and the Mediterranean*. Vol. 3 of *The Political Economy of Agricultural Pricing Policy*. Baltimore: Johns Hopkins University Press; Washington, DC: World Bank.

Lerner, Abba P. 1936. "The Symmetry between Import and Export Taxes." *Economica* 3 (11): 306–13.

Limão, Nuno M., and Anthony J. Venables. 2001. "Infrastructure, Geographical Disadvantage, Transport Costs, and Trade." *World Bank Economic Review* 15 (3): 451–79.

Lin Yifu, Tao Ran, Liu Mingxing, and Zhang Qi. 2002. "Rural Direct Taxation and Government Regulation in China: Economic Analysis and Policy Implications." CCER Working Paper, August, China Center for Economic Research, Peking University, Beijing.

Little, Ian M. D., Richard N. Cooper, W. Max Corden, and Sarath Rajapatirana, eds. 1993. *Boom, Crisis and Adjustment: The Macroeconomic Experience of Developing Countries*. World Bank Comparative Macroeconomic Studies. New York: Oxford University Press; Washington, DC: World Bank.

Lloyd, Peter J. 1974. "A More General Theory of Price Distortions in Open Economies." *Journal of International Economics* 4 (4): 365–86.

Martin, Will. 1993. "Modeling the Post-Reform Chinese Economy." *Journal of Policy Modeling* 15 (5–6): 545–79.

Matthews, Alan, and Jacob Opolot. 2006. "Agricultural Distortions in Uganda." Unpublished working paper, Agricultural Distortions Research Project, World Bank, Washington, DC.

Michaely, Michael, Demetris Papageorgiou, and Armeane M. Choksi, eds. 1991. *Lessons from Experience in the Developing World*. Vol. 7 of *Liberalizing Foreign Trade*. Oxford: Basil Blackwell.

Moser, Christine, Christopher B. Barrett, and Bart Minten. 2005. "Missed Opportunities and Missing Markets: Spatio-Temporal Arbitrage of Rice in Madagascar." Paper prepared for the American Agricultural Economics Association Annual Meeting, Providence, RI, July 24–27.

OECD (Organisation for Economic Co-operation and Development). 2005. *Looking Beyond Tariffs: The Role of Non-Tariff Barriers in World Trade*. OECD Trade Policy Studies. Paris: OECD.

————. 2007a. *Agricultural Policies in Non-OECD Countries: Monitoring and Evaluation 2007*. Paris: OECD.

————. 2007b. *Agricultural Policies in OECD Countries: Monitoring and Evaluation 2007*. Paris: OECD.

OECD PSE-CSE Database (Producer Support Estimate–Consumer Support Estimate Database). Organisation for Economic Co-operation and Development. http://www.oecd.org/document/58/0,2340,en _2649_37401_32264698_1_1_1_37401,00.html (accessed October 2007).

Orden, David, Fuzhi Cheng, Hoa Nguyen, Ulrike Grote, Marcelle Thomas, Kathleen Mullen, and Dongsheng Sun. 2007. *Agricultural Producer Support Estimates for Developing Countries: Measurement Issues and Evidence from India, Indonesia, China, and Vietnam*. IFPRI Research Report 152. Washington, DC: International Food Policy Research Institute.

Productivity Commission. 1999. *Trade and Assistance Review, 1998–99*. Annual Report Series 1998–99. Canberra: Productivity Commission, Commonwealth of Australia.

Rajan, Raghuram G., and Luigi Zingales. 2004. *Saving Capitalism from the Capitalists: Unleashing the Power of Financial Markets to Create Wealth and Spread Opportunity*. Princeton, NJ: Princeton University Press.

Rausser, Gordon C. 1982. "Political Economic Markets: PERTs and PESTs in Food and Agriculture." *American Journal of Agricultural Economics* 64 (5): 821–33.

Reardon, Thomas, and C. Peter Timmer. 2007. "Transformation of Markets for Agricultural Output in Developing Countries since 1950: How Has Thinking Changed?" In *Agricultural Development: Farmers, Farm Production, and Farm Markets*. Vol. 3 of *Handbook of Agricultural Economics*, ed. Robert E. Evenson and Prabhu Pingali, 2807–55. Handbooks in Economics 18. Amsterdam: Elsevier North-Holland.

Rodrik, Dani, ed. 2003. *In Search of Prosperity: Analytic Narratives on Economic Growth*. Princeton, NJ: Princeton University Press.

Salter, W. E. G. 1959. "Internal and External Balance: The Role of Price and Expenditure Effects." *Economic Record* 35 (71): 226–38.

Sandri, Damiano, Ernesto Valenzuela, and Kym Anderson. 2006. "Compendium of Economic and Trade Indicators by Region, 1960 to 2004." Agricultural Distortions Working Paper 01, World Bank, Washington, DC.

Shatz, Howard J., and David G. Tarr. 2000. "Exchange Rate Overvaluation and Trade Protection: Lessons from Experience." Policy Research Working Paper 2289, World Bank, Washington, DC.

Tarr, David G. 1990. "Second-Best Foreign Exchange Policy in the Presence of Domestic Price Controls and Export Subsidies." *World Bank Economic Review* 4 (2): 175–93.

Valdés, Alberto. 1996. "Surveillance of Agricultural Price and Trade Policy in Latin America during Major Policy Reforms." World Bank Discussion Paper 349, World Bank, Washington, DC.

_____, ed. 2000. "Agricultural Support Policies in Transition Economies." World Bank Technical Paper 470, World Bank, Washington, DC.

Venables, Anthony J. 2004. "Small, Remote and Poor?" *World Trade Review* 3 (3): 453–57.

Venables, Anthony J., and Nuno M. Limão. 2002. "Geographical Disadvantage: A Heckscher-Ohlin-von Thunen Model of International Specialization." *Journal of International Economics* 58 (2): 239–63.

Vousden, Neil. 1990. *The Economics of Trade Protection.* Cambridge: Cambridge University Press.

WGI (Worldwide Governance Indicators) Database. World Bank. http://info.worldbank.org/governance/wgi2007/home.htm (accessed October 2007).

World Bank. 2006a. *Assessing World Bank Support for Trade, 1987–2004: An IEG Evaluation.* Washington, DC: Knowledge Programs and Evaluation Capacity Development, Independent Evaluation Group, World Bank.

_____. 2006b. *Information and Communications for Development 2006: Trends and Policies.* Washington, DC: World Bank.

ANNUAL ESTIMATES OF ASIAN DISTORTIONS TO AGRICULTURAL INCENTIVES

Ernesto Valenzuela, Marianne Kurzweil,
Johanna Croser, Signe Nelgen, and Kym Anderson

This appendix summarizes the estimates of the key distortion indicators defined in appendix A (see also Anderson et al. 2008). The estimates refer to our focus economies of Asia. Specifically, three tables are provided for each economy: (a) the nominal rates of assistance (NRAs) for the individual farm products we cover in the study, including averages weighted according to the value of production at undistorted prices; (b) the relative rates of assistance (RRAs) for producers of agricultural tradables relative to nonagricultural tradables, including the components of the RRA calculations and averages weighted according to the value of production at undistorted prices; and (c) the individual weights, shown as percentages so they sum to 100 percent of the covered farm products and the residual noncovered group of products.

If only the output price of a product is distorted by government policies, the NRAs represent the percentage by which the domestic producer price exceeds the price that would prevail under free market conditions, that is, the price at the border appropriately adjusted to account for differences in product quality, transport costs, processing costs, and so on. A negative value indicates that the domestic price is below the comparable border price. If producers of the product are also affected by a distortion in product-specific input prices, this distortion is accounted for by subtracting the ad valorem input price distortion, times the related input-output coefficient, from the farm industry's output NRAs to obtain the total NRA for the production of the farm product.

473

The RRA is defined as follows:

$$100*[(100 + NRAag^t)/(100 + NRAnonag^t) - 1],$$

where $NRAag^t$ and $NRAnonag^t$ are the percentage NRAs for the tradables parts of the agricultural and nonagricultural sectors, respectively.

The sources of these tables are the working paper versions of the chapters in this volume (and the associated spreadsheets), each of which is downloadable in the working papers section of the project Web site, at http://www.worldbank.org/agdistortions. The specific references are provided following the tables.

Table B.1. Annual Distortion Estimates, Republic of Korea, 1955–2004

(percent)

a. NRAs for covered products

Year	Barley	Beef	Cabbages	Eggs	Garlic	Milk	Peppers	Pig meat	Poultry	Rice	Soybeans	Wheat	All
1955	−11	7	—	—	—	—	—	—	—	−42	−33	−56	−38
1956	36	36	—	—	—	—	—	—	—	−6	−28	−41	−3
1957	90	54	—	—	—	—	—	−15	—	26	−5	−32	28
1958	63	62	—	−16	—	—	—	29	—	−6	−11	−43	3
1959	27	35	—	−38	—	—	—	−8	—	−12	12	−43	−7
1960	65	53	—	−45	—	—	—	−2	—	−4	29	−41	1
1961	19	−3	—	−50	—	—	—	−41	−33	−44	−33	−56	−36
1962	19	21	—	−40	—	—	—	16	−13	−44	−23	−45	−32
1963	144	61	—	−13	—	—	—	68	12	25	61	−8	36
1964	171	40	—	25	—	—	—	67	62	32	60	16	52
1965	61	39	—	25	—	—	—	108	81	−2	44	−19	16
1966	43	26	—	24	—	—	—	114	81	−10	55	−15	7
1967	68	30	—	34	—	105	—	145	134	−14	104	−10	10
1968	85	87	—	30	—	210	—	235	203	−11	38	−6	19
1969	105	143	—	2	—	205	—	191	158	9	53	−6	32
1970	144	119	—	28	—	216	—	207	152	39	131	10	64
1971	149	120	—	9	—	133	—	286	153	63	76	17	82
1972	198	85	—	−8	—	41	—	222	80	88	102	25	95
1973	74	18	—	−7	—	60	—	193	52	11	48	−20	23
1974	36	28	—	−21	—	94	—	112	80	−44	43	−31	−27
1975	59	80	—	−17	—	133	—	154	107	−4	59	−20	13
1976	76	128	—	−14	—	187	—	189	144	48	108	−4	60
1977	112	218	—	−11	—	189	—	169	182	65	118	53	76

(Table continues on the following page.)

Table B.1. Annual Distortion Estimates, Republic of Korea, 1955–2004 (continued)

a. NRAs for covered products

Year	Barley	Beef	Cabbages	Eggs	Garlic	Milk	Peppers	Pig meat	Poultry	Rice	Soybeans	Wheat	All
1978	131	224	—	-2	—	175	—	270	212	66	174	61	89
1979	129	162	—	6	—	261	—	232	164	123	152	42	131
1980	57	137	—	12	—	223	—	181	90	109	199	89	112
1981	125	186	—	4	—	194	—	285	122	98	252	86	119
1982	170	190	—	8	—	169	—	196	90	122	290	92	131
1983	241	159	—	36	—	153	—	106	87	130	292	110	129
1984	238	144	—	14	—	160	—	78	82	133	232	84	123
1985	293	68	—	23	—	128	—	164	75	169	275	69	144
1986	399	97	30	11	250	211	175	144	64	196	302	99	158
1987	417	93	30	3	250	238	175	100	57	222	415	171	161
1988	336	178	30	7	250	162	175	119	112	226	410	204	177
1989	341	195	30	54	250	187	175	97	126	259	407	178	195
1990	363	207	30	39	250	152	175	190	142	276	459	222	209
1991	494	223	30	9	250	289	175	172	136	254	461	265	200
1992	461	206	30	40	250	158	175	95	138	254	508	201	184
1993	534	171	30	12	310	197	281	116	165	283	554	195	198
1994	769	197	30	39	383	222	421	173	198	262	559	197	219
1995	632	223	30	59	210	154	204	130	171	340	734	200	214
1996	403	200	29	15	44	128	108	138	185	336	604	134	186
1997	635	144	29	17	232	147	153	88	161	284	453	99	177
1998	449	71	29	7	373	118	87	60	135	199	393	64	127
1999	596	162	29	35	207	157	176	166	206	313	945	116	210
2000	740	139	28	30	30	205	192	124	220	390	908	157	216
2001	412	175	28	42	8	105	221	93	201	374	702	137	194
2002	561	254	28	40	88	154	144	122	164	422	780	130	221
2003	572	142	27	55	205	139	267	134	131	395	750	129	211
2004	528	129	27	105	282	145	162	199	180	350	647	124	226

476

b. Agricultural NRAs and RRAs: All products, tradables, and relative to nonagricultural tradables

Year	NRA, total agriculture[a]				NRA, agricultural tradables			NRA, nonagricultural tradables[b]	RRA
	Covered products		Noncovered products	All products, including NPS	Exportables[b]	Import-competing[b]	All		
	Inputs	Outputs							
1955	0	−38	−19	−28	n.a.	−36	−36	48	−57
1956	0	−3	1	−2	n.a.	−2	−2	35	−27
1957	0	28	11	17	n.a.	26	26	35	−6
1958	0	3	2	2	n.a.	3	3	41	−27
1959	0	−7	−4	−5	n.a.	−7	−7	69	−45
1960	0	1	0	1	n.a.	1	1	66	−39
1961	0	−36	−17	−27	n.a.	−33	−33	37	−51
1962	0	−32	−15	−23	n.a.	−29	−29	34	−47
1963	0	36	15	27	n.a.	35	35	26	7
1964	0	52	21	42	n.a.	51	51	23	23
1965	0	16	7	13	n.a.	15	15	27	−9
1966	0	7	4	6	n.a.	7	7	23	−13
1967	0	10	5	8	n.a.	9	9	23	−11
1968	0	19	10	15	n.a.	19	19	21	−2
1969	0	32	15	25	n.a.	31	31	18	11
1970	0	64	25	48	n.a.	61	61	17	38
1971	0	82	31	61	n.a.	78	78	12	59
1972	0	95	33	72	n.a.	90	90	12	70
1973	0	23	10	18	n.a.	22	22	9	12
1974	0	−27	−8	−21	n.a.	−23	−23	8	−29
1975	0	13	6	10	n.a.	12	12	9	2
1976	0	60	27	48	n.a.	58	58	11	43
1977	0	76	35	59	n.a.	75	75	17	50
1978	0	89	38	66	n.a.	85	85	12	65

(Table continues on the following page.)

Table B.1. Annual Distortion Estimates, Republic of Korea, 1955–2004 (*continued*)

b. Agricultural NRAs and RRAs: All products, tradables, and relative to nonagricultural tradables

| Year | NRA, total agriculture[a] | | | | NRA, agricultural tradables | | | NRA, nonagricultural tradables | RRA |
| | Covered products | | Noncovered products | All products, including NPS | Exportables[b] | Import-competing[b] | All | | |
	Inputs	Outputs							
1979	0	131	52	98	n.a.	127	127	10	106
1980	0	112	44	79	n.a.	105	105	8	90
1981	0	119	48	90	n.a.	114	114	6	101
1982	0	131	52	96	n.a.	125	125	7	111
1983	0	129	53	93	n.a.	123	123	7	108
1984	0	123	52	89	n.a.	117	117	6	104
1985	0	144	59	101	n.a.	136	136	6	124
1986	0	158	69	126	n.a.	156	156	6	141
1987	0	161	67	125	n.a.	155	155	6	140
1988	0	177	69	138	n.a.	169	169	6	155
1989	0	195	70	141	n.a.	180	180	4	169
1990	0	209	76	155	n.a.	196	196	4	185
1991	0	200	77	145	n.a.	187	187	4	177
1992	0	184	81	143	n.a.	179	179	3	170
1993	0	198	96	153	n.a.	200	200	3	192
1994	0	219	109	168	n.a.	226	226	3	217
1995	0	214	87	148	n.a.	198	198	2	191
1996	0	186	50	117	n.a.	145	145	3	139
1997	0	177	77	129	n.a.	164	164	2	158
1998	0	127	75	105	n.a.	129	129	2	124
1999	0	210	83	150	n.a.	188	188	2	183
2000	0	216	60	133	n.a.	166	166	2	161
2001	0	194	56	123	n.a.	150	150	2	145
2002	0	221	66	133	n.a.	168	168	2	163
2003	0	211	85	142	n.a.	181	181	2	176
2004	0	226	91	155	n.a.	196	196	1	191

c. Value shares of the primary production of covered[c] and noncovered products

Year	Barley	Beef	Cabbages	Eggs	Garlic	Milk	Peppers	Pig meat	Poultry	Rice	Soybeans	Wheat	Noncovered
1955	5	1	0	0	0	0	0	3	0	37	1	1	51
1956	6	1	0	0	0	0	0	4	0	30	1	1	57
1957	4	1	0	0	0	0	0	3	0	29	1	1	61
1958	4	1	0	1	0	0	0	3	0	34	1	1	56
1959	5	2	0	2	0	0	0	4	1	32	1	1	53
1960	4	2	0	3	0	0	0	3	1	31	1	1	54
1961	6	1	0	1	0	0	0	2	1	38	1	1	49
1962	7	1	0	2	0	0	0	1	1	37	1	1	50
1963	5	1	0	2	0	0	0	1	1	46	1	1	42
1964	9	2	0	2	0	0	0	2	1	50	2	1	31
1965	11	2	0	2	0	0	0	2	1	44	2	1	36
1966	11	2	0	2	0	0	0	2	1	46	1	1	35
1967	9	2	0	2	0	0	0	2	1	45	1	1	37
1968	10	2	0	2	0	0	0	1	1	45	2	1	36
1969	7	2	0	4	0	0	0	2	1	46	1	1	36
1970	7	2	0	4	0	0	0	2	1	39	1	1	41
1971	8	3	0	5	0	0	0	2	1	38	2	1	40
1972	7	3	0	6	0	0	0	2	2	39	2	1	38
1973	7	4	0	4	0	0	0	2	1	42	2	0	38
1974	4	2	0	3	0	0	0	1	1	51	1	0	35
1975	7	3	0	4	0	0	0	2	1	49	1	0	32
1976	7	3	0	4	0	0	0	2	1	43	1	0	37
1977	3	2	0	5	0	0	0	3	1	44	2	0	40
1978	3	2	0	4	0	1	0	3	1	41	1	0	44
1979	4	5	0	4	0	1	0	5	1	39	1	0	40
1980	3	5	0	4	0	1	0	6	2	31	1	0	47
1981	2	5	0	4	0	1	0	5	1	40	1	0	41
1982	2	4	0	4	0	1	0	6	1	36	1	0	43

(Table continues on the following page.)

Table B.1. Annual Distortion Estimates, Republic of Korea, 1955–2004 (continued)

c. Value shares of the primary production of covered[c] and noncovered products

Year	Barley	Beef	Cabbages	Eggs	Garlic	Milk	Peppers	Pig meat	Poultry	Rice	Soybeans	Wheat	Noncovered
1983	2	4	0	4	0	2	0	7	2	33	1	0	46
1984	2	5	0	4	0	2	0	7	2	31	1	0	46
1985	1	7	0	4	0	2	0	6	2	28	1	0	48
1986	1	7	3	4	2	2	4	6	3	31	1	0	36
1987	1	7	4	5	1	2	3	6	3	27	1	0	38
1988	1	5	5	4	2	3	4	6	3	30	1	0	36
1989	1	4	5	4	2	3	1	6	3	26	1	0	44
1990	1	4	4	4	3	4	2	7	3	26	1	0	41
1991	1	5	4	5	3	2	3	7	3	23	0	0	45
1992	1	6	3	4	3	3	5	9	3	22	0	0	40
1993	1	6	3	4	2	3	3	10	3	19	0	0	44
1994	0	6	4	4	2	3	2	8	3	21	0	0	46
1995	0	5	3	4	4	3	4	8	3	15	0	0	52
1996	0	4	3	4	4	3	5	7	3	16	0	0	51
1997	0	5	3	4	2	3	3	9	3	19	0	0	48
1998	0	6	3	5	2	3	4	10	3	21	0	0	43
1999	0	6	3	4	2	3	3	9	3	19	0	0	47
2000	0	5	3	3	3	3	3	7	2	16	0	0	54
2001	0	4	3	4	4	4	3	8	2	16	0	0	51
2002	0	3	3	4	2	4	3	8	3	13	0	0	56
2003	0	5	4	4	1	4	2	9	3	14	0	0	55

Sources: Author compilation; Honma and Hayami 2007; chapter 2 of this volume.

Note: — = no data are available. n.a. = not applicable.

a. Including assistance for nontradables and non-product-specific assistance (NPS).

b. Including product-specific input subsidies.

c. The covered products are calculated at undistorted farmgate prices in U.S. dollars.

Table B.2. Annual Distortion Estimates, Taiwan, China, 1955–2002
(percent)

a. NRAs for covered products

Year	Beef	Eggs	Pig meat	Poultry	Rice	Wheat	All
1955	−23	0	−39	−68	−49	96	−47
1956	52	0	10	−37	−11	31	−6
1957	47	0	9	−30	−3	38	1
1958	−10	0	−20	−55	−48	53	−41
1959	3	0	−1	−46	−37	23	−25
1960	20	0	14	−34	−9	31	−3
1961	49	0	24	−14	3	34	8
1962	48	0	73	2	−13	32	2
1963	51	0	120	4	−7	41	16
1964	39	0	88	25	−7	42	13
1965	66	0	118	20	−8	43	16
1966	51	0	112	14	−14	30	11
1967	4	0	87	18	−21	36	2
1968	0	0	113	31	−24	43	2
1969	24	0	69	23	−21	45	1
1970	14	0	82	19	0	55	21
1971	29	0	109	29	0	39	31
1972	50	0	114	39	2	65	35
1973	−4	0	111	27	−24	8	16
1974	22	0	74	22	−25	−6	0
1975	105	0	125	22	−15	0	15
1976	73	0	57	20	3	29	20
1977	89	0	45	42	−10	84	13
1978	91	0	49	35	−19	90	9
1979	41	0	28	31	3	83	15
1980	54	0	46	39	17	81	29
1981	72	0	48	65	8	81	27
1982	75	0	44	63	29	115	37
1983	88	1	41	85	46	—	46
1984	96	2	33	66	63	—	47
1985	95	9	41	57	73	—	53
1986	104	19	56	70	84	—	64
1987	108	17	72	87	110	—	81
1988	102	27	90	98	108	—	93
1989	97	61	123	110	142	—	122
1990	97	9	112	107	146	—	112
1991	97	−1	76	112	144	—	93

(Table continues on the following page.)

Table B.2. Annual Distortion Estimates, Taiwan, China, 1955–2002 (*continued***)**

a. NRAs for covered products

Year	Beef	Eggs	Pig meat	Poultry	Rice	Wheat	All
1992	95	41	93	149	170	—	115
1993	99	30	100	168	191	—	126
1994	106	40	138	178	156	—	140
1995	66	33	108	167	208	—	131
1996	97	2	124	167	174	—	126
1997	101	−1	94	195	149	—	114
1998	85	11	108	242	134	—	128
1999	63	44	221	372	174	—	212
2000	44	33	201	347	189	—	202
2001	95	22	168	254	195	—	169
2002	79	19	150	237	226	—	164

b. Agricultural NRAs and RRAs: All products, tradables, and relative to nonagricultural tradables

Year	NRA, total agriculture[a]				NRA, agricultural tradables			NRA, nonagricultural tradables	RRA
	Covered products		Noncovered products	All products, including NPS	Exportables[b]	Import-competing[b]	All		
	Inputs	Outputs							
1955	0	-47	0	-22	-35	-7	-30	7	-35
1956	0	-6	0	-3	-4	-3	-4	8	-11
1957	0	1	0	0	1	-2	0	8	-7
1958	0	-41	0	-20	-31	-3	-27	10	-33
1959	0	-25	0	-14	-21	-3	-18	10	-26
1960	0	-3	0	-1	-2	-1	-2	9	-10
1961	0	8	0	4	7	-1	5	9	-3
1962	0	2	0	1	1	1	1	10	-8
1963	0	16	0	8	13	1	11	9	1
1964	0	13	0	6	10	2	8	9	-1
1965	0	16	0	7	12	2	10	9	0
1966	0	11	0	5	8	2	7	10	-2
1967	0	2	0	1	1	2	1	8	-7
1968	0	2	0	1	1	3	1	9	-7
1969	0	1	0	1	0	3	1	8	-7
1970	0	21	0	10	16	2	13	8	5
1971	0	31	0	14	23	3	18	7	10
1972	0	35	0	16	26	5	20	8	11
1973	0	16	0	7	12	3	9	8	1
1974	0	0	0	0	-1	3	0	7	-6
1975	0	15	0	7	12	3	9	7	2
1976	0	20	0	10	16	4	13	7	6
1977	0	13	0	7	9	8	8	7	1
1978	0	9	0	4	5	6	5	7	-2

(Table continues on the following page.)

483

Table B.2. Annual Distortion Estimates, Taiwan, China, 1955–2002 (*continued*)

b. Agricultural NRAs and RRAs: All products, tradables, and relative to nonagricultural tradables

| Year | NRA, total agriculture[a] | | | | NRA, agricultural tradables | | | NRA, nonagricultural tradables | RRA |
| | Covered products | | Noncovered products | All products, including NPS | Exportables[b] | Import-competing[b] | All | | |
	Inputs	Outputs							
1979	0	15	0	7	10	5	9	7	2
1980	0	29	0	12	21	6	15	5	9
1981	0	27	0	11	17	9	14	5	8
1982	0	37	0	14	25	8	19	5	13
1983	0	46	0	19	31	12	23	5	17
1984	0	47	0	19	33	10	23	5	17
1985	0	53	0	20	37	9	25	5	19
1986	0	64	0	23	44	11	29	5	23
1987	0	81	0	26	53	13	33	5	27
1988	0	93	0	28	58	13	35	4	30
1989	0	122	0	38	53	45	47	4	41
1990	0	112	0	41	60	45	50	4	45
1991	0	93	0	34	57	34	41	3	37
1992	0	115	0	37	56	40	45	2	41
1993	0	126	0	38	61	41	46	2	43
1994	0	140	0	41	51	50	50	2	47
1995	0	131	0	39	60	43	47	2	45
1996	0	126	0	42	55	48	50	2	47
1997	0	114	0	43	58	48	50	2	48
1998	0	128	0	45	51	54	53	2	50
1999	0	212	0	63	61	79	74	2	72
2000	0	202	0	69	70	83	80	1	78
2001	0	169	0	60	66	70	69	1	67
2002	0	164	0	55	75	60	63	1	62

c. Value shares of the primary production of covered[c] and noncovered products

Year	Beef	Eggs	Pig meat	Poultry	Rice	Wheat	Noncovered
1955	0	0	12	1	34	0	52
1956	0	0	15	1	40	0	43
1957	0	0	16	1	35	0	48
1958	0	0	12	1	36	0	50
1959	0	1	17	1	37	0	43
1960	0	1	13	1	33	0	53
1961	0	1	13	2	35	0	49
1962	0	1	8	1	40	0	49
1963	0	1	9	2	38	0	50
1964	0	1	9	1	35	0	54
1965	0	1	9	1	36	0	53
1966	0	1	9	1	37	0	52
1967	0	1	10	2	37	0	51
1968	0	1	9	1	39	0	50
1969	0	1	11	2	35	0	50
1970	0	1	12	2	32	0	53
1971	0	1	12	2	29	0	55
1972	0	2	12	3	28	0	55
1973	0	1	12	3	29	0	54
1974	0	1	12	2	38	0	46
1975	0	2	10	2	36	0	50
1976	0	2	15	3	31	0	49
1977	0	2	17	4	26	0	51
1978	0	3	16	4	26	0	52
1979	0	2	18	4	22	0	54
1980	0	2	14	4	21	0	58
1981	0	2	14	4	21	0	59
1982	0	2	15	4	18	0	61
1983	0	3	16	5	17	—	59
1984	0	3	16	5	15	—	60
1985	0	3	16	5	14	—	62
1986	0	3	17	5	11	—	64
1987	0	2	16	5	9	—	68
1988	0	2	14	5	10	—	69
1989	0	2	14	6	9	—	69
1990	0	3	17	6	10	—	63
1991	0	3	19	5	9	—	64

(Table continues on the following page.)

Table B.2. Annual Distortion Estimates, Taiwan, China,
1955–2002 (*continued*)

c. Value shares of the primary production of covered[c] and noncovered products

Year	Beef	Eggs	Pig meat	Poultry	Rice	Wheat	Noncovered
1992	0	3	17	5	7	—	68
1993	0	3	15	5	7	—	70
1994	0	3	14	5	7	—	70
1995	0	3	16	5	6	—	70
1996	0	4	17	6	7	—	67
1997	0	5	17	7	8	—	62
1998	0	5	14	7	8	—	65
1999	0	5	11	6	8	—	70
2000	0	5	14	7	8	—	66
2001	0	5	16	7	7	—	64
2002	0	5	14	7	7	—	67

Sources: Author compilation; Honma and Hayami 2007; chapter 2 of this volume.

Note: — = no data are available.

a. Including assistance for nontradables and non-product-specific assistance (NPS).
b. Including product-specific input subsidies.
c. The covered products are calculated at undistorted farmgate prices in U.S. dollars.

Table B.3. Annual Distortion Estimates, China, 1955–2005

a. NRAs for covered products, 1981–2005

Year	Cotton	Fruits	Maize	Milk	Pig meat	Poultry	Rice	Soybeans	Sugar	Vegetables	Wheat	All
1981	−38	−37	−54	124	−74	24	−66	−12	30	−37	−15	−53
1982	−28	−32	−43	114	−81	33	−62	−3	33	−29	−10	−53
1983	−38	−34	−39	124	−80	31	−56	10	36	−50	5	−52
1984	−31	−12	−5	152	−80	13	−38	9	76	−51	27	−45
1985	−20	−5	6	160	−36	32	−23	30	82	−43	31	−24
1986	−33	0	−3	88	−55	−53	−25	13	33	−58	36	−39
1987	−46	−25	−11	38	−62	−62	−37	−13	27	−67	27	−50
1988	−44	−7	−36	4	−53	−46	−47	−19	37	−63	10	−49
1989	−30	−10	−36	2	−37	−7	−38	−4	45	−56	8	−40
1990	−27	−8	−39	−6	−30	−5	−36	5	3	−45	−4	−34
1991	−25	−6	−31	22	−22	−4	−33	14	29	−34	26	−24
1992	−28	−4	−37	−18	−15	−3	−46	−4	3	−22	−5	−24
1993	−32	−2	−27	−22	−7	−1	−32	−11	−3	−11	−7	−16
1994	−19	0	9	2	0	0	−5	19	25	0	46	3
1995	0	0	−7	−5	0	0	−2	33	23	0	53	3
1996	2	0	−7	−3	0	0	−6	40	24	0	28	1
1997	3	0	11	15	0	0	−9	35	33	0	28	3
1998	−6	0	23	44	0	0	−5	28	18	0	29	4
1999	−17	0	7	40	0	0	−11	11	35	0	13	0
2000	22	0	9	45	0	0	−8	20	67	0	13	2
2001	−21	0	16	4	0	0	−6	21	11	0	−1	0
2002	2	0	7	11	0	0	−15	14	30	0	−3	−1
2003	0	0	20	27	0	0	0	23	10	0	−1	2
2004	−13	0	6	30	0	0	−2	10	25	0	8	1
2005	14	0	17	32	0	0	−12	10	34	0	8	1

(Table continues on the following page.)

Table B.3. Annual Distortion Estimates, China, 1955–2005 (continued)

b. Agricultural NRAs and RRAs: All products, tradables, and relative to nonagricultural tradables, 1955–2005

Year	NRA, total agriculture[a]				NRA, agricultural tradables			NRA, nonagricultural tradables	RRA
	Covered products		Noncovered products	All products, including NPS	Exportables[b]	Import-competing[b]	All		
	Inputs	Outputs							
1955–80c	—	—	—	−40	—	—	—	—	−54
1981	0	−54	−35	−48	−58	−28	−48	43	−54
1982	0	−53	−32	−47	−58	−19	−47	42	−63
1983	0	−52	−31	−46	−59	−12	−46	40	−62
1984	0	−45	−19	−39	−52	15	−39	39	−57
1985	0	−25	−1	−17	−31	34	−17	24	−40
1986	0	−39	−11	−33	−45	32	−33	25	−46
1987	0	−50	−23	−45	−56	20	−45	26	−56
1988	0	−50	−24	−46	−54	9	−46	27	−57
1989	0	−41	−18	−36	−45	6	−36	28	−50
1990	0	−34	−21	−29	−37	−16	−29	27	−45
1991	0	−24	−6	−18	−28	13	−18	26	−36
1992	0	−24	−12	−20	−26	−6	−20	24	−36
1993	0	−16	−9	−12	−17	−5	−12	19	−29
1994	0	3	11	7	0	25	7	13	−10
1995	0	3	7	6	0	17	6	12	−6
1996	1	0	4	4	−2	10	4	9	−7
1997	1	2	11	7	−1	23	7	9	−2
1998	1	3	11	10	1	21	10	7	1
1999	1	0	6	5	−2	13	5	6	−1
2000	1	1	9	8	0	17	8	6	2
2001	1	0	1	4	0	1	4	5	−1
2002	1	−2	1	4	−2	4	4	4	−1
2003	1	2	4	7	2	6	7	3	2
2004	0	1	4	7	0	8	7	3	3
2005	0	0	6	7	−1	12	7	3	3

c. Value shares of the primary production of covered[d] and noncovered products, 1981–2005

Year	Cotton	Fruits	Maize	Milk	Pig meat	Poultry	Rice	Soybeans	Sugar	Vegetables	Wheat	Noncovered
1981	1	1	7	0	20	1	27	2	0	18	6	16
1982	1	1	5	0	26	1	25	2	0	16	6	16
1983	2	1	6	0	23	1	21	1	0	24	6	15
1984	2	1	5	0	26	1	19	1	0	25	6	12
1985	1	2	5	0	14	1	18	1	0	32	6	18
1986	1	2	5	0	18	2	16	2	1	37	5	11
1987	1	2	4	0	19	2	15	2	1	39	4	9
1988	1	2	4	0	19	3	18	2	1	38	4	8
1989	1	2	5	0	16	2	18	1	1	40	5	8
1990	1	2	6	0	14	3	17	1	1	34	6	14
1991	2	3	7	0	15	4	17	1	1	30	5	15
1992	1	3	7	1	14	3	19	2	1	32	7	13
1993	1	3	8	1	15	2	19	3	1	21	7	19
1994	2	4	7	1	18	4	19	2	1	24	6	13
1995	1	5	8	1	19	6	17	2	1	23	6	11
1996	1	3	9	1	18	5	17	1	1	21	7	15
1997	1	3	6	1	22	6	16	2	1	18	7	19
1998	1	3	6	0	18	6	15	1	1	18	6	25
1999	1	3	5	1	16	6	13	1	1	16	6	33
2000	1	3	4	1	16	6	11	1	1	19	5	34
2001	1	3	4	1	16	5	9	1	1	18	5	35
2002	1	3	4	1	15	5	9	1	1	18	4	37
2003	1	4	4	1	18	6	9	1	1	19	4	33
2004	1	4	5	1	19	5	10	2	1	17	4	32
2005	1	4	4	1	17	5	11	1	1	17	4	34

Sources: Author compilation; Huang et al. 2007; chapter 3 of this volume.

Note: — = no data are available.

a. Including assistance for nontradables and non-product-specific assistance (NPS).

b. Including product-specific input subsidies.

c. The estimates for China before 1981 are based on the assumption that the NRAs in agriculture in those years were the same as the average NRAs for 1981–89.

d. The covered products are calculated at undistorted farmgate prices in U.S. dollars.

Table B.4. Annual Distortion Estimates, Indonesia, 1970–2004

(percent)

a. NRAs for covered products

Year	Coconuts	Coffee	Maize	Palm oil	Poultry	Rice	Rubber	Soybeans	Sugar	Tea	All
1970	−17	−9	−7	−33	—	—	12	2	26	10	−2
1971	−2	−11	−21	−30	89	—	12	2	27	9	7
1972	2	−14	−22	26	62	—	21	−4	1	−10	2
1973	−2	1	−5	7	50	—	27	−20	−32	−18	−10
1974	−11	−3	−22	−41	89	—	3	−9	−11	−21	−10
1975	−5	−2	−24	−15	107	22	15	27	28	−9	15
1976	10	−1	−3	7	92	19	21	28	62	−10	21
1977	14	−4	22	−3	187	22	1	29	37	−8	20
1978	9	−5	30	−13	220	−1	−28	35	4	17	3
1979	−17	−7	25	−22	115	8	−26	40	−14	0	−4
1980	−4	−8	11	10	138	−10	−29	32	25	3	−4
1981	9	−5	10	14	183	−6	−21	50	58	17	9
1982	8	−4	13	65	186	33	−13	77	30	9	27
1983	−18	−13	50	36	132	11	−14	42	66	−10	17
1984	−26	−13	10	−14	99	10	−3	45	90	−10	11
1985	−16	−9	9	4	144	15	−8	31	39	4	14
1986	0	−4	24	48	108	7	−25	37	20	3	11

1987	−19	6	32	−13	58	−4	−35	14	−1	−11	−5
1988	−24	1	50	−33	68	−9	−19	0	−8	−4	−9
1989	−51	−6	−5	−12	56	−14	−15	2	−7	−3	−12
1990	−43	−2	−3	17	69	−10	−23	20	14	−8	−5
1991	−45	1	28	0	147	−16	−28	18	15	−2	−7
1992	−47	1	35	4	69	−8	−33	14	4	−3	−5
1993	−44	0	21	23	86	−4	−37	16	−6	−5	−5
1994	−50	−2	31	14	103	−6	−38	19	−7	6	−6
1995	−47	−2	37	−18	102	−12	−31	28	−7	6	−11
1996	−47	6	29	2	136	−15	−21	19	−12	−13	−10
1997	−16	5	19	−12	71	−7	56	16	−29	−23	−7
1998	−26	−1	36	−57	−9	−34	58	0	67	−23	−24
1999	−11	4	2	−6	139	4	123	24	37	−16	6
2000	−8	7	23	−3	107	15	56	1	60	−19	16
2001	−9	4	−3	12	70	21	38	−5	26	−18	17
2002	−10	1	1	−12	120	23	0	5	42	−15	15
2003	−6	0	25	−13	101	25	−4	4	68	−12	18
2004	—	3	9	—	—	9	−6	0	51	−14	12

(Table continues on the following page.)

Table B.4. Annual Distortion Estimates, Indonesia, 1970–2004 (*continued*)

b. Agricultural NRAs and RRAs: All products, tradables, and relative to nonagricultural tradables

	NRA, total agriculture[a]				NRA, agricultural tradables			NRA, nonagricultural tradables	RRA
	Covered products		Noncovered products	All products, including NPS	Exportables[b]	Import-competing[b]	All		
Year	Inputs	Outputs							
1970	6	−8	−4	−3	−11	10	−8	28	−28
1971	6	1	6	6	−2	19	7	28	−16
1972	7	−5	1	2	5	−1	2	28	−20
1973	6	−16	−7	−9	2	−25	−10	28	−30
1974	5	−16	−7	−9	−11	−10	−10	28	−30
1975	9	6	6	12	−3	21	13	28	−11
1976	6	14	12	18	10	26	20	28	−6
1977	6	14	12	17	9	27	20	28	−6
1978	6	−3	2	3	1	4	3	28	−19
1979	7	−10	−4	−4	−18	5	−4	28	−25
1980	7	−10	−4	−4	−11	0	−4	28	−25
1981	7	2	5	8	3	12	9	28	−15
1982	8	20	13	22	7	34	25	28	−2
1983	8	9	5	12	−12	27	14	28	−11
1984	7	4	2	7	−21	25	9	28	−15
1985	7	7	4	10	−12	24	12	28	−12
1986	6	4	4	8	−3	15	9	28	−14

1987	6	-11	-6	-6	-20	1	-7	28	-27
1988	6	-15	-9	-9	-21	-5	-10	26	-29
1989	5	-17	-12	-12	-27	-9	-14	24	-30
1990	4	-9	-7	-6	-21	-1	-6	22	-23
1991	4	-11	-10	-8	-26	-3	-9	20	-24
1992	4	-9	-9	-7	-28	0	-7	18	-21
1993	2	-7	-8	-6	-23	0	-7	16	-19
1994	2	-8	-8	-7	-25	0	-8	14	-19
1995	2	-13	-11	-11	-28	-4	-12	12	-21
1996	2	-12	-9	-10	-21	-7	-11	11	-20
1997	2	-9	-4	-6	-5	-7	-7	11	-16
1998	3	-27	-17	-22	-30	-21	-25	10	-31
1999	3	3	3	5	-1	10	6	10	-4
2000	2	13	8	13	0	23	14	9	5
2001	2	15	9	14	4	22	16	9	7
2002	2	14	7	12	-8	29	14	8	5
2003	1	16	9	14	-8	34	16	8	8
2004	3	9	3	8	-5	15	10	8	2

(Table continues on the following page.)

Table B.4. Annual Distortion Estimates, Indonesia, 1970–2004 (*continued*)

c. Value shares of the primary production of covered[c] and noncovered products

Year	Coconuts	Coffee	Maize	Palm oil	Poultry	Rice	Rubber	Soybeans	Sugar	Tea	Noncovered
1970	32	3	5	1	—	—	7	2	15	1	34
1971	31	2	5	1	1	—	5	2	20	1	32
1972	22	2	5	1	1	—	4	2	24	1	38
1973	27	1	4	1	1	—	5	2	22	1	36
1974	34	1	4	2	1	—	4	2	16	0	35
1975	12	1	4	1	1	34	2	1	11	0	31
1976	14	2	3	1	1	36	3	1	8	0	30
1977	18	3	2	1	0	30	3	1	9	1	33
1978	15	2	2	1	0	32	4	1	11	0	32
1979	15	2	2	1	1	28	5	1	11	0	33
1980	11	2	2	1	1	34	6	1	7	0	35
1981	10	1	2	1	1	35	3	1	11	0	35
1982	9	1	2	1	1	31	3	0	14	0	38
1983	11	1	2	1	1	33	3	1	10	0	36
1984	13	1	3	2	1	31	3	1	7	0	38
1985	10	1	3	2	1	30	3	1	10	0	40
1986	7	2	3	1	1	29	3	1	11	0	41
1987	8	2	2	2	1	27	5	1	11	0	40
1988	8	2	1	2	1	30	5	1	12	0	37
1989	4	1	2	2	1	35	4	1	12	0	36
1990	3	1	4	2	2	35	4	1	11	0	37

Year											
1991	4	1	3	2	1	35	4	1	11	0	37
1992	5	1	2	3	2	34	4	2	14	0	34
1993	4	1	2	2	2	29	5	1	14	0	39
1994	5	2	2	4	2	29	6	1	13	0	35
1995	5	2	2	4	1	30	6	1	10	0	39
1996	5	1	3	4	1	33	5	1	10	0	37
1997	8	1	3	5	2	30	2	1	10	0	38
1998	9	2	2	9	1	36	2	1	3	0	33
1999	13	2	3	4	1	35	1	1	4	0	36
2000	11	2	2	6	2	33	2	1	4	0	37
2001	9	1	3	6	2	29	2	1	7	0	39
2002	8	1	3	8	2	27	3	0	5	0	42
2003	8	1	3	7	2	23	4	0	4	0	46
2004	—	1	4	—	—	35	5	1	6	0	46

Sources: Author compilation; Fane and Warr 2007; chapter 4 of this volume.

Note: — = no data are available.

a. Including assistance for nontradables and non-product-specific assistance (NPS).

b. Including product-specific input subsidies.

c. The covered products are calculated at undistorted farmgate prices in U.S. dollars.

Table B.5. Annual Distortion Estimates, Malaysia, 1960–2004
(percent)

a. NRAs for covered products

Year	Cocoa	Palm oil	Rice	Rubber	All
1960	—	−11	29	−14	−11
1961	—	−11	21	−13	−8
1962	—	−9	11	−9	−6
1963	—	−10	14	−9	−6
1964	—	−16	21	−15	−11
1965	—	−10	25	−10	−5
1966	—	−12	11	−11	−8
1967	−1	−11	−10	−9	−10
1968	−3	−9	−19	−7	−10
1969	−2	−11	−16	−11	−12
1970	−1	−10	3	−9	−7
1971	−1	−17	20	−16	−10
1972	−1	−12	19	−9	−4
1973	−7	−11	−3	−11	−10
1974	−4	−26	−23	−19	−22
1975	1	−22	−17	−15	−18
1976	−1	−12	74	−18	−8
1977	−1	−22	83	−24	−16
1978	−6	−11	27	−26	−17
1979	−2	−9	30	−29	−18
1980	−2	−7	29	−29	−17
1981	−1	−7	33	−22	−10
1982	−1	−5	81	−13	0
1983	−1	−3	160	−15	1
1984	−3	−7	167	−13	−2
1985	4	1	192	−4	8
1986	−1	−3	171	−8	4
1987	−7	−8	253	−13	−3
1988	−4	−5	112	−12	−2
1989	1	0	63	−6	2
1990	−1	−2	123	−7	5
1991	−1	−2	100	−7	4
1992	−6	−6	147	−12	1
1993	−2	−3	165	−8	5
1994	−2	−3	101	−7	2
1995	−1	−3	117	−5	2
1996	−1	−2	86	−5	3

a. NRAs for covered products

Year	Cocoa	Palm oil	Rice	Rubber	All
1997	−8	−9	6	−13	−8
1998	0	−1	26	−5	1
1999	0	−1	52	−6	2
2000	0	−1	54	−5	3
2001	0	−2	89	−6	3
2002	0	−1	82	−5	2
2003	0	−1	65	−4	1
2004	0	−1	65	−3	1

(*Table continues on the following page.*)

Table B.5. Annual Distortion Estimates, Malaysia, 1960–2004 (continued)

b. Agricultural NRAs and RRAs: All products, tradables, and relative to nonagricultural tradables

| Year | NRA, total agriculture[a] | | | | NRA, agricultural tradables | | | NRA, nonagricultural tradables | RRA |
| | Covered products | | Noncovered products | All products, including NPS | Exportables[b] | Import-competing[b] | All | | |
	Inputs	Outputs							
1960	0	−11	0	−10	−14	16	−10	8	−17
1961	0	−8	0	−7	−12	15	−8	8	−14
1962	0	−6	0	−5	−9	8	−6	8	−12
1963	0	−6	0	−5	−9	11	−5	7	−11
1964	0	−11	0	−9	−15	16	−9	7	−15
1965	0	−5	0	−4	−9	18	−4	6	−10
1966	0	−8	0	−7	−10	8	−7	6	−12
1967	0	−10	0	−8	−9	−8	−9	8	−15
1968	0	−10	0	−9	−7	−15	−9	8	−16
1969	0	−12	0	−10	−10	−12	−10	8	−17
1970	0	−7	0	−6	−9	2	−6	7	−12
1971	0	−10	0	−9	−15	16	−9	7	−15
1972	0	−4	0	−3	−9	15	−4	9	−12
1973	0	−10	0	−8	−10	−3	−9	8	−16
1974	0	−22	0	−19	−20	−18	−19	4	−23
1975	0	−18	0	−15	−17	−14	−16	6	−21
1976	0	−8	0	−7	−15	45	−7	6	−12
1977	0	−16	0	−13	−22	44	−14	7	−20

Year									
1978	0	−17	0	−15	−20	15	−15	6	−21
1979	0	−18	0	−15	−21	18	−16	7	−21
1980	0	−17	0	−14	−20	16	−15	6	−20
1981	0	−10	0	−8	−14	20	−8	5	−13
1982	0	0	0	0	−8	43	0	5	−5
1983	0	1	0	1	−9	60	1	5	−4
1984	0	−2	0	−2	−8	45	−2	5	−6
1985	0	8	0	6	−1	56	6	4	2
1986	0	4	0	3	−5	56	3	4	−1
1987	0	−3	0	−2	−10	55	−2	5	−7
1988	0	−2	0	−2	−7	32	−2	4	−5
1989	0	2	0	2	−2	22	2	3	−1
1990	0	5	0	4	−3	40	4	3	1
1991	0	4	0	3	−3	32	3	3	0
1992	0	1	0	1	−7	38	1	3	−2
1993	0	5	0	3	−4	35	3	3	1
1994	0	2	0	1	−3	21	1	3	−1
1995	0	2	0	1	−3	19	1	2	−1
1996	0	3	0	2	−2	18	2	3	−1
1997	0	−8	0	−5	−8	3	−6	2	−8
1998	0	1	0	0	−1	5	0	1	−1
1999	0	2	0	1	−1	9	1	2	0
2000	0	3	0	2	−1	13	2	1	1
2001	0	3	0	2	−2	17	2	1	1
2002	0	2	0	1	−1	13	1	1	0
2003	0	1	0	1	−1	9	1	1	0
2004	0	1	0	1	−1	9	1	1	0

(Table continues on the following page.)

Table B.5. Annual Distortion Estimates, Malaysia, 1960–2004
   (*continued*)

c. Value shares of the primary production of covered[c] and noncovered products

Year	Cocoa	Palm oil	Rice	Rubber	Noncovered
1960	—	2	6	78	14
1961	—	3	11	72	14
1962	—	3	13	70	14
1963	—	4	13	69	14
1964	—	4	11	70	14
1965	—	6	12	68	14
1966	—	6	13	67	14
1967	0	7	17	62	14
1968	0	6	21	59	14
1969	0	5	16	65	14
1970	0	11	16	58	14
1971	0	16	14	56	14
1972	0	17	17	52	14
1973	0	11	17	57	14
1974	0	23	17	46	14
1975	0	29	18	37	15
1976	1	21	8	55	15
1977	0	30	6	49	15
1978	0	27	6	52	15
1979	0	26	7	51	15
1980	0	25	7	51	17
1981	1	29	9	41	19
1982	1	37	8	33	21
1983	1	30	5	41	23
1984	2	46	3	25	25
1985	2	43	3	27	25
1986	3	31	4	37	25
1987	3	29	2	41	25
1988	3	37	3	31	27
1989	2	40	5	23	29
1990	2	37	5	25	31
1991	2	39	5	21	33
1992	1	41	4	18	35
1993	1	41	3	18	37
1994	1	38	3	19	39
1995	1	42	3	14	41
1996	1	43	4	13	41
1997	0	44	5	10	41

c. Value shares of the primary production of covered[c] and noncovered products

Year	Cocoa	Palm oil	Rice	Rubber	Noncovered
1998	0	49	3	5	42
1999	0	49	3	6	42
2000	0	47	4	5	43
2001	0	44	4	9	43
2002	0	45	3	9	43
2003	0	45	2	10	43
2004	0	48	2	11	38

Sources: Author compilation; Athukorala and Loke 2007; chapter 5 of this volume.

Note: — = no data are available.

a. Including assistance for nontradables and non-product-specific assistance (NPS).

b. Including product-specific input subsidies.

c. The covered products are calculated at undistorted farmgate prices in U.S. dollars.

Table B.6. Annual Distortion Estimates, the Philippines, 1962–2004
(percent)

a. NRAs for covered products

Year	Bananas	Beef	Coconuts	Maize	Pig meat	Poultry	Rice	Sugar	All
1962	0	15	−24	−14	−30	−13	−18	38	−13
1963	0	15	−25	8	−27	6	−6	−39	−8
1964	0	15	−25	8	−34	34	14	−24	1
1965	0	15	−25	42	−23	49	10	103	16
1966	0	15	−20	29	−4	48	12	157	22
1967	0	15	−23	39	10	66	−5	134	15
1968	0	15	−18	44	44	80	−14	142	14
1969	0	15	−16	38	40	92	−10	67	16
1970	−4	15	−28	−10	13	67	−8	38	5
1971	−4	15	−27	49	25	35	29	16	24
1972	−4	10	−29	43	−10	25	23	−31	4
1973	−4	10	−23	−8	−18	−1	−39	−48	−31
1974	−4	10	−19	−3	6	18	−53	−34	−32
1975	−4	10	−21	6	−23	13	−29	−44	−23
1976	−4	10	−18	22	−12	5	0	−19	−5
1977	−4	10	−14	41	−9	42	−4	14	1
1978	−4	10	−12	37	−15	42	−32	24	−11
1979	−4	10	−18	16	31	38	−24	16	−6
1980	−4	5	−25	25	48	48	−38	−18	−16
1981	−4	5	−21	28	42	46	−36	−15	−13
1982	−4	5	−31	42	30	44	3	73	12
1983	−4	5	−36	−2	21	27	−10	64	−3
1984	−4	5	−23	7	39	26	0	193	12
1985	−4	5	−37	41	59	50	43	273	26
1986	0	20	−27	62	32	40	26	114	26
1987	0	20	−17	96	43	44	11	126	27
1988	0	20	−14	46	65	43	−9	70	13
1989	0	20	−9	54	56	37	2	33	17
1990	0	20	−17	51	25	34	16	29	16
1991	0	30	−15	24	24	39	1	56	10
1992	0	30	−19	88	16	84	21	75	24
1993	0	30	−15	69	24	68	46	51	32
1994	0	30	−10	82	36	57	21	35	24
1995	0	30	−9	94	−2	50	55	80	36
1996	0	30	−4	48	31	37	71	80	47
1997	0	30	−22	84	53	39	63	60	45
1998	0	30	−5	66	−2	25	21	95	20
1999	0	20	2	100	23	60	53	171	41
2000	0	10	−23	96	6	66	73	77	39
2001	0	10	−23	72	0	51	69	67	36
2002	0	10	−5	45	−7	55	54	105	27
2003	0	10	−8	25	−22	49	41	84	15
2004	0	10	−11	35	−19	40	17	64	7

b. Agricultural NRAs and RRAs: All products, tradables, and relative to nonagricultural tradables

	NRA, total agriculture[a]				NRA, agricultural tradables			NRA, nonagricultural tradables	RRA
	Covered products		Noncovered products	All products, including NPS	Exportables[b]	Import-competing[b]	All		
Year	Inputs	Outputs							
1962	0	-13	-3	-11	3	-15	-8	19	-23
1963	0	-8	-1	-6	-11	-6	-3	19	-19
1964	0	1	3	2	-10	5	7	19	-10
1965	0	16	8	14	27	12	19	19	0
1966	0	22	8	19	44	15	21	22	-1
1967	0	15	5	13	40	8	13	20	-6
1968	0	14	4	12	40	6	9	19	-9
1969	0	16	4	13	27	10	10	21	-9
1970	0	5	1	4	14	1	3	20	-14
1971	0	24	8	21	4	31	19	24	-4
1972	0	4	2	4	-20	17	5	15	-9
1973	0	-31	-11	-27	-30	-28	-27	11	-35
1974	0	-32	-12	-28	-19	-35	-31	10	-37
1975	0	-23	-8	-19	-25	-19	-20	13	-29
1976	0	-5	-1	-4	-14	3	-3	17	-17
1977	0	1	2	2	-3	5	2	18	-13
1978	0	-11	-3	-8	-1	-14	-8	17	-21
1979	0	-6	-2	-5	-6	-5	-8	17	-22
1980	0	-16	-7	-13	-15	-14	-17	16	-29
1981	0	-13	-6	-11	-12	-13	-15	13	-25
1982	0	12	7	11	5	17	9	13	-3

(Table continues on the following page.)

503

Table B.6. Annual Distortion Estimates, the Philippines, 1962–2004 (continued)

b. Agricultural NRAs and RRAs: All products, tradables, and relative to nonagricultural tradables

	NRA, total agriculture[a]				NRA, agricultural tradables			NRA, nonagricultural tradables	RRA
	Covered products		Noncovered products	All products, including NPS	Exportables[b]	Import-competing[b]	All		
Year	Inputs	Outputs							
1983	0	−3	1	−2	−6	0	−4	11	−14
1984	0	12	7	11	10	13	8	12	−4
1985	0	26	17	24	2	44	22	12	9
1986	0	26	12	22	7	35	21	10	10
1987	0	27	11	23	11	33	21	11	9
1988	0	13	4	11	5	17	6	13	−6
1989	0	17	5	14	5	21	10	9	0
1990	0	16	7	14	0	24	12	11	1
1991	0	10	3	8	5	11	6	9	−3
1992	0	24	10	21	8	30	20	11	9
1993	0	32	13	28	6	43	27	9	17
1994	0	24	8	21	4	31	18	10	8
1995	0	36	15	31	−4	44	34	7	26
1996	0	47	19	41	−2	58	44	8	33
1997	0	45	20	39	4	60	42	9	31
1998	0	20	8	17	−2	25	19	8	10
1999	0	41	18	36	1	53	39	11	25
2000	0	39	17	34	−9	50	37	9	25
2001	0	36	15	32	−8	45	34	8	24
2002	0	27	11	24	−2	34	26	7	18
2003	0	15	6	14	−3	19	15	5	10
2004	0	7	3	6	5	7	6	3	3

c. Value shares of the primary production of covered[c] and noncovered products

Year	Bananas	Beef	Coconuts	Maize	Pig meat	Poultry	Rice	Sugar	Noncovered
1962	5	7	2	8	11	5	37	3	22
1963	5	4	3	9	12	4	37	4	22
1964	5	4	3	9	14	4	34	5	22
1965	4	4	3	8	13	4	34	7	22
1966	4	4	2	8	14	4	36	5	22
1967	4	3	2	7	12	4	42	6	19
1968	4	3	2	7	9	3	45	6	20
1969	5	3	2	8	9	3	38	10	22
1970	4	4	3	11	11	2	31	12	22
1971	5	2	3	11	12	3	30	15	19
1972	4	3	4	9	11	2	27	17	23
1973	2	2	4	10	8	2	34	17	22
1974	3	3	5	10	6	1	41	11	21
1975	2	2	9	10	6	1	29	15	24
1976	2	2	12	10	6	1	25	15	25
1977	2	2	15	7	8	1	26	10	29
1978	3	2	15	7	9	1	28	7	28
1979	3	2	21	7	6	1	25	9	25
1980	4	3	14	6	6	1	28	10	28
1981	3	3	12	7	6	1	29	11	28
1982	4	4	15	8	8	1	25	9	27
1983	4	4	16	9	8	1	23	6	29
1984	4	3	22	9	9	1	21	5	26
1985	4	3	24	10	7	1	23	4	25
1986	5	3	14	9	9	1	24	5	30
1987	4	3	15	8	9	1	26	5	28
1988	5	3	17	9	8	1	26	6	24
1989	4	3	13	8	9	1	27	9	26
1990	4	3	14	8	12	2	23	9	26
1991	4	3	10	7	11	1	35	5	22
1992	4	3	13	7	13	1	31	6	22
1993	4	4	12	7	13	1	29	7	22
1994	4	3	10	6	12	1	35	6	22
1995	4	3	9	5	18	1	32	6	21
1996	4	3	9	7	14	2	33	6	22
1997	5	4	11	5	12	2	32	6	23
1998	4	5	10	5	16	2	28	5	25
1999	6	6	11	5	14	1	31	3	22
2000	5	7	8	5	18	1	29	5	21
2001	5	6	7	6	19	2	29	6	20
2002	5	5	9	6	21	1	30	4	19
2003	5	5	8	6	23	1	29	4	20
2004	4	4	10	6	21	1	30	4	20

Sources: Author compilation; David, Intal, and Balisacan 2007; chapter 6 of this volume.

a. Including assistance for nontradables and non-product-specific assistance (NPS).

b. Including product-specific input subsidies.

c. The covered products are calculated at undistorted farmgate prices in U.S. dollars.

Table B.7. Annual Distortion Estimates, Thailand, 1970–2004
(percent)

a. NRAs for covered products

Year	Cassava	Maize	Palm oil	Pig meat	Poultry	Rice	Rubber	Soybeans	Sugar	All
1970	−10	−2	—	−5	—	−26	−5	—	33	−20
1971	−25	−3	—	16	−37	−29	5	—	30	−24
1972	−33	5	—	−17	−43	−22	11	—	12	−23
1973	−39	−8	—	−35	−32	−21	−5	—	5	−22
1974	−8	−2	—	18	−19	−52	−8	—	−17	−41
1975	0	−5	—	−7	30	−40	2	—	−11	−28
1976	0	−3	—	−9	24	−21	−3	—	−3	−12
1977	−10	0	—	19	3	−26	−11	—	−2	−16
1978	−13	−2	—	−13	8	−31	−14	—	2	−22
1979	19	−4	—	19	15	−24	−18	—	−2	−13
1980	−2	−4	−25	83	45	−25	−21	—	6	−12
1981	−22	−7	−33	60	12	−29	−28	—	21	−17
1982	−7	0	−20	19	34	−16	−14	—	1	−7
1983	7	0	−19	68	27	−9	−8	—	7	0
1984	−21	0	−31	29	16	−12	−19	−18	28	−7
1985	−29	−7	−22	−5	16	−20	−14	−27	41	−13
1986	0	−12	12	−5	−9	−18	−11	−20	41	−11
1987	−21	−9	68	3	−13	−11	−15	−16	38	−10
1988	−20	−4	71	53	−13	−9	−14	−7	43	−5
1989	−13	−6	32	58	−17	−17	−13	−12	21	−9
1990	−11	−5	67	14	−5	−14	−4	−44	24	−7
1991	−16	−4	39	−6	−12	−14	−7	−16	35	−8
1992	−12	−13	18	15	−17	−10	−2	35	45	−4
1993	−17	0	22	−20	−10	−20	−8	21	37	−10
1994	1	−1	−14	5	−11	−24	−2	27	29	−9
1995	3	6	−13	60	17	−10	−2	22	21	3
1996	−19	−10	−3	32	18	−2	2	25	37	5
1997	−20	−37	−18	3	8	−17	−4	7	37	−8
1998	−11	−7	−19	19	23	−16	4	17	14	−4
1999	−22	−10	−11	67	23	−11	−6	37	2	−1
2000	−14	1	−11	−10	21	−13	−1	36	16	−3
2001	−8	−2	−38	−16	15	−9	1	30	8	−3
2002	−5	−2	−9	21	33	−6	4	33	12	5
2003	−13	0	−15	−3	13	−3	3	28	9	1
2004	−10	0	—	—	—	−6	−6	22	18	−2

Year	NRA, total agriculture[a]				NRA, agricultural tradables			NRA, nonagricultural tradables	RRA
	Covered products		Noncovered products	All products, including NPS	Exportables[b]	Import-competing[b]	All		
	Inputs	Outputs							
1970	-1	-18	-9	-15	-21	-5	-18	16	-29
1971	-1	-22	-3	-16	-26	16	-18	16	-30
1972	-1	-21	-13	-19	-23	-17	-22	16	-33
1973	-1	-21	-19	-21	-21	-35	-23	16	-34
1974	-1	-40	-8	-30	-43	18	-34	16	-43
1975	-1	-27	-12	-23	-29	-7	-26	16	-36
1976	-1	-11	-7	-10	-13	-9	-12	16	-24
1977	-1	-15	0	-10	-18	19	-12	16	-24
1978	-1	-21	-12	-18	-23	-13	-21	16	-32
1979	-1	-12	2	-8	-15	19	-9	16	-22
1980	-1	-11	21	-1	-16	78	-1	16	-15
1981	-1	-16	11	-8	-21	55	-9	15	-21
1982	-1	-6	3	-4	-8	17	-4	14	-16
1983	-1	1	18	6	-3	56	7	13	-6
1984	-1	-5	4	-3	-8	21	-4	12	-14
1985	-3	-10	-7	-11	-14	-7	-13	11	-22
1986	-2	-9	-5	-9	-11	-4	-10	11	-19
1987	-3	-6	0	-7	-11	11	-8	11	-17
1988	-2	-3	16	0	-9	56	0	11	-10

(Table continues on the following page.)

Table B.7. Annual Distortion Estimates, Thailand, 1970–2004 (*continued*)

b. Agricultural NRAs and RRAs: All products, tradables, and relative to nonagricultural tradables

Year	NRA, total agriculture				NRA, agricultural tradables			NRA, nonagricultural tradables	RRA
	Covered products		Noncovered products	All products, including NPS	Exportables[b]	Import-competing[b]	All		
	Inputs	Outputs							
1989	−3	−7	13	−4	−13	53	−4	11	−14
1990	−3	−3	4	−4	−9	22	−4	10	−13
1991	−2	−6	−3	−7	−9	−1	−8	10	−16
1992	−1	−3	4	−2	−7	18	−2	10	−11
1993	−2	−9	−7	−9	−10	−10	−10	10	−18
1994	−1	−8	−2	−7	−11	4	−8	10	−16
1995	−1	4	18	7	−1	54	7	9	−2
1996	0	5	11	6	2	31	7	9	−2
1997	0	−8	−2	−7	−10	3	−8	9	−15
1998	−2	−1	4	−2	−5	19	−2	9	−10
1999	−3	2	19	4	−5	64	4	8	−4
2000	−1	−2	−3	−3	−3	−6	−3	8	−11
2001	−1	−3	−5	−4	−2	−14	−4	8	−11
2002	−2	7	8	6	4	22	7	8	−1
2003	0	0	0	0	1	−1	0	8	−7
2004	−1	−2	7	−1	−3	22	−1	8	−8

c. Value shares of the primary production of covered[c] and noncovered products

Year	Cassava	Maize	Palm oil	Pig meat	Poultry	Rice	Rubber	Soybeans	Sugar	Noncovered
1970	3	4	—	4	—	44	3	—	1	40
1971	3	4	—	3	9	40	3	—	1	37
1972	6	2	—	4	9	39	3	—	1	35
1973	4	5	—	5	7	42	4	—	2	31
1974	1	4	—	2	4	50	2	—	2	34
1975	2	5	—	3	3	47	2	—	3	35
1976	4	4	—	3	3	39	3	—	5	37
1977	6	2	—	3	5	38	4	—	7	36
1978	4	3	—	4	4	42	4	—	3	34
1979	5	4	—	3	4	39	7	—	6	33
1980	7	4	0	3	3	41	6	—	3	33
1981	6	4	0	3	4	42	5	—	5	32
1982	7	4	0	4	4	35	5	—	8	33
1983	7	5	0	3	5	36	6	—	4	33
1984	8	6	1	4	4	35	6	1	4	32
1985	6	5	1	5	4	34	7	1	3	33
1986	7	5	0	5	6	30	10	2	2	33
1987	10	3	1	5	6	28	11	1	3	31
1988	7	5	1	3	6	36	13	2	3	25
1989	6	5	1	3	6	38	10	2	4	24
1990	7	4	1	5	7	29	11	3	5	28
1991	7	4	1	6	9	30	9	1	4	28
1992	6	4	1	6	11	27	11	1	4	29
1993	5	3	1	7	11	24	12	1	4	31
1994	4	4	2	6	9	29	14	1	4	28
1995	5	4	2	4	8	28	18	1	5	25
1996	5	5	2	6	9	27	16	1	4	24
1997	4	6	2	7	9	31	12	1	4	24
1998	5	4	3	4	9	36	10	1	4	25
1999	4	5	2	4	10	33	11	1	6	25
2000	3	5	2	6	10	31	13	1	6	23
2001	4	4	2	9	12	27	12	0	5	25
2002	4	4	3	6	11	27	16	0	5	23
2003	4	4	3	6	9	24	21	0	6	21
2004	5	4	—	—	—	29	31	0	11	20

Sources: Author compilation; Warr and Kohpaiboon 2007; chapter 7 of this volume.

Note: — = no data are available.

a. Including assistance for nontradables and non-product-specific assistance (NPS).

b. Including product-specific input subsidies.

c. The covered products are calculated at undistorted farmgate prices in U.S. dollars.

Table B.8. Annual Distortion Estimates, Vietnam, 1986–2005
(percent)

a. NRAs for covered products

Year	Coffee	Pig meat	Poultry	Rice	Rubber	Sugar	All
1986	−58	−45	—	1	—	—	−11
1987	−74	−73	—	−7	—	—	−29
1988	−36	−27	—	2	—	—	−3
1989	−30	−22	—	−7	—	—	−11
1990	−34	−52	−3	−37	92	26	−36
1991	−27	−46	−4	−20	14	37	−23
1992	−21	−50	−4	−35	−5	38	−34
1993	−12	−32	−4	−25	5	67	−23
1994	−12	−8	−4	−16	0	80	−11
1995	−10	5	−4	−8	1	61	−4
1996	0	16	5	−7	2	79	0
1997	−2	−37	5	0	8	80	−6
1998	−15	−22	6	−9	33	105	−8
1999	−8	8	6	22	50	239	21
2000	−7	−4	2	19	24	99	14
2001	−16	−14	2	35	50	97	20
2002	−16	45	2	4	23	160	14
2003	−9	—	2	34	−6	218	31
2004	—	—	2	22	−6	227	24
2005	—	—	2	9	—	162	12

b. Agricultural NRAs and RRAs: All products, tradables, and relative to nonagricultural tradables

| Year | NRA, total agriculture[a] | | | | NRA, agricultural tradables | | | NRA, nonagricultural tradables | RRA |
| | Covered products | | Noncovered products | All products, including NPS | Exportables[b] | Import-competing[b] | All | | |
	Inputs	Outputs							
1986	0	−11	−16	−13	−19	50	−15	7	−21
1987	0	−29	−24	−27	−32	53	−31	6	−35
1988	0	−3	−11	−6	−8	44	−7	7	−13
1989	0	−11	−7	−9	−10	2	−10	−2	−8
1990	0	−36	−35	−36	−37	17	−37	−15	−26
1991	0	−23	−19	−22	−24	21	−23	−8	−17
1992	0	−34	−33	−34	−36	18	−35	−16	−22
1993	0	−23	−23	−23	−25	31	−24	−11	−15
1994	0	−11	−15	−12	−14	41	−13	−7	−7
1995	0	−4	−7	−4	−6	41	−6	−8	3
1996	0	0	−6	−2	−3	50	−3	−8	5
1997	0	−6	0	−5	−8	52	−5	3	−8
1998	0	−8	−8	−8	−10	66	−7	−2	−6
1999	0	21	22	21	17	119	21	23	−1
2000	0	14	19	15	12	50	14	16	−2
2001	0	20	33	24	19	54	21	27	−4
2002	0	14	5	11	11	70	13	8	5
2003	0	31	33	32	28	79	31	31	1
2004	0	24	22	23	19	84	23	22	1
2005	0	12	9	11	8	56	11	11	1

(Table continues on the following page.)

511

Table B.8. Annual Distortion Estimates, Vietnam, 1986–2005 (*continued*)

c. Value shares of the primary production of covered[c] and noncovered products

Year	Coffee	Pig meat	Poultry	Rice	Rubber	Sugar	Noncovered
1986	1	14	—	43	—	—	42
1987	1	22	—	47	—	—	29
1988	1	10	—	57	—	—	32
1989	1	14	—	56	—	—	29
1990	1	14	2	56	1	2	24
1991	1	13	3	53	1	2	28
1992	1	12	3	44	1	1	39
1993	2	13	3	45	1	1	35
1994	2	11	3	45	1	2	36
1995	5	12	3	54	1	2	23
1996	4	11	3	55	1	2	24
1997	5	18	3	46	2	2	24
1998	4	13	3	55	1	2	22
1999	5	14	3	49	1	1	26
2000	6	14	4	42	2	2	31
2001	4	16	4	37	1	3	34
2002	2	12	4	47	2	1	33
2003	2	—	5	43	4	1	45
2004	—	—	4	47	4	1	44
2005	—	—	3	49	—	1	47

Sources: Author compilation; Athukorala, Huong, and Thanh 2007; chapter 8 of this volume.

Note: — = no data are available.

a. Including assistance for nontradables and non-product-specific assistance (NPS).

b. Including product-specific input subsidies.

c. The covered products are calculated at undistorted farmgate prices in U.S. dollars.

Table B.9. Annual Distortion Estimates, Bangladesh, 1974–2004
(percent)

a. NRAs for covered products

Year	Jute	Potatoes	Rice	Sugar	Tea	Wheat	All
1974	−30	1	−26	74	1	39	−21
1975	−53	1	105	−9	−4	140	78
1976	−33	2	−5	−19	−14	−6	−8
1977	−43	2	−26	65	−14	18	−23
1978	−38	2	−28	209	−23	9	−24
1979	−19	2	−13	213	−17	−9	−10
1980	−30	0	−12	137	−24	1	−10
1981	−40	1	−36	−13	−14	−19	−33
1982	−37	1	5	56	−5	−11	4
1983	−17	2	3	270	−9	−1	6
1984	−22	2	14	236	−2	1	14
1985	−21	2	39	715	−12	7	32
1986	−54	2	8	688	−59	14	2
1987	−44	1	42	338	−8	24	38
1988	−20	2	12	298	−9	16	10
1989	−38	2	1	140	−12	−5	2
1990	−28	3	−4	124	0	3	−1
1991	−33	3	2	137	−14	32	4
1992	−42	2	−2	194	−12	5	0
1993	−46	0	−11	205	−13	−3	−7
1994	−44	2	−12	171	−21	−14	−8
1995	−29	3	−1	124	−33	6	2
1996	15	3	−19	111	−18	−14	−14
1997	−3	3	−24	131	−21	−4	−17
1998	21	3	−15	138	−5	9	−11
1999	−32	2	−1	192	−26	16	2
2000	−37	1	2	308	−16	19	5
2001	−41	2	9	180	−18	−1	9
2002	−29	2	3	149	−27	−5	4
2003	−40	2	6	271	−22	−15	6
2004	−46	2	−8	212	−19	1	−5

(Table continues on the following page.)

Table B.9. Annual Distortion Estimates, Bangladesh, 1974–2004 (*continued*)

b. Agricultural NRAs and RRAs: All products, tradables, and relative to nonagricultural tradables

| Year | NRA, total agriculture[a] | | | | NRA, agricultural tradables | | | NRA, nonagricultural tradables | RRA |
| | Covered products | | Noncovered products | All products, including NPS | Exportables[b] | Import-competing[b] | All | | |
	Inputs	Outputs							
1974	1	−21	0	−16	−29	−21	−22	46	−46
1975	0	78	0	57	−48	93	82	29	42
1976	1	−9	0	−6	−32	−6	−8	27	−27
1977	1	−24	0	−18	−39	−22	−23	28	−40
1978	1	−25	0	−19	−36	−24	−25	29	−42
1979	2	−11	0	−7	−19	−9	−10	30	−31
1980	1	−11	0	−7	−29	−8	−10	18	−24
1981	1	−34	0	−27	−36	−34	−34	24	−47
1982	1	3	0	3	−32	7	4	22	−15
1983	1	5	0	5	−16	8	6	23	−13
1984	1	13	0	11	−17	18	15	25	−8
1985	1	31	0	22	−19	43	33	25	7
1986	1	2	0	2	−55	16	2	29	−21
1987	1	37	0	26	−37	47	40	33	5
1988	1	8	0	7	−18	13	10	29	−15
1989	2	−1	0	1	−33	4	2	26	−20

Year									
1990	2	−3	0	0	−23	1	−1	29	−23
1991	2	3	0	3	−30	7	4	32	−21
1992	1	−1	0	0	−36	3	0	35	−26
1993	0	−8	0	−5	−39	−5	−8	32	−30
1994	1	−9	0	−5	−37	−6	−8	39	−34
1995	2	−1	0	1	−30	4	2	29	−21
1996	2	−16	0	−9	5	−15	−14	30	−34
1997	3	−19	0	−11	−8	−18	−17	30	−36
1998	2	−13	0	−8	13	−13	−12	32	−33
1999	2	0	0	1	−30	4	2	25	−18
2000	2	3	0	4	−31	8	6	25	−16
2001	2	7	0	6	−34	12	9	25	−12
2002	3	1	0	3	−28	6	4	21	−14
2003	3	3	0	5	−35	9	7	26	−15
2004	3	−8	0	−4	−37	−4	−6	20	−21

(*Table continues on the following page.*)

Table B.9. Annual Distortion Estimates, Bangladesh, 1974–2004 (*continued*)

c. Value shares of the primary production of covered[c] and noncovered products

Year	Jute	Potatoes	Rice	Sugar	Tea	Wheat	Noncovered
1974	9	3	61	3	0	1	23
1975	5	4	57	7	0	0	27
1976	5	3	64	5	1	1	22
1977	7	2	67	3	1	1	19
1978	6	2	68	1	1	1	21
1979	8	2	60	1	1	1	26
1980	6	2	63	1	1	2	25
1981	4	2	69	4	1	3	18
1982	5	3	62	4	1	4	22
1983	5	2	64	1	1	4	22
1984	5	3	61	1	2	4	25
1985	9	3	52	1	2	4	29
1986	11	2	52	1	2	3	29
1987	4	3	54	1	1	3	33
1988	5	3	62	0	1	3	26
1989	4	3	63	2	1	3	24
1990	4	3	62	2	1	2	27
1991	5	2	60	2	1	2	27
1992	4	3	61	2	1	3	27
1993	3	3	58	2	1	3	30
1994	3	4	56	2	1	3	31
1995	3	3	58	2	1	3	30
1996	2	3	58	2	1	4	31
1997	3	3	56	2	1	4	32
1998	3	3	59	0	1	5	29
1999	2	5	58	1	1	4	29
2000	2	7	57	1	1	4	29
2001	3	4	56	1	1	4	30
2002	3	4	58	1	1	4	28
2003	2	6	58	1	1	3	28
2004	2	7	61	1	1	3	26

Sources: Author compilation; Ahmed et al. 2007; chapter 9 of this volume.

a. Including assistance for nontradables and non-product-specific assistance (NPS).

b. Including product-specific input subsidies.

c. The covered products are calculated at undistorted farmgate prices in U.S. dollars.

Table B.10. Annual Distortion Estimates, India, 1965–2004

(percent)

a. NRAs for covered products

Year	Chickpeas	Cotton	Fruits and vegetables	Groundnuts	Maize	Milk	Rapeseeds	Rice	Sorghum	Soybeans	Sugar	Sunflower	Wheat	All
1965	5	33	0	54	85	—	66	0	46	—	171	—	47	21
1966	4	6	0	24	81	—	40	-34	25	—	181	—	11	-2
1967	39	16	0	6	59	—	83	-37	65	—	126	—	19	-5
1968	0	0	0	16	36	—	64	-44	12	—	224	—	42	-13
1969	75	34	0	18	57	—	62	-35	60	—	90	—	39	0
1970	0	85	0	0	23	—	56	-16	35	—	52	—	58	8
1971	0	90	0	0	34	—	65	0	97	—	29	—	53	17
1972	0	122	0	8	106	—	72	0	39	—	59	—	41	19
1973	0	107	0	0	55	—	0	-34	48	0	0	—	0	-6
1974	7	-12	0	0	28	—	1	-67	56	0	-51	—	0	-36
1975	0	0	0	-31	-31	130	0	-58	0	-16	-69	0	0	-29
1976	0	30	0	-14	0	171	0	-36	0	-14	-16	0	-3	-1
1977	0	0	0	-21	20	176	27	-29	45	-6	8	0	18	5
1978	0	15	0	-18	24	137	34	-43	8	-28	30	0	0	-6
1979	0	0	0	0	0	149	22	-29	5	-10	0	0	0	3
1980	26	8	0	0	0	93	50	-45	0	0	-24	1	0	-9
1981	9	-9	0	25	0	68	46	-54	16	0	-18	3	-2	-15
1982	0	9	0	35	4	97	34	-30	10	0	25	28	0	6
1983	0	8	0	21	9	146	47	-13	4	0	21	0	0	13
1984	3	-14	0	28	-20	164	15	-13	2	-6	44	7	11	15

(Table continues on the following page.)

Table B.10. Annual Distortion Estimates, India, 1965–2004 (*continued*)

a. NRAs for covered products

Year	Chickpeas	Cotton	Fruits and vegetables	Groundnuts	Maize	Milk	Rapeseeds	Rice	Sorghum	Soybeans	Sugar	Sunflower	Wheat	All
1985	34	6	0	41	4	186	12	6	24	9	93	52	12	29
1986	3	34	0	95	10	192	60	4	66	35	76	117	8	32
1987	5	90	0	124	86	178	136	8	56	44	68	65	14	43
1988	12	25	0	18	33	79	113	−21	19	5	37	5	18	14
1989	7	14	0	31	−1	49	53	−16	13	4	6	40	−6	8
1990	15	10	0	39	8	91	113	−18	6	5	6	45	29	16
1991	9	1	−17	36	11	48	77	−27	7	4	8	32	−5	0
1992	9	6	−32	4	−15	16	48	−30	−3	3	7	4	−9	−12
1993	6	31	−17	4	3	24	49	−13	−25	1	8	4	17	1
1994	7	65	−13	6	9	23	37	−17	51	3	8	5	21	4
1995	16	−6	−21	7	11	0	22	−9	2	4	−5	7	−13	−7
1996	11	−6	−9	6	−5	21	19	−31	9	3	9	11	−15	−7
1997	24	12	−17	8	−12	20	21	−21	13	0	11	10	35	−2
1998	10	14	−2	6	8	26	67	0	33	3	10	18	34	11
1999	14	16	−19	12	11	44	56	−5	50	5	37	21	31	8
2000	18	22	−13	13	12	14	53	15	13	7	29	17	38	9
2001	35	−1	0	11	12	31	36	18	16	7	9	19	36	17
2002	16	7	−5	17	16	59	72	29	16	10	44	16	47	26
2003	11	17	−14	15	9	40	89	19	15	−2	51	11	34	16
2004	13	15	−13	9	10	17	75	22	18	−8	63	10	37	11

b. Agricultural NRAs and RRAs: All products, tradables, and relative to nonagricultural tradables

Year	NRA, total agriculture				NRA, agricultural tradables			NRA, nonagricultural tradables[c]	RRA
	Covered products		Noncovered products	All products, including NPS	Exportables[b]	Import-competing[b]	All		
	Inputs	Outputs							
1965	0	21	20	20	—	55	54	113	−56
1966	0	−2	−3	−2	−34	33	−4	113	−55
1967	0	−5	−5	−5	−37	35	−6	113	−56
1968	0	−13	−13	−13	−44	39	−17	113	−61
1969	0	0	0	0	−35	46	0	113	−53
1970	0	8	8	8	−16	53	12	79	−37
1971	0	17	17	17	0	61	61	85	−13
1972	0	19	19	19	0	53	53	81	−16
1973	0	−6	−6	−6	−34	73	−13	83	−52
1974	0	−36	−36	−36	−61	24	−50	87	−73
1975	0	−29	−28	−28	−57	77	−39	66	−64
1976	0	−1	−1	−1	−25	110	−2	57	−38
1977	0	5	5	5	−28	58	6	64	−35
1978	0	−6	−6	−6	−40	59	−9	61	−43
1979	0	3	3	3	−29	69	7	76	−39
1980	0	−9	−9	−9	−43	57	−15	82	−53
1981	0	−15	−15	−15	−39	42	−18	63	−50
1982	0	6	5	6	−30	46	9	54	−29
1983	0	13	13	13	−13	54	21	56	−22

(Table continues on the following page.)

Table B.10. Annual Distortion Estimates, India, 1965–2004 (*continued*)

b. Agricultural NRAs and RRAs: All products, tradables, and relative to nonagricultural tradables

Year	NRA, total agriculture[a]				NRA, agricultural tradables			NRA, nonagricultural tradables[c]	RRA
	Covered products		Noncovered products	All products, including NPS	Exportables[b]	Import-competing[b]	All		
	Inputs	Outputs							
1984	3	11	15	15	−14	95	23	42	−13
1985	5	24	29	29	4	99	85	49	25
1986	3	29	32	32	0	102	102	52	32
1987	5	38	43	43	0	122	123	59	40
1988	5	9	14	14	−21	49	18	46	−19
1989	5	3	8	8	−13	35	10	37	−20
1990	7	9	16	16	−14	72	21	35	−11
1991	5	−5	0	0	−19	42	−1	13	−12
1992	5	−17	−12	−12	−25	19	−15	2	−16
1993	5	−4	1	1	−10	27	0	11	−9
1994	7	−2	4	4	−9	31	4	19	−13
1995	7	−14	−7	−7	−13	2	−9	19	−24
1996	6	−13	−7	−7	−19	21	−9	15	−22
1997	7	−9	−2	−2	−18	20	−7	11	−16
1998	8	3	11	11	0	26	9	10	−1
1999	8	0	8	8	−12	44	5	8	−2
2000	9	1	9	9	−2	18	7	4	3
2001	10	7	17	17	−1	31	29	0	28
2002	12	14	26	26	−4	55	24	4	19
2003	9	7	16	16	−13	42	12	13	−1
2004	9	2	11	11	−12	25	5	—	—

c. Value shares of the primary production of covered[d] and noncovered products

Year	Chickpeas	Cotton	Fruits and vegetables	Groundnuts	Maize	Milk	Rapeseeds	Rice	Sorghum	Soybeans	Sugar	Sunflower	Wheat	Noncoverd
1965	3	3	15	4	2	—	1	21	3	—	2	—	4	43
1966	2	3	13	3	2	—	1	22	3	—	2	—	4	45
1967	3	3	13	3	2	—	1	28	3	—	1	—	6	39
1968	2	3	12	3	1	—	1	30	3	—	1	—	5	39
1969	2	3	16	4	1	—	1	26	2	—	2	—	6	38
1970	3	2	15	5	2	—	1	24	3	—	2	—	7	37
1971	3	3	16	5	2	—	1	22	2	—	2	—	8	36
1972	3	3	18	4	1	—	1	19	2	—	2	—	7	38
1973	2	2	13	5	1	—	1	24	2	0	3	—	5	40
1974	2	3	9	3	1	—	1	32	2	0	3	—	5	39
1975	2	2	8	3	2	4	1	31	2	0	7	0	6	32
1976	2	3	13	4	2	5	1	23	3	0	3	0	8	33
1977	2	4	13	5	1	5	1	25	3	0	3	0	7	31
1978	2	3	12	4	1	5	1	29	2	0	2	0	8	30
1979	1	4	14	4	1	5	1	21	3	0	3	0	8	34
1980	2	3	12	3	1	6	1	25	2	0	3	0	7	35
1981	2	3	11	3	1	7	1	28	2	0	4	0	6	32
1982	2	3	14	2	1	7	1	20	2	0	4	0	9	34
1983	2	3	14	4	1	6	1	20	3	0	3	0	9	34
1984	2	4	16	3	2	6	2	19	2	0	2	0	8	33
1985	3	3	19	2	1	7	1	19	2	0	2	0	9	31

(Table continues on the following page.)

Table B.10. Annual Distortion Estimates, India, 1965–2004 (continued)

c. Value shares of the primary production of covered[d] and noncovered products

Year	Chickpeas	Cotton	Fruits and vegetables	Groundnuts	Maize	Milk	Rapeseeds	Rice	Sorghum	Soybeans	Sugar	Sunflower	Wheat	Noncoverd
1986	2	2	22	2	2	7	1	18	1	0	2	0	9	32
1987	2	3	20	2	1	8	1	15	2	1	3	0	8	34
1988	2	2	15	3	1	9	1	19	2	1	3	0	6	33
1989	2	3	14	3	1	12	1	19	2	1	4	0	7	31
1990	2	3	15	3	1	9	1	20	2	1	5	1	6	30
1991	1	3	15	2	1	11	1	19	1	1	4	0	6	32
1992	1	2	17	3	1	12	1	18	1	1	4	0	6	32
1993	2	3	16	3	1	13	1	18	2	1	3	0	6	30
1994	2	3	16	3	1	14	2	19	1	2	3	1	7	27
1995	1	3	17	2	1	16	2	14	1	1	5	0	7	29
1996	1	3	15	2	1	13	2	19	1	2	4	0	7	30
1997	2	3	21	2	1	14	1	19	1	2	4	0	6	26
1998	2	3	20	3	1	15	1	17	1	1	3	0	6	27
1999	1	2	22	1	1	13	1	18	1	1	3	0	7	29
2000	1	2	22	1	1	18	1	13	1	1	4	0	6	29
2001	2	2	20	2	1	16	1	14	1	1	5	0	7	29
2002	1	1	23	1	1	16	1	11	1	1	4	0	7	32
2003	2	2	23	2	1	15	1	11	1	2	3	0	6	31
2004	1	2	22	2	1	17	1	10	1	2	2	0	6	31

Sources: Author compilation; Pursell, Gulati, and Gupta 2007; chapter 10 of this volume.

Note: — = no data are available.

a. Including assistance for nontradables and non-product-specific assistance (NPS).

b. Including product-specific input subsidies.

c. The NRAs for nonagricultural tradables in 1965–69 are based on author assumptions.

d. The covered products are calculated at undistorted farmgate prices in U.S. dollars.

Table B.11. Annual Distortion Estimates, Pakistan, 1962–2005
(percent)

a. NRAs for covered products

Year	Cotton	Maize	Milk	Rice	Sugar	Wheat	All
1962	−22	−17	—	−52	193	−7	7
1963	−17	−16	—	−42	191	−16	6
1964	−18	−27	—	−45	27	−17	−16
1965	−3	−14	63	−42	84	6	15
1966	−19	−26	63	−42	266	−11	17
1967	−24	−4	60	−53	228	31	24
1968	−19	6	81	−53	296	18	22
1969	−23	−11	85	−31	296	12	29
1970	−11	−11	140	−14	199	19	45
1971	9	−21	143	2	140	19	47
1972	1	19	241	6	192	7	42
1973	−8	−41	26	−62	11	−69	−48
1974	−22	−44	70	−68	25	−57	−38
1975	−2	−11	67	−59	−35	−14	−19
1976	−8	−24	18	−46	−18	−13	−15
1977	−40	−32	38	−20	26	−26	−11
1978	2	−8	43	−36	92	−23	−4
1979	22	9	108	−44	102	−29	−11
1980	−8	−14	59	−48	63	−36	−20
1981	−17	−19	68	−46	−14	−30	−22
1982	32	18	47	−34	61	−2	7
1983	−5	5	14	−34	123	−21	−8
1984	14	−20	49	−34	129	−23	−4
1985	−20	−20	46	−42	178	−18	−6
1986	4	−22	43	−51	155	−15	−5
1987	24	−10	45	−40	115	−24	−1
1988	−18	43	78	−40	124	−18	0
1989	−20	14	59	−47	45	−33	−16
1990	−43	−23	15	−46	21	−46	−32
1991	−31	−9	22	−9	21	−26	−13
1992	−17	15	22	−5	78	−17	−2
1993	−1	11	44	3	85	−23	0
1994	−8	−6	24	−3	56	−23	−4
1995	−18	3	25	1	33	−19	−5
1996	−13	2	24	2	43	−32	−7
1997	−6	−21	1	−2	75	−35	−14
1998	−4	0	9	9	51	−13	1
1999	1	7	25	−1	70	−2	12
2000	17	8	26	−15	145	9	17
2001	5	−15	14	−11	107	−15	1
2002	18	−17	4	−13	62	−27	−7
2003	−2	−12	44	−13	82	−29	−2
2004	3	−15	18	−18	51	−13	−1
2005	0	−13	13	−21	73	−9	−2

(Table continues on the following page.)

Table B.11. Annual Distortion Estimates, Pakistan, 1962–2005 (*continued*)

b. Agricultural NRAs and RRAs: All products, tradables, and relative to nonagricultural tradables

	NRA, total agriculture[a]				NRA, agricultural tradables			NRA, nonagricultural tradables	RRA
	Covered products		Noncovered products	All products, including NPS	Exportables[b]	Import-competing[b]	All		
Year	Inputs	Outputs							
1962	−4	11	0	5	−36	20	7	164	−59
1963	−5	11	0	4	−27	15	6	175	−61
1964	−4	−13	0	−11	−36	−8	−16	185	−71
1965	−1	17	0	11	−30	31	15	227	−65
1966	−1	18	0	12	−33	38	17	199	−61
1967	−2	26	0	17	−43	53	24	214	−61
1968	−5	28	0	16	−43	48	22	232	−63
1969	−1	31	0	22	−28	55	29	250	−63
1970	−2	47	0	33	−13	64	45	236	−57
1971	−6	53	0	35	5	59	47	261	−59
1972	−13	54	0	30	3	56	42	153	−44
1973	5	−54	0	−36	−43	−49	−48	51	−66
1974	7	−45	0	−29	−53	−33	−38	33	−54
1975	7	−26	0	−14	−46	−8	−19	25	−35
1976	5	−20	0	−11	−35	−9	−15	44	−41
1977	2	−13	0	−8	−29	−6	−11	53	−42
1978	3	−7	0	−3	−25	3	−4	47	−35
1979	5	−16	0	−7	−32	−2	−11	51	−41
1980	4	−24	0	−14	−37	−14	−20	55	−49
1981	5	−27	0	−15	−38	−16	−22	55	−50

1982	4	3	0	5	−20	18	7	45	−26
1983	2	−10	0	−5	−26	−1	−8	41	−35
1984	2	−5	0	−2	−24	4	−4	46	−34
1985	4	−10	0	−4	−35	6	−6	45	−35
1986	3	−8	0	−3	−35	7	−5	50	−37
1987	2	−4	0	−1	−22	6	−1	46	−32
1988	3	−3	0	0	−31	16	0	41	−30
1989	3	−19	0	−11	−37	−8	−16	44	−42
1990	2	−34	0	−22	−45	−28	−32	48	−54
1991	2	−15	0	−9	−22	−10	−13	41	−38
1992	3	−5	0	−1	−12	2	−2	38	−29
1993	2	−2	0	0	1	0	0	34	−25
1994	2	−6	0	−3	−5	−4	−4	35	−29
1995	2	−7	0	−3	−12	−3	−5	34	−29
1996	3	−10	0	−5	−7	−7	−7	32	−29
1997	2	−16	0	−10	−4	−16	−14	26	−32
1998	2	−1	0	1	2	1	1	24	−19
1999	1	12	0	9	0	16	12	19	−5
2000	1	16	0	12	−5	23	17	17	0
2001	2	−1	0	1	−3	2	1	15	−12
2002	1	−9	0	−5	−1	−9	−7	11	−16
2003	1	−3	0	−2	−9	0	−2	15	−15
2004	1	−2	0	−1	−10	2	−1	15	−14
2005	2	−4	0	−1	−14	2	−2	14	−14

(Table continues on the following page.)

Table B.11. Annual Distortion Estimates, Pakistan, 1962–2005
    (*continued*)

c. Value shares of the primary production of covered[c] and noncovered products

Year	Cotton	Maize	Milk	Rice	Sugar	Wheat	Noncovered
1962	9	4	—	8	7	42	31
1963	8	4	—	6	8	43	31
1964	7	4	—	14	11	34	31
1965	6	3	12	12	8	28	31
1966	7	3	14	12	5	27	31
1967	7	5	12	14	4	27	30
1968	6	3	10	14	3	33	30
1969	8	3	12	15	5	31	27
1970	8	3	10	11	7	35	26
1971	8	4	12	9	9	34	26
1972	10	3	7	9	5	39	27
1973	4	2	7	8	6	47	25
1974	7	2	6	14	6	40	26
1975	4	2	7	16	13	30	27
1976	4	2	11	12	13	30	28
1977	7	3	11	10	9	34	27
1978	5	2	10	13	6	35	29
1979	4	2	5	16	4	39	30
1980	5	2	6	14	5	38	30
1981	5	2	5	13	12	32	31
1982	4	2	8	16	8	30	31
1983	5	2	9	13	4	34	31
1984	4	2	8	14	5	33	33
1985	6	2	9	14	3	33	33
1986	5	2	9	14	3	33	33
1987	5	2	10	13	6	32	32
1988	10	2	9	14	4	31	30
1989	7	2	8	12	5	34	32
1990	9	2	9	10	5	33	33
1991	11	2	11	7	6	33	29
1992	11	2	11	6	4	31	35
1993	7	2	10	6	4	35	36
1994	7	2	12	7	5	31	36
1995	11	2	10	5	5	30	36
1996	9	2	16	5	4	29	36
1997	7	2	19	6	3	32	30
1998	6	2	19	5	6	31	30

Table B.11. (*continued*)

Year	Cotton	Maize	Milk	Rice	Sugar	Wheat	Noncovered
1999	7	2	20	9	6	28	29
2000	5	2	20	11	3	31	27
2001	7	2	19	7	3	33	28
2002	5	2	19	8	5	32	29
2003	6	2	14	10	5	34	30
2004	7	2	16	11	5	30	30
2005	6	3	16	11	3	31	30

Sources: Author compilation; Dorosh and Salam 2007; chapter 11 of this volume.

Note: — = no data are available.

a. Including assistance for nontradables and non-product-specific assistance (NPS).
b. Including product-specific input subsidies.
c. The covered products are calculated at undistorted farmgate prices in U.S. dollars.

Table B.12. Annual Distortion Estimates, Sri Lanka, 1955–2004
(*percent*)
a. NRAs for covered products

Year	Chilies	Coconuts	Onions	Potatoes	Rice	Rubber	Tea	All
1955	—	−35	—	—	42	−18.0	−23	−14
1956	—	−24	—	—	51	−3.6	−18	−8
1957	—	−28	—	—	70	−19.0	−23	−10
1958	—	−29	—	—	95	−24.9	−25	−9
1959	—	−28	—	—	54	−13.5	−22	−11
1960	—	−32	—	—	42	−38.5	−32	−21
1961	—	−37	—	—	32	−45.6	−35	−26
1962	—	−23	—	—	−7	−53	−40	−31
1963	—	−26	—	—	4	−59	−44	−34
1964	—	−30	—	—	−11	−62	−46	−38
1965	—	−31	—	—	−16	−59	−43	−38
1966	—	−18	—	—	−23	−70	−51	−44
1967	—	−19	—	—	−9	−57	−44	−32
1968	—	−34	—	—	1	−25	−28	−20
1969	—	−23	—	—	18	−34	−30	−15
1970	—	−22	—	—	15	−48	−36	−19
1971	—	−48	—	—	7	−60	−41	−7
1972	—	−33	—	—	3	−56	−44	−31

(*Table continues on the following page.*)

Table B.12. Annual Distortion Estimates, Sri Lanka,
1955–2004 (*continued*)

a. NRAs for covered products

Year	Chilies	Coconuts	Onions	Potatoes	Rice	Rubber	Tea	All
1973	—	−26	—	—	42	−45	−30	−10
1974	—	−34	—	—	−22	−72	−33	−35
1975	—	−30	—	—	−12	−61	−39	−31
1976	—	−4	—	91	−16	−70	−40	−35
1977	—	−37	—	23	38	−38	−15	−11
1978	36	−53	−36	150	−18	−61	−45	−38
1979	69	−58	13	46	−29	−67	−48	−45
1980	52	−52	−9	−41	−12	−55	−36	−33
1981	36	−25	97	164	−4	−53	−35	−18
1982	48	−9	16	25	−1	−48	−30	−12
1983	35	1	11	28	−10	−48	−26	−15
1984	−5	−13	28	40	−2	−54	−25	−17
1985	22	−14	51	70	8	−30	−30	−7
1986	0	26	59	80	23	−31	−25	5
1987	−22	25	−62	−39	7	−30	−21	−8
1988	30	−21	−87	14	−29	−54	−33	−33
1989	5	−42	−25	38	−10	−43	−20	−20
1990	41	−45	−47	67	4	−46	−25	−14
1991	47	−33	3	178	−1	−40	−28	−8
1992	32	−34	−42	146	8	−15	−5	−5
1993	73	−26	68	144	18	−4	−2	9
1994	118	−35	236	253	14	−4	−2	10
1995	102	−42	61	177	29	−5	−2	10
1996	59	−30	86	66	15	−7	−2	0
1997	74	10	65	83	22	−7	−1	13
1998	83	35	108	149	6	−3	−1	16
1999	67	20	78	150	23	0	−2	18
2000	71	25	65	160	3	0	−1	11
2001	81	50	78	225	7	0	−2	19
2002	63	19	37	181	23	0	−1	17
2003	54	1	34	257	−5	0	−1	2
2004	—	−10	—	—	−9	−1	−1	−6

b. Agricultural NRAs and RRAs: All products, tradables, and relative to nonagricultural tradables

Year	NRA, total agriculture[a]				NRA, agricultural tradables			NRA, nonagricultural tradables	RRA
	Covered products		Noncovered products	All products, including NPS	Exportables[b]	Import-competing[b]	All		
	Inputs	Outputs							
1955	0	−14	6	−7	−25	42	−8	105	−55
1956	0	−8	12	−1	−16	51	−1	105	−52
1957	0	−10	16	−1	−23	70	−2	105	−52
1958	0	−9	23	2	−26	95	2	105	−50
1959	0	−11	10	−4	−23	54	−4	104	−53
1960	0	−21	3	−13	−34	42	−14	103	−58
1961	0	−26	−2	−18	−38	32	−20	114	−63
1962	0	−31	−15	−26	−39	−7	−29	130	−69
1963	0	−34	−13	−27	−44	4	−30	135	−70
1964	0	−38	−19	−31	−46	−11	−36	142	−73
1965	0	−38	−20	−32	−43	−16	−36	158	−75
1966	0	−44	−24	−37	−50	−23	−42	172	−79
1967	0	−32	−17	−26	−41	−9	−30	165	−74
1968	0	−20	−10	−17	−30	1	−19	124	−64
1969	0	−15	−3	−11	−29	18	−12	73	−50
1970	0	−19	−6	−15	−35	15	−17	77	−53
1971	0	−7	−14	−9	−48	7	−11	93	−54
1972	0	−31	−14	−24	−44	3	−28	93	−63
1973	0	−10	3	−4	−34	42	−5	52	−38
1974	0	−35	−22	−29	−45	−22	−34	39	−53
1975	0	−31	−18	−25	−43	−12	−30	43	−51
1976	0	−35	−20	−29	−45	−13	−33	65	−60
1977	0	−11	3	−5	−28	37	−7	55	−40
1978	0	−38	−22	−31	−52	−13	−37	51	−58
1979	0	−45	−25	−37	−58	−17	−43	51	−62
1980	0	−33	−19	−26	−48	−8	−32	51	−55

(Table continues on the following page.)

Table B.12. Annual Distortion Estimates, Sri Lanka, 1955–2004 (*continued*)

b. Agricultural NRAs and RRAs: All products, tradables, and relative to nonagricultural tradables

Year	NRA, total agriculture				NRA, agricultural tradables			NRA, nonagricultural tradables	RRA
	Covered products		Noncovered products	All products, including NPS	Exportables[b]	Import-competing[b]	All		
	Inputs	Outputs							
1981	0	−18	−10	−11	−34	5	−17	56	−47
1982	0	−12	−7	−8	−25	4	−12	56	−43
1983	0	−15	−9	−11	−22	−4	−14	56	−45
1984	0	−17	−9	−13	−26	0	−16	68	−50
1985	0	−7	−3	−4	−23	15	−7	68	−44
1986	0	5	4	6	−10	22	5	68	−37
1987	0	−8	−5	−6	−6	−10	−8	53	−40
1988	0	−33	−22	−29	−35	−32	−33	53	−56
1989	0	−20	−13	−17	−33	−5	−20	53	−48
1990	0	−14	−9	−13	−35	7	−14	45	−41
1991	0	−8	−6	−7	−32	15	−8	45	−37
1992	0	−5	−4	−4	−23	12	−5	52	−38
1993	0	9	7	8	−14	34	10	50	−27
1994	0	10	9	10	−18	44	11	43	−23
1995	0	10	9	11	−20	47	11	37	−19
1996	0	0	4	3	−16	29	2	40	−27
1997	0	13	12	14	3	32	14	36	−16
1998	0	16	11	16	13	20	16	35	−14
1999	0	18	14	18	10	32	19	33	−11
2000	0	11	8	11	10	14	11	21	−8
2001	0	19	13	19	17	22	19	23	−3
2002	0	17	13	17	8	32	17	23	−4
2003	0	2	2	4	0	6	3	25	−18
2004	0	−6	−5	−4	−4	−9	−6	22	−23

c. Value shares of the primary production of covered[c] and noncovered products

Year	Chilies	Coconuts	Onions	Potatoes	Rice	Rubber	Tea	Noncovered
1955	—	15	—	—	11	12	27	34
1956	—	16	—	—	9	13	28	34
1957	—	16	—	—	9	13	27	34
1958	—	18	—	—	9	12	27	34
1959	—	21	—	—	10	11	24	34
1960	—	15	—	—	11	14	26	34
1961	—	15	—	—	11	12	28	34
1962	—	12	—	—	15	12	26	34
1963	—	12	—	—	14	13	27	34
1964	—	14	—	—	15	13	25	34
1965	—	16	—	—	12	13	25	34
1966	—	11	—	—	14	18	23	34
1967	—	11	—	—	18	13	21	36
1968	—	20	—	—	21	8	19	32
1969	—	17	—	—	20	12	18	32
1970	—	16	—	—	21	13	18	31
1971	—	5	—	—	48	4	7	36
1972	—	12	—	—	17	11	22	38
1973	—	12	—	—	19	13	16	39
1974	—	14	—	—	31	11	12	33
1975	—	10	—	—	23	10	15	43
1976	—	9	—	1	20	17	16	37
1977	—	21	—	1	16	8	21	33
1978	2	18	2	0	21	9	16	32
1979	2	19	1	1	18	14	11	35
1980	2	19	1	1	18	10	11	37
1981	2	16	1	1	23	8	12	38
1982	2	14	1	1	23	7	13	38
1983	2	12	1	1	21	8	16	38
1984	3	16	1	1	16	8	20	36
1985	6	16	1	1	20	7	17	32
1986	8	11	1	2	21	9	15	34
1987	6	12	2	4	18	7	15	35
1988	4	10	7	2	22	9	13	32
1989	6	13	1	2	23	7	15	34
1990	5	11	3	1	24	6	18	31
1991	7	13	1	1	24	5	16	33
1992	6	18	4	1	24	4	9	34
1993	5	15	1	1	23	4	13	37

(Table continues on the following page.)

Table B.12. Annual Distortion Estimates, Sri Lanka, 1955–2004
    (*continued*)

c. Value shares of the primary production of covered[c] and noncovered products

Year	Chilies	Coconuts	Onions	Potatoes	Rice	Rubber	Tea	Noncovered
1994	4	16	1	1	21	6	12	39
1995	4	15	1	1	21	7	11	40
1996	4	18	1	1	15	6	14	41
1997	2	19	1	1	16	5	17	40
1998	3	16	1	0	20	4	19	38
1999	3	20	2	0	22	3	16	34
2000	2	15	1	0	22	3	19	36
2001	2	14	1	1	21	3	21	37
2002	2	17	1	1	20	4	19	36
2003	2	14	1	1	23	5	18	36
2004	—	16	—	—	22	6	21	36

Sources: Author compilation; Bandara and Jayasuriya 2007; chapter 12 of this volume.

Note: — = no data are available.
a. Including assistance for nontradables and non-product-specific assistance (NPS).
b. Including product-specific input subsidies.
c. The covered products are calculated at undistorted farmgate prices in U.S. dollars.

Table B.13. Annual Distortion Estimates, Asian Focus Economies, 1955–2005
(percent)

a. NRAs for covered products

Year	Barley	Beef	Cassava	Chickpeas	Cocoa	Coconuts	Coffee	Cotton	Eggs	Fruits and vegetables[a]	Jute	Maize
1955	−11	6	—	—	—	−35	—	—	—	0	—	—
1956	36	36	—	—	—	−24	—	—	—	0	—	—
1957	90	54	—	—	—	−28	—	—	—	0	—	—
1958	63	61	—	—	—	−29	—	—	−16	0	—	—
1959	27	35	—	—	—	−28	—	—	−33	0	—	—
1960	65	53	—	—	—	−32	—	—	−41	0	—	−20
1961	19	−2	—	—	—	−37	—	—	−40	0	—	−15
1962	19	16	—	—	—	−23	—	−22	−31	0	—	0
1963	144	29	—	—	—	−26	—	−17	−10	0	—	−5
1964	171	26	—	50	—	−28	—	−18	19	0	—	65
1965	61	25	—	5	—	−29	—	28	21	0	—	57
1966	43	19	—	4	—	−19	—	2	20	0	—	47
1967	68	21	—	39	−1	−20	—	9	27	0	—	34
1968	85	45	—	0	−3	−31	—	−3	24	0	—	45
1969	105	63	—	75	−2	−21	—	24	2	0	—	8
1970	144	60	−10	0	−1	−17	−9	63	23	0	—	8
1971	149	77	−25	0	−1	−6	−11	77	7	0	—	16
1972	198	52	−33	0	−1	−1	−14	97	−6	0	—	52
1973	74	14	−39	0	−7	−3	1	93	−6	0	—	17

(Table continues on the following page.)

Table B.13. Annual Distortion Estimates, Asian Focus Economies, 1955–2005 (*continued*)

a. NRAs for covered products

Year	Barley	Beef	Cassava	Chickpeas	Cocoa	Coconuts	Coffee	Cotton	Eggs	Fruits and vegetables[a]	Jute	Maize
1974	36	19	-8	7	-4	-12	-3	-13	-17	-27	-30	4
1975	59	49	0	0	1	-9	-2	0	-13	-21	-53	-18
1976	76	79	0	0	-1	4	-1	26	-11	-40	-33	3
1977	112	115	-10	0	-1	7	-4	-5	-9	-40	-43	20
1978	131	123	-13	0	-6	3	-5	13	-1	-33	-38	24
1979	129	110	19	0	-2	-19	-7	2	4	-42	-19	9
1980	57	79	-2	26	-2	-11	-8	6	8	-52	-30	5
1981	125	116	-22	9	-1	2	-5	-21	3	-48	-40	-41
1982	170	115	-7	0	-1	-1	-4	-6	6	-46	-37	-30
1983	241	96	7	0	-1	-21	-13	-18	24	-34	-17	-27
1984	238	100	-21	3	-3	-25	-13	-23	10	-25	-22	-5
1985	293	55	-29	34	4	-22	-9	-9	18	-20	-21	7
1986	399	78	0	3	-1	-5	-8	-2	14	-8	-54	3
1987	417	76	-21	5	-7	-16	1	17	7	1	-44	2
1988	336	134	-20	12	-4	-21	-2	-10	13	-2	-20	-19
1989	341	128	-13	7	1	-34	-9	-7	56	0	-38	-25
1990	363	132	-11	15	-1	-32	-9	-14	29	-3	-28	-28

1991	494	163	−16	9	−1	−34	−5	−16	6	1	−33	−20
1992	461	163	−12	9	−6	−35	−5	−12	41	−4	−42	−24
1993	534	125	−17	6	−2	−32	−3	4	18	−3	−46	−16
1994	769	141	1	7	−2	−36	−3	23	39	1	−44	13
1995	632	151	3	16	−1	−36	−4	−5	49	0	−29	1
1996	403	133	−19	11	−1	−34	4	−4	10	−3	15	−3
1997	635	99	−20	24	−8	−16	2	6	9	−3	−3	10
1998	449	54	−11	10	0	−17	−7	3	9	1	21	22
1999	596	94	−22	14	0	−7	0	3	39	22	−32	9
2000	740	73	−14	18	0	−9	0	21	31	22	−37	13
2001	412	87	−8	35	0	−7	−6	−10	34	20	−41	16
2002	561	115	−5	16	0	−7	−4	6	32	24	−29	8
2003	572	78	−13	11	0	−6	−2	7	55	26	−40	19
2004	528	72	−10	13	0	−11	3	1	105	18	−46	7
2005	—	205	—	—	0	−18	—	11	—	19	—	17

(Table continues on the following page.)

Table B.13. Annual Distortion Estimates, Asian Focus Economies, 1955–2005 (*continued*)

a. NRAs for covered products

Year	Milk	Oilseeds[a]	Palm oil	Pig meat	Poultry	Rice	Rubber	Sorghum	Sugar	Tea	Wheat
1955	—	−33	—	−39	−52	−37	−18	—	—	−23	−56
1956	—	−28	—	10	−34	−4	−4	—	—	−18	−29
1957	—	−5	—	4	−15	18	−19	—	—	−23	−32
1958	—	−11	—	−8	−16	−15	−25	—	—	−25	−22
1959	—	12	—	−3	−10	−15	−14	—	—	−22	−26
1960	—	29	−11	10	−10	1	−17	—	—	−32	−27
1961	—	−33	−11	7	−23	−21	−16	—	—	−35	−38
1962	—	−23	−9	10	−11	−26	−14	—	151	−40	−8
1963	—	61	−10	31	6	6	−14	—	124	−44	−16
1964	—	24	−16	20	37	9	−20	82	14	−46	28
1965	63	56	−10	37	48	−1	−15	46	140	−43	31
1966	63	28	−12	47	46	−26	−18	25	192	−51	3
1967	60	24	−11	51	66	−32	−14	65	151	−44	21
1968	82	25	−9	90	94	−38	−9	12	220	−28	34
1969	86	26	−11	69	91	−27	−13	60	113	−30	31
1970	141	13	−18	47	79	−11	−6	35	56	−25	46
1971	142	11	−20	76	4	4	−11	97	37	−28	44
1972	230	20	−3	48	−5	7	−3	39	23	−34	31
1973	27	0	−6	35	−4	−28	−4	48	−22	−26	−28
1974	72	1	−29	46	16	−57	−16	56	−28	−27	−17
1975	123	−18	−21	47	49	−24	−10	0	−40	−25	−3
1976	144	−5	−8	42	50	−8	−11	0	7	−26	−6
1977	155	−5	−19	41	64	−7	−17	45	22	−12	6
1978	126	−1	−11	42	71	−22	−27	8	19	−22	−5
1979	147	10	−11	65	57	−5	−29	5	0	−26	−9
1980	92	16	−4	79	70	−23	−29	0	4	−21	−11
1981	71	15	−3	−64	43	−44	−23	16	16	−16	−13
1982	95	20	5	−74	51	−30	−14	10	31	−15	−6
1983	129	21	5	−73	47	−25	−15	4	50	−18	0
1984	151	19	−9	−73	30	−14	−14	2	83	−18	16
1985	168	31	1	−28	46	2	−8	24	74	−18	19
1986	169	47	7	−46	−18	−1	−14	66	50	−25	18
1987	157	51	−7	−53	−30	−4	−21	56	37	−17	14
1988	76	17	−10	−43	−21	−16	−16	19	21	−21	9
1989	51	20	−2	−27	11	−13	−12	13	11	−14	−2
1990	78	36	5	−17	13	−12	−12	6	13	−18	−3
1991	49	32	0	−11	15	−11	−16	7	19	−20	7
1992	18	11	−3	−3	15	−16	−16	−3	15	−6	−8

a. NRAs for covered products

Year	Milk	Oilseeds[a]	Palm oil	Pig meat	Poultry	Rice	Rubber	Sorghum	Sugar	Tea	Wheat
1993	26	8	4	4	32	−6	−19	−25	8	−5	−2
1994	26	18	2	12	23	2	−18	51	9	−3	26
1995	5	22	−8	8	16	7	−15	2	7	−5	21
1996	22	22	−1	10	20	−1	−9	9	11	−7	7
1997	19	22	−11	5	16	1	10	13	6	−9	19
1998	26	24	−22	3	12	−2	16	33	30	−7	23
1999	44	22	−3	9	20	7	24	50	46	−10	16
2000	20	22	−2	7	19	19	14	13	50	−7	20
2001	28	20	2	5	14	21	10	16	22	−8	8
2002	48	24	−6	6	17	16	1	16	45	−8	7
2003	40	26	−6	1	8	22	−1	15	50	−7	5
2004	21	18	−1	2	4	14	−5	18	49	−7	13
2005	33	19	—	0	0	−10	—	—	40	−29	4

(Table continues on the following page.)

Table B.13. Annual Distortion Estimates, Asian Focus Economies, 1955–2005 (*continued*)

b. Agricultural NRAs and RRAs: All products, tradables, and relative to nonagricultural tradables

	NRA, total agriculture[b]				NRA, agricultural tradables			NRA, nonagricultural tradables	RRA
	Covered products		Noncovered products	All products, including NPS	Exportables[c]	Import-competing[c]	All		
Year	Inputs	Outputs							
1955	0	-33	-8	-28	-30	-21	-25	78	-58
1956	0	-5	2	-27	-10	8	-1	132	-57
1957	0	6	9	-27	-10	28	11	155	-57
1958	0	-15	5	-27	-29	13	-6	121	-58
1959	0	-15	0	-28	-22	1	-9	116	-58
1960	0	-5	0	-27	-15	6	-6	118	-57
1961	0	-14	-9	-28	-11	-20	-16	98	-57
1962	-1	-9	-7	-27	-12	-11	-11	107	-57
1963	-1	6	3	-26	-10	15	6	140	-56
1964	0	1	3	-26	-15	33	6	136	-55
1965	0	-3	16	-20	-7	42	34	199	-55
1966	0	-11	-3	-27	-29	27	-1	119	-55
1967	0	-13	-4	-26	-33	30	-3	117	-55
1968	0	-14	-10	-28	-38	32	-11	108	-57
1969	0	-10	1	-24	-29	39	3	122	-54
1970	0	-7	5	-21	-14	42	10	107	-47
1971	0	6	12	-18	-9	49	30	115	-40
1972	0	1	13	-20	-6	44	29	120	-41
1973	1	-24	-6	-29	-25	7	-13	84	-53
1974	1	-29	-26	-37	-50	-8	-37	53	-59
1975	1	-11	-16	-30	-45	31	-18	66	-51
1976	1	0	2	-23	-17	35	5	84	-43
1977	1	1	7	-20	-17	35	9	88	-42

1978	1	−5	−1	−24	−26	23	−2	75	−44
1979	2	0	3	−22	−21	32	5	86	−44
1980	2	−9	−2	−26	−29	23	−6	80	−48
1981	1	−23	−12	−25	−45	4	−27	30	−44
1982	1	−18	−5	−19	−46	19	−22	29	−39
1983	1	−19	−3	−19	−46	21	−22	28	−39
1984	1	−17	2	−15	−41	38	−18	25	−34
1985	2	−2	11	2	−26	51	1	19	−15
1986	1	−10	10	−6	−38	52	−8	10	−16
1987	1	−19	11	−11	−47	56	−14	8	−21
1988	2	−22	2	−16	−42	34	−19	20	−32
1989	1	−16	1	−15	−36	27	−16	20	−30
1990	2	−11	0	−8	−30	20	−11	19	−25
1991	2	−7	1	−4	−23	30	−5	16	−18
1992	1	−7	−5	−7	−24	23	−8	12	−18
1993	2	−1	1	1	−14	23	1	13	−11
1994	2	6	8	9	−4	34	10	14	−4
1995	2	1	4	6	−5	24	6	12	−5
1996	2	4	2	5	−7	21	5	11	−6
1997	2	4	7	7	−5	25	7	10	−3
1998	3	3	9	9	−1	21	9	9	0
1999	2	10	9	11	−3	32	11	7	4
2000	3	10	10	13	0	30	13	6	7
2001	3	9	7	12	1	21	12	2	10
2002	3	10	8	12	−2	27	12	4	7
2003	3	8	10	12	−1	27	12	7	5
2004	2	5	9	10	−2	22	10	3	6
2005	1	2	6	6	−1	14	7	4	2

(Table continues on the following page.)

Table B.13. Annual Distortion Estimates, Asian Focus Economies, 1955–2005 (*continued*)

c. Value shares of the primary production of covered[d] and noncovered products

Year	Chickpeas	Coconuts	Cotton	Fruits and vegetables[a]	Maize	Milk	Oilseeds[a]	Palm oil	Pig meat
1955	—	4	—	—	—	—	0	—	4
1956	—	4	—	—	—	—	0	—	5
1957	—	4	—	—	—	—	0	—	6
1958	—	4	—	—	—	—	0	—	5
1959	—	6	—	—	—	—	0	—	7
1960	—	3	—	—	—	—	0	1	4
1961	—	2	—	—	1	—	0	1	4
1962	—	2	2	1	2	—	0	0	4
1963	—	2	2	1	3	—	0	1	4
1964	5	1	1	24	1	—	10	0	2
1965	2	0	3	11	2	1	4	0	1
1966	1	0	3	10	2	1	3	0	1
1967	2	0	3	11	2	1	3	0	1
1968	1	0	3	9	1	1	3	0	1
1969	1	0	2	12	1	1	3	0	1
1970	2	3	2	10	2	1	4	0	1
1971	2	3	2	10	2	1	4	1	1
1972	2	2	2	11	2	0	4	1	1
1973	1	4	2	8	2	0	4	0	1
1974	1	4	2	5	2	0	3	1	1
1975	1	2	1	5	2	2	2	1	1
1976	1	3	2	7	2	3	3	1	1
1977	1	4	2	6	2	3	3	1	1
1978	1	4	2	6	2	3	2	1	1
1979	1	4	2	7	2	3	2	1	1
1980	1	3	2	6	2	3	2	1	1
1981	0	2	1	12	4	2	2	1	10
1982	0	1	1	13	4	2	2	1	14
1983	0	1	2	17	4	2	2	1	13
1984	1	2	2	18	4	2	2	1	15
1985	1	2	1	22	3	2	2	1	8
1986	0	1	1	25	3	2	2	1	10
1987	0	1	1	26	3	2	2	1	11
1988	1	1	1	24	3	3	2	1	11
1989	0	1	1	26	3	3	2	1	10
1990	0	1	2	22	4	2	2	1	9
1991	0	1	2	20	4	3	2	1	8

c. Value shares of the primary production of covered[d] and noncovered products

Year	Chickpeas	Coconuts	Cotton	Fruits and vegetables[a]	Maize	Milk	Oilseeds[a]	Palm oil	Pig meat
1992	0	1	1	20	4	4	2	1	8
1993	0	1	1	15	4	4	3	1	8
1994	1	1	2	16	4	4	3	1	9
1995	0	1	2	17	4	4	2	2	10
1996	0	1	1	15	5	4	2	1	10
1997	0	1	1	15	4	4	2	1	12
1998	0	1	1	16	4	4	2	2	11
1999	0	1	1	15	4	4	1	1	9
2000	0	1	1	17	3	5	1	1	10
2001	0	1	1	17	3	4	2	1	10
2002	0	1	1	17	3	4	1	2	10
2003	0	1	1	17	3	4	2	2	10
2004	0	0	1	17	4	5	2	1	12
2005	—	0	1	19	4	2	1	—	15

Year	Poultry	Rice	Rubber	Sorghum	Sugar	Wheat	Noncovered	Covered
1955	0	30	3	—	—	0	48	52
1956	0	28	3	—	—	1	48	52
1957	0	26	3	—	—	1	51	49
1958	0	29	3	—	—	0	49	51
1959	0	28	3	—	—	1	46	54
1960	0	21	25	—	—	1	39	61
1961	1	26	18	—	—	0	39	61
1962	1	26	10	—	2	8	36	64
1963	1	28	11	—	2	9	33	67
1964	1	14	5	5	2	12	15	85
1965	0	23	2	2	2	5	40	60
1966	0	24	2	2	2	5	42	58
1967	0	28	2	2	1	6	37	63
1968	0	30	1	3	1	6	38	62
1969	0	27	2	2	2	6	36	64
1970	0	24	2	2	3	6	36	64
1971	1	23	2	1	4	7	35	65
1972	1	20	2	2	5	7	37	63
1973	1	23	3	1	5	6	37	63
1974	0	31	2	1	5	4	36	64
1975	0	34	1	1	7	5	31	69

(Table continues on the following page.)

Table B.13. Annual Distortion Estimates, Asian Focus Economies, 1955–2005

c. Value shares of the primary production of covered[d] and noncovered products
(*continued*)

Year	Poultry	Rice	Rubber	Sorghum	Sugar	Wheat	Noncovered	Covered[d]
1976	1	29	3	2	5	5	32	68
1977	1	28	3	1	4	5	32	68
1978	1	32	3	1	4	5	31	69
1979	1	26	4	1	5	5	33	67
1980	1	29	3	1	4	5	34	66
1981	1	29	1	1	3	5	25	75
1982	1	25	1	0	3	6	25	75
1983	1	22	1	1	2	6	24	76
1984	1	21	1	1	2	6	23	77
1985	1	20	1	0	2	6	26	74
1986	1	19	1	0	2	6	23	77
1987	2	18	2	0	2	5	22	78
1988	2	21	1	0	2	4	21	79
1989	2	21	1	0	3	5	20	80
1990	2	21	1	0	3	5	23	77
1991	2	21	1	0	3	5	25	75
1992	2	21	1	0	3	5	25	75
1993	2	21	1	0	3	6	28	72
1994	3	21	2	0	3	5	25	75
1995	4	19	2	0	3	5	24	76
1996	3	21	1	0	3	6	25	75
1997	3	20	1	0	3	6	25	75
1998	4	19	1	0	2	5	28	72
1999	3	18	0	0	2	5	32	68
2000	4	15	1	0	2	5	33	67
2001	4	14	1	0	2	5	34	66
2002	4	13	1	0	2	4	36	64
2003	4	13	1	0	2	5	34	66
2004	3	14	1	0	2	4	33	67
2005	5	11	—	—	1	5	34	66

Sources: Author compilation; chapters 2–12 of this volume.

Note: — = no data are available.

a. Fruits and vegetables include bananas, cabbages, chilies, garlic, onions, peppers, potatoes, and fruit and vegetable aggregates. Oilseeds include groundnuts, rapeseeds, soybeans, and sunflower seeds.

b. Including assistance for nontradables and non-product-specific assistance (NPS).

c. Including product-specific input subsidies.

d. The covered products are calculated at undistorted farmgate prices in U.S. dollars. Products representing less than 0.5 percent of the gross value of regional production beginning in 1965 are excluded because of the low shares. These products include barley, beef, cassava, cocoa, coffee, eggs, jute, and tea.

Table B.14. Gross Subsidy Equivalents of Assistance to Farmers, Asian Focus Economies, 1955–2005

(constant 2000 US$, millions)

Year	Bangladesh	China	India	Indonesia	Korea, Rep. of	Malaysia	Pakistan	Philippines	Sri Lanka	Taiwan, China	Thailand	Vietnam
1955	—	-7,101	6	—	-269	—	—	—	-40	-150	—	—
1956	—	-11,171	10	—	-14	—	—	—	-5	-19	—	—
1957	—	-11,081	10	—	175	—	—	—	-7	2	—	—
1958	—	-11,488	10	—	21	—	—	—	9	-134	—	—
1959	—	-11,533	10	—	-49	-87	—	—	-22	-87	—	—
1960	—	-13,026	11	—	5	-53	—	—	-64	-9	—	—
1961	—	-14,654	13	—	-357	—	—	—	-81	30	—	—
1962	—	-15,694	14	—	-313	-35	45	-103	-116	7	—	—
1963	—	-16,644	15	—	315	-32	43	-58	-108	61	—	—
1964	—	-15,061	13	—	485	-62	-149	15	-129	57	—	—
1965	—	-14,382	3,361	—	157	-29	165	144	-141	69	—	—
1966	—	-16,418	-463	—	86	-49	175	218	-135	53	—	—
1967	—	-17,322	-1,158	—	119	-55	278	166	-96	9	—	—
1968	—	-17,729	-3,203	—	233	-63	308	160	-102	13	—	—
1969	—	-18,498	10	—	447	-102	388	186	-61	8	—	—
1970	—	-19,674	1,802	-88	777	-53	612	52	-77	121	-366	—
1971	—	-20,624	3,818	230	985	-79	611	255	-124	167	-370	—
1972	—	-24,468	4,538	64	1,154	-30	545	64	-88	209	-439	—
1973	—	-37,675	-2,437	-655	487	-151	-1,081	-803	-21	141	-741	—
1974	-661	-48,394	-22,142	-941	-1,144	-556	-978	-1,375	-298	0	-1,879	—
1975	3,267	-47,489	-15,816	1,453	476	-391	-482	-937	-189	229	-1,332	—

(Table continues on the following page.)

Table B.14. Gross Subsidy Equivalents of Assistance to Farmers, Asian Focus Economies, 1955–2005 (continued)

Year	Bangladesh	China	India	Indonesia	Korea, Rep. of	Malaysia	Pakistan	Philippines	Sri Lanka	Taiwan, China	Thailand	Vietnam
1976	−256	−45,680	−560	2,862	2,138	−171	−396	−153	−181	330	−560	—
1977	−766	−49,751	2,231	3,492	2,929	−468	−307	71	−41	238	−593	—
1978	−1,188	−56,535	−3,610	733	4,170	−571	−116	−483	−343	168	−1,378	—
1979	−436	−64,676	1,923	−1,064	5,780	−788	−378	−329	−501	307	−604	—
1980	−553	−75,983	−6,769	−1,084	4,323	−815	−894	−942	−391	601	−116	—
1981	−2,210	−67,295	−12,122	2,606	6,011	−377	−1,148	−859	−168	616	−754	—
1982	149	−72,898	3,722	6,377	6,127	1	287	607	−97	837	−272	—
1983	236	−77,539	8,907	3,190	6,087	25	−346	−117	−144	1,054	454	—
1984	588	−64,979	9,188	2,082	6,090	−95	−142	645	−215	1,051	−251	—
1985	1,236	−23,694	16,977	2,735	6,478	276	−265	1,201	−65	1,039	−824	—
1986	100	−45,633	19,306	2,043	8,053	115	−231	1,028	81	1,292	−589	−535
1987	1,343	−64,588	25,295	−1,483	8,807	−111	−60	1,089	−86	1,758	−511	−833
1988	417	−74,357	10,633	−2,745	12,019	−102	−17	732	−431	2,143	−26	−340
1989	80	−73,545	6,157	−3,959	14,054	83	−855	1,070	−234	3,094	−376	−440
1990	−34	−55,293	11,885	−1,860	15,230	172	−2,086	1,061	−211	3,008	−308	−1,826
1991	230	−28,451	−26	−2,682	15,524	135	−720	695	−122	2,791	−753	−1,193
1992	15	−29,938	−10,411	−2,072	15,409	55	−98	1,794	−71	3,308	−200	−2317

1993	−345	−15,303	881	−2,246	15,618	206	6	2,321	138	3,578	−954	−1,565
1994	−335	10,701	4,020	−2,920	18,332	101	−224	2,181	175	3,931	−911	−865
1995	88	12,964	−7,749	−5,789	19,976	133	−356	3,598	221	4,130	1,007	−378
1996	−850	9,834	−8,224	−5,415	18,836	156	−576	4,973	63	4,284	891	−151
1997	−931	16,352	−1,751	−2,929	17,450	−395	−1,226	4,354	281	3,681	−905	−410
1998	−547	22,510	11,094	−7,179	10,847	32	85	1,660	292	3,258	−224	−719
1999	108	13,165	8,756	1,984	16,166	83	879	3,622	318	4,500	430	1,621
2000	288	19,443	9,395	4,098	16,075	107	1,135	3,041	207	4,448	−292	1,205
2001	429	11,679	16,333	3,960	13,887	122	73	2,600	290	3,642	−369	1,734
2002	171	9,746	22,641	4,607	14,671	116	−506	2,269	288	3,300	633	955
2003	370	18,471	17,720	6,632	15,611	92	−187	1,380	67	—	47	2,428
2004	−295	22,044	14,295	2,975	19,266	83	−77	740	−64	—	−72	2,038
2005	—	24,641	—	—	—	—	−179	—	—	—	—	1121

Sources: Author compilation; chapters 2–12 of this volume.

Note: — = no data are available.

Table B.15. Share of the Regional Value of Agricultural Production, Asian Focus Economies, 1955–2004
(*percent*)

Year	Bangladesh	China	India	Indonesia	Korea, Rep. of	Malaysia	Pakistan	Philippines	Sri Lanka	Taiwan, China	Thailand	Vietnam
Five-year average												
1955–59	—	59.7	34.6	—	2.6	—	—	—	1.4	1.7	—	—
1960–64	—	58.5	33.9	—	2.1	1.3	1.4	1.5	0.8	1.4	—	—
1965–69	—	56.8	32.8	—	2.3	1.2	2.6	1.9	0.7	1.7	—	—
1970–74	2.0	55.4	27.7	4.5	2.1	1.2	2.0	1.8	0.7	1.5	2.7	—
1975–79	2.4	52.1	23.5	9.0	2.5	1.6	1.8	2.3	0.4	1.6	2.8	—
1980–84	2.0	52.0	23.3	9.6	2.3	1.6	2.1	2.1	0.5	1.8	2.7	—
1985–89	1.9	51.7	22.2	9.4	2.6	1.7	2.2	1.9	0.5	2.2	2.7	1.4
1990–94	2.1	45.4	24.3	10.4	3.1	1.9	2.5	2.5	0.5	2.5	3.1	1.8
1995–99	1.7	48.6	22.9	10.0	2.9	2.1	2.5	2.3	0.4	1.9	2.8	1.9
2000–04	1.5	56.1	21.4	7.5	2.5	1.9	2.1	2.0	0.4	1.4	2.2	1.6
Yearly average												
1955	—	58.2	33.8	—	3.4	—	—	—	2.1	2.5	—	—
1956	—	60.3	34.9	—	2.1	—	—	—	1.3	1.4	—	—
1957	—	59.9	34.7	—	2.6	—	—	—	1.2	1.6	—	—
1958	—	60.1	34.8	—	2.4	—	—	—	1.2	1.6	—	—
1959	—	60.0	34.8	—	2.3	—	—	—	1.4	1.4	—	—
1960	—	59.3	34.4	—	2.0	1.8	—	—	1.0	1.4	—	—
1961	—	59.4	34.5	—	2.5	1.3	0.1	—	0.8	1.3	—	—
1962	—	57.9	33.6	—	2.2	1.1	1.6	1.6	0.8	1.3	—	—
1963	—	58.4	33.8	—	1.9	1.1	1.5	1.4	0.6	1.2	—	—
1964	—	57.3	33.2	—	2.1	1.2	2.3	1.6	0.7	1.6	—	—

Year												
1965	—	58.6	30.4	—	2.4	1.3	2.9	1.9	0.8	1.7	—	—
1966	—	59.4	30.4	—	2.4	1.2	2.4	1.9	0.6	1.7	—	—
1967	—	56.1	34.1	—	2.3	1.0	2.4	1.8	0.5	1.7	—	—
1968	—	54.4	35.3	—	2.1	1.0	2.7	1.8	0.9	1.7	—	—
1969	—	55.4	33.9	—	2.5	1.4	2.4	1.9	0.8	1.7	—	—
1970	—	54.4	29.4	4.0	2.1	1.1	2.3	1.6	0.7	1.5	3.0	—
1971	—	55.6	27.3	4.4	2.1	1.1	2.1	1.5	1.6	1.5	2.8	—
1972	—	58.8	26.1	4.2	1.9	0.9	1.9	1.8	0.4	1.5	2.5	—
1973	—	57.2	26.4	5.1	1.9	1.3	2.1	2.1	0.4	1.4	2.4	—
1974	2.0	51.2	29.1	4.9	2.4	1.4	1.6	2.3	0.5	1.4	3.0	—
1975	2.8	51.5	27.3	5.9	2.3	1.3	1.7	2.4	0.4	1.5	2.9	—
1976	2.3	53.6	22.7	8.4	2.5	1.4	2.0	2.3	0.3	1.7	2.8	—
1977	2.0	52.4	23.0	9.5	2.5	1.7	1.9	2.2	0.4	1.7	2.7	—
1978	2.5	50.1	23.5	10.7	2.7	1.6	1.6	2.3	0.4	1.6	3.0	—
1979	2.3	53.0	21.1	10.2	2.4	2.0	1.9	2.3	0.5	1.7	2.7	—
1980	2.3	52.0	23.7	9.4	1.9	1.8	2.0	2.2	0.5	1.6	2.7	—
1981	2.6	45.5	26.7	11.0	2.4	1.6	2.5	2.5	0.5	1.8	3.0	—
1982	1.7	52.8	23.0	9.8	2.4	1.4	2.1	1.9	0.4	2.0	2.6	—
1983	1.6	54.8	22.6	8.5	2.4	1.4	2.1	1.9	0.4	1.8	2.4	—
1984	1.8	54.7	20.7	9.3	2.5	1.8	2.0	2.0	0.6	1.9	2.6	—
1985	2.0	52.2	22.1	9.9	2.6	1.7	2.3	1.9	0.6	2.0	2.7	—
1986	2.1	51.4	22.5	9.5	2.4	1.5	2.4	1.7	0.5	2.1	2.5	1.5
1987	1.9	51.6	21.6	9.5	2.7	1.9	2.2	1.7	0.5	2.4	2.8	1.1
1988	1.8	49.8	23.3	9.3	2.8	1.8	1.9	2.0	0.5	2.3	2.8	1.8
1989	1.7	53.7	21.4	8.6	2.7	1.4	2.1	2.0	0.4	2.2	2.5	1.2
1990	2.1	52.5	20.9	9.2	2.8	1.3	2.7	2.1	0.5	2.0	2.4	1.4

(Table continues on the following page.)

Table B.15. Share of the Regional Value of Agricultural Production, Asian Focus Economies, 1955–2004 (*continued*)

Year	Bangladesh	China	India	Indonesia	Korea, Rep. of	Malaysia	Pakistan	Philippines	Sri Lanka	Taiwan, China	Thailand	Vietnam
1991	2.2	46.6	23.9	10.1	3.2	1.5	2.3	2.5	0.5	2.5	3.2	1.6
1992	2.2	44.9	25.3	9.2	3.3	1.8	2.5	2.5	0.5	2.7	3.2	2.0
1993	2.1	41.1	25.8	11.7	3.3	2.1	2.6	2.5	0.5	2.9	3.2	2.1
1994	1.7	41.7	25.4	11.8	3.1	2.5	2.3	2.9	0.5	2.6	3.5	1.9
1995	1.6	44.9	23.0	11.9	3.1	2.5	2.4	2.5	0.4	2.3	3.3	1.9
1996	1.8	45.3	23.9	11.4	3.4	2.0	2.6	2.4	0.4	2.1	2.9	1.8
1997	1.7	48.7	22.1	10.8	3.0	1.7	2.7	2.4	0.4	1.8	2.8	1.9
1998	1.6	52.2	22.3	7.4	2.5	2.3	2.6	2.2	0.4	1.6	2.7	2.1
1999	1.7	51.9	23.1	8.6	2.5	2.0	2.2	2.2	0.4	1.5	2.3	1.6
2000	1.7	53.8	22.8	7.3	3.0	1.5	2.1	2.0	0.4	1.5	2.2	1.8
2001	1.5	57.4	21.5	6.3	2.6	1.5	2.1	1.8	0.3	1.3	2.1	1.6
2002	1.4	57.6	18.5	8.3	2.5	2.0	2.1	2.0	0.4	1.3	2.2	1.8
2003	1.6	53.6	22.3	9.5	2.3	2.4	2.2	2.0	0.4	—	2.3	1.5
2004	1.4	58.0	21.7	6.3	2.2	2.2	2.2	2.2	0.3	—	2.0	1.5

Sources: Author compilation; chapters 2–12 of this volume.

Note: — = no data are available.

Table B.16. Summary of NRA Statistics, Asian Focus Economies

Economy	Data, years	Products, maximum in a year	Observations	NRA, weighted average[a]	Standard deviation[b]	Gross value of production[c]
					2000–04	
Bangladesh	32	6	187	2.7	101.2	7.4
China	25	11	275	5.9	15.3	276.6
India	41	13	499	15.8	21.5	105.3
Indonesia	35	10	346	12.0	33.3	37.1
Korea, Rep. of	51	12	459	137.3	225.4	12.2
Malaysia	46	4	174	1.2	40.1	9.6
Pakistan	45	6	262	1.2	43.1	10.6
Philippines	44	8	346	22.0	37.6	9.8
Sri Lanka	50	7	280	9.5	69.1	1.7
Taiwan, China	48	6	275	61.3	109.0	6.2
Thailand	35	9	287	–0.2	16.7	10.6
Vietnam	20	6	102	21.2	74.3	8.0
Total	51	35	3,492	12.0	64.4	495.2

Sources: Author compilation; chapters 2–12 of this volume.

a. The weights are based on the gross value of the production of the covered products at undistorted prices.
b. The standard deviation is a simple average.
c. At undistorted prices in current US$, billions.

Table B.17. Summary of NRA Statistics, by Major Product, Asian Focus Economies, 2000–04

Product	Economies, number	2000–04		Gross value of production[a]	Economy
		NRA, unweighted average	NRA, weighted average		
Bananas	1	0.0	0.0	0.47	PH
Barley	1	562.8	562.8	0.04	KR
Beef	3	83.5	85.2	1.66	KR, PH, TW
Cabbages	1	27.6	27.6	0.39	KR
Cassava	1	−10.0	−10.0	0.42	TH
Chickpeas	1	18.7	18.7	1.43	IN
Chilies	1	67.2	67.2	0.03	LK
Cocoa	1	0.0	0.0	0.02	MY
Coconuts	3	−2.0	−7.9	3.80	ID, MY, PH, LK
Coffee	2	−3.0	−1.7	0.68	ID, VN
Cotton	3	6.1	5.1	4.79	CH, IN, PK
Eggs	2	50.5	51.3	0.64	KR, TW
Fruits and vegetables	1	−8.9	−8.9	23.10	IN
Fruits	1	0.0	0.0	9.23	CH
Garlic	1	122.6	122.6	0.26	KR
Groundnuts	1	12.9	12.9	1.79	IN
Jute	1	−38.7	−38.7	0.18	BD
Maize	6	13.1	12.6	16.30	CH, IN, ID, PK, PH, TH
Milk	4	56.6	31.6	22.00	CH, IN, KR, PK, TW

Onions	1	53.4	53.4	0.02	LK
Palm oil	3	−6.4	−2.6	6.66	ID, MY, TH
Peppers	1	197.0	197.0	0.28	KR
Pig meat	6	46.8	4.2	52.10	CH, KR, PH, TW, VN
Potatoes	2	83.4	6.2	0.44	BD, LK
Poultry	7	77.1	12.2	17.50	CH, KR, PH, TW, VN
Rapeseeds	1	64.8	64.8	1.09	IN
Rice	12	57.4	18.5	67.10	BD, CH, IN, ID, KR, MY, PK, PH, LK, TW, TH, VN
Rubber	5	5.8	3.9	4.47	ID, MY, LK, TH, VN
Sorghum	1	15.7	15.7	0.83	ID
Soybeans	5	161.8	16.9	5.22	CH, IN, ID, KR, TH
Sugar	8	85.3	43.1	9.18	TH, CH, IN, ID, PK, PH, TH, VN
Sunflower	1	14.6	14.6	0.26	IN
Tea	3	−12.4	−7.5	0.56	BD, ID, LK
Vegetables	1	0.0	0.0	49.90	CH
Wheat	6	32.4	10.7	22.50	BD, CH, IN, KR, PK, TW
All		44.1	12.0	325.33	

Sources: Author compilation; chapters 2–12 of this volume.

Note: BD = Bangladesh. CH = China. IN = India. ID = Indonesia. KR = Rep. of Korea. LK = Sri Lanka. MY = Malaysia. PK = Pakistan. PH = the Philippines. TH = Thailand. TW = Taiwan, China. VN = Vietnam.

a. The average annual gross value of covered production at undistorted prices in current US$, billions.

Table B.18. Share of the Global Value of Production and Consumption, Key Covered Products, Asian Focus Economies, 2000–04

(percent)

Product	Q, C[a]	Bangladesh	China	India	Indonesia	Korea, Rep. of	Malaysia	Pakistan	Philippines	Thailand	Sri Lanka	Vietnam	Regional[b]
Grains, etc.	Q	1.6	18.5	8.2	4.3	0.6	0.1	1.7	1.2	1.4	0.1	1.3	39.1
	C	1.8	18.8	10.0	4.8	1.2	0.2	1.6	1.4	0.7	0.1	0.9	41.6
Rice	Q	5.2	32.1	15.2	13.1	2.1	0.3	1.2	3.5	3.6	0.5	4.2	81.0
	C	5.2	30.0	18.3	13.6	2.0	0.7	0.7	3.6	1.8	0.5	3.0	79.4
Wheat	Q	0.4	17.5	9.5		0.0		4.8					32.2
	C	0.8	18.0	12.6		2.0		4.7					38.1
Maize	Q		19.9	2.0	1.9			0.3	0.9	0.7			25.7
	C		24.9	2.9	2.8			0.5	1.2	0.9			33.1
Cassava	Q									2.0			2.0
	C									0.1			0.1
Barley	Q					0.2							0.2
	C					0.5							0.5
Sorghum	Q			9.5									9.5
	C			14.1									14.1
Chickpeas	Q			61.2									61.2
	C			—									—
Oilseeds	Q		4.9	6.5	3.8	0.0	6.3			0.5			22.0
	C		11.8	8.5	2.1	3.7	0.3			0.7			27.0
Soybeans	Q		10.0	4.2	0.6	0.1				0.1			15.1
	C		21.7	5.0	1.6	6.8				0.7			35.9
Groundnuts	Q			17.2									17.2
	C			17.9									17.9
Palm oil	Q				28.1		49.3			3.1			80.5
	C				7.8		1.7			1.9			11.5

Rapeseeds	Q			12.6								12.6
	C			—								—
Sunflower seeds	Q			4.7								4.7
	C											
Sesame	Q			5.2								5.2
	C											
Tropical crops	Q	0.2	5.7	8.5	10.9	1.4	1.6	1.9	4.2	1.0	0.9	36.4
	C	0.2	5.2	8.3	9.7	0.7	1.6	1.6	0.4	0.4	0.2	28.3
Sugar	Q	0.4	7.8	17.1	9.0		2.1	2.1	3.4		0.6	42.5
	C	0.5	6.6	16.9	15.0		2.4	2.3	1.0		0.6	45.3
Cotton	Q		13.6	12.1			4.0					29.7
	C		13.2	13.1			3.6					29.9
Coconuts	Q				45.6			10.6			3.6	59.7
	C				42.3			8.8			2.9	54.0
Coffee	Q				7.3						4.6	11.8
	C				3.0						0.1	3.1
Rubber	Q				21.0	14.8			33.4	1.2	3.3	73.7
	C				1.9	8.7			0.7	0.8	0.1	12.1
Tea	Q	1.3			2.9					6.3		10.5
	C	1.4			1.4					0.4		3.1
Cocoa	Q					0.4						0.4
	C					0.1						0.1

(Table continues on the following page.)

Table B.18. Share of the Global Value of Production and Consumption, Key Covered Products, Asian Focus Economies, 2000–04 (continued)

Product	Q, C[a]	Bangladesh	China	India	Indonesia	Korea, Rep. of	Malaysia	Pakistan	Philippines	Thailand	Sri Lanka	Vietnam	Regional[b]
Livestock products	Q		12.4	3.3	0.1	0.5		0.4	0.5	0.3		0.3	17.8
	C		16.5	4.3	0.2	0.9		0.5	0.7	0.4		0.4	23.7
Pig meat	Q		43.9			0.9			1.9	0.7		1.0	48.3
	C		48.7			1.1			2.1	0.7		1.2	53.8
Milk	Q		2.5	16.4		0.4		1.8					21.0
	C		3.1	19.2		0.5		2.1					24.8
Beef	Q					0.5			0.6				1.1
	C					2.1			1.2				3.3
Poultry	Q		23.0		1.1	0.4			0.2	1.6		0.5	26.8
	C		31.6		1.4	0.7			0.3	1.4		0.6	36.0
Eggs	Q					0.4							0.4
	C					0.6							0.6
Total, all products	Q	0.5	13.2	5.3	2.4	0.5	0.6	0.8	0.8	0.9	0.1	0.6	25.7
	C	0.6	15.9	6.9	2.7	1.1	0.2	0.9	1.0	0.5	0.1	0.5	30.4
Production													
All covered	Q	0.6	21.2	8.5	2.5	0.6	0.6	0.9	0.9	1.0	0.1	0.6	37.5
Noncovered	Q	0.5	23.1	7.9	3.9	1.5	1.0	0.8	0.5	0.6	0.2	0.7	40.7
All agriculture	Q	0.6	21.8	8.3	2.9	0.9	0.8	0.8	0.8	0.8	0.1	0.6	38.5

Sources: Author compilation; FAO SUA-FBS Database 2008.

Note: World = 100. — = no data are available.

a. C = consumption. Q = production.
b. There are no data on Taiwan, China in the FAO SUA-FBS Database.

Table B.19. Share of the Global Value of Exports and Imports, Key Covered Products, Asian Focus Economies, 2000–03

(percent)

Product	M, X[a]	Bangladesh	China	India	Indonesia	Korea, Rep. of	Malaysia	Pakistan	Philippines	Thailand	Sri Lanka	Vietnam	Regional[b]
Grains, etc.	X	0.0	4.7	3.4	0.0	0.0	0.0	0.2	0.0	5.8	0.0	1.9	16.0
	M	0.9	2.6	0.2	1.1	1.5	0.3	0.2	0.5	0.0	0.0	0.0	7.4
Rice	X	0.0	6.7	12.7	0.0	0.0	0.0	0.0	0.0	24.5	0.0	10.0	53.9
	M	1.6	1.7	0.0	4.0	0.6	2.0	0.0	2.3	0.0	0.1	0.0	12.3
Wheat	X	0.0	0.6	2.1		0.0		0.4					3.2
	M	1.4	1.9	0.0		3.2		0.4					6.8
Maize	X		11.9	0.3	0.1			0.0	0.0	0.3			12.6
	M		5.7	0.0	1.3			0.1	0.4	0.1			7.6
Cassava	X									72.6			72.6
	M									0.0			0.0
Barley	X					0.0							0.0
	M					0.6							0.6
Sorghum	X			0.1									0.1
	M			0.0									
Chickpeas	X			0.2									0.2
	M			23.5									23.5

(Table continues on the following page.)

Table B.19. Share of the Global Value of Exports and Imports, Key Covered Products, Asian Focus Economies, 2000–03 (*continued*)

Product	M, X[a]	Bangladesh	China	India	Indonesia	Korea, Rep. of	Malaysia	Pakistan	Philippines	Thailand	Sri Lanka	Vietnam	Regional[b]
Oilseeds	X		0.4	1.2	9.9	0.0	20.7			0.2			32.4
	M		6.9	0.2	1.1	1.1	0.5			1.2			11.1
Soybeans	X		1.1	2.4	0.0	0.0				0.0			3.6
	M		17.4	0.0	2.7	2.7				3.1			25.9
Groundnuts	X			8.3									8.3
	M			0.0									0.0
Palm oil	X				27.0		56.8			0.6			84.4
	M				0.0		1.3			0.0			1.4
Rapeseeds	X			0.1									0.1
	M			0.0									
Sunflower seeds	X			0.1									0.1
	M												
Sesame	X												
	M			3.2									3.2
Tropical crops	X	0.0	0.6	1.2	3.0		1.4	0.2	0.3	6.4	2.7	2.7	18.6
	M	0.3	2.4	0.6	1.0		1.1	0.8	0.2	0.0	0.0	0.0	6.5
Sugar	X	0.0	0.7	2.8	0.0			0.0	0.4	7.4		0.2	11.4
	M	0.8	2.8	0.1	2.5			1.3	0.4	0.0		0.1	8.0
Cotton	X		2.5	0.7				1.0					4.2
	M		9.4	4.4				2.4					16.2
Coconuts	X				15.0				30.3		16.9		62.2
	M				0.1				0.0		0.0		0.2
Coffee	X				3.2							11.2	14.4
	M				0.1							0.0	0.1
Rubber	X				23.7		15.6			41.6	0.7	11.7	93.3
	M				0.2		6.3			0.0	0.1	0.1	6.7

		1	2	3	4	5	6	7	8	9	10	Total
Tea	X	0.3				3.7					23.9	27.9
	M	0.0				0.1					0.3	0.4
Cocoa	X						0.6					0.6
	M						4.3					4.3
Livestock products	X		1.7	0.1	0.0	0.1	0.0	0.0	1.3		0.1	3.3
	M		1.4	0.0	0.0	1.7	0.0	0.2	0.0		0.0	3.3
Pig meat	X		2.2	0.1	0.0	0.3					0.4	3.0
	M		0.6	0.0	0.2	1.4					0.0	2.2
Milk	X		0.2	0.2		0.0		0.0				0.4
	M		1.7	0.1		0.6		0.0				2.3
Beef	X				0.0	0.0						0.0
	M				0.6	5.2						5.8
Poultry	X		7.9		0.0	0.0			8.6		0.0	16.6
	M		4.5		0.0	1.0		0.1	0.0		0.0	5.7
Eggs	X					0.0						0.0
	M					0.1						0.1
Total, all products	X	0.0	2.1	1.1	1.6	0.0	2.5	0.1	3.1	0.5	0.9	12.1
	M	0.3	2.5	0.2	0.6	1.3	0.3	0.2	0.2	0.0	0.0	5.8
All covered products	X	0.0	3.2	1.2	1.3	0.4	1.6	0.4	1.8	0.2	0.5	10.8
	M	0.3	3.8	0.8	0.9	1.9	0.9	0.6	0.6	0.2	0.3	10.6

Sources: Author compilation; FAO SUA-FBS Database 2008; chapters 2–12 of this volume.

Note: World = 100.

a. M = imports. X = exports.

b. There are no data on Taiwan, China in the FAO SUA-FBS Database.

Table B.20. Share of Production for Export, Consumption of Imports, and Domestic Production, Key Covered Products, Asian Focus Economies, 2000–03

(percent)

Product	C, M, Q, X[a]	Bangladesh	China	India	Indonesia	Korea, Rep. of	Malaysia	Pakistan	Philippines	Thailand	Sri Lanka	Vietnam	Total[b]
Grains, etc.	X/Q	0	4	4	0	1	2	13	0	42	0	16	7
	M/C	10	2	0	5	36	26	2	9	1	3	0	8
	Q/C	98	99	101	95	103	73	119	95	293	99	137	119
Rice	X/Q	0	2	4	0	0	2	45	0	43	0	16	6
	M/C	3	1	0	4	3	26	0	10	0	3	0	1
	Q/C	102	99	102	96	104	73	186	95	196	99	137	105
Wheat	X/Q	0	2	5		2,038		5					3
	M/C	61	2	0		101		2					4
	Q/C	49	96	102		0		101					96
Maize	X/Q		10	2	0			0	0	5			8
	M/C		5	0	11			0	8	2			5
	Q/C		101	101	89			96	95	103			100
Cassava	X/Q									75			75
	M/C									0			0
	Q/C									1,181			1,181
Barley	X/Q					1							1
	M/C					44							44
	Q/C					56							56
Sorghum	X/Q			0									0
	M/C			0									0
	Q/C			100									100
Oilseeds	X/Q		2	2	66	1	98			24			32
	M/C		52	0	27	93	61			71			51
	Q/C		50	99	331	7	2,804			136			571

	Measure	1	2	3	4	5	6	7	8	9	10
Soybeans	X/Q	2		2		0	1	2			2
	M/C	52		0		61	93	119			49
	Q/C	50		94		39	7	22			53
Groundnuts	X/Q			3							3
	M/C			0							0
	Q/C			102							102
Palm oil	X/Q			71		98		28			85
	M/C			1		61		13			11
	Q/C			355		2,804		157			661
Sunflower seeds	X/Q			0							0
	M/C			0							0
	Q/C			104							104
Sesame	X/Q			0							
	M/C			0							
	Q/C			104							
Tropical crops	X/Q	7	3	22	1	105	9	92	63	75	38
	M/C	21	9	18	7	110	6	1	5	5	18
	Q/C	97	97	270	96	192	107	3,855	1,250	4,171	1,024
Sugar	X/Q	0	6	2	12		6	68		5	12
	M/C	34	16	39	12		12	1		4	9
	Q/C	79	97	62	92		93	328		102	109
Cotton	X/Q	1	1		1		3	1			1
	M/C	4	5		3						4
	Q/C	97	96		99						97
Coconuts	X/Q	5					12		17		9
	M/C	0					0		2		0
	Q/C	106					114		120		110
Coffee	X/Q			50						101	78
	M/C			3						0	3
	Q/C			196						5,130	413

(Table continues on the following page.)

Table B.20. Share of Production for Export, Consumption of Imports, and Domestic Production, Key Covered Products, Asian Focus Economies, 2000–03 (*continued*)

Product	C, M, Q, X[a]	Bangladesh	China	India	Indonesia	Korea, Rep. of	Malaysia	Pakistan	Philippines	Thailand	Sri Lanka	Vietnam	Total[b]
Rubber	X/Q				90		99			101	38	94	96
	M/C				14		97			3	6	47	71
	Q/C				1,189		162			5137	150	6,069	657
Tea	X/Q	14			64						97		78
	M/C	0			6						31		6
	Q/C	117			263						2,166		431
Cocoa	X/Q						448						448
	M/C						2,434						2,434
	Q/C						1,009						1,009
Livestock products	X/Q		3	0	0	3		0	0	22			4
	M/C		4	0	1	38		0	9	0			7
	Q/C		99	100	100	74		100	92	133			100
Pig meat	X/Q		1			3			0	3		—	1
	M/C		1			15			3	0		—	2
	Q/C		100			88			97	103		—	99
Milk	X/Q		2	0		0		0					0
	M/C		7	0		0		0					1
	Q/C		95	100		100		100					99
Beef	X/Q					5			0				2
	M/C					61			26				48
	Q/C					41			74				53

Product	Measure	Values (left to right)
Poultry	X/Q	9, 0, 1, 0, 35, 10
	M/C	12, 1, 18, 3, 0, 11
	Q/C	96, 100, 83, 97, 153, 99
	X/Q	—, 10
	M/C	—, 11
	Q/C	—, 99
Eggs	X/Q	0, 0, 2, 0
	M/C	1, 1, 9, 1
	Q/C	99, 99, 96, 99
Total, all products	X/Q	0, 3, 2, 15, 2, 94, 8, 2, 51, 42, 25, 22
	M/C	10, 6, 0, 10, 40, 63, 2, 9, 7, 4, 0, 14
	Q/C	98, 97, 101, 181, 84, 2,256, 111, 96, 1,234, 867, 762, 535

Sources: Author compilation; FAO SUA-FBS Database 2008.

Note: — = no data are available.

a. C = consumption. M = imports. Q = production. X = exports.

b. There are no data on Taiwan, China in the FAO SUA-FBS Database.

References

Ahmed, N., Z. Bakht, P. A. Dorosh, and Q. Shahabuddin. 2007. "Distortions to Agricultural Incentives in Bangladesh." Agricultural Distortions Working Paper 32, World Bank, Washington, DC.

Anderson, K., M. Kurzweil, W. Martin, D. Sandri, and E. Valenzuela. 2008. "Measuring Distortions to Agricultural Incentives, Revisited." *World Trade Review* 7 (4): 675–704.

Athukorala, P.-C., P. L. Huong, and V. T. Thanh. 2007. "Distortions to Agricultural Incentives in Vietnam." Agricultural Distortions Working Paper 26, World Bank, Washington, DC.

Athukorala, P.-C., and W.-H. Loke. 2007. "Distortions to Agricultural Incentives in Malaysia." Agricultural Distortions Working Paper 27, World Bank, Washington, DC.

Bandara, J., and S. Jayasuriya. 2007. "Distortions to Agricultural Incentives in Sri Lanka." Agricultural Distortions Working Paper 31, World Bank, Washington, DC.

David, C. C., P. Intal, and A. M. Balisacan. 2007. "Distortions to Agricultural Incentives in the Philippines." Agricultural Distortions Working Paper 28, World Bank, Washington, DC.

Dorosh, P. A., and A. Salam. 2007. "Distortions to Agricultural Incentives in Pakistan." Agricultural Distortions Working Paper 33, World Bank, Washington, DC.

Fane, G., and P. Warr. 2007. "Distortions to Agricultural Incentives in Indonesia." Agricultural Distortions Working Paper 24, World Bank, Washington, DC.

FAO SUA-FBS Database (Supply Utilization Accounts and Food Balance Sheets Database, FAOSTAT). Food and Agriculture Organization of the United Nations. http://faostat.fao.org/site/354/default.aspx (accessed May 2008).

Honma, M., and Y. Hayami. 2007. "Distortions to Agricultural Incentives in Korea and Taiwan." Agricultural Distortions Working Paper 30, World Bank, Washington, DC.

Huang, J., S. Rozelle, W. Martin, and Y. Liu. 2007. "Distortions to Agricultural Incentives in China." Agricultural Distortions Working Paper 29, World Bank, Washington, DC.

Pursell, G., A. Gulati, and K. Gupta. 2007. "Distortions to Agricultural Incentives in India." Agricultural Distortions Working Paper 34, World Bank, Washington, DC.

Warr, P. G., and A. Kohpaiboon. 2007. "Distortions to Agricultural Incentives in Thailand." Agricultural Distortions Working Paper 25, World Bank, Washington, DC.

INDEX

Figures, notes, and tables are indicated by *f*, *n*, and *t*, respectively.